INTRODUCTION TO
GROUP
COUNSELING

SECOND EDITION

Edited by

DAVID CAPUZZI
Portland State University

DOUGLAS R. GROSS
Arizona State University

LOVE PUBLISHING COMPANY®
Denver • London • Sydney

Acknowledgment is made to the American Counseling Association for permission to reprint the Professional Standards for the Training of Group Workers, Ethical Guidelines for Counselors, Code of Ethics, and Standards of Practice that are the appendices of this book.

Published by Love Publishing Company
Denver, Colorado 80222

Second Edition

Library of Congress Catalog Card Number 98-65330

ISBN 0-89108-259-X

Contents

WITHDRAWN

Part One: Foundations for Group Counseling   1

Part Two: Professional Issues   99

Part Three: Theme Focused Groups   205

Foreword

The history and influence of group work theory and practice represent one of the major contributions to the counseling profession during the 20th century. This history, rich with evidence of the efficacy of groups, has been shaped by the pioneering and sustaining efforts of a number of exemplary practitioners and researchers. During this century we have witnessed the power of the group process for enhancing personal growth, interpersonal competencies, and skill development, and for offering healing to a wide diversity of people across multiple settings. The second edition of *Introduction to Group Counseling* is an insightful text to continue the influence of this counseling specialty by transporting students of group counseling into the complex challenges and unique opportunities that await us in the 21st century.

Topics range from definitions of group work, group dynamics, leadership, and membership issues to ethics, research, training standards, and the application of group work methods to a wide array of populations and issues. Capuzzi and Gross begin the text by presenting the history of group work and making important connections to the next frontier: what they refer to as the interaction of the individual with the machine. Indeed, counselors will be well positioned to help people cope with the realities of technology and their continuing and evolving interpersonal needs and challenges. In this fast-paced, transient world, the need for interpersonal skills, social contact, and a sense of connectedness with others is more crucial than ever.

This book helps readers move toward being effective, competent, and compassionate group leaders. The editors take ample time in the beginning chapters to set the stage for group work. They attend carefully to concepts indigenous to group work practice and impart a real flavor of what group work is all about. Although this text is designed for group counseling, it gives the reader information that can be applied to groups with varying purposes. The early focus on group work concepts is a major strength of this text. Capuzzi and Gross interact with the literature and arrive at their own perspective about stages of group work practice. This is effective because all students eventually will take the information and knowledge gleaned from others and develop their own approaches and styles. The linking of stages to member and leader behaviors keeps the connection between concepts and practice alive. The editors also link the ASGW Training Standards to effective leader behavior. The blending of knowledge competencies with skill competencies precludes the need to provide a cookbook approach. The reader can appreciate the practical suggestions and options for leaders to consider while maintaining some breathing room to adapt their own personal style. The focus on concepts is especially helpful because group leaders need a conceptual map to guide their practice.

In Chapter 4 Capuzzi and Gross address the vexing challenge of applying individual theories to group work practice. Their opening vignette captures the confusion and struggle of many students and teachers who try to apply individual approaches to groups. In addressing this issue, Capuzzi and Gross provide an overview of the six theoretical approaches and their applications to group work. The discussion of variables that reflect both content and process is refreshing. This presentation offers the student of group counseling some useful illustrations of how one might select and utilize individual theories in serving the group's purpose, goals, and setting.

Group counseling is both an art and a science, and effective group leaders need to know how to maximize the success of the group experience for their members. The chapter on the efficacy of group work builds on earlier chapters by presenting the research on group counseling with special populations. The reader quickly recognizes how groups can be helpful and when groups are unhelpful and, at times, harmful. The tone conveyed in this chapter is one of thoughtfulness, patience, and a respect for taking time to learn how to be an effective leader. The chapter on ethical considerations and ethical decision making continues this tone and encourages the reader to take time to understand and appreciate the magnitude of the responsibilities facing competent and effective group leaders.

Energy builds throughout this text as subsequent chapters provide snapshots of the multiple possibilities inherent within group counseling settings. Following the opening four chapters, which set the stage for understanding group goals, purposes, dynamics, stages, leadership, theory, and applications, the contributors present compelling issues that interact with these elements—creating an overlay that conveys to the reader the magic, complexity, reward, challenge, and multifaceted nature of group counseling.

The discussions about multicultural issues challenge the reader to become thoughtful and open to learning. One major theme throughout this text is that of taking the risk to really explore oneself—one's values, worldviews, and perspectives—in order to be accessible and effective with a wide range of people and issues. This exploration is necessary to enhance a therapeutic group process when examining issues of loss and suicide; when designing and implementing groups for people with physical disabilities, addictions, eating disorders, and career decision-making concerns; and when preparing groups for gay, lesbian, and bisexual people, elderly members and their caregivers, and the diverse multicultural populations in our society.

By using the group process to openly discuss diversity issues, leaders can help foster important learning for themselves and for their members. Readers moving through this text soon will realize that group dynamics and theories are not enough; effective leaders need to recognize and understand the complex interaction of setting, philosophies, populations, and counseling and administrative issues. As the complexity and multifaceted nature of group counseling is presented, one feels comforted by the excellent resources and maps that guide the individual who is ready to embark on the journey of becoming an effective group leader.

Another resounding theme is that of leadership as a shared function. The chapters describing group work with multiple populations convey a strong sense of honoring the contributions of group members. The notion of leaders sharing their skills and functions is at the heart of helping members become more active and contributing resources in groups and is a key factor in members' ability to take learning from the group to their world outside the group. Shared leadership is especially underscored in the discussion of self-help groups and how aspects of these groups can be incorporated into professionally led groups.

In all of the application chapters one gets a sense of how the group process can be used to enhance growth and skill development across a range of settings. These chapters give the reader a glimpse of what is conceptually possible and provide helpful, practical outlines that can guide the group leader's actions. The attention to these populations mirrors the realities of the society we live in today and reflects the pluralistic society we can expect in the next century. The application chapters take the reader beyond the usual discussion about whether groups do or do not work to more specific and useful discussions about how people do change in these groups.

In reading this text, we learn where we have been and receive important information about the challenges and issues facing leaders of group counseling and other groups as we enter the next millennium. Counselors in a range of work settings will find information, guides, resources, and perspectives to enhance their effectiveness as group leaders. The vast amount of learning during this century has paved the way for an understanding of what does and does not work in groups. We can use these learning points to guide us into our future group encounters.

We know that groups work best when the purpose and goals are clear and when the group process is utilized in the service of the group experience. Readers of this text will sense that, to be an effective group leader, they must have the courage and patience to slow down and view their learning as a process, a journey that will include integrating theory, group process, research, ethics, knowledge, and skill competencies with a strong commitment to tackling their own personal growth. Effective leaders must know themselves and utilize all opportunities for practice and supervision to enable them to offer group experiences that will serve the needs of the people who seek their help. This text is an effective guide for such a journey. It is a usable and engaging text that honors the complexity and power of group counseling.

Diana Hulse-Killacky
Professor of Counseling
University of New Orleans

Preface

The therapeutic elements of a positive group experience have been documented through empirically based research, client self-reports, descriptions by group leaders, and the emergence of paradigms derived from a variety of theoretical perspectives. These curative factors have been identified by such terms as acceptance, altruism, universalization, belonging, security, instillation of hope, increased awareness of emotional dynamics, interpersonal learning, and many other descriptors. The role of professional counselors in educational, corporate, mental health, private practice, and rehabilitation settings calls for knowledge, experience, and competence in facilitating groups. Therefore, the aspiring group leader has to start developing the knowledge and competencies necessary to provide a powerful, growth-enhancing opportunity for clients involved in group counseling.

Group work is demanding. To effectively lead groups, the professional counselor must acquire knowledge and skills beyond the foundation in individual counseling provided by course work and supervised practice. Individuals who are trying to decide if group work is the specialization they want will find the information in this text helpful as a point of departure in the decision-making process.

The book is unique in format and content. The contributed-authors format allows for the provision of state-of-the-art information by experts in their respective group work specializations. The content goes beyond that usually addressed in introductory group work texts. Chapters on group work with clients who have eating disorders, suicidal clients, gay, lesbian, and bisexual clients, clients with disabilities, and people with addictions are cases in point. The first four chapters provide prerequisite information on the foundational aspects of group work that makes subsequent chapters on group work easier to assimilate. This format and content are intended to increase the book's readability, interest level, and provision of knowledge needed in today's world.

Students enrolled in a beginning course in group work will find the book useful for the future as well as the present. The book provides a comprehensive overview of major issues connected with group work, as well as insight and practical guidelines for group work in general, for theme-focused groups, and for group work with specialized populations. Although the special populations addressed are primarily adult, the overall developmental focus encompasses younger populations as appropriate. The concept of cultural diversity, certainly a major issue in group work, is incorporated throughout the book and also is accorded a chapter of its own (Chapter 8), "Multicultural Group Counseling: Cross-Cultural Considerations." We know that one book cannot cover all the factors involved in preparing a person to be a group leader. Rather, we are attempting to give readers a broad perspective on group work.

With few exceptions, each chapter contains information specific to a topic and includes discussion of age-specific variations, where appropriate, for special populations (e.g., clients with eating disorders). The many case studies are intended to help the reader identify with and make applications to current or future clients. The text is divided into four parts: Foundations for Group Counseling; Professional Issues; Theme-Focused Groups; and Group Work With Special Populations.

Part One, Foundations for Group Counseling (Chapters 1 through 4), leads off with information dealing with the historical, definitive, theoretical, research, and practical perspectives that provide the foundation for all types of group work. These chapters are entitled "Group Counseling: An Introduction," "Group Counseling: Stages and Issues," "Group Counseling: Elements of Effective Leadership," and "Group Counseling: Theory and Application."

Part Two, Professional Issues, discusses the efficacy of group work, group counseling in special settings, and both ethical and cross-cultural considerations.

Parts Three and Four deal with theme-focused groups and group work with special populations, respectively.

Acknowledgments ~

We would like to thank the 20 authors who contributed their time, expertise, and experience to the development of this textbook for the beginning group work specialist. We would also like to thank our families, who provided the support to make our writing and editing efforts possible, as well as the counselor education faculties and staffs at Portland State University and Arizona State University. Our thanks are also directed to Stan Love and the staff of Love Publishing Company for their encouragement, understanding, and editing. Recognition is given to Nila Epstein, graduate assistant in Counselor Education at Portland State University, who worked so diligently and so competently to make this task less difficult.

Meet the Editors ~

David Capuzzi, Ph.D., N.C.C., L.P.C., is a past president of the American Counseling Association and professor of counselor education for the School of Education at Portland State University in Portland, Oregon. From 1980 to 1984, Dr. Capuzzi was editor of *The School Counselor.* He has authored a number of textbook chapters and monographs on the topic of preventing adolescent suicide. He has also authored or co-authored books dealing with family interventions, youth at risk, and counseling theories and interventions. He has authored or co-authored articles in a number of ACA and related journals.

A frequent speaker and keynoter at professional conferences and institutes, Dr. Capuzzi has also consulted with a variety of school districts and community agencies interested in initiating counseling and intervention strategies for adolescents at risk for suicide. He has facilitated the development of suicide prevention, crisis management, and postvention programs in communities in 24 states. He also provides trainings on the topics of youth at risk and counseling and teaching youth at risk.

Douglas R. Gross, PH.D., N.C.C., C.P.C., is a professor emeritus of counselor education at Arizona State University in Tempe. His professional work history includes public school teaching, counseling, and administration. He has served in several leadership positions with the counseling profession including president of the Western Association for Counselor Education and Supervision and president of the Association for Humanistic Education and Development. Dr. Gross has co-authored four textbooks and contributed chapters in numerous other books. His research has been published in several of the major scholarly journals.

Dr. Gross also serves as a consultant to several alcohol and drug programs in the state of Arizona and does training in the area of grief and loss.

Meet the Authors ~

Valerie Appleton, Ed.D., is an Associate Professor of Applied Psychology at Eastern Washington University, Spokane, Washington. She is the director of counselor education at Eastern. Dr. Appleton is a licensed Marriage, Family, and Child Counselor and a Registered Art Therapist. She is also serving as the President of the Washington State Chapter of the American Art Therapy Association.

G. Miguel Arciniega, Ph.D., is an associate professor in the Division of Psychology in Education, Program of Counseling, at Arizona State University, Tempe. Dr. Arciniega has been director of minority counseling projects and institutes, teacher corps, and centers for bilingual/bicultural education. He has written several articles in multicultural counseling and has served on several editorial journal boards. He has also consulted extensively with federal, state, and local agencies with respect to counseling minorities in addition to working with A.I.D. (Aid for International Development) in Central and South America.

Melissa Blanchard, M.Ed., obtained a master of educational psychology degree from the University of Utah, Salt Lake City, with a concentration in rehabilitation counseling. As the clinical director at the New Arizona Family, she oversees three residential sites focusing on substance abuse, the dually diagnosed (substance abuse and serious mental illness), and stabilization/referral of serious mentally ill clients, respectively. She teaches college-level courses in chemical dependency counseling.

Jack Clark, ACSW, CISW, is Chief of Mental Health at Arizona State University, Student Health and is an adjunct faculty member at the Graduate School of Social Work. In addition to his University position, Jack consults nationally with social service, mental health, and substance abuse treatment agencies. Jack received a Masters in Social Work from the Jane Adams College of Social Work, University of Illinois at Chicago. A longtime member of the National Association of Social Workers, Jack holds the Diplomate in Clinical Social Work certification.

Cass Dykeman, Ph.D., is an Associate Professor of Applied Psychology at Eastern Washington University in Spokane, WA. He is the director of the school counseling preparation program at Eastern. Dr. Dykeman is a National Certified Counselor, Master Addictions Counselor, and National Certified School Counselor. He has served as president of the Washington State Association for Counselor Education and Supervision.

Mary Lou Bryant-Frank, Ph.D., is a counseling psychologist who has also been trained in family therapy. At Arizona State University, she coordinated the eating disorders program, co-coordinated practicum training, and concurrently taught in the Counseling Department. She has contributed a chapter to *Counseling and Psychotherapy: Theories and Interventions* (1995) and has published in the *Journal of Counseling and Development* and *Psychological Reports*. Dr. Frank served as Associate & Lead Professor of Psychology and Assistant Academic Dean at Clinch Valley College. Currently, she is a Professor and the Department Head of Psychology at North Georgia College.

Ardis Sherwood-Hawes, M.S., is a counselor in private practice in Beaverton, Oregon and instructor for Human Development at Clark College, Vancouver, Washington. She received her masters in counseling degree from the counselor education program at Portland State University. Her professional interests and expertise include issues related to women, survivors of sexual abuse, life-skills training, parent skills training and adolescent pregnancy and parenthood. Her publication history includes chapters on adolescent pregnancy and childbearing, suicide, counseling children and adolescents, and group therapy.

Reese M. House, Ed.D., N.C.C., is a professor in the Counselor Education Program at Oregon State University. His areas of expertise include working with gay, lesbian, and bisexual clients; death, dying, and loss issues; AIDS education and counseling; and group work in counseling. He has served as a consultant on AIDS education and prevention strategies throughout Asia. Dr. House has a doctorate in counseling from Oregon State University.

Rolla E. Lewis, Ed.D., is an assistant professor in the School of Education at Portland State University. Dr. Lewis has taught, led groups, and counseled students in alternative and public school settings for over 15 years. His approaches with groups range from teaching communication skills to teaching juggling to enhance self-perception.

Hanoch Livneh, Ph.D., is professor of Counselor Education and coordinator of the Rehabilitation Counseling Specialization at Portland State University, Portland, Oregon. He received his M.A. and Ph.D. degrees in rehabilitation counseling psychology from the University of Wisconsin at Madison. Before joining the faculty at Portland State University, he served as the director of the rehabilitation counseling program, department of counseling and educational psychology, at Rhode Island College.

Virginia Martin, Ed.D., L.P.C., is an associate professor of counselor education in the Department of Instructional Support Programs at Alabama State University in Montgomery, Alabama. She is also a counselor and clinical supervisor in the AUM Counseling Center at Auburn University at Montgomery. Dr. Martin earned her Ed.D. in counselor education from Auburn University (1985). Her teaching specialties are developmental and abnormal psychology, group counseling, and helping relationships. Her publications are concerned with group counseling for shy persons and older persons, and treatment of specific anxiety disorders.

Russell D. Miars, Ph.D., is an assistant professor in the counselor education program at Portland State University. Previously Dr. Miars was director of the Counseling and Student Development Center and adjunct associate professor in clinical psychology at Indiana University of Pennsylvania. His research and scholarly interests include counselor supervision, legal and ethical issues, life-span human development, career development, and assessment in counseling.

Holly Forester-Miller, Ph.D., is an Associate Professor and Counselor Education Coordinator at North Carolina Central University, Durham, North Carolina. She has published and presented internationally in the areas of group work, ethics, and the mind-body connection. Holly has served as member and chair of both the Association for Specialists in Group Work and the American Counseling Association's (ACA) Ethics Committees. Dr. Forester-Miller has published several books dealing with ethics and most recently *Issues and Challenges for Group Practitioners* (1997).

Betty J. Newlon, Ed.D., is a member of the graduate faculty at Chapman University, Davis-Monthan Academic Center in Tucson, Arizona. She has written and lectured in the areas of career counseling and counseling women.

Richard E. Pearson, Ph.D., is a faculty member in the Counselor Education program at Syracuse University. His long-standing involvement in group work intersects with his interest in social support, in the area of support groups. Dr. Pearson believes that support groups represent an exciting opportunity for professional and non-professional collaboration and cross-fertilization of ideas.

Robert E. Pullo, Ph.D. is a professor and coordinator of the Rehabilitation Services Program, Department of Health & Rehabilitation, University of Maine at Farmington. He received his Ph.D. in rehabilitation counseling psychology from the University of Wisconsin, Madison. Dr. Pullo's interests focus primarily on the psychosocial impact of disability in the areas of vocational rehabilitation and substance abuse rehabilitation.

Conrad Sieber, Ph.D., is a postdoctoral fellow in the counselor education program at Portland State University and is involved in teaching courses as well as the training and supervision of graduate students. Dr. Sieber received his doctoral degree from Colorado State University. He has 5 years experience in university counseling centers where he coordinated and developed group programs, did program evaluation of clinical services, and was actively involved in the training and supervision of graduate student trainees.

M. Carolyn Thomas, Ph.D., L.P.C., is a professor and coordinator of counselor education and director of the AUM Counseling Center at Auburn University at Montgomery in Montgomery, Alabama. She is also a clinical supervisor at the Family Sunshine Center. Dr. Thomas earned her Ph.D. in counselor education from the University of Iowa (1973). Her specialties include group work, career development, and supervision, and her publications are concerned with group work for older persons or victims of family abuse.

Virginia Tyler, M.S., N.C.C., is the Social Services Coordinator for Evergreen Hospice in Albany, Oregon, working with individuals and families coping with terminal illness. Her areas of expertise include: group counseling with children and adults around issues of loss; providing hospice care to HIV/AIDS patients; and ethical dilemmas involving end-of-life decisions. She has a particular interest in bisexuality throughout the lifespan. She received her M.S. in counseling from Western Oregon State/Oregon State University.

Ann Vernon, Ph.D., is professor and coordinator of counseling in the Department of Educational Administration and Counseling at the University of Northern Iowa. In addition, she maintains a private practice where she works primarily with children, adolescents, and their parents. Dr. Vernon presents workshops in the U.S. and Canada on a variety of topics such as counseling techniques with children and adolescents, effective parenting and rational emotive therapy. Dr. Vernon is the author of numerous books and articles, including *Thinking, Feeling, Behaving, Counseling Children and Adolescents,* and *Developmental Assessment.*

Part One

Foundations for
Group Counseling

Group counseling encompasses many knowledge and skill modalities in which the group leader must be proficient. The first part of this text provides an overview of the historical context of group work as well as basic knowledge and skill areas pertinent to group facilitation.

Chapter 1, "Group Counseling: An Introduction," leads off with basic information and terminology. This is followed by an overview of the history of group work, examples of goals for groups, a discussion of different types of groups, other models for group work, therapeutic factors in groups, personal characteristics of effective group leaders, and myths connected with group work.

The stages and transitions inherent in the group experience, as well as the issues these stages and transitions present for the leader and the members of a group, are analyzed in Chapter 2, "Group Counseling: Stages and Issues." After the presentation of a case study, revisited at the end of the chapter, the early and current conceptualizations of stage theory and member behavior are discussed. A composite conceptualization of the developmental stages of groups incorporates definitive, personal involvement, group involvement, and enhancement and closure stages. In conjunction with descriptions of each of the four stages, member and leader behaviors are identified.

Chapter 3, "Group Counseling: Elements of Effective Leadership," explores leadership style: authoritarian, democratic, laissez-faire, leader centered, group centered, interpersonal, intrapersonal, and charismatic. It also covers skills related to pre-group screening and organizing for groups. Various member roles are outlined. The authors set forth the skills the group leader must master to facilitate the definitive, personal involvement, group involvement, and enhancement and closure stages discussed in Chapter 2. Chapter 3 concludes with a consideration of techniques for dealing with difficult members.

Chapter 4, "Group Counseling: Theory and Application," takes six selected theoretical/therapeutic approaches and applies them to groups: Adlerian, Gestalt, person centered, rational-emotive behavior therapy, transactional analysis, and psychodrama. Rather than reiterating theory available in texts on individual counseling and psychotherapy, the authors translate these theoretical concepts into group leader behaviors and techniques. The chapter concludes with an integrative theme considering relationship, leader role, member role, process, and outcome variables in light of the six theoretical approaches.

1

Group Counseling:
An Introduction

David Capuzzi and Douglas R. Gross

As noted by Gladding (1997), a group can be defined as "two or more people interacting together to achieve a goal for their mutual benefit" (p. 170). Most people spend a considerable amount of time in groups, whether at home, at work, at school, at social gatherings, at church, or at civic, professional, or political meetings. Counselors have become increasingly aware of the fact that many of the problems that bring clients to counseling are interpersonally based (Corey & Corey, 1997) and that, for many clients, group counseling or therapy may be the treatment of choice because of the interpersonal learning opportunities groups provide. Group counseling fits well into the current emphasis on managed care (Sleek, 1995) because many groups can be facilitated in ways that provide brief and cost-effective assistance for participants.

Like other institutions and training activities, group counseling reflects both the culture and the history of the moment as influenced by national, regional, and local concerns (Klein, 1985). Of importance today, the transition from the 20th to the 21st century in the United States poses challenges and possibilities for those who are considering work in group counseling. If the 1950s symbolized the "individual in society," the 1960s "the individual against society," the 1970s "the individual's conflict with self," and the 1980s "the individual's integration into the family," the 1990s and beyond may symbolize "the individual's integration with the machine" (Shapiro & Bernadett-Shapiro, 1985).

In the 21st century, much of the work in educational, career, and day-to-day living situations will be done by computers; connections among colleagues, friends, and family members will be maintained by telephone lines, word processors, and modems (Capuzzi & Gross, 1997). The replacement of consistent social contact with friends and co-workers by the video display terminal and telecommunication networks will create a much greater need for interpersonal communication on a person-to-person basis. Groups will provide an antidote to isolation, and more and more counselors, therapists, and other human development specialists will be called upon to serve as group facilitators. The counseling and human development professional faces crescendoing opportunities and escalating responsibilities in group work.

The History of Group Work~

Beginnings

Group counseling can be traced back to the first decade of the 20th century (Gazda, 1985). In 1905, Joseph Hersey Pratt, a physician, applied the "class" method in providing assistance to patients with tuberculosis in Boston, Massachusetts. A few years later in 1909, Cody Marsh began to offer psychiatric inpatients what could be called inspirational group lectures (Scheidlinger, 1994). He soon became known for his motto "By the crowd they have been broken; by the crowd they shall be healed." During the 1920s, Edward Lazell, a psychiatrist, used a similar lecture method when working with severely disturbed inpatients suffering from schizophrenic and manic-depressive psychoses. In later years, Lazell applied this didactic approach to outpatients relying upon concepts from Jungian psychology (Scheidlinger, 1994).

As noted by Rudolf Dreikurs (1932), Alfred Adler used collective therapy with families and children in Vienna in the 1920s in his child guidance clinics. Dreikurs brought these methods with him to America. His work with groups complemented that of early American group "pioneers" such as Jesse B. Davis, who used public school classrooms in Michigan as forums for vocational guidance, and the followers of Frank Parsons, who worked with vocationally undecided individuals in small groups via the Vocational Bureau of Boston (Gladding, 1991). By the middle of the 1920s, Trigant Burrow, one of the founders of the American Psychoanalytic Association, had begun conducting groups for his patients, members of his patients' families, and mental health professionals (Scheidlinger, 1994). The experience was termed *group analysis* and replaced Sigmund Freud's emphasis on individual intrapsychic themes with a focus on interactive themes.

From 1908 to 1925, Jacob L. Moreno, known as the founder of psychodrama, used group action techniques in Vienna. Following his arrival in the United States, Moreno continued developing his psychodramatic techniques, and his ideas influenced later American Gestalt, existential, and encounter group movements (Gladding, 1991; Scheidlinger, 1994).

The 1930s

A number of psychoanalytic clinicians began to apply Freudian principles to group work in hospitals in the 1930s (Scheidlinger, 1994). One of these individuals, Louis Wender, facilitated small groups in a private hospital and differentiated his approach from those of Pratt, Lazell, and Marsh by emphasizing family transference manifestation. Paul Schilder, a colleague of Louis Wender and a research professor of psychiatry at New York University School of Medicine, also helped legitimize the growing interest in group modalities.

Among the first to employ group work with children was Loretta Bender. She pioneered the use of children's cathartic expression in groups with the use of puppets. She was followed by Betty Gabriel, who was the first American to use groups with adolescents (Scheidlinger, 1994). S. R. Slavson, a contemporary of both Bender and Gabriel and founder of the American Group Psychotherapy Association, also pioneered the use of groups for children (Slavson & Schiffer, 1975). His groups, which he called activity therapy groups, consisted of about eight children of the same sex and similar ages. Handicrafts, games, and food served to focus interactions, and the groups were conducted in the context of a nondirective climate. Slavson's approach was welcomed by counselors and therapists of the day, who had found it difficult to engage children in one-to-one "talking" sessions. Variations of activity group therapy, directed at more seriously disturbed youth, were soon introduced. This early emphasis on group work with children provided the basis for the use of psychoeducational groups with children in elementary schools. In recent years, elementary school counselors have seen children in groups focused on divorce, substance abuse, self-esteem enhancement, conflict resolution, and other concerns.

It should also be noted that the 1930s bore witness to the development of Alcoholics Anonymous (AA), which provides self-help support group experiences to help alcoholics maintain sobriety (Gladding, 1991). Currently, AA groups are found in most communities in the United States.

The 1940s

During World War II, large numbers of American military personnel who were "psychiatric casualties" of the war experience were seen by military psychiatrists (Scheidlinger, 1994). As a result of sheer necessity, more and more of these psychiatrists adopted the use of group methods. Indeed, many of the subsequent leaders of the American group work movement gained their experience in military hospitals. Among these American army psychiatrists were Samuel Hadden, Harris Pick, Irving Berger, and Donald Shaskan. William C. Menninger, America's chief of military psychiatry during the war, believed that the practice of group work during that time period constituted a major contribution of military psychiatry to civilian psychiatry. Great Britain also contributed to the emerging interest in the use of groups during the era of World War II. Joshua Bierer, S. H. Foulkes, Wilfred R. Bion, and Thomas Main all provided leadership (Scheidlinger, 1994).

Another influential promoter of group work during the 1940s was Kurt Lewin, who emphasized field theory and the interaction between individuals and their environments (Gladding, 1991). Much of his work was based on the ideas of Gestalt psychology, in which the relationship of the part to the whole is emphasized. Lewin was influential in establishing a workshop on intergroup relations in New Britain, Connecticut, in 1946 (Gladding, 1991). Later, with the help of Ron Lippitt, Lee

Bradford, and Ken Benne, he founded the National Training Laboratories in Bethel, Maine (now called NTL: The Institute for Applied Behavioral Science) (Schmuck & Schmuck, 1997). The laboratories focused research on groups directed at improving personal learning and organizational process. An important derivation of the work of these individuals was the training group, or T-group (Bradford, Gibb, & Benne, 1964). Participants in T-groups learn to understand themselves and others better and to develop the skills of collaboration. T-groups popularized in later decades emphasized individual and personal growth goals, understanding of interpersonal relations, and the application of group dynamics to social change.

Two important group organizations were established in the 1940s. The American Society of Group Psychotherapy and Psychodrama (ASGPP) was established by J. L. Moreno, and, as noted earlier in this chapter, the American Group Psychotherapy Association (AGPA) was founded by Samuel R. Slavson. Two important journals, *Group Psychotherapy* and the *International Journal of Group Psychotherapy,* were founded by Moreno and Slavson, respectively. Both journals were characterized by the philosophies of their founders (Gladding, 1991).

The 1950s

One of the first references to group work with the elderly appeared in 1950 with the work of J. J. Geller (1950). Early efforts in this area dealt with the use of groups in residences for older adults. Reports of this work were often anecdotal in nature and most often appeared in social work and nursing journals (Scheidlinger, 1994). The reports described groups for well functioning elderly, for those experiencing widowhood or retirement, and for those with physical and emotional disabilities. They emphasized that older adults often responded well to group experiences aimed at anxiety and pain reduction and social skills training. As time has passed, more and more journals have published either research or practice articles for professionals interested in group work with the elderly. A subsequent chapter in this textbook is entirely focused on this topic.

The 1950s were also characterized by the application of group procedures to family counseling (Gladding, 1997). Rudolph Dreikurs, John Bell, Nathan Ackerman, Gregory Bateson, and Virginia Satir are just a few of the notables who addressed group work with families. Most practitioners who are licensed as marriage and family therapists are familiar with the growing body of literature that addresses aspects of group work with families.

The 1960s and 1970s

The 1960s were a time of great social upheaval and questioning. There were riots on university campuses and in cities as civil rights groups struggled to raise the consciousness of the nation after years of unfair discrimination and prejudice. Charismatic leaders such as John F. Kennedy and Martin Luther King, Jr., became the idolized champions and international symbols of a people's determination to change a society and to promote social responsibility. The nation united in grief-stricken disbelief as its heroes were martyred, and determination to counter the human rights violations of the decades escalated. As the 1960s ended, the encounter group movement, emphasizing personal consciousness and closer connection with others, reached its zenith. It gradually waned in the 1970s as events such as the Watergate scandal, the first presidential resignation in the history of the United States, the Charles Manson killings, the group killings at the Munich Olympics, and the rise of fanatic cults made people in all parts of the country question the extent to which permissiveness and "human potential" should be allowed to develop (Janis, 1972; Rowe & Winborn, 1973).

An important influence on group work in the 1960s was the federal legislation that created a national network of community mental health centers. Administrators, in their attempts to fill newly created positions intended to provide counseling and mental health services to the less affluent members of communities, often resorted to less than advisable solutions (Scheidlinger, 1994). They frequently assigned counselors and therapists whose education and supervised practice was limited to one-to-one counseling and psychotherapy to facilitate groups. When poorly run groups proved ineffective, and sometimes harmful, a frantic search began for counselors and therapists trained in group work.

In addition to the group work conducted by the community mental health centers, the youth revolt kindled by the Vietnam War gave rise to many nontraditional group models that flourished outside the auspices of the mental health profession. Among the most publicized of these groups were the encounter and transcendental meditation groups. Because they functioned without adequate pre-group screening, these commercial undertakings often attracted disturbed and emotionally vulnerable participants. Many participants were harmed by membership in these groups and a protest by qualified mental health professionals resulted in the elimination of the most serious abuses by individuals who organized such community programs.

Granted, the use and misuse of group approaches were sensationalized by the journalists of the era; however, a number of important developments in the use of groups did occur (Gladding, 1991). Fritz Perls' applications of Gestalt theory in groups at the Esalen Institute in California, Eric Berne's application of transactional analysis to groups, William C. Schutz's contributions that stressed aspects of non-verbal communication in groups, Jack Gibb's study of competitive versus cooperative behavior in groups, Irvin Yalom's work on curative factors in groups, and Carl Rogers' encounter group philosophy all provided important insights and methods for group counselors and therapists.

As the decade of the 1970s progressed, counselor education, counseling psychology, psychology, and social work departments on university campuses instituted more and more course work and supervised experiences in aspects of group work. In 1973, the Association for Specialists in Group Work (ASGW) was chartered, and by 1974 it had become a division of the American Counseling Association (ACA) (at that time known as the American Personnel and Guidance Association). ASGW publishes *The Journal for Specialists in Group Work,* which provides group work specialists with information on research, practice, and supervision as related to group work. Similar developments also took place during the 1970s in the context of other large professional groups such as the American Psychological Association (APA) and the National Association of Social Workers (NASW).

The 1980s

Interest in group work and in working with specialized populations grew during the 1980s. Groups sprang up for alcoholics, adult children of alcoholics, incest victims, adults molested as children, overweight people, underassertive individuals, and victims of violent crimes. There were groups for the elderly, people dealing with death and other losses, individuals with eating disorders, smokers, and victims of the Holocaust (Shapiro & Bernadett-Shapiro, 1985). This increasing specialization brought with it a need for higher standards for the preparation of group leaders, as evidenced by the development of ethical standards for group work specialists (Association for Specialists in Group Work [ASGW], 1989) and the inclusion of specific group work specialist preparation guidelines for the graduate-level university educator in the standards of the Council for the Accreditation of Counseling and Related Educational Programs (CACREP, 1994).

The 1990s and Beyond

The escalating interest in group work and in working with special populations so evident in the 1980s continued into the last decade of the century. The 1983 ASGW standards for the training of group counselors were revised, and a new set of standards was adopted in 1991 (ASGW, 1991). Although the 1991 standards built on the 1983 standards, emphasizing the knowledge, skills, and supervised experience necessary for the preparation of group workers, the newer standards broadened the conception of group work, clarified the difference between core competencies and specialization requirements, defined the four prominent varieties of group work, and eliminated the previously made distinctions among different kinds of supervised field experience (Conyne, Wilson, Kline, Morran, & Ward, 1993). In addition, CACREP, in its 1994 revision of accreditation standards, reemphasized the importance of group work by identifying principles of group dynamics, group leadership styles, theories of group counseling, group counseling methods, approaches used for other types of group work, and ethical considerations as essential curricular elements for all counselor education programs (CACREP, 1994).

The use of groups has expanded to virtually all settings connected with counseling and therapy, as well as to schools, hospitals, and corporate environments. Group programs for individuals suffering from chronic diseases (e.g., cancer, heart disease, AIDS), for people suffering from eating disorders, and for people involved in the recovery process connected with substance abuse, sexual abuse, and other traumas are just beginning to capture the attention of the general public. In conjunction with the escalating number of older adults in this and other countries, group approaches for working with older individuals are bound to expand (Scheidlinger, 1994). Given the current emphasis on managed care and cost containment, the interest in group work will continue to grow and the qualified group work specialist will be in high demand.

Goals for Groups ~

In the early "or definitive stage" of a group, it is important for each member to develop a clear understanding of the goals of the group experience. Members who have not really developed some ownership of the reasons they are group participants may not make constructive use of the group experience (Corey & Corey, 1997). There are a number of ways in which group goals can be addressed: (a) general goals for groups, (b) goals for specialized groups, (c) goals based on theoretical perspectives, and (d) goals developed by individual members.

General Goals for Groups

Although many group work leaders believe that the goals for each counseling group should be established by the members and leaders of those groups, there has been some consensus on general group goals (George & Dustin, 1988). As early as 1957, J. Frank proposed a general statement defining group goals as helping members to:

- release their feelings constructively.
- strengthen self-esteem.
- face and resolve their problems.
- improve their skills in recognizing and resolving interpersonal and intrapersonal conflicts.
- fortify their ability to consolidate and maintain therapeutic gains.

In 1963, H. C. Kelman proposed a similar set of general goals, which added the dimensions of helping members to overcome feelings of isolation, develop hope for increased adjustment, learn to accept responsibility, develop new relationship skills, and enhance commitment to change.

Corey, Corey, Callahan, and Russell (1982) suggested that group facilitators have two kinds of goals: general and process. General goals have to do with establishing a psychological environment within the context of a group that is conducive to supporting members as they work toward their personal goals. Process goals relate to teaching members appropriate methods of sharing their own concerns and providing feedback to others in the group. This differentiation provides a helpful guideline. Carroll and Wiggins (1990) identified the general goals of helping the group member:

1. Become a better listener.
2. Develop sensitivity and acceptance of others.
3. Increase self-awareness and develop a sense of identity.
4. Feel a sense of belongingness and overcome feelings of isolation.
5. Learn to trust others as well as self.
6. Recognize and state areas of belief and values without fear of repression.
7. Transfer what is learned in the group to the outside by accepting responsibility for solving one's own problems. (p. 25)

In addition, Carroll and Wiggins (1997) proposed the following process goals helpful to group members:

1. Help members stay in the here and now.
2. Prevent story telling related to the there and then.
3. Help members to confront others with care and respect.
4. Learn to give nonevaluative feedback.
5. Learn to risk by speaking from the first person. (p. 29)

Both of the above lists are only partial and could be modified depending on the group leader's style and philosophy, and on the type of group. For example, a group of adults molested as children would modify the process goals so the members could disclose some there-and-then information relative to their own experiences as victims of sexual abuse, because they may not have been able to verbalize their thoughts and feelings in the past. In any case, these goals provide general guidelines only, and the different experience and different process of each group call for flexibility in goals. As noted by Corey and Corey (1997), there are dozens of generic goals that can be applied to the group experience. Such goals always need to be selected based on the needs of those who constitute a particular group.

Goals for Specialized Groups

Specialized groups often have specific goals based on the issues of individual members of the groups. The goals for a weight loss group, for example, might be for members to identify individual reasons for why food has become such an important aspect of everyday life; to discuss nutrition, exercise, and motivation; to provide understanding and support for one another's efforts; and to learn to avoid using food to manage stress. The goals for a group of incest survivors might be for members to tell about incidences of sexual abuse; to learn that other members have similar feelings of hurt, shame, and anger; to develop trust; and to identify ways in which their earlier experiences affect their friendships and relationships with significant others. Goals for a men's group might include discussion of gender role expectations, transitions, overworking, or enhancement of self-esteem. Regardless of the specific purpose for which a number of individuals meet as a group, it is important that goals are thoroughly discussed and understood by every group member.

Goals Based on Theoretical Perspectives

As noted by Gibson and Mitchell (1995), the theoretical orientation of the group leader can be a primary influence on the establishment of group goals. The psychoanalytic, Adlerian, psychodramatic, existential, person-centered, Gestalt, transactional analysis, behavior therapy, rational-emotive behavior therapy, and reality therapy conceptual frames of reference all provide perspectives for the establishment of group goals. The following examples illustrate the point:

The Adlerian group leader may focus on:

- establishing a working relationship in which the leader and members are equal.
- aiding the members in exploring the personal goals, beliefs, feelings, and motives that are determining factors in the development of their lifestyle.
- helping members to enhance their involvement with others and to extend their social interest as it applies to self and others.

- aiding members in considering alternative lifestyles and assisting them in strengthening their commitment to change.

The Gestalt group leader may focus on:

- allowing members to find their own way in life and accept the responsibility that goes with this.
- aiding members in accepting all aspects of themselves and encouraging their sharing of hidden and self-disguised aspects of self.
- helping members to recognize the blocks/barriers that impede their growth.
- helping members recognize the splintered parts of self and work toward integrating those parts.

The person-centered group leader may focus on:

- establishing a facilitative climate within the group characterized by congruence, unconditional positive regard, and empathic understanding.
- providing an environment in which all group members perceive the constructs of safety and mutual trust.
- supporting members in finding their own way in life and accepting the responsibility that goes with this.
- refraining from giving advice and direction and allowing members to positively activate their organismic valuing process.

Chapter 4 of this book provides a more comprehensive overview of theoretical perspectives as related to group counseling.

Goals Developed by Individual Members

Group participants often need assistance in personalizing their reasons for wanting to be part of a group (Corey & Corey, 1997); often, their goals need to be refined and clarified. The goal of "wanting to get in touch with feelings," for example, might relate to feelings of loss, anger, or guilt. The member who says she is "having trouble with assertiveness" might be talking about the workplace, the home, or the responsibilities of parenting. "Having trouble with depression" could stem from difficult circumstances, a long-term approach to problem solving, or a chemically based, genetically linked, endogenous problem. It is important for group leaders to help individual members continuously analyze their reasons for participating in a group to ensure that personalized goals are stated and realized.

Types of Groups ～

Most textbooks for introduction to counseling courses begin the discussion of group work by attempting to make distinctions between group therapy, group counseling, and group guidance. In general, *group therapy* is described as being longer term, more remedially and therapeutically focused, and more likely to be facilitated by someone with doctoral-level preparation and a more "clinical" orientation. *Group counseling* is usually differentiated from group therapy by its focus on conscious problems, by the fact that it is not aimed at major personality changes, by an orientation toward short-term issues, and by the fact that it is not as concerned with the treatment of the more severe psychological and behavioral disorders. *Group guidance* is used to describe a classroom group in a K through 12 setting in which the leader presents information or conducts mental health education. In contrast to group therapy and group counseling, which generally involve no more than 8 to 10 participants, a group guidance experience could involve 20 to 40 group participants, lessening the opportunities for individual participation and facilitator observation and intervention.

For the purposes of this chapter, ASGW's definitions of the four group work specialty types are presented as a point of departure for classifying groups (Conyne et al., 1993). Good sources for additional reading on group "types" include Corey and Corey (1997), Dinkmeyer and Muro (1979), Gazda (1984), and Ohlsen (1977).

Task/Work Groups

The group worker who specializes in promoting the development and functioning of task and work groups seeks to support the members of such groups in the process of improving group function and performance. Task and work group specialists employ principles of group dynamics, organizational development, and team building to enhance group members' skills in group task accomplishment and group maintenance. The scope of practice for these group work specialists includes normally functioning individuals who are members of naturally occurring task or work groups operating within a specific organizational context.

Graduate course work for specialists in task and work groups should include at least one specialization course in organizational management and development. Ideally, course work should also be taken in the broad area of organizational psychology, management, and development to foster an awareness of organizational life and how task and work groups function within an organization. In addition, a task/work group specialist would benefit from developing skill in organizational assessment, training, program development, consultation, and program evaluation.

Clinical instruction for training specialists for working with task and work groups should include a minimum of 30 clock hours (45 clock hours recommended) of supervised practice in leading or co-leading a task/work group appropriate to the age and clientele of the group leader's specialty area(s) (e.g., school counseling, community counseling, mental health counseling).

Guidance/Psychoeducational Groups

The psychoeducational group specialist educates group participants in a particular area (e.g., how to cope with external threats, developmental transitions, or personal and interpersonal crises). Such participants may be informationally deficient in that area. The scope of practice of psychoeducational group leaders includes essentially normally functioning individuals who are "at risk" for, but currently unaffected by, an environmental threat (e.g., AIDS), who are approaching a developmental transition point (e.g., new parents), or who are in the midst of coping with a life crisis (e.g., the suicide of a loved one). The primary goal in psychoeducational group work is to prevent the future development of dysfunctional behaviors.

Course work for specialization in psychoeducational groups should include at least one specialization course that provides information about community psychology, health and wellness promotion, and program development and evaluation. Ideally, psychoeducational group specialists would also take courses in curriculum design, group training methods, and instructional techniques. Further, they should acquire knowledge about the topic areas in which they intend to work (e.g., AIDS prevention, substance abuse prevention, grief and loss, coping with transition and change, parent effectiveness training).

Clinical instruction for preparing to facilitate psychoeducational groups should include a minimum of 30 clock hours (45 clock hours recommended) of supervised practice in leading or co-leading a psychoeducational group appropriate to the age and clientele of the group leader's specialty area(s) (e.g., school counseling, community counseling, mental health counseling).

Counseling Groups

The group worker who specializes in group counseling focuses on assisting group participants to resolve the usual, yet often difficult, problems of living by stimulating interpersonal support and group problem solving. Group counselors support participants in developing their existing interpersonal problem-solving competencies so that they may become more able to handle future problems of a similar nature to those they are currently experiencing. The scope of practice for these group work specialists includes essentially normally functioning individuals with nonsevere career, educational, personal, interpersonal, social, or developmental concerns.

Graduate course work for specialists in group counseling should include multiple courses in human development, health promotion, and group counseling. Group counseling specialists should have in-depth knowledge in the broad areas of normal human development, problem identification, and treatment of normal personal and interpersonal problems of living.

Clinical instruction for preparing to facilitate counseling groups should include a minimum of 45 clock hours (60 clock hours recommended) of supervised practice in leading or co-leading a counseling group appropriate to the age and clientele of the group leader's specialty area(s) (e.g., community counseling, mental health counseling, school counseling).

Psychotherapy Groups

The specialist in group psychotherapy helps individual group members remediate in-depth psychological problems or reconstruct major personality dimensions. The group psychotherapist differs from specialists in task/work groups, psychoeducational groups, or counseling groups in that his or her scope of practice is focused on individuals with acute or chronic mental or emotional disorders characterized by marked distress, impairment in functioning, or both.

Graduate course work for training in group psychotherapy should include multiple courses in the development, assessment, and treatment of serious or chronic personal and interpersonal dysfunction. The group psychotherapist must develop in-depth knowledge in the broad areas of normal and abnormal human development, diagnosis, treatment of psychopathology, and group psychotherapy.

Clinical instruction for training specialists to work with psychotherapy groups should include a minimum of 45 clock hours (60 clock hours recommended) of supervised practice in leading or co-leading a psychotherapy group appropriate to the age and clientele of the group leader's specialty area(s) (e.g., mental health counseling, community counseling).

Other Models for Group Work

Various other distinctions are made between types of groups (Corey & Corey, 1997; Gibson & Mitchell, 1995). For example, *T-groups* help members develop self-awareness and sensitivity to others through the verbalization of feelings. *Encounter groups*, initiated by Carl Rogers, became known as "personal growth groups" because of their emphasis upon the individual personal development of each of their members (Gladding, 1991). Both T-groups and encounter groups are sometimes called *sensitivity groups*.

In J. L. Moreno's *psychodrama* groups, participants stage a production in which they sometimes play themselves and sometimes play the alter egos of others. Through acting out their issues and concerns and "processing" the experience afterward, members progress to higher levels of self-awareness and begin to exert better control over their emotions and behaviors.

Marathon groups, introduced in the 1960s by George Bach and Fred Stoller, are intense experiences lasting 24 hours, 48 hours, or even longer, and requiring that group members stay together for the duration of the experience. Because fatigue and intensity are aspects of the marathon, participants' defenses break down, truthfulness and openness increase, and personal growth can take place differently than in groups conducted once a week for an hour and a half. (Provisions are generally made for participants to receive individual or small-group follow-up counseling after participating in a marathon group.)

"Self-help" groups are widely utilized as adjunct support for individual or group counseling or therapy conducted by professionally prepared, licensed counselors and therapists. As noted by Gladding (1997), self-help groups take at least two forms: those that are organized by an established professional helping organization (e.g., Alcoholics Anonymous) and those that emerge spontaneously. These groups are composed of members who share something in common; they can be psychoeducational, therapeutic, or task focused. Self-help groups can be powerful catalysts in the process of helping people take charge of their lives. Some of these groups lack the advantage of having professional leaders but often compensate through the contribution of committed and experienced lay leaders.

Closed and *open groups* are subcategories for most groups. A closed group is characterized by having members who remain together until the group terminates. In an open group, new members are added during the life cycle of the group (Gruner, 1984).

Both the closed and open group models have advantages and disadvantages. Open-ended groups permit members to resolve problems and issues in their own time frame and then leave the group. New members may enter the groups as openings occur. Although new members coming in at various times may be viewed as adding stimulation to the group, the group as a whole may go through a process of regression, with accompanying fluctuations in cohesion and trust, when a new member is added. In contrast, closed groups offer stability of membership and facilitate cohesion and trust. Because all members of a group do not progress at the same rate, however, some group members might lose the advantage of being able to work hard and terminate in a manner consistent with their own ability to learn, resolve intrapersonal or interpersonal issues, and obtain closure based on an appropriate resolution (Gruner, 1984).

Composition of Groups～

The composition of a group influences many aspects of how the group functions (Waltman & Zimpfer, 1988; Yalom, 1985). Two general approaches to combining members of a group are the heterogeneous approach and the homogeneous approach.

Heterogeneous or Mixed-Gender Group Composition

Beasley and Childers (1985) discussed five fundamental assumptions for creating groups composed of both men and women:

1. This kind of group is a microcosm of society.
2. Self-defeating behavior can be identified and confronted more easily in a group approximating the composition of society.
3. The group focus is on the present rather than on the past.
4. Reality testing can and does occur.
5. The heterosexual group situation generates anxiety that produces change.

These assumptions are discussed in more detail in the sections that follow.

Social Microcosm   Creating a group environment representative of the world in which an individual interacts on a daily basis is said to maximize opportunities for learning and the realization of potential (Hansen, Warner, & Smith, 1980). However, not all group research supports the assumption that creating such a microcosm through heterogeneous grouping promotes personal growth for both women and men.

In some studies, women in a mixed-gender group, compared with those in all-female groups, have been seen to talk less, talk primarily to the men, share less personal information, and be less involved in topics (Carlock & Martin, 1977). Although some studies have indicated that men in heterogeneous groups are more personal and self-disclosing and initiate and receive more interaction than they do in all-male groups (Aries, 1976; Carlock & Martin, 1977; Reed, 1981), it will be interesting to see if these findings continue to be reported with the same frequency as researchers begin to study the group phenomenon created by Robert Bly and other proponents of the men's movement.

Confrontation of Self-Defeating Behavior   Based on the premise that a person's true self will emerge in a group reflecting society in general, this assumption pre- supposes that group members' dysfunctional behavior will become more clearly evi- dent in a heterogeneous group than in a homogeneous group. Once the behavior sur- faces, other group members, as well as the group leader, can confront the behavior and provide constructive feedback (Beasley & Childers, 1985). Some evidence sup- ports this assumption. A person's self-perception evolves from the feedback the per- son receives through the years on his or her interactions with both men and women, so a mixed-gender group would seem to be the best avenue for clarifying self-per- ception. But the evidence is not unanimously supportive. For example, women could risk negative feedback by revealing such characteristics as assertiveness, competi- tiveness, and independence in the group (Broverman, Broverman, Clarkson, Rosenkrantz, & Vogel, 1970). Further, the concern has been voiced that heteroge- neous groups may tend to reinforce stereotypical behavior for men and for women (Reed, 1981); group leaders should be alert to that possibility when facilitating a mixed-gender group.

Focus on the Present   Yalom (1985) maintained that a focus on the present aug- ments a group's potency and effectiveness. Such a focus aids the development of each group member's social microcosm and promotes feedback, self-disclosure, and the acquisition of social skills. Focusing on the present may be easier in heteroge- neous than homogeneous groups (Aries, 1973), a factor that should be considered when making decisions about group composition.

Reality Testing   In groups, participants can discuss new alternatives and test the reality of those alternatives by having other group members provide feedback. Reactions from both genders, in the context of a safe and well-facilitated group, may help a group member gain confidence and accept responsibility for behavior in a way that will transfer to heterosexual relationships outside the group (Beasley & Childers, 1985). However, if women's behaviors are circumscribed in a mixed-gen- der group, the group composition may limit women's communication and explo- ration of new options.

Generation of Gender-Based Anxiety   Much research shows that heterogeneous groups produce more anxiety in the members than do homogeneous groups (Aries, 1973; Carlock & Martin, 1977; Hansen et al., 1980; Melnick & Woods, 1976). Yalom (1985) contended that this anxiety is positive because change usually follows a period of anxiety and a state of ambiguity. This anxiety ideally propels members to participate in problem solving, in the consideration of new behaviors, and so on. Active participation and interest in self-enhancement are generally valued in the con- text of the group experience.

Homogeneous or Same-Gender Group Composition

A homogeneous group consists entirely of members of a given population or mem- bers who share a specific need, concern, or situation (Beasley & Childers, 1985). The cohesiveness theory underlies this approach to group composition and supports the idea that similarity of members can lead to a great deal of cohesion, openness, and exploration of issues.

All-Female Groups   Some feminist groups have excluded men from membership because of the perception that men tend to dominate the conversation and the decision-making process (Bardwick, 1971). When women are in the presence of men in a group, they tend to withdraw, become passive, defer to more dominant men, and assume other patterns of communication that are different from those seen in all-female groups (Aries, 1973; Carlock & Martin, 1977).

According to some group leaders (Halas, 1973), groups composed solely of women are more conducive to change for women than are mixed-gender groups. In summarizing the research on women's consciousness groups, Kravetz (1980) reported the following consistent outcomes:

- Increased self-awareness, self-respect, and self-esteem.
- Greater awareness of the effects of traditional sex roles and sexism.
- More awareness of a commonality with other women.
- Improved relationships and a sense of solidarity with other women.
- Positive changes in interpersonal relationships and roles.
- Participation in work and community activities to change the options and opportunities of women.

All-Male Groups   Washington (1982) suggested that men's groups provide opportunities for members to share the stress and anger they experience, to discuss concerns and insecurities, and to develop the confidence they need to change behaviors. Research such as that done by Twentyman and McFall (1975) and MacDonald, Lindquist, Kramer, McGrath, and Rhyne (1975) has indicated that all-male groups helped members improve and rehearse behaviors and confront personal issues, which resulted in improving their relationships with women. Some research (Aries, 1973; Reed, 1981) has suggested that men's self-disclosures in all-male groups frequently take the form of storytelling and metaphors with frequent references to competition, self-aggrandizement, and aggression.

Therapeutic Factors in Groups～

A therapeutic factor in a group is "an element occurring in group therapy that contributes to improvement in a patient's condition and is a function of the actions of a group therapist, the patient, or fellow group members" (Bloch, 1986, p. 679). This definition is important because it helps distinguish between therapeutic factors and necessary conditions for change in a group as well as group interventions or techniques. An example of a condition for change is the presence of a group leader and group members to listen and provide feedback. "Making the rounds" is an example of a Gestalt intervention or technique that a group leader might employ. Conditions and interventions or techniques increase the impact of therapeutic factors in groups.

As George and Dustin (1988) noted, Corsini and Rosenberg (1955) published the first major work that presented a unifying paradigm of factors considered therapeutic by group leaders from a variety of theoretical perspectives. After clustering statements reflecting therapeutic factors, they formed the following nine-category classification system:

1. Acceptance: a sense of belonging.
2. Altruism: a sense of being helpful to others.
3. Universalization: the realization that one is not unique in one's problems.
4. Intellectualization: the process of acquiring knowledge about oneself.
5. Reality testing: recognition of the reality of issues such as defenses and family conflicts.
6. Transference: a strong attachment either to therapist or to co-members.
7. Interaction: relating within the group that brings benefits.
8. Spectator therapy: gaining from the observation and imitation of fellow members.
9. Ventilation: the release of feelings and expression of previously repressed ideas.

In 1957, Hill interviewed 19 group leaders in an attempt to further refine the classification of therapeutic elements in groups. He proposed the six elements of catharsis, feelings of belongingness, spectator therapy, insights, peer agency (universality), and socialization. Berzon, Pious, and Farson (1963) used group members rather than group leaders as a source of information about therapeutic factors. Their classification included:

1. Becoming more aware of emotional dynamics.
2. Recognizing similarity with others.
3. Feeling positive regard, acceptance, sympathy for others.
4. Seeing self as seen by others.
5. Expressing self congruently, articulately, or assertively in the group.
6. Witnessing honesty, courage, openness, or expressions of emotionality in others.
7. Feeling warmth and closeness in the group.
8. Feeling responded to by others.
9. Feeling warmth and closeness generally in the group.
10. Ventilating emotions.

A very different set of therapeutic factors connected with group experiences was proposed by Ohlsen (1977). His list differs from earlier proposals in that it emphasizes group members' attitudes about the group experience. Ohlsen's paradigm includes 14 elements, which he labeled "therapeutic forces":

1. Attractiveness of the group.
2. Acceptance by the group.
3. Clear expectations.
4. Sense of belonging.
5. Security within the group.

6. Client readiness.
7. Client commitment.
8. Client participation.
9. Client acceptance of responsibility.
10. Congruence.
11. Feedback.
12. Openness.
13. Therapeutic tension.
14. Therapeutic norms.

In what is now considered a landmark classification of "curative factors," Yalom (1970, 1975, 1985) proposed a list of therapeutic elements based on research he and his colleagues conducted:

1. Instillation of hope: receiving reassurance that the group experience will be constructive and helpful.
2. Universality: developing an awareness that what seems to be a unique problem may be similar to the experience of another member of the group.
3. Imparting of information: learning about mental health and mental illness via group discussion.
4. Altruism: sharing with others and being willing to reach out.
5. The corrective recapitulation of the primary family group: reliving family-of-origin conflicts and resolving them through the group.
6. Development of socializing techniques: learning social skills.
7. Imitative behavior: imitating positive behaviors modeled by other group members.
8. Interpersonal learning: developing new insights and correcting past interpretations.
9. Group cohesiveness: developing bonds of trust, support, and caring.
10. Catharsis: sharing feelings and experiences.
11. Existential factors: accepting responsibility for one's life, including decisions, meaning making, and spiritual dimensions.

These listings represent only a few of the many possibilities for viewing the therapeutic elements of a positive group experience. Jacobs, Harvill, and Masson (1988) pointed out that a number of factors can work for or against a group. Size, session length, the setting, member composition, level of goodwill, level of commitment, level of trust, members' attitudes toward one another, members' attitudes toward the leader, leader's attitude toward members, interaction pattern of members and leader, and stage of the group were all cited and identified as possible contributors to a positive or negative group experience for members. Gladding (1991) stressed the importance of identification with the groups' structure, norms, power roles, group interaction, length of group, attitude, here-and-now variables, and racial and gender issues in his discussion of factors influencing group dynamics. Marianne Schneider Corey and Gerald Corey (1997) discussed therapeutic factors that operate in groups. Their discussion of this topic focused on self-disclosure, confrontation, feedback, cohesion and universality, hope, willingness to risk and trust, caring and acceptance, power, catharsis, the cognitive component, commitment to change, freedom to experiment, and humor. It is our belief that the beginning group worker should spend time reading these and other resources on therapeutic factors in groups because of the importance of this aspect of working with groups.

Personal Characteristics of Effective Group Leaders ~

Many professionals in the field have described the personal traits and characteristics of effective group leaders (Corey & Corey, 1997; Dinkmeyer & Muro, 1979; Kottler, 1983). As expressed by Gerald Corey (1985):

> It is my belief that group leaders can acquire extensive theoretical and practical knowledge of group dynamics and be skilled in diagnostic and technical procedures yet be ineffective in stimulating growth and change in the members of their groups. Leaders bring to every group their personal qualities, values, and life experiences. In order to promote growth in the members' lives, leaders need to live growth-oriented lives themselves. In order to foster honest self-investigation in others, leaders need to have the courage to engage in self-appraisal themselves. In order to inspire others to break away from deadening ways of being, leaders need to be willing to seek new experiences themselves. In short, the most effective group direction is found in the kind of life the group members see the leader demonstrating and not in the words they hear the leader saying. (p. 39)

Like Corey, we believe that the group leader must possess certain characteristics to be effective. Arbuckle (1975), Carkhuff and Berenson (1977), Jourard (1971), Truax and Carkhuff (1967), and Yalom (1975) have also presented their views on this topic. Corey and Corey's (1997) orientation is summarized here as a starting point for the beginning group work specialist.

Presence

The group leader's capacity to be emotionally present as group members share their experience is important. Leaders who are in touch with their own life experiences and associated emotions are usually better able to communicate empathy and understanding because they can relate to similar circumstances or emotions. Group leaders must not lose perspective by being overly focused on their own reactions, but they must allow themselves to be connected with the experience of group members in such a way that they can communicate compassion and concern and still facilitate constructive personal growth.

Personal Power

Personal power is derived from a sense of self-confidence and a realization of the group leader's influence on a group. Personal power channeled in a way that enhances the ability of each group member to identify and build upon his or her strengths, overcome problems, and cope more effectively with stressors is both essential and curative. Leaders who have the most power are acceptant of their own strengths and weaknesses and do not expend energy attempting to prevent others from seeing them as they are.

Courage

Group leaders have to be courageous. They take risks when they express their reactions to aspects of group process, confront members, share life experiences, act on a combination of intuition and observation, and direct group movement and discussion. These risks are the same risks group members are expected to take; the leader's role-modeling, in this regard, can help make a group more productive and better able to communicate and bond.

Self-Awareness

Serving in any kind of a counseling role would be difficult without a highly developed sense of self-awareness. Personal needs, defenses, apprehensions, relationship conflicts, and unresolved issues of any kind all come into play in the process of facilitating a group. These can enhance or detract from one's ability to lead the group, depending upon the group leader's level of awareness and the extent to which these factors make the leader's role more difficult. Many counselor education departments require graduate students to obtain personal counseling outside the department, to resolve "unfinished business," so personal issues do not impede their ability to serve constructively in a counseling role.

Belief in Group Process

Group leaders must be positive about the healing capacity of groups and must believe in the benefits of the group experience. If they are unsure, tentative, or unenthusiastic about the healing capacity of the group experience, the same tenor will develop among group members. Although the outcome of a group experience does not totally depend on its leader, the leader does convey messages, both verbally and nonverbally, that impact the overall benefit of the experience.

Inventiveness

Group leaders who can be spontaneous about their approach to a group can often catalyze better communication, insight, and personal growth than those who rely on structured interventions and techniques. Creative leaders usually accept those who are different from themselves and are flexible about approaching members and groups in ways that seem congruent with the particular group. In addition, a certain amount of creativity and spontaneity is necessary to cope with the unexpected. In a group situation the leader is continuously presented with comments, problems, and reactions that cannot be anticipated before a given session.

Stamina and Energy

Unlike an individual counseling session, during which the counselor listens to and interacts with one client, the group experience requires the leader to "track," remember, and diagnose several clients simultaneously. This set of circumstances requires more alertness, observation, responsiveness, proactivity, and energy. Therefore, a group leader should not overschedule groups. Many leaders prefer the co-facilitation model, in which the co-facilitator or co-leader assumes part of the responsibility for group process and observation.

Goodwill and Caring

Group leaders must place the welfare of group members first. It is essential that they make sure members are achieving the goals that have been established for the group experience. Caring about those in a group is also vital to successful outcomes. If, for some reason, a group leader has difficulty in this regard, he or she must evaluate what is blocking this capacity and what steps can be taken to ensure that member needs will be met.

Openness

Group leaders must be open with and about themselves, open to experiences and lifestyles different from their own, and open to how the group is affecting them. Openness does not mean that the leader should reveal every aspect of his or her personal life; it can mean being open enough to give members an understanding of who he or she is as a person. The leader's willingness to be open helps promote a corresponding spirit of openness and willingness to communicate among group members.

Awareness of One's Own Culture and That of Group Members

It is important that the group leader be aware of diversity issues. They must understand that just as their culture influences their worldview and decision making, the same is true of the culture of each member of a given group. Diversity encompasses more than ethnic influences; it encompasses age, gender, sexual orientation, disability, and numerous other factors. Effective group leaders are sensitive to aspects of diversity and respect the differences individual members of a group bring to group experiences.

Nondefensiveness in Coping With Attacks

Members of a group often test the leader by being critical or confrontational with him or her. Such attacks can occur if the leader has made a mistake or has been insensitive; they can also occur if a member is jealous, wishes to control, or is projecting feelings about someone else to the leader. Regardless of the reason for an attack, it is important for the leader to remain nondefensive and explore the reasons for such member behavior. To do so, the leader must have a strong sense of ego integrity and confidence. To become angry or to refuse to explore reasons for the "attack" role-models behavior that can interfere with openness, trust, and positive outcomes.

Sense of Humor

Humor can be crucial to the success of a group. Laughter can help release tension and help members retain perspective on their problems. As long as humor does not become a roadblock to doing the therapeutic work that needs to be accomplished, it can be a tremendous asset to a group.

Personal Dedication and Commitment

To be effective, the group leader must be dedicated to the value of group process and be committed to continuing to develop his or her leadership skills. If the group leader has the belief that group membership can empower and benefit participants, his or her enthusiasm and energy will come through to participants and contribute to some of the therapeutic elements of group work discussed earlier in this chapter.

Myths Connected With Group Work∼

Counselors who are group leaders are usually quite enthusiastic about the benefits to clients who participate in a small-group experience. A competently facilitated group experience can engender personal growth (Capuzzi & Gross, 1997) that affects clients well into the future. However, group work, like other forms of therapeutic assistance (e.g., individual or family therapy), can be for better or for worse (Carkhuff, 1969). Many group leaders adhere to a belief system that can be challenged by empirical facts. The following myths connected with group work are given quite a bit of attention here, with the hope that group leaders will not base their practices on a belief system that is not supported by research (Anderson, 1985; Capuzzi & Gross, 1997).

Myth #1: Everyone Benefits From Group Experience

Groups do provide benefits. Research on the psychosocial outcomes of groups demonstrates that groups are a powerful modality for learning, the results of which can be used outside of the group experience itself (Bednar & Lawlis, 1971; Gazda & Peters, 1975; Parloff & Dies, 1978). At times, however, membership in a group can be detrimental. Some research shows that 1 out of every 10 group members can be hurt by the experience (Lieberman, Yalom, & Miles, 1973).

The research findings that seem to relate most to individuals who are harmed by group experience suggest two important principles: (a) those group members who have the greatest potential to be hurt by the experience have unrealistic expectations, and (b) these expectations seem to be reinforced by leaders who coerce the group members to meet them (DeJulio, Bentley, & Cockayne, 1979; Lieberman et al., 1973; Stava & Bednar, 1979). To prevent harm, members' expectations for the group have to be realistic, and the leader must maintain a reasonable perspective.

Myth #2: Groups Can Be Composed in a Way That Assures Success

The fact is that we do not know enough about how to compose groups via the pre-group screening interview. In general, objective criteria (age, gender, socioeconomic status, presenting problem, and so forth) can be applied to keep groups homogeneous in some respects, but behavioral characteristics should be selected on a heterogeneous basis (Bertcher & Maple, 1979). The most consistent finding is that groups should be composed so that each member is compatible with at least one other member (Stava & Bednar, 1979). This seems to prevent the evolution of neglected isolates or scapegoats in a group. The essence of group process in terms of benefit to members and effective outcomes is perceived mutual aid (helping others, a feeling of belonging, interpersonal learning, instillation of hope, and so on) (Butler & Fuhriman, 1980; Long & Cope, 1980; Yalom, 1975).

Myth #3: The Group Revolves Around the Leader's Charisma

Although leaders do influence groups tremendously, two general findings in the research on groups should be noted. First, the group, independent of the leader, has an impact on outcomes. Second, the most effective group leaders are those who help the group develop so that members are primary sources of help to one another (Ashkenas & Tandon, 1979).

As noted by Anderson (1985), research on leadership styles has identified four leader functions that facilitate the group's functioning:

(1) *Providing:* This is the provider role of relationship and climate-setting through such skills as support, affection, praise, protection, warmth, acceptance, genuineness, and concern.

(2) *Processing:* This is the processor role of illuminating the meaning of the process through such skills as explaining, clarifying, interpreting, and providing a cognitive framework for change, or translating feelings and experiences into ideas.

(3) *Catalyzing:* This is the catalyst role of stimulating interaction and emotional expression through such skills as reaching for feelings, challenging, confronting, and suggesting; using program activities such as structured experiences; and modeling.

(4) *Directing:* This is the director role through such skills as setting limits, roles, norms, and goals; managing time; pacing; stopping; interceding; and suggesting procedures. (p. 272)

Providing and processing seem to have a linear relationship to outcomes: The higher the providing (or caring) and the higher the processing (or clarifying), the higher the positive outcomes. Catalyzing and directing have a curvilinear relationship to outcomes. Too much or too little catalyzing or directing results in lower positive outcomes (Lieberman et al., 1973).

Myth #4: Leaders Can Direct Groups Through Structured Exercises or Experiences

Structured exercises create early cohesion (Levin & Kurtz, 1974; Lieberman et al., 1973); they help to bring about the early expression of positive and negative feelings. At the same time, they restrict members from dealing with such group themes as affection, closeness, distance, trust, mistrust, genuineness, and lack of genuineness. All of these areas form the basis for group process and should not be hampered by too much structure. The best principle around which to plan and use structured exercises to get groups started and to keep them going can best be stated as "Overplan and underuse."

Myth #5: Therapeutic Change in Groups Comes About Through Here-and-Now Experiences

Much of the research on groups indicates that corrective emotional experiences in the here-and-now of the group increase the intensity of the members' experience (Levine, 1971; Lieberman et al., 1973; Snortum & Myers, 1971; Zimpfer, 1967). The intensity of emotional experiences, however, does not seem to be related to outcomes. Higher level outcomes are achieved by group members who develop insight or cognitive understanding of emotional experiences in the group and can transfer that understanding into their lives outside the group. The Gestaltists' influence on groups in the 1960s and 1970s (Perls, 1969) suggested that group members should "lose their mind and come to their senses" and "stay with the here and now." Research, however, suggests that members "use their mind and their senses" and "focus on the there and then as well as the here and now."

Myth #6: Major Member Learning in Groups Is Derived From Self-Disclosure and Feedback

Most of the learning of members in a group is assumed to come from self-disclosure made in exchange for feedback (Jacobs, 1974). To a large extent, this statement is a myth. Self-disclosure and feedback per se make little difference in outcome (Anchor, 1979; Bean & Houston, 1978). Rather, the use of self-disclosure and feedback seems to make the difference (Martin & Jacobs, 1980). Self-disclosure and feedback seem useful only when deeply personal sharing is understood and appreciated and the feedback is accurate (Berzon et al., 1963; Frank & Ascher, 1951, Goldstein, Bednar, & Yanell, 1979). The actual benefit of self-disclosure and feedback relates to how these processes generate empathy among group members. Empathy, or the experience of being understood by other members, is what catalyzes personal growth and understanding in the context of a group.

Myth #7: A Leader Does Not Have to Understand Group Process and Group Dynamics

In all groups, there is a natural evolution and unfolding of processes and dynamics. Anderson (1979) labeled these processes and dynamics as trust, autonomy, closeness, interdependence, and termination (TACIT). Tuckman (1965) suggested the more dramatic terminology of forming, storming, norming, performing, and adjourning. Chapter 2 of this book suggests four stages in the evolution of a group: the definitive stage, the personal involvement stage, the group involvement stage, and the enhancement and closure stage. Two reviews covering more than 200 studies of group dynamics and group process (Cohen & Smith, 1976; La Coursiere, 1980) revealed remarkably similar patterns (despite differences in the terms chosen as descriptors) in the evolution of group processes. Group leaders must understand group processes and dynamics to do a competent job of enhancing benefits from group participation.

Myth #8: Changes in Group Participants Are Not Maintained

Groups can be powerful! Members can maintain changes for as long as 6 months to a year after a group has disbanded, even when the group met for only three or four months (Lieberman et al., 1973). The positive effects of having participated in a group can be subtle but pervasive. For example, graduate students at Portland State University who took part in a 10-week off-campus personal growth group focusing on art therapy reported that skills they learned in the group, such as the need for creativity in their lives, relaxation techniques, insight into personal family dynamics, and ways of working with daily stress, continued to be relevant and useful a year later.

Myth #9: A Group Is a Place to Get Emotionally High

As noted by Corey (1985), feeling good after a group session is a positive outcome, but it is not the main reason for being in a group. Some group members have periods of depression after their group has disbanded because they don't find, on a daily basis, the kind of support they had received from members of the group. Group members should be prepared for this possibility and assisted in their ability to obtain support, when appropriate, from those around them.

Myth #10: A Group's Purpose Is to Make Members Close to Every Other Member

Although genuine feelings of intimacy and cohesiveness develop in effective groups, intimacy is the by-product and not the central purpose of the group. Intimacy develops as individual members risk self-disclosure and problem solving and other group members reach out in constructive ways (Corey & Corey, 1997).

Myth #11: Group Participation Results in Brainwashing

Professional groups do not indoctrinate members with a particular philosophy of life or a set of rules about how each member "should be." If this does occur in a group, it is truly a breach of professional ethics and an abuse of the group. Group participation should encourage members to look within themselves for answers and to become as self-directed as possible (Corey & Corey, 1997).

Myth #12: To Benefit From a Group, a Member Has to Be Dysfunctional

Group counseling is as appropriate with individuals who are functioning relatively well and who want to enhance their capabilities as it is for those who are having difficulty with certain aspects of their lives. Groups are not for dysfunctional people only (Corey & Corey, 1997).

Summary〜

Group counseling has its roots in the early 1900s, when it was applied in medical settings and with children, adults, and families. The first "laboratory" group, or T-group, emerged in 1947, and groups later branched out to university and other settings. Interest in group work has increased dramatically over time, illustrated by the recent flood of self-help groups led by either professionals or lay people.

Among the goals for groups are to facilitate the release of feelings, to strengthen members' self-esteem, to help members face and resolve their problems, to help them learn how to recognize and solve interpersonal and intrapersonal conflicts, and to facilitate their maintenance of their therapeutic gains. There are a number of ways in which group goals can be addressed: (a) general goals for groups, (b) goals for specialized groups, (c) goals based on theoretical perspectives, and (d) goals developed by individual members.

Distinctions can be made between group therapy (more likely to be longer term and have a therapeutic emphasis), group counseling (having a focus on conscious problems and an orientation toward short-term issues), and group guidance (in which the leader presents information or conducts mental health education to a larger group). Specialized types of group experiences include sensitivity groups, psychodrama groups, marathon groups, and task groups, among others. Based on ASGW's definitions, groups can be classified into four primary categories: task/work groups, guidance/psychoeducational groups, counseling groups, and psychotherapy groups. All of these types of groups can be either heterogeneous (mixed gender) or homogeneous (same gender) and can be closed (members stay together until the group is terminated) or open (new members are added as others leave).

Therapeutic factors in a group include acceptance, altruism, universalization, intellectualization, reality testing, transference, interaction, spectator therapy, and ventilation. Translated into leader qualities, these factors entail presence, personal power, courage, self-awareness, belief in group process, inventiveness, stamina and energy, goodwill and caring, openness, becoming aware of one's own culture and that of group members, nondefensiveness in coping with attacks, sense of humor, and personal dedication and commitment. Numerous myths commonly connected to group work, by group leaders and others, can actually detract from group effectiveness. Among these misconceptions are that everyone benefits from group experience, groups always have advantageous outcomes, the group revolves around the leader's charisma, group members should be limited to discussion of here-and-now experiences, and dysfunctional people are the only ones who can benefit from groups. Groups can be either powerful and growth enhancing or stifling and hindering. The more a leader is aware of the goals, purposes, and dynamics of groups, the better equipped he or she will be to provide an optimal experience for group members.

References ~

Anchor, K. N. (1979). High- and low-risk self-disclosure in group psychotherapy. *Small Group Behavior, 10,* 279–283.

Anderson, J. D. (1979). Social work with groups in the generic base of social work practice. *Social Work With Groups, 2,* 281–293.

Anderson, J. D. (1985). Working with groups: Little known facts that challenge well-known myths. *Small Group Behavior, 16,* 267–283.

Arbuckle, D. (1975). *Counseling and psychotherapy: An existential-humanistic view.* Boston: Allyn & Bacon.

Aries, E. J. (1973). Interaction patterns and themes of male, female and mixed groups. *Dissertation Abstracts International, 35,* 3084. (University Microfilms No. 74–27, 772)

Aries, E. J. (1976). Interactional patterns and themes of male, female and mixed groups. *Small Group Behavior, 7,* 718.

Ashkenas, R., & Tandon, R. (1979). Eclectic approach to small group facilitation. *Small Group Behavior, 10,* 224–241.

Association for Specialists in Group Work. (1989). *Ethical guidelines for group counselors.* Alexandria, VA: Author.

Association for Specialists in Group Work. (1991). *Professional standards for the training of group workers* (rev. ed.). Alexandria, VA: Author.

Bardwick, J. M. (1971). *Psychology of women.* New York: Harper & Row.

Bean, B. W., & Houston, B. K. (1978). Self-concept and self-disclosure in encounter groups. *Small Group Behavior, 9,* 549–554.

Beasley, L., & Childers, J. H., Jr. (1985). Group counseling for heterosexual, interpersonal skills: Mixed or same-sex group composition. *Journal for Specialists in Group Work, 10*(4), 192–197.

Bednar, R., & Lawlis, G. (1971). Empirical research in group psychotherapy. In S. L. Garfield & A. E. Bergin (Eds.), *Handbook of psychotherapy and behavior change* (2nd ed., pp. 420–439). New York: Wiley.

Bertcher, H. J., & Maple, F. F. (1979). *Creating groups.* Beverly Hills, CA: Sage Publications.

Berzon, B., Pious, C., & Farson, R. (1963). The therapeutic event in group psychotherapy: A study of subjective reports by group members. *Journal of Individual Psychology, 19,* 204–212.

Bloch, S. (1986). Therapeutic factors in group psychotherapy. In A. J. Frances & R. E. Hales (Eds.), *Annual review* (Vol. 5, pp. 678–698). Washington, DC: American Psychiatric Press.

Bradford, L. P., Gibb, J. R., & Benne, K. D. (Eds.). (1964). *T-group theory and laboratory method: Innovation in re-education.* New York: Wiley.

Broverman, I. K., Broverman, D. M., Clarkson, F. E., Rosenkrantz, P., & Vogel, S. R. (1970). Sex role stereotypes and clinical judgments of mental health. *Journal of Consulting Psychology, 34,* 17.

Butler, T., & Fuhriman, A. (1980). Patient perspective on the curative process: A comparison of day treatment and outpatient psychotherapy groups. *Small Group Behavior, 11,* 371–388.

Capuzzi, D., & Gross, D. R. (1997). *Introduction to the counseling profession* (2nd ed.). Boston: Allyn & Bacon.

Carkhuff, R. R. (1969). *Helping and human relations: A primer for lay and professional helpers: Vol. 2. Practice and research.* New York: Holt, Rinehart & Winston.

Carkhuff, R. R., & Berenson, B. G. (1977). *Beyond counseling and therapy* (2nd ed.). New York: Holt, Rinehart & Winston.

Carlock, C. J., & Martin, P. Y. (1977). Sex composition and the intensive group experience. *Journal of the National Association of Social Workers, 22,* 27–32.

Carroll, M. R., & Wiggins, J. (1990). *Elements of group counseling: Back to the basics.* Denver: Love Publishing.

Carroll, M. R., & Wiggins, J. (1997). *Elements of group counseling: Back to the basics* (2nd ed.). Denver: Love Publishing.

Cohen, A. M., & Smith, D. R. (1976). *The critical incident in growth groups: Theory and techniques.* La Jolla, CA: University Associates.

Conyne, R. K., Wilson, F. R., Kline, W. B., Morran, D. K., & Ward, D. E. (1993). Training group workers: Implications of the new ASGW training standards for training and practice. *Journal for Specialists in Group Work, 18,* 11–23.

Corey, G. (1985). *Theory and practice of group counseling* (2nd ed.). Pacific Grove, CA: Brooks/Cole.

Corey, M. S., & Corey, G. (1997). *Groups: Process and practice* (5th ed.). Pacific Grove, CA: Brooks/Cole.

Corey, G., Corey, M. S., Callahan, P. J., & Russell, J. M. (1982). *Group techniques.* Pacific Grove, CA: Brooks/Cole.

Corsini, R., & Rosenberg, B. (1955). Mechanisms of group psychotherapy: Processes and dynamics. *Journal of Abnormal & Social Psychology, 51,* 406–411.

Council for the Accreditation of Counseling and Related Educational Programs. (1994). *Accreditation procedures manual and application.* Alexandria, VA: Author.

DeJulio, S. J., Bentley, J., & Cockayne, T. (1979). Pregroup norm setting: Effects on encounter group interaction. *Small Group Behavior, 10,* 368–388.

Dinkmeyer, D. C., & Muro, J. J. (1979). *Group counseling: Theory and practice* (2nd ed.). Itasca, IL: Peacock.

Dreikurs, R. (1932). Early experiments with group psychotherapy. *American Journal of Psychotherapy, 13,* 882–891.

Frank, J. (1957). Some determinants, manifestations, and efforts of cohesiveness in therapy groups. *International Journal of Group Psychotherapy, 7,* 53–63.

Frank, J., & Ascher, E. (1951). The corrective emotional experience in group therapy. *American Journal of Psychiatry, 108,* 126–131.

Gazda, G. (1984). *Group counseling* (3rd ed.). Dubuque, IA: Wm. C. Brown.

Gazda, G. M. (1985). Group counseling and therapy: A perspective on the future. *Journal for Specialists in Group Work, 10*(2), 74–76.

Gazda, G. M., & Peters, R. W. (1975). An analysis of research in group psychotherapy, group counseling and human relations training. In G. M. Gazda (Ed.), *Basic approaches to group psychotherapy and group counseling* (pp. 38–54). Springfield, IL: Charles C Thomas.

Geller, J. J. (1950). Proposed plan for institutionalized group psychotherapy. *Psychiatric Quarterly Supplement, 24,* 270–277.

George, R. L., & Dustin, D. (1988). *Group counseling: Theory and practice.* Englewood Cliffs, NJ: Prentice-Hall.

Gibson, R. L., & Mitchell, M. M. (1995). *Introduction to counseling and guidance* (4th ed.). Columbus, OH: Merrill.

Gladding, S. T. (1991). *Group work: A counseling specialty.* Columbus, OH: Merrill.

Gladding, S. T. (1997). *Community and agency counseling.* Columbus, OH: Merrill.

Goldstein, M. J., Bednar, R. L., & Yanell, B. (1979). Personal risk associated with self-disclosure, interpersonal feedback, and group confrontation in group psychotherapy. *Small Group Behavior, 9,* 579–587.

Gruner, L. (1984). Membership composition of open and closed groups. *Small Group Behavior, 15,* 222–232.

Halas, C. (1973). All-women's groups: A view from inside. *Personnel & Guidance Journal, 52,* 91–95.

Hansen, J. C., Warner, R. W., & Smith, E. J. (1980). *Group counseling: Theory and process* (2nd ed.). Chicago: Rand McNally.

Hill, W. F. (1957). Analysis of interviews of group therapists' papers. *Provo Papers, 1,* 1.

Jacobs, A. (1974). The use of feedback in groups. In A. Jacobs & W. W. Spradline (Eds.), *The group as an agent of change* (pp. 31–49). New York: Behavioral Publications.

Jacobs, E. E., Harvill, R. L., & Masson, R. L. (1988). *Group counseling: Strategies and skills.* Pacific Grove, CA: Brooks/Cole.

Janis, I. L. (1972). *Victims of group think: A psychological study of foreign-policy decisions and fiascos.* Boston: Houghton Mifflin.

Jourard, S. (1971). *The transparent self* (rev. ed.). New York: Van Nostrand Reinhold.

Kelman, H. C. (1963). The role of the group in the induction of therapeutic change. *Journal of Group Psychotherapy, 13,* 399–432.

Klein, E. B. (1985). Group work: 1985 and 2001 [Special issue]. *Journal for Specialists in Group Work, 10*(2), 108–111.

Kottler, J. A. (1983). *Pragmatic group leadership.* Pacific Grove, CA: Brooks/Cole.

Kravetz, D. (1980). Consciousness-raising and self-help. In A. M. Brodsky & R. Hare-Mustin (Eds.), *Women and psychotherapy* (pp. 267–281). New York: Guilford.

La Coursiere, R. (1980). *The life-cycle of groups: Group development stage theory.* New York: Human Sciences.

Levin, E. M., & Kurtz, R. P. (1974). Participant perceptions following structured and nonstructured human relations training. *Journal of Counseling Psychology, 21,* 514–532.

Levine, N. (1971). Emotional factors in group development. *Human Relations, 24,* 65–89.

Lieberman, M. A., Yalom, I. D., & Miles, M. B. (1973). *Encounter groups: First facts.* New York: Basic Books.

Long, L. D., & Cope, C. S. (1980). Curative factors in a male felony offender group. *Small Group Behavior, 11,* 389–398.

MacDonald, M. L., Lindquist, C. V., Kramer, J. A., McGrath, R. A., & Rhyne, L. D. (1975). Social skills training: Behavior rehearsal in groups and dating skills. *Journal of Counseling Psychology, 22,* 224–230.

Martin, L., & Jacobs, M. (1980). Structured feedback delivered in small groups. *Small Group Behavior, 1,* 88–107.

Melnick, J., & Woods, M. (1976). Analysis of group composition research and theory for psychotherapeutic and group oriented groups. *Journal of Applied Behavioral Science, 12,* 493–512.

Ohlsen, M. M. (1977). *Group counseling* (2nd ed.). New York: Holt, Rinehart & Winston.

Parloff, M. B., & Dies, R. R. (1978). Group therapy outcome instrument: Guidelines for conducting research. *Small Group Behavior, 9,* 243–286.

Perls, F. (1969). *Gestalt therapy verbatim.* New York: Bantam.

Reed, B. G. (1981). Gender issues in training group leaders. *Journal for Specialists in Group Work, 6,* 161–170.

Rowe, W., & Winborn, B. B. (1973). What people fear about group work: An analysis of 36 selected critical articles. *Educational Technology, 13*(1), 53–57.

Scheidlinger, S. (1994). An overview of nine decades of group psychotherapy. *Hospital and Community Psychiatry, 45*(3), 217–225.

Schmuck, R. A., & Schmuck, P. A. (1997). *Group process in the classroom* (7th ed.). Madison, WI: Brown & Benchmark.

Shapiro, J. L., & Bernadett-Shapiro, S. (1985). Group work to 2001: Hal or haven (from isolation)? [Special issue]. *Journal for Specialists in Group Work, 10*(2), 83–87.

Slavson, S. R., & Schiffer, M. (1975). *Group psychotherapy for children: A textbook.* New York: International Universities Press.

Sleek, S. (1995, July). Group therapy: Tapping the power of teamwork. *APA Monitor, 26*(1), 38–39.

Snortum, J. R., & Myers, H. F. (1971). Intensity of T-group relations as function of interaction. *International Journal of Group Psychotherapy, 21,* 190–201.

Stava, L. J., & Bednar, R. L. (1979). Process and outcome in encounter groups: The effect of group composition. *Small Group Behaviour, 10,* 200–213.

Truax, C. B., & Carkhuff, R. R. (1967). *Toward effective counseling and psychotherapy: Training and practice.* Chicago: Aldine.

Tuckman, B. W. (1965). Developmental sequences in small groups. *Psychological Bulletin, 63,* 384–389.

Twentyman, C. J., & McFall, R. M. (1975). Behavioral training of social skills in shy males. *Journal of Counseling & Clinical Psychology, 43,* 384–395.

Waltman, D. E., & Zimpfer, D. G. (1988). Composition, structure and duration of treatment: Interacting variables in counseling groups. *Small Group Behavior, 19*(2), 171–184.

Washington, D. S. (1982). Challenging men in groups. *Journal for Specialists in Group Work, 7,* 132–136.

Yalom, I. D. (1970). *The theory and practice of group psychotherapy.* New York: Basic Books.

Yalom, I. D. (1975). *The theory and practice of group psychotherapy* (2nd ed.). New York: Basic Books.

Yalom, I. D. (1985). *The theory and practice of group psychotherapy* (3rd ed.). New York: Basic Books.

Zimpfer, D. G. (1967). Expression of feelings in group counseling. *Personnel & Guidance Journal, 45,* 703–708.

2

Group Counseling:
Stages and Issues

Douglas R. Gross and David Capuzzi

As George left the group counseling classroom that evening, he could not help but think of all of the issues the class had been discussing during the past few weeks. He would finish his program within the next year, and he knew that the expectations of any position he might take would require both group and individual counseling. He felt comfortable with his individual skills, and his practicum experience had substantiated his ability in this domain. His current concern centered on his ability to work with groups. This was his second class in groups, and there seemed to be so many things to remember, so many factors to consider, and so many issues to be addressed. As he drove home that evening, George felt overwhelmed. In talking with others in his class, he felt that many shared his concern. He wondered if he would ever feel comfortable in this area and what would happen in his internship when he was asked to lead or co-lead groups. "Will I be able to function effectively as a group leader?" is a question that continued to plague him.

Many concerns and questions arise for both students and trainers in the group counseling or therapy area. According to Gill and Barry (1982) "Every trainer of group counselors and most group counseling trainees have been either the sender or receiver of these statements" (p. 302). They address the anxiety surrounding group counseling for the experienced and novice group leader alike. The individuals selected to lead groups are immediately struck by the complexity and the challenge groups present. In addressing this issue, Ward (1985) stated:

31

> Group work is challenging and complex because groups are complex because each group member has complex thoughts, feelings, and behaviors. The complexity is magnified many times because most group members who have psychological exploration, growth, and change as their goals interact with one another and with the group leaders in intricate patterns. In addition, if members have an opportunity to interact over a period of time, the group develops a set of overt and covert guidelines or group norms that help regulate individual behavior and interactions between and among members. (p. 59)

The challenge and complexity of group work have been further substantiated in the literature by Gladding (1991), Hershenson, Power, and Waldo (1996), Hulse-Killacky and Page (1994), and Kottler (1994). Each of these authors, although addressing different aspects of group work, arrived at similar conclusions related to issues of challenge and complexity. They highlighted such areas as group membership, leadership styles, group methods, issues surrounding confidentiality, resistance, silence, conflict, termination and follow-up, and stages and transitions inherent in the group experience. Add to these the complexity of each individual involved, and it is easy to see why group work generates anxiety for the leader and for the members and sets forth a challenge for both.

Adding to this challenge is the fact that groups are often designed around special themes and populations, as identified in Parts Three and Four of this text. Such theme- and population-specific groups often carry with them special directives related to membership, leadership, methods, process, dynamics, multicultural issues, ethics, and stages and transitions. Current group journals are replete with theme and special population research, as illustrated by the following article topics: single father groups (Gregg, 1994); solution-focused groups (LaFountain & Garner, 1996); interracial groups (McRae, 1994); AIDS groups (Norsworthy & Horne, 1994); male sex offender groups (Rich, 1994); total quality groups (Samby, Peterson, & Houland, 1994); children and family groups (Sayger, 1996); and classroom groups (Schmuck & Schmuck, 1997). Such specialized groups together with their directives add to the complexity of group work and raise the question: Is it possible to approach group work from a generic perspective, or should all groups be viewed in terms of their specialized members and purpose? The answer to this question is not readily available. It is dependent on the philosophical and theoretical viewpoint of the group leader.

In this chapter we explore one aspect of the complex process of group counseling or therapy, namely, the stages and transitions through which groups move from initiation through termination. We believe that the information presented has application across both generic and specialized approaches to group work. We begin the chapter by discussing both early and current conceptualizations of stage development and then present the reader with our own view of this developmental process based on our literature review and our experience in working with groups. Member and leader behaviors are discussed for each stage. We conclude the chapter with recommendations for how group leaders can use this knowledge of stage development for the enhancement of both member growth and leader effectiveness.

Stages and Transitions～

The distinct stages that groups move through as they pass from opening to closure are difficult to describe in definitive terms. The nature of the group, the membership, and the leadership style all influence this developmental process. Another set of factors arises from the open or closed nature of the group. A closed group, which maintains the same membership through its lifetime, is more easily described in terms of stages of development than is an open group, in which members come and go. The addition of new members as old members leave complicates the developmental process. Any developmental scheme, therefore, is based more upon experience than upon hard-and-fast rules governing a group's development.

Readers must also be aware that, due to a myriad of factors, group stage development is not a discrete and neatly separated process. In discussing this point, George and Dustin (1988) stated:

> The stages described do not occur in discrete and neatly separated points in the life of a real group. There is considerable overlap between the stages, as groups move from one stage to the other in a somewhat jerky, hesitant manner. As a result, there may be some movement toward the next stage and then regression to the previous stage. (p. 102)

In spite of these caveats, recent authors have been in apparent agreement about a generalized pattern of stages and transitions in groups (Berg & Landreth, 1990; Corey, 1990; Gazda, 1989; Gladding, 1996; Tuckman, 1965; Tuckman & Jensen, 1977; Yalom, 1995). The stages and transitions identified within this pattern are outlined in Table 2.1. Before we discuss these stages, however, we present the following background information as significant foundational material.

Early Conceptualizations

A great deal has been written about the stages through which groups progress from inception to closure. Much of the early work in this area stems from such authors as Thelen and Dickerman (1949), Bales (1950), and Miles (1953). They conceptualized stages of groups based on the problem-solving behaviors exhibited in task groups. In these early developmental schemas, the emphasis was on tasks the group was expected to accomplish, such as getting organized, sharing ideas and opinions, and reaching solutions through suggestions. From this task orientation, specific member roles in groups were examined. Researchers then began to translate group maintenance behaviors (member behaviors utilized to either promote or impede the progress of the group) into interactional behaviors, which added a dimension to the early emphasis on task behaviors. Subsequent approaches to stage development in small groups combined task and member behaviors into descriptions of group process over time.

An example of how task and member behaviors have been combined is found in the work of Bennis and Shepard (1956). Integrating the work of Bales (1953) with their own concepts, these authors developed a conceptualization of group movement based upon their observations while teaching group dynamics to graduate students.

Table 2.1 ～
Stages/Transitions of Group Development

Author	Stages/Transitions				
	1	2	3	4	5
Tuckman (1965) Tuckman & Jensen (1977)	Forming	Storming	Norming	Performing	Adjourning
Gazda (1989)	Exploratory	Transition	Action	Termination	
Corey (1990)	Initial	Transition	Working	Consolidation/Termination	
Berg & Landreth (1990)	—Precommitment—		—Commitment—		
Yalom (1995)	Orientation	—Conflict—		—Cohesiveness—	
Gladding (1996)	Forming	Norming	Working	Terminating	

As a result of those observations, they proposed that groups generally move through six developmental phases from beginning to termination:

1. Dependence-flight.
2. Counterdependence-fight.
3. Resolution-catharsis.
4. Enchantment-flight.
5. Disenchantment-fight.
6. Consensual validation.

This conceptualization indicates that groups begin in a somewhat dependent stage and that growth takes place as group members strive to move toward interdependent functioning.

Expanding on the work of Bennis and Shepard, Reid (1965) discussed the developmental stages of groups in terms of an "authority cycle." He viewed the growth and development of the group in direct relationship to the leader's authority. Groups move from dependence upon an established leader through counterindependence and counterdependence until interdependence with the original authority leader has been established. According to Reid, a crisis within the group may cause it to fall back to dependence on the established leader and begin the circular developmental pattern again. Like Bennis and Shepard, he stressed that growth occurs in groups as the members move from degrees of dependence to degrees of interdependence.

Other writers (Bion, 1961; Gazda, 1971; Gibb, 1964; Kaplan & Roman, 1963; Mills, 1964; Ohlsen, 1970; Schutz, 1958) also aided in the early development of stage theories applied to the group process. Each described the various stages through which groups progress. Their descriptions cover not only the content of each of the stages but also the behaviors individual group members display at each of these stages.

Current Conceptualizations

The authors listed in Table 2.1 expanded upon the early theories, viewing the movement of groups from origination to termination from a stage/transition perspective. A perusal of the table indicates that the authors differ in the terminology used to describe each stage and also in the number of stages delineated. They do show, however, a good deal of consistency in their descriptions of group members' behaviors in these stages.

Stage 1   Labeled by terms such as forming, exploratory, initial, precommitment, and orientation, Stage 1 has been described by the following member behaviors:

- Orienting.
- Testing the environment.
- Identifying boundaries.
- Coming together.
- Seeking acceptance.
- Seeking approval.
- Developing commitment.
- Searching for structure and meaning.
- Getting acquainted.
- Defining goals.
- Building a culture.
- Exploring expectations.
- Learning group functioning.
- Seeking one's place in the group.
- Reviewing and defining power.

Whether these behaviors are viewed from an individual's perspective or from the group's perspective, Stage 1 in group development seems to be a period of definition for both the individual member and the group. Individuals seem to be defining for themselves where and, perhaps, if they fit in the group, what role they will take in the group, degrees of acceptance and approval within the group, and expectations both for themselves and for others as these relate to the group process.

If the "group" can be viewed as an entity unto itself separate from its individual parts, other aspects of definition appear. This entity called "group" is seeking to define its structure and meaning, its functions, its goals, and its boundaries. Through such definition, the "group" attempts to build a networking system connecting its individual parts, its members. The degree of success in this endeavor often rests in the strength of the constructed network and the skills of the group leader in building this network.

In addition to being a period of definition, this stage is also characterized by anxiety. The amount of anxiety seems to be related to perceptions of risk, threat, power, member behaviors, leader behaviors, and expectations, either perceived or real. The degree of anxiety varies from member to member and from group to group, but it does seem to be present, to some extent, in the beginning stages of all groups.

Another characteristic is dependence. Aspects of dependence seem much more pronounced during this initial stage than in the other stages identified. Perhaps the unknown elements of the new group are responsible for this response. Perhaps the testing, seeking, and exploring to find one's place in the group are the catalysts for this type of behavior. Perhaps a more dependent stance is necessary in attempting to reach a definition of self in relationship to the group.

Stage 2   Labeled by such terms as storming, transition, norming, precommitment, and conflict, Stage 2 is characterized by active personal involvement in which the individual begins to test his or her position and power in the group and also the behavioral parameters of the group and its members. The following behaviors are descriptive of Stage 2:

- Conflict.
- Polarization.
- Resistance.
- Dominance
- Control
- Power
- Anxiety
- Defensiveness
- Struggle
- Confrontation

These terms depict not only action and reaction but also interaction on the part of the individual members as they attempt to establish themselves within the group structure. Such words as struggle, conflict, and confrontation attest to the individual's need to move from the safety of passive involvement to the more risk-oriented position of active involvement. Most of the descriptors for Stage 2 signify a movement from observation to participation, and this participation is generally viewed as action oriented.

Stage 3   In describing Stage 3, terms such as norming, action, working, and commitment are applied. Yalom (1995) noted that conflict is part of both Stages 2 and 3 but that the conflict associated with Stage 3 is a more productive interaction out of which group cohesion develops. Berg and Landreth (1990) have viewed this period of group development as one of transition in which greater degrees of commitment develop, leading to more productive interactions within the group. The following behaviors are descriptive of Stage 3:

- Cohesiveness.
- Standardization.
- Role clarification and adoption.
- Intimacy.
- Problem exploration.
- Action exploration.

- Development of belonging.
- Development of inclusion.
- Development of solidarity.
- Conflict resolution.
- Development of helping skills.
- Enhanced risk-taking.
- Decreased aggression.
- Increased compromise.

Activities in Stage 3 involve blending and merging. In this move from independence to more interdependence, individuality is not lost but instead becomes enmeshed in the group. Stage 3 encompasses behaviors and activities that are more group specific than member specific. Whereas in Stage 2 the individual, through testing, checking, and confrontation, was striving for greater self-involvement, members in Stage 3 are most accurately viewed as involved in the group. The group, its purposes, processes, and membership, is put ahead of the individual maximizing its development.

Stages 4 and 5   For the purposes of discussion, Stages 4 and 5 are presented here as overlapping, because the authors cited in Table 2.1 vary in whether they view these as one or two stages and also in the words they use to describe these stages. Such words as performing/adjourning, termination, consolidation, commitment, and cohesiveness are applied. In his early conceptualization, Tuckman (1965) discussed only four stages. He added a fifth stage, adjournment, in his later work (Tuckman & Jensen, 1977). Corey (1990) delineated four stages, and described Stage 4 in terms of consolidation. Yalom (1995) has described three stages, labeling the last stage as cohesiveness. In the views of Gazda (1989), Corey (1990), and Gladding (1996), the last stage is termination. In the view of Berg and Landreth (1990), the last stage is commitment, with several phases within this stage. Whether viewed as being one or two stages, the final phase of group development has been characterized by the following behaviors:

- Developing roles.
- Channeling energy.
- Resolving issues.
- Increasing self-disclosure.
- Increasing honesty.
- Increasing spontaneity.
- Increasing responsibility.
- Increasing integration.
- Increasing interpretation.
- Increasing behavioral reaffirmations.
- Increasing intensification of feelings.
- Increasing sadness, anxiety, and dependence.
- Preparing for separation.

- Evaluating.
- Ending.

With group members drawing upon the growth and development that have taken place during the previous stages, the final segment is best viewed in terms of self- and group-enhancement and closure. Enhancement is seen in more group involvement and personal development as these apply to the group and to the individual. Group development is furthered by greater depth of problem exploration, action orientation, solidarity, integration, and problem resolution. Personal change is seen when areas such as honesty, spontaneity, intimacy, feelings of belonging, inclusion, and integration come to fruition.

The cyclical nature of group development (Capuzzi & Gross, 1997) becomes obvious as the group approaches culmination. As individuals begin to see closure as a reality, loss anxiety and dependence evolve, evidenced by such questions as: Will I be able to take what I have learned and apply it outside the group? Will I be able to function without the group? The loss anxiety and dependence inherent in these questions are characteristic of Stage 1 behaviors, and the leader will have to be skilled to turn this anxiety and dependence into positive attributes as members leave the group. In discussing the closure process, Berg and Landreth (1990) made the following observations:

> A certain ambiguity of feelings can be anticipated that approximates the grieving process. Leave taking will produce denial and withdrawal in some and elation in others. Overriding these natural feelings of loss and anticipation should be a general optimism and a sense of completion. The group leader needs to take special care in dealing fully with feelings of anxiety associated with leaving the group. (p. 109)

Composite Conceptualizations ∼

Based upon the preceding information, and calling upon our own collective experience, we developed our own view of the developmental stages of groups. In our view, this developmental process consists of four stages: (a) definitive stage, (b) personal involvement stage, (c) group involvement stage, and (d) enhancement and closure stage. These are addressed in the following sections.

Definitive Stage

The duration of this stage varies with the group. The stage involves the individual group members defining for themselves the purpose of the group, their commitment to it, their potential involvement in it, and the degree of self they are willing to share. Characterizing this stage of development are such questions as: Whom can I trust? Where will I find support? Will I be hurt by others knowing about me? and How much of myself am I willing to share? Dealing with these questions and the lack of immediate answers, members in the definitive stage show increased anxiety, excitement, and nervousness. The dialogue during this stage tends to be self-protective and of a social nature (small talk) as the members test the waters of group involvement.

To help group members deal effectively with the definitive stage, the group leader needs skills in dealing with such issues as trust, support, safety, self-disclosure, and confidentiality.

In the definitive stage in group development, individuals define, demonstrate, and experiment with their own role definitions; they test out the temperament, personality, and behaviors of other group members; and they arrive at conclusions about how personally involved they are willing to become. The individual's movement through this stage can be enhanced or impeded by the group's makeup (age, gender, number, values, attitudes, socioeconomic status, and so on), the leadership style (active, passive, autocratic, democratic), the group's setting (formal, informal, comfortable, relaxed), the personal dynamics the individual brings to the group (shy, aggressive, verbal, nonverbal), and the individual's perceptions of trust and acceptance from other group members and from the group leader.

The definitive stage is crucial in group development and can determine for the individual, and, therefore, for the group, future involvement, commitment, and individual and group success or failure in the long run. The following are member and leader behaviors descriptive of the definitive stage:

Member Behaviors
- Members evaluate the leader in terms of skill, ability, and capacity to trust.
- Members evaluate other members in terms of commitment, safety, and confidentiality.
- Members evaluate themselves in terms of risk-taking, sharing of themselves with others, and their willingness to fully participate.
- Members search for meaning and structure within the group.
- Members search for approval from members and from the leader.
- Members define themselves in relationship to other members and the leader.
- Members define the group experience in terms of their other life experiences.

Leader Behaviors
- The leader attempts to foster inclusion of all group members.
- The leader explains the rules and regulations that will operate within the group.
- The leader attempts to draw from the members rules and regulations that will aid their participation in the group.
- The leader explains the structure, timelines, and leader behaviors that members can expect within the group.
- The leader attempts to model the behaviors expected of the group members.
- The leader attempts to deal effectively with the various emotions within the group.
- The leader discusses issues of confidentiality, behavior, and goals and expectations for the group.
- The leader attempts to draw from the members their goals and expectations for the group.
- The leader attempts to provide an environment that facilitates growth.

Personal Involvement Stage

Once individuals have drawn conclusions about their commitment and role in the group, they move into the personal involvement stage of group development. This stage is best described as a period of member-to-member interactions, the sharing of personal information, confrontation with other group members, power struggles, and the individual's growing identity as a group member. Statements such as "I am," "I need," and "I care" are characteristic of this stage of group involvement. Through speech and behaviors, the individual member demonstrates the degree of personal sharing he or she is willing to invest and confirms the commitment made during the definitive stage.

The personal involvement stage is one of action, reaction, and interaction. Both fight and flight are represented in this stage as individuals strive to carve their place within the group. This carving or creating process often involves heated member-to-member interactions followed by retreat to regroup and battle again. The battles that ensue not only enhance the member's place within the group but also aid in firmly establishing the group as an entity in its own right.

The personal involvement stage offers the individual the opportunity to try out various behaviors, affirm or deny perceptions of self and other, receive feedback in the form of words or behaviors, and begin the difficult process of self-evaluation. Individual involvement in this stage of group development is critical to the eventual outcome of the group. The following member and leader behaviors are descriptive of the personal involvement stage:

Member Behaviors

- Members openly challenge other members and the leader as they strive to find their place in the group.
- Members test their personal power within the group in attempts at manipulation and control.
- Members struggle as they try to find safety and comfort in sharing themselves with others.
- Members resist integrating the feedback they receive, as the suggested changes may be too painful to implement.
- Members join with other selected members in attempts to build safety and security.
- Members increase their commitment to themselves and also to the group and its goals and purposes.
- Members become more willing to share themselves with others and take a more active role in the group process.
- Members expand their ability to share feelings, ideas, and needs as these relate to the group process.

Leader Behaviors

- The leader demonstrates awareness of the emotional makeup of the group and encourages affective expression.

- The leader participates in the struggle, confrontation, and conflict that are part of this stage.
- The leader communicates to the members the appropriateness of their member-to-member reactions and interactions.
- The leader allows members to move through this stage at their own pace, knowing the dangers of rushing the process.
- The leader provides an environment conducive to increased comfort and safety.
- The leader encourages members to explore new ways of behaving within the group.
- The leader acknowledges his or her own struggles as the group moves to deeper levels of interaction.
- The leader stresses the importance of all members of the group aiding in the transition from definition to involvement.

Group Involvement Stage

With the information about themselves gained in the personal involvement stage, group members move into the group involvement stage, characterized by a self-evaluation and self-assessment of behavior, attitudes, values, and methods used in relating to others and also by members channeling their energies to better meet group goals and purposes. During this stage, the member and the group become somewhat more synonymous.

Degrees of cooperation and cohesiveness replace conflict and confrontation as members, more confident in their role in the group, direct more of their attention to what is best for the group and all of its members. This stage reveals increasing role clarification, intimacy, problem exploration, group solidarity, compromise, conflict resolution, and risk taking.

The group, with its purposes and goals, is merging with the individual purposes and goals of its members. Individual agendas are being replaced by group agendas, and the members are identifying more with the group. Bonding is taking place between members as they join forces to enhance the group and, in turn, enhance their individual selves in relation to the group. References to "insider" and "outsider" differentiate the group and others in the members' lives outside the group. Members grow protective of other group members and also of the group itself. The group and its membership take on special significance unique to those who are part of the process. The melding of member and group purposes and goals is necessary to the group's ongoing success. The following member and leader behaviors are descriptive of the group involvement stage:

Member Behaviors

- Members develop confidence in themselves and their ability to relate effectively in the group environment.
- Members develop better helping skills and apply these to working with other group members and to themselves.

- Members devote increasing energy to aiding the group to meet its purposes and goals.
- Members direct more attention to cooperation and cohesiveness and less to conflict and confrontation.
- Members take more of a perspective of belonging and inclusion and less of nonbelonging and exclusion.
- Members operate more in a problem exploration/solution mode than in a problem developmental mode.
- Members provide support for other members and the group as a whole.
- Members demonstrate more solidarity, as in their view of members and the group.

Leader Behaviors

- The leader encourages and facilitates the development of individual strengths within the group.
- The leader encourages members in their development of group identity and solidarity.
- The leader provides more opportunity for members to serve in a leadership role within the group.
- The leader gives positive direction as the members move from individual to group-directed purposes and goals.
- The leader demonstrates, in verbalization and behaviors, the benefits to be derived from individuals working cooperatively.
- The leader demonstrates, in words and through his or her behaviors, the benefits to be derived, for individual members and for the group, from reinforcement of positive change.
- The leader involves himself or herself to a greater extent as a participant, sharing in the changing dynamics of the group.
- The leader involves himself or herself more in a helping capacity than in a leader capacity to enhance the development of individual members and the group.

Enhancement and Closure Stage

The final stage in a group's life is often described as the most exhilarating but also the saddest aspect of group work. The exhilaration stems from the evaluation and reevaluation that are so much a part of the final stage. The evaluative aspect consists of reevaluation of the group process and individual and group assessment of change, in conjunction with individual and group reinforcement of individual member change, and a commitment to continue self-analysis and growth. Members have an opportunity to share what they feel have been significant growth experiences during the group tenure, and they receive feedback, generally positive, from other group members and the leader. Members are encouraged to review the process of the group and to measure changes within themselves that have taken place from the time they entered the group to this period just before closure. Members' statements at this stage of group development tend to be along the line of: "I was...now I am," "I felt...now I feel," "I didn't...now I do," and "I couldn't...now I can." The following member and leader behaviors are descriptive of the enhancement and closure stage:

Member Behaviors

- Members evaluate the amount of self-progress they have made during the life of the group.
- Members evaluate the extent to which the group accomplished its purposes and goals.
- Members share their perceptions of the strengths and weaknesses of other members and the leader.
- Members share their concerns about what will happen after the group ends.
- Members attempt to evaluate the group experience in terms of their other life experiences.
- Members try to build contacts with group members and the leader that will continue after closure.
- Members start to deal with the loss that group closure will bring.
- Members consider alternative actions to take the place of what the group provided.

Leader Behaviors

- The leader assists group members in evaluating their growth and development during the tenure of the group.
- The leader aids group members in resolving any issues that remain.
- The leader facilitates closure by initiating certain activities, such as structured ways of saying goodbye, early in this last stage.
- The leader makes sure each member in the group receives appropriate feedback.
- The leader reviews the dynamics of the group and its members based upon his or her perception.
- The leader reviews, for each member, the member's strengths and weaknesses from his or her perspective.
- The leader encourages the emotional venting that is necessary in the closure process.
- The leader encourages each member to discuss what he or she plans to do after the group ends.

The movement of a group from its initiation to its termination varies. Groups and their individual members differ in this movement process for a myriad of reasons. No one conceptualization has all the answers or addresses all the issues inherent in this developmental process of groups. The various conceptualizations do, however, provide guidelines and directions for working with groups. According to Hershenson et al. (1996):

> The group as a whole can be seen as passing though different periods in its life, similar to the way individuals pass through periods in their lives. When a group first forms

it is in childhood, then moves into adolescence, followed by young adulthood, then adulthood, and then maturity as it is about to disband. (p. 211)

Summary ⌇

The concerns expressed at the beginning of this chapter by our hypothetical student, George, are quite legitimate. The process of group work is both complex and challenging, and the information that has been written about this process often results in more questions than definitive answers. Group leaders, whether novice or experienced, search to increase their degrees of comfort in the leadership role. The following recommendations for group leaders are presented to summarize the information covered in this chapter and to assist in enhancing leader comfort:

1. Knowledge of group stages and transitions provides information on typical member behaviors and the developmental process of groups as they move from initiation to termination.
2. Knowledge of group stages and transitions provides the following directives to those in a leadership role:
   a. During the early stages of group development, the leader has to address the anxiety and dependence of group members.
   b. During the early stages of group development, the leader should establish operating procedures and structures that will help alleviate some of this anxiety and dependence.
   c. During the middle stages of group development, the leader should facilitate empowerment of group members as they work on personal and group issues. These are the working stages, the productive stages, of the group, and the stages that foster both individual and group development.
   d. During the final stages, the leader must be aware of the dichotomy of exhilaration and sadness the group members feel. Allowing members to discuss and deal with both ends of this emotional continuum will facilitate positive closure.
3. Knowledge of group stages and transitions allows the leader to plan and structure the group to better meet the needs of its members.
4. Knowledge of group stages and transitions enables the leader to instruct and orient the members in regard to possible experiences in moving from initiation to termination of the group.
5. Knowledge of group stages and transitions helps the leader to better judge the types of individuals who would benefit most from the group experience and, accordingly, enhance the group outcome.
6. Knowledge of group stages and transitions enables the leader to better understand the cyclical nature of groups and be better prepared to deal with forward and backward movement within the group and with the behaviors and emotional reactions that can be expected throughout the group's life.
7. Knowledge of group stages and transitions allows the leader to integrate his

or her experiences in a group with information from past and current research. By doing so, he or she is able to restructure or reconceptualize the group process to the best advantage for all.

8. Knowledge of group stages and transitions permits the leader to measure or evaluate the developmental process within his or her groups by comparing it with what others in the field have reported.

9. Knowledge of group stages and transitions allows the leader to become comfortable with the overall process of group work through an understanding of certain dynamics that are generally predictable.

10. Knowledge of group stages and transitions offers the leader the freedom to work within the known parameters of the group process and also to create and develop his or her own conceptualizations within the process.

References ~

Bales, R. F. (1950). *Interaction process analysis: A method for the study of small groups.* Cambridge, MA: Addison-Wesley.

Bales, R. F. (1953). The equilibrium problem in small groups. In T. Parson, R. F. Bales, & E. A. Shils (Eds.), *Working papers in the theory of action* (pp. 111–161). Glencoe, IL: Free Press.

Bennis, W. G., & Shepard, H. A. (1956). A theory of group development. *Human Relations, 9,* 415–437.

Berg, R., & Landreth, G. (1990). *Group counseling: Concepts and procedures* (2nd ed.). Muncie, IN: Accelerated Development.

Bion, R. W. (1961). *Experiences in groups.* New York. Basic Books.

Capuzzi, D., & Gross, D. (1997). *Introduction to the counseling profession* (2nd ed.). Boston, MA: Allyn & Bacon.

Corey, G. (1990). *Theory and practice of group counseling* (2nd ed.). Pacific Grove, CA: Brooks/Cole.

Gazda, G. (1971). *Group counseling: A developmental approach.* Boston: Allyn & Bacon.

Gazda, G. (1989). *Group counseling: A developmental approach* (4th ed.). Boston: Allyn & Bacon.

George, R. L., & Dustin, D. (1988). *Group counseling: Theory and practice.* Englewood Cliffs, NJ: Prentice-Hall.

Gibb, J. R. (1964). Climate for trust formation. In L. P. Bradford, J. R. Gibb, & K. D. Benne (Eds.), *T-group theory and laboratory method: Innovation in re-education* (pp. 279–300). New York: Wiley.

Gill, S. J., & Barry, R. A. (1982). Group-focused counseling: Classifying the essential skills. *Personnel and Guidance Journal, 60,* 302–305.

Gladding, S. T. (1991). *Group work: A counseling speciality.* New York: Macmillan.

Gladding, S. T. (1996). *Counseling: A comprehensive profession.* Englewood Cliffs, NJ: Prentice-Hall.

Gregg, C. (1994). Group work with single fathers. *Journal for Specialists in Group Work, 19*(2), 95–101.

Hershenson, D., Power, P. L., & Waldo, M. (1996). *Community counseling: Contemporary theory and practice.* Boston: Allyn & Bacon.

Hulse-Killacky, D., & Page, B. (1994). Development of the corrective feedback instrument: A tool for use in counselor training groups. *Journal for Specialists in Group Work, 19*(4), 197–210.

Kaplan, S. R., & Roman, M. (1963). Phases of development in an adult therapy group. *International Journal of Group Psychotherapy, 13,* 10–26.

Kottler, J. (1994). Working with different group members. *Journal for Specialists in Group Work, 19*(1), 3–10.

LaFountain, R., & Garner, N. (1996). Solution-focused counseling groups: The results are in. *Journal for Specialists in Group Work, 21*(2), 128–143.

McRae, M. (1994). Interracial group dynamics: A new perspective. *Journal for Specialists in Group Work, 19*(3), 168–174.

Miles, M. B. (1953). Human relations training: How a group grows. *Teachers College Record, 55,* 90–96.

Mills, T. M. (1964). *Group transformation*. Englewood Cliffs, NJ: Prentice-Hall.

Norsworthy, K., & Horne, A. (1994). Issues in group work with HIV-infected gay and bisexual men. *Journal for Specialists in Group Work, 19*(2), 112–119.

Ohlsen, M. M. (1970). *Group counseling*. New York: Holt, Rinehart & Winston.

Reid, C. (1965). The authority cycle in small group development. *Adult Leadership, 13*(10), 308–331.

Rich, K. (1994). Outpatient group therapy with adult male sex offenders: Clinical issues and concerns. *Journal for Specialists in Group Work, 19*(2), 120–128.

Samby, M., Peterson, T., & Houland, J. (1994). Total quality groups in business: Opportunity and challenges for specialists in group work. *Journal for Specialists in Group Work, 19*(4), 217–226.

Sayger, T. (1996). Creating resilient children and empowering families using a multifamily group process. *Journal for Specialists in Group Work, 21*(2), 81–89.

Schmuck, R., & Schmuck, P. (1997). *Group processes in the classroom* (7th ed.). Madison, WI: Brown & Benchmark.

Schutz, W. D. (1958). *FIRO: Three dimensional theory of interpersonal behavior*. New York: Rinehart.

Thelen, H., & Dickerman, W. (1949). Stereotypes and the growth of groups. *Educational Leadership, 6*, 309–316.

Tuckman, B. W. (1965). Developmental sequence in small groups. *Psychological Bulletin, 63*, 384–399.

Tuckman, B. W., & Jensen, M. S. (1977). Stages of small group development revisited. *Groups & Organizational Studies, 2*, 419–427.

Ward, D. E. (1985). Levels of group activity: A model for improving the effectiveness of group work. *Journal of Counseling and Development, 64*(1), 59–64.

Yalom, I. D. (1995). *The theory and practice of group psychotherapy* (4th ed.). New York: Basic Books.

3

Group Counseling: Elements of Effective Leadership

David Capuzzi and Douglas R. Gross

Many factors contribute to the outcomes of group counseling (Conyne, Harvill, Morganett, Morran, & Hulse-Killacky, 1990; Zimpfer & Waltman, 1982). Studies have focused on the relationship between group counseling outcomes and counselor personality (Cooper, 1977; Kellerman, 1979), counselor experience (Heikkinen, 1975; Wittmer & Webster, 1969), group membership (Heslin, 1964; Shaw, 1981), leader directiveness (Brown, 1969; Chatwin, 1972), counselor self-disclosure (Dies, 1973, 1977), and counselor-group interaction (MacLennan, 1975). In an interesting analysis of the bases of influence in groups, Richard and Patricia Schmuck (1997) concluded that group outcomes are influenced by the following aspects of the power of the group leader:

1. *Expert power*—the extent of expertise and knowledge attributed to the leader by group members.
2. *Referent power*—the extent to which group members identify with and feel close to the group leader.
3. *Legitimate power*—the power attributed to the leader by group members because the "leader" is in the position of facilitating the group.
4. *Reward power*—the extent to which group members view the leader as having the ability to reward them through providing reinforcement and attention during group sessions.
5. *Coercive power*—the extent to which the group leader is seen as having the ability to move the group in a certain direction or even "punish" group members.

6. *Informational power*—the amount of information the leader has about the members of the group.

7. *Connection power*—the number of close relationships the leader has developed with other professionals outside the group.

Because the leader of a group can influence the outcome of a group counseling experience in a number of ways, elements of effective leadership are important considerations for anyone interested in leading or co-leading a group.

Leadership Styles ~

Lewin's Three "Classics"

Discussing elements of effective leadership is not possible without understanding the contributions of Kurt Lewin and his colleagues. In the late 1930s, Lewin studied the influences of different leadership styles or patterns on groups and group members. He observed small groups of 10- and 11-year-old children who met for a period of weeks under the leadership of adults who behaved in one of three ways: democratically, autocratically, or in a laissez-faire manner (Johnson & Johnson, 1994). The impact of these leadership styles on the members of the groups was dramatic and definite. A great deal of scapegoating, for example, occurred in groups led by autocratic leaders. Further, in some of the autocratic groups, the children destroyed the items they had been making when the groups terminated. Lewin's studies made it clear that the leader's style can greatly influence the outcomes experienced by group members.

Lewin's (1944) identification of authoritarian, democratic, and laissez-faire leadership styles provided the group leader with a point of departure for understanding this element of group leadership. *Authoritarian* group leaders assume a position as the "expert" and direct the movement of a group. They may interpret, give advice, explain individual and group behavior, and generally control most aspects of group process. This style of leadership may be preferred by professionals with strong psychoanalytic, medical, or teaching backgrounds. Generally, the leader does little self-disclosing. Authoritarian leaders wield a great deal of power and are usually quite safe from being personally vulnerable (Gladding, 1991). In directing and controlling the group they typically create structure that protects them from being self-disclosing or being confronted by group members.

Democratic group leaders are more group and person centered in the way they interact with group members. They place more stress upon the responsibility of each participant to create a meaningful individual and group experience. Their trust in the ability of members and the phenomenon of the group experience is implicit. Professionals who subscribe to a Rogerian frame of reference or who align themselves with humanistic or phenomenological viewpoints are more likely than others to adopt a democratic leadership style. They are more accessible and self-disclosing than authoritarian leaders.

In contrast to authoritarian and democratic leaders, laissez-faire group leaders do not provide structure or direction to a group. Group members are expected to take responsibility for making the group experience beneficial. As Gladding (1991) noted, some group leaders (usually inexperienced) select this style in an attempt to be "nondirective" (a misnomer in and of itself), as a way to avoid decision making and enhance their likability, or because they believe a completely unstructured group works best. Some evidence shows that many laissez-faire groups accomplish little during the life of the group.

Several studies, as identified by Zimpfer and Waltman (1982), have investigated the relationship between the extent to which the group leader takes an active, directive role and success with certain group members. The studies showed that low-anxiety members, for example, may do well in a group with little structure, whereas low-trust members may prefer a distinctly leader-centered group.

Leader-Centered and Group-Centered Styles

Another way to conceptualize leadership styles is based on the degree to which the group is leader centered or group centered (Gladding, 1991). In a leader-centered group, the leader is the center of focus, and he or she determines what will most benefit group members. In this kind of group, the leader may emphasize a predetermined theme, a sequence of structured exercises, or a format for each group session and will likely direct interaction quite assertively at times. Group members are expected to cooperate with the leader and to deal with personal issues as they fit into the leader's agenda. In contrast, a more group-centered style would encourage members to establish the agenda for the group and to more freely discuss personal concerns, issues, and plans. Each of these styles can facilitate growth of group members, depending upon the group's purpose, the expectations and personalities of group members, and the leader's ability to apply techniques and interventions in a comfortable, congruent, and sensitive manner.

Interpersonal and Intrapersonal Styles

In 1978, Shapiro described two leadership styles: interpersonal and intrapersonal. Leaders with an *interpersonal* style (Corey, 1990) emphasize the importance of understanding and processing interactions among group members and relationships that develop within a group as group sessions progress. Interest centers on the nature, quality, and dynamics of the interaction among members and what is occurring in the here and now of the group. Leaders with an *intrapersonal* orientation are likely to explore why group members make certain responses by focusing upon individual members and the conflicts, concerns, and dynamics within them. This style is directed more toward the past, and it facilitates insight and resolution of internal conflicts. At times, leaders with an intrapersonal orientation may engage in individual counseling or therapy in the context of the group experience.

Charismatic Leadership Style

Group members have a tendency to admire and respect the group leader, particularly in the early stages of a group (Rutan & Rice, 1981). The group leader may derive some of his or her power from a combination of traits that are particularly appealing to group members, such as personableness, appearance, and verbal ability. Group leaders with this type of charisma may inspire group members, who become almost devoted to them (Schmuck & Schmuck, 1997).

Group leaders whom members perceive as charismatic may have an advantage during the early stages of a group in terms of their ability to facilitate the work occurring at that time. However, if group members view the leader as an ego ideal, they may become dependent upon his or her leadership and initiatives. Some charismatic leaders may begin to enjoy the admiration of group members to such an extent that they fail to encourage autonomy of the participants (Rutan & Rice, 1981). Group leaders, it must be stressed, should work to develop the skills needed to promote the personal growth of group members and to guide the group from the beginning to middle and later stages of the group's life.

The Importance of Leadership Style ∿

Leadership styles do make a difference in how groups function. Lewin's pioneering study was mentioned earlier in this chapter. After reviewing numerous studies, Stogdill (1974) reached these conclusions:

1. Person-centered styles of leadership are not always related to group productivity.
2. Socially distant, directive, and structured leadership styles that tend to promote role differentiation and clear member expectations are consistently related to group productivity.
3. Person-centered styles of leadership that provide for member involvement in decision making and show concern for the welfare of members are consistently related to group cohesiveness.
4. Among task-focused leadership styles, only the structuring of member expectations is consistently related to group cohesiveness.
5. All person-centered leadership styles seem to be related to high levels of member satisfaction.
6. Only the structuring of member expectations is positively related to member satisfaction with task-focused leadership styles.

As noted by Johnson and Johnson (1994), initiating structure by being clear about one's role as a leader and what one expects from members is the single aspect of leadership style that contributes positively to group productivity, cohesiveness, and satisfaction. The most effective group leaders may be those who not only show concern for the well-being and disclosures of members, but also structure member role responsibilities. The importance of taking time during the definitive stage of a group to establish goals, as discussed in Chapter 2, cannot be overstated.

Developing Your Own Leadership Style~

Before professionals are in the position of providing leadership to a group, they should acquire an understanding of their own inherent qualities, characteristics, and inclinations. But the leader has to go far beyond assessing his or her personal qualities before leading a group. In addition to gaining self-awareness and an understanding of how personality traits and personal qualities can enhance or detract from what the leader contributes to a group experience, he or she must master a set of core knowledge and skill competencies in the process of developing a personalized leadership style.

In 1990, the Association for Specialists in Group Work (ASGW), a division of the American Counseling Association, published a revised version of its training standards, entitled *Professional Standards for Training of Group Work Generalists and of Group Work Specialists.* (Parts of these standards were overviewed in Chapter 1 in conjunction with the discussion of group types.) These standards specify knowledge and skill competencies as well as education and supervision requirements. Some examples of the specified *knowledge* competencies are an understanding of the basic principles of group dynamics, an awareness of the specific ethical issues unique to group work, an understanding of the specific process components in typical stages of a group's development, and a comprehension of the therapeutic factors inherent in a group experience. Examples of specified *skill* competencies are the ability to explain and clarify the purpose of a particular group, the ability to encourage the participation of group members, the ability to open and close sessions effectively, and the ability to help group members integrate and apply what they have learned in the group. Depending upon whether the group leader wishes to be prepared at a beginning (generalist) or an advanced (specialist) level, *education* requirements range from a minimum of two group work courses to a wide range of related course work in such areas as organizational development, sociology, community psychology, and consultation. *Supervision* requirements involve group observation, co-leading, and leading expectations, ranging from 30 to 55 clock hours (minimum) depending on the type of group work under study. (Appendix A gives the complete set of ASGW training standards. It should be carefully studied by anyone thinking about becoming a specialist in group work.)

The point is that professionals interested in becoming competent group leaders must develop a leadership style that integrates personal qualities with a myriad of knowledge and skill competencies engendered through master's or doctoral course work, as well as through meeting requirements for group observation and supervised practice. In many ways, developing a leadership style is an integrative, sequential, and creative endeavor resulting in the group leader's ability to transmit knowledge and skill competencies in a unique, individualized way, linked and integrated with a variety of personal characteristics, to encourage emotional, cognitive, and behavioral changes on behalf of each member of a group.

Leadership Skills ~

Conducting Pre-Group Screening

Group leaders have to develop expertise in screening potential group members. As noted in the *Ethical Guidelines for Group Counselors* (Association for Specialists in Group Work, 1989), leaders must screen prospective members of a group to select individuals whose needs and goals are congruent with the group goals, who will not be detrimental to the group, and whose well-being will not be jeopardized by the group experience. As noted by Corey and Corey (1997):

> We are concerned that candidates benefit from a group but even more concerned that they might be psychologically hurt by it or might drain the group's energies excessively. Certain members, while remaining unaffected by the group, sap its energy for productive work. This is particularly true of hostile people, people who monopolize, extremely aggressive people, and people who act out. The potential gains of including certain of these members must be weighed against the probable losses to the group as a whole. We also believe that group counseling is contraindicated for individuals who are suicidal, extremely fragmented, or acutely psychotic, sociopathic, facing extreme crises, highly paranoid, or extremely self-centered. (pp. 112–113)

Screening may be accomplished through individual interviews, group interviews of potential group members, an interview as part of a team staffing, or completion and review of a written questionnaire. The pre-group screening process must provide prospective members with information about participation expectations, goals, payment methods and fee schedules, termination and referral procedures, client rights, and so on. The group leader also must inquire about prospective members' current and past experience with counseling and provide clients with a written disclosure statement of his or her qualifications and the nature of the services to be provided. (See Appendix B for a complete statement of the *Ethical Guidelines for Group Counselors*, which addresses screening procedures.) George Gazda (1989) made some interesting screening recommendations that also serve to establish "ground rules" for prospective group members. He suggested providing group candidates with the following guidelines as part of the screening process:

1. It is important to establish personal goals before you attend the first group session. These goals can be refined and clarified as the group progresses.
2. Be as honest and straightforward about yourself as possible whenever you contribute during a group session. Success and lack of success with respect to aspects of your behavior may be important topics for you to discuss.
3. Listen carefully when other members of the group are contributing and try to communicate nonjudgmental understanding and caring.
4. Do not discuss any information about other group members outside the group.
5. Be sure to attend all sessions and arrive on time.
6. Respect your counselor's right to suggest that you terminate participation in the group if the counselor feels it is best for you and best for the group.

7. Respect the fact that no one group member can control the group and that group decisions are made by consensus.
8. Let the group counselor know if there is someone in your group who poses a barrier, because of a prior relationship, to your open participation as a member of the group.
9. If you request an individual meeting with your group counselor, you may be asked to share the content of the discussion with the total group.
10. Be sure to be aware of the amount and schedule of fee payment for membership in the group prior to committing to group participation.

As Gladding (1991) noted, selection of group members through pre-group screening also grants potential members the opportunity to assess their readiness and interest in being a group member. Group leaders who have not conducted a group before should conduct pre-group screening under the supervision of an experienced group work specialist.

Organizing for Groups

The Physical Setting   Group sessions may be conducted in a variety of settings, as long as the room allows privacy and relative freedom from distraction for participants (Yalom, 1985). Some leaders seat participants around a circular table; others prefer placing chairs in a circle so members' nonverbal or body language responses are more readily observed. If group sessions are to be observed or videotaped, group members must give permission ahead of time and must have the opportunity to ask questions about and discuss the purposes of observation and taping procedures.

Length and Frequency of Meetings   As noted by George and Dustin (1988), the agency or the setting may dictate the duration and frequency of group sessions. However, the group leader also has to consider the purpose of the group when determining scheduling. Some groups require longer time periods and more frequent scheduling than do others. Typical groups require 1½-hour sessions to provide for a "warm-up" period and for the participation of each person in the group. Sessions scheduled for more than 2 hours, unless they are specifically designed as part of a marathon group, generally become nonproductive and fatiguing for all concerned. Groups conducted in educational settings, such as high schools or middle schools, may of necessity be limited to a 40- or 50-minute time period based upon the school's standard class schedule. Ideally, groups should meet once or twice a week to promote the continuity of the group experience.

Size of the Group   Yalom (1985) suggested that the ideal size of a counseling/therapy group is 7 or 8 members, with 5 to 10 members constituting an acceptable range. He noted that a minimum number is required for a group to function and interact as a group; a group of fewer than 5 members often results in a sequence of individual therapy or counseling sessions within the group context. Many of the advantages of a group, particularly the opportunity to receive validation and feedback from a microcosm of society, are lost as the size of the group diminishes.

Other Aspects of Organization   Several additional possibilities for group leaders to consider in conjunction with groups they lead or co-lead are as follows (Yalom, 1985):

1. Weekly, written summaries, describing some aspects of the group experience during a given week could be mailed to group members, providing a means of maintaining reinforcement and continuity.
2. In addition to the disclosure statement mentioned earlier, written material describing the ground rules, purposes, expectations, and so on, of the group could be distributed. Material of this nature not only provides important information, it also reinforces group participants. It may be particularly helpful to provide this written material after the first session, because members, due to anxiety, may not have been able to totally integrate information about what a group experience would be like.
3. Group members might be afforded an opportunity to see a movie or a videotape presenting information about group participation that is similar to the information described in item #2.
4. Group members could be given the option of watching videos of their own group after each session. This would give members a chance to evaluate their participation and to obtain additional feedback from other group members. As noted earlier, group members must have provided written permission before filming.
5. Group members could be offered pre-group training sessions during which they would be taught skills for self-disclosure, expressing feelings, staying in the here and now, and so forth. Obviously, this suggestion depends upon the time and resources available to the group leader and group participants and may work better in the context of "inpatient" rather than "outpatient" situations.

Recognizing Membership Roles ~

As emphasized by Vander Kolk (1985), when a group is formed and begins to meet, all of the members have just one role, that of group member. As time passes, however, role differentiation occurs as members interact and become more comfortable about being themselves in the group. In most groups, a combination of roles exists. This combination results in a dynamic interaction among members that energizes or de-energizes the group in some way. For example, a group composed of a number of task-oriented members might focus on identifying objectives for the group experience and monitoring interactions to ensure movement and progress during each session. Another group might consist of several task-oriented members and several process-oriented members who value spontaneous interaction and disclosure. This group might find itself in conflict from time to time if task-oriented members feel time is being spent nonproductively and process-oriented members feel they are not always able to complete interactions or express deep feelings without others pressuring them to refocus on the original objectives established for the session.

The group leader has to recognize the types of roles group members are taking and make appropriate interventions to maintain balanced interaction and movement through the definitive, personal involvement, group involvement, and enhancement and closure stages of a group (described in Chapter 2). One way of conceptualizing membership roles in groups is to view roles as facilitative, maintenance, or blocking in nature.

Facilitative Roles

Facilitative roles serve to keep the group on task and to clarify aspects of communication. Members who behave in facilitative ways contribute to the group constructively and increase the likelihood of participation and cooperation. Table 3.1 presents some examples of facilitative roles in groups.

Maintenance Roles

Maintenance roles help develop social-emotional bonds among members of a group and usually contribute to cohesiveness and feelings of connectedness. Group members who fill maintenance roles usually are quite sensitive to the affective components of a group experience and respond in ways that either escalate or reduce tensions related to affective aspects of intra- and interpersonal communication. Table 3.2 summarizes selected maintenance roles.

Blocking Roles

Individual needs of group members (Vander Kolk, 1985) often inhibit a group's progress. Group leaders must recognize these blocking roles and learn to recognize and diffuse problematic behaviors in individuals so the entire group does not become unproductive. Table 3.3 outlines some of the possible blocking roles that members of a group might bring to a group experience.

Facilitating the Group Stages

Facilitating the Definitive Stage

As discussed in Chapter 2, in the definitive stage of the developmental process of a group, group members define for themselves and each other the purpose of the group, the quality of their commitment to it, and their involvement level. Members have questions about trust, support, safety, self-disclosure, confidentiality, and many other aspects of group participation. The group leader has to be sensitive to members' questions and uncertainties during initial sessions and be able to model behavior that encourages constructive communication and gradual movement toward achieving individual and group goals. Several group specialists (Corey, 1990; Gladding, 1991; Nolan, 1978) have discussed the importance of mastering special skills that are unique to group work. Among the skills vital to the definitive stage of a group are:

Table 3.1 ~
Facilitative Roles in Groups

Role	Description
Initiator	Energizes the group; presents new ideas, new ways of looking at things, stimulates the group to move toward some sort of action. Responses to the initiator may be positive, if the group is ready to move ahead, or negative, if it prefers inaction.
Information Seeker Opinion Seeker	Both request data of a factual or judgmental nature from the group. Information seeker simply requires cognitive information for clarification; opinion seeker focuses on values and the group's affective aspect. Each can be facilitative when data would be helpful to the group. An information seeker, however, can dwell on data to the exclusion of affective concerns; and the opinion seeker can put people on the defensive by pressing for value judgments and self-disclosure before a member is ready.
Information Giver Opinion Giver	An information giver may spontaneously provide cognitive data or respond to the information seeker. An opinion giver may also offer values or judgments on his/her own or in response to the opinion seeker.
Elaborator	Explains and gives examples of the topic, thus developing a meaning for what the group discusses; a rationale for group ideas evolves and the elaborator suggests how the ideas might work out.
Coordinator	Acts as a reality base for the group; ties ideas to practicality, prevents meandering into unrealistic discussions; pulls together group ideas; tries to have the group organize its activities.
Orienter	Tells the group where it is in regard to goals and direction; summarizes what group has done and whether it is "on course."
Evaluator	Describes group's accomplishments and how well it is functioning; may evaluate usefulness or logic of a procedure, suggestion, or group discussion.
Procedural Technician	Carries out technical tasks (arranging chairs, brewing coffee).
Recorder	Writes down or remembers the group's decisions, plans, and suggestions.

Source: From *Introduction to Group Counseling and Psychotherapy* (p. 139) by C. J. Vander Kolk, 1985, Columbus, OH: Charles E. Merrill. Copyright © 1985 by Charles E. Merrill. Reprinted by permission of Merrill, an imprint of Macmillan Publishing Company and the author.

Table 3.2 ～
Vitalizing and Maintenance Roles

Role	Description
Encourager	Accepts others' ideas by praising, agreeing with, or stimulating ideas from participants; wants good feelings and a sense of security for the group. Excessive use of this role may direct attention from this person to the others.
Harmonizer	Attempts to mediate conflict and tension to keep group in harmony rather than polarized. May deal with subgroups in conflict. May brush real conflicts aside without a thorough working through.
Compromiser	Contracts with the harmonizer in cognitive orientation toward resolving group issues; may seek alternatives acceptable to the participants. When compromiser is part of the conflict, is often willing to give up status, see other points of view, or compromise in a way that resolves the problem.
Expediter	Oversees establishing group norms and guiding adherence to those norms. May try to get everyone to participate or suggest length of individual contributions. Role is similar to a leader's assistant or referee. Group members can become annoyed with someone who takes this role too seriously.
Standard Setter	Wants group process and goals to meet a criterion for acceptance by others. Sets high standards for norms and objectives. May evaluate quality of interactions. Often unsure of himself/herself; wants high standards as a means of reassurance.
Group Observer and Commentator	Notes group process, relates observations or conclusions. Contributions may be descriptive, interpretive, or evaluative. In the extreme, this member may be distancing himself/herself from the group, becoming a less involved participant.
Follower	Goes along with whatever group wants; quiet; offers little of self, preferring to be friendly observer. Usually too insecure and fearful to initiate ideas or discussion; not really a vitalizer.

Source: From *Introduction to Group Counseling and Psychotherapy* (p. 140) by C. J. Vander Kolk, 1985, Columbus, OH: Charles E. Merrill. Copyright © 1985 by Charles E. Merrill. Reprinted by permission of Merrill, an imprint of Macmillan Publishing Company and the author.

Table 3.3 ~	
Anti-Group Roles	

Role	Description
Aggressor	Disagrees with ideas and discussion. May disapprove of behavior, feelings, and values. May impose beliefs or ways of doing things on others. May be jealous, insecure, need attention. Some groups fight back; others react passively.
Blocker	Stubborn about what should and should not be discussed; resists wishes of total group. Negativism can impede group progress.
Recognition Seeker	Boasts; engages in other behavior to attract group attention.
Self-Confessor	Reveals feelings and insights unrelated to group's immediate dealings. Personal expressions distract group from concentrating on its task.
Playboy	Nonchalant or cynical toward group; engages in horseplay or other behaviors that communicate lack of involvement, thus disrupting group cohesiveness.
Dominator	Tries to manipulate others to recognize his/her authority; less aggressive than manipulative. Behaviors include interrupting, flattery, asserting status, giving directions. Interferes with sense of equality among participants.
Help Seeker Rescuer	Elicits sympathy from group by excessively dwelling on personal problems, confusions, and inadequacies. Giving attention may reinforce dependent behavior. Rescuers may meet own needs by accommodating help seekers, but both roles are unproductive.
Self-Righteous Moralist	Has need to always be right and to think others are always wrong. Authority on moral issues. Does not care to be liked; wants to be respected for moral integrity. Imposes moral standards on others. Will at first be quiet, then assert position persistently without conceding or admitting error. Projects image of moral superiority that soon alienates participants. Yalom (1970) suggested these people are disturbed by feelings of shame and anger but usually believe they have no problems.
Do-Gooder	May be a modified form of self-righteous moralist who wants to do what is "right." Is helpful, kind, understanding toward others. Does not usually impose "good" behavior on others, but wants acceptance from others.

(continued)

Table 3.3~
Anti-Group Roles (continued)

Role	Description
Informer	Possible variation on the do-gooder. Occurs when group members interact and know each other outside group sessions; informer shares information about someone's behavior outside the group. Purpose of "squealing" is to enhance one's status with and acceptance by others, or as act of revenge.
Seducer	Uses manipulations, usually in the form of active or subtle attempts to control others by getting others to reach out to him/her or pretending to be fragile. Seductive behavior also avoids genuine closeness.
Hostile or Angry Member	Manipulates others by intimidation or avoids needs such as affection. Joking, sarcasm, and ridicule are signs of hostility. Result is greater self-protection on part of other participants to avoid attacks.
Monopolist	Talks incessantly about experiences, ideas, and information that is usually only tangentially related to group goals. Self-centered talk may be set off by similarity of another member's problems with an experience of the monopolist. May tell stories, relate what he/she has read, or relate personal upheavals in great detail. At first, group is relieved to have someone carry the ball; after several sessions, there is often fighting, absenteeism, and dropouts. Leader and group must deal with underlying anxiety of the monopolist.
Withdrawn, Nonparticipating, Silent Member	Opposite end of continuum from monopolist. Nonfacilitative group members may resent these members' seeming noninvolvement or resent attention they get when other members try to draw them out.

Source: From *Introduction to Group Counseling and Psychotherapy* (p. 142–143) by C. J. Vander Kolk, 1985, Columbus, OH: Charles E. Merrill. Copyright © 1985 by Charles E. Merrill. Reprinted by permission of Merrill, an imprint of Macmillan Publishing Company and the author.

1. *Active listening.* Paying attention to and paraphrasing the verbal and non-verbal aspects of communication in a way that lets members know they have been listened to and have not been evaluated.
2. *Supporting.* Providing reinforcement and encouragement to members to create trust, acceptance, and an atmosphere in which self-disclosure can occur when appropriate.
3. *Empathizing.* Communicating understanding to members by being able to assume their frames of reference.

4. *Goal setting.* Assisting with the planning process by helping members define concrete and meaningful goals.
5. *Facilitating.* Opening up communication between and among group members so that each person contributes in some way to the group experience and begins to feel some involvement with others and with the group experience.
6. *Protecting.* Preventing members from taking unnecessary psychological risks in the group.
7. *Modeling.* Teaching members the elements of constructive communication by demonstrating desired behavior in conjunction with each interaction with group members.

Certain practical tasks also must be accomplished. Establishing ground rules, for example, is something the group leader usually does during the first and, if necessary, subsequent sessions, even if some of this material has been addressed as part of the pre-group screening process. Some examples of ground rules that may be established are attendance at all meetings, no physical violence, no smoking during meetings, no sexual relationships with other members of the group, and no coming late (Vander Kolk, 1985). The leader should explain all of the ground rules and the rationale behind each. Group members may add ground rules as the group continues to meet, as long as none of these rules endangers the well-being of group members.

Confidentiality is another aspect of group participation that should be discussed during the definitive stage. The group leader must stress the importance of confidentiality and possible violations (for example, talking about the disclosures of group members outside the group, telling individuals outside the group the identity of those participating in the group). This topic will receive more attention in Chapter 7.

During the definitive stage of a group, members' uncertainties about what the group experience may be like are often related to their individual fears and apprehensions. Group leaders can anticipate some of the following misgivings and should help members address any that might interfere with participation (Corey and Corey, 1997):

- Concern about being accepted by other members of the group.
- Uncertainty about whether honesty will be accepted by other group members or whether contributions must be carefully framed so others won't be upset.
- Questions about how communication in the group will be different from communication outside the group.
- Apprehension about being judged by other group members.
- Wondering about similarities to other group members.
- Concern about pressure to participate.
- Uncertainty about whether to take risks.
- Apprehension about appearing to be inept.
- Confusion about how much to self-disclose.
- Fear about being hurt by other members of the group.
- Fear of being attacked by the group.

- Wondering about becoming dependent on the group experience.
- Apprehension about facing new insights about oneself.
- Uncertainty about changing and whether significant others will accept these changes.
- Concern about being asked to do something that would be uncomfortable to do.

In addition to establishing ground rules, discussing confidentiality, and addressing individual member's apprehensions, the leader may wish to provide structural elements, such as leader and member introductions, exercises to be completed in dyads or triads followed by sharing in the total group, guided fantasies followed by discussion of the experience, sentence completion exercises, and written questionnaires with subsequent discussion. Such structural elements can promote involvement and productivity. The amount of structure needed to catalyze group interaction will always depend on pre-group screening, the purpose of the group, the age and functionality of group members, and the leader's style. As a rule of thumb, we recommend that the leader provide and use structure when needed but not depend on group exercises to the extent that members are unable to express their concerns, desires, and issues. The special population chapters of this text provide numerous examples of how to structure group sessions.

Finally, the leader should think about how he or she will close the group sessions in a way that provides time for reflection, summarization, and integration. Corey and Corey (1987) recommended setting aside at least 10 minutes at the end of each session for this purpose so group members do not feel frustrated by a lack of closure or what might be perceived as an abrupt ending. This might be an ideal time to suggest introspection, behavioral rehearsal, or other homework, if applicable.

Facilitating the Personal Involvement Stage

The personal involvement stage of a group is best depicted as one of member-to-member interactions, the sharing of personal information, confrontation with other members of the group, power struggles, and the individual's growing identity as a member of the group. It is a stage of action, reaction, and interaction and requires the group leader to demonstrate awareness of the emotional makeup of the group and the intra- and interpersonal struggles that are part of this stage of a group. In addition to the skills discussed for the definitive stage, the following skills are also required of the leader during this challenging stage of group life:

1. *Clarifying.* Helping members sort out conflicting feelings and thoughts to arrive at a better understanding of what is being expressed.
2. *Questioning.* Asking questions to gain additional information or promote members' self-exploration and description of feelings and thoughts.
3. *Interpreting.* Providing tentative explanations for feelings, thoughts, and behaviors that challenge members to explore in more depth their motivations and reactions.
4. *Reflecting feelings.* Letting members know they are being understood in a way that goes beyond the content of their communication.

5. *Confronting.* Challenging members to become aware of discrepancies between words and actions or current and previous self-disclosures.
6. *Initiating.* Being proactive to bring about new directions in individual sharing or interpersonal communication.
7. *Giving feedback.* Offering an external view of how a member appears to another by describing concrete and honest reactions in a constructive way.
8. *Self-disclosing.* Describing here-and-now reactions to events in the group.
9. *Blocking.* Preventing counterproductive behavior by one or more group members.

Some practical considerations also must be dealt with during the personal involvement stage of any group. As self-disclosure becomes more open and interactions among members become more straightforward and more focused on the here and now, some group members may become threatened and remain silent to avoid taking risks. When this happens, the group leader should use his or her skills to acknowledge the way those members may be feeling and encourage them to participate without demanding more participation than they are able to contribute at the time. The longer members remain silent, the more difficulty they may have entering into dialogue and spontaneous interaction. Also, the silent member often engenders suspicions and criticisms by other group members who begin to wonder why the silent members are not involved in the group.

Silence is not the only way members who become threatened by the dynamics of the personal involvement stage react. Benjamin (1981), Corey (1990), Corey and Corey (1997), Sack (1985), and Yalom (1985) offered these additional possibilities the group leader should recognize:

1. *Intellectualization.* Members who are feeling threatened by the openness of communication may focus completely on their thoughts to avoid making connections with either their own or others' emotions. Use of a cognitive pattern of communication should signal the leader that these members may not be comfortable with their feelings.
2. *Questioning.* Questions by members can direct the discussion to why something was said or has happened rather than on how members are feeling and what they are experiencing now. Questions are often asked to avoid dealing with true feelings.
3. *Advice giving.* Advice rarely helps another group member resolve personal issues or solve problems independently, but it does provide a means for the advice giver to avoid struggling with internal issues, empathizing, and adopting the internal frame of reference of other group members.
4. *Band-aiding.* Band-aiding is the misuse of support for the purpose of alleviating painful feelings. Group members who band-aid prevent themselves and others from fully expressing their emotions.
5. *Dependency.* Dependent group members invite advice giving and band-aiding by presenting themselves as helpless and "stuck." This, too, prevents

complete and accurate self-disclosure by those who feel threatened by aspects of group interaction.

6. *Behaviors related to struggles for control.* Struggles for control are common during this stage of group development. Some of the behaviors that might surface include competition and rivalry, jockeying for position, jealousies, affronts to leadership, and arguing about the division of responsibility and decision-making procedure. The leader must recognize these issues and help members talk about them.

7. *Conflict and anger.* Conflict and anger are other common responses to feeling threatened. However, when conflict and anger are recognized, expressed, and discussed, cohesion in a group usually increases. Participants learn that it is safe to openly disagree and express intense feelings. In addition, group members learn that bonds and relationships are strong enough to withstand honest levels of communication.

8. *Confrontation.* Confrontations in a group are not helpful when the focus is on criticizing others, providing negative feedback and then withdrawing, or assaulting others' integrity or inherent personality traits. If, however, confrontations are presented in a caring and helpful way, change can be catalyzed. Group leaders should provide members with guidelines such as the following for responsible confrontation:

   - Know why you are confronting.
   - Avoid dramatic statements about how another member appears to be.
   - Include description of both observable behaviors and the impact they have on you.
   - Imagine being the recipient of what you are saying to another member.
   - Provide the recipient of a confrontive statement with time to integrate and reflect. Do not expect an immediate change in behavior.
   - Think about whether you would be willing to consider what you are expecting another group member to consider.

9. *Challenges to the group leader.* Although a leader may feel uncomfortable when challenges to his or her leadership are expressed, it is important for the leader to recognize that confrontations are often the members' first significant steps toward realizing their independence and trust in the group. The way the leader responds to a challenge by a group member can have a powerful effect on member willingness to trust and to take risks. Leaders can be excellent role models if they respond to challenges nondefensively and ask members to talk about the thoughts and feelings behind them.

   The group leader may be verbally attacked by one or more members. Such attacks are usually the result of the leader modeling some inappropriate behavior or members feeling threatened by the energy or the interactions in the group. The leader has to work through the criticism, during the session, by encouraging those who have negative feelings toward him or her to describe those feelings. A give-and-take discussion may lead to acceptable resolution of the difficulty. If a leader does not provide an opportunity for the members to describe and resolve their feelings, the feelings may escalate to the point that group sessions become counterproductive.

Facilitating the Group Involvement Stage

As explained in Chapter 2, the group involvement stage is characterized by much self-evaluation and self-assessment of behavior, attitudes, values, and methods in relating to others, and also by members channeling their energies toward meeting the group's goals and purposes. During this stage, the terms *members* and *group* become somewhat more synonymous. The group, with its purposes and goals, is merging with members' individual purposes and goals. Individual agendas are replaced by group agendas, and the members identify more with the group.

Facilitating this stage of the group's life requires the leader to use all of the skills needed during the definitive stage and, from time to time, some of the skills important to positive resolution of the personal involvement stage. Additional skills that may be needed include:

1. *Linking.* Stressing the importance of interpersonal communication within the group by connecting what one member is feeling or doing to what another member is feeling or doing.
2. *Providing group identity.* Encouraging members in their development of a group identity.
3. *Suggesting direction.* Providing suggestions as the members progress from individual to group-directed purposes and goals.
4. *Sharing leadership.* Encouraging members to assume leadership responsibility within the group when appropriate.
5. *Participating in the group.* Involving oneself as a member of the group and sharing leadership as opportunities arise.
6. *Reinforcing cooperation.* Demonstrating, on verbal and nonverbal levels, the benefits of cooperative participation.

Practical considerations for constructive leadership during this stage relate to the higher level of self-disclosure and intimacy that members have developed. One situation that often arises comes from sudden insights that a member gains as another member self-discloses and problem-solves. Because members are now readily able to put aside personal agendas and listen and empathize as others in the group share during this stage, they may become aware of incidents in their own lives (e.g., interactions designed to prevent intimacy from occurring) that are emotionally laden. At times, these memories may be extremely difficult to share and then integrate into a new perspective or set of behaviors. During these circumstances, the leader must provide the safety and support needed to guide resulting disclosure and group response and interaction. Insights about previously denied experience can be powerful and quite difficult for an individual to handle.

Risk-taking in the group may be high during the group involvement stage, and self-disclosure may progress more rapidly than is necessary or appropriate for the participant or the group as a whole. The leader may have to slow down the rate and intensity of self-disclosure to safeguard members from unnecessary psychological risks. Because of the cohesive atmosphere that has developed during this stage, other members may reinforce a participant's self-disclosure or offer suggestions that the leader might have to ward off so the risk is not escalated.

Group efforts to help a member with a problem sometimes become detrimental during this stage. Unlike the advice giving and band-aiding in the personal involvement stage, these efforts are not meant to direct the group away from discussing emotional or painful issues. Instead, they derive from the strong feelings of closeness that have developed, and they occur following intense discussions and thorough exploration. The problem arises when a participant receives so many suggestions for resolving a problem that he or she begins to feel confused and at a loss to deal with the many options presented. The group leader needs to intervene so an option or two can be carefully considered and then either adopted or discarded. Or the leader might more appropriately encourage participants to discuss a specific problem or area in future sessions after they have identified their own solutions.

During the group involvement stage, group members begin discussing their desire to establish on the "outside" the same kind of cooperation, cohesiveness, and communication patterns they enjoy during these group sessions. The leader should encourage discussion of this topic, helping members to understand that they should not expect the same level of cooperation and the same degree of self-disclosure in all groups. Still, they should not assume that nothing can improve in established outside circles. Members may also express how much they look forward to group sessions and how much they dislike the idea of their group terminating at some future point. This latter sentiment, which may begin to be expressed as the group moves toward the enhancement and closure stage, must be addressed.

Facilitating the Enhancement and Closure Stage

This final stage in group development is often described simultaneously as the most exhilarating and the saddest aspect of group work. The exhilaration stems from evaluation and reevaluation as members are encouraged to review the group process and to measure changes from the time they entered the group to this period just before closure and termination. The sadness centers on leaving an environment that has provided safety, security, and support and individuals who have offered encouragement, friendship, and positive feedback related to one's growth potential.

Facilitation of this stage requires the leader to draw upon the following skills in addition to any of those used during previous stages:

1. *Evaluating.* Assessing both individual and group process during the group's tenure.
2. *Resolving issues.* Assisting individual members and the group to achieve closure on remaining issues.
3. *Reviewing progress.* Helping group members obtain an overview of the progress and change that have taken place since the group was initiated.

4. *Identifying strengths and weaknesses.* Encouraging members to pinpoint the strengths they have developed in the group, as well as the weaknesses they have acknowledged and begun to overcome, so they can apply this learning outside the group after it terminates.

5. *Terminating.* Preparing group members to finalize the group's history, assimilate the experience, and separate from the group as sessions come to an end.

6. *Referring.* Recommending possibilities for individual or group counseling after the group ends.

Practical considerations for the group leader are numerous. Corey (1990), Corey and Corey (1997), George and Dustin (1988), Gladding (1991), Jacobs, Harvill, and Masson (1988), Ohlsen, Horne, and Lawe (1988), Vander Kolk (1985), and others have discussed aspects of effective leadership connected with closure and termination. The following are some suggestions the leader can draw on for facilitating closure and termination, although these are by no means an exhaustive listing of possibilities:

1. *Reminders.* Make sure members are aware of the approaching termination date, to enable them to achieve the essential review and closure. This suggestion applies to groups that have a predetermined closure date established by the members themselves or by a set of external circumstances.

2. *Capping.* During the last few sessions of a group, do not encourage members to initiate discussions of intensely emotional material or to facilitate powerful emotional interchange in the group as a whole. Capping means easing members and the group out of affective expression and into intellectual consideration of progress, change, and strengths, because time is running out for the processing of new emotional material.

3. *Logs.* If members have been keeping written logs chronicling the group experience, suggest that they share particularly meaningful segments as the group reaches its conclusion. This can be an excellent vehicle for evaluation, review, and providing feedback.

4. *Unfinished business.* Ask group members to share and work on the resolution of any unfinished business (whether individual or group focused). Allow enough time for members to adequately achieve resolution.

5. *Homework.* Suggest that each group member identify, discuss, and commit to some homework to be completed after the group ends. This may help group members integrate learning and develop perspectives for the future.

6. *Making the rounds.* Offer members the opportunity to look at each person in the group and provide some final feedback (or to hand each person some written feedback). This can provide the basis for one or more sessions aimed at easing the emotions sometimes associated with the end of a positive group experience. To allow feedback to be adequately discussed and processed, the leader should allow more than one group session for this activity.

7. *Saying good-bye.* Allow each member to express his or her unique personality and perspective in saying good-bye when a group is ending. Suggest that members frame this good-bye as it relates to the group as a whole, to each participant, or both.

8. *Future planning.* Discuss how group members can approach the future in a proactive way. This helps participants integrate new learning and plan to meet future needs. Members need plenty of time to think about how they will function in the absence of the support of the group.

9. *Referrals.* Make arrangements for members who need further counseling, whether group or individual. Discuss the possibilities during a specifically scheduled group session. Members may decide to share with the group their decision for follow-up counseling.

10. *Questionnaires.* If desired, use questionnaires to assess the strengths and weaknesses of a particular group experience. If these questionnaires are filled out before the group ends, share excerpts with the group, with advance permission of the members.

11. *Follow-up interviews.* Ease the apprehension often associated with the end of a group by offering the opportunity for individual follow-up sessions. Members can utilize the follow-up meeting to discuss post-group progress, difficulties, or issues and to obtain the support needed to continue in productive ways.

12. *Group reunions.* Organize a group reunion. The reunion might be in the form of a group session, a potluck dinner or picnic, or group attendance at a lecture, as examples. The purpose of the follow-up is to give members a chance to reconnect, share, and provide support and encouragement.

Dealing With Difficult Members〜

Counselors at times face some difficult group members. These are members who attempt to control or take over the group in some way. Typical patterns, presented by Carroll, Bates, and Johnson (1997), Dyer and Vriend (1973), Kottler (1994), and Milgram and Rubin (1992), are listed here with suggestions for how the group leader might respond (Capuzzi & Gross, 1997). The 14 examples that follow concretize the use of skills discussed for facilitating the four stages of a group.

1. A group member speaks for everyone.

A group member commonly says something like, "We think we should...," "This is how we all feel," or "We were wondering why... ." Often this happens when a member does not feel comfortable making statements such as, "I think we should..." or "I'm wondering why..." or when a group member is attempting to garner support for a point of view. The difficulty with allowing the "we" syndrome to operate in a group is that it inhibits members from expressing their individual feelings and thoughts. The group leader might give *feedback* ("You mentioned 'we' a number of times. Are you speaking for yourself or for everyone?") or engage in *linking* ("What do each of you think about the statement that was just made?").

2. A member speaks for another member in the group.

"I think I know what he means" and "She's not really saying how she feels; I can explain it for her" are examples of one group member speaking for another. One member speaking for another often connotes a judgment about the ability of the other member to communicate or a judgment that the other member is about to share uncomfortable information. Regardless of the motivation behind the statement, the group member who permits another group member to do the talking for him or her needs to assess the reason for this and whether the same communication patterns happen outside the group. The "talker" needs to evaluate his or her inclination to make decisions for or rescue others.

Appropriate leader skills here include *questioning* ("Did Jim state your feelings more clearly than you can?" or "How does it feel to have someone rescue you?") and making *interpretive statements* ("Did you feel June needed your assistance?" or "Do you find it difficult to hold back when you think you know what someone else is going to say?").

3. A group member behaves in an "entitled" manner.

The entitled group member is someone who attempts, in a variety of ways, to keep the focus of the group on himself or herself. This member may monopolize the conversation, tell stories that are only tangentially related to the topic under discussion, arrive late or miss sessions and then expect everyone to accommodate him or her by using most of the time to bring him or her up to date, or be needy and demanding of attention a great deal of the time. As long as such a member can control the proceedings of the group, he or she can demonstrate a sense of power. Such a client must be taught the capacity for empathy and attentiveness to the needs of others; groups can be ideal for teaching those skills.

Possible leader interventions include *modeling* ("I realize that what you are saying is important to you; perhaps we can provide you with more time after others have had an opportunity to participate in today's session") and giving *feedback* ("Have you noticed how much time you have taken today, and how restless some other group members appear to be?"). Another option is to cue another group member to do the work ("John, you seem to be getting progressively restless as Bonnie has been speaking; tell her how you feel.").

4. A group member remains silent.

As noted earlier in this chapter, silent group members can create difficulties for groups. There are many different reasons for a group member's silence. Sometimes a member is silent because he or she cannot find the words to describe a subjective experience; sometimes silence occurs because the member is observing and taking things in. If a group member lacks self-confidence and generally avoids taking initiative in conversations, he or she may be behaving in his or her normal pattern and not mean to be resistant or difficult. However, at times, a group may have a member who is not committed to participation and uses the silence as a means of manipulation.

In any case, when a group member *remains* silent, the possibility increases that this member will eventually be confronted, or even attacked, by other group members. Group members may begin to imagine that the silent member does not approve, has definite opinions that ought to be shared, or simply does not care about others in the group. Group leaders may need to *empathize* ("I get the feeling that it is difficult for you to speak up in a group.") or *facilitate* ("Jim, is there anything you can add to the discussion at this time?"). Although *questioning* ("I'm wondering what you are thinking and feeling right now?") and *blocking* ("I don't think it is a good idea for you to remain so silent. Others may wonder why you don't participate.") may be used by the leader to elicit participation, these actions may engender even more resistance. It can be quite difficult to work with the silent group member.

5. A group member identifies a scapegoat.

Scapegoating is a common and difficult problem for the group leader. Often, the person who is scapegoated is the focus of the displaced anger of another member of the group. Something in his or her behavior has, however, elicited the attack. Although leaders sometimes encourage group members to give feedback to the scapegoat so that this member can better understand the reason others are upset with his or her behavior, caution must be employed so that the scapegoat is not unnecessarily attacked. Leaders who are not experienced group work specialists often allow the attention to remain on the scapegoat because of the interaction and participation that is occurring in the group. Even if the feedback being given is accurate, the leader is responsible for seeing that the rights of the scapegoated member are not being violated. At times, a silent member may be inclined to support the scapegoat but may need the help of the leader to vocalize a minority point of view. The leader might also ask the group members to focus upon how they would feel if they were in the place of the scapegoat so that a constructive resolution of the process can be reached.

6. A group member challenges the leader's authority.

Since this topic is one of such importance to the group leader, it merits additional attention in this chapter. Group members who challenge the competence of the leader sometimes do so in a nonaggressive way, suggesting how the leader might be more effective. On the other end of the continuum of member behavior is the angry, hostile member who overtly attacks the leader's competency and expertise. Since members usually view the leader as a source of authority, norm setting, and leadership during the first few sessions, such challenges often do not occur until the group has met two or three times.

The most important things for a group leader to remember when coping with a challenger is to stay calm and avoid responding with defensiveness. A response like, "I am glad you are able to express those feelings; can you tell me more about what has led up to this?" implies that the leader is willing to listen to the challenger, is not going to withdraw from the confrontation, and is not going to abdicate the leadership role. Once some interchange occurs, the conflict may be seen as a misunderstanding and resolved in a way that makes the group even more cohesive and able to function constructively. In any event, the behavior the leader *models* for the group when facing a challenge is crucial to the future productivity and comfort levels of the group.

7. A group member focuses on persons, conditions, or events outside the group.

Many times group counseling sessions can turn into gripe sessions. Group members tend to enjoy complaining about a colleague, a friend, or a partner if they are allowed to reinforce one another. The difficulty with this type of interaction is that it might erroneously substantiate that others are at fault and that group members do not have to take responsibility for those aspects of their behavior contributing to their complaints.

The group leader might use skills in *initiating* ("You keep talking about your wife as the cause of your unhappiness. Isn't it more important to ask yourself what contributions you can make to improve your relationship?") or *clarifying* ("Does complaining about others really mean you think you would be happier if they could change?").

8. A member seeks the approval of the leader or a group member before or after speaking.

Some group members nonverbally seek acceptance by nodding, glancing, or smiling at the leader or another group member. These members may be intimidated by authority figures or by personal strength or have low self-esteem, causing them to seek sources of support and acceptance outside themselves. When a group member glances at the leader for approval when speaking, one tactic is for the leader to look at another member, forcing the speaker to change the direction of his or her delivery. Another is to give *feedback* ("You always look at me as you speak, almost as if you're asking permission.").

9. A member says, "I don't want to hurt her feelings, so I won't say what I'd like to say."

Especially in the early stages of a group, this sentiment is common. Sometimes it happens when a member believes another member of the group is too fragile for feedback. Other times the member is revealing apprehension about being liked by other group members. The group leader should explore reasons for the reticence to offer feedback. In doing so, the leader may reinforce cooperation, asking the member to check with the person to whom feedback may be directed to validate his or her fears.

10. A group member suggests that his or her problems are someone else's fault.

This example may seem to overlap with the seventh one, but it presents a different problem than a group gripe session. When a group member periodically attributes difficulties and unhappiness to another person, the leader might use *blocking*

("Who is really the only person who can be in charge of you?" or "How can other people determine your mood so much of the time?"). We are not suggesting a stance that would be perceived as lacking empathy and acceptance, but the leader should facilitate members' taking responsibility for themselves.

11. A member might suggest that "I've always been that way."

This suggestion indicates irrational thinking and lack of motivation to change. Believing that the past determines all of one's future can limit one's future growth. The group leader must help these members identify irrational thoughts that cause them to be ineffective in specific areas and learn that they are not doomed to repeat the mistakes of the past. *Interpreting* ("You're suggesting that your past has such a hold over you that you will never be any different") and *questioning* ("Do you feel that everyone has certain parts of his life over which he has no control?") are possible responses to stimulate the examination of faulty thinking and assumptions.

12. A member of the group suggests, "I'll wait, and it will change."

Frequently, group members are willing to discuss their self-defeating behavior during a group session but are not willing to make an effort to change outside the group. At times they take the position that if they postpone action, things will correct themselves. A competent group leader will use *initiating* to help members develop strategies for doing something about their problems outside the group and will assign *homework* as a means of tracking or checking in with members to evaluate progress.

13. A member shows discrepant behavior.

When discrepancies appear in a member's behavior, the group leader must intervene. Discrepancies may occur between what a member is currently saying and what he or she said earlier, in a lack of congruence between what a member is saying and what he or she is doing in the group, in a difference between how a member sees himself or herself and how others in the group see him or her, or in a difference between how a member reports feelings and how his or her nonverbal cues communicate what is going on inside. The statements a leader uses to identify discrepancies may be *confrontational* in nature because the leader usually has to describe the discrepancies so the group member can begin to identify, evaluate, and change aspects of the behavior.

14. A member bores the group by rambling.

Sometimes members use talking as a way of seeking approval, and it may become "overtalk." In response, the leader might ask other members to give *feedback* to the "intellectualizer" to let him or her know how the rambling affects them. If this behavior is not addressed, other members may become angry and hostile toward the offender and toward the leader.

Summary ∼

The group leader's style, personality, experience, and skills have many ramifications for group experiences and outcomes. The three classic leadership styles identified by Lewin are authoritarian, democratic, and laissez-faire, which may relate somewhat to the purpose of the group and its composition. In another conceptualization, groups can be seen as leader centered or group centered. A third way of looking at leader style is to characterize it as interpersonal or intrapersonal. Group members tend to admire leaders who have charisma, though this carries the danger of the leader's relying too much on this characteristic and failing to facilitate the autonomy of group members. Leaders are encouraged to develop their own unique style through self-awareness, an understanding of their own personal traits and qualities, and the acquisition of specific skills common to all group needs.

In planning for a group experience, leaders should conduct pre-group screening, which may be done through interviews or completion of questionnaires, to select members whose needs and goals are compatible with those of the intended group and who will not be detrimental to other group members or themselves. During pre-group screening, potential members should receive full information about all aspects of the group and what to expect.

When organizing for a group, the leader has to consider the physical setting, the length and frequency of the meetings, and the size of the group (within a recommended range of 5 to 10). Other organizational aspects may include weekly summaries, written material, movies or videotapes, and pre-group training sessions.

Members assume various roles within a group, including maintenance, blocking, and facilitative, and subroles of each. The leader must be able to recognize these roles and make appropriate interventions. The leader also has to apply a repertoire of skills in leading each of the stages in a group's development. In a group's life, the leader is likely to encounter difficult members and behaviors, which he or she must counteract to ensure that the group progresses as intended from beginning to termination.

References ∼

Association for Specialists in Group Work. (1989). *Ethical guidelines for group counselors.* Alexandria, VA: Author.

Association for Specialists in Group Work. (1990). *Professional standards for training of group work generalists and of group work specialists.* Alexandria, VA: Author.

Benjamin, A. (1981). *The helping interview* (3rd ed.). Boston: Houghton Mifflin.

Brown, R. (1969). Effects of structured and unstructured group counseling with high- and low-anxious college underachievers. *Journal of Counseling Psychology, 16,* 209–214.

Capuzzi, D., & Gross, D. R. (1997). *Introduction to the counseling profession.* Boston: Allyn & Bacon.

Carroll, M., Bates, M., & Johnson, C. (1997). *Group leadership: Strategies for group counseling leaders* (3rd ed.). Denver: Love Publishing.

Chatwin, M. (1972). Interpersonal trust and leadership style in group counseling. *Dissertation Abstracts International, 32,* 6120A.

Conyne, R. K., Harvill, R. L., Morganett, R. S., Morran, D. K., & Hulse-Killacky, D. (1990). Effective group leadership: Continuing the search for greater clarity and understanding. *Journal for Specialists in Group Work, 15*(1), 30–36.

Cooper, G. L. (1977). Adverse and growthful effects of experimental learning groups: The role of the trainer, participant, and group characteristics. *Human Relations, 30,* 1103–1109.

Corey, G. (1990). *Theory and practice of group counseling* (3rd ed.). Pacific Grove, CA: Brooks/Cole.

Corey, M. S., & Corey, G. (1987). *Groups: Process and practice* (3rd ed.). Pacific Grove, CA: Brooks/Cole.

Corey, M. S., & Corey, G. (1997). *Groups: Process and practice* (5th ed.). Pacific Grove, CA: Brooks/Cole.

Dies, R. R. (1973). Group therapist self-disclosure: An evaluation by clients. *Journal of Counseling Psychology, 20,* 344–348.

Dies, R. R. (1977). Group therapist transparency: A critique of theory and research. *International Journal of Group Psychotherapy, 27,* 177–200.

Dyer, W. W., & Vriend, J. (1973). Effective group counseling process interventions. *Educational Technology, 13*(1), 61–67.

Gazda, G. M. (1989). *Group counseling: A developmental approach* (4th ed.). Boston: Allyn & Bacon.

George, R. L., & Dustin, D. (1988). *Group counseling: Theory and practice.* Englewood Cliffs, NJ: Prentice-Hall.

Gladding, S. T. (1991). *Group work: A counseling specialty.* Columbus: Merrill.

Heikkinen, C. A. (1975). Another look at teaching experience and closed-mindedness. *Journal of Counseling Psychology, 22,* 79–83.

Heslin, R. (1964). Predicting group task effectiveness from members' characteristics. *Psychological Bulletin, 62,* 248–256.

Jacobs, E. E., Harvill, R. L., & Masson, R. L. (1988). *Group counseling: Strategies and skills.* Pacific Grove, CA: Brooks/Cole.

Johnson, D. W., & Johnson, F. P. (1994). *Joining together: Group theory and group skills* (5th ed.). Boston: Allyn & Bacon.

Kellerman, H. (1979). *Group psychotherapy and personality: Intersecting structures.* New York: Grune & Stratton.

Kottler, J. A. (1994). Working with difficult group members. *Journal for Specialists in Group Work, 19,* 3–10.

Lewin, K. (1944). The dynamics of group action. *Educational Leadership, 1,* 195–200.

MacLennan, B. W. (1975). The personalities of group leaders: Implications for selection and training. *International Journal of Group Psychotherapy, 25,* 177–184.

Milgram, D., & Rubin, J. S. (1992). Resisting resistance: Involuntary substance abuse group therapy. *Social Work With Groups, 15,* 95–110.

Nolan, E. J. (1978). Leadership interventions for promoting personal mastery. *Journal for Specialists in Group Work, 3,* 132–138.

Ohlsen, M. M., Horne, A. M., & Lawe, C. F. (1988). *Group counseling* (3rd ed.). New York: Holt, Rinehart & Winston.

Rutan, J. S., & Rice, C. A. (1981). The charismatic leader: Asset or liability? *Psychotherapy: Theory, Research and Practice, 18,* 487–492.

Sack, R. T. (1985). On giving advice. *AMHCA Journal, 7,* 127–132.

Schmuck, R. A., & Schmuck, P. A. (1997). *Group process in the classroom* (7th ed.). Dubuque, IA: Brown & Benchmark.

Shapiro, J. L. (1978). *Methods of group psychotherapy and encounter: A tradition of innovation.* Itasca, IL: Peacock.

Shaw, M. E. (1981). *Group dynamics: The psychology of small group behavior.* New York: McGraw-Hill.

Stogdill, R. M. (1974). *Handbook of leadership.* New York: Free Press.

Vander Kolk, C. J. (1985). *Introduction to group counseling and psychotherapy.* Columbus, OH: Merrill.

Wittmer, J., & Webster, G. B. (1969). The relationship between teaching experience and counselor trainee dogmatism. *Journal of Counseling Psychology, 16,* 499–504.

Yalom, I. D. (1985). *The theory and practice of group psychotherapy* (3rd ed.). New York: Basic Books.

Zimpfer, D., & Waltman, D. (1982). Correlates of effectiveness in group counseling. *Small Group Behavior, 13*(3), 275–290.

4

Group Counseling: Theory and Application

Douglas R. Gross and David Capuzzi

The group procedures class was just beginning, and Dr. Burns asked if anyone had questions about the material that was to have been read prior to class. Greg, a first-year student, raised his hand and said he was confused about the information dealing with theory applied to groups. When Dr. Burns asked Greg to be more specific in his question, Greg said that when he had taken the counseling theory class last semester, he had understood that the various counseling theories had been developed to work with the individual, that the research done in developing these theories was all completed on individual cases. His confusion stemmed from the fact that the author of the assigned material seemed to be simply transferring these theoretical concepts from the individual to the group.

His question was, "How do I transfer these individual concepts into a group of 8 or 10 members?" Dr. Burns's response of "carefully" brought laughter from the class. He continued, however, by stating that Greg had a good question, one that continues to concern even the most experienced group leaders. The class spent most of the period discussing the issue. As with many such questions, the class arrived at no definitive answers, and every student left that evening with several questions regarding the relationship of counseling theory to group interaction and how to use individual-based approaches with groups.

This scenario has probably taken place, in one form or another, in every group class. The confusion surrounding the issue of how to transfer individual counseling theory to groups plagues not only students but also professionals who operate in the broad arena of group counseling. Addressing this issue in 1978, Shapiro made the following statement:

> There is an apparent paradox in the notion of group psychotherapy. The locus of therapy is the group, and yet the group is not in need of treatment. Unless the group in question is a natural group (family, management, etc.), group therapists are using a group format to treat individuals. The goal of the leader is not to alter the group per se but to provide treatment and growth for the members of the group. This problem is reflected in the development of therapeutic approaches to groups. Most of the extant group therapies are in fact individual therapies which subsequently were applied in group settings for reasons of economy. (pp. 44–45)

This statement encapsulates one of the major dilemmas emanating from discussions of theoretical/therapeutic systems applied to groups. The dilemma revolves around the transferability of concepts, techniques, and approaches originally developed for and directed toward the individual into a group modality. Authors such as Capuzzi and Gross (1992, 1995), Corey (1990), Gladding (1996), and Yalom (1995) have all addressed the difficulties and cautions that the counselor or therapist, making the transition from individual to group counseling or therapy, has to face. These difficulties and cautions should not be interpreted to mean that transferability is impossible. On the contrary, current practice indicates that all theoretical/therapeutic systems have been applied, with varying degrees of success, across both individual and group counseling or therapy. Based upon statements by Lakin (1985), Shaffer and Galinsky (1989), and Wright (1989), many of the factors that dictate the selection of one or more theoretical/therapeutic systems in the individual realm have applicability in the group domain. The selection of a theoretical system is often based upon the counselor's or therapist's philosophical position and what he or she believes regarding the nature of the individual as this relates to development and change. It also may stem from an experiential position based upon the counselor's or therapist's education and working background in selected theoretical systems. Regardless of the reasons for the selection of a theoretical system, those who choose to work with groups should do so with a basis in theory. To do otherwise places the individual and group in the following situation described by Corey and Corey (1987):

> Attempting to lead groups without having an explicit theoretical rationale is like flying a plane without a flight plan. Though you may eventually get there (and even find detours exciting), you're equally likely to run out of patience and gas and do nothing but fly aimlessly in circles. Group leaders without any theory behind their interventions will probably find that their groups never reach a productive stage. (p. 7)

Responding to the issue raised in the preceding quotation, we present in this chapter selected concepts of theoretical/therapeutic systems and their application to groups. This discussion is followed by an integration of the concepts and systems based on similarities in the variables of relationship, leader role, member role, process, and outcome.

Theoretical Systems ～

This chapter covers six theoretical systems that have gained wide acceptance in the group setting: Adlerian, Gestalt, person-centered, rational-emotive behavior theory, transactional analysis, and psychodrama. The basic concepts of each theory are presented followed by leader dynamics and techniques drawn from these concepts that are applicable to a discussion of group therapy or counseling.

Adlerian Theory

Basic Concepts   Adlerian psychology is both an individual and a social psychology. The individual aspects define humans as unified organisms whose behaviors are purposeful and goal directed and not necessarily determined by genetic endowment, environmental press, or early sexual impressions. Individuals give meaning to their lives. They have the creative power and the self-determination to influence not only their personal/social development but also certain events. Through their unique powers, individuals strive to achieve an identity and to belong.

The social aspects emphasize the importance of the individual's interaction with the rest of society and depend on the premise that individuals are motivated primarily by social interest. This is translated into a "need to belong." According to Sweeney (1995), social interest is possibly the most distinctive and valuable concept in Adlerian psychology. It involves individuals' attitudes in dealing with the social world and includes a concern and striving for a better world for all humans. The social connectedness and individuals' needs to be useful to others are what give people measures of happiness and success. Based upon this social interest, individuals strive to master three main tasks as they move through life: their relationships with society, work, and love.

Adler (1938) believed that feelings of inferiority are common in children because of the dependent, small, and socially inferior position they hold in the family and in society. This position provides motivational forces according to Adlerians. These forces are best described as striving from a perceived negative to a hoped for positive position in life, striving in the direction of a unique goal or ideal self, striving to belong in one's social world, striving to understand one's spiritual nature, and striving to better comprehend the "I" and "Me" aspects of self. None of these motivating forces stands alone. They are interrelated, and movement in one area impacts movement in another.

These motivating forces are influenced by a number of factors, any one of which may encumber individuals in their development and movement toward goals:

1. Fictional goals (unconscious assumptions regarding what must be done to develop worth as an individual, such as striving for superiority).
2. Birth order (the individual's chronological and psychological position within the family).
3. The family constellation/atmosphere (variables related to personality, relationships, developmental issues, structural factors, attitudes and values within the family).

This planned and orchestrated movement toward goals is termed one's "style of life" and, based upon the factors identified above, may lead individuals to a lifestyle characterized by positive growth and development or to one characterized by maladjustment. The key rests with individuals and their perceptions and interpretations, which translate into assumptions and goals that direct the formation of their "style of life."

In summarizing the major concepts underlying Adlerian psychology, Gilliland, James, Roberts, and Bowman (1984) identified the following seven attributes:

1. *Humanistic.* Individual and society valued over the organization.
2. *Holistic.* Individual is indivisible.
3. *Phenomenological.* Importance of the individual's perspective.
4. *Teleological.* Future orientation and striving for goal attainment.
5. *Field theoretical.* Interactional nature of the individual with the social and physical environment.
6. *Socially oriented.* Individual responds to and contributes to society.
7. *Operational.* Methodology in place.

Concepts/Leader Behaviors   The following theoretical concepts are presented as group leader behaviors. The Adlerian group leader needs to be able to:

- establish a working relationship in which the leader and members are equal.
- communicate to the members feelings of mutual trust and respect.
- aid the members in exploring the personal goals, beliefs, feelings, and motives that are determining factors in the development of the members' "style of life."
- assist the members in gaining insight into their fictitious goals and the self-defeating behaviors that impede them from formulating effective life goals.
- help members accept responsibility for their freedom and personal effectiveness so that they can develop feelings of self-worth.
- aid members in considering alternative lifestyles and assist them in strengthening their commitment to change.
- help members to enhance their involvement with others and to extend their social interest as this applies to self and others.
- aid members in accepting self with the assets and the liabilities that make up the self.
- assist members in developing a sense of belonging and a sense of community, because their self-meaning is tied closely to their social purpose.
- aid members in exploring alternative behaviors and gaining new insights, and empower them to put these behaviors and insights into action.

Group Stages and Techniques   According to Gladding (1991), the Adlerian approach to working with groups has four stages:

1. Developing and maintaining the proper therapeutic relationship.
2. Analyzing the dynamics that operate within the individual.

3. Fostering the individual's insight into understanding self.
4. Helping the individual to discover new alternatives and make new choices.

In each of these stages, certain techniques have been found to enhance group members' growth and development. These techniques, however, are not limited to only one stage. Their use throughout the group process is highly effective in bringing forth positive group interaction. The following techniques will aid the Adlerian leader in enhancing both the growth and development within the group:

- Model appropriate social skills and show interest to demonstrate acceptance.
- Contract to demonstrate the equality of the leader-member relationship.
- Make use of active listening skills (e.g., restatement, reflection, summarization).
- Employ visual imagery to help members clarify and put into concrete terms some of the absurdities of their thinking and behavior.
- Call upon early recollections to aid members in identifying emotional patterns and feelings and discovering the basis for negatives carried from childhood into adulthood.
- Make use of paradoxical intention by having members attempt to increase debilitating thoughts and behaviors.
- Use confrontation, in a constructive fashion, to point out discrepancies between what group members say and their actions.
- Assess members' current functioning in work and social relationships.
- Assess members' goals and how these translate into individual lifestyles.
- Observe members' interactions, as they may be descriptive of their feelings regarding self and their social skills development.
- Observe members' nonverbal behaviors, and do not hesitate to interpret from these observations.

These are examples of the techniques that have application in an Adlerian group. Special techniques, as reported by Sharf (1996) and Sweeney (1995), with names such as "The Question," "Catching Oneself," "Spitting in the Client's Soup," "Push Button," "Avoiding the Tar Baby," "Paradoxical Intention," and "Acting As If," are specific to Adlerians and are used in both individual and group modalities. Each technique is designed to deal with the identified group stages discussed earlier.

Gestalt Theory

Basic Concepts   Gestalt counseling or therapy is rooted in Gestalt psychology, a school of perception that originated in Europe before World War I. Gestalt psychology began with studies of the perceptual field as a whole. Gestaltists then broke this field down into parts (figure and background), identifying the characteristics of each of these parts and their relationships. Using the body of knowledge collected in this academic field, Fritz Perls translated the perceptual approach to psychology into Gestalt therapy, which moved it from the primarily academic realm into the arena of counseling and therapy.

As applied to counseling and therapy, Gestalt theory views the individual (organism) as being fully responsible for determining the essence of his or her being and his or her reality. In this sense, Gestalt theory may be viewed as both phenomenological and existential. This view credits individuals with the ability to find their own way in life and to accept the responsibilities that come from the decisions made in this journey. Individuals must accept responsibility for the problems created by their decisions and at the same time accept the responsibility of dealing effectively with these problems. The major goal of counseling is to aid individuals in attaining greater awareness of their potential, which will, in turn, allow the individuals to exercise their potential in positive growth and change.

According to Maples (1995), the process of change in Gestalt therapy involves experience and activity. Contributing to the process of change are what Perls (1969) defined as five layers of neurosis that the client passes through. The five layers include the cliche layer, described as one in which the individual has no contact with others and interactions are generally routine and superficial; the phony layer, described as one in which the individual plays a role or a game to avoid contact with others; the impasse layer, described as the point at which the individual is "stuck" and unable to change or move; the implosive layer, described as the point at which the individual begins to experience himself or herself and develop an awareness of who he or she really is but may not act on these new perceptions; and the explosive layer, described as the point at which the individual becomes alive, authentic, and without pretense and has the motivation to act upon this new awareness.

Gestalt theory explains motivation as striving toward some degree of balance or equilibrium. This striving is natural and is represented by movement between the polarities of equilibrium and disequilibrium. According to Polster and Polster (1973), this striving for balance provides the organism with perceptual order, which is best viewed in terms of a figure set against a background. When the individual perceives a need (figure), a state of disequilibrium exists. When that need is met, the figure melds into the background and a new need (figure) takes its place. Therefore, the individual tends to remain in a constant state of flux.

To further understand the individual, the principle of holism, the individual's interdependent combination of body and spirit and his or her relationship to the environment, must be taken into consideration. The individual is viewed as a physical and psychological totality, and this totality is also unified with the environment. Through the individual's aggressive capacity, he or she is able to interact with the environment and assimilate from that environment what is needed for growth and change. Gilliland et al. (1984) commented about the individual's integration of body, spirit, and aggressive capacity:

> Connecting these three aspects of personality theory together presupposes that a person exists in a field that includes the self and environment. Although the individual and the environment are separate, the process of interaction between them cannot be split (holism). Moreover, human aggressive capacity comes into play at the contact boundary between the organism and the environment by means of contact or withdrawal (the opposite of contact). More specifically, when an object has been contacted or with-

drawn from in a way satisfying to the individual, both the object and the need associated with it disappear into the background. The situation is finished; another Gestalt is completed. (p. 96)

These same three aspects play a role in the development of dysfunctional behavior. Instead of using these aspects for growth, the individual uses them to protect the organism, and in so doing develops defense structures that prevent positive growth and change. Words such as introjection, projection, retroflection, and confluence describe these nonproductive defensive behaviors, which render the individual's perceptions unclear so that he or she is in danger of erecting rigid, artificial boundaries that do not permit the successful completion of need satisfaction.

Gestaltists believe that to remove these artificial boundaries, counseling or therapy must approach the individual from an experiencing perspective through which the individual can deal with the boundaries that detract from effective functioning. This is done through a here-and-now orientation that deals with present functioning, because current behavior is more representative of the boundaries than is past behavior. By dealing with behaviors in the here and now, through sensing, feeling, and experiencing the boundaries, the individual is able to move through the impasse and reformulate his or her life for more productive results.

To enhance the counselor's or therapists' effectiveness in aiding clients in this experiential process, implied direction can be found in Naranjo's (1970) listing of nine "moral injunctions for the individual," which he stated are implicit in Gestalt counseling:

1. Live now. Be concerned with the present rather than the past.
2. Live here. Deal with what is present rather than with what is absent.
3. Stop imagining. Experience the real.
4. Stop unnecessary thinking. Rather, taste and see.
5. Express rather than manipulate, explain, justify, or judge.
6. Give in to unpleasantness and pain just as to pleasure. Do not restrict your awareness.
7. Accept no should or ought other than your own. Adore no graven image.
8. Take full responsibility for your actions, feelings, and thoughts.
9. Surrender to being as you are. (pp. 49–50)

Concepts/Leader Behaviors   The following theoretical concepts are presented as group leader behaviors. The Gestalt group leader needs to be able to:

- establish an environment in which leader and members share equally in the process of change.
- allow members to find their own way in life and accept the responsibility that goes with this.
- focus members on their experiences in the present moment (the here and now).
- recognize the blocks/boundaries that impede members' growth, and be willing to bring them to the members' attention.
- aid members in accepting all aspects of themselves, and encourage their sharing of hidden and self-disguised aspects of self.

- assist members in understanding, accepting, and dealing with the concept that they are responsible for their existence.
- confront members with their defensive structures and their unwillingness to take responsibility for self.
- aid members, through exercises, in addressing the unfinished business in their lives.
- help members try out new forms of behavior, to open them up to the full spectrum of their being.
- help members recognize the splintered parts of self and work toward integrating these parts.

Group Stages and Techniques   Gestalt counseling or therapy does not lend itself well to the concept of group stages. The techniques identified here have special significance in Gestalt counseling or therapy, but their use is not limited to one stage. One attempt at defining group stages for Gestalt counseling or therapy that has been made was posed by Kepner (1980). In his description, he identified the following:

- *Stage 1: Identity and dependence.* This involves setting limits and boundaries for the group and encouraging member-to-member contact.
- *Stage 2: Influence and counterdependence.* This involves group members coming to terms with authority, influence, and control and the challenge that this entails.
- *Stage 3: Intimacy and interdependence.* This involves the development of closeness within the group. This often takes a long time to develop, and not all groups reach this stage.

As stated previously, the following techniques should not be viewed as stage specific but should aid the Gestalt leader in enhancing both growth and development within the group:

- Become actively involved with members of the group.
- Demonstrate, through exaggeration, the meanings of gestures, posture, and movement in communication.
- Experiment with exercises that will help group members gain greater awareness.
- Demonstrate, through dialogue and exercises, willingness and ability to stay in the here and now.
- Apply active listening skills (e.g., restating, paraphrasing, summarizing).
- Enlist other members of the group in providing feedback.
- Demonstrate intensive interaction with one member as a learning model for all members.
- Use confrontational skills to startle or shock members into greater awareness of their self-defeating behaviors.
- Be a creative agent of change to enhance members' self-awareness.
- Observe and give direct feedback on group members' nonverbal behaviors.

These are examples of leader techniques that have application in a Gestalt-oriented group. Special techniques identified by Gladding (1991), Maples (1995), and

Sharf (1996), such as "Awareness Statements and Questions," "Awareness Through Self-Dialogue," "Dream Work," "Empty Chair or Two Chair Strategy," "Making the Rounds," and "Unfinished Business," are specific to Gestalt counseling and are used in both individual and group settings.

Person-Centered Theory

Basic Concepts   Person-centered counseling or therapy arose from the work of Carl Rogers. Based upon its major tenets and belief structures, it may be viewed as both phenomenological (human behavior is based on the individual's perception of reality and the values and attitudes attached to that perception) and holistic (human existence is best understood by viewing individuals as a whole and in relationship to the contexts in which they live their lives). The theory sets forth an optimistic view of human potential. The "organismic valuing process" Rogers described is, according to the theory, inborn and provides the individual with the capacity to make wise choices that will maintain and enhance the organism. People make bad choices, choices that are self-destructive, not because of a failure of the organismic valuing process but, rather, because this process has been subverted by the individual's accepting (introjecting) the values, beliefs, and experiences of others.

The uniqueness of the individual, which is stressed in person-centered theory, is explained developmentally through the potential that exists within the organism. The organism enters the world with both an organismic valuing process and the tendency toward self-actualization. The infant is able to evaluate what feels good (what actualizes self) and through this process forms a self-concept from experiences, values, meanings, and beliefs that enhance the "I" or "Me" of self. With self-concept come perceptions of relationships with others and the values attached to them.

As the organism matures, the self becomes identified as an entity separate from others and from the environment. With this awareness, a new need appears: the need for positive regard. This need initially can be fulfilled only through interaction with others and is, fortunately, reciprocal. The need is fulfilled by receiving positive regard from others or by perceiving that a person's own behavior has met another's need.

With the emergence of self-awareness and the need for positive regard, the individual becomes concerned with self-regard and seeks experiences that result in positive valuing of the self by others. When a person receives unconditional positive regard from others, the need for positive self-regard is almost automatically fulfilled and no problems are likely to arise. The individual remains congruent and bases his or her behavior on his or her organismic valuing process (Hazler, 1995).

In the course of human development, trouble arises when significant others negatively value some of the individual's positive self-experiences. When this happens, the need for positive regard and the organismic valuing process are thrown into conflict and "conditions of worth" develop. To maximize the positive regard received from others and to feel personally worthwhile, the individual is forced to deny or distort the value of some of these experiences. In doing so, the individual becomes incongruent and no longer simply assimilates and symbolizes experiences. The person now denies or distorts experiences that are threatening to the distorted self-concept, and hence to the need for positive self-regard, in order to be accepted into the unrealistic self-structure. This defensive pattern becomes circular. More and more behavior is based on the need for positive regard rather than on the organismic valuing process, and the person becomes increasingly incongruent, defensive, and rigid, compulsively acting to protect his or her erroneous self-image (Noble, 1977).

Rogers (1959) identified the changes he expected successful counseling or therapy to produce:

1. People come to see themselves differently.
2. People accept themselves and their feelings more fully.
3. People become more self-confident and more self-directing.
4. People become more the person they would like to be.
5. People become more flexible, less rigid, in their perceptions.
6. People adopt more realistic goals for themselves.
7. People behave in a more mature fashion.
8. People change maladjustive behaviors.
9. People become more accepting of others.
10. People become more open to the evidence of what is going on within them and outside of themselves.
11. People change basic personality characteristics in constructive ways. (p. 232)

Rogers (1959) stated that the following "core conditions" were necessary and sufficient for bringing about personal changes in counseling or therapy:

- *Psychological contact.* A relationship between two persons in which impact between the two persons is possible.
- *Incongruence.* A condition in which clients are fearful, anxious, or distressed due to differing perceptions of self and their experiences.
- *Congruence/genuineness.* A condition describing the counselor's/therapist's ability to be himself or herself.
- *Unconditional positive regard.* A condition describing the counselor's or therapist's ability to accept the client without conditions.
- *Empathy.* A condition that enables the counselor/therapist to step into the world of the client without being influenced by the client's personal attitudes and values.

Rogers felt that if these core conditions were present and if the client perceived the existence of these conditions, change would occur.

Concepts/Leader Behaviors   The following theoretical concepts are presented as group leader behaviors. The person-centered group leader needs to:

- establish a facilitative climate within the group characterized by congruence, unconditional positive regard, and empathic understanding.
- provide an environment in which all group members perceive the constructs of safety and mutual trust.

- establish an environment in which leader and members share equally in the process of change.
- be congruent (genuine) in relationships with members and be able to communicate this to the members.
- have unconditional positive regard for all members and be able to communicate this to the members.
- have empathic understanding and be able to communicate this to all members.
- support members' finding their own way in life and accepting the responsibility that goes with this.
- refrain from giving advice and direction and allow members to positively activate their organismic valuing process.
- use one's being as a catalyst for change within the group.

Group Stages and Techniques   Person-centered counseling or therapy is not presented in terms of stages or listings of techniques. According to Gilliland et al. (1984):

> Since person-centered counseling is essentially a "being" and a relationship-oriented approach, it is important to note that Rogerian-based strategies for helping people are devoid of techniques that involve doing something to or for the client. There are no steps, techniques, or tools for inducing the client to make measured progress toward some goal; instead the strategies are geared to the experiential relationship. (p. 78)

With this caveat in mind and the knowledge that the core conditions identified earlier need to be met, the person-centered group leader should benefit from the use of:

- silence as a way of communicating acceptance and understanding.
- active listening skills (e.g., restatement, paraphrasing, summarizing).
- confrontation to demonstrate congruence and positive regard for group members.
- attending behaviors to focus fully on group members.
- communication skills to verbally and nonverbally communicate the depth of empathic understanding for group members.
- self-disclosures, when appropriate, to communicate willingness to be real and to model safety and trust within the group.
- members' resources to enable and promote self-empowerment.

Rational-Emotive Behavior Theory

Basic Concepts   Rational-emotive behavior therapy (REBT), a cognitive approach to human development and counseling, stems from the work of Albert Ellis. Ellis assumed that many types of emotional problems result from irrational patterns of thinking. People with emotional problems develop belief systems that lead to implicit verbalizations, or self-talk, resting on faulty logic and assumptions. What individuals tell themselves is intimately related to the way they feel and act.

As reported in Ellis (1991), the basic foundation of REBT is the application of the A-B-C-D-E therapeutic approach. In this approach:

 A = *Activating event.* An external event to which a person is subjected.

 B = *Belief.* A sequence of thoughts or self-verbalizations in which the person engages in response to the external event.

 C = *Consequence.* The feelings and behaviors that result from B.

 D = *Disputing.* The counselor's/therapist's attempt to modify the sequence of thoughts or self-verbalizations.

 E = *Effect.* The presumed affective and behavioral consequences resulting from intervention by the counselor or therapist.

Undergirding this therapeutic approach is the belief that human problems are not based in the actual situation or event that triggers the discomfort but, instead, are based in the thinking (views, beliefs, attitudes) that individuals attach to the situation or event. For example, someone who is rejected in attempting to develop a relationship (situation) cognitively processes the rejection (interprets) according to views, beliefs, and attitudes and, based upon that interpretation, reacts in an irrational manner. The person blows the situation out of proportion (catastrophizes), moves beyond the situation, feels both rejected and rejectable, and, therefore, will not be able to establish a meaningful relationship in the future.

Ellis (1991) contended that people are born with the ability to think and respond both rationally and irrationally. As a result of individuals' interactions with the environment and the significant persons who frequent that environment, too often the propensity for irrational thinking surfaces as a more consistent mode of operating. This should not be interpreted to mean that external forces exert total control. According to Ellis, individuals, based upon instinctual influences, tend to desire that all things will happen for the best and that they will get whatever they desire. Therefore, both internal and external factors operate in influencing individuals, whose behaviors are determined more from irrational than rational approaches to problem solving. In Ellis's view, this is the basis for human maladjustment.

Rational-emotive behavior therapy also posits a hopeful view, holding that individuals have a strong growth/actualizing potential and that this potential facilitates their ability to replace irrational approaches to problem solving with more rational ones. This same potential facilitates their seeking counseling or therapy and provides the counselor or therapist with what he or she may need to facilitate change (Livneh & Wright, 1995).

In facilitating this change, counselors or therapists operating within the REBT framework are highly active, somewhat didactic, and purposely seek to persuade, confront, de-indoctrinate, direct, and lead clients to more rational ways of thinking and behaving. Rational-emotive behavior theory views the client as learner and the counselor/therapist as teacher.

The following statement from Ellis (1982) incorporates the basic tenets of REBT and also provides direction for the group leader who is operating from this theoretical viewpoint:

> In RET group therapy, the therapist not only actively and directively shows members bringing up their emotional problems that they are largely creating these problems

themselves by devoutly and rigidly inventing and holding on to irrational beliefs, not only vigorously questions and challenges these beliefs and helps rip them up, but he or she also encourages and pushes all the group members to look for and dispute the shoulds, oughts, and musts of the other members and to help them give up their perfectionism and dictatorialness. All group participants are steadily taught to use the scientific method with themselves and others: to phrase logically, to vigorously undermine, and to empirically contradict the disordered disturbance-creating cognitions of the other members. (pp. 384–385)

Concepts/Leader Behaviors The following theoretical concepts are presented as group leader behaviors. The REBT group leader needs to be able to:

- develop a group climate characterized as instructional, didactic, confrontational, and challenging.
- instruct group members as to the nature of their faulty thinking and the reasons behind such thinking and provide them with directions for changing.
- separate the behavior of group members from their personhood and focus on the behaviors reported.
- set aside his or her need for a warm personal relationship with members of the group, as this may be counterproductive to change and growth.
- confront members with their thinking and resulting behaviors and encourage other members of the group to do the same, to aid in the reeducative process of REBT.
- detect the irrational belief structures of group members and cause the group members to reach this same type of understanding.
- dispute the "crooked" thinking of members and teach them ways of disputing or challenging this same thinking.
- teach group members the fundamental principles of REBT (A-B-C-D-E formulation), which will empower them to strive for greater self-direction.
- provide relevant experiences, outside of the group through homework, to reinforce and enhance learning and change.
- use principles of contingency management and skill training as viable options for growth and change.

Group Stages and Techniques Rational-emotive behavior therapy is not presented in terms of stages of group development but, instead, in terms of levels of perspectives. According to Gilliland et al. (1984), the techniques that have application in REBT may be viewed from three perspectives: (a) cognitive-explicatory, (b) evocative-emotive, and (c) behavioristic-active-directive. Techniques that derive from all three of these perspectives include:

- presentation, instruction, demonstration, and modeling to help members gain an understanding of their behaviors.
- role-playing as a form of behavioral rehearsal within the group for members' effective operation outside the group.
- distracting methods to get the members involved in activities that will stop them from dealing solely with their self-defeating thinking and behaving.

- humor directed at members' behaviors so they can begin to see how ridiculous their current ways of thinking and behaving are.
- emotionally charged language, which will have impact on the members and which they, in turn, can use on themselves.
- shame-attacking exercises, which force group members to place themselves in embarrassing situations and then show that others' reactions are not what the members expected.
- exaggeration to get points across to group members and alert members to their tendencies to exaggerate the end results of their behaviors.
- exhortation and persuasion to convince members to relinquish illogical thinking and acquire more efficient and adaptive ideas.

These are examples of techniques that have application to the REBT group. Other techniques, reported by Livneh and Wright (1995), include cognitive distraction/diversion procedures (thought stopping), reframing (changing negative thoughts to positive thoughts), referenting (changing viewpoints from fragmatic to holistic), and analogies, parables, and stories (using verbal images to dramatize rational ideas).

Transactional Analysis

Basic Concepts Transactional analysis (TA) is based on ideas and concepts originally developed by Eric Berne (1964) and popularized in his book, *Games People Play*. Building on the early work of Berne, TA proponents have added structure and concepts that continue to expand this evolving view of human development and change (Dusay & Dusay, 1979; Goulding, 1987; Karpman, 1981; Stewart & Jaines, 1987; Thompson & Rudolph, 1992; Zalcman, 1990).

Addressing TA from a global perspective brings into clear focus the significance of early decision making, which sets the parameters for future behavior. The three ego states (parent, adult, child) form early in life, and each carries with it a script on how one is to behave, think, and feel. The developing individual takes in messages, verbal and nonverbal, delivered by the environment and by significant persons within that environment, processes them, and develops from them a set of scripts that form the framework for the individual's behavior. Individuals are not passive in this process; they make decisions and develop their own life script. Because the individual is able to decide and, therefore, determine the original life script, he or she also can re-decide and change the script. This redecision and rescripting become central issues in the process of counseling or therapy.

According to Poidevant and Lewis (1995), TA does not present a set of developmental stages through which individuals proceed. The development of an individual's personality is best understood through analyzing the following structures of TA:

- Ego states
- Strokes
- Injunctions
- Decisions

- Script formation
- Life positions

The ego states (parent, adult, child) are the foundation for the personality, from which individuals build the cognitive, affective, and behavioral dynamics that direct their lives. The first ego state to develop is that of the child. This development begins shortly after birth. During the first few years of life, the child incorporates within this ego state rudimentary configurations of the adult ego state and the parent ego state. This "early adult," called the "little professor," processes information and makes decisions based on this processing. The "early parent" incorporates the infant's perception of parental behaviors and the messages this behavior transmits. As development proceeds, the fully developed adult ego state and parent ego state emerge from these early configurations. Each is separate and distinct, but the interplay of the three, based upon the scripts written for each, forms the basis of behavior.

Strokes, the second key concept, are units of attention that stimulate the individual and serve as a motivational force for human interaction. This attention may be positive or negative. The rule seems to be that even negative strokes are better than no strokes at all. Strokes may stem from both internal and external sources, and if strokes are not readily available, the individual may devise "games" and "rackets" (transactions that allow the individual to gain needed strokes) to provide this motivational force. Transactions are generally described in three forms: complementary (two persons operating from the same ego state); crossed (two persons interacting, but one is operating from an ego state that draws a response from an inappropriate ego state of the other person); and ulterior (two persons interacting, one from an appropriate ego state and the other from an inappropriate one).

Injunctions, decisions, and script formation, the next three concepts, are most easily understood in combination. Injunctions are parental messages that children receive at an early age. These messages are generally prescriptive in terms of ways of being: "Don't be, don't feel, don't love, don't trust." Upon hearing and processing these messages, the child makes decisions regarding them. Based upon those decisions, he or she forms a script for living his or her life. If the messages are reinforced and repeated, the foundation for this early scripting becomes strong.

Life positions, the last of the major concepts, represent the resolution of the three-part process of injunctions, decisions, and script formation. Life positions form the framework within which individuals structure and operate the behavioral, cognitive, and affective domains of their lives. According to Harris (1967), individuals adopt one of the following four life positions:

1. I'm OK—You're OK.
2. I'm OK—You're not OK.
3. I'm not OK—You're OK.
4. I'm not OK—You're not OK.

Each position is descriptive of the individual's developmental process and also how he or she interacts with the environment and the people who frequent that environment. The boundaries between the positions are not hard and fast. Even though individuals usually operate more in one position than the others, movement across all four positions is possible. The life position "I'm OK—You're OK" is considered a "winner's script." The other life positions are viewed as "losers' scripts" and set the stage for maladjustment in later life.

In summary, transactional analysis is based on the philosophy that individuals are inherently okay and have potential and desire to move toward a positive growth-oriented position. This potential is often stifled because of early decisions, and a redecision process is necessary for individuals to realize their growth potential. Awareness seems to be a key to this change process. Individuals need to become aware first of their current scripting and how it impacts on their way of being, and then of their power and ability to change the scripts and create for themselves a more positive and productive way of living.

Concepts/Leader Behaviors The following theoretical concepts are presented as group leader behaviors. The TA group leader needs to be able to:

- develop a therapeutic contract with the group members that stresses equality and identifies the goals to which leader and members mutually agree.
- instruct group members in the specific tenets and specialized terminology of transactional analysis.
- analyze at least four elements for group members: (a) structures, (b) transactions, (c) games, and (d) scripts.
- establish a working relationship with group members that is best described as a partnership in which equality is a key ingredient.
- enhance group members' awareness of their scripts, resulting from early decisions, and their power and ability to change these scripts.
- provide positive strokes to group members and instruct them in the significance these strokes play in motivating behavior.
- reinforce the redecisions group members make during the group process and encourage them to act upon these redecisions.
- function in the cognitive/rational domain of human behaviors, as these are major forces for change in the redecision process.
- challenge group members to change current patterns of thinking/feeling/behaving and to move to more growth-producing patterns.
- enhance group members' autonomy to reduce dependence on the leader or on other group members.

Group Stages and Techniques Although stages for groups are not specified in transactional analysis, a TA group probably would follow a pattern of (a) establishing a facilitative climate, (b) developing contracts that identify goals, (c) working through various analyses of structures, transactions, games, and scripts, and (d) terminating with specific directives for action-oriented change. In each of these stages, the TA group leader would:

- use active listening skills to encourage member participation.

- confront members to challenge them in the redecision process.
- role-play to encourage members to try out their new scripts.
- develop therapeutic contracts to keep members on target in reaching their goals.
- enhance the redecision process, drawing upon members' commitment to change.
- make use of self-scripting to model more positive ways of being.
- give strokes to motivate members to change.

These are examples of leader techniques that have application in a TA-oriented group. Special techniques identified by Poidevant and Lewis (1995), such as "Reparenting," "Analysis of Rituals and Pastimes," and "Egograms: Shifting the Energy," are specific to TA counseling or therapy and are used in both individual and group settings.

Psychodrama

Basic Concepts With the exception of transactional analysis, the theoretical approaches discussed in this chapter were primarily designed for individual counseling and therapy. Applications to group work are extensions of this individual frame of reference. Psychodrama, conversely, was designed specifically for groups, and its application is group specific.

Created and developed by Jacob L. Moreno in the 1920s and 1930s (Ohlsen, Horne, & Lawe, 1988), psychodrama is an approach that requires a group member (protagonist) to spontaneously act out his or her problems(s) with the assistance of the group leader (director) and other members of the group (auxiliaries, audience). This acting out takes place on a stage and involves a three-step process that includes warm-up (preaction), action, and integration (Blatner, 1989).

The precursor of psychodrama was the Theater of Spontaneity created by Moreno in Vienna in 1921. It was developed out of Moreno's own creativity and his passion for the theater. Believing the conventional theater to be too structured, he encouraged his young actors to develop improvisational presentations on current issues of the day that were designed to entertain a variety of Viennese audiences. Outcomes of these productions, over and above their entertainment value, were cathartic experiences for both the actors and the audiences (Corey, 1990).

Moreno moved to New York in 1925, where he began to use the processes of spontaneous drama in working with groups of patients in hospitals. According to Sharf (1996), Moreno opened a sanitarium in Beacon, New York, in 1936 that included a theater for both treatment through the use of psychodrama and training in the use of psychodrama as a therapeutic tool.

A basic concept of psychodrama rests in role theory and the relationships individuals have with others, their views of others, and the psychological distance between individuals based upon both their relationships and their viewpoints. The roles and the interactions that stem from these roles lead to what Corey (1990) referred to as the encounter. According to Gladding (1991), this encounter is "an existentialist concept that involves total physical and psychological contact between persons on an intense, concrete, and complete basis in the here and now" (pp. 110–111).

It is this encountering, through role-playing, that rests at the heart of psychodrama. This experiencing in the here and now provides the individual with the opportunity to play someone else, to play something else, or to play him- or herself in different circumstances.

Greenberg (1974), in discussing Moreno's emphasis on this here-and-now experiencing, identified the following precepts that undergird this role-play process:

- *Spontaneity/creativity.* Individual responses that provide a degree of "newness" to a past situation.
- *Situation.* A present orientation through which past and future concerns/problems can be reexperienced.
- *Tele.* Total emotional communication between two or more people.
- *Catharsis.* Emotional purging.
- *Insight.* New perspectives.

In psychodrama, a group member is asked to script and act out a situation, relationship, or other area of concern before the other group members. The member selected is the protagonist and with the assistance of the group leader (director) identifies the situation, relationship, or concern, creates the scenario to be acted out, selects other group members (auxiliaries) to play roles in the scenario, and assigns the rest of the group to serve as the audience.

Once the scenario has been established, the group leader (director) facilitates the first phase (warm-up) of the psychodrama process. Its purpose is to make sure that the group leader is ready to lead the group and that the group members (protagonist, auxiliaries, audience) are ready to be led. According to Blatner (1989), the warm-up, done either verbally or through structured activities, is designed to develop the right frame of mind, for both the leader and the group members, to conduct the psychodrama and to develop trust and spontaneity.

The second phase, action, involves the acting out of the group member's (protagonist) situation, relationship, or other concerns. The group leader (director) aids in setting the scene, aids the other members (auxiliaries) with their roles, encourages role change within the acting-out phase of the scenario, aids the protagonist to expand his or her emotional response pattern, and encourages the protagonist to work through the situation by trying out alternative attitudes, behaviors, and emotional response patterns. This may mean that the scenario is re-acted several times.

The third phase, the integration phase, involves feedback, discussion, and closure. The group (audience and auxiliaries) is encouraged to provide the protagonist with personal, supportive, and constructive affective feedback. The emphasis is initially on the emotional aspects of the enactment. Later in the feedback session, emphasis may be directed to the cognitive aspects of the enactment. The goal of this phase is to provide the protagonist with ways to act differently in the future if similar situations arise (Gladding, 1991).

Concepts/Leader Behaviors   The following theoretical concepts are presented as group leader behaviors. The group leader in psychodrama needs to be able to:

- establish a working relationship within the group based upon equality.
- develop trust in the group members.
- develop spontaneity in group members.
- establish a group atmosphere that is accepting and tolerant of change.
- establish a format within the group that allows group members to identify and work on significant issues in their lives.
- encourage group members to be willing to risk aspects of self in the playing out of the psychodrama.
- provide protection for group members from abuse that may arise from the playing out of the psychodrama.
- utilize his or her creativity as a model for members of the group and encourage group members in their own creative development.
- utilize his or her knowledge and skill in directing all aspects of the psychodramatic enactment.

Group Stages and Techniques The group stages for psychodrama, as presented previously, carry with them various directives related to group leader techniques. The following techniques should aid the psychodrama leader in enhancing both growth and development across all three stages. These techniques are presented from a developmental perspective based on the fact that, according to Z. Moreno (1987), Jacob L. Moreno's wife, individuals need approximately 2 years of training and experience in psychodrama prior to taking on the role of director:

- Develop comfort in effectively working with all of the theatrical aspects of psychodrama.
- Develop the ability to assess all aspects of the members' behaviors as the psychodrama unfolds.
- Develop the ability to determine which problems, concerns, relationships, and so forth, are best dealt with through psychodrama.
- Develop the ability to actively direct an ongoing emotional drama that could entail but not be limited to actor movement, role switching, role creation, and drama reconstruction.
- Develop the ability to effectively cast various group members in roles that will enhance the ongoing process of the psychodrama.
- Develop the ability to effectively weave, when indicated by the psychodrama, members of the audience into roles as auxiliaries or alter egos for the protagonist.
- Develop the ability to know which of the myriad of techniques available within psychodrama are best suited to which types of presenting problems, relationships, and concerns.
- Develop the ability to aid all participants in desensitizing the emotional impact of the psychodrama enactment during closure.

These are examples of leader techniques that have application in psychodrama groups. Special techniques identified by Gladding (1991) and Sharf (1996), such as

"Monodrama," "Role Reversal," "The Double," "The Mirror Technique," "Act Fulfillment," "The Magic Shop," "The Soliloquy Technique," "Sculpting," and "Future Projection," are specific to psychodrama counseling.

An Integration of Theoretical Approaches〰

The six theories presented in this chapter offer the group leader options in working with groups. At first glance, each of these approaches seems to represent a unique underpinning for group process. But the six approaches actually have many aspects in common, which enhances the possibility for integrating these theories and applying them to the ongoing group process. The following five factors, common to all of the approaches, address this integrative theme: (a) relationship variables, (b) leader role variables, (c) member role variables, (d) process variables, and (e) outcome variables.

Relationship Variables

A working relationship is basic to all six theoretical approaches. Although the terms describing this working relationship vary, each approach presents a need for trust, safety, mutual respect, and leader competence, and five of the six approaches present a need for "equality" as this relates to leader-member interaction. In all six, the working relationship is the foundational building block on which all other aspects of group dynamics rest. Each approach stresses the importance of taking time to build this foundational structure and to assure that group members understand the nature of this relationship. From the integrative perspective, a working relationship must be established first, regardless of which of the theoretical positions is followed. All other aspects of the group process stem from this relationship.

Leader Role Variables

In all six theoretical positions, the leader's role is an active one. Action-oriented descriptors such as develop, instruct, analyze, establish, enhance, provide, reinforce, demonstrate, aid, confront, communicate, direct, and observe give the leader specific directions to take an active role in his or her interaction with the group. (It could be argued that the person-centered approach does not call for leader action, but the person-centered leader does have an active role. He or she must be able to communicate unconditional positive regard and empathy and be congruent in his or her interactions with group members.) Therapeutic conditions are, in themselves, action-oriented, for the leader must possess these "conditions" and then demonstrate and communicate them to group members. From the integrative perspective, then, active leader participation is necessary in all six theoretical approaches. The type of action may vary, but action-oriented leadership seems to be a key element in all six.

Member Role Variables

Similar themes related to the role members are to play in the groups permeate all six theoretical approaches. These themes focus on being responsible; committed to change; willing to risk; willing to try out new behaviors; willing to share oneself with others; able to deal with affect, cognitions, and behaviors; willing to do the "hard work" that change demands; willing to express creativity through role-play; and open to new information, insights, and awareness. These themes stress the active role that members must take and also the concept that if change is to occur, members must assume major responsibility for this change. From the integrative perspective, each theoretic approach has the same underlying message with regard to the role of members: If you desire change, you must be willing to take major responsibility for that change and be willing to take the necessary action to make that change possible.

Process Variables

The area that seems to have the most variability across the six theoretical approaches is the process dimension. It encompasses the various experiential activities that take place within groups to attain the desired goals. Even here, however, the six approaches have some similarity. Self-disclosure, role-playing, giving and receiving feedback, observing others, using active listening skills, modeling, demonstrating, encountering, and dialoguing are common to all six approaches. The differences are not as much in terms of process as in the unique way these processes are employed in each of the six approaches. For example, in the person-centered approach, giving and receiving feedback is seen as an ongoing means of facilitating group interaction and member growth. From the Gestalt orientation, giving and receiving feedback might be structured to give group members exaggerated exposure to the various affective responses associated with giving and receiving feedback. The group may be directed to engage in this process at a specific time to emphasize a specific point. In psychodrama, giving and receiving feedback centers on the encounter between individuals or with self acted out in a staged scenario. All group members participate actively in the feedback process.

From the integrative perspective, for all six theoretical approaches, the process variable dimension is not nearly as diverse as one might expect. The diversity is not so much in the "what" of process as in the "how" and perhaps the "why" of process. All six approaches provide a process to expand the affective, cognitive, and behavioral realms of group members.

Outcome Variables

The greatest similarity across the theoretical approaches is in intended group outcomes. Such concepts as increasing awareness, changing dysfunctional behaviors, enhancing self-concept, fostering insight, accepting responsibility, and increasing degrees of trust in self and with others are common to all six approaches. Regardless of theoretical approach, the desired outcomes all center on change. The words used to describe this change vary from theory to theory, but the end result is to have group members function more effectively in affective, cognitive, and behavioral domains. From the integrative perspective, although outcome variables for the different perspectives are directed in different areas of positive change—change in the way group members feel about themselves and their world, change in the way group members think about themselves and their world, and change in the way group members behave as a result of changes in the way they feel and think—all have the same end result. Differences exist in some of the fundamental principles of the six theoretical approaches presented, but fundamental differences do not exist in terms of outcome variables.

Implementation

The following suggestions are provided to aid group leaders in effectively integrating individual counseling approaches in their work with groups:

- Be familiar with all theoretical approaches, even though most were originally developed for work with the individual. Each will provide insight into human development and change and how to apply this insight in the group setting.
- Attempt to integrate aspects of various theoretical approaches in working with groups. An eclectic approach will prove beneficial to you and consequently to group members.
- Apply theoretical approaches as they were intended to be used—as facilitative guides to better understand individual dynamics and to assist individuals in the change process. They were not conceived as the true and only way of explaining the human condition.
- Do not rely solely on one approach to the exclusion of the others. Base your approach in working with groups on a broad knowledge base, and take from this base what will make your group work most effective.
- Experiment with many approaches to group work until you find the combination of principles and techniques that best fits your personal philosophy regarding people and your personal style of being with people. The approach you finally develop should be much more a reflection of you than of any single theoretical position.

Summary ～

Group approaches are derived largely from theories and therapies developed for individuals. Because theory has to form the foundation for group counseling or therapy, group leaders should become knowledgeable about the major theories and learn how to integrate them and apply them within the group modality. The six individual theories highlighted in this chapter were Adlerian, Gestalt, person-centered, rational-emotive behavior therapy, transactional analysis, and psychodrama.

Commonalities in five dimensions enable leaders to blend these theories in their work with groups: relationship, leader role, member role, process, and outcome. In all six theories, the working relationship is the basis for the group dynamic, and most advocate equality in leader-member interactions. All six theories propel the leader into an active role, particularly in providing optimum therapeutic conditions. Similarities in member role permeate all the theoretical precepts, and all agree that individuals ultimately have to take responsibility to change whatever they want to change. Process presents the most diversity of the five dimensions, but the differences are more in the "why" and "how" than in the "what" of the process. The theories are similar in the outcome variable: all center on evoking positive change in people.

Most important, group leaders should take their knowledge of various theories, experiment with different approaches, and strive to find the way that works best for them and for their groups. The approach developed should reflect the leaders' personal philosophy and personal style.

References ~

Adler, A. (1938). *Social interest.* London: Faber & Faber.

Berne, E. (1964). *Games people play.* New York: Grove Press.

Blatner, A. (1989). Psychodrama. In R. J. Corsini & D. Wedding (Eds.), *Current psychotherapies* (4th ed., pp. 561–571). Itasca, IL: Peacock.

Capuzzi, D., & Gross, D. (1992). *Introduction to group counseling.* Denver, CO: Love Publishing.

Capuzzi, D., & Gross, D. (1995). *Counseling and psychotherapy: Theories and interventions.* Englewood Cliffs, NJ: Prentice-Hall.

Corey, G. (1990). *Theory and practice of group counseling* (3rd ed.). Pacific Grove, CA: Brooks/Cole.

Corey, M. S., & Corey, G. (1987). *Groups: Process and practice* (3rd ed.). Pacific Grove, CA: Brooks/Cole.

Dusay, J., & Dusay, K. M. (1979). Transactional analysis. In R. Corsini (Ed.), *Current psychotherapies* (2nd ed., pp. 374–427). Itasca, IL: Peacock.

Ellis, A. (1982). *Rational emotive therapy and cognitive behavior therapy.* New York: Springer.

Ellis, A. (1991). The philosophical basis of rational-emotive therapy (RET). *Psychotherapy in Private Practice, 8,* 97–106.

Gilliland, B., James, R., Roberts, G., & Bowman, J. (1984). *Theory and strategies in counseling and psychotherapy.* Englewood Cliffs, NJ: Prentice-Hall.

Gladding, S. T. (1991). *Group work: A counseling speciality.* New York: Merrill.

Gladding, S. T. (1996). *Counseling: A comprehensive profession.* Englewood Cliffs, NJ: Prentice-Hall.

Goulding, M. (1987). Transactional analysis and redecision therapy. In J. L. Zeig (Ed.), *The evolution of psychotherapy* (pp. 285–299). New York: Brunner/Mazel.

Greenberg, I. A. (1974). Moreno: Psychodrama and the group process. In I. A. Greenberg (Ed.), *Psychodrama: Theory and therapy* (pp. 11–28). New York: Behavioral Publications.

Harris, T. (1967). *I'm OK—you're OK.* New York: Harper & Row.

Hazler, R. J. (1995). Person-centered theory. In D. Capuzzi & D. Gross (Eds.), *Counseling and psychotherapy: Theories and interventions* (pp. 237–265). Englewood Cliffs, NJ: Prentice-Hall.

Karpman, S. (1981). The politics of theory. *Transactional Analysis Journal, 11*(1), 68–75.

Kepner, E. (1980). Gestalt group process. In B. Feder & R. Ronall (Eds.), *Beyond the hot seat* (pp. 5–24). New York: Brunner/Mazel.

Lakin, M. (1985). Helping groups in our times. In M. Lakin (Ed.), *The helping group: Therapeutic principles and issues* (pp. 21–28). Reading, MA: Addison-Wesley.

Livneh, H., & Wright, P. E. (1995). Rational-emotive theory. In D. Capuzzi & D. Gross (Eds.), *Counseling and psychotherapy: Theories and interventions* (pp. 325–352). Englewood Cliffs, NJ: Prentice-Hall.

Maples, M. F. (1995). Gestalt theory. In D. Capuzzi & D. Gross (Eds.), *Counseling and psychotherapy: Theories and interventions* (pp. 267–295). Englewood Cliffs, NJ: Prentice-Hall.

Moreno, Z. T. (1987). Psychodrama, role theory, and the concept of the social atom. In J. K. Zeig (Ed.), *The evolution of psychotherapy* (pp. 341–366). New York: Brunner/Mazel.

Naranjo, C. (1970). Present centeredness techniques, prescriptions and ideals. In J. Fogan & I. Shepherd (Eds.), *Gestalt therapy now* (pp. 45–55). Palo Alto, CA: Science and Behavior Books.

Noble, F. (1977). Procedure for promoting behavior change: Humanistic approach. In G. Blackham (Ed.), *Counseling theory, process and practice* (pp. 165–183). Belmont, CA: Wadsworth.

Ohlsen, M. M., Horne, A. M., & Lawe, C. F. (1988). *Group counseling* (3rd ed.). New York: Holt, Rinehart & Winston.

Perls, F. S. (1969). *Gestalt therapy verbatim.* Moab, UT: Real People Press.

Poidevant, J. M., & Lewis, H. A. (1995). Transactional analysis theory. In D. Capuzzi & D. Gross (Eds.), *Counseling and psychotherapy: Theories and interventions.* Englewood Cliffs, NJ: Prentice-Hall.

Polster, E., & Polster, M. (1973). *Gestalt therapy integrated.* New York: Brunner/Mazel.

Rogers, C. R. (1959). Significant learning in therapy and in education. *Educational Leadership, 16*(4), 232–242.

Shaffer, J. B. P., & Galinsky, M. D. (1989). The Gestalt therapy workshop. In J. B. P. Shaffer & M. D. Galinsky (Eds.), *Methods of group therapy* (pp. 118–140). Englewood Cliffs, NJ: Prentice-Hall.

Shapiro, J. L. (1978). Major theoretical orientations. In J. L. Shapiro (Ed.), *Methods of group psychotherapy and encounter: A tradition of innovation* (pp. 40–63). Itasca, IL: Peacock.

Sharf, R. S. (1996). *Theories of psychotherapy and counseling: Concepts and cases.* Pacific Grove, CA: Brooks/Cole.

Stewart, I., & Jaines, V. S. (1987). *TA today: A new introduction to transactional analysis.* Nottingham, England: Lifespace.

Sweeney, T. J. (1995). Adlerian theory. In D. Capuzzi & D. Gross (Eds.), *Counseling and psychotherapy: Theories and interventions* (pp. 171–206). Englewood Cliffs, NJ: Prentice-Hall.

Thompson, C. L., & Rudolph, L. B. (1992). *Counseling children.* Pacific Grove, CA: Brooks/Cole.

Wright, H. (1989). Therapeutic properties of group. In H. Wright (Ed.), *Group work: Perspectives and practice* (pp. 89–99). London: Scutan Press.

Yalom, I. D. (1995). *The theory and practice of group psychotherapy* (4th ed.). New York: Basic Books.

Zalcman, M. J. (1990). Game analysis and racket analysis: Overview, critique and future development. *Transactional Analysis Journal, 20,* 4–19.

Part Two

Professional

Issues

~

Building upon the foundational informa-
tion presented in the first four chapters of this book, the chapters in this section raise
professional issues all counselors and therapists interested in group work need to
address as they initiate their study of group work. The efficacy of group work, issues
associated with leading groups in specific settings, ethical considerations for the
group work specialist, and cross-cultural considerations are all addressed in Part Two
of the text. In the opinion of the co-authors/co-editors of this text, all four of these
areas require careful consideration by all of those wishing to base their work with
groups on current thinking about best, safe, and ethical practices.

Chapter 5, "Group Counseling: The Efficacy of Group Work," is a keystone contribution to the education of the group work specialist. This chapter takes a hard look
at what the research indicates about whether or not group counseling or group therapy works. First, the chapter provides a definition of efficacy and discusses the professional importance of efficacy questions. Second, it explores how efficacy is measured in counseling or therapy. Third, it analyzes effective practices in group counseling. Fourth, it discusses group counseling or therapy efficacy with select client
populations. At the end of the chapter, unanswered questions about group counseling or therapy are addressed. The highlight of the chapter is a discussion of what the
research reveals about effective, ineffective, and harmful interventions with select
client populations.

Chapter 6, "Group Work in Specific Settings," examines the practice of group
work in six real-world settings. A variety of settings, each creating a context that
influences group work practices, are explored. The settings include an alternative
high school, a nonprofit community organization serving at-risk urban youth, an
urban university, a private practice, a private hospital adult day treatment program,

and a nonprofit organization contracting services in a community mental health setting. The intent of this chapter is to expand understanding of group counseling through the specific examples of the contextual factors that influence the development of group programs. Like Chapter 5, it promises to be an eye-opener for the beginning group work specialist.

Ethics is at the heart of the counseling process; this is especially so in group counseling. For many clients, membership in a group provides the first opportunity ever available to them to be open, honest, and safe as they share who they are with others. The group leader is responsible for setting the norm of ethical behavior, not only for him- or herself but also for the group as a whole. It is important that the leader limit the possibilities of trust being broken. Chapter 7, "Group Counseling: Ethical Considerations," presents the ACA ethical codes specific to group work, the ASGW Standards of Best Practice, an ethical decision-making model, and other important issues the group work specialist must consider. No one should attempt to lead a group prior to mastering the material in this chapter.

This section of the text concludes with Chapter 8, "Multicultural Group Counseling: Cross-Cultural Considerations." If counseling professionals are to act with integrity and commitment to their changing profession, they must begin to take steps to change the existing mainstream cultural paradigm. Although there has been an increase in the multicultural knowledge base, it has been directed toward a more general and individual base and not toward groups. Until recently, the area of multicultural group counseling has received little attention in the development of strategic approaches and specific empirical research. Chapter 8 presents an overview of the factors and cultural considerations that are important in developing effective multicultural groups. Perspectives of Afro-American, Hispanic, Asian/Pacific Islander, and American Indian groups are discussed to enhance the sensitivity and respect with which group leaders approach culturally diverse groups. Other topics covered in the chapter include acculturation, languages, cultural identity, generational factors, cultural custom styles, geographical location and neighborhoods, family constituency, psychohistorical and religious traditions, and individuality.

5

Group Counseling:
The Efficacy of Group Work

Cass Dykeman and Valerie E. Appleton

In professional training, the curriculum is usually determined by an accreditation agency. In counselor preparation, the main accreditation agency is the Council for the Accreditation of Counseling and Related Educational Programs (CACREP). In CACREP's accreditation manual (CACREP, 1994), eight curricular areas are designated as core to the training of any counselor. These areas are (a) human growth and development, (b) social and cultural foundations, (c) helping relationships, (d) group work, (e) career and lifestyle development, (f) appraisal, (g) research and program evaluation, and (h) professional orientation. Of most relevance to readers of this textbook is item d. The other counselor preparation accreditation agency is the Council on Rehabilitation Education (CORE), which accredits rehabilitation counseling programs. Like CACREP, CORE mandates group counseling training (CORE, 1994).

Counseling students have often raised the question of whether group counseling or therapy courses should be required. If no scientific evidence exists that group counseling or therapy works, then this book and the group counseling or therapy courses required of counseling students appear to be nothing more than "hoops to jump through" imposed by some scholastic bureaucracy.

In this chapter, we will help the reader develop his or her own answers to the preceding question in four steps. First, we will provide a definition of efficacy and discuss the professional importance of efficacy questions. Second, we will review how efficacy is measured in counseling or therapy. Third, we will detail the scientific knowledge concerning effective practices in group counseling or therapy. Fourth, we will present the scientific knowledge concerning group counseling or therapy efficacy with select client populations. Finally, at the end of the chapter, we will discuss the unanswered questions about group counseling or therapy efficacy that still exist. Please note that the term counseling will be used to refer to both counseling and therapy throughout the remainder of this chapter.

What Is Efficacy? ~

The key term in this chapter is efficacy. Without a clear understanding of this term, the rest of this chapter is meaningless. In the human services professions, the term efficacy refers to "the degree to which desired goals or projected outcomes are achieved" (Barker, 1995, p. 116). A sample group counseling efficacy question one could ask is: To what extent does cognitive group counseling impact people with bulimia? Such a question, however, would be difficult to answer, because each of the three terms in the question (i.e., cognitive counseling, group counseling, and bulimia) can mean many things. For example, does the term bulimic refer to people with nonpurging bulimia or purging bulimia? When possible, we will consider in this chapter more fine-grained efficacy questions, such as the following: To what extent does challenging shape and weight distortions in a small group counseling setting decease the number of eating binges per week in nonpurging bulimic individuals?

Importance of Efficacy Questions ~

At first glance, efficacy questions such as that just posed may seem more the domain of researchers than clinicians. However, efficacy questions are critical to counselors in "the trenches." Specifically, efficacy questions play an important role in the areas of ethics, professionalism, and economics.

Ethics

Nonmaleficence   One of the oldest ethical dictates in health care is, "Above all else, do no harm." The dictate captures the spirit of the moral principle of nonmaleficence, which prohibits counselors from implementing interventions that risk harm to others (Forester-Miller, 1998; Forester-Miller & Davis, 1996). Later in this chapter we review what is known about group counseling "casualties" with the goal of teaching group counselors how to prevent such casualties.

Beneficence   This ethical principle contains the imperative that the counselor engage in activities that will benefit the client. Thus, counselors must seek out efficacious interventions and avoid or discard interventions found inefficacious. For instance, a number of rational-emotive therapy psychoeducational programs have been developed for classroom use by school counselors. However, as will be discussed later in this chapter, researchers have not found these interventions to be efficacious. While there is no evidence that these large group interventions harm children, they do waste instructional time that could be spent upon more fruitful activities.

Professionalism

One behavior that separates a professional from a lay person in any activity is that the professional bases his or her actions upon scientific knowledge rather than upon personal preference or whim. The specific term for this professional behavior is *informed practice*. Indeed, the psychologist's code of conduct demands that a clinician's work reflect the pragmatic application of scientific knowledge based upon research (American Psychological Association, 1992). Thus, it is incumbent upon the group counselor to seek out and use such knowledge.

Economics

Spiraling expenses have prompted both business and government to impose cost-control mechanisms upon the health care system (Budman, Demby, Feldstein, & Gold, 1984; Mone, 1994). The generic term for these mechanisms is *managed care*. In a recent historical overview of group counseling, Scheidlinger (1995) commented that the advent of managed health care will force counselors to demonstrate the cost-effectiveness of their group methods. Thus, efficacy issues are becoming paramount in the practice settings that professional counselors inhabit. Such issues are no longer the sole domain of university-based researchers.

How Efficacy Is Measured~

A wide range of research methods are used to study group counseling outcomes. In contrast to individual counseling outcome research, group counseling outcome research involves complex interactions of member, leader, and treatment factors (Stockton & Morran, 1982). To provide a better understanding of how group research is conducted, we will examine two major research methods: quantitative and qualitative.

Quantitative Methods

Correlational, causal-comparative, true experimental, quasi-experimental, and action research are all quantitative research methods (Isaac & Michael, 1985). In quantitative studies, outcome is determined through statistical analyses of the numerical data for targeted behaviors. In this frame, group counseling outcomes are those behavioral, role, or process phenomena that can be defined and counted.

Quantitative researchers focus on client and group characteristics that can vary. These characteristics are called *variables*. In quantitative research, there are two types of variables: independent and dependent. The independent variable is the component of the group counseling treatment manipulated by the researcher. An example of an independent variable is the introduction of a cognitive disputation exercise to a body-image enhancement group (see Grant & Cash, 1995). The variable measured to determine the effects of the independent variable is called the *dependent* variable (Borg & Gall, 1989). In the previous example, an example of a dependent variable would be the pretest to posttest score differences on the Private Body Talk Questionnaire (see Grant & Cash, 1995).

Also important to quantitative researchers is the issue of control. The term *control* refers to the researcher's efforts to eliminate the influence of factors other than the independent variable upon the dependent variable. Examples of factors that quantitative researchers usually try to control include age, sex, IQ, socioeconomic status, education, and motivation. The best way to employ control in a study is through the use of a control group. In a quantitative study, the control group is matched as closely as possible to the experimental group except that it is not exposed to the independent variable (Reber, 1986).

Qualitative Methods

Qualitative assessment is based on interpretable data generated through "thick description" of client or group phenomena (Guba & Lincoln, 1989; Patton, 1990). Such thick description is built through narratives, surveys, interviews, and observations. Outcome data in this type of research can include assessments of change in such things as worldview or personal idiosyncracy.

Yalom (1985) developed his seminal group counseling ideas predominately through thick description. For example, he developed his curative factors theory from an application of qualitative research methods to group counseling. Interestingly, his qualitative applications spawned a major thrust of quantitative research in group counseling.

Outcome Measurement

One of the most important things a group counseling researcher must determine is whether the tools chosen for studying the behaviors of interest will obtain a measurement that is complete and accurate. To determine accuracy in group measurement, reliability and validity must be considered. In general, *reliability* concerns the issue of whether a measurement device produces consistent results across observations. *Validity* concerns the issue of whether an assessment tool measures what it is supposed to assess.

Reliability   Because quantitative researchers rely on the indirect measurement of targeted features and qualitative researchers rely on narratives rather than numerical data, they can be understood to view reliability quite differently (Martella, Nelson, & Marchand-Martella, in press). Martella et al. emphasized that qualitative researchers view reliability as the match between what they observe happening and the data that are recorded. In contrast, quantitative researchers view reliability as the consistency found across different observations.

Validity   Quantitative and qualitative researchers view the issue of validity differently as well. Quantitative researchers concern themselves with issues of measurement validity. That is, does a particular assessment tool measure what it claims to measure? In quantitative research, standard procedures exist for the establishment of measurement validity. In contrast, qualitative researchers do not rely on empirical means to judge the validity of an assessment tool. Instead, they ask whether the assessment process has "credibility." Guba and Lincoln (1989) stated that credibility occurs when a match exists between the constructed realities of the participants and the constructed reality of the researcher. The methods to establish credibility are less well developed than are methods for measurement validity. Methods currently used to establish credibility include participant review of findings and researcher peer debriefing (Guba & Lincoln, 1989; Patton, 1990).

Effective Counselor Practices in Group Work

The components of effective group counseling have been defined specifically by the Association for Specialists in Group Work (ASGW). In fact, ASGW developed 15 knowledge competencies for counselors. The sixth of these competencies addresses research knowledge. This competency directs students to discover what is efficacious in group counselor practice and apply it (ASGW, 1990). In this section, we review the general group counseling literature, discussing those counseling practices that have been found to be especially effective, to help counselors improve their work with their clients. The research will be considered in terms of specific factors, "nonspecific" factors, and group counseling modes.

Specific Factors and Outcome

The term *specific factors,* as used here, refers to a counselor's acts that are unique to a particular theory of counseling. An example is the use of cognitive distortion refutation to combat body imagery problems. Commonly employed specific factors in group counseling include applying structure and providing alternatives and instruction.

The Use of Structure   In his analysis of the research literature, Gazda (1989) found a definite trend toward the use of structured group strategies. This trend stands in opposition to the traditional unstructured group approach. Structured groups developed as a result of the influence of behavioral counseling and skills training. Rohde and Stockton (1994) reviewed the 40-year controversy over the role and efficacy of structure in therapeutic groups. Early group counseling theorists recommended that group leaders avoid influencing the natural development of group culture. However, group counseling researchers later found that the lack of structure actually created the following undesired client phenomena: cognitive distortion, interpersonal fear, subjective distress, and premature termination.

While applying structure to groups has been found to be beneficial, counselors should exercise caution in this regard. All types of structure are not beneficial to all groups. For example, although the application of self-disclosure contracts can increase attraction to a group, it can decrease the members' "mutual liking" (Ribner, 1974). It is important to note that the positive impact of structure may be related to the clients' ability to engage in risk-taking behavior (Evensen & Bednar, 1978). Specifically, higher levels of structure tend to be associated with more negative evaluations of counseling by low risk-takers. Also, high levels of structure may result in lower levels of group cohesion (Lee & Bednar, 1977). The practitioner is encouraged to match the techniques utilized with the personalities of the group members.

Providing Alternatives and Instruction   The power of instruction in group counseling lies in the counselor's ability to be clear with clients about the tasks and goals of counseling. The power of providing alternatives to clients is that it will often prevent client reactance (Brehm, 1966). The judicious application of instruction and the judicious provision of alternatives have been identified as causal factors of client behavior change with certain populations.

Flowers (1979) discovered that trained group counselors produced more improvement in their clients than did student counselors because they gave less advice and offered more alternatives and instruction in their feedback to group members. Also, student counselors who used alternatives and instruction produced more improvement in their clients than those who did not. However, the student counselors used these interventions less frequently and produced less client improvement overall. Interestingly, alternatives and instruction were often viewed as superior therapeutically by the group clients but often not by the group counselors. Flowers' study showed that counselors who are not specifically trained to avoid the use of advice may be inclined to use it to the detriment of their clients.

Nonspecific Factors and Outcome

Nonspecific factors of counseling are those change-producing elements present in counseling regardless of theoretical orientation. Gelso and Carter (1994) identified a number of nonspecific factors they felt operated in all counseling. The most studied of these factors is working alliance. Other nonspecific factors mentioned in the group counseling literature include curative factors, group development, and leadership.

Working Alliance   Substantial empirical evidence exists that the development of a working alliance (also called a working relationship) is an important component in all counseling. In fact, working alliance scores are the best known predictor of counseling outcomes (Horvath, 1994). Bordin (1994) defined the working alliance as having three equal and interacting components: goal (collaboration between counselor and client on the goals of counseling), task (collaboration between counselor and client on the tasks of counseling), and bond (mutual affective bonding between client and counselor). Glatzer (1978) noted that group process stimulates the unfolding of the working alliance in all clients.

Curative Factors   While working alliance theory has had an enormous impact upon individual counseling research, its impact upon group counseling research has been limited. The majority of the literature on the nonspecific factors in group counseling has focused on Yalom's curative factor theory. Yalom (1985) postulated that 12 curative factors operated in group counseling: self-understanding, interpersonal learning (input), interpersonal learning (output), universality, instillation of hope, altruism, recapitulation of primary family group, catharsis, cohesiveness, existential factors, identification, and guidance.

Butler and Fuhriman (1983) reviewed 10 years of research on Yalom's curative factors. In the studies they reviewed, clients were asked to rank the 12 factors with regard to their curative value. Butler and Fuhriman's research supported Yalom's own idea that there was a triad of highly curative factors. This triad included self-understanding, catharsis, and interpersonal interaction (input).

More than 10 years later, Shaughnessy and Kivlighan (1995) suggested that the analyses in these early studies were not sufficiently complex. Instead of ranking the clients' views of the 12 factors, Shaughnessy and Kivlighan utilized cluster analysis. They described three clusters of client responders. These clusters were broad-spectrum responders, self-reflective responders, and other-directed responders. The broad-spectrum responders, the largest cluster, endorsed all 12 curative factors evenly. The next largest cluster, the self-reflective responders, valued a specific curative factor triad most highly. Based on the results of their analysis, Shaughnessy and Kivlighan recommended that group counselors include a broad range of curative factors in their group counseling rather than focus on a few factors that appeal to a minority of clients.

Group Development Fundamental to the assessment of group progress and outcome is understanding the stages of group development (Zimpfer, 1984). Most group development research has been based upon Tuckman's (1965) five-stage theory. The five stages Tuckman identified are forming, storming, norming, performing, and adjourning. Maples (1988) refined Tuckman's work through 5 years of data collection. From analysis of her data, she developed a 20-substage model designed as a star. At each stage, or point of the star, Maples offers definitions that can be used in practice to better evaluate clinical progress.

Leadership Group leadership research fills the counseling literature. Group leadership involves the interaction of so many features of group counseling that it defies any simple definition (Stockton & Morran, 1982). Furthermore, confusion continues to exist surrounding leadership functions and their relationship to the therapeutic gains made by group members (Conyne, Harvill, Morganett, Morran, & Hulse-Killacky, 1990). However, regardless of counselor technique, when the counselor's attitudes are acceptable to the client, the client is more likely to report positive therapeutic outcomes (Beutler, Jobe, & Elkins, 1974). In addition to counselor attitude, the literature has pointed to the following as being important nonspecific leadership factors: sense of hope, leadership style, and personal characteristics.

Sense of Hope Effective leaders were found to project a sense of hope to their clients. This hope was manifested in such behaviors as acknowledging client resources and the client's potential to change, conveying a clear and strong belief in the effectiveness of group counseling, and communicating a sense of confidence or personal power (Couch & Childers, 1987). Although the literature indicates that hope is a curative factor in group counseling, it is devoid of strategies for its use.

Leadership Style Abramowitz, Roback, Abramowitz, and Jackson (1974) found that matching counselor leadership style with client personality promotes positive group counseling outcomes. They described client personality based on Rotter's (1966) research on internal and external locus of control. Clients described as having an internally oriented locus of control believe that life events are the result of initiative. In contrast, clients who believe that luck or powerful forces determine life outcomes are described as having an externally oriented locus of control. Abramowitz et al. found that nondirective techniques were more effective than directive techniques with internally oriented clients. The reverse was true for clients with an external orientation.

Personal Characteristics   Certain personal characteristics may distinguish effective from ineffective group leaders (Combs, Avila, & Purkey, 1978). The literature indicates that effective leaders are more positive than less effective leaders. For example, effective leaders hold more positive perceptions of clients. Also, effective group counselors display emotionally supportive behaviors (e.g., care, listening, and flexibility) more often than ineffective counselors do during group interactions (Stockton, Morran, & Velboff, 1987).

Group Counseling Modes and Outcome

The group counseling literature is replete with reviews of outcome research for different types of groups. These reviews can be more easily digested when the types of groups are categorized into four modes:

- Task/Work (TSK).
- Guidance/Psychoeducational (EDU).
- Counseling/Interpersonal Problem Solving (IPR).
- Psychotherapy/Personality Reconstruction (REC).

These modes are the ones officially recognized by the ASGW (1990).

Task/Work Mode   The TSK classification includes the following types of groups: task forces, committees, planning groups, and study circles. All focus on identification and completion of specific goals. Because this focus is not a therapeutic one, persons other than professional counselors usually lead these groups. However, counselors may at times work in a consultant role with these groups. Given the nontherapeutic nature of TSK groups, the literature on these groups will not be reviewed in this chapter. For an excellent review of the TSK literature, see Bettenhausen (1991).

Guidance/Psychoeducational Mode   The purpose of EDU groups is to prevent psychological maladjustment (ASGW, 1990). EDU interventions were originally developed for educational settings. However, the use of EDU groups has expanded beyond schools and students. EDU interventions are currently used to educate all types of clients about potential threats (e.g., AIDS), developmental life events (e.g., the empty nest), and life skills (e.g., assertiveness).

Counseling/Interpersonal Problem-Solving Mode   IPR interventions focus on interpersonal growth and problem solving (ASGW, 1990). T-groups, sensitivity groups, and encounter groups are examples of IPR interventions. The emphasis in IPR groups is on growth promotion and the resolution of normative life crises. As such, pathology remediation is typically not addressed in IPR groups.

Psychotherapy/Personality Reconstruction Mode   REC groups are designed to remediate psychopathology through in-depth personality reconstruction (ASGW, 1990). Budman et al. (1984) provides an excellent example of research on an REC intervention. In this study, Budman et al. found their psychodynamically oriented group approach effective in the treatment of clients with severe characterological problems.

Group Counseling Efficacy With Select Client Populations~

Regardless of the mode, group counseling outcomes with specific client populations fall along a single continuum. The main points on this continuum are effective interventions, ineffective interventions, and harmful interventions (see Figure 5.1). In this section, we relay the scientific knowledge on what works, what does not work, and what has been found harmful in reference to specific client populations.

Effective Interventions

The literature indicates that group counseling is effective with several different client populations. In general, clients enter group counseling for many reasons. These reasons fall into three broad categories: mental health problems, physical health problems, and personal growth. The discussion in this section, concerning effective interventions for specific client populations, is structured in accordance with these categories. Drawing on the taxonomic work of Achenbach and Edelbrock (1989), we further divided the mental health problems category into two subcategories: internalizing disorders and externalizing disorders. For the present discussion, internalizing disorders are those in which a client's aggression is directed against himself or herself. Externalizing disorders are those in which the client's aggression is directed against others.

Mental Health Problems

Internalizing Disorders   The majority of efficacy studies in the group counseling literature have focused on internalizing disorders. The prototypical disorder of this subcategory is depression.

Depression. Researchers have examined group counseling efficacy with depression in pediatric, adult, and geriatric client populations. Beeferman and Orvaschel (1994) reported that the efficacy of group counseling with depressed adolescent clients is well documented in the research literature. They noted that the most effective interventions blended skills training, cognitive restructuring, and a supportive group process. In a rare head-to-head comparison study, Reynolds and Coats (1986) compared the effectiveness of cognitive group counseling and group relaxation training for depressed adolescents. They found that the adolescents in both groups moved from moderate depression levels at pretest to nondepression levels at posttest.

The efficacy of group counseling with depressed adult clients is also well established (Vandervoort & Fuhriman, 1991). Scott and Stradling (1991) explored the

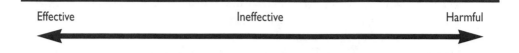

Effective	Ineffective	Harmful

Figure 5.1 ~
Intervention Continuum

question of whether an individual or group approach has been more efficacious in cognitive behavioral counseling for depression. They found that both approaches have been equally effective. Nezu (1986) examined the effectiveness of the social problem-solving approach to depression. He noted that this approach contains five separate components: problem orientation (i.e., cognitive and motivation view of problem), problem definition and formulation, generation of alternatives, decision making, and solution implementation and verification. Nezu found that the groups in which this approach was applied showed more improvement than both unstructured problem-solving groups and wait-list control groups.

Kanas (1993) reviewed the use of group counseling for bipolar depression and reported that the research supports the use of group counseling for this client population. Specifically, group counseling helped clients with bipolar depression learn about their disease, gain coping skills, and elicit support on related interpersonal issues. Group counseling also has been discovered to be a useful adjunct to the pharmacological treatment of bipolar depression. Cerbone, Mayo, Cuthbertson, and O'Connell (1992) reported that their group counseling intervention, which blended EDU and IPR group approaches, promoted greater social functioning and lowered relapse rates in this client group.

Depression is the most common mental illness suffered by older adults (Dhooper, Green, Huff, & Austin-Murphy, 1993). Dhooper et al. conducted research to determine whether their "Coping Together Group" intervention could impact depression among geriatric nursing home residents. The Coping Together Group program was based upon an amalgam of counseling strategies, including reminiscing, problem solving, communication training, and education. At posttesting, depression in the members of the Coping Together Groups had decreased significantly compared with depression in the members of the control group.

Eating disorders. Professional counselors have made extensive use of group counseling in the treatment of clients with eating disorders. Zimpfer (1990b) reviewed 31 studies on group treatment of bulimia. He reported the following:

> In every group study, regardless of the specific type of treatment, the group intervention was successful on whatever criteria were used. That is to say, binge/purge behavior was reduced or eliminated at a significant level among the participants, and depression was reduced and body image improved. (p. 247)

Specific group treatment approaches for eating disorders mentioned in the literature as effective include cognitive (Levey, McDermott, & Lee, 1989), cognitive and behavioral blend (Davis, Olmstead, & Rockert, 1992), and interpersonal (Agras et al., 1995; Wilfley et al., 1993).

Research has shown that group counseling is also an effective approach to the remediation of distorted body imagery. A study reported in 1995 by Grant and Cash represents a long line of quality studies that have shown cognitive group interventions to be an efficacious treatment for body image distortion. Core to these interventions were the identification, monitoring, and cognitive reconstructing of body image errors. Other researchers have found that both group cognitive and group behavioral interventions were efficacious with weight control issues (Lewis, Blair, & Booth, 1992; McNamara, 1989).

Other internalizing disorders. Researchers have found group counseling efficacious with a variety of other internalizing disorders. These disorders include divorce adjustment (Pedro-Carroll, Albert-Gillis, & Cowen, 1992; Zimpfer, 1990a), loneliness (Brough, 1994), sex abuse trauma (Alexander, Neimeyer, Follette, Moore, & Harter, 1989; Cahill, Llewelyn, & Pearson, 1991; Hiebert-Murphy, De Luca, & Runtz, 1992; Silovsky & Hembree-Kigin, 1994; Winick & Levene, 1992), obsessive-compulsive disorders (Krone, Himle, & Nesse, 1991), addictive disorders (McAuliffe, 1990), encopresis (Stark, Owens-Stively, Spirito, Lewis, & Guevremont, 1990), grief (McCallum & Piper, 1990; Zimpfer, 1991), anxiety (Eayrs, Rowan, & Harvey, 1984; Meichenbaum, Gilmore, & Fedoravicius, 1971; Powell, 1987), schizophrenia (McFarlane, Link, Dushay, Marchal, & Crilly, 1995), personality disorders (Linehan, Heard, & Armstrong, 1993; Nehls, 1991), and sexual dysfunctions (Hurlbert, White, Powell, & Apt, 1993).

Two of the reports just cited deserve special attention given their usefulness to practicing group counselors. Pedro-Carroll et al.'s study on a divorce adjustment group intervention for children (Pedro-Carroll et al., 1992) represents a good example of efficacy research in an applied setting. In addition, their article describes their protocol in detail. Thus, professional counselors can use the article to replicate this effective intervention at their work sites.

Stark, Owens-Stively, Spirito, Lewis, and Guevremont (1990) represents a good example of a group behavioral counseling intervention outcome study. The target of this intervention, which included group work with both children and their parents, was retentive encopresis. While treatment of encopretic children is not widely discussed in the counseling literature, this problem is commonly encountered by professional counselors who work with children. The researchers provided a clear explication of their treatment steps as well as an articulate rationale for the delivery of their intervention in a group setting. They postulated that:

> the group format may have enhanced treatment effectiveness by providing support to both parents and children in complying with the treatment regimen. Often parents reported feeling a great deal of relief and support in meeting other families with encopretic children. Further, the children reported enjoying the group and feeling of relief upon meeting other children with the same problem. The group format may have enhanced the parents' and children's compliance to the treatment protocol because they

were required to report back to the group on their success or failure with each aspect of treatment. (p. 669)

As for outcome, the researchers reported that during the intervention phase, soiling was reduced by 83%. Furthermore, at the 6-month follow-up, the average number of soiling incidents per week among the participants had dropped from the baseline of 14 to .021. Efficacy studies with high clinical utility are a goldmine for practicing counselors. Pedro-Carroll et al. (1992) and Stark, Owens-Stively, Spirito, Lewis, and Guevremont (1990) represent two of the best examples of this rare research literature genre.

Externalizing Disorders

Spouse battering. Following a review of the research literature on group counseling and spouse battering, Tolman and Bennett (1990) reported that most spouse battering groups use a cognitive approach. They also noted that research on these groups showed that "the majority of men stop their physically abusive behavior subsequent to intervention. Percentages of successful outcome ranged from 53% to 85%" (p. 104). Of the programs Tolman and Bennett reviewed, the most successful ones contained the following elements: cognitive techniques, profeminist components woven into the content, and highly structured group process. A professional counselor who anticipates working with this population should start his or her preparation by reading this comprehensive review.

Dutton (1986) studied the outcome of a court-mandated group counseling program for wife assault. This IPR program also utilized a cognitive approach, which Dutton defined as follows:

[It] has as its main objective the decrease or elimination of the use of violence by the husband as a means of resolving conflict with his wife. A variety of sub-goals exist that includes (a) recognition of one's personal responsibility for the use of violence, (b) termination of externalizing causes of violence to one's wife and minimizing the destructive effects of one's violence, (c) improved ability to detect the warning signs of violence, such as increased arousal or anger, and (d) an expanded behavioral repertoire for dealing with conflict. (p. 164)

The recidivism rate for the clients who completed the program was only 4%. This rate stands in stark contrast to the 40% recidivism rate for the comparison group that did not receive this treatment.

Disruptive behavior disorders and delinquency. Group counseling has long been the favored approach to working with disruptive and delinquent youth. As early as 1943, Slavson, in his seminal work on group counseling, reported protocols and case studies of group counseling with disruptive and delinquent youth. Strangely, there has been little solid research on group counseling with this population. In the rest of this subsection, we will outline the few exceptions to this research dearth.

Braswell (1993) reviewed the small research literature on cognitive interventions with children with disruptive disorders. She found that cognitive interventions have produced clinically meaningful and durable treatment effects. The article also described a detailed counseling protocol that Braswell developed. The key goal of her cognitive intervention was to change the children's primary response to conflict, instilling in its place a "think first—act later" orientation.

Truax, Wargo, and Volksdorf (1970) examined the impact of a nondirective REC intervention on institutionalized juvenile delinquents. They found that their twice-weekly, 24-session intervention positively influenced client personality factors and decreased reinstitutionalization rates. Smets and Cebula (1987) examined an eclectic five-step group counseling program for adolescent sex offenders. In a detailed report on their intervention, they recounted the behaviors associated with each step. These behaviors ranged from "admission of responsibility" (Step 1) to "restitution planning" (Step 5). The structure of the group was such that the group continued until all participants reached Step 5. At the 3-year follow-up assessment, only 1 of the 21 treatment participants had re-offended.

Physical Health Problems   In addition to mental health problems, physical health problems have been treated through group counseling interventions. The counseling has occurred both within and outside medical settings with a variety of client populations.

Geriatric Cognitive Dysfunction   McCrone (1991) noted that among institutionalized older adults, a major presenting problem is confusion. She commented that among these adults, the number with confusion can run as high as 70%. In a well-crafted experimental study, McCrone examined the use of "resocialization" group counseling with this population. She used the term *resocialization* to refer to a "formal group method which encourages interaction among members by introducing a focal stimulus or topic to facilitate reminiscence" (p. 30). McCrone stated that resocialization is thought to remediate both cognitive and social confusion by reinforcing small group participation and decreasing social isolation. Her positive findings supported the efficacy of resocialization as a group treatment modality with confused older adults. Other researchers have also commented on the efficacy of group approaches with institutionalized older adults (Christopher, Loeb, Zaretsky, & Jassani, 1988; Gilewski, 1986).

Insomnia   Group counseling interventions also have been applied to the problem of insomnia. Davies (1989) reported finding success with an approach that incorporated both cognitive and behavioral strategies. These strategies included cognitive restructuring, problem solving, anxiety management, and sleep education. Davies reported that treatment gains were maintained through a 1-year follow-up assessment. In a subsequent study, Davies (1991) examined the interaction of sedative medicines with the same group treatment. He found no difference in treatment efficacy between the group counseling clients who took sedative medicines and the group counseling clients who did not take such medicines. Davies has not been the only researcher to examine cognitive and behavioral treatments of insomnia. Kupych-Woloshyn, MacFarlane, and Shapiro (1993) also found such a blended approach to be effective in alleviating insomnia. Their clients reported that they valued both the educational and the support components of the intervention.

Other Physical Health Problems   Researchers have found group counseling effica-cious with a variety of other physical health problems. These problems include can-cer (Harman, 1991), respiratory diseases (Pattison, Rhodes, & Dudley, 1971; Stark, Bowen, Tyc, Evans, & Passero, 1990), and chronic headaches (Kneebone & Martin, 1992).

Personal Growth   Professional counselors use group work for more than the remediation of physical and mental health problems. Group counseling has also been used to help clients optimize their role performance at work and at home.

Career Development   The literature on group counseling as a career development intervention extends back to the turn of the twentieth century (Gazda, 1989). Zimpfer and Carr (1989), outlining the research literature on group counseling pro-grams for midlife career changers, reported finding evidence that group counseling helps this population. They noted that successful adult career interventions pos-sessed a different focus than that of typical youth career development programs. They felt that this different focus resulted from the view held by adults that job changing is a cyclical rather than a linear process. Consequently, for adults, career development components beyond interests and ability require assessment. These components include needs, values, goals, and role salience.

Baker and Popowicz (1983) conducted a meta-analysis of 18 research studies examining the efficacy of EDU career interventions with school-aged youth. The settings for these interventions included both small group counseling and large group (classroom) counseling. Across the studies, Baker and Popowicz found an average effect size of .50. They noted that such an effect size indicates that a person at the mean of the control group would be expected to rise to the 69th percentile if he or she were to receive the intervention. Another positive review of the career EDU research appears in Herr and Cramer's (1996) influential career counseling text.

Finally, group counseling interventions have been found to increase work per-formance. Kanas (1991), for example, found that support group activities enhanced the performance of first-year medical residents.

Parent Education   Parents seeking to enhance their parenting skills have also been helped through group counseling. In the finest research literature review we read, Dembo, Sweitzer, and Lauritzen (1985) examined the differential efficacy of three approaches to parent education EDU interventions. These approaches were behav-ioral, Adlerian, and client centered. The specific client-centered approach was par-ent effectiveness training (PET). When they reviewed studies that focused on a sin-gle approach, they found that the research literature supported behavioral interven-tions as being efficacious. In contrast, they found little evidence that the PET inter-ventions were effective. The research findings on Adlerian approaches were mixed. When they reviewed research that compared the three approaches, however, they uncovered no differential effectiveness among the approaches. Other literature reviews also reported finding mixed results among these three approaches (Polster, Dangel, & Rasp, 1987; Todres & Bunston, 1993).

Given the mixed findings of the literature reviews, what is a counselor to do when faced with running a parent education EDU intervention? A study by Sutton (1992) may provide some clues. Sutton conducted a well-designed study of a parent education EDU intervention using behavioral principles. The acting-out behavior of children whose parents were in the EDU group significantly declined. The acting-out behavior of children whose parents were in the control group did not change. Although none of the three approaches (behavioral, Adlerian, or client centered) offers a 100% guarantee, we feel it is justifiable for professional counselors to be asked to conduct such parent education EDU interventions. Our recommendation to such counselors is that they select a program based upon behavioral principles given the extant positive evidence for this approach in the literature.

Interpersonal Relations   Historically, the improvement of interpersonal relations has been a primary goal in growth-focused group counseling experiences. Indeed, group counseling, by its very nature, offers a unique laboratory for the development of new interpersonal skills. The research literature documents numerous efficacious group counseling initiatives designed to improve such skills. In an outstanding series of studies, Shechtman (1994a) examined the ability of group counseling to improve interpersonal relations among school-aged children. Her counseling protocol (Shechtman, 1994b) included both structured group activities (e.g., therapeutic games) and open-ended group process (e.g., disclosing disturbing feelings and receiving group feedback). One interesting finding from Shechtman's research was the differential effect of the group counseling treatment between genders. Concerning this differential effect, Shechtman (1994a) commented that "the results suggest that preadolescent girls grow in intimacy in a friendship relationship, whether treated or not, in a somewhat naturalistic developmental fashion. In contrast, only treated boys significantly grow in this domain" (p. 833). Shechtman (1994a) emphasized that the development of interpersonal relations skills such as the mutual discussion of feelings and needs is critical to the development of cross-gender attachment. Shechtman's protocol represents an efficacious intervention for professional counselors that is completely consistent with the developmental focus and ethic of the counseling profession. The group counseling literature needs more applied-setting outcome research like the work of Shechtman.

Children are not the only clients that benefit from the experience of counseling groups focused on the promotion of interpersonal skills. Adults can grow from these experiences as well. In their classic study of encounter groups, Lieberman, Yalom, and Miles (1973) reported that such groups can promote better interpersonal skills. In this study, Lieberman et al. classified the clients in reference to outcome, labeling those that benefited the most from the group experiences as "high learners." In reference to high learners, they stated:

> [They] changed in their methods of relating to others: They behaved in a more trusting, open, honest manner; they hid less of themselves; they expressed their opinions more forthrightly; they gave feedback to others, and requested it for themselves. They also

perceived that adaptive openness is curvilinear; too much as well as too little can jeopardize human relationships. (p. 139)

Despite the benefits of growth-oriented group counseling cited by Lieberman et al. and other researchers, we wonder what the future is for this type of counseling in the current managed-care environment. Will a person have to be labeled dysfunctional in some way to receive a group counseling experience? Will professional counselors have to abandon the growth-promoting segment of their work to earn a place within the health care market?

Ineffective Interventions

One popular setting for EDU interventions is the classroom. This type of EDU intervention is commonly called "large group guidance" (LG-EDU). In fact, LG-EDU interventions have long been a staple of professional counselors who work in schools. School counselors have designated LG-EDU work as an essential activity of their profession. The school counselor role definition published by the American School Counselor Association (1990) specifically states that LG-EDU offers "the best opportunity to provide guidance to the largest number of students in a school" (p. 2). Gysbers and Henderson's (1994) influential text on school counseling suggests that LG-EDU should occupy between 25% and 40% of a school counselor's time. The purpose of this type of intervention is to promote student knowledge and self-efficacy concerning learning, interpersonal skills, listening skills, decision making, and self-management (American School Counselor Association, 1995).

The research literature contains several literature reviews that support the efficacy of LG-EDU (e.g., Baker, Swisher, Nadenichek, & Popowicz, 1984; Borders & Drury, 1992; Cartledge & Milburn, 1978; Gerler, 1985; Gerler & Anderson, 1986). These reviews have led to the inclusion of LG-EDU in the role definitions of many counseling specialities. However, except for career development LG-EDU interventions, the results from rigorous research studies cast doubt on the efficacy of this intervention. For example, Laconte, Shaw, and Dunn (1993), who used an experimentally rigorous research design to study the impact on middle school students of an LG-EDU intervention based on rational-emotive therapy, found no significant outcome differences between the students receiving the LG-EDU intervention and the students not receiving this intervention. Wiggins and Wiggins (1992) studied school counselors' ability to improve student self-esteem and classroom behavior. They compared school counselors who primarily used individual counseling to school counselors who primarily used LG-EDU. They found that student improvement was greater with the individual-counseling-oriented school counselors. Considering their findings, the researchers commented that "although counselors have long been urged to do more classroom guidance, hard data are difficult to find to support this viewpoint; however, assertions that this is the road to take are plentiful" (p. 380).

Recent LG-EDU literature reviews also have raised doubts about the efficacy of LG-EDU. Strein (1988) reviewed all experimental and quasi-experimental research published on LG-EDU from 1970 on. He reported that only 103 of the 344 comparisons (29%) he found in the literature reached statistical significance. Moreover, Strein reported that the most rigorous studies showed a strong tendency toward non-significant results.

Gossette and O'Brien (1993) reviewed the research literature LG-EDU interventions based on rational-emotive therapy. Like Strein (1988), they found dismal support for the efficacy of these interventions. Only 70 of the 278 treatment comparisons they reviewed favored the LG-EDU intervention. Given these results, Gossette and O'Brien stated:

> A total of 1344 children received an average of 10.5 hours of classroom instruction in the philosophy of RET. How have their lives benefited? At best, we must conclude, very little. The justification most commonly cited for classroom intervention was that it would be "preventive," forestalling future maladjustment and presumably facilitating academic performance. Yet no evidence was ever offered to show that the incidence of maladjustment either within the time frame of the intervention, usually about 2–3 months, or even within the school year, was high enough to warrant such an expenditure of school time. (p. 22)

Despite enthusiastic endorsement by both professional associations and influential theorists, the utility of LG-EDU remains a troubling question. Professional counselors must ask themselves: Given the plethora of proven group counseling interventions, what justification is there to engage in interventions like LG-EDU that lack such proven efficacy?

Other than the literature on LG-EDU, there is surprisingly little contemporary literature reporting ineffective group counseling interventions. However, there are two articles detailing inefficacy that merit mentioning. Joanning, Quinn, Thomas, and Mullen (1992) compared three different interventions for adolescent drug abuse: family counseling, adolescent group counseling, and family drug education. The group counseling intervention was a client-centered, process-oriented IPR intervention. The family drug education intervention was an information-only EDU intervention. The researchers reported that neither the EDU nor the IPR intervention influenced adolescent drug abuse.

Kneebone and Martin (1992) found that a combined cognitive and behavioral group intervention was efficacious with chronic headache sufferers. However, when they added a partner involvement (PI) component to this group intervention, treatment efficacy was diminished. Kneebone and Martin hypothesized:

> If PI subjects in this study shared responsibility for the program with their partners, they may have considered success to be not just a function of their own efforts. Positive changes in internal locus of control and self-efficacy would have been less likely under such circumstances, and efforts to cope with headache related stresses would have remained stable or even declined leading to reduced treatment efficacy. (p. 213)

Kneebone and Martin went on to detail how their findings supported their hypothesis.

On the surface, partner involvement seems like a sound idea. However, professional counselors must constantly remain vigilant to the hidden messages contained in their interventions. In particular, counselors must ask whether their actions contain noxious hidden messages. In the case of the PI intervention, the hidden message appears to have been, "Your partner is here because I do not think you can do this on your own." While this message was wholly unintended, its impact was nevertheless felt.

Harmful Interventions

As we have discussed in this chapter, group counseling offers the professional counselor a powerful tool to apply to many mental and physical health issues. However, any potent therapeutic tool also contains the potential to harm clients (Hadley & Strupp, 1976). Thus, the potency of group counseling can produce casualties. By "casualty," we mean a client who experiences a lasting deterioration of psychological functioning directly attributable to a counseling intervention (Crown, 1983).

Bergin (1963) introduced the idea into the research literature that counseling can produce negative as well as positive results for clients. Concerning the production of negative results, Bergin (1966) suggested that counselors should be more cautious and critical of their practices—careful to eliminate ineffective or harmful therapeutic techniques. Later, Bergin and his colleagues examined the research literature on negative effects. They reported that the general casualty rate in counseling was somewhere between 9% and 11% (Lambert, Shapiro, & Bergin, 1986).

Group counseling researchers have not ignored the ongoing casualty-rates debate in the general counseling literature. Their first focus was on personal growth group interventions (e.g., T-groups, encounter groups, and marathon groups). The reported casualty rates for such interventions varied widely (Hartley, Roback, & Abramowitz, 1976; Kaplan, 1982). However, careful studies on these group interventions did not find casualty rates to be any higher than the general counseling casualty rate (Cooper, 1975, Kaplan, 1982; Lambert et al., 1986; Lieberman et al., 1973).

While group counseling does not appear to be any more dangerous than other counseling interventions, it still does produce casualties. Thus, in light of the ethical imperative of nonmaleficence, professional counselors must learn how to minimize group counseling casualties. Such casualties result from two sources: poor pre-group screening and counselor actions.

Screening   Professional counselors cannot conduct a proper pre-group screening without a knowledge of group counseling contraindications. *Contraindication* refers to a symptom, condition, or circumstance of the client that warns against taking some course of action (Barker, 1995). Fortunately, group counseling researchers have catalogued a number of such contraindications for IPR and REC interventions. In reference to the IPR and REC modalities, Toseland and Siporin (1986) detailed three types of contraindications: practical barriers, particular treatment needs, and client personality functioning. To aid practitioners in screening clients for IPR and REC group counseling interventions, we will now examine these three areas in greater detail.

Contraindication Types

Barriers and needs. Toseland and Siporin (1986) listed the following as practical barriers to prescribing group counseling: lack of clients with similar issues, client resistance to a group counseling prescription, scheduling problems, lack of qualified counselors, and lack of agency or school support. In terms of *client treatment needs*, some clients, such as those in crisis and those with a high suicide potential, need more immediate one-on-one attention than group counseling can provide (Gazda, 1989; Horwitz, 1976; Toseland & Siporin, 1986). Also, some clients may have an authentic need for a private therapeutic setting in which to discuss a highly sensitive issue or critical decision (Toseland & Siporin, 1986).

Client personality factors. Many client personality factors can contraindicate an assignment to group counseling. In their study of group counseling outcomes, Budman, Demby, and Randall (1980) encountered one treatment casualty. This casualty was a client who had scored high on scales measuring interpersonal sensitivity, paranoid thinking, and psychotic thinking. Similarly, other researchers have commented that strong contraindicators for group counseling include the presence of extreme interpersonal sensitivity (Hartley et al., 1976; Lieberman et al., 1973), paranoid thinking (Budman et al., 1980; Crown, 1983; Horwitz, 1976; Toseland & Siporin, 1986), and psychoticism (Gazda, 1989; Gurman, 1971; Smets & Cebula, 1987).

Researchers have also consistently indicated that low motivation for change is a strong contraindicator for group counseling (Crown, 1983). Consequently, professional counselors should take care to assess this obvious but often forgotten client characteristic. Another obvious client characteristic that group counselors often forget to assess is the client's tolerance for anxiety and frustration. A low tolerance for anxiety and frustration puts a client at risk to become a group counseling casualty. In reference to this tolerance, Horwitz (1976) commented that:

> a group often tends to induce frustration due to competition among members for its time and attention. A common wish is to become the favorite "child." Although support is also an important dimension of the group experience, it may be overshadowed by anxiety in the opening phases of group membership. Patients who deal with heightened tension by engaging in self-destructive actions, who tend to take flight in reaction to anxiety, are best excluded from a group. (p. 506)

One specific type of anxiety that has been mentioned as a contraindicator is acute self-disclosure fear (Gazda, 1986).

Personality issues that contraindicate a group counseling placement include borderline personality disorder (Lambert et al., 1986) and psychopathy (Slavson & Schiffer, 1975). Also, the presence of severe schizophrenia contraindicates a group counseling placement (Bergin, 1980; Kanas, 1991; Slavson & Schiffer, 1975; Toseland & Siporin, 1986). Marked emotional liability is an additional contraindicator (Gazda, 1989).

Finally, we feel it is important to note two contraindications specific to children and adolescents. First, Sugar (1993) advised that encounter and marathon group interventions are contraindicated for these populations. These group interventions can present material too intense for nascent egos. Second, Baider and De Nour (1989) cautioned that adolescent cancer patients need to be medically stable before they begin any group counseling. They exerted this caution because of their finding that group counseling can strip away denial defense mechanisms that cancer patients who are medically unstable need to function adaptively and with hope.

The information presented herein on client contraindications for group counseling can be a lot to digest at once. As an aid, we have constructed an alphabetical listing of client contraindicators (see Table 5.1). Also, we have found that reviewing case studies can make counseling facts "come alive." Therefore, we recommend the following rich descriptions of group counseling casualties: Brandes (1977), Budman et al. (1980), and Kaplan (1982).

Best Practice   We have two caveats about our research review on contraindications. First, our discussion pertained solely to the IPR and REC modalities. The research literature gave us no indication if the contraindications listed in Table 5.1 would hold true for EDU interventions. For example, we know an IPR group would be contraindicated for a client with extreme self-disclosure fears. However, the same client might find an EDU group very helpful (Gazda, 1989). Indeed, an EDU group experience might "set the stage" for an effective IPR intervention or might be in itself a sufficient intervention.

Second, there is growing evidence that homogeneous EDU interventions are effective with clients who suffer from borderline personality disorder (see, e.g., Linehan et al., 1993) or schizophrenia (see, e.g., Hayes, Halford, & Varghese, 1995). (The term *homogeneous* denotes groups in which all clients share the same diagnosis. The term *heterogeneous* refers to groups that contain clients with a mixture of diagnoses.) Also, in general, treating clients with schizophrenia or borderline personality disorder in homogeneous group settings is gaining in popularity (Hayes et

Table 5.1 ∼
Client Contraindicators for Group Counseling

Acute self-disclosure fears
Borderline disorder
Extreme interpersonal sensitivity
Low anxiety tolerance
Low frustration tolerance
Low motivation for change
Marked emotional lability
Paranoia
Psychopathy
Psychotic thinking
Schizophrenia
Severe depression
Severe impulse-control problems
Unstable medical condition

al., 1995; Hyde & Goldman, 1992; Kanas, 1993; MacKenzie, 1986; Nehls, 1991; O'Neill & Stockell, 1991).

Given unanswered and conflicting information about contraindicators, what is a counselor to do? Currently, we feel the "best practice" when screening for group counseling is to consider, but not slavishly apply, the contraindicators listed in Table 5.1. We cannot emphasize enough that counselors best serve clients through a case-by-case application of contraindicators.

Counselor Actions   While the research on client contraindicators for group counseling is somewhat muddled, the research on counselor actions and group counseling casualties is crystal clear. Counselor behaviors are a primary source of group counseling casualties (Cooper, 1975; Hadley & Strupp, 1976; Kaplan, 1982). Hadley and Strupp (1976) discussed two sources of counselor behaviors that can lead to counseling casualties: training/skills deficits and counselor noxious personality traits.

Training/Skills Issues   Counselor skill or knowledge deficits can lead to client casualties. For example, counselors who are unaware of client contraindicators for group counseling will put clients in ill-advised therapeutic situations. Also, counselors may select to work with client populations or employ counseling techniques for which they have had little training. Finally, counselors may possess the proper skills but rigidly apply those skills regardless of the clinical situation (Crown, 1983). For example, a psychoanalytically oriented counselor may make an accurate transference interpretation to a client during a session. However, despite his or her skillful application of this technique, the intervention will fall flat if the client does not possess the observing ego needed to use the insight contained in the interpretation. To speak metaphorically, when all that a counselor has in his or her professional toolbox is a hammer, the whole world becomes just a collection of nails. Builders of good counseling experiences always possess and use a variety of tools in their work.

Counselor Personality Issues   Hadley and Strupp (1976) detailed 12 personality traits that can generate counseling casualties: coldness, obsessiveness, excessive need to make people change, excessive unconscious hostility, seductiveness, lack of interest or warmth (neglect), pessimism, absence of genuineness, sadism, narcissism, greed, and dearth of self-scrutiny. Combinations of these traits can lead to destructive behaviors by leaders. In their classic examination of group casualties in which they identified five group counseling leadership styles, Lieberman et al. (1973) found that one leadership style produced almost one half of the casualties, including the most severe ones. They called this style "Aggressive Stimulator." It is characterized by the following behaviors: high stimulus input, intrusiveness, confrontation, challenging but demonstrating, and high positive caring (Cooper, 1975; Lieberman et al., 1973). Hartley et al. (1976) has pointed to leadership characteristics as the critical causal factor of group counseling casualties.

How can group counselors prevent themselves from producing casualties? Taking a group counseling class is a start, for it helps counselors to build their skills.

As for personality traits, access to quality supervision is the key to recognizing and remediating noxious personality traits. In fact, quality supervision is so important that CACREP standards mandate one hour per week of individual supervision for all practicum and internship students. Also, both CACREP and CORE set strict faculty to student ratios (1:5) for practicum and internship supervision classes (CACREP, 1994; CORE, 1994).

Unanswered Questions About Group Counseling Effectiveness〜

The research on group counseling casualties has focused exclusively on the IPR and the REC types of group counseling interventions. To date, researchers have not addressed the issue of casualty production by EDU interventions. Quality research on classroom-level EDU interventions only suggested that these interventions were ineffective but not harmful. However, the relationship of harm to other EDU interventions remains an open question. Specifically, do certain mixes of EDU interventions and client characteristics produce counseling casualties? If so, what are the contraindicating signs that counselors can look for when screening clients for EDU interventions?

Another open question concerns how best to compose a group—homogeneously or heterogeneously—with respect to client diagnosis. The traditional thought among group counseling researchers was that with certain diagnoses (e.g., borderline personality disorder and schizophrenia), homogeneous groups are contraindicated. This prohibition existed because of the fear that clients in a diagnostic homogeneous group would actually model and reinforce their pathology. However, as noted earlier, some researchers have had success working with difficult mental health problems in homogeneous groups (e.g., Kanas, 1993). Unfortunately, we do not have detailed answers concerning the interaction of *outcome* (effective, ineffective, or harmful), *group composition* (heterogeneous or homogeneous), *group modality* (TSK, EDU, IPR, or REC), and *theoretical orientation* (cognitive, behavioral, psychodynamic, or client centered). Answers concerning these interactions could help professional counselors deliver more effective group counseling services.

Scheidlinger (1995) noted the lack of research on group counseling interventions with children and adolescents. With three exceptions (depression, career development, and sex abuse trauma), no consensus exists in the research that group counseling is efficacious with any particular child or adolescent population. Other researchers have commented on the mixed evidence supporting the efficacy of group counseling with youth (Abramowitz, 1976; Sugar, 1993). Sugar (1993) presented an extensive listing of research needs concerning group counseling with youth. These needs included the differentiation of treatment from maturation effects, the impact of different demographic variables, the impact of working alliance, the identification of family factors, and outcome effects for open versus closed groups. Given the wide application of group methods to children and adolescents, this research dearth needs to be remedied if counselors are going to argue for the existence of group interventions in a managed-care environment.

Summary ～

A common experience of nascent professionals in any field is an enthusiasm to apply their newly learned skills. These skills can be used to heal pain and promote peak performance; however, like any powerful tool, group counseling skills can cause harm as well as good. Therefore, the purpose of this chapter was to help beginning group counselors temper and focus their enthusiasm for their newly gained group counseling skills. To that end, we first defined efficacy and discussed how it was measured. Then we covered the influence of specific and nonspecific factors on group counseling outcomes. Finally, we detailed the efficacy of group counseling with specific client populations.

We also aimed in this chapter to instill a sense of respect for the counseling research literature. All group counselors will face many situations during their careers in which they are unsure of what to do to help their clients. Time and human complexity inevitably outstrip even the best counselor preparation training. In confusing clinical circumstances, the counseling research literature can serve as an invaluable resource. In their article entitled "Building on an Empirical Foundation: Strategies to Enhance Good Practice," Nelson and Neufeldt (1996) presented a very readable guide for counselors on how to use research to improve their clinical practice. We recommend that all group counselors read and reread this article.

As we have noted throughout this chapter, the group counseling research literature contains a rich panoply of strategies and techniques available for the asking. Our question to all of our readers is: Will you ask, or instead curse in the darkness?

References ～

Abramowitz, C. V. (1976). The effectiveness of group psychotherapy of children. *Archives of General Psychiatry, 33*, 320–326.

Abramowitz, C. V., Roback, H. B., Abramowitz, S. I., & Jackson, C. (1974). Differential effectiveness of directive and nondirective group therapies as a function of client internal-external control. *Journal of Consulting and Clinical Psychology, 42*, 849–853.

Achenbach, T. M., & Edelbrock, C. (1989). Diagnostic, taxonomic, and assessment issues. In T. H. Ollendick & M. Hersen (Eds.), *Handbook of childhood pathology* (pp. 53–69). New York: Plenum.

Agras, W. S., Telch, C. F., Arnow, B., Eldredge, K., Detzer, M. J., Henderson, J., & Marnell, M. (1995). Does interpersonal therapy help patients with binge eating disorder who fail to respond to cognitive-behavioral therapy? *Journal of Consulting and Clinical Psychology, 63,* 356–360.

Alexander, P. C., Neimeyer, R. A., Follette, V. M., Moore, M. K., & Harter, S. (1989). A comparison of group treatments of women sexually abused as children. *Journal of Consulting and Clinical Psychology, 57,* 479–483.

American Psychological Association. (1992). *Ethical principles of psychologists and code of conduct.* Washington, DC: Author.

American School Counselor Association. (1990). *Role statement: The school counselor.* Alexandria, VA: Author.

American School Counselor Association. (1995). *The professional school counselor's role in educational reform.* Alexandria, VA: Author.

Association for Specialists in Group Work. (1990). *Professional standards for training of group work generalists and of group work specialists.* Alexandria, VA: Author.

Baider, L., & De Nour, A. K. (1989). Group therapy with adolescent counselor patients. *Journal of Adolescent Health Care, 10,* 35–38.

Baker, S. B., & Popowicz, C. L. (1983). Meta-analysis as a strategy for evaluating effects of career education interventions. *Vocational Guidance Quarterly, 31,* 178–186.

Baker, S. B., Swisher, J. D., Nadenichek, P. E., & Popowicz, C. L. (1984). Measured effects of primary prevention strategies. *Personnel and Guidance Journal, 62,* 459–463.

Barker, R. L. (1995). *The social work dictionary.* Washington, DC: NASW Press.

Beeferman, D., & Orvaschel, H. (1994). Group psychotherapy for depressed adolescents: A critical review. *International Journal of Group Psychotherapy, 44,* 463–473.

Bergin, A. E. (1963). The effects of psychotherapy: Negative results revisited. *Journal of Counseling Psychology, 10,* 244–250.

Bergin, A. E. (1966). Some implications of psychotherapy research for therapeutic practice. *Journal of Abnormal Psychology, 71,* 235–246.

Bergin, A. E. (1980). Negative effects revisited: A reply. *Professional Psychology, 11,* 93–100.

Bettenhausen, K. L. (1991). Five years of groups research: What we have learned and what needs to be addressed. *Journal of Management, 17,* 345–381.

Beutler, L. E., Jobe, A. M., & Elkins, D. (1974). Outcomes in group psychotherapy: Using persuasion therapy to increase treatment efficacy. *Journal of Consulting and Clinical Psychology, 42,* 547–553.

Borders, L. D., & Drury, S. M. (1992). Comprehensive school counseling programs: A review for policymakers and practitioners. *Journal of Counseling and Development, 70,* 487–501.

Bordin, E. S. (1994). Theory and research on the therapeutic working alliance: New directions. In A. O. Horvath & L. S. Greenberg (Eds.), *The working alliance* (pp. 13–37). New York: Wiley.

Borg, W. R., & Gall, M. D. (1989). *Educational research.* New York: Longman.

Brandes, N. S. (1977). Group therapy is not for every adolescent: Two case illustrations. *International Journal of Group Psychotherapy, 27,* 507–510.

Braswell, L. (1993). Cognitive-behavioral groups for children manifesting ADHD and other disruptive behavior disorders. *Special Services in the Schools, 8,* 91–117.

Brehm, J. W. (1966). *A theory of psychological reactance.* New York: Academic Press.

Brough, M. F. (1994). Alleviation of loneliness: Evaluation of an Adlerian-based group psychotherapy. *Individual Psychology, 50,* 40–51.

Budman, S. H., Demby, A., Feldstein, M., & Gold, M. (1984). The effects of time-limited group psychotherapy: A controlled study. *International Journal of Group Psychotherapy, 34,* 587–603.

Budman, S., Demby, A., & Randall, M. (1980). Short-term group psychotherapy: Who succeeds, who fails? *Group, 4,* 3–16.

Butler, T., & Fuhriman, A. (1983). Curative factors in group therapy: A review of recent literature. *Small Group Behavior, 14,* 131–142.

Cahill, C., Llewelyn, S. P., & Pearson, C. (1991). Treatment of sexual abuse which occurred in childhood: A review. *British Journal of Clinical Psychology, 30,* 1–12.

Cartledge, G., & Milburn, J. F. (1978). The case for teaching social skills in the classroom: A review. *Review of Educational Research, 48,* 133–156.

Cerbone, M. J. A., Mayo, J. A., Cuthbertson, B. A., & O'Connell, R. A. (1992). Group therapy as an adjunct to medication in the management of bipolar affective disorder. *Group, 16,* 174–187.

Christopher, F., Loeb, P., Zaretsky, H., & Jassani, A. (1988). A group psychotherapy intervention to promote the functional independence of older adults in a long term rehabilitation hospital: A preliminary study. *Physical and Occupational Therapy in Geriatrics, 6,* 51–61.

Combs, A. W., Avila, D. L., & Purkey, W. W. (1978). *Helping relationships: Basic concepts for the helping professions.* Boston: Allyn & Bacon.

Conyne, R. K., Harvill, R. L., Morganett, R. S., Morran, D. K., & Hulse-Killacky, D. (1990). Effective group leadership: Continuing the search for greater clarity and understanding. *Journal for Specialists in Group Work, 15*, 30–36.

Cooper, C. L. (1975). How psychologically dangerous are T-groups and encounter groups? *Human Relations, 28*, 249–260.

Couch, R. D., & Childers, J. H. (1987). Leadership strategies for instilling and maintaining hope in group counseling. *Journal for Specialists in Group Work, 12*, 138–143.

Council for the Accreditation of Counseling and Related Educational Programs. (1994). *Accreditation standards and procedures manual.* Alexandria, VA: Author.

Council on Rehabilitation Education. (1994). *Accreditation manual for rehabilitation counselor education programs.* Rolling Hills, IL: Author.

Crown, S. (1983). Contraindications and dangers in psychotherapy. *British Journal of Psychiatry, 143*, 436–441.

Davies, D. R. (1989). A multiple treatment approach to the group treatment of insomnia: A follow-up study. *Behavioural Psychotherapy, 17*, 323–331.

Davies, D. R. (1991). A comparison of hypnotic and non-hypnotic users in the group psychotherapy of insomnia. *Behavioural Psychotherapy, 19*, 193–204.

Davis, R., Olmstead, M. P., & Rockert, W. (1992). Brief group psychoeducation for bulimia nervosa: II. Prediction of clinical outcome. *International Journal of Eating Disorders, 11*, 205–211.

Dembo, M. H., Sweitzer, M., & Lauritzen, P. (1985). An evaluation of group parent education: Behavioral, PET, and Adlerian programs. *Review of Educational Research, 55*, 155–200.

Dhooper, S. S., Green, S. M., Huff, M. B., & Austin-Murphy, J. (1993). Efficacy of a group approach to reducing depression in nursing home elderly residents. *Journal of Gerontological Social Work, 20*, 87–100.

Dutton, D. G. (1986). The outcome of court-mandated treatment for wife assault: A quasi-experimental evaluation. *Violence and Victims, 1*, 163–175.

Eayrs, C. B., Rowan, D., & Harvey, P. G. (1984). Behavioural group training for anxiety management. *Behavioural Psychotherapy, 12*, 117–129.

Evensen, E. P., & Bednar, R. L. (1978). Effects of specific cognitive and behavioral structure on early group behavior and atmosphere. *Journal of Counseling Psychology, 25*, 66–75.

Flowers, J. V. (1979). The differential outcome effects of simple advice, alternatives and instructions in group psychotherapy. *International Journal of Group Psychotherapy, 29*, 305–316.

Forester-Miller, H. (1998). Group counseling: Ethics and professional issues. In D. Capuzzi & D. R. Gross (Eds.), *Introduction to group counseling* (2nd ed., pp.159–179). Denver: Love Publishing.

Forester-Miller, H., & Davis, T. E. (1996). *A practitioner's guide to ethical decision making.* Alexandria, VA: American Counseling Association.

Gazda, G. M. (1986). Discussion of "When to recommend group treatment: A review of the clinical and research literature." *International Journal of Group Psychotherapy, 36*, 202–206.

Gazda, G. M. (1989). *Group counseling: A developmental approach.* Boston: Allyn & Bacon.

Gelso, C. J., & Carter, J. A. (1994). Components of the psychotherapy relationship: Their interaction and unfolding during treatment. *Journal of Counseling Psychology, 41*, 296–306.

Gerler, E. R. (1985). Elementary school counseling research and the classroom learning environment. *Elementary School Counseling and Guidance, 20*, 39–48.

Gerler, E. R., & Anderson, R. F. (1986). The effects of classroom guidance on children's success in school. *Journal of Counseling and Development, 65*, 78–81.

Gilewski, M. J. (1986). Group therapy with cognitively impaired older adults. *Clinical Gerontologist, 5*, 281–296.

Glatzer, H. T. (1978). The working alliance in analytic group psychotherapy. *International Journal of Group Psychotherapy, 28*, 147–161.

Gossette, R. L., & O'Brien, R. M. (1993). Efficacy of rational emotive therapy (RET) with children: A critical re-appraisal. *Journal of Behavioural Therapy and Experimental Psychiatry, 24*, 15–25.

Grant, J. R., & Cash, T. F. (1995). Cognitive-behavioral body image therapy: Comparative efficacy of group and modest-contact treatments. *Behavior Therapy, 26*, 69–84.

Guba, E. G., & Lincoln, Y. S. (1989). *Fourth generation evaluation.* Newbury Park, CA: Sage Publications.

Gurman, A. S. (1971). Group marital therapy: Clinical and empirical implications for outcome research. *International Journal of Group Psychotherapy, 21,* 174–189.

Gysbers, N. C., & Henderson, P. (1994). *Developing and managing your school guidance program.* Alexandria, VA: American Counseling Association.

Hadley, S. W., & Strupp, H. H. (1976). Contemporary views of negative effects in psychotherapy. *Archives of General Psychiatry, 33,* 1291–1302.

Harman, M. J. (1991). The use of group psychotherapy with cancer patients: A review of recent literature. *Journal for Specialists in Group Work, 16,* 56–61.

Hartley, D., Roback, H. B., & Abramowitz, S. I. (1976). Deterioration effects in encounter groups. *American Psychologist, 31,* 247–255.

Hayes, R. L., Halford, W. K., & Varghese, F. N. (1995). Generalization of the effects of activity therapy and social skills training on the social behavior of low functioning schizophrenia patients. *Occupational Therapy in Mental Health, 11,* 3–20.

Herr, E. L., & Cramer, S. H. (1996). *Career guidance and counseling through the life span.* New York: Harper Collins.

Hiebert-Murphy, D., De Luca, R. V., & Runtz, M. (1992). Group treatment for sexually abused girls: Evaluating outcome. *Families in Society, 73,* 205–213.

Horvath, A. O. (1994). Research on the alliance. In A. O. Horvath & L. S. Greenberg (Eds.), *The working alliance* (pp. 259–286). New York: Wiley.

Horwitz, L. (1976). Indications and contraindications for group psychotherapy. *Bulletin of the Menninger Clinic, 40,* 505–507.

Hurlbert, D. F., White, L. C., Powell, R. D., & Apt, C. (1993). Orgasm consistency training in the treatment of women reporting hypoactive sexual desire: A comparison of women-only groups and couples-only groups. *Journal of Behavior Therapy and Experimental Psychiatry, 24,* 3–13.

Hyde, A. P., & Goldman, C. R. (1992). Use of multi-modal multiple family group in the comprehensive treatment and rehabilitation of people with schizophrenia. *Psychosocial Rehabilitation Journal, 15,* 77–86.

Isaac, S., & Michael, W. B. (1985). *Handbook in research and evaluation for the behavioral sciences.* San Diego: EDits.

Joanning, H., Quinn, W., Thomas, F., & Mullen, R. (1992). Treating adolescent drug abuse: A comparison of family systems therapy, group therapy, and family drug education. *Journal of Marital and Family Therapy, 18,* 345–356.

Kanas, N. (1991). University of California, San Francisco: Group Therapy Research Program. In L. E. Beutler & M. Crago (Eds.), *Psychotherapy research* (pp. 305–308). Washington, DC: American Psychological Association.

Kanas, N. (1993). Group psychotherapy with bipolar patients: A review and synthesis. *International Journal of Group Psychotherapy, 43,* 321–333.

Kaplan, R. E. (1982). The dynamics of injury in encounter groups: Power, splitting, and the mismanagement of resistance. *International Journal of Group Psychotherapy, 32,* 163–187.

Kneebone, I., & Martin, P. R. (1992). Partner involvement in the treatment of chronic headaches. *Behaviour Change, 9,* 201–215.

Krone, K. P., Himle, J. A., & Nesse, R. M. (1991). A standardized behavioral group treatment program for obsessive-compulsive disorder: Preliminary outcomes. *Behaviour Research and Therapy, 29,* 627–631.

Kupych-Woloshyn, N., MacFarlane, J. G., & Shapiro, C. M. (1993). A group approach for the management of insomnia. *Journal of Psychosomatic Research, 37*(Suppl. 1), 39–44.

Laconte, M. A., Shaw, D., & Dunn, I. (1993). The effects of a rational-emotive affective education program for high-risk middle school students. *Psychology in the Schools, 30,* 274–281.

Lambert, M. J., Shapiro, D. A., & Bergin, A. E. (1986). The effectiveness of psychotherapy. In S. L. Garfield & A. E. Bergin (Eds.), *Handbook of psychotherapy and behavior change* (pp. 157–212). New York: Wiley.

Lee, F., & Bednar, R. L. (1977). Effects of group structure and risk taking deposition on group behavior, attitudes, and atmosphere. *Journal of Counseling Psychology, 24,* 191–199.

Levey, J., McDermott, S., & Lee, C. (1989). Current issues in bulimia nervosa. *Australian Psychologist, 24,* 171–185.

Lewis, V. J., Blair, A. J., & Booth, D. A. (1992). Outcome of group therapy for body-image emotionality and weight-control self-efficacy. *Behavioural Psychotherapy, 20,* 155–165.

Lieberman, M. A., Yalom, I. D., & Miles, M. B. (1973). *Encounter groups: First facts.* New York: Basic Books.

Linehan, M. M., Heard, H. L., & Armstrong, H. E. (1993). Naturalistic follow-up of a behavioral treatment for chronically parasuicidal borderline patients. *Archives of General Psychiatry, 50,* 971–974.

MacKenzie, K. R. (1986). Commentary: "When to recommend group treatment." *International Journal of Group Psychotherapy, 36,* 207–210.

Maples, M. (1988). Group development: Extending Tuckman's theory. *Journal for Specialists in Group Work, 13,* 17–23.

Martella, R., Nelson, J. R., & Marchand-Martella, N. (in press). *Research methods.* Boston: Allyn & Bacon.

Mays, D. T., & Franks, C. M. (1980). Getting worse: Psychotherapy or no treatment—the jury should still be out. *Professional Psychotherapy, 11,* 78–92.

McAuliffe, W. E. (1990). A randomized controlled trial of recovery training and self-help for opioid addicts in New England and Hong Kong. *Journal of Psychoactive Drugs, 22,* 197–209.

McCallum, M., & Piper, W. E. (1990). A controlled study of effectiveness and patient suitability for short-term group psychotherapy. *International Journal of Group Psychotherapy, 40,* 431–452.

McCrone, S. H. (1991). Resocialization group treatment with the confused institutionalized elderly. *Western Journal of Nursing Research, 13,* 30–45.

McFarlane, W. R., Link, B., Dushay, R., Marchal, J., & Crilly, J. (1995). Psychoeducational multiple family groups: Four-year relapse outcome in schizophrenia. *Family Process, 34,* 127–144.

McNamara, K. (1989). Group counseling for overweight and depressed college women: A comparative evaluation. *Journal for Specialists in Group Work, 14,* 211–218.

Meichenbaum, D. H., Gilmore, J. B., & Fedoravicius, A. (1971). Group insight versus group desensitization in treating speech anxiety. *Journal of Consulting and Clinical Psychology, 36,* 410–421.

Mone, L. C. (1994). Managed care cost effectiveness: Fantasy or reality? *International Journal of Group Psychotherapy, 44,* 437–448.

Nehls, N. (1991). Borderline personality disorder and group therapy. *Archives of Psychiatric Nursing, 5,* 137–146.

Nelson, M. L., & Neufeldt, S. (1996). Building on an empirical foundation: Strategies to enhance good practice. *Journal of Counseling and Development, 74,* 609–615.

Nezu, A. M. (1986). Efficacy of social problem-solving therapy approach for unipolar depression. *Journal of Consulting and Clinical Psychology, 54,* 196–202.

O'Neill, M., & Stockell, G. (1991). Worthy of discussion: Collaborative group therapy. *Australian and New Zealand Journal of Family Therapy, 12,* 201–206.

Pattison, E. M., Rhodes, R. J., & Dudley, D. L. (1971). Response to group treatment in patients with severe chronic lung disease. *International Journal of Group Psychotherapy, 21,* 214–225.

Patton, M. Q. (1990). *Qualitative evaluation and research methods.* Newbury Park, CA: Sage Publications.

Pedro-Carroll, J. L., Albert-Gillis, L. J., & Cowen, E. L. (1992). An evaluation of the efficacy of a preventive intervention for 4th-6th grade urban children of divorce. *Journal of Primary Prevention, 13,* 115–130.

Polster, R. A., Dangel, R. F., & Rasp, R. (1987). Research in behavioral parent training in social work: A review. *Journal of Social Service Research, 10,* 37–51.

Powell, T. J. (1987). Anxiety management groups in clinical practice: A preliminary report. *Behavioural Psychotherapy, 15,* 181–187.

Reber, A. S. (1986). *Dictionary of psychology.* New York: Penguin Books.

Reynolds, W. M., & Coats, K. I. (1986). A comparison of cognitive-behavioral therapy and relaxation training for the treatment of depression in adolescents. *Journal of Consulting and Clinical Psychology, 54,* 653–660.

Ribner, N. G. (1974). Effects of explicit group contract on self-disclosure and group cohesiveness. *Journal of Counseling Psychology, 21,* 116–120.

Rohde, R. I., & Stockton, R. (1994). Group structure: A review. *Journal of Group Psychotherapy, Psychodrama, and Sociometry, 46,* 151–158.

Rotter, J. B. (1966). Generalized expectancies for internal versus external locus of control reinforcement. *Psychological Monographs, 80* (1, Whole No. 609).

Scheidlinger, S. (1995). The small healing group—A historical overview. *Psychotherapy, 32,* 657–668.

Scott, M. J., & Stradling, S. G. (1991). The cognitive-behavioural approach with depressed clients. *British Journal of Social Work, 21,* 533–544.

Shaughnessy, P., & Kivlighan, D. M. (1995). Using group participants' perceptions of therapeutic factors to form client typologies. *Small Group Research, 26,* 250–268.

Shechtman, Z. (1994a). The effects of group psychotherapy on close same-gender friendships among boys and girls. *Sex Roles, 30,* 829–834.

Shechtman, Z. (1994b). Group counseling/psychotherapy as a school intervention to enhance close friendships in preadolescence. *International Journal of Group Psychotherapy, 44,* 377–391.

Silovsky, J. F., & Hembree-Kigin, T. L. (1994). Family and group treatment for sexually abused children: A review. *Journal of Child Sexual Abuse, 3,* 1–20.

Slavson, S. R. (1943). *An introduction to group therapy.* New York: Commonwealth Fund.

Slavson, S. R., & Schiffer, M. (1975). *Group psychotherapies for children.* New York: International Universities Press.

Smets, A. C., & Cebula, C. M. (1987). A group treatment program for adolescent sex offenders: Five steps toward resolution. *Child Abuse and Neglect, 11,* 247–254.

Stark, L. J., Bowen, A. M., Tyc, V. L., Evans, S., & Passero, M. A. (1990). A behavioral approach to increasing calorie consumption in children with cystic fibrosis. *Journal of Pediatric Psychology, 15,* 309–326.

Stark, L. J., Owens-Stively, J., Spirito, A., Lewis, A., & Guevremont, D. (1990). Group behavioral treatment of retentive encopresis. *Journal of Pediatric Psychology, 15,* 659–671.

Stockton, R. M., & Morran, D. K. (1982). Review and perspective of critical dimensions in therapeutic small group research. In G. Gazda (Ed.), *Basic approaches to group psychotherapy and group counseling* (pp. 37–83). Springfield, IL: Charles C Thomas.

Stockton, R., Morran, D. K., & Velboff, P. (1987). Leadership of therapeutic small groups. *Journal of Group Psychotherapy, Psychodrama, & Sociometry, 39,* 157–165.

Strein, W. (1988). Classroom-based elementary school affective education programs: A critical review. *Psychology in the Schools, 25,* 288–296.

Sugar, M. (1993). Research in child and adolescent group psychotherapy. *Journal of Child and Adolescent Group Therapy, 3,* 207–226.

Sutton, C. (1992). Training parents to manage difficult children: A comparison of methods. *Behavioural Psychotherapy, 20,* 115–139.

Todres, R., & Bunston, T. (1993). Parent education: A review of the literature. *Canadian Journal of Community Mental Health, 12,* 225–257.

Tolman, R. M., & Bennett, L. W. (1990). A review of quantitative research on men who batter. *Journal of Interpersonal Violence, 5,* 87–118.

Toseland, R. W., & Siporin, M. (1986). When to recommend group treatment: A review of the clinical and the research literature. *International Journal of Group Psychotherapy, 36,* 171–201.

Truax, C. B., Wargo, D. G., & Volksdorf, N. R. (1970). Antecedents to outcome in group counseling with institutionalized juvenile delinquents. *Journal of Abnormal Psychology, 76,* 235–242.

Tuckman, B. (1965). Developmental sequence in small groups. *Psychological Bulletin, 63,* 384–399.

Vandervoort, D. J., & Fuhriman, A. (1991). The efficacy of group therapy for depression. *Small Group Research, 22,* 320–338.

Wiggins, J. D., & Wiggins, M. M. (1992). Elementary students' self-esteem and behavioral rating related to counselor time-task emphases. *The School Counselor, 39,* 377–381.

Wilfley, D. E., Agras, W. S., Telch, C. F., Rossiter, E. M., Schneider, J. A., Cole, A. G., Sifford, L., & Raeburn, S. D. (1993). Group cognitive-behavioral therapy and group interpersonal therapy for the nonpurging bulimic: A controlled comparison. *Journal of Consulting and Clinical Psychology, 61*, 296–305.

Winick, C., & Levene, A. (1992). Marathon therapy: Treating rape survivors in a therapeutic community. *Journal of Psychoactive Drugs, 24*, 49–56.

Yalom, I. (1985). *The theory and practice of group psychotherapy* (3rd ed.). New York: Basic Books.

Zimpfer, D. G. (1984). Patterns and trends in group work. *Journal for Specialists in Group Work, 9*, 204–208.

Zimpfer, D. G. (1990a). Groups for divorce/separation: A review. *Journal for Specialists in Group Work, 15*, 51–60.

Zimpfer, D. G. (1990b). Group work for bulimia: A review of outcomes. *Journal for Specialists in Group Work, 15*, 239–251.

Zimpfer, D. G. (1991). Groups and grief and survivorship after bereavement: A review. *Journal for Specialists in Group Work, 16*, 46–55.

Zimpfer, D. G., & Carr, J. J. (1989). Groups for midlife career change: A review. *Journal for Specialists in Group Work, 14*, 243–250.

6

Group Work in Specific Settings

Conrad Sieber and Rolla E. Lewis

The literature on group counseling explores research and practice in a variety of settings, ranging from hospitals and community mental health centers to schools and universities. In a review of nine decades of group therapy, Scheidlinger (1994) traced the origins of group practice in the United States from its beginning in a Boston medical setting, where groups of tuberculosis patients were taught proper home care, to the present, in which group counseling is recognized as an effective treatment for addressing developmental concerns and mental disorders in children, adolescents, adults, and the elderly. Economic necessity has often been a catalyst for group counseling's evolution. For instance, in World War II, military hospitals with limited psychiatric resources turned to group work as a cost-effective means of service delivery. During the community mental health center movement in the 1960s, groups were used as a means of providing remedial and preventative counseling (Scheidlinger, 1994); and in the late 1980s, university counseling centers, experiencing increased demand for clinical service and diminished resources, expanded group programs (Sieber, 1994). In the present era of managed care, group therapy is once again being seen as a potentially cost-effective means of treatment (Scheidlinger, 1994).

This chapter examines the practice of group counseling in six real-world settings.* The focus is on the application of group interventions and the way in which the development of a group program is affected by organizational issues such as the

* We are thankful to the following individuals for sharing their expertise and providing information about their group practices: Dapo Sobomehin, Ph.D.; Perry Roth, L.C.S.W.; Etta Martin, L.C.S.W.; Bruce Neben, M.A., M.F.C.C.; and Mary Baker, M.S., L.P.C.

client population, the training and expertise of group leaders, the staff philosophy on service delivery, and budgetary constraints. Each setting creates its own context, which affects practice and program development. The group programs examined here include those at an alternative high school, an African American church-based program, university counseling centers, a private practice, a nonprofit organization contracting services to a community mental health center, and an adult day treatment program. Two voices are evident in the pages that follow: that of the practitioner and that of the researcher/theoretician. These sometimes divergent voices are contrasted, blended, and finally integrated. The learning that can take place through examination of the similarities and differences in the practice of group counseling in these diverse settings may be surprising.

Psychoeducational Groups for Alternative High School Students ~

The high attrition rate for teens seeking help at mental health clinics makes school-based programs attractive as an efficient and cost-effective treatment. Developing an effective group program in a traditional or alternative high school requires an understanding of group and organizational behavior, because the efficacy of the intervention itself depends on the support of teachers and administrators. Serving troubled and/or vulnerable adolescents also demands an effective approach to training and consulting with teachers, who make the group referrals (Litvak, 1991). Adolescents may prefer groups over individual counseling because of their desire for peer interaction and the fact that they rarely enter counseling willingly. In group counseling there is greater psychological distance from the adult authority figure and easy access to peer support (Scheidlinger, 1994).

Based on adolescent developmental needs, common goals for teenagers in groups include improving self-understanding, exploring personal identity, learning problem-solving skills, enhancing social skills, developing the ability to relate to authority figures, and learning coping skills to manage the emotional, physical, and behavioral changes inherent in maturation (Ohlsen, 1970). Of course, school administrators are most interested in students' academic performance and dealing with disruptive behavior that interferes with the educational process. Therefore, school-based group programs must demonstrate their relevance in addressing these issues. Many researchers have noted the role group counseling can play in helping students at risk for dropping out (e.g., Muha & Cole, 1991; Page & Chandler, 1994; Praport, 1993). These researchers, among others, have pointed out that group counseling can address emotional and psychological issues to create behavioral change (Litvak, 1991); improve academic performance (Litvak, 1991; Page & Chandler, 1994); increase insight into ineffective behavior and the need to focus more on choice and self-responsibility (Page & Chandler, 1994); and enhance self-esteem (Muha & Cole, 1991). Often, group counseling can accomplish these goals more effectively than individual treatment because teenagers typically value peer feedback more highly than adult feedback (Muha & Cole, 1991).

The continuation high school selected for this discussion is located in a rural, agricultural area in a rapidly growing community in the western United States. Continuation high schools are alternative schools designed to help students who have experienced frustration and failure in the traditional school setting. This school had four full-time teachers and an enrollment of 110 students.

The psychoeducational group described in this section was structured to meet 40 minutes per day, 5 days a week, over 6 weeks. The effectiveness of this group, like all adolescent psychoeducational groups, depended on such issues as attendance, group cohesion, and the degree to which the group was conducted as intended (Rice & Meyer, 1994). Group goals were to assist students in four areas: (a) establishing social and personal comfort in group settings (see, e.g., Praport, 1993), (b) building self-trust and self-respect (see, e.g., Muha & Cole, 1991; Page & Chandler, 1994), (c) teaching active listening skills (see, e.g., Ohlsen, 1970), and (d) teaching respectful response skills (see, e.g., Ohlsen, 1970). The group ranged in size from 10 to 16 students who were 16 to 19 years of age. All members were required to have parental consent to participate. Students with conduct disorders were screened out and referred to individual counseling.

Group membership was consistent with school enrollment, having approximately 71% Euro-American and 29% Hispanic members and generally more males than females. Students in this continuation high school were customarily characterized as having oppositional and passive-aggressive traits. Their behaviors commonly led them to confront the role, behaviors, and hypocrisy of authority figures such as teachers and school administrators. As a population within the community, the continuation students were viewed as inferior to traditional high school students and frequently labeled dropouts, druggies, and failures. Thus, these students often had little faith in their ability to learn and succeed.

The group's guiding principle was celebrating personal differences and the cultural pluralism inherent in the community. Otto Rank (1941) captured this principle in saying, "There is no other equality possible than the equal right of every individual to become and to be himself, which actually means to accept his own difference and have it accepted by others" (p. 241). Group members were encouraged to explore and discuss what it meant to be students, and to view group members, the leader, and the supervisor as simultaneously being students and teachers (Freire, 1970).

The group leader, the second author and formerly a teacher in the school, was supervised by a therapist from the county mental health center, who sat in with the group on a regular basis. Videotaping of the sessions was frequently done for group, teaching, and supervision purposes. The videotapes were used with group members to assist them in observing their own behavior and interactions with others. A primary goal of the group was to teach communication skills; access to videotapes of group meetings allowed students to observe and critique themselves as they interacted with other group members. Students who used denial as a primary defense found it difficult to persist in this behavior in the face of incontrovertible evidence of their actions.

Dies (1992) described leader behaviors that facilitate adolescent group development, recommending anticipatory, directive, and interpersonally focused strategies for each stage. In the present group, the definition stage was the most challenging for the leader. Parent permission slips were collected first. Although initial screening for group participation may take place prior to parental approval, acquiring parental consent is essential in these groups and helps prevent unexpected or premature termination. This contributes to group stability, often a concern in adolescent groups (Litvak, 1991).

Trust rapidly became a central concern in the group. Defining the limits of confidentiality and child abuse reporting requirements were important initial considerations among group members. It is significant to note that dealing with confidentiality issues is different in a school setting than in others. For instance, in a community mental health center, clients are less likely to share the same environment outside of treatment. In a school, violations of confidentiality among group members must be addressed quickly and directly. By addressing possible breaches in confidentiality from the standpoint of group norms, the group is allowed to proceed and function appropriately (Litvak, 1991). A related issue is what information, if any, does the group leader share with the faculty who made the initial group referral. Discussion of this issue involves, among other things, probing students' expectations and fantasies about this concern. It should be evident that alternative school students are likely to come from backgrounds in which they have felt violated and taken advantage of by people they should be able to trust. Dealing effectively with issues of confidentiality and the consequences for potential breaches is an important step in building trust in the mistrustful and moving toward group cohesion.

The initial group structure was critical for these students. In fact, research has shown that lack of structure or ambiguity in purpose can actually increase group members' cognitive distortions, fear of relating to others, and distress and can lead to premature termination (Rohde & Stockton, 1994). It is probably self-evident that students from chaotic backgrounds are likely to have a high degree of anxiety in beginning a new group where they may be vulnerable.

When told by the leader, "This is your group. Each of you is my teacher," some members felt threatened. Exercises such as a blind trust walk, creating magazine collages, and journaling were used to help group members explore the outside world and its influences. Gibbs (1994) and Vernon (1989) served as primary catalysts for generating group topics. Gender differences were a regular theme. During the collage exercise, cutouts made by males depicted deep cleavage, cars, weapons, alcohol, drugs, and power over others. Collages made by females showed flowers, babies, dogs, houses, teddy bears, handsome men, and wedding rings. Thus, these collages revealed gender differences that created debate and a desire by some to establish one gender as superior. The group struggled with accepting differences between the sexes and other cultural diversity issues. As the group developed, hostility toward the world and toward peers was examined and a sense that differences were not necessarily evil emerged.

During the personal involvement stage, appropriate personal boundaries were explored by group members. As the group progressed, the leader was challenged to gently confront anger, fear, and negativity among members. During this stage, members also began to voluntarily form their chairs into a circle instead of needing direction from the leader. The members became more invested in allowing one person to speak at a time and listened more attentively to others. During this stage, they became less dependent on the leader to provide daily techniques to prompt conversation.

The group involvement stage began when juggling was introduced by one member who taught three-bag juggling to the others. Reluctant members began to let their bodies show them that they could learn. In one instance, a very timid female avoided the lesson. She said, "I can't," as she was frozen in her primary fear of failure. While being shown the most basic juggling toss, she was encouraged to "let go of the 'I can't' in your head. Let your body show that you can learn." During five lessons she tried halfheartedly but continued to feel and act like she was a failure. Finally, with persistence and encouragement from the leader and peers, she completed her first jug, a difficult step in successful juggling. After that, she improved dramatically and made a major learning breakthrough. She discovered that she was capable of doing much more than she assumed.

Juggling was used as a learning metaphor. Members began to see themselves as capable of learning and able to do something constructive at school. They began to teach others outside the group how to juggle. They organized a Jugglers for Peace Celebration. Successfully organizing a school event led the group to believe they had power within the school community.

During one session, when the teacher described himself as the group leader, a student confronted him by saying, "This is our group. We're all equal." The leader asked, "If I'm not a teacher and I'm not a leader, what is my role?" The student replied, "You're a guide." The students had truly become owners of the group. Although the group was described as a psychoeducational intervention, it is clear that there were therapeutic elements to the group process that were welcomed by the leader. This blending of psychoeducational skill building and therapy is not uncommon in groups offered in the schools (see, e.g., Litvak, 1991). Furthermore, the dynamic of a successful experience of interacting with an authority figure, the teacher and group leader, is an important aspect of this intervention for students who by definition have difficulties with authority (e.g., Ohlsen, 1970).

Since the group was structured in a 6-week format, the enhancement and closure stage was described to members from the beginning. During the final week, termination was addressed directly and members were invited to participate in the next 6-week group. As a closure activity, students were asked to give feedback about their reactions to the group experience. One student wrote, "I like this class because kids get to know one another better. I also like this class so much because the students run the class, not just the teacher... . I also...learned active listening skills, and you [sic] learn to deal with some of the problems that come up in life." Another student wrote, "I found out that the students in the class are really great people. At first I didn't think much of them but they kind of grow on you... . I learned I didn't have to be afraid to share things with people... . If we want something done or to happen we should go for it. I have also learned that as a team we can do much more." Thus, the group achieved its goal of building cohesion and promoting a sense of empowerment and trust in self and others. The goals of improving communication skills and encouraging students to take responsibility for themselves while engaging in a constructive relationship with a trustworthy authority figure were also accomplished.

During termination students also met individually with the leader. At these meetings, they were given specific feedback about the changes they had made by accepting responsibility and learning to see themselves as teachers. Thus, personal responsibility, the power to be effective, and the power to make decisions—important concepts to convey in adolescent groups—were explicitly reinforced at termination (Page & Chandler, 1994). Closure was also used as an opportunity to assess and review individual achievements. For students returning for the next 6-week session, termination became a chance to define specific goals for learning communication skills and leadership qualities that would enhance member participation. Students who functioned as saboteurs were met with privately and referred to individual counseling for 6 weeks before being considered for reentry to the group.

Psychoeducational groups are used in this continuation high school to empower individuals and build community. Working with continuation high school students is a challenge. They are frequently angry, alienated, and hurting from real or perceived negative experiences in relationships with peers and adults. Therefore, creating a group in which students learn to trust peers and the adult leader by listening to one another and showing mutual respect can provide a powerful healing experience. These students became part of a learning community in which each person is encouraged to take risks to grow. In the end, successful group members became more empowered as individuals and community members. These points are exemplified by the words of an early pioneer in the use of group interventions who said, "By the crowd they have been broken, by the crowd they shall be healed" (Marsh, 1931, p. 330).

Thus, group interventions with adolescents in school settings have much to offer. As previously mentioned, they may be more efficacious than individual counseling because teenagers desire peer interactions and often give greater weight to feedback from peers than from adults (Muha & Cole, 1991; Scheidlinger, 1994). Group interventions can also address adolescent development tasks that are salient to school performance. These tasks include enhancing one's sense of self; developing coping, problem-solving, and social skills for negotiating the academic environment; learning to work effectively as part of a team; and changing behaviors that are disruptive to others (Ohlsen, 1970).

Attention to the interplay between group and organizational behavior in the school community is an important component in developing an effective adolescent group program. Having clear criteria for referral and screening that can be communicated to teachers and administrators is essential (Litvak, 1991). Also, counselors must be prepared to manage administrative issues raised by group interventions and have an effective conceptualization of training and supervision for both educational and counseling professionals, who work together toward common goals in the group program.

Nonprofit Community Organization Psychoeducational Groups for At-Risk Urban Youth~

Operation E.A.S.Y. (Efforts Aimed at Sensitizing Youth) is a nonprofit community organization affiliated with a church that provides on-site psychoeducational groups focused on the needs of at-risk, inner-city African American youth. African American churches have historically played a significant role in providing outreach programs to youth. These programs often include group discussions, seminars, and workshops (Rubin, Billingsley, & Caldwell, 1994).

Operation E.A.S.Y. does more than work directly with youth. It functions as a center for care in the community (Benard, 1993). Parents, grandparents, and other community members utilize its services to address the challenges to the psychological well-being of the community's children brought about by poverty and despair. Because African American inner-city youth frequently lack mentors or other adults with the time and resources to encourage their growth, building positive relationships between youth and the church, community agencies, parents, siblings, and the extended family is a primary goal of organizations like Operation E.A.S.Y. In fact, findings of a study on patterns of violence among African American youth suggest that upward mobility for these children is related to strong family ties and church activities (Rubin et al., 1994).

The leader of the Operation E.A.S.Y. groups is advised by a psychologist and works collaboratively with several community mental health agencies (D. Sobomehin, personal communication, July 11, 1996). His knowledge of the community, African American culture, and adolescent development, and his upbringing in a Nigerian Yoruba village, contribute to his group leadership abilities. The phrase "It takes a whole village to raise a child" is more than rhetoric to him. He stated, "I was raised by a whole people—the extended family and community. In my village we used the term *oba*. *Oba* means king or queen. No matter what you call me, I am *oba*. I teach them *oba*. We are kings. We are queens" (D. Sobomehin, personal communication, July 11, 1996). This group leader has been characterized as a community wizard (McLaughlin, Irby, & Langman, 1994) who raises expectations and provides "settings where youth can gain the attitudes, confidence, and expertise necessary to remove themselves from the inner city's despair" (p. 98). Operation E.A.S.Y. is a place of hope where supportive and caring relationships accentuate efforts to help community members to take responsibility for building social capital and showing children that their life trajectories may be changed from despair and hopelessness to hope and success. Program objectives are consistent with the social and behavioral science literature that supports the important role community institutions play in socializing youth (Rubin et al., 1994).

These psychoeducational groups emphasize social skills, self-awareness, and respect building. Seating is usually in a circle to ensure that members "look at each other's faces, become more attached, and empathize," with the aim of creating a resiliency-enhancing atmosphere in which youth will learn to love and accept themselves and others (D. Sobomehin, personal communication, July 11, 1996). The group leader has found that the greatest challenge is encouraging self-respect and sensitivity to others. He addresses violence in terms of messing up. He stated, "I do not want to mess up who I am, and I want them to know that messing with each other is hurtful" (D. Sobomehin, personal communication, July 11, 1996). The key lessons emphasize respect, doing the right thing, and knowing who you are. Youth are encouraged to think about things before they do them. Standard questions posed regularly include Who am I? and What is my purpose? Group members are told, "You must like yourself and take yourself seriously; otherwise, you treat yourself in a worthless way" (D. Sobomehin, personal communication, July 11, 1996).

Group members range in age from kindergarten through high school students. Groups are normally divided into K-6, middle school, and high school. Occasionally, more mature, younger students will be placed with older members. For instance, a mature fifth grader may meet with the middle school group. Groups are open and range in size from 6 to 10 members. However, one-time educational programs may include as many as 50 members. Poverty is one thing all the children have in common. Some of these children do not know their fathers. Many of the youth do not have family members who are working or even know others who are working. The youth are exposed to alcohol, drugs, and other forms of abuse arising from hopelessness. One child, for instance, came to a group session with $10 and shared how he had gotten the money from his grandfather who made money selling drugs. Many of the youth are unsupervised at home, left to do whatever they want. One 5-year-old child, damaged through neglect, swore so much it made working with him difficult. It was hard to be close to him and his anger.

Children such as these have no village, because the village has thrown them away. Their school might provide a community, but they may get into trouble and be thrown out of school. Such children learn a sense of victimization that disables them and exacts a toll on the community. The group intervention at Operation E.A.S.Y. provides opportunity screens, described as a process in which negative family and peer influences are transcended by community-based institutional opportunities. Although parents may not have attachment to important community institutions, children can be connected in constructive ways to the primary institution in the African American community, the church (Billingsley, 1968; Rubin et al., 1994).

To be effective with this population, cultural sensitivity is required. The group leader stated:

> You must become part of them and their community. I am black, but I have an accent and I act differently. I ask them to do what I do. I teach them to show respect or to show some social limits. I ask them, "If I go into your house and go into your stuff without your permission, what do you think?" I get to the basics. If you have the basics under control, then you have it. You have to have those basics. I had those before my degrees. That's what kids need. I'm training myself as I grow with the kids and review the basics with them. What are the basics? What do you do in the morning? Are you going to brush your teeth? Comb your hair? Are you going to take care of the basics? You do

those things that have to be done. Life is built on those basics. These kids have frequently been deprived of their childhood. They did not get those basics. If we do not go
back and take care of that, they are lost. We have to give them the basics. You must build
your house on a solid foundation. Kids tell me that they do not eat dinner at home. They
say, "We eat at 7-11 or McDonald's." They do not eat [with their families]. I take them
out as a family and serve them and teach them how to eat with others (D. Sobomehin,
personal communication, July 11, 1996).

Storytelling and listening are the dominant methods used in the group. The
group leader shares family stories from Africa, especially those of the Yoruba people in Nigeria, to emphasize connection to something larger than one's self. Some of
the stories encourage youth to focus on developing a positive attitude. The children
are told, "You never know what angel is flying by and is going to grant what you are
asking. If you are asking for tennis shoes or something bad to happen to someone
else, what does that really do for you? What do you want?" (D. Sobomehin, personal communication, July 11, 1996) In telling such stories, the group leader points out
to the youth that thoughts precede and guide actions. "Drug selling can be attractive
in the short run" he tells them, "but how does it really help you and your family?"
(D. Sobomehin, personal communication, July 11, 1996)

Group sessions sometimes focus on careers, relationships, or the possibilities
inherent in using heart, head, and hands. The group leader tries to connect with
school-to-work programs and to help prepare the children for what they will do when
they leave school. "Sometimes their patience is lacking," he said, "and they think the
[school] training is too long. That's why drug selling can be attractive. They need
mentors" (D. Sobomehin, personal communication, July 11, 1996). The program
uses community members who want to be teachers or counselors as mentors and
models. "They help show the kids other ways," the group leader told us. Clearly, this
perspective would be supported by Benard (1993), who stated that positive child-
adult relationships with parents, grandparents, neighbors, teachers, and other concerned adults are a "protective factor for youth growing up in stressful family and
community environments" (p. 21).

Trust is difficult to build in this community, and the lack of trust of the community members creates ethical dilemmas for the group leader. The group leader
consults with counselors about specific group members and makes referrals, but the
group members often don't go. He said, "They don't trust. The level of trust is very
low in this community. [So] I go to the home and talk to the family. They tell me
what's going on. I end up working with families" (D. Sobomehin, personal communication, July 11, 1996). These anecdotal reports are consistent with research showing that ethnic minorities tend to underutilize mental health services and terminate
prematurely when they do seek help (see, e.g., Sue & Sue, 1990). This characteristic makes a community outreach program anchored in an African American institution like the church that much more important. It challenges the counselor to extend
his or her practice beyond the counseling office.

The group leader is also a member of the Citizen Review Committee that oversees child abuse cases and out-of-home placement, which creates some challenging

situations. "I have a grandmother with a 15-year-old grandson who babysat his 7-year-old niece," the group leader told us. "It was found out that he molested the niece. He confessed to the police after being interrogated. I try to support the grandmother and [am working to get] all parties help. The boy is now with the Youth Authority. This boy's brother was shot and killed a few months ago. Now the family comes to me" (D. Sobomehin, personal communication, July 11, 1996).

Through these youth, the group leader becomes connected to the family and community. To him, youth, family, and community are interconnected. Each needs support and care in confronting hopelessness and despair. The community members who help him in mentoring the youth add to the social capital and hope in the economically impoverished inner city. With their help, the group leader took his groups to visit a nearby metropolitan city. They slept in classrooms at a local school where they were asked to show respect for property and each other. They did. The group leader summed up the experience by saying, "It takes time to teach the beauty of being human. We are all god's creation and we are good" (D. Sobomehin, personal communication, July 11, 1996). The group leader's outreach work with citizens, teachers, counselors, and families helps him show the youth that goodness does exist, for there are community wizards who keep hope alive. In fact, a study of black churches and family-oriented community outreach concluded that the integration and cooperation of social institutions, of which the church is one, is necessary to improve the lives of African American youth. These programs are challenged to address such issues as alcohol and drug abuse, teen pregnancy, prenatal care for pregnant adolescents, life skills, self-esteem enhancement, and the creation of educational, vocational, and professional advancement opportunities (Rubin et al., 1994). Declining federal support for social services increases the importance of church-based community outreach programs such as Operation E.A.S.Y.

Group Counseling in University Settings ~

Many university counseling centers have expanded group counseling programs to decrease the demand for individual counseling. Groups have also joined in popularity because they can be the treatment of choice for traditional-aged college students negotiating the developmental tasks of developing identity and intimacy (Chickering, 1969). The literature on group interventions in colleges and universities is replete with examples of psychoeducational, support, and counseling groups. Types of groups include those for problem solving and interpersonal communication skills (e.g., McMillon, 1994), life skills enhancement (e.g., Clark, 1993), assertiveness training (e.g., Ernst & Heesacker, 1993), self-defeating perfectionism (Richards, Owen, & Stein, 1993), career exploration (Anderson, 1995), ethnic minority students (e.g., Brown, Lipford-Sanders, & Shaw, 1995; Fukuyama & Coleman, 1992; Rollock, Westman, & Johnson, 1992), learning disabilities (e.g., Wilczenski, 1992), grief (e.g., Janowiak, Mei-tal, Drapkin, 1993), women with eating disorders (e.g., Brouwers, 1994; Weiss & Orysh, 1994; Zimmerman & Shepherd,

1993), and incest/sexual abuse survivors (e.g., Axelroth, 1991; Thomas, Nelson, & Sumners, 1994).

The first author has coordinated group programs in two university counseling centers. University programs usually offer psychoeducational, support, and time-limited therapy groups that are scheduled to fit the academic calendar. Groups typically range in size from 6 to 10 students. Many counseling groups may be organized around a theme, such as women's, family-of-origin, and men's issues. Although many of these groups may function as standard counseling groups with an interpersonal process focus, students seem to respond favorably to themes. These themes can provide a means for early identification with other members and diminish anxieties about joining a group. That is, many students feel anxious about joining a general counseling group with no explicit focus or structure. Attending a men's group, or another theme group, may feel less threatening than going to discuss one's problems in an unstructured process-oriented therapy group. Groups with themes appear to alleviate anxiety about the unpredictability of open-ended counseling groups and buffer against the expectation of detriment, two issues found to be significant negative expectations held by prospective group members (Slocum, 1987). Thus, a theme can provide some clarity concerning the purpose of the group and diminish negative expectations.

Organizing around a theme also helps create homogeneity. However, debate exists about whether homogeneity or heterogeneity is best for group functioning. Some researchers and clinicians believe that groups should be formed with clients who are homogeneous in terms of some salient factor such as diagnosis, while others believe that groups should be heterogeneous. Traditionally, clinicians and researchers of group counseling assumed that with certain problems, such as borderline personality disorder, homogeneous groups were detrimental because clients would model and reinforce one another's pathology. This in turn would prevent clients from working through their problems (see, e.g., Corazzini, 1994). Recently some counselors and researchers have reported success in working with clients with difficult mental disorders, including borderline personality disorder, in homogeneous groups (see Chapter 5 of this text; also Nehls & Diamond, 1993). Furthermore, those who advocate time-limited or brief therapy groups have noted that homogeneity is an important factor in promoting connectedness and rapid development of cohesion. For instance, Budman (1981) described success with a time-limited group for adolescents coping with the developmental issues of separation and individuation from family. Here, the homogenous group was organized around life stage and developmental tasks, not diagnosis. Elsewhere, it was reported that an important advantage of single diagnosis groups is that members readily see they are not alone and that others have similar problems. The resulting increased potential for empathy, understanding, and acceptance can increase the efficacy of treatment (Friedman, 1989). Advocates of heterogeneity not only fear that clients with similar problems will reinforce one another's negative behavior but also believe that group members with divergent background and experiences can learn from addressing their own sense of difference. For instance, they may discover that those group members they initially perceive as fundamentally different actually have concerns and life difficulties similar to their own (Yalom, 1985). Thus, when theme groups are led in a university setting, careful consideration should be given to issues of homogeneity and heterogeneity of group membership. The possibility that members of a homogeneous group will reinforce negative behaviors should be taken into account, while the benefits to rapid development of cohesion should be acknowledged.

The resurgence in popularity of group counseling in university settings over the past 10 years has brought together professionals with different levels of training and expertise in group leadership. Some were prepared in their graduate programs, while others learned through briefer in-service training opportunities within the university's counseling department. Thus, staff share a variety of philosophies and skills in group leadership. For some, group work is seen as an important means of providing clinical service that is different from, but equivalent to, individual counseling; to others, it is viewed as a secondary treatment option. This can create challenges in referring clients to groups and in coordinating concurrent individual and group treatments. For instance, a counselor who truly believes in the efficacy of group counseling is more likely to refer a client directly from intake to an appropriate group, whereas a counselor who sees group as second best is more likely to assign this same client to individual counseling. One advocate of university counseling center group programs recommended that counseling staff must change their irrational belief that individual treatment is superior to group counseling for a program to be successful (Corazzini, 1994). Another difficulty can occur in cases in which a client is seen by both an individual and a group counselor whose philosophies concerning the role and/or efficacy of group treatment differ. For example, the individual counselor may be cautious about consulting with the group leader concerning the client because of their concern for maintaining the sanctity of the individual therapy relationship, while the group leader may appreciate and desire the opportunity to consult. These differences can affect group program functioning and need to be addressed directly to ensure the success of group practice in university counseling centers (Sieber & Kettler, 1994).

Students seen in university counseling center groups present difficulties ranging from developmental issues focused on relationship and identity formation to more serious conditions such as anxiety, depression, substance abuse, and personality disorders. Nontraditional-aged students or adult learners often seek counseling for help in coping with difficulties related to the life transitions that brought them back to college (e.g., divorce, job loss) and handling the stress of multiple roles. One of the advantages of university group programs is access to clients. Students seeking university counseling services place a high demand on centers with limited resources; therefore, the opportunity to develop a meaningful group program is supported by the need to deliver timely, cost-effective services (Sieber, 1994).

Referral of students to group counseling is often done in one of two ways. Evaluation of referral decisions in one group program revealed that 50% of clients were referred to groups directly from intake, while the other 50% were referred from counselors' individual caseloads (Sieber, 1992). During an intake appointment a counselor who believes group is the treatment of choice for a student's concerns will make a group referral. At this time, he or she would educate the student about the difference between individual and group counseling, since most students expect referral to individual therapy and/or have a limited and sometimes negative view of group work (Broday, Gieda, Mullison, & Sedlacek, 1989; Sieber & Kettler, 1994). Of course, it is ideal for intake workers to make treatment recommendations based on client needs. Oddly enough, this is often not the case. One study of referral decisions in a university counseling center found that many times so-called nonclinical factors such as financial resources and staff availability were the primary consideration in the referral process. The researchers found that there were no significant differences between individual and group counseling referral decisions based on clinical factors, while pragmatic considerations such as long waiting lists and availability of outside referral did differentiate between individual and group assignment. However, client characteristics did play a role in these decisions. Those clients perceived as socially skilled and capable of intimacy were referred more often to group counseling, while those seen as more severely disturbed were more often referred to individual therapy. Finally, the area of expertise of the intake counselor impacted referral decisions. Intake counselors with expertise relevant to a particular client's dilemmas often referred the client to their group (Quintana, Kilmartin, Yesenosky, Macias, 1991). In counseling centers using brief therapy models many clients are also referred to a group once their quota of individual sessions has been met (e.g., after 12 sessions). Clients referred from individual to group counseling may utilize insights developed in individual therapy in the counseling group, where the focus shifts from individual concerns to an interpersonal focus.

In university settings and elsewhere, pre-group screenings are required for counseling groups, while psychoeducational and support groups usually do not require them. Once a counseling group referral has been made, the leaders conduct a pre-group screening that typically lasts 30 minutes. During the meeting, the client's readiness and appropriateness for group work are assessed. The ideal group candidate defines his or her problems as relational, commits to change in interpersonal behavior, accepts the idea of being influenced by the group, engages readily but not inappropriately in self-disclosure, and is willing to help others (Friedman, 1989). During the screening meeting, the client will usually describe his or her difficulties in terms of a personal problem such as depression or loneliness. When this happens, the group leader helps the client redefine the personal problem in relationship terms so the client begins to learn that the power of the group is in the interpersonal process (Yalom & Yalom, 1990). For example, a depressed client may be helped to understand his or her difficulty as a lack of assertiveness and problems in getting his or her needs met. Such a client would enter a group with the goal of being more assertive and speaking up for him- or herself. During the pre-group screening, the group leader may encourage this client to watch other members who are assertive about their needs, take risks to practice new behaviors, request feedback, and observe the effect of increased assertiveness on the quality of their group relationships. The screening interview also provides the opportunity to orient clients to group counseling. Research has shown that clients who enter groups with a specific problem to address will report greater benefit and satisfaction at termination than those with global expectations of change. Thus, the initial goals of the client developed during the pregroup screening should be as close as possible to his or her presenting concern, should be specific, and should be attainable in a few months (Friedman, 1989).

Brief interactive counseling groups offered in university counseling centers provide an excellent opportunity for students to learn new behaviors, such as assertiveness or limit setting, and are relatively low-risk venues in which direct and honest feedback can be solicited. In these groups, clients become aware of their maladaptive interpersonal behavior and beliefs while they begin to make corrections with support and feedback from peers. The leader attends to group process and creates opportunities for constructive here-and-now interactions while helping clients stay focused on their treatment goals. The leader also continuously reminds the group that time is limited within any one session and to a specific number of sessions overall. In these ways, the leader encourages members to be active in the pursuit of specific goals and to take risks in the present. Brief interactive groups do not provide time to analyze or work through resistance to treatment; therefore, members must simply be encouraged to experiment with new behaviors even though they may maintain certain fears about doing so (Yalom & Yalom, 1990).

Counselors working with university students should have expertise in leading psychoeducational, support, and time-limited counseling groups. It is also helpful to have knowledge of the developmental issues of traditional-aged students, those of identity and intimacy (Chickering, 1969), and of adult learners, who often return to college after an extended absence. Many staff members who lead groups in the university setting make use of a blend of expertise in facilitating long-term interpersonal process groups and time-limited groups, where being more active/directive is necessary.

University counseling centers often provide unique opportunities for training in group counseling because they can bring together a substantial pool of prospective group counseling clients, trained professionals, and counseling graduate students completing practica and internships. Graduate students in these settings often co-lead groups with senior staff members. This provides the students with opportunities to work closely with an experienced group leader who usually provides supervision after each group meeting. In this format, trainees observe the experienced group leader in action, have the opportunity to provide leadership within the group while being observed by a professional, and can discuss their learning experiences in supervision meetings.

Group counseling in university counseling centers can be an effective means of service delivery. The catalyst for developing group programs at many centers is the common economic issue of limited resources. The hope has been that group work would serve more clients for less cost. However, one research study indicated that this expectation has not been met, as only 20% of clients seeking assistance in university counseling centers were receiving some form of group intervention (Golden,

Corazzini, & Grady, 1993). Hindrances to the more effective use of groups include staff beliefs that individual therapy is superior to group therapy (Corazzini, 1994), client preference for individual attention and skepticism about groups (Broday et al., 1989; Sieber & Kettler, 1994), and pragmatic concerns that impede group referrals, such as scheduling (Sieber & Kettler, 1994; Quintana et al., 1991).

Group Counseling in Private Practice ～

The literature on group counseling rarely addresses issues specific to group work in private practice. However, many articles discuss specific groups typically conducted in private practice and the client populations they serve. These include group therapy for adult children of alcoholics using an object relations orientation (Mahon & Flores, 1992), short-term modern analytic group therapy (Kirman, 1991), intensive psychotherapy of clients with borderline personality disorder (Finn & Shakir, 1990), Gestalt groups for HIV-positive clients (Siemens, 1993), and the use of genograms in latency-aged children's groups (Fink, Kramer, Weaver, & Anderson, 1993).

The private practitioners who develop and lead the group program described here are both certified group psychotherapists offering groups in a metropolitan area (P. Roth & E. Martin, personal communication, August 12, 1996). Their group therapy room is located in a professional office building and is an oversized individual therapy office. A video camera can be mounted on the wall, allowing observers to view these groups via a monitor. The client population consists of people with difficulties ranging from borderline personality to obsessive-compulsive and depressive disorders. Clients are predominantly white and middle class with an age range of 25 to 70 years. There are several gay and lesbian clients. Most groups are heterogeneous in composition and evenly balanced between men and women. The therapists' philosophy is that honoring diversity is important and that clients learn from differences.

It should be obvious that leading private practice groups requires knowledge of how to develop a client referral base. This involves connecting with other health care professionals and teaching them the purpose of group therapy. Often, health care professionals have the bias that individual counseling is superior. Once they have been taught to overcome this bias, they will likely refer clients for group therapy in the future.

The philosophy shared with clients at pre-group screenings is that group psychotherapy is a special type of therapy in which the focus is on the interactional/interpersonal process. The group leaders work with their clients during the meeting to identify both constructive and problematic interactional patterns and personality traits. Those that lead to difficulties can be addressed and worked through within the group. The focus is on the interpersonal part of clients' lives, how the clients relate to others, the difficulties that interfere with their relationships, and the opportunity they will have in group to learn from one another. The group leaders use the metaphor coined by Malcolm Pines, who described the group as a "hall of mirrors" where individuals receive several images of themselves from others.

Those interested in Pines work are referred to a description of the practice of group analysis (Roberts & Pines, 1991).

Both long- and short-term groups are offered. These leaders view group work as an adjunct to or graduation from individual counseling. Clients enter groups to apply what has been learned in individual work to the group experience. Hence, pre-group screening also involves a discussion of personality structure. Clients are asked to describe what they have learned about themselves and who they are in individual therapy and then to identify those issues they want to continue to address in group. Previous group experiences of any kind are also examined. Some clients may have distortions concerning their expectations of group counseling based on previous negative experiences (e.g., Broday et al., 1989). By discussing these in the screening appointment, leaders correct clients' distortions and/or prepare themselves for the possibility that clients may reenact previous negative experiences in the group. Goals are set for group members, including addressing relationship concerns, identifying projections, and understanding that there are other more adaptive ways to cope. Thus, clients will be helped in group sessions to be better communicators, to learn to give and receive feedback, and to remove obstacles that have created difficulties in their relationships.

Most groups in this practice are long-term and are co-led. The focus is on the interpersonal process, what it reveals about each client, and how it can be used to the client's benefit. A special challenge is faced in leading groups with clients who have personality disorders. The group leaders must deal with group members who project their own difficulties onto others, often perceive feedback as personal criticism, and may have a pattern of becoming stuck in self-defeating behaviors. An example of a client using projection is the group member who sees herself as the neglected child and often assumes that other members suffer from the same fear of rejection. Another group member, who grew up with a psychotic mother, exhibits signs of distress when any group member becomes emotionally aroused; while a male client tends to eroticize relationships and presumes that others respond in a similar way. Often it is necessary to prevent groups from becoming stuck in obsessional thinking that blocks their progress. For instance, one male member had a pattern of getting involved with two women simultaneously and then obsessing on choosing between the two. One evening he brought a current example of this dilemma to group. The group engaged in an extended discussion of his handling of the two relationships and the choices he needed to make. After some time, one of the leaders asked the group to examine its interactions with this person and the ways in which it had become stuck on the details of his latest romantic escapades. Slowly but surely, the group members acknowledged that it was easier to focus on the details of the romance than address the concerns each of them had brought to group. This intervention initiated a shift from the focus being excessively on this one man to other members participating more fully (P. Roth & E. Martin, personal communication, August 12, 1996). It is important for leaders to see group process and to know how to intervene using a group as opposed to an individual-level intervention.

The group leaders focus in the here and now on the interpersonal process and encourage clients in their long-term groups to give and receive feedback. For instance, within the first two sessions clients are asked to share their impressions of one another. The leaders ask, "Who is willing to give feedback to one of the other members?" (P. Roth & E. Martin, personal communication, August 12, 1996) The leaders also take an active role in teaching clients how to be effective group members. One concept clients are taught is metacommunication (i.e., that there are overt and covert messages in every interaction). Clients are assisted in identifying when and how metacommunication occurs and ways to make use of these insights. Focus is also placed on the group as a whole as the leaders pay attention to its progression through developmental phases. The question why now is often asked. Why is this particular event happening now in this group, and is it moving the group toward or away from its goals? This sort of exploration when a group is stuck in its development may uncover defenses against anger or resentment that are blocking progress. This anger can then be addressed, directly freeing the group to move on. When the leaders have been effective, members become good therapists for one another.

Twelve-week time-limited therapy groups are also offered in this practice. Important aspects of these groups are client selection and preparation. Much of an initial individual orientation session is devoted to teaching clients how to use time-limited groups. Leaders are more active-directive, placing the focus on member interactions in the here and now (Yalom & Yalom, 1990), facilitating discussion, and using bridging techniques to help clients see similarities in one another's dilemmas.

These clinicians recommend that students training to be group leaders in private practice seek out as many different group leadership experiences as possible with professionals having different styles (P. Roth & E. Martin, personal communication, August 12, 1996). They encourage students to earn American Group Psychotherapy Association certification as group psychotherapists following graduation and to take part in ongoing consultation concerning their practice. The practitioners highlighted in this discussion, for instance, run a group therapy training institute in which practicing counselors are trained in leading counseling groups. By participating in a training group, counselors learn more about leading groups themselves. They also receive the opportunity for ongoing clinical supervision of group leadership and share professional readings on relevant topics.

Multiple Family Groups in a Private, Nonprofit Setting ~

The group described in this section is led by a private, nonprofit organization contracting mental health services to the county (B. Neben, personal communication, July 18, 1996). Working as a group of licensed counselors, the practitioners have common assumptions about practice. In developing the group program, the leaders consulted with the Mental Research Institute (MRI) and Kaiser Hospital to integrate a number of interventions, especially those of Jay Haley and MRI. Finding training on multiple family group process was difficult, as few practitioners were conducting these groups. Thus, the leaders were dependent on books, theory, and professional conversations to develop their practice. Their research led to the creation of training seminars for other health care professionals. The therapeutic groups serve families with identified patients who suffer from severe mental disorders, such as schizophrenia and bipolar disorder. Groups are conducted in an old house with a comfortably furnished carpeted living room, which creates an informal atmosphere. The goal is to help families feel as comfortable as possible because they are usually nervous about seeing counselors. In this friendlier, less clinical environment, groups are arranged in an oval to make sure no one is looking at anyone else's back. Sessions are frequently videotaped for supervision and training. Once video equipment has been discussed, clients are not distracted by the camera, as their problems are severe enough to keep them focused on their own difficulties.

The guiding principle of the group leaders is to distance themselves from the medical model and to help identified patients and their families live normal or as close to normal lives as soon as possible. The counselors' philosophy is that everyone has a good chance to live in a more normal way, and interventions are designed to help the clients live in less restricted settings, such as a halfway house. The focus is on every member of the family, not merely the identified patient. In helping families find ways to lead more normal lives, the group leaders encourage them to support one another. Because the groups are heterogeneous in degree of pathology, one family can get ideas from another about what works in a specific situation. These are open groups, so that when one family leaves another enters. Thus, more experienced families can help the newcomers, thereby enhancing the theme of families helping families.

Referrals to the program are usually made by hospitals, community mental health centers, halfway houses, day treatment facilities, homeless programs, private psychiatrists, or the National Alliance for the Mentally Ill. The primary criterion for entry to the group program is that clients have families who are willing to become involved due to their concern about the situation. Although no specific commitments for change are required, an assessment of family flexibility and willingness to change is made.

During screening interviews, the key is to select clients who will be cooperative and not disruptive. Clients with personality disorders are screened out. Screening interviews take place with the identified patient, then with the parents and other possibly influential people in these clients' lives. Rules about confidentially, not criticizing other group members, and being helpful are reviewed. Families are asked to commit to weekly meetings for at least 1 month.

Due to the isolation these families feel, they frequently organize around the client's dysfunction. Often, the family designates a specified member to take care of the identified patient and his or her career often changes as a result. For example, one mother was very worried about what her schizophrenic son was going to do. Her entire life was consumed with worry about whether he would break a window or something else in the house. She found herself cutting short phone conversations, taking showers with the door open, and being preoccupied with caring for her son. This parent's goal was to find help for making changes necessary to lead a more functional life.

Because families are exposed regularly to the medical model, the leaders eschew it in favor of a more psychosocial approach. The leaders focus more on family relationships than on brain chemistry, because focusing on brain chemistry frequently takes responsibility away from the client. When asked about medication, the leaders play dumb, saying, "I'm not a psychiatrist. Maybe you should talk to your psychiatrist," and reframe the concern in terms of the psychosocial issues of the family (B. Neben, personal communication, July 18, 1996). However, the groups are intentionally designed to complement, not undermine, the medical system in helping disturbed clients become more functional. Although medication can be necessary and/or helpful, there are no chemical quick fixes that are going to make clients' lives 100% better. Thus, families have to sacrifice and make changes to help bring about more normal lives.

The identified patients are adolescents, young adults, and middle-aged adults. Groups are designed to be homogeneous according to age of the client and socioeconomic status of the family. The groups are divided by ages (14–19, 19–30, and 30–45) because age-appropriate life goals vary. For instance, the group leader said, "Teenagers need to be in school; a real, comprehensive high school rather than a hospital school. Adults should work. For some, competitive paid work is not realistic but can be approximated. In any case, the issue of occupation needs to be addressed" (B. Neben, personal communication, July 18, 1996). Groups are also divided by socioeconomic status, as the group leaders discovered that upper- and lower-income families did not have much understanding of each other's needs. In mixed groups, socioeconomic issues too often became the dominant focus, rather than what the family could do to help normalize itself. The overt theme of the groups is to help the identified patient get back on track, getting sidetracked with insurmountable social issues is detrimental. Covertly, the counselors try to restructure family relationships to improve levels of mutual support, help the families stop patterns of behavior that have repeatedly been unsuccessful, and arrange contingencies to increase successful behavioral interactions.

For their young adult clients, the team members recognize that many severe problems do not occur until the client thinks about leaving home. Jay Haley's (1973) work helped the counselors formulate the view that in the process of leaving home some adolescents or young adults go "crazy." Although the team members have found their work harder than Haley described, his ideas have been useful in providing guidance for coordinating treatment with psychiatrists, social workers, and vocational rehabilitation counselors. They also recognize the importance of family therapists maintaining some control over the treatment plan so that health care professionals are not working at cross-purposes.

Substance abuse has proven to be a special challenge, since identified patients often have another diagnosis in addition to substance abuse. The team members view substance abuse as partially the attempts of a severely disturbed person to self-medicate. Being a little drunk or high dulls the voices or other painful symptoms. It is therefore important to look at the reasons the clients are using drugs or alcohol. The rationale is to avoid laying another major problem upon the client, and to avoid pathologizing, while injecting hopefulness. However, people who are clearly addicted are confronted more directly.

Clear, concise, concrete, and realistic behavioral goals are clarified and defined early in the group process for the identified patients. Sometimes it takes a few sessions to define these goals. Family members are also asked how they will know when the family reaches its goals. Miracle questions are posed, such as, "How would the family relations be different if your son was not having this depression?" (B. Neben, personal communication, July 18, 1996) If the parent states that the family would go on more vacations, the leaders may negotiate that as a goal.

The multiple family group is viewed as a counseling, support, and psychotherapeutic effort to help clients get back on their feet. Success is stressed, since everybody has had some success. Individuals are asked to think about where they have been successful and are encouraged to share their successful experiences with others. If group members see self-defeating behaviors, they are encouraged to confront them and suggest possible alternatives. Thus, client strengths are utilized whenever possible.

Regardless of the extent of the individual client or family pathology, strengths can be elicited from family members or other group members and utilized for change. Some interventions are indirect. Counselors may talk to one person when the actual target is another, or group members may help each other. For instance, a father who has discovered that positive solutions exist may work with a mother or father in another family who is more negative or discouraged. Sometimes, artificial familial subsets are created. Children from different families can be placed together to role-play siblings; parents and spouses from different families can be put together to role-play parents of a member of the group or spouses; parent-child relationships can be created from parents and children from different families. The artificial relationships last for the length of the intervention. These subgroups can be reformed at a later time if the pairing resulted in a particularly useful intervention or if the point needs to be made again. These pairings are created to address real or hypothetical problems. The following examples illustrate this point:

For parents who cannot work together to help their daughter, the leaders might ask the role-playing parent: "If you two were the parents of Gail, how would you help her to get out of the house and be less isolated?" Then, to the actual parents the leaders would ask, "Why don't you give it a try?" Other examples include: "Gail can't seem to get out of bed in the morning to go to her (college) classes. What would you suggest if you were her parents?" or "What approaches could a family make to help a young adult who is stuck at home and can't get out to work or see friends?" (B. Neben, personal communication, July 18, 1996)

Parents who want to get tough with their child are paired with parents who want to use only love and understanding. Feedback is sought from children. Family members give feedback to one another and to other families. Sometimes this process is achieved or accentuated by splitting the group into two or more groups of different configurations and moving small subgroups to other rooms with overt or covertly targeted tasks. Parents and children may be split off into separate subgroups, or groups may be formed of men and sons, women and daughters. There may be a sibling group. The groups may come back together that session or they may not. When they do, they sometimes make a report or statement to the larger group.

Co-leaders work closely with each other to utilize the power of the entire group. Often this leads them to take different roles. When one leader is working with an individual, the other leader can be working with others. Or, when one leader is working with a parent, the other can be supporting the children in the group. These roles can switch at any time if a leader feels that his or her partner is missing something important. It is crucial for leaders to avoid doing the same things in different ways. Although separate but similar interventions may be therapeutic, it is not nearly as effective or powerful as a clear, whole-group strategy devised by the co-leaders together.

Clearly, multiple family groups present a number of dilemmas. First, there may be clients who are better suited for individual family work and must be referred. Second, the issue of termination brings out the need for follow-up. Relapse is not uncommon. To prepare for probable relapse, questions such as, "What would happen if ...?" and "What would you do if your parents argued again?" can be asked (B. Neben, personal communication, July 18, 1996). Plans should be made in preparation for relapse. Families should be told there is no cure and that problems will come up again but that they have learned some skills and gained some tools. They should be told that situations will arise that will test their resolve and that the best they can do is to be prepared. Third, ethical concerns are always difficult with groups and with families. Bringing the two together creates even more concerns. When individual family members call the counselor with an issue that would be addressed more effectively in group, the counselor is put in a bind. In the end, counselors are served best by telling the group about the limits of confidentiality during the screening process and reminding them of those limits when necessary.

Multiple family groups are clearly a challenge. At the same time, such groups offer families an avenue to lead more normal lives. Anecdotal reports of therapeutic success achieved by using multiple family groups in nonmedical settings, encourages continued exploration and development of innovative approaches to using group process with families.

Group Counseling in an Adult Day Treatment/Partial Hospitalization Program ∼

The literature on group work in day treatment programs provides examples of various types of groups created for specific purposes, such as cognitive therapy for chronically mentally ill patients (Albert, 1994), parenting groups for recovering addicts (Plasse, 1995), groups for psychiatrically ill elderly patients (Plotkin &

Wells, 1993), those focused on gender issues (Sirkin, Maxey, Ryuan, & French, 1988), and groups for adolescents (Mendel, 1995). Day treatment programs serve individuals who are to some extent in remission from acute illnesses requiring hospitalization and those who would otherwise be treated in outpatient settings. Many programs can be viewed as a form of time-limited therapy. Typical goals are improved psychological functioning and symptom reduction (Rosie & Azim, 1990). Also known as partial hospitalization programs, day treatment programs provide "half time in plus half time out" treatment in which the clients maintain contact with the community outside of therapy (Weil, 1984, p. 165).

In this section, an adult outpatient day treatment program at a metropolitan hospital is examined (M. Baker, personal communication, August 5, 1996). The staff of the program is made up primarily of master's level counselors and social workers who work as part of a treatment team providing psychoeducational and therapy groups. The program is located in an office building adjacent to the hospital and has five group rooms. Videotaping is available through the use of a camcorder and live observation can be done in one room through a two-way mirror. It is interesting to note that taping and observation of groups for training purposes are reported to be limited by client complaints.

Three populations of clients who are predominantly white and have a wide range of socioeconomic status are served. Through a state contract with the Justice Department, the hospital works with adjudicated clients found not guilty by reason of insanity who have Axis I disorders. These clients usually have schizophrenia, bipolar, or substance abuse disorders. Clients with Axis II disorders, in particular those diagnosed with borderline personality disorder, make up another client population. This is consistent with another day treatment program which also reported a significant percentage of clients (i.e., 60%) having Axis II or personality disorders (Rosie & Azim, 1990). The third group consists of geriatric clients, who most often have depression or bipolar disorder. Treatment goals for all groups are stabilization, skill building, and improved functioning.

Individual counseling is considered an adjunct to group work, which is the primary treatment modality. This approach is consistent with the observation that the key ingredients in a successful adult day treatment group program are an emphasis on groups throughout the program and staff expertise in group therapy (Rosie & Azim, 1990). Groups are viewed as the most efficacious treatment modality because of the opportunities they provide for peer interaction. Learning from peers is thought to be as valuable as treatment by professionals because peers are often able to confront one another more effectively than a counselor can. Group work also provides a sense of belonging for these clients, who often feel isolated and alone.

Most groups are psychoeducational and address such topics as daily living skills, self-image, impulse control, and self-defeating behaviors. At the time of intake, clients are evaluated and assigned to appropriate psychoeducational groups. These groups usually meet 1 to 3 times weekly for 1 hour and are led by a counselor. Psychoeducational groups range in size from 4 to 12 members.

A few psychotherapy groups are offered to selected clients and have 6 to 8 members. Pregroup screenings are done for acting-out behaviors, substance abuse, and eating disorders that require additional attention. Axis I therapy groups meet once a week for 1 hour. They are led by an active-directive group leader who helps clients identify themes such as maintaining relationships when one has a mental disorder. The unique characteristics and challenges of working with Axis I clients in groups are that they are usually mandated to treatment and have little motivation to change, that they may at times be actively psychotic, and that they may also experience difficulties with side effects from medications that interfere with their functioning. Getting and keeping these clients' attention in skill-building groups and encouraging interaction in therapy groups can be a challenge requiring patience and flexibility. Given these limitations, another adult day treatment program that emphasizes group work as the primary treatment modality excludes psychotic patients and those recovering from a recent psychosis including schizophrenia (Rosie & Azim, 1990).

Therapy groups offered for Axis II disordered clients are part of the disorders of self program guided by Masterson's work (see, e.g., Masterson & Klein, 1995). Group leaders use an object relations perspective within the group. These groups meet twice a week for 1½ hours. Clients are referred to therapy groups by their case managers and then screened by the group leaders. Criteria for entry into the Axis II disorder group includes the ability to give and receive feedback and the willingness to strive for nondefensiveness.

Conducting groups in line with a theoretical orientation that is based on treating individuals has a long history. Groups utilizing a number of diverse theoretical orientations have been described, such as Yalom's interpersonal orientation, based on Sullivanian principles, psychodynamic, self-psychology, systems, object relations, and existential orientations, to name a few. This interaction between group process and leader's theoretical orientation makes categorizing the principal dimensions of the group treatment modality difficult (Scheidlinger, 1994).

In the Axis II disorder therapy group leaders assume that clients' outer behaviors are reflections of distorted inner conclusions (Masterson & Klein, 1995). Therefore, group experience is used to help clients clarify these distortions, develop a better relationship with themselves, and enhance their self-concept. At times, counselors feel that clients are working against them, instead of viewing the counselor as an ally. The clients sometimes see the therapists as authority figures trying to impose their will on them. This population is also chronically suicidal and may share stories of self-injurious behavior for their shock value. Thus, group leaders must be able to tolerate their own anxiety about these behaviors without overreacting. They also must resist the temptation to rescue clients who are working through particularly difficult problems, and help other members to do the same. Sometimes the counselors also need to cope with clients who are prone to misinterpretations of others' behavior toward them. Their cognitive distortions often interfere with client's tolerance for feedback. Sometimes leaders help the group cope with clients who become agitated and leave before a meeting ends or drop out all together.

Group clients with borderline personality disorder are viewed as having developed a false self. Clients are believed to have learned to curry parents' support by being the good boy or girl who was rewarded for compliance and punished for act-ing autonomously. Punishment often came in the form of parental withdrawal and the experience of abandonment (Masterson & Klein, 1995). Using this conceptual-ization, group leaders reward self-care and are cautious not to reward behavior that is merely an attempt to please the counselors. In the group setting, the counselors recognize that there are several people for the client to be in relationship with and encourage group members to support one another in acting capably and in their own best interest. Affirming one another's self-defeating behavior is discouraged. Involving these clients in group therapy also diffuses the potential for the malignant transferences that can occur in individual counseling. These transferences involve simultaneously devaluing and idealizing the counselor to such a degree that produc-tive counseling is difficult.

Obviously, leadership in these groups requires good communication and coop-eration between co-leaders to prevent splitting, a thorough understanding of the dynamics of borderline personality disorder, and knowledge of the ways this dis-order manifests itself in interpersonal interactions. The capacity to assist clients in observing their own process, in voicing and then examining their assumptions about others, and in understanding the meaning of their interactions is also neces-sary.

In recent years, group therapy has been identified as having an important role in treating clients with borderline personality disorder. Members of one group program viewed these interventions as helpful for attaining self-defined goals, decreasing hostility and depression (Nehls & Diamond, 1993). This finding is interesting in light of the fact that these clients have often been excluded from therapy groups because of their potential for disrupting group process. In leading groups for clients with borderline personality disorder, it is recommended that group leaders be part of the overall treatment team and if possible be the group members' case managers, since this decreases the probability of splitting. Successful client outcomes in these groups have been associated with two interventions: leaders' providing information to and seeking information from members. Common discussion themes include anger, self-destructiveness, loneliness, and poor relationships. Leaders' sharing ideas in a noninterpretive way about coping with loneliness, self-destructive impulses, relationships, housing, jobs, and negotiating the health care system has seemed to help enable women with borderline personality disorder to accept alternative ways of understanding their concerns. It has also empowered them with important infor-mation and the means to manage multiple problems (Nehls, 1992). Areas for further research in group treatment of borderline personality disorder include communica-tion, identifying the most effective group modality for treating borderline personal-ity disorder with special consideration of clients having histories of childhood trau-ma, and determining whether group counseling alone or in tandem with individual treatment is best (Nehls & Diamond, 1993).

Recommendations for students who wish to pursue group counseling in adult treatment programs include doing a practicum or internship that provides opportu-nities to experience supervised practice of group work. Gaining experience in leading psychoeducational groups and those that focus on interpersonal process is also helpful (M. Baker, personal communication, August 5, 1996).

Summary ～

This chapter provided a brief review of group programs in a variety of real-world settings. These programs demonstrate the unique way group work can be adapted to serving clients. Two programs, an inner-city program serving at-risk African American youth and a teacher-led psychoeducational group for alternative high school students, illustrate the effective use of psychoeducational groups and community-building principles. The description of groups for borderline clients in an adult day treatment program is interesting especially in its application of Masterson's work on disorders of self to group process (Masterson & Klein, 1995). In these groups, a strong theoretical base is used to guide the group leaders in their interactions with group members who traditionally have been seen as undesirable candidates for group therapy (see, e.g., Nehls, 1992). In a similar vein, principles of structural and strategic therapy are applied to the multiple family groups for clients with severe mental disorders. These examples illustrate that group program development is influenced by the leader's training, his or her theoretical orientation, and the setting in which the group is offered. Effective group leaders often combine knowledge of a specific theoretical orientation with an understanding of general principles of group process and development. For instance, a group leader who uses Masterson's theories on disorders of self is likely to have a different style of leadership than one with a background in strategic therapy, while both will likely share a common knowledge of group process and group intervention skills.

Groups offered in private practice present the unique challenge of identifying and nurturing a referral base. Often the group counselor finds him- or herself in the role of teaching the merits of group work to other health care professionals. Thus, it is not only the clients who must be educated about group interventions but also the professionals who are likely to refer these clients in the first place.

Comprehensive group programs that provide a wide spectrum of interventions, from psychoeducational through counseling groups, were also examined. University counseling center programs often offer psychoeducational groups such as stress management and relationship building and counseling groups focusing on themes such as men's, women's, and family-of-origin issues. Although general process oriented counseling groups may be utilized college students seem to respond more favorably to groups with themes because they provide a means for early identification and seem to allay client anxieties about open-ended therapy groups (see, e.g., Broday et al., 1989). Issues of homogeneity versus heterogeneity of group membership in the university counseling setting were also discussed (see Chapter 5 of this text; also see Corazzini, 1994). The other comprehensive group program examined here was an adult day treatment program that focused mainly on skill-building (e.g., daily living skills) but also offered a few counseling groups to selected clients. Comprehensive group programs in agency settings require staff members to address such issues as client referral, opportunities for consultation between group leaders and individual counselors seeing the same client, and offering the best groups for the client population being served (see, e.g., Sieber & Kettler, 1994).

It should be evident that each setting—school, nonprofit-church-based, university, private practice, community, and hospital—provides a unique set of circumstances that help define the group program. Some of these contextual factors are the training, expertise, and philosophy of the group leaders, the client population itself, administrative issues shaped by setting, and organizational constraints related to the availability of clients, the degree of support for group interventions, and funding. This chapter has revealed the influence setting and context have on shaping the formation of group practice.

References

Albert, J. (1994). Rethinking difference: A cognitive therapy group for chronic mental patients. *Social Work with Groups, 17*(1–2), 105–121.

Anderson, K. J. (1995). The use of structured career development group to increase career identity: An exploratory study. *Journal of Career Development, 21*(4), 279–291.

Axelroth, E. (1991). Retrospective incest group therapy for university women. *Journal of College Student Psychotherapy, 5*(2), 81–100.

Benard, B. (1993). *Turning the corner: From risk to resiliency*. Portland, OR: Northwest Regional Educational Laboratory.

Billingsley, A. (1968). *Black families in white America.* Englewood Cliffs, NJ: Prentice-Hall.

Broday, S. F., Gieda, M. J., Mullison, D. D., & Sedlacek, W. E. (1989). Factor analysis and reliability of the Group Therapy Survey: *Educational and Psychological Measurement, 49*, 457–459.

Brouwers, M. (1994). Bulimia and the relationship with food: A letters to food technique. *Journal of Counseling and Development, 73*(2), 220–222.

Brown, S. P., Lipford-Sanders, J., & Shaw, M. (1995). Kujichagulia: Uncovering the secrets of the heart. Group work with African American women on predominantly white campuses. *Journal for Specialists in Group Work, 20*(3), 151–158.

Budman, S. H. (1981). *Forms of brief therapy.* New York: Guilford.

Chickering, A. W. (1969). *Education and identity*. San Francisco: Jossey-Bass.

Clark, C. A. (1993). Life-skills enhancement groups as an alternative for waiting-list clients. *Journal of College Student Development, 34*(5), 382.

Corazzini, J. G. (1994). Staff beliefs which hinder the use of group treatment. *American College Personnel Association. Commission VII Counseling and Psychological Services Newsletter. Theme Issue: Group Work in Counseling Centers, 21*(2), 3.

Dies, K. R. (1992). Leadership in adolescent psychotherapy groups: Strategies for effectiveness. *Journal of Child and Adolescent Group Therapy, 2*(3), 149–159.

Ernst, J. M., & Heesacker, M. (1993). Application of the elaboration likelihood model of attitude change to assertion training. *Journal of Counseling Psychology, 40*(1), 37–45.

Fink, A. H., Kramer, L., Weaver, L. L., & Anderson, J. (1993). More on genograms: Modifications to a model. *Journal of Child and Adolescent Group Therapy, 3*(4), 203–206.

Finn, B., & Shakir, S. A. (1990). Intensive group psychotherapy of borderline patients. *Group, 14*(2), 99–110.

Freire, P. (1970). *Pedagogy of the oppressed.* New York: Continuum.

Friedman, (1989). *Practical group therapy: A guide for clinicians*. San Francisco: Jossey-Bass.

Fukuyama, M. A., & Coleman, N. C. (1992). A model for bicultural assertion training with Asian Pacific American college students: A pilot study. *Journal for Specialists in Group Work, 17*(4), 210–217.

Gibbs, J. (1994). *Tribes: A new way of learning together.* Santa Rosa, CA: Center Source.

Golden, B. R., Corazzini, J. G., & Grady, P. (1993). Current practice of group therapy at university counseling centers: A national survey. *Professional Psychology Research and Practice, 24*(2), 228–230.

Haley, J. (1973). *Uncommon therapy.* New York: Norton.

Janowiak, S. M., Mei-tal, R., & Drapkin, R. G. (1995). Living with loss: A group for bereaved college students. *Death Studies, 19*(1), 55–63.

Kirman, W. J. (1991). Short-term modern analytic group therapy. *Modern Psychoanalysis, 16*(2), 151–159.

Litvak, J. J. (1991). School based group psychotherapy with adolescents: Establishing an effective group program. *Journal of Child and Adolescent Group Therapy, 1*(3), 167–176.

Mahon, L., & Flores, P. (1992). Group psychotherapy as the treatment of choice for individuals who grew up with alcoholic parents: A theoretical review. *Alcoholism Treatment Quarterly, 9*(3–4), 113–125.

Marsh, C. L. (1931). Group treatment of the psychoses by the psychological equivalent of revival. *Mental Hygiene, 15*, 328–349.

Masterson, J. F., & Klein, R. (1995). *Disorders of self: New therapeutic horizons.* New York: Brunner/Mazel.

McLaughlin, M., Irby, M., & Langman, J. (1994). *Urban sanctuaries: Neighborhood organizations in the lives and futures of inner-city youth.* San Francisco: Jossey-Bass.

McMillon, H. G. (1994). Developing problem solving and interpersonal communication skills through intentionally structured groups. *Journal of Specialists in Group Work, 19*(1), 43–47.

Mendel, S. (1995). An adolescent group within a milieu setting. *Journal of Child and Adolescent Group Therapy, 5*(1), 47–51.

Muha, D. G. & Cole, C. (1991). Dropout prevention and group counseling: A review of the literature. *High School Journal, 74*(2), 76–80.

Nehls, N. (1992). Group therapy for people with borderline personality disorder: Interventions associated with positive outcomes. *Issues in Mental Health Nursing, 13,* 255–269.

Nehls, N., & Diamond, R. J. (1993). Developing a systems approach to caring for persons with borderline personality disorder. *Community Mental Health Journal, 29*(2), 161–172.

Ohlsen, M. M. (1970). *Group counseling.* New York: Holt, Rinehart & Winston.

Page, R. C., & Chandler, J. (1994). Effects of group counseling on ninth-grade at-risk students. *Journal of Mental Health Counseling, 16*(3), 340–351.

Plasse, B. R. (1995). Parenting groups for recovering addicts in a day treatment center. *Social Work, 40*(1), 65–74.

Plotkin, D. A., & Wells, K. B. (1993). Partial hospitalization (day treatment) for psychiatrically ill elderly patients. *American Journal of Psychiatry, 150*(2), 266–271.

Praport, H. (1993). Reducing high school attrition: Group counseling can help. *School Counselor, 40*(4), 309–311.

Quintana, S. M., Kilmartin, C., Yesenosky, J., & Macias, D. (1991). Factors affecting referral decisions in a university counseling center. *Professional Psychology Research and Practice, 22*(1), 90–97.

Rank, O. (1941). *Beyond psychology.* New York: Dover.

Rice, K. G., & Meyer, A. L. (1994). Preventing depression among young adolescents: Preliminary process results of a psycho-educational intervention program. *Journal of Counseling and Development, 73*(2), 145–152.

Richards, S. P., Owen, L., & Stein, S. (1993). A religiously oriented group counseling intervention for self-defeating perfectionism: A pilot study. *Counseling and Values, 37*(2), 96–104.

Roberts, J. P., & Pines, M. (1991). *The practice of group analysis. The international library of group psychotherapy and group process.* London, England; Tavistock/Routledge.

Rohde, R. I., & Stockton, R. (1994). Effects of explicit group contract on self-disclosure and group cohesiveness. *Journal of Counseling Psychology, 21*, 116–120.

Rollock, D. A., Westman, J. S., & Johnson, C. (1992). A black student support group on a predominantly white university campus: Issues for counselors and therapists. *Journal for Specialists in Group Work, 17*(4), 243–252.

Rosie, J. S., & Azim, H. F. A. (1990). Large-group psychotherapy in a day treatment program. *International Journal of Group Psychotherapy, 40*(3), 305–321.

Rubin, R. H., Billingsley, A., & Caldwell, C. H. (1994). The role of the black church in working with black adolescents. *Adolescence, 29*(114), 251–266.

Scheidlinger, S. (1994). An overview of nine decades of group psychotherapy. *Hospital and Community Psychiatry, 45*(3), 217–225.

Sieber, C. (1992). *Group referral decisions in one university counseling center.* Unpublished manuscript, Illinois State University, Normal.

Sieber, C. (1994). From the guest editor. *American College Personnel Association. Commission VII Counseling and Psychological Services Newsletter. Theme Issue: Group Work in Counseling Centers, 21*(2), 2.

Sieber, C., & Kettler, J. (1994). Group coordinators survey results. *American College Personnel Association. Commission VII Counseling and Psychological Services Newsletter. Theme Issue: Group Work in Counseling Centers, 21*(2), 5.

Siemens, H. (1993). A Gestalt approach in the care of persons with HIV. *Gestalt Journal, 16*(1), 91–104.

Sirkin, M., Maxey, J., Ryuan, M., & French, C. (1988). Gender awareness group therapy: Exploring gender-related issues in a day treatment population. *International Journal of Partial Hospitalization, 5*(3), 263–272.

Slocum, Y. S. (1987). A survey of expectations about group psychotherapy. *International Journal of Group Psychotherapy, 32*, 309–325.

Sue, D. W., & Sue, D. (1990). *Counseling the culturally different: Theory and practice.* New York: Wiley.

Thomas, C. M., Nelson, C. S., & Sumners, C. M. (1994). From victims to victors: Group process as the path to recovery for males molested as children. *Journal for Specialists in Group Work, 10*(2), 102–111.

Vernon, A. (1989). *Thinking, feeling, behaving: An emotional education curriculum for adolescents. Grades 7–12.* Champaign, IL: Research Press.

Weil, F. (1984). Day hospitalization as a therapeutic tool. *Psychiatric Journal of the University of Ottawa,. 9*, 165–169.

Weiss, C. R., & Orysh, L. K. (1994). Group counseling for eating disorders: A two-phase treatment program. *Journal of College Student Development, 35*(6), 487–488.

Wilczenski, F. L. (1992). Coming to terms with an identity of "learning disabled" in college. *Journal of College Student Psychotherapy, 7*(1), 49–61.

Yalom, I. (1985). *The theory and practice of group psychotherapy* (3rd ed.) New York: Basic Books.

Yalom, V. J., & Yalom, I. (1990). Brief interactive group psychotherapy. *Psychiatric Annals, 20*(7), 362–367.

Zimmerman, T. S., & Shepherd, S. D. (1993). Externalizing the problem of bulimia: Conversation, drawing and letter writing in group therapy. *Journal of Systemic Therapies, 12*(1), 22–31.

7

Group Counseling:
Ethical Considerations

Holly Forester-Miller

Ethics lies at the heart of the counseling process. (Van Hoose, 1980, p. 2)

Ethics is truly at the heart of the coun-
seling process. This is especially so in group counseling. For many people group
counseling is the first opportunity they have had to be open and honest and feel safe
in sharing who they are with others. The group leader is responsible for setting the
norm of ethical behavior, not only for the counselor but also for the group as a whole,
to limit the possibilities of that trust being broken.

The following quote from the first page of the preamble to the Association for
Specialists in Group Work's (ASGW) Ethical Guidelines for Group Counselors
(since 1996 referred to as Standards of Best Practice) stresses the role of group leaders as "ethical agents":

> Group counselors, by their very nature in being responsible and responsive to their
> group members, necessarily embrace a certain potential for ethical vulnerability. It is
> incumbent upon group counselors to give considerable attention to the intent and con-
> text of their actions because the attempts of counselors to influence human behavior
> through group work always have ethical implications. (Association for Specialists in
> Group Work [ASGW], 1989, p. 1)

As Van Hoose (1980) pointed out, counseling is affected by much more than the
techniques and information in the counseling process, although these are important.
It is influenced by "attitudes, beliefs, personal behavior, and views about right and
wrong acts" (p. 2), and group members bring many differences, attitudes, beliefs,

behaviors, and views to the group. The leader has to assist the group in facilitating each member's growth and development, without imposing any one person's values on any other member. When one throws into the mix all the additional aspects of group leaders' responsibilities, some of which may have conflicting demands, such as professional codes, institutional policies, societal expectations, client needs, and state and federal laws, it gets even more confusing. Group leaders must make ethical decisions that satisfy all of the areas just mentioned and at the same time satisfy their own sense of ethics and morality. According to Kottler (1994), "The awesome responsibility of group leadership is that practitioners must answer ultimately to themselves for their actions" (p. 307).

Each group leader will eventually formulate an individual method of making ethical decisions, based on a personal view of human nature and the process of change. Van Hoose and Paradise (1979) suggested that ethical theory is a systematic way of organizing the "principles or norms that ought to govern one's conduct" (p. 23) and that these norms are based on institutional, societal, and professional policies. By studying ethical principles, guidelines, and decision making, group leaders should be able to form methods of ethical decision making congruent with professional codes and societal expectations. A study by Robinson and Gross (1989) showed that participants who had taken a university course in ethics were better able than those who had not taken a university ethics course to recognize what ethical issues were pertinent in a given situation and to suggest ethical behaviors to correct those situations.

In 1995, the American Counseling Association (ACA) approved a newly revised and expanded code of *Ethics and Standards of Practice*. In addition to revising the earlier ACA codes, the intent was to reduce the number of codes of ethics for which ACA members were responsible by eliminating the necessity for ACA divisions to each maintain an additional code of ethics. In 1996, the Executive Committee of the Association for Specialists in Group Work formally adopted the ACA Code of Ethics and Standards of Practice as its sole code of ethics and agreed to develop a "Standards of Best Practice" document for group workers. The document will further explain the ACA Code and its application to group work. In the interim, the ASGW 1989 *Ethical Guidelines for Group Counselors* will serve as the *Standards of Best Practice* (ASGW, 1989, 1996). To avoid confusion this document will be referred to as the *Standards of Best Practice* throughout the rest of this chapter.

This chapter presents the ACA ethical codes specific to group work, the *Standards of Best Practice* (ASGW, 1989, 1996), an ethical decision-making model, and ethical issues of importance to group workers. The overall theme is ethical decision making and forming a personal ethical stance.

Codes of Ethics ⁓

Many professional organizations have established codes of ethics or standards of best practice for their memberships. In the mental health field these organizations include the American Counseling Association, the Association for Specialists in

Group Work, the American Psychological Association (APA), the American Group Psychotherapy Association (AGPA), the American Mental Health Counselors Association (AMHCA), the National Board for Certified Counselors (NBCC), the American School Counselors Association (ASCA), the National Association of Social Workers (NASW), and the American Association for Marriage and Family Therapy (AAMFT). Each association's guidelines are designed to cover the major areas of concern for its constituency and their realm of practice.

As Kibler and Van Hoose (1981) indicated, a counselor can approach "ethical decision making with a whole set of rules and regulations but with few principles to guide his or her behavior" (p. 225). Knowing the ethical standards that affect practice is not enough. Professionals need to understand the moral principles upon which the ethical standards are based. Unfortunately, not all counselor education programs go beyond the introduction of ethical codes and guidelines to examine the moral principles that apply in various situations (Corey, Corey, & Callanan, 1992; Strom & Tennyson, 1989).

Though important, ethical guidelines are limited in their use in professional decision making (Gumaer & Scott, 1985; Mabe & Rollin, 1986; Strom & Tennyson, 1989; Tarvydas, 1987; Van Hoose, 1980; Welfel & Lipsitz, 1984). Ethical guidelines do not provide specific directives for all potential situations; they are not meant to do so. They are meant to provide parameters to "guide" behavior, rather than to give right or wrong answers to difficult questions.

Professionals need to be able to utilize the guidelines as a starting place to explore ethical dilemmas; they also need a set of moral principles and an ethical decision-making model to use when the guidelines are in conflict or do not address the issue at hand. As Mabe and Rollin (1986) pointed out, "There is a limited range of topics covered in the code, and because a code approach is usually reactive to issues already developed elsewhere, the requirement of consensus prevents the code from addressing new issues and problems at the 'cutting edge'" (p. 295). Here, we approach ethics first by examining the guidelines, then by exploring moral principles, and, last, by presenting an ethical decision-making model.

Purposes of Ethical Guidelines

Codes of ethics serve several purposes (Van Hoose, 1980; Van Hoose & Kottler, 1985).

1. They present standards to aid in ethical decision making.
2. They provide some measure of self-regulation and give some assurance that individual counselor's behaviors will not be detrimental to the profession.
3. They clarify the various areas of counselor responsibilities to clients, to society, and to the profession.
4. They offer some protection to clients that professionals will supposedly function in accordance with social mores and expectations.
5. They help counselors safeguard their freedom and integrity by setting acceptable standards of care.

As Gumaer and Scott (1985) stated, "Knowledge of the profession's ethical codes is the key to informed behavior" (p. 199).

As mentioned, the sets of ethical codes in the mental health field are many and varied. Although I have chosen to focus on the American Counseling Association's *Code of Ethics and Standards of Practice* (ACA, 1995) and the Association for Specialists in Group Work's *Standards of Best Practice* (1989, 1996), the other codes also affect professionals in the field and group leaders should be familiar with them. All group leaders should spend time thinking about the issues and the morals inherent in them. As Kibler and Van Hoose (1981) pointed out, the key to appropriate ethical conduct is internalizing morality. "Novices and established professionals alike," they wrote, "need to weigh their moral decisions, not in light of legal mandates, but in relation to their personally responsible codes of conduct" (p. 226).

Ethical Codes for Group Workers

Here I will spotlight and discuss the ACA codes that are directed specifically at group work and all 16 ASGW standards to aid readers in understanding their purposes and implications. Understanding, I hope, will lead to internalization. The standards of the Association for Specialists in Group Work (1989, 1996) are reprinted in their entirety in Appendix A. The American Counseling Association's (1995) *Code of Ethics and Standards of Practice* are reprinted in their entirety in Appendices C and D.

Code of Ethics and Standards of Practice (ACA, 1995)

Although group workers are required to adhere to the entire ACA *Code of Ethics and Standards of Practice*, here I will address only the codes that feature ethical issues specific to group work.

A.4. Clients Served by Others   Although this issue is not solely related to group counseling, it is a very important guideline of which group counselors should be aware. Quite often a group member is also in individual counseling with another professional. In such instances, group leaders, with the permission of the client, should contact the other professional to assure they are not confusing the client or working at cross-purposes.

A.9.a. Group Work—Screening   The group counselor needs to confirm that the group members' goals for counseling/therapy groups are compatible with the proposed group experience. This is important in protecting the well-being of all the group members. It is important to note that this code specifically refers to "group counseling/therapy participants." This wording reflects the differences in the types of groups and indicates that it is not usually appropriate to screen members for task/work groups or guidance groups. Screening is addressed further in the ASGW *Standards of Best Practice*.

A.9.b. Group Work—Protecting Clients   It is the group counselor's responsibility to ensure that members are not harmed in the group setting either physically or psychologically. Since the members are not trained professionals, the leader needs to teach them how to be group members and model appropriate behaviors. The leader needs to be ready to intercede if a member's well-being is threatened.

B.2.a. Confidentiality—Group Work   In individual counseling, the counselor can assure confidentiality to the client and clearly define any limitations. It is an agreement that involves only the counselor and the client. In group counseling the issue of confidentiality becomes much more complicated. Counselors cannot assure confidentiality on the part of the many members of the group; they can do so only for themselves. Counselors need to clearly communicate to group members that confidentiality cannot be guaranteed. More discussion of this issue and an example of a member nonmaliciously breaking confidentiality follow in the discussion of ASGW Standard 3: Confidentiality.

Ethical Guidelines for Group Counselors/Standards of Best Practice (ASGW, 1989, 1996)

Standard 1: Orientation and Providing Information   Following this standard ensures informed consent from group members, as is specified in ACA code A.3.a. Disclosure to Clients. *Informed consent* means defining and discussing the participation expectations for group members, the limits of confidentiality, the process of group counseling, the specifics of the particular group, and any ramifications of nonparticipation.

Group leaders might consider developing an "orientation-information checklist" that includes the pertinent information from items *a* through *k* of the ASGW standard and ACA code A.3.a. To make a record of having covered these issues with each participant, the leader might first explain each item, then have prospective members sign a statement at the bottom of the checklist acknowledging that the group leader has explained each item and that the individual acknowledges an understanding of the content presented. Gregory and McConnell (1986) stressed the importance of using informed consent with children over age 7. They recommend that group leaders briefly question children under 7 after explaining informed consent to be sure the children understand this concept.

Standard 2: Screening of Members   This standard directly relates to ACA code A.9.a. Screening. It offers four possible ways to do screening. The preferred screening format is the private, individual session, because this allows both the group leader and the group member the greatest opportunity for interaction and information exchange. The better the understanding of the group and its purpose, and the more information the counselor has about the member's purpose and goals, the better is the potential for matching the group to the person, and vice versa.

Effective pre-group screening can eliminate many potential difficulties that might arise if a group member's goals do not correlate with the group's stated purpose—difficulties not only for the leader but also for the group members. Screening is necessary to establish an effective group. The ideal of one-on-one screening interviews may not always be feasible, but the group leader has to find creative methods of conducting screening in some manageable form. This is vital to protecting the rights of all group members.

Standard 3: Confidentiality   Confidentiality in any counseling setting is essential, but in a group setting it takes on a few interesting twists. There is no way of guaranteeing that group members will keep confidentiality. Rosenbaum (1982) discussed how Jacob Moreno, the developer of psychodrama, used to have group members take an oath of confidentiality but contended that this practice was "probably unnecessary since clinical experience indicates that patients learn to trust one another, care for one another, and come to realize that if any patient exposes another outside of the group the same act may in turn be visited upon him" (p. 238). What Rosenbaum seemed to overlook is the nonmalicious, accidental breaking of confidentiality. A group member rarely will go out and intentionally breach confidentiality, but the potential for accidentally breaking confidentiality is fairly high.

Mary is so excited about her own realization and growth that she can hardly wait to go home and tell her husband about it. In talking to her husband, Mary is careful not to mention any names, but she does share the details of Sue's story in explaining how she has acquired this new insight.

Several weeks later, Mary's husband, John, is telling his best friend how things are so much better sexually between him and Mary. He mentions that it all stems from a story someone told Mary, and John proceeds to tell his friend the story. As he is telling the story in the locker room at the fitness club, a stranger walks in. John continues to tell his friend the story about this other couple without realizing that the stranger is Sue's husband, Mark. Upon arriving home that evening, Mark is quite upset, explaining to his wife that he did not appreciate hearing strangers discuss the intimate details of their sex life.

Obviously, Mary was not maliciously breaking confidentiality. Nonetheless, confidentiality was broken, resulting in some potential difficulties for Sue.

Examples such as this should be shared with group members to help them truly understand their part in maintaining confidentiality and to reduce the risk of something similar happening in their group. Participants need to be advised that they can share only their own growth and insights and are obligated to do so in a way that does not mention what anybody else in the group has said or done. Thus, Mary might have said to her husband, "I realized several things about myself tonight that I think may make a difference in our sexual relationship." She could then have told him about her insights without mentioning the group or other members' issues.

All of Section B of the ACA Code deals with confidentiality. Codes B.1.g. Explanation of Limitations and B.2.a. Group Work reflect some of the specific concerns for group work demonstrated by this example.

Standard 4: Voluntary/Involuntary Participation   Participation in a group can be challenging. The degree of control the members have in choosing to participate in the group can directly influence early interactions between the group leader and members. This is especially important with groups in which membership is involuntary. In the orientation and information phase of a group, informed consent is one method to assist members, whether they are voluntary or involuntary participants, to understand group goals. It further ensures that members are aware of the voluntary or involuntary construct of the group. It allows for involuntary members to discuss their feelings about being required to participate and to decide at what level they are willing to actively take part in the group. ACA codes A.3.a. Disclosure to Clients, A.3.b. Freedom of Choice, and B.1.g. Explanation of Limitations are all relevant here.

Standard 5: Leaving a Group   Members have the right to exit a group at any time, but a member's leaving has ramifications for the individual if he or she leaves prematurely and for the group as a whole, whether the member's leaving is premature or not. The group leader must advise a departing member of the potential risks involved in early departure and offer appropriate referrals for the individual. The group leader also has a responsibility to assist the remaining group members in processing the departure of the group member.

Whenever an individual leaves a group, for whatever reason, the dynamics of the group change. Ideally, the departing member will discuss his or her decision to leave the group, and this expectation should be shared with members in pre-group screening interviews. If a member indicates to the group that he or she wishes to leave, the leader should make sure that other members do not pressure the individual to stay but do have an opportunity to say good-bye and wind up any unfinished business. If a member leaves without discussing his or her decision in the group, the leader should allow the group members time to process their feelings and thoughts about how the individual's departure affects them and the group. These issues are related to ACA codes A.11.c. Appropriate Termination and A.9.b. Protecting Clients.

Standard 6: Coercion and Pressure   Group members will probably not truly understand how coercion and pressure directly or indirectly affect them unless the group leader openly admits that these forces do operate in groups. Both the group members and the leader have the potential for exerting pressure on members. Kottler (1982) explained that the group leader has a natural tendency to exert pressure and persuasion on people to become and remain group members. The real ethical issue, he asserted, is to control the degree to which these behaviors surface.

During the course of the group experience, members should be reminded that they have the right to participate or refuse to participate in any specific group activity. The group leader should support their decisions regarding participation. Such support fosters the feeling of safety and control within the group. In turn, it increases the possibility of growth and exploration of difficult issues and enhances the transference of the knowledge gained to the extended environment (society). ACA codes A.3.a. Disclosure to Clients and A.9.b. Protecting Clients are operating here.

Standard 7: Imposing Counselor Values   The ACA code represented by this standard is A.5.b. Personal Values. Group leaders have values, and no group leader can act as if he or she does not. Rosenbaum (1982) noted, "The psychotherapist, more than any other student of behavior, presents values to his patients by his very commitment to the affirmation of life" (p. 244). So leaders have to be sure they do not impose their values on the group members, even subtly. Their response in a given situation or the focus they take in questioning a member can be a subtle way of imposing values. For example, if a group member is pregnant and mentions abortion as a possible option, a leader might choose one of the following three basic response categories: (a) to present abortion as a plausible option, and possibly the primary option; (b) to mention all options other than abortion (subtle) or clearly indicate that abortion is not a viable option; and (c) to ask the group member what options she sees open to herself and wants to explore, leaving the decision up to the person.

How aware leaders are of their own values will certainly make a difference in how they respond in group sessions. When they are aware of their values, they can reduce the possibility of unintentionally imposing their values on others, no matter how subtly. Corey, Corey, and Callanan's (1990) article on group leaders' values gives examples of many subtle ways in which leaders might impose their values on group members and demonstrates "how easy it is to steer clients toward a particular path" (p. 73).

Standard 8: Equitable Treatment   Corey et al. (1990) stated that group leaders must "be able to identify some types of clients with whom they cannot work well, for whatever reason" (p. 69). This identification process is important because group leaders will encounter a variety of lifestyle, cultural, religious, racial, age, and gender issues. By maintaining a level of awareness of their biases toward individual group members, leaders can attempt to limit any negative effects from these biases.

Using a variety of skills and techniques designed to build group trust and cohesiveness, the group leader can involve all group members, regardless of their personal, social, or emotional experience. By encouraging active participation and guarding against inappropriate involvement, the group leader can construct an atmosphere of balance for participants. The ACA codes addressed here are A.2.a. Nondiscrimination and A.2.b. Respecting Differences.

Standard 9: Dual Relationships   As stated by Kitchener and Harding (1990), "In a dual role relationship, one person simultaneously or sequentially plays two or more roles with another person" (p. 147). Not all dual role relationships are problematic, but group leaders should understand what causes dual relationships to be difficult and, therefore, how to avoid potentially harmful or high-risk relationships.

Kitchener identified three factors to differentiate potentially high-risk dual relationships from those with little or no risk: (a) incompatibility of expectations between roles, (b) divergence of obligations associated with the roles, and (c) the professional's power and prestige (Kitchener, 1988; Kitchener & Harding, 1990, p. 147). A good example of the difference between high-risk and low-risk relationships is apparent in bartering for goods and for services. Typically, "goods" and "services" are discussed as though they are one in the same, but the risk levels are significantly different. Exchanging counseling for *services* such as painting or household repairs represents a high risk. If the repairs are not done properly or prove not to hold up, the group leader has to deal with the member not only with regard to his or her psychological well-being but also with regard to the leader's dissatisfaction with the work performed. In bartering *goods* for services with group members, a group leader might accept a blanket for "x" number of counseling sessions, as long as both parties agree that this trade constitutes a reasonable exchange. Many low-income people have a strong sense of pride and will not allow themselves to receive services for which they cannot pay (even if they had been asked to pay only a nominal amount). Bartering for goods allows these individuals to receive the desired counseling services and keep their pride intact, without all the potential complications involved in exchanging services. In guideline 9(d), the term goods was purposely omitted. ACA code A.10.c. discourages bartering due to the "potential for conflicts, exploitation, and distortion of the professional relationship" but does allow it when certain arrangements are made and if it is an accepted practice in the community, as is the case in many rural communities. ACA code A.6.a. Dual Relationships—Avoid When Possible is also represented by this standard.

Standard 10: Use of Techniques   No set of techniques exists from which a group leader can select the most appropriate technique for each situation encountered. Therefore, group leaders must continually expand their knowledge and understanding of various techniques and be open to altering them to fit the unique needs of individuals in a group. Leaders can create their own techniques when necessary. In doing this, leaders must have a sound rationale and a reasonable idea of what to expect from the techniques utilized. This concept is tied to having a sound theoretical orientation to guide one's practice. Corey, Corey, Callanan, and Russell (1982) "urge group leaders to strike a balance between creativity and irresponsible lack of caution" (p. 140).

In pointing out that even the factors typically considered curative or therapeutic in groups can possibly have counter-therapeutic effects on participants, Lakin (1986) warned:

> Ethical practice is not merely adherence to a professional code, but rather is based on understanding...how the modality itself—the group mode in this case—and the techniques that one uses are likely to affect a range of participants. (p. 456)

It is crucial that group leaders know the boundaries of their competence, monitor their effectiveness, receive appropriate training for speciality areas, and keep current through continuing education. The ACA codes that address these issues are C.2.a., C.2.d., C.2.b., and C.2.f., respectively.

Standard 11: Goal Development   Coaches at every level of athletic participation know that the design, implementation, and ongoing evaluation of a game plan are all important determinants of the team's overall success. The same is true for groups. The leader and the members must, together, periodically review the group's and individuals' goals. Goal setting helps each member in identifying and dealing with personal issues. As the group progresses, goals need to be reevaluated and redefined. This is reflective of ACA code A.1.c. Counseling Plans.

Standard 12: Consultation   The group leader has two roles in regard to consultation as addressed in this guideline: (a) consultant to group members, and (b) consultee with other professionals. It is important that during orientation and information sharing the counselor apprise the members regarding the circumstances under which he or she will have individual consultations with group members.

When group leaders have questions regarding their professional practice or ethical obligations, they may choose to consult with competent professionals. The related ACA codes are B.6.a. Consultation—Respect for Privacy, C.2.e. Ethical Issues Consultation, D.2.a. Consultation as an Option, and D.2.b. Consultant Competency.

Standard 13: Termination From the Group   Leaders must not foster dependency in group members. Kottler (1982) reminded us that there comes a point when participating in a group "no longer results in significant progress, except further dependency on the leader" (p. 185). As part of the group leader's role, he or she is to promote the autonomy of members and help them transfer what they have learned in the group into their everyday lives. ACA code A.11.c. addresses appropriate termination.

Standard 14: Evaluation and Follow-Up   During the termination phase of a group, there are a variety of questions the group leader needs to address. For example, should a member be referred for further counseling? When, where, and how will follow-up services be offered? Group leaders need to discuss these questions with the members prior to the last session. At the termination stage the leader helps members determine where they are in relation to their individual and group goals, where they want to be, and how they can continue to progress toward their goals. This is an aspect of the ongoing development of counseling plans presented in ACA code A.1.c.

Standard 15: Referrals   At any time during the group experience, the group leader may have to refer a group member for individual counseling or other related services. To make these referrals to the most appropriate and highly qualified professionals, I suggest that the group leader maintain a referral directory, listing each professional's areas of specialization, qualifications, fee structure, and treatment modalities. Having this type of information at hand enables the group leader to make conscientious referrals according to the unique needs of the group members. ACA code A.11.b. Termination and Referral—Inability to Assist Clients addresses the referral process.

Standard 16: Professional Development   This standard and ACA code C.2.f. Continuing Education both clearly recommend that group leaders participate in ongoing professional development activities. Because of rapid growth and changes in technologies and information delivery systems, professionals in all mental health areas must attempt to stay abreast of new discoveries so they can provide the best services possible. Emerging theories of personality development, growing understanding of the relationship between physiological and psychological factors, and studies of genetic influences on behavior are but a few of the concepts that will directly impact the counseling profession into the 21st century. Professional involvement in development activities at local, regional, and national levels is imperative to keep up to date and provide the best possible assistance to those served.

Cases and Applicable Ethical Codes and Standards ~

Each of the following three cases represents an actual ethical dilemma experienced by a group leader. For each of the cases, identify which of the ACA ethical codes address the primary issues. You might also assess which ASGW standards are pertinent to the case. Later, I will ask you to apply an ethical decision-making model to each case; but for now, simply review the codes and standards in Appendices C and D and identify which ones are primary in discussing each case.

Case 1: To support or not to support parents? You are leading a personal growth group for 10th- and 11th-graders, consisting of 12 members. One of the female members comes to the group with visible bruises. She indicates that she had been in a fight with another student. She had talked to her parents about it, and they had advised her how to handle it. She will ambush the student and then fight, so she can beat her adversary this time. The leader and the group members all seem to feel this was poor advice.

Case 2: The qualified co-leader? You are leading a group for sex offenders in a mental health center. All of the group members have been required by court order to participate in your treatment group. For some, the participation requirement is part of their parole; for others, it is part of their probation agreement—treatment in place of prison. All of the court orders require that they be "active participants" in the group process, and the group leader has to sign forms each month verifying that the parolee or probationer is in fact "actively participating in therapy."

The mental health center often hires part-time people to assist with the groups it offers. A part-time person has been hired as co-leader for your offenders' group. This co-leader has a master's degree in counseling with special training in group counseling, and his full-time job is as a probation officer. He is the probation officer for two of the current group members. Several of the members have approached you about their discomfort with this co-leader. They are afraid that information they share in the group will be used against them in the probation review process or in future court hearings. They also are concerned that if they do not continue to "actively participate," this will be considered a violation of their probation or parole.

Case 3: What to do about a confidentiality breach? You are a school counselor co-leading, with a teacher, an interpersonal problem-solving group. The group consists of 12 eighth-graders. This teacher is one of only a few in the school who will allow you to run a group with her class. During the initial stages, each group member, including the teacher, contracted to maintain confidentiality. Around the eighth session, several group members approach you about a suspected breach of confidentiality. They say the teacher/co-leader has been using inside information she heard in the group to entrap and discipline students and has been leaking information to the school principal. You know that this teacher is experiencing stress on the job as well as at home. The teacher has a history of retaliating against students.

Applicable ACA Codes and ASGW Standards

The ACA ethical codes and ASGW standards that address the primary issues in each case are:

Case 1: ACA codes B.1.c. Confidentiality/Exceptions; B.2.a. Confidentiality/ Group Work; A.2.b. Respecting Differences; A.5.b. Personal Values

ASGW standards 3(a); 6(a, b, c); 7(a, e); 10(d)

Case 2: ACA codes A.3.a. and A.3.b. Client Rights/Disclosure; A.6.a. and A.6.b. Dual Relationships; B.1.g. Confidentiality/Explanation of Limitations; A.9.a. Group Work/Screening

ASGW standards 3(g); 4(a, c, d); 9

Case 3: ACA codes A.1.a. Client Welfare; A.9.b. Group Work/Protecting Clients; A.6.a. and A.6.b. Dual Relationships; B.1.a. Confidentiality/Respect for Privacy; B.1.g. Confidentiality/Explanation of Limitations; B.2.a. Confidentiality/Group Work

ASGW standards 1(c); 3(b, c, d, f, g); 7(c); 8(b); 9(a); 12(d); 14(c)

Ethical Decision Making ~

As group leaders develop their own method of making ethical decisions, they should explore the applicable ethical guidelines, the moral principles inherent in those guidelines, and the existing ethical decision-making models.

Moral Principles

Kitchener (1984) identified five moral principles that she saw as critical to evaluating ethical concerns in psychology and counseling. Ethical codes do not address all situations; however, the moral principles inherent in these codes can offer direction in ethical dilemmas and provide a consistent framework for ethical decision making (Kitchener, 1984; Stadler, 1986). The five principles Kitchener (1984) identified are autonomy, justice, beneficence, nonmaleficence, and fidelity.

1. The principle of *autonomy* is basic to the concept of promoting independence. It means allowing individuals both freedom of choice and freedom of action. As Kitchener (1984) pointed out, autonomy has two limitations. The first limitation to the individual's freedom is based on the concept of not impinging on anyone else's

freedom. No one has the right to deprive someone else of autonomy. The second limitation is tied to whether the individual has the ability to make rational decisions. If an individual is not competent to make reasonable choices, such as small children and people with mental handicaps, that person should not be allowed to act on decisions that could harm themselves or others.

2. The principle of *justice*, when traced to its formal meaning, means "treating equals equally and unequals unequally but in proportion to their relevant differences" (Kitchener, 1984, p. 49). One starts by assuming that everyone is equal. If individuals are not going to be treated as equals, it is necessary to give a rationale for why these individuals warrant different treatment.

3. The principle of *beneficence* means to do good, to provide services beneficial to the other person. Providing beneficial service is what counseling is all about; it is the crux of the profession. As Stadler (1986) indicated, this principle requires counseling professionals to be proactive and to actively do good and prevent harm.

4. The principle of *nonmaleficence*, which can be most easily understood as "above all do no harm" (Kitchener, 1984, p. 47), includes not inflicting intentional harm and not engaging in actions that risk harming others.

5. The principle of *fidelity* addresses the issues of loyalty, faithfulness, and fulfilling obligations. Codes regarding confidentiality stem from this principle. Trust is the foundation on which effective counseling is built, because it is the basic ingredient in a helping relationship. Any actions that threaten this trust or leave obligations unfulfilled have serious implications for the helping relationship and are in conflict with the principle of fidelity.

As indicated by the wording "*above all* do no harm," the principle of nonmaleficence is considered by some to be the most important of the moral principles (Kitchener, 1984; Rosenbaum, 1982; Stadler, 1986). According to moral philosophers, though, each of these principles is considered to be an absolute truth. Each is of primary importance. Each is indicative of the ultimate path to follow in making a moral decision. However, at times these moral principles are in conflict with one another—which is the definition of an ethical dilemma. Obviously, each principle cannot be regarded as absolutely binding when two or more of them are in conflict in a given situation. Therefore, a true ethical dilemma exists, and the counselor must have a means of deciding which course to follow.

Decision-Making Model

Most authors in the field of ethics acknowledge the importance of having a model for making ethical decisions (Forester-Miller & Rubenstein, 1992; Gladding, 1995; Herlihy & Corey, 1996; Paradise & Siegelworks, 1982; Van Hoose & Kottler, 1985; Van Hoose & Paradise, 1979). In the mental health field, the American Counseling Association's Ethics Committee developed a *Practitioner's Guide to Ethical Decision Making* (Forester-Miller & Davis, 1996) to provide counselors with a framework for sound ethical decision making.

The ACA ethical decision-making model (Forester-Miller & Davis, 1996) is a practical, sequential, seven-step model that incorporates the work of Van Hoose and Paradise (1979), Kitchener (1984), Stadler (1986), Haas and Malouf (1989), Forester-Miller and Rubenstein (1992), and Sileo and Kopala (1993). The steps of the model are:

1. Identify the problem.
2. Apply the ACA Code of Ethics.
3. Determine the nature and dimensions of the dilemma.
4. Generate potential courses of action.
5. Consider the potential consequences of all options and determine a course of action.
6. Evaluate the selected course of action.
7. Implement the course of action.

The ACA ethical decision-making model follows:

1. *Identify the problem.* Gather as much information as you can that will illuminate the situation. In doing so, it is important to be as specific and objective as possible. Writing ideas on paper may help you gain clarity. Outline the facts, separating out innuendoes, assumptions, hypotheses, and suspicions. There are several questions you can ask yourself: Is it an ethical, legal, professional, or clinical problem? Is it a combination of more than one of these? If a legal question exists, seek legal advice.

Other questions that may be useful are: Is the issue related to me and what I am or am not doing? Is it related to a client and/or the client's significant others and what they are or are not doing? Is it related to the institution or agency and its policies and procedures? If the problem can be resolved by implementing one of the institution's or agency's policies, look to the agency's guidelines. Because the dilemmas you face in counseling are often complex, a useful guideline is to examine the problem from several perspectives. It is wise to avoid searching for a simplistic solution.

2. *Apply the ACA Code of Ethics.* After you have clarified the problem, refer to the ACA Code of Ethics (ACA, 1995) to see if the issue is addressed there. If an applicable standard or standards exist, following the course of action indicated should lead to a resolution of the problem. To be able to apply the ethical standards, it is essential that you have read them carefully and that you understand their implications.

If the problem is more complex and a resolution does not seem apparent, then the problem is probably a true ethical dilemma. In such cases, it is necessary to proceed with further steps in the ethical decision-making process.

3. *Determine the nature and dimensions of the dilemma.* There are several avenues you must follow to examine the problem in all of its various dimensions.

- Consider the moral principles of autonomy, nonmaleficence, benefi-cence, justice, and fidelity. Decide which principles apply to the specific situation, and determine which principle takes priority for you in this case. In theory, each principle is of equal value. Thus, it is up to you to determine the priorities when two or more of the principles are in conflict.
- Review the relevant professional literature to ensure that you are using the most current professional thinking in reaching a decision.
- Consult with experienced professional colleagues and/or supervisors. As they review with you the information you have gathered, they may see other issues that are relevant or provide a perspective you have not considered. They may also be able to identify aspects of the dilemma that you are not viewing objectively.
- Consult your state or national professional associations to see if they can provide help with the dilemma.

4. *Generate potential courses of action.* Brainstorm as many possible courses of action as possible. Be creative; consider all options. If possible, enlist the assistance of at least one colleague to help you generate options.

5. *Consider the potential consequences of all options and determine a course of action.* Evaluate each option in light of the information you have gathered and the priorities you have set and assess the potential consequences of each course of action for all the parties involved. Ponder the implications for the client, for others who will be affected, and for yourself as a counselor. Eliminate the options that clearly do not give the desired results or cause even more problematic consequences. Review the remaining options to determine which option or combination of options best fits the situation and best address-es the priorities you have identified.

6. *Evaluate the selected course of action.* Review the selected course of action to see if it presents any new ethical considerations. Stadler (1986) sug-gested applying three simple tests to the selected course of action to ensure that it is appropriate: the test of justice, the test of publicity, and the test of uni-versality. The test of justice requires that you judge the fairness of the intend-ed action by determining whether you would treat other clients the same way in the same situation. The test of publicity requires that you ask yourself whether you would want your behavior reported in the press. The test of uni-versality asks you to assess whether you could recommend the same course of action to another counselor in the same situation.

If the course of action you have selected seems to present new ethical issues, it is necessary to go back to the beginning and reevaluate each step of the process. Perhaps you have chosen the wrong option, or perhaps you have identified the problem incorrectly.

If, however, the course of action you have selected passes each of the tests suggested by Stadler and you are satisfied that it is an appropriate course of action, you are ready to move on to Step 7, implementation.

7. *Implement the course of action.* Taking the appropriate action in an ethical dilemma is often difficult. It involves identifying the concrete steps needed to implement the plan and strengthening your ego to allow you to carry out the plan. After implementing your course of action, it is good practice to follow up on the situation to assess whether your actions had the anticipated effect and consequences.

It is important to realize that different professionals may implement different courses of action in the same situation. There is rarely one right answer to a complex ethical dilemma. However, if you follow a systematic model, you can be assured that you will be able to give a professional explanation for the course of action you have chosen. Van Hoose and Paradise (1979) suggested that a counselor "is probably acting in an ethically responsible way concerning a client if (1) he or she has maintained personal and professional honesty, coupled with (2) the best interests of the client, (3) without malice or personal gain, and (4) can justify his or her actions as the best judgment of what should be done based upon the current state of the profession" (p. 58). Following the model outlined here will help to ensure that all four of these conditions have been met (Forester-Miller & Davis, 1996).

Cases in Relation to the Model ∼

Let's go back to the cases presented earlier. Reread the cases, then utilize the ethical decision-making model to answer the following questions about them. As you follow the steps of the model, be sure to answer all of the questions posed.

Case 1: How should the leader handle this situation? Would you call the parents or in some other way involve them?

Case 2: What would you do if you were the original leader of this group? What would you do if you were the new co-leader and found out that the members were concerned?

Case 3: How would you handle this situation? Typically, in cases of a breach in confidentiality, the breach is discussed in the group. Would you do so in this case? Why or why not?

Issues to Consider ∼

Several ethical issues specific to group counseling warrant further discussion. Among them are the importance of (a) clearly defining the purpose of the groups, (b) obtaining permission for minors to participate in groups, (c) understanding cultural diversity, and (d) cultivating a personal ethical stance.

Purpose of the Group

Group counselors in all settings (mental health centers, private practice, public schools, residential facilities) should clearly define the purpose of the groups they lead. In doing so, the counselor must clearly state the reason the group is meeting and the specific goals and objectives to be met. If the leader clearly defines the purpose of the group from the first planning stages, he or she will be able to select members whose needs and goals are compatible with the goals of the group. In addition, by defining the purpose of the group to prospective members in the orientation and information-giving phase, the group leader can establish for the group members the parameters in which difficult issues can be explored safely and ethically.

Keeping the group attuned to the purpose allows members to know what is expected of them. Not keeping the group attuned to the purpose can have ethical implications. For example, if members join an educational group and then after several meetings many of the group members and the leader start dealing with therapy issues, the members have not given informed consent. The consent forms they originally signed were for a very different purpose. Appropriately planning groups around a purpose and staying consistent to that purpose will help to preclude such ethical dilemmas and will help to ensure successful group experiences for the members.

Permission to Participate

When working with minors, group counselors need to be aware of the issues related to participation. In agency settings, the parents (or the state as custodian) typically bring the child in for services and the appropriate permission forms are signed. In the school setting, the issue is more complex. School counselors need to be aware of the policies of their school district related to securing parental permission for children to participate in individual or group counseling. Policies regarding parental permission vary drastically, sometimes differing from school to school within the same district. Some school administrators believe that counseling is part of the school curriculum and believe that because no special permission is needed for math, none should be needed for counseling. Others require counselors to obtain signed permission slips before they even set up an intake interview.

Three methods of securing permission for minors to participate in counseling are:

1. Send home a form that is specific to the activity offered. This form is to be signed by a parent or guardian and returned to the school before the student can participate.
2. Send home a form that is specific to the activity, requiring parents or guardians to notify the school "only if they do not want their child to participate."
3. Develop a policy booklet, newsletter, or information sheet, and give it to all parents or guardians at the beginning of the school year. This should contain information about the variety of counseling services offered to students and specify that it is the students' right to use the services unless the parent or guardian notifies the school in writing of any objections.

Before applying any specific method, the counselor should review local, regional, and state policies to be sure the method selected is in compliance with them.

Cultural Diversity

Group counselors need to understand how their cultural background and experiences influence their values and beliefs and therefore influence their thinking and behavior. They must be careful to not assume that their values are the norm and unwittingly impose them on their clients (Forester-Miller, 1997). Wittmer (1992) pointed out that counselors must be open to learning about others and to being aware of their own personal experiences when working with them.

In planning a group, the counselor must ensure that the basic assumptions underlying the group purpose and process fit the culture of the group being served (Corey & Corey, 1997). The counselor must also be sensitive to the ways in which the members' cultural background may influence their reactions to the group process (Johnson, Torres, Coleman, & Smith, 1995).

The ACA Code (ACA, 1995) addresses these issues directly in section A.2.b. Respecting Differences, which states: "Counselors will actively attempt to understand the diverse cultural backgrounds of the clients with whom they work. This includes, but is not limited to, learning how the counselor's own cultural/ethnic/racial identity impacts her/his values and beliefs about the counseling process" (p. 2).

In the past, people often associated the terms *multicultural awareness* and *cultural diversity* with issues related to color alone. Although this aspect of cultural diversity is important, there are other aspects to be considered as well. ACA code A.2.a. Respecting Diversity refers to nondiscrimination regarding "age, color, culture, disability, ethnic group, gender, race, religion, sexual orientation, marital status, or socioeconomic status" (ACA, 1995). Group counselors must be truly open to the worldviews and experiences of others, whether that entails being open to differences between the values of the urban versus the rural dweller (Forester-Miller, 1997) or understanding the lack of trust and low self-esteem of racial or ethnic minority group members who are marginalized and disempowered (Brinson & Lee, 1997). Group counselors need to work to learn ways to be culturally responsive and to respect diversity in all of its forms.

Cultivating a Personal Ethical Stance

Knowledge of the codes of ethics and standards of practice is not enough. Group counselors need to cultivate and work from their own personal ethical stance. Several authors have suggested supervision for practicing counselors as a means of developing ethical group practice (Gladding, 1995; Gumaer & Forrest, 1995). Kibler and Van Hoose (1981) wrote that internalizing morality is the key to appropriate ethical conduct. Herlihy and Corey (1996) recommended that counselors develop their own personal ethical stance based on aspirational ethics, which goes beyond the profession's codes of ethics.

All group counselors need to go further than the ethical codes and challenge themselves to explore their behaviors and examine in what subtle ways they may not be acting as ethically as possible. Kottler (1982) challenged group counselors to look at these nuances in a classic article titled "Unethical Behaviors We All Do and

Pretend We Do Not." He encouraged group counselors to examine their little white lies, such as "I neither like nor dislike you; you're a client"; "This [group] is a safe place"; and "No pressure will be put on you to participate unless you want to" (Kottler, 1982, 1994).

Galanes and Brilhart (1997) discussed ethics in groups from a more personal perspective. They asked group counselors to address communication in groups that are part of everyday life, such as local service committees, the school board, and business meetings. They indicated that the leaders of these groups should act as models for other members to follow and presented the following guidelines to help leaders maintain the highest standards of ethical behavior (Galanes & Brilhart, 1997):

1. Do not lie or intentionally send deceptive or harmful messages.
2. Place your concern for the group and others ahead of your own personal gain.
3. Be respectful of and sensitive to the other members.
4. Stand behind the other members when they carry out policies and actions approved by the leader and the group.
5. Treat members with equal respect, regardless of sex, ethnicity, or social background.
6. Establish clear policies that all group members are expected to follow.
7. Follow the group rules, just as you expect the others to do. (190–191)

Group counselors must look beyond the ethical codes and internalize the moral principles inherent in them, applying those principles to best serve their clients and their communities. They must develop a personal ethical stance based not on simply obeying rules but on the idea of being the best they can be as a counselor and as a person.

Summary ∼

If "ethics lies at the heart of the counseling process" (Van Hoose, 1980, p. 2), every group leader has a responsibility to be ethically fit so the "heart" beats strong. To be ethically fit, the group leader must:

- have a working knowledge of the ACA *Code of Ethics and Standards of Practice* (ACA, 1995) and the ASGW *Ethical Guidelines for Group Counselors/Standards of Best Practice* (ASGW, 1989,1996).
- be able to apply these guidelines to the variety of situations that may arise in group counseling.
- understand the moral principles inherent in ethical behavior.
- be able to implement an ethical decision-making model.
- be aware of the issues specific to his or her work setting and do what is necessary to deliver group counseling with maximum results and minimum disruptions.
- keep abreast of research, new techniques, and theories, and upgrade counseling skills continually.

- be involved with professional organizations in which all of the issues mentioned in this chapter are routinely addressed.
- internalize the moral principles and form a personal ethical stance.

With these guidelines as an ethical foundation, group counseling can be an exciting and rewarding experience for group leaders and participants alike.

References ∿

American Counseling Association. (1995). *Code of ethics and standards of practice*. Alexandria, VA: Author.

Association for Specialists in Group Work. (1989, 1996). *Ethical guidelines for group counselors*. Alexandria, VA: Author. (1996 referred to as the *Standards of Best Practice*).

Brinson, J. A., & Lee, C. C. (1997). Culturally responsive group leadership: An integrative model for experienced practitioners. In H. Forester-Miller & J. Kottler (Eds.), *Issues and challenges for group practitioners* (pp. 43–56). Denver, CO: Love Publishing.

Corey, G., Corey, M. S., & Callanan, P. (1990). Role of group leader's values in group counseling. *Journal for Specialists in Group Work, 15,* 68–74.

Corey, G., Corey, M. S., & Callanan, P. (1992). *Issues and ethics in the helping professions* (4th ed.). Pacific Grove, CA: Brooks/Cole.

Corey, G., Corey, M. S., Callanan, P., & Russell, J. M. (1982). Ethical considerations in using group techniques. *Journal for Specialists in Group Work, 7,* 140–148.

Corey, M. S., & Corey, G. (1997). *Groups: Process and practice* (5th ed.). Pacific Grove, CA: Brooks/Cole.

Forester-Miller, H. (1997). Rural communities—Can dual relationships be avoided? In B. Herlihy & G. Corey (Eds.), *Boundary issues in counseling: Multiple roles and responsibilities* (pp. 99–100). Alexandria, VA: American Counseling Association.

Forester-Miller, H., & Davis, T. E. (1996). *A practitioner's guide to ethical decision making*. Alexandria, VA: American Counseling Association.

Forester-Miller, H., & Rubenstein, R. L. (1992). Group counseling: Ethics and professional issues. In D. Capuzzi & D. R. Gross (Eds.), *Introduction to group counseling* (pp. 308–323). Denver, CO: Love Publishing.

Galanes, G. J., & Brilhart, J. K. (1997). *Communicating in groups: Applications and skills* (3rd ed.). Madison, WI: Brown & Benchmark.

Gladding, S. T. (1995). *Group work: A counseling speciality* (2nd ed.). Englewood Cliffs, NJ: Prentice-Hall.

Gregory, J. C., & McConnell, S. C. (1986). Ethical issues with psychotherapy in group contexts. *Psychology in Private Practice, 4*(1), 51–62.

Gumaer, J., & Forrest, A. (1995). Avoiding conflict in group therapy: Ethical and legal issues in group training and practice. *Directions in Mental Health Counseling, 5*(5), 1–16.

Gumaer, J., & Scott, L. (1985). Training group leaders in ethical decision making. *Journal for Specialists in Group Work, 10,* 198–204.

Haas, L. J., & Malouf, J. L. (1989). *Keeping up the good work: A practitioner's guide to mental health ethics*. Sarasota, FL: Professional Resource Exchange.

Herlihy, B., & Corey, G. (1996). *ACA ethical standards casebook* (5th ed.). Alexandria, VA: American Counseling Association.

Johnson, I. H., Torres, J. S., Coleman, V. D., & Smith, M. C. (1995). Issues and strategies in leading culturally diverse counseling groups. *Journal for Specialists in Group Work, 20,* 143–150.

Kibler, R. D., & Van Hoose, W. H. (1981). Ethics in counseling: Bridging the gap from theory to practice. *Counseling and Values, 25,* 219–226.

Kitchener, K. S. (1984). Intuition, critical evaluation and ethical principles: The foundation for ethical decisions in counseling psychology. *Counseling Psychologist, 12*(3), 43–55.

Kitchener, K. S. (1988). Dual role relationships: What makes them so problematic? *Journal of Counseling & Development, 67,* 217–221.

Kitchener, K. S., & Harding, S. S. (1990). Dual role relationships. In B. Herlihy & L. B. Golden (Eds.), *Ethical standards casebook* (pp. 146–154). Alexandria, VA: American Association for Counseling and Development.

Kottler, J. A. (1982). Unethical behaviors we all do and pretend we do not. *Journal for Specialists in Group Work, 7,* 182–186.

Kottler, J. A. (1994). *Advanced group leadership.* Pacific Grove, CA: Brooks/Cole.

Lakin, M. (1986). Ethical challenges of group and dyadic psychotherapies: A comparative approach. *Professional Psychology: Research & Practice, 17,* 454–461.

Mabe, A., & Rollin, S. A. (1986). The role of a code of ethics in counseling. *Journal of Counseling & Development, 64,* 294–297.

Paradise, L. V., & Siegelworks, B. J. (1982). Ethical training for group leaders. *Journal for Specialists in Group Work, 7,* 162–166.

Robinson, S. E., & Gross, D. R. (1989). Applied ethics and the mental health counselor. *Journal of Mental Health Counseling, 11,* 289–299.

Rosenbaum, M. (1982). Ethical problems of group psychotherapy. In M. Rosenbaum (Ed.), *Ethics and values in psychotherapy: A guidebook* (pp. 237–257). New York: Free Press.

Sileo, F., & Kopala, M. (1993). An A-B-C-D-E worksheet for promoting beneficence when considering ethical issues. *Counseling and Values, 37,* 89–95.

Stadler, H. A. (1986). Making hard choices: Clarifying controversial ethical issues. *Counseling & Human Development, 19,* 110.

Strom, S. M., & Tennyson, W. W. (1989). Developing moral responsibleness through professional education. *Counseling and Values, 34,* 33–44.

Tarvydas, V. M. (1987). Decision-making models in ethics: Models for increased clarity and wisdom. *Journal of Applied Rehabilitation Counseling, 18*(4), 50–52.

Van Hoose, W. H. (1980). Ethics and counseling. *Counseling & Human Development, 13,* 112.

Van Hoose, W. H., & Kottler, J. A. (1985). *Ethical and legal issues in counseling and psychotherapy* (2nd ed.). San Francisco: Jossey-Bass.

Van Hoose, W. H., & Paradise, L. V. (1979). *Ethics in counseling and psychotherapy: Perspectives in issues and decision-making.* Cranston, RI: Carroll Press.

Welfel, E. R., & Lipsitz, N. E. (1984). The ethical behavior of professional psychologists: A critical analysis of the research. *Counseling Psychologist, 12*(3), 31–42.

Wittmer, J. (1992). *Valuing diversity and similarity: Bridging the gap through interpersonal skills.* Minneapolis, MN: Educational Media Corporation.

8

Multicultural Group Counseling: Cross-Cultural Considerations

Miguel Arciniega and Betty J. Newlon

The United States contains more ethnically diverse and regional subcultures than any nation in history. The many physically identifiable minority groups, and others not so apparent, make the United States a complex, heterogeneous society. However, this complexity has not heightened Americans' ability to tolerate, much less understand, cultural differences. Society continues to see the nation as a melting pot, which has devalued cultural diversity. The move to homogenize society and encourage common norms has blinded us to ways that capitalize on and encourage the development of the culturally diverse groups (Pedersen, 1988).

Each minority group has a unique cultural heritage making it distinct from other groups. Cultural distinction, however, has often been interpreted erroneously as evidence of cultural conformity, which has tended to result in a monolithic view of minority group attitudes and behaviors. Clearly, uniformity of attitudes and behaviors is no more true for minority individuals than it is for members of the dominant culture. Not only do intragroup differences exist, but attitudes and behaviors within individuals can fluctuate greatly as their identification with one culture or another changes.

The most readily identifiable minority groups in the United States are Asian Americans, African Americans, Hispanics, and American Indians. These groups have all witnessed exclusionist legislation and discriminatory practices. Racial/ethnic groups that have come from other countries or were here before colonization of the United States have been thrust, voluntarily or by force, into a dominant majority culture that routinely has subordinated nonwhite people. Only recently has multicultural counseling been acknowledged and endorsed by the American Association for Multicultural Counseling and Development. The context of counseling preparation and application now refers to the groups just cited in addition to the Caucasian/Euro-American group (Arredondo et al., 1996).

Until the mid-1960s the counseling profession showed little interest or concern for the status of racial, ethnic, and other minority groups. Counseling was directed toward the needs of average people. Minority clients, by virtue of their skin color, physical characteristics, and socioeconomic status, were seen as disadvantaged in a world designed for white, middle-class people.

In both overt and covert ways, equal access to counseling and psychological care has been denied. Until recently, the training of counselors and psychologists has not weighed the special needs of unique cultural and ethnic groups. Until the early 1990s, few training programs addressed multicultural issues in their courses and curricula (D'Andrea & Daniels, 1991). Schools and mental health agencies have not been sufficiently prepared to be culturally responsive to the large and increasing ethnic populations (Padilla, 1980). Indeed, even today, counseling theories do not adequately address nonwhite, non-Euro-American groups. Hence, many of the diverse cultural groups are being underserved because of lack of training, understanding, and awareness.

Considering the demographic realities and the rapid growth of minority groups in the United States, counselors cannot operate without cultural information and awareness. They have to understand the culture of those they are serving, including their history, beliefs, values, and worldviews. Not only do counselors need to develop an awareness of the cultural factors and their effect on the counselee, they must also develop an awareness of the effects of the counselee's interaction with the dominant culture and, more important, with their own views and biases. Rather than demanding that a person adapt to the counselor's culture, the counselor has to learn to adjust to and work within the culture of those he or she serves. This adjustment means that group leaders who come from the dominant culture must recognize that their own values have been shaped by a particular cultural environment and that this environment is significantly different from the cultural environment of multicultural group members. The same is true for counselors of specific ethnicity.

Cultural considerations have to be integrated into a systematic process as a basis for effective group leadership with members from minority cultures. The process of cultural integration involves (Arciniega & Newlon, 1995):

- confronting and challenging personal stereotypes held about cultural groups.
- acquiring knowledge and appreciation of the group's culture and, more important, the heterogeneous response of the group.
- understanding the effects of institutional racism and stereotypes on minority people.
- understanding the traditional, institutional interaction of the dominant society with minorities, and vice versa.

- acquiring firsthand experience with minority groups.
- challenging normative traditional counselor approaches and understanding their cultural implications for minority groups.
- utilizing a culturally pluralistic model in its counseling approach.

Unless group leaders follow a process incorporating these factors, they will not be effective with minority groups. This cultural integrative process is not easy, as it requires, beyond a cultural knowledge base, a shift in thinking and a cultural paradigm shift toward broader thinking that incorporates other worldviews. The influences of institutional mind-sets conditioned over a lifetime by mainstream institutions have made a major impact on counselors' thinking, at conscious and unconscious levels alike. This mind-set has shaped the frame of reference—the historically evolved mainstream paradigms, the cognitive maps of how counselors perceive other groups. These paradigms are the source of attitudes, values, beliefs, and behaviors that are difficult to modify and change.

If counseling professionals are to act with integrity and commitment to their changing profession, they must begin to take specific steps to shift the existing mainstream cultural paradigm. This will take careful study and examination of a body of knowledge at both cognitive and experiential levels. Only recently have authors begun to address a theoretical shift that involves issues, approaches, and strategies (Ivey, Ivey, & Simek-Morgan, 1993). To aid counselors in developing effective multicultural groups, we provide in this chapter an overview of a cultural knowledge base and cultural considerations by which counselors can begin the shift to integrate cognitive understanding with experiential application. In light of the potential for cultural diversity in group counseling, the format presented here represents a vehicle for group leaders to become culturally competent and foster a greater understanding of cultural differences.

Definitions Used in this Chapter ~

Acculturation: the degree to which minority individuals incorporate, add, or synthesize the dominant culture's values, customs, language, beliefs, and ideology with their own.

Cultural paradigm shift: the ability to integrate ethnic and racial paradigms with one's own view.

Culture: the values, beliefs, and practices shared by groups identified by such variables as ethnicity, traditions, and foods.

Ethnic group: a body of people who think of themselves as alike by virtue of their common ancestry and who are regarded so by others.

Ethnicity: a group classification in which members share a unique social and cultural heritage that includes similarities of religion, history, and common ancestry.

Minority: a racial/ethnic group receiving differential and unequal treatment because of collective discrimination.

Multicultural group counseling: group counseling situations in which counselors and clients are distinguished by their cultural, ethnic, or racial differences (D'Andrea & Daniels, 1996).

Race: a pseudobiological system of classifying people by a shared genetic history or physical characteristics such as skin color (Pedersen, 1988).

Although there has been an increase in the multicultural counseling knowledge base, it has been directed toward a more general and individual approach and not toward groups. Until recently, the area of multicultural group counseling has received little attention in the development of strategic approaches and specific empirical research (Merta, 1995). The studies and articles that have been published, although lacking in empirical data, do point to the potential benefits that multicultural group counseling can have. Much of the information presented here has been gleaned from the general literature on multicultural counseling and a few articles on multicultural group counseling. Several studies conducted in the late 1980s and the 1990s provided evidence that groups made up of individuals from multicultural backgrounds could be used to increase client's tolerance, respect for cultural diversity, and self-concept and to address cultural/racial issues (Avila & Avila, 1988; Greeley, Garcia, Kessler, & Gilchrest, 1992; Merta, 1995).

Developing Cultural Awareness ∼

Developing cultural awareness is a process that addresses stages, characteristics, assumptions, and biases. The group leader who is interested in developing cultural awareness proceeds from (a) more awareness of a person's culturally learned opinions, attitudes, and assumptions to (b) more knowledge and relevant facts and information about the culture in question, and finally to (c) better skills for making integrative changes and taking appropriate measures (Lopez et al., 1989).

Group leaders begin by assessing their own cultural values, beliefs, and personal strengths and weaknesses and then become knowledgeable about other cultural worldviews and values, which leads to the beginning of the development of an awareness of a broader worldview. Having cultural awareness means having the ability to accurately judge a cultural situation from one's own as well as the other's cultural viewpoint and to be able to describe a situation in a culture so that a member of that culture will verify one's perception. Cultural awareness has the following characteristics (Pedersen, 1988):

1. Ability to recognize different communication styles.
2. Sensitivity to cultural nonverbal cues.
3. Awareness and recognition of cultural and linguistic differences.
4. Sensitivity to the myths and stereotypes of different cultures.
5. Concern for the welfare of people from another culture.
6. Ability to articulate elements of one's own culture.
7. Appreciation of the importance of cultural diversity.
8. Awareness and recognition of the relationships between cultural groups.
9. Ability to determine functional and dysfunctional factors in other cultures.

For the group leader to be able to accurately reflect or paraphrase a situation in a multicultural group, his or her responses must have a basis in knowledge and awareness. In addition, the group leader needs specific knowledge about the diverse historical experiences, adjustment styles, feelings about the role of education, socioeconomic backgrounds, preferred values, typical attitudes, honored behaviors, inherited customs, slang, learning styles, and ways of thinking of the culturally diverse people in the group (Pedersen, 1988).

Basic assumptions determine how people see the world, and each person sees the world more or less differently. Knowledge of one's basic assumptions, values, and beliefs is the first step in clarifying one's perceptual paradigm. The next step is integration and expansion of one's knowledge base to include other cultural world-views, which results in a cultural paradigm shift. People tend to see evidence that supports their assumptions more clearly than evidence that challenges those assumptions. However, people often misread, among other things, nonverbal communications, such as gesture, posture, tone of voice, and timing, which are often perceived differently by groups with different perceptual paradigms (Pedersen, 1988).

It is important to recognize that Western cultural biases in our conventional thinking have little to do with geography and a great deal to do with social, economic, and political perceptions. The consequences of these unexamined assumptions perpetuate institutionalized racism, ageism, and sexism.

Culturally Biased Assumptions

Some of the unexamined, institutionalized assumptions that group leaders should critically evaluate are (Pedersen, 1988):

1. Normal behavior is seen from one measure.
2. The individual is the basic component of society.
3. Problems are defined by mainstream society.
4. Everyone will understand the dominant culture's abstractions.
5. Independence is desirable and interdependence is undesirable.
6. All individuals are helped more by formal counseling than by natural support systems.
7. All people use linear thinking to understand the world around them.
8. Group leaders need to change the individual to fit the system and not change the system to fit the individual.
9. History is not relevant for a proper understanding of contemporary events.
10. We already know all of our assumptions, and they are correct.

Group leaders need to challenge not only the assumptions and the content of what they are thinking but also the way and process by which they handle that content. Perhaps the biggest struggle for group leaders who attempt to consider cultural factors is to know when to apply specific norms for a particular group member and when to apply universal norms. This conflict has been identified as the etic-emic conflict: *Etic* refers to universal norms, and *emic* to group-specific norms (Draguns, 1981). Group leaders sometimes err on the side of assuming that certain behaviors have the same meaning for all people, when in fact the meaning of these behaviors is quite different for certain cultural group members.

In addition to becoming culturally competent in knowledge of self and other minority groups, group leaders have the responsibility of interpolating this knowledge in the multicultural group counseling process. Group leaders must be aware of the institutionalized racism and ethnocentrism in the counseling profession as manifested in the lack of attention directed at multicultural issues, multicultural group counseling, and current counseling theories that reflect only a Euro-American point of view (Parham, 1989; Sue, Ivey, & Pedersen, 1996). Further, because of the lack of information of the multicultural group process in counseling curricula, group leaders need to actively seek out literature, information, experts, workshops, seminars, and courses that address these areas.

Cultural Groups ~

This chapter does not attempt to provide a comprehensive analysis of all minority groups. Rather, it presents a brief overview of information on and cultural considerations of four minority groups: African American, Hispanic, Asian/Pacific Islander, and American Indian. It deals more with the traditional cultures than with differences within those cultures. Caution is advised to be aware that differences exist in various groups, such as level of acculturation, geographical location, language, and other variables. These differences exist on a continuum and are not fixed. Additional cross-cultural readings are given at the end of this chapter to assist in obtaining more specific information.

African American

To understand the African American experience before initiating intervention approaches, group leaders have to know the psychohistorical experiences of this group. This involves knowledge of historical figures; omissions and bias of books; the social, political, and economic climate; development of the militant movement of the 1960s and 1970s; and evolution of demographic data of the African American population.

Group leaders must recognize (a) that no prescriptive approaches can be applied in dealing with African American group members, and (b) that it is a myth that the problems of African American group members are their own sole responsibility. Group leaders must incorporate a systemic view, one that looks at all of the interacting systems in the individual's life, to gain a more comprehensive understanding of the African American individual's history with self, family, institutions, and economic and political factors. As with all groups, cultural stereotyping is endemic, and group leaders must exercise caution to separate the culture of poverty from the culture of the group itself.

The following general characteristics of African American group members may help group leaders develop a systemic view (Vacc & Wittmer, 1980). The reader is cautioned that these characteristics are given as a framework to consider and not as fact.

1. African Americans have differential access to the resources of society.
2. As contrasted with white society, a group of internal factors operating within the African American community to maintain cohesiveness keeps African Americans' cultural system intact.
3. Older African Americans are treated with respect, and often addressed as "uncle" or "aunt."
4. Turning the head and putting the hand over the mouth when laughing, or averting the eyes and perhaps even the face when speaking to elders or other respected persons, is considered a mark of respect.
5. The African American mother must teach her child appropriate gender and age roles as well as the racial role.
6. The cultural values associated with this African American worldview are cooperation, interdependence, and collective responsibility.
7. The church offers a kind of extended family fellowship.

Although these characteristics are general, group leaders need to take into account the level of acculturation of individual group members and the historical impact of the dominant society on the culture. African American group members may come from situations in which they feel powerless, hostile, and lacking specific direction. Because the dominant societal systems and institutions are often insensitive and unresponsive to change, African American group members may want concrete responses from the group leader much like they would receive from respected family members or friends. In addition, the heterogeneity and initial cultural paranoia of this group need to be taken into consideration.

Hispanic

Perhaps the first step in effectively counseling Hispanic individuals from a culturally relevant perspective is to acknowledge the group's tremendous intracultural diversity. The many Hispanic groups have distinct differences as well as similarities. The Spanish language is the most common cultural artifact even though it, too, varies widely in its dialect and linguistic nuances. Other similarities include religious and family values and some traditions. But major historical and traditional differences are present among as well as within the various groups.

For example, the history of the Mexican American is tied to the history of the land. Some Mexicans were already present in the Southwest when the Anglo-Americans arrived in the East, others migrated later. Other Hispanic groups, such as Cubans and Central Americans, immigrated to the United States for political or economic reasons. Puerto Ricans' uniqueness comes from their territorial relationship with the United States. They have retained their cultural ties to preterritorial days.

Many Hispanics have chosen to remain identified with their own ethnic group rather than to be categorized under the aggregate Hispanic/Latino label. To understand the diversity of Hispanics, each group must be examined historically.

When the Spanish explorers came to the North American continent in the early 16th century, they intermarried with the Indians and produced the Mestizo. In Puerto Rico, the Spaniards also intermarried with many of the native peoples. In Cuba, as in many of the Central and South American countries, some cultural fusion occurred with imported African slaves, and some Spanish colonists maintained their European lineage. Thus, the population labeled Hispanic is very heterogeneous and diverse.

Because of this diversity, common characteristics of Hispanic group members are often difficult to determine. The group leader must be cautious in acknowledging the uniqueness of each Hispanic group. Keeping in mind the strong loyalty each group ties to ethnic identification, group leaders should consider, when working with Hispanics, the following characteristics that many of the Hispanic groups may share to various degrees (Ruiz & Padilla, 1977; Sue & Sue, 1990):

1. More than 50% of Hispanics report that Spanish is their native language.
2. The extended family structure is still an important factor in Hispanic group members' backgrounds. They place a high value on the family over the self.
3. The concept of respect is a value, particularly respect for authority figures.
4. Unwavering love and respect for the mother, who is a unifying force in the family, is a prominent feature.
5. Formalized kinships, such as the *compadrazgo* (godfather) system, operate to varying degrees.
6. Loyalty to the family takes precedence over loyalty to social institutions. The family fosters a spirit of cooperation, as contrasted with competition with siblings and relatives. Hispanic people learn to share.
7. Sex roles traditionally have been more rigid, but this norm is currently undergoing some change.
8. The concept of *personalismo* (personal contact) is a preferred relating style.
9. Traditional Hispanics have a collectivist worldview—one that entails looking at a situation from a family and group point of view.

In attempting to understand these characteristics, group leaders must recognize how the concept of acculturation affects each member. The characteristics listed here are not static and do not hold for all Hispanics. Each group member's perceptions must be acknowledged individually and the heterogeneity of the Hispanic population kept in mind. Acculturated Hispanics will more likely respond to regular group counseling approaches, whereas the traditional immigrants (or first generation) will be more hesitant to accept participation in group approaches that rely on individual responsibility and abstract thinking. They will more likely respond to the group leader as an authority figure who will help interpret the system (Arciniega & Newlon, 1995).

Asian/Pacific Islander

The Asian American population in the United States consists mainly of people from China, Japan, Korea, Malaysia, Myanmar (formerly Burma), Cambodia, Indonesia, Thailand, the Philippines, Samoa, and Vietnam. Most are from Japan and China. Like the Hispanics, the diversity among Asian American groups is vast. Each group has its own cultural norms, values, language, and traditions.

The first Asian American group to immigrate to the United States were the

Chinese in the 1840s. This immigration resulted from the discovery of gold in California, and many Chinese people came with the idea of returning home once they had made their fortune. These Chinese immigrants who came to work as laborers in the gold mines and the railroads were subject to massive acts of discrimination (Sue & Sue, 1990).

Japanese immigration began in the late 1800s. The early Japanese immigrants filled a demand for cheap agricultural labor and were not initially treated with the same anti-Oriental disrespect that the Chinese were. The Japanese people's success in agriculture, however, antagonized the white citizens, contributing to the threat of yellow peril. By the beginning of World War II, acts of racism toward Asians had increased and were fanned by the press. This resulted in more than 110,000 Japanese being sent to relocation camps (Daniels, 1971).

The Chinese and Japanese cultures have many similar values and traditions, and scholars have found similar psychological characteristics for Asian Americans of Chinese and Japanese descent. Following is a synthesized list of some of the psychological characteristics of Japanese and Chinese Americans (Atkinson, Morten, & Sue, 1993). Again, caution is advised about not assuming that all Japanese and Chinese Americans have these characteristics. The characteristics listed are more traditional than modern and must be viewed on an acculturation continuum.

1. Chinese and Japanese people feel a great sense of obligation toward the family and parents.
2. Family expectations of obedience are strong and produce problems when people are exposed to white values.
3. Asian Americans tend to evaluate ideas on the basis of practical application. Consequently, they are apt to be more intolerant of ambiguities than their white counterparts.
4. Asian Americans seem to be more obedient, conservative, conforming, and inhibited than their white counterparts.
5. They tend to exhibit the cultural values of emotional restraint, dependence on family, and formality in interpersonal relations.
6. Asian Americans generally feel more comfortable in structured than unstructured situations.
7. They are more reluctant to self-disclose than are their white counterparts.
8. Because of their minority status and potential discrimination from white society, Asian Americans may be suspicious of people who are not Asian.
9. Asian Americans seem to have a need to feel guilty and accept personal blame when things go wrong.
10. Asian Americans are less verbal about their feelings with non-Asians than with Asians.

Cultural differences of Southeast Asians (people from Myanmar, Cambodia, Indonesia, Laos, Malaysia, Philippines, Singapore, Thailand, and Vietnam) include time orientation, role of the family and its individual members, value system, and social behavior (Fernandez, 1988).

1. *Time orientation.* In their time orientation, Southeast Asians tend to stress the past and the future; they see the present as a transitory period. Although individuals are perceived as in control of their destiny, lineage and familial background are extremely important in establishing an individual's sense of honor and character (Fernandez, 1988).
2. *Role of the family and its individual members.* The family is the basic foundation in the lives of most individuals. The continuous affective and social bonds with immediate family members validate individuals' self-esteem and secure their future. Social control is exerted through shame and guilt. Clearly specified roles for family members dictate demands that have to be met to ensure that the family network functions. The father is the head of the family; the mother is the emotionally devoted, nurturant parental figure. Children are socialized into a network in which filial piety and deference to elders are stressed (Shon & Ja, 1982).
3. *Value system.* The primary emphasis in the Asian ethical system is upon social obligation. The family is the fundamental unit of society and the major emotive support. This society disapproves of individual independence and autonomy. Family needs supersede those of the individual (Shon & Ja, 1982; Sue & Sue, 1990).
4. *Social behavior.* The Asian cultural emphasis on formality in interpersonal relations often makes Asians uncomfortable when relating to Americans, who have a much more informal and spontaneous nature (Sue & Sue, 1990).

Southeast Asians are conservative and reticent about expressing their personal problems because of their fear of being looked down upon. Openness, genuineness, and honesty may be construed by Southeast Asian group members, who value reserved and modest self-disclosure, as an invasion of privacy or as an affront to their dignity (Church, 1982). Asians have an external locus of control because of their perception of being just a part of the larger whole. Expecting Asian group members to make decisions independent of their families would go against their disposition (Sue & Sue, 1990).

When Southeast Asians seek group counseling, they typically desire a guidance-nurturant oriented intervention. They want the leader to take an active-directive role and give them explicit directions on how to solve problems and bring immediate relief from disabling distress. They are looking for straightforward solutions to concrete and immediate problems that are generating stress in their lives. Asian group members value modesty and are often ashamed to admit having any problems. They view group leaders as experts and authorities. They do not initiate conversations and are comfortable with silence. They seldom maintain much eye contact because it is considered rude to stare (Fernandez, 1988).

For some specific applications see Leong (1992), "Guidelines for Minimizing Premature Termination Among Asian American Clients in Group Counseling."

American Indian

One of the most neglected areas in the counseling literature has been counseling and the American Indian culture. The literature that does exist has been limited largely to historical or philosophical treatises on the American Indian. This neglect may be attributed to several causes (Arciniega & Newlon, 1995):

1. The monolithic tradition of Western training is prevalent in most counselor training institutions, leaving little room for American Indian worldviews.
2. Limited information is available about the psychology of the American Indian. More important, there are few Indian counselors and psychologists to assist in interpreting counseling information.
3. There are 511 federally recognized Indian nation entities and an additional 365 state-recognized tribes with 200 distinct languages (LaFramboise, 1988).

Of all the minority groups, leaders often have the most difficulty working with American Indian members, partially because of the strong existing stereotypes and partially because most Western modes of group counseling are not compatible with the traditional Indian cultures. Further, many American Indians have become bicultural or have acculturated within the dominant society. The process of acculturation is a major counseling factor with all minority groups, and group leaders will encounter American Indian group members on all points of the acculturation continuum (Newlon & Arciniega, 1983).

To gain some understanding of the American Indian group member, it is necessary to examine the culture of origin of this group. The following list, compiled from an examination of the traditional American Indian cultures, provides some basic guidelines for the group leader of general characteristics that may manifest in group situations (Sanders, 1987; Vacc & Wittmer, 1980):

1. Sharing is a major value in family life.
2. Time is seen more as a natural phenomenon.
3. Nature is a part of living and is part of such happenings as death, birth, and accidents.
4. Acceptance of life is a style of being in harmony with the world.
5. Family, including extended family, is of major importance.
6. The basic worth of the individual resides in his or her family and tribe. Individual responsibility is only a part of the total responsibility concept.
7. Harmony and cooperative behavior are valued.
8. Tradition is important; it adds to the quality of life.
9. Assertive or aggressive behavior is seen as impinging on others' dignity.
10. Respect for elders is valued, and the elders play an important part in family life.
11. American Indians tend to speak softly and slowly and interject less.
12. American Indians use fewer physical signs of acknowledgment.
13. American Indians treat auditory messages differently, giving responses that may appear delayed.
14. The orientation is to the present time.
15. American Indians participate verbally after observation.
16. American Indians encourage patience and allowing others to go first.

It cannot be stressed enough that the group leader exercise caution and not assume that all American Indians have these characteristics.

American Indian history is replete with failures of intervention programs. Before considering group counseling with the American Indian, group leaders must develop an understanding of the culture of origin, of what occurred between Indian cultures and U.S. society, and, more important, of the effect culture, history, economics, and politics have had on the American Indian. Leaders also must be aware of the erroneous institutional mind-set that has permeated the literature about "Indian problems." It is a mind-set that developed from an inability to understand a distinct and different view of the nature of the world and what impact the dominant society has had.

As with all minority groups, a generic understanding of American Indian cultures is essential. Of equal importance is learning about the differences between each member, family, and tribe. Counseling as it is now in the United States has not been successful with traditional Indian cultures. Therefore, group counseling will have to assume a contextual frame of reference compatible with the view of the individual American Indian group member. Only through increased awareness of cultural influences and expanded counselor education can effective group counseling with American Indians become a reality.

For more specific application see Dufrene and Coleman (1992), "Counseling Native Americans: Guidelines for Group Process."

Cross-Cultural Factors 〜

Much of the criticism of minority group counseling has been directed at the barriers to communication between the group counselor from the dominant white group and the group's multicultural members. Counseling is seen as a process of interpersonal interaction and communication requiring accurate sending and receiving of verbal and nonverbal messages. When the group counselor and the member(s) come from different cultural backgrounds, barriers to communication are likely to develop, leading to misunderstandings that destroy rapport and render counseling ineffective.

Beyond specific cultural factors, some theoretical considerations need to be noted. Sue, Ivey, and Pedersen (1996), in their recent book *A Theory of Multicultural Counseling and Therapy (MCT),* proposed several theoretical propositions that have great implications for multicultural group counseling. They argued for a meta-theory of counseling that will provide the counselor with an overall professional competence when working with persons from diverse populations and for the need to derive helping models from indigenous non-Western cultures. They also proposed that counselors address clients' identity from individual, group, and universal levels, which include all systems affecting them. They emphasized the need for understanding cultural identity development, which affects the counselor's and clients' attitude toward themselves, their own cultural group, other minority groups, and members of the dominant society. Further, they noted that effective multicultural counseling may actually enhance the group counseling experience by teaching the group members multicultural skills that are within their worldview. Finally, Sue et al. contended that the goal of multicultural counseling is the liberation of consciousness; it is being able to expand the clients' understanding of their personal, family, group, and organizational consciousness, which includes a relational perspective. Readers are strongly encouraged to read this book, as it has major implications for multicultural group counseling.

Several cross-cultural factors that should be considered by all group counselors include acculturation, language, cultural identity, generational issues, cultural custom styles, geographical location and neighborhoods, family constituency, psychohistorical and religious traditions, and individuality. The group leader should take these factors into account when gathering information and should integrate them into the group counseling process (Newlon & Arciniega, 1983).

Acculturation

Acculturation is more than a continuum from traditional to nontraditional modes of operation. It is a multifaceted phenomenon encompassing many dimensions, such as values, ideologies, beliefs, and attitudes. In addition, it incorporates language, ethnic identity, cultural customs, practices, and ethnic interaction. This complex phenomenon might be best understood in terms of the extent to which minority individuals uniquely incorporate, add, or synthesize the values, customs, languages, beliefs, and ideology of the dominant culture with their own yet are still able to operate from a contextual point on the continuum.

The group leader needs an understanding of this complex issue because it has vast implications in terms of the member's identity, style of communication, and interactional worldview. The group member's identity is tied historically to his or her culture of origin. Though some view it as a continuum from traditional culture of origin to a nontraditional dominant culture, it demands far more than a linear explanation.

Many minority group members assume a contextual identity that depends on the social circumstances. Thus, they may manifest behaviors and language from their culture of origin, from a totally Americanized style and language, or from a mixed synthesis. The group leader needs some understanding of contextual identity and where and how it operates with the members. To facilitate groups more effectively, group leaders need to be aware of the nature of acculturation and the manifestations of members' behaviors.

Language

In group counseling with minority members who continue to speak in their language of origin, the group leader must understand more than the content and the contextual meaning of the language. In addition, the leader must be able to assess the language abilities of the various group members; all members may not have the same degree of fluency in the language of origin or in English. Group leaders must be cognizant of the fact that it is in the language of origin where much of the affect is first learned. Although members may be fluent in English, they may not realize that the affect of the English words they use may have a different meaning than the words did in the language of origin.

Code switching, mixing words, and combining words in new and creative expressions that operate from a distinct cultural base occurs when two languages come in contact. The linguistic style of symbolic meaning and cadence, as well as familial context, are factors the group leader needs to assess.

Cultural Identity

Group leaders must be aware of the self-referent labels that members choose. Self-referent labels are a sensitive issue for many people and may be different even for various members of a family. For example, identifiers for individuals of Mexican or Latin American descent may be Mexican American, Hispanic, Chicano, Americans of Mexican descent, or Latinos. For members of African descent, the identifiers may be Afro-American, Negro, black, or West Indian. For American Indians, they may be Indian, Native American, Red, or a tribal name. For Asian Americans, the identifiers may be Asian, Asian American, Oriental, or an identifier derived from the name of the specific country of origin. In many cases, clients may use different self-referent labels depending on the contextual situation.

Generational Issues

Group leaders should consider generational factors (whether the group member is from the first, second, third generation in this country) to assist in assessing the extent of acculturation that might have taken place. First-generation members may have more ties to the traditional culture than members of later generations, and these ties may be reflected in the nuclear and extended family dynamics. The acculturation process is unique for each minority person. Contrary to some current beliefs, as members become acculturated, they do not drop their former cultural ways but, rather, add new ones and creatively synthesize the new and the old.

Cultural Custom Styles

In addition to the obvious cultural customs of foods, dress, and traditions, several cultural styles of responsibility and communication have to be considered. For example, the Mexican, American Indian, and Asian cultures emphasize the responsibility of the oldest child to younger siblings. Oldest children assume this responsibility as part of tradition. As another example, the Asian family's expectations of unquestioning obedience may produce problems when exposed to American values emphasizing independence and self-reliance in group counseling.

The style of communication in traditional American Indian and Mexican American people stresses patience and personal respect. Group members from traditional families may show respect by looking down and not looking into the eyes of authority figures. When doing group counseling with members from these groups, the verbal question/answer approach is often ineffective in obtaining behavior cues. These group members typically appear to be slow in responding but are actually observing and waiting to determine if the group will be accepting. For the same reason, confrontational group counseling approaches are often ineffectual. Cultural contextualizing (cultural interpretation) by a group member who is more bicultural than the group leader may provide much needed information. Respect is the key to sensitive probing with these groups.

With African American group members, verbal interaction moves at a faster pace, and sensitive confrontation is accepted more readily, than with traditional Hispanics, American Indians, and Asian Americans. Group leaders need to be aware of their own interactional style to determine any contradictory differences in interactions.

Geographical Location and Neighborhoods

Ethnic groups from different geographical locations have distinct geocultural traditions and customs. Group leaders cannot assume that the same customs apply to seemingly similar cultural groups. An African American family from the South manifests its culture in a different way than an African American family from the West Coast does. This concept of geographical differences also applies to Asian American, Hispanic, and American Indian groups. The group leader should also note rural and urban influences in the group member's present situation within the family history.

The neighborhoods in which the minority group members reside have a great deal to do with how they see themselves. Minority members living in a totally ethnic area have a different view than members living in an integrated neighborhood or members living in a neighborhood in which theirs is the only minority family. Thus, it is essential that group leaders obtain information about members' neighborhood.

Family Constituency

In most racial/ethnic groups, family kinship networks help to satisfy important cultural needs for intimacy, belonging, and interpersonal relations. Extended families, in which more than one generation lives in the same household, with formalized kinship relations, are common among these groups. The culturally sensitive group leader must be able to comprehend this concept within each culture. In many Hispanic and American Indian families, significant adults may extend to uncles, grandparents, cousins, close friends, and godparents. These adults often play a significant part in child rearing and perhaps should be considered in identifying the significant adult models in the group counseling process.

Family occupies a special place with racial/cultural minority group members. Love, protection, and loyalty to the family are pronounced, creating an environment in which members can develop strong feelings of self-worth despite the lingering effects of discrimination and racism. In some instances, the family functions as a buffer against society's attempt to impose a negative self-image. Effective group leaders have to be aware of this dynamic.

Psychohistorical and Religious Traditions

The history of the ethnic group's origin and of the ethnic group in the United States is essential information for group leaders. Racial/ethnic members reflect the psychohistory of the family through, among other things, child-rearing practices. Many facets of child rearing are rooted in the history of minority groups and are distinct from the dominant culture in which the members presently live.

Spiritual and religious practices traditionally have been strong within most of these groups. These, too, affect group dynamics. Religion and spirituality provide the medium through which minority group members deal with forces and powers beyond their control. They also provide a basis for social cohesion and support. Historically, the church has been a resource for personal counseling and a refuge from a hostile environment. Group leaders must take these factors into account in working with individuals who are more traditionally bound in their religion and history.

Individuality

Many racial/ethnic groups view the concept of individual responsibility differently than the majority group does. American Indians, for instance, judge their worth primarily in terms of whether their behavior serves to better the tribe. Tribal culture places a high value on the harmonious relationship between an individual and all other members of the tribe. The importance of cooperation within Hispanic groups has also been documented (Kagan & Madsen, 1971).

Group leaders must be wary of assuming that individual responsibility for these groups is primarily at the expense of cooperation, which is of value and manifests itself in thinking and behaving. Responsibility to the family is a major value found in minority groups and should be considered and encouraged. In traditional families, individual responsibilities are of secondary value. Therefore, group leaders need to carefully consider how confrontation about taking responsibility will impact group participants.

Counselor Awareness ∼

Why should group leaders make the effort to increase their understanding of minority groups and their cultures? The number and variety of individuals whom group leaders impact, especially in today's world, are staggering. Projected demographics, especially in the West, Southwest, Northeast, and Southeast, show and will continue to show a dramatic and significant increase in the minority populations. Subsequently, the world of work and all societal institutions, including mental health services, will be greatly affected. Thus, group leaders have a special and unique responsibility to understand the cultural frame of reference of minority group members and to become more acutely aware of their own views and beliefs.

Currently, most group leaders are white and middle class. In addition to having cultural differences, group leaders and members may have class differences in attitudes, behaviors, beliefs, and values. The impact of social class differences on counseling in general acquires added significance when one considers that existing group counseling techniques are middle- and upper-class based.

Group leaders frequently impose their own cultural values upon minority members without intending to. For example, one of the most highly valued strategies for group cohesion entails members' self-disclosure. Self-disclosure may be contrary to the basic cultural values of some minorities. Chinese American clients who are taught at an early age to restrain from emotional expression will likely feel threatened by direct and subtle demands for self-disclosure. Hispanic and Native American group members have reported similar conflicts (Sue & Sue, 1990). Thus, group leaders need to be aware of the implications of self-disclosure.

Other factors group leaders need to consider because of their impact on groups are stereotyping and self-concept.

Stereotyping

Stereotyping is a major problem in all forms of group counseling. It may be defined as rigid preconceptions applied to all members of a group or to an individual over time, regardless of individual variation. Stereotypes are often institutionalized, and group leaders have to be conscious of this process. Most counselor training institutions do not train group counselors from a culturally pluralistic model. Therefore, a process is lacking for the confrontation and sensitive awareness of self- and institutional stereotypes.

The preconceived notions group leaders may have about group members who differ from them ethnically, racially, and socioeconomically affect their reactions to these group members. Leaders may unwittingly act upon these beliefs, approaching members from a monolithic, dominant point of view. Or, in an attempt to avoid stereotyping and to treat members as just other human beings, leaders may demonstrate color or culture blindness. This blindness shows a lack of respect in acknowledging that culture is an inherent part of group members' personhood. The leader may avoid discussing members' cultural identity, and the content of the group counseling may disavow their uniqueness. The content of the counseling may also be restricted by the group leaders' fear that the members will detect conscious or unconscious stereotyping on their part.

In addition to stereotyping on the part of group leaders, each participant in group situations brings his or her own stereotypes to the group. Group counselors need to be able to recognize and address stereotyping by group members when it occurs.

Self-Concept

Group counseling inherently deals closely with members' self-concepts, including their cultural self-concepts. Leaders should be aware that the development of minority members' self-concepts has distinct characteristics not found in the self-concept development of people in the dominant culture. The unique cultural values of minority members are part of their identity and part of their self-concept. These are cognitively and effectively learned through interaction of the family culture and the dominant group environment. Thus, a bicognitive self-concept (concept of self within family and concept of self in relation to the dominant group) may become evident and may be manifested in cultural conflict. Group leaders should be aware of this issue so they can provide, in the group, a place of acceptance, confirmation, and encouragement to resolve this conflict and enhance healthy minority self-concept development.

Attributes of Effective Counselors

Some studies have shown that the ethnicity of counselors is not always the significant variable in determining the efficacy of their counseling. If a counselor is culturally competent, sensitive, caring, and genuine with participants, his or her ethnicity becomes secondary. As with any group the process of trust is even more important with minority groups where group counseling is not a part of their experience. It is acceptable to acknowledge distrust of the situation and if the counselor is white even more so. It is essential that the development of trust be established before sensitive issues are addressed. Therefore, a culturally sensitive development of trust is of paramount importance as a prerequisite to any attribute.

Group counselors who facilitate positive interaction with minority groups (Newlon & Arciniega, 1983):

- personally acknowledge that cultural diversity exists within the United States and that diversity implies difference, not inferiority.
- confront and resolve personal cultural diversity through learning about themselves.
- increase their knowledge of cultural variation through study and interpersonal contact.
- examine the historical and present interaction between minorities and the dominant culture.
- expand interactions with people from minority and dominant cultural groups.

Characteristics of culturally sensitive group leaders also include (Sue et al., 1982):

- the ability to generate a wide variety of verbal and nonverbal responses. The wider the repertoire of responses, the greater the chances for understanding the presenting problems.
- the ability to send and receive verbal and nonverbal messages appropriately. Some ethnic groups have a high regard for subtlety and indirectness of communication; others prize directness and confrontation. To respond appropriately, the group leader must understand the communication style of the ethnic member.
- the ability to exercise appropriate institutional intervention skills on behalf of the group member. This sensitivity requires a perspective that views many problems and barriers to member success as problems of the institutional system's inability to respond appropriately.

Group Composition ~

Due to the differences that exist within and between cultures, when deciding on the composition of a group, the group leader needs to consider various dimensions of group membership dynamics, race and ethnicity, gender, and socioeconomic status.

Membership

Although the data on cultural diversity and its effects on group membership are scarce, DeLucia, Coleman, and Jensen-Scott (1992) proposed that cultural diversity should enhance the heterogeneity of multicultural group counselors. However, group leaders cannot just incorporate different cultural backgrounds into groups without also understanding the values and worldviews of the different cultures. In terms of group size, research has not indicated a specific number for groups, but it has suggested that there be no more than 6-8 members in a group.

It has also been found that the proportion of members of different racial groups may influence the character of the group. Davis (1981) purported that whites tend to be most comfortable in racially heterogeneous groups when the proportion of whites to blacks is about 70% to 30%, whereas blacks are rarely comfortable when the proportion is 50% to 50%. It has also been suggested that a person from a minority racial or cultural group never be placed in a group where he or she is the only representative from that racial or cultural group.

In addition to culture and race, it is obvious that potential group members should be screened to provide for an equal number, if possible, in terms of gender as well as to provide for homogeneity in socioeconomic status and stage of identity development.

Race and Ethnicity

Race and ethnicity affect not only the assumptions drawn about others but also the comfort levels experienced in interpersonal relationships. Minority individuals are often most comfortable in groups with people who are racially and ethnically similar to them and are most likely to be anxious in groups with a larger number from the dominant white group. To induce trust, which is a major interpersonal dynamic in mixed groups, the leader should make a deliberate and sensitive effort to address the issue of diversity right away. It is important that diversity also be acknowledged in groups as a part of the process of examining communication.

Gender

The gender composition of a group seems to influence members' attraction to that group. Males and females prefer different sizes of groups, depending on whether they are mixed- or single-gender groups. In general, members of both genders seem to view the other sex more favorably in situations where gender balances are equitable.

Gender affects the dynamics of small groups by influencing the extent to which groups are cooperative or competitive. In general, males are more competitive than females in groups, and males tend to be more competitive in all-male groups than in mixed-gender groups. This is even more apparent in traditional minority groups.

Because women significantly outnumber men as recipients of social and mental health services, group leaders must understand the clear role of social gender roles when they attempt to address women's problems. In group and family situations, gender roles influence members' communication, expectations, and evaluations of one another (Davis & Proctor, 1989).

Socioeconomic Status

Contrary to popular opinion, minority individuals who participate in group counseling may be from varied socioeconomic groups. Consideration of whether groups should be heterogeneous or homogeneous with respect to socioeconomic status (SES) is as important as consideration of their ethnic and racial makeup. Inherent in this assessment is the need for group leaders to be aware of the differences in the culture of poverty and the culture of ethnicity and race. Many professionals advocate against including only one person of a particular SES group in an otherwise homogeneous SES group. Doing so places that individual in a deviant status, requiring him or her to become a representative of his or her income group (Davis & Proctor, 1989).

Research literature suggests that groups composed of individuals of different SES are at great risk for communication problems. Difficulties in communication spring from the lack of a common experiential base and the difference in social status. Therefore, balanced group communication might be difficult to achieve in groups consisting of individuals from different status groups (Davis & Proctor, 1989).

SES seems to be more important to group composition when the group's purpose requires that members have some *a priori* understanding of the values and customs of the other members.

Strategies and Recommendations

A number of strategies have been proposed. They are similar to regular group counseling modalities but have valid multicultural theoretical backing.

1. Multicultural counselors need to conduct self-assessment of their level of multicultural counseling competency to determine areas in which they may need more training. One method of doing this is to review the multicultural competencies outlined by the Association for Multicultural Counseling and Development (AMCD) (Arredondo et al., 1996; Sue, Arredondo, & McDavis, 1992).
2. Multicultural group counselors need to be aware of the current cultural identity models that offer insight into this issue. They include minority identity development models (Atkinson et al., 1993; Cook, 1994; Cross, 1995; Helms, 1984) and the white identity development model (Sabnani, Ponterotto, & Borodovsky, 1991). These models can assist counselors by explaining how racial/ethnic cultural background influences psychological development. They can also be used as preassessment tools to determine the level of each member and the group leader.
3. Multicultural counselors need to become knowledgeable about, utilize, and integrate the helping role models that have evolved out of nonwhite cultural groups to expand the group leader role.
4. Multicultural counselors need to address ethnic/cultural/racial diversity as part of group process without walking on eggshells (Locke, 1996).

5. Multicultural counselors need to be cognizant of the extended family ties, acculturation, and individualistic or collectivistic view of each group member as well as their own views.

6. Multicultural counselors need to develop trust slowly. It is important for group leaders to discuss trust and what it means in the group with the group members.

7. Multicultural counselors need to ask group members periodically how they think the differences in their and the clients' ethnic/racial background, or such differences among the clients, might affect the ways in which members interact (D'Andrea & Daniels, 1996).

8. Multicultural counselors need to use psychoeducational techniques to explain emotionally laden words like racism and oppression, stereotypes, and the stage development model.

9. Multicultural counselors need to provide structure for the group and explain the purpose of the group process at the beginning of the group experience.

10. Multicultural counselors need to assist group members to examine assumptions and statements made about attitudes and beliefs.

11. Multicultural counselors need to be cognizant of communication patterns, as proposed by Helms' model, and integrate racial identity stage (Helms, 1990).

12. Multicultural counselors need to become aware of all of the instruments that assess racial identity, white racial consciousness, and cross-cultural counseling, such as the Crosscultural Counseling Inventory, the Racial Identity Attitude Scale, and individual and collectivistic assessment scales.

13. Multicultural counselors need to provide themselves with the opportunity to consult with supervisors or colleagues with expertise.

Summary ~

The four minority groups discussed in this chapter—Asian Americans, African Americans, Hispanics, and American Indians—will, in a short time, become a majority portion of the U.S. population. In leading groups with members of any cultural group, effective counselors have to be aware of the racial/cultural uniqueness of the members and actively seek to be more understanding. Leaders have to recognize direct and indirect communication styles, be sensitive to nonverbal cues, recognize cultural linguistic differences, have an interest in the culture, be sensitive to the myths and stereotypes surrounding the culture, appreciate and have concern for the well-being of people from other cultures, recognize the relationships between cultural groups, and apply accurate criteria when viewing function and dysfunction. In doing this, leaders have to search out and face attitudes in themselves that may detract from their effectiveness.

Differences exist not only between cultures but also within cultures, related to language, cultural identity, customs, family makeup, geography and neighborhood, psychohistorical and religious traditions, views on individuality, and generational differences and acculturation. When deciding on group composition, the leader has to consider race and ethnicity, gender, socioeconomic status, and group membership dynamics.

Developing cultural sensitivity is an ongoing process that requires a respectful dialogue of mutual education. Group leaders need to take the necessary steps to continue this dialogue by sharing their questions, thoughts, and feelings about cultural issues with supervisors, colleagues, and, to some extent, their group members. Willingness to face these issues openly will likely lead to a reduction in the stereotypes, misunderstandings, and prejudices that can adversely affect the quality of group counseling. Genuineness and respect, above all, have to be part of the attitudinal makeup of group leaders. Although this perspective is not different in theory from that for any group, the focus and process with minorities requires a paradigm shift that integrates other cultural worldviews to provide for more effective communication with group participants.

As group counselors cross cultures, they must realize that the theories, the techniques, and the profession itself are cultural phenomena reflecting the majority culture's history, beliefs, and values. Without this awareness, in the process of trying to respect and be sensitive to different cultures, group counselors will likely end up totally ineffective.

The challenge for group leaders who want to be sensitive to cultural pluralism in group counseling settings is to accurately clarify their own values, acquire knowledge of focus cultural groups, and learn the systems and helping strategies applicable to or designed for those groups. This task is by no means easy. It takes courage to venture outside one's habitual ways of construing and interpreting events, and time to learn about different cultures, that entails more than reading articles and participating in workshops. Ideally, one should be actively and purposely involved in relationships within other cultures, trying new methods, making mistakes, and correcting errors, to learn what is necessary to be a culturally sensitive counselor. The purpose of this chapter was not to present a "how-to" but to present an overview and background of cultural factors and considerations that are important in developing effective multicultural groups. The difficult part now lies with those who have read the chapter and are working with, or aspire to work with, multicultural groups.

References ∽

Arciniega, G. M., & Newlon, B. (1995). Counseling and psychotherapy multicultural considerations. In D. Capuzzi, & D. Gross (Eds.), *Counseling and psychotherapy: Theories and interventions* (pp. 557–587). Englewood Cliffs, NJ.: Prentice-Hall.

Arredondo, P., Toporek, R., Brown, S. P., Jones, J., Locke, D. C., Sanchez, J., & Stadler, H. (1996). Operationalization of the multicultural counseling competencies. *Journal of Multicultural Counseling & Development, 24,* 42–78.

Atkinson, D. R., Morten, G., & Sue, D. W. (1993). *Counseling American minorities* (4th ed.). Dubuque, IA: Brown & Benchmark.

Avila, D. L., & Avila, A. L. (1988). Mexican Americans. In N. A. Vacc, J. Wittmer, & S. Devaney (Eds.), *Experiencing and counseling multicultural and diverse populations* (2nd ed., pp. 289–316). Muncie, IN: Accelerated Development.

Church, A. T. (1982). Sojourner adjustment. *Psychological Bulletin, 91,* 540–572.

Cook, D. A. (1994). Racial identity in supervision. *Counselor Education and Supervision, 34,* 132–1412.

Cross, W. E. (1995). The psychology of nigrescence: Revising the Cross model. In J. G. Ponterotto, J. M. Casas, L. A. Suzuki, & C. M. Alexander (Eds.), *Handbook of multicultural counseling* (pp. 93–124). Thousand Oaks, CA: Sage Publications.

D'Andrea, M., & Daniels, J. (1991). Exploring the different levels of multicultural counseling training in counselor education. *Journal of Counseling and Development, 70*(1), 78–85.

D'Andrea, M. & Daniels, J. (1996). What is multicultural group counseling? Identifying its potential benefits, barriers, and future challenges. *Counseling & Human Development,* (28) 6.

Daniels, R. (1971). *Concentration camps, U.S.A.* New York: Harper & Rocul.

Davis, L. E. (1981). Racial composition of groups. *Social Work, 24,* 208–213.

Davis, L. E., & Proctor, E. K. (1989). *Race, gender, and class: Guidelines for practice with individuals, families, and groups.* Englewood Cliffs, NJ: Prentice-Hall.

DeLucia, J., Coleman, V., & Jenson-Scott, R. (1992). Cultural diversity in group counseling (editorial). *Journal for Specialists in Group Counseling, 174,* 194–195.

Draguns, J. G. (1981). Counseling across cultures: Common themes and distinct approaches. In P. Pedersen et al. (Eds.), *Counseling across cultures* (rev. ed., pp. 3–21). Honolulu: East-West Center.

Dufrene, P., & Colman, V. (1992). Counseling Native Americans: Guidelines for group process. *Journal for Specialists in Group Work, 17*(4), 229–234.

Fernandez, M. S. (1988). Issues in counseling Southeast-Asian students. *Journal of Multicultural Counseling and Development, 16*(4), 157–166.

Greeley, A. T., Garcia, V. L., Kessler, B. L., & Gilchrest, G. (1992). Training effective multicultural group counselors: Issues for a training course. *Journal for Specialists in Group Work, 17*(4), 197–209.

Helms, J. E. (1984). Toward a theoretical explanation of the effects of race on counseling: A black and white model. *Counseling Psychologist, 12*(4), 153–165.

Helms, J. E. (Ed.). (1990). *Black and white racial identity: Theory, research, and practice.* New York: Greenwood Press

Ivey, A. E., Ivey, M. B., & Simek-Morgan, L. (1993). *Counseling and psychotherapy: A multicultural perspective.* Boston: Allyn & Bacon.

Kagan, S., & Madsen, M. (1971). Cooperation and competition of Mexican, Mexican American, and Anglo American children of two ages under four instructional sets. *Developmental Psychology, 5,* 32.

LaFromboise, T. D. (1988). American Indian Mental Health Policy. *American Psychologist, 43,* 388–397.

Leong, F. (1992). Guidelines for minimizing premature termination among Asian American clients. *Journal for Specialists in Group Work, 17*(4), 219–227.

Locke, D. C. (1996, April). *Multicultural group work.* Paper presented at the meeting of the American Counseling Association, Pittsburgh, PA.

Lopez, S., Grover, K., Holland, D., Johnson, M., Kain, C., Kanel, K., Mellins, C., & Rhyne, M. (1989). Development of culturally sensitive psychotherapists. *Professional Psychology: Research and Practice, 20*(6), 369–376.

Merta, R. J. (1995). Group work: Multicultural perspectives. In J. G. Ponterotto, J. M. Casas, L. A. Suzuki, & C. M. Alexander (Eds.), *Handbook of multicultural counseling* (pp. 567–585). Thousand Oaks, CA: Sage Publications.

Newlon, B., & Arciniega, M. (1983). Counseling minority families: An Adlerian perspective. *Counseling & Human Development, 16*(4), 1–12.

Padilla, A. M. (1980). The role of cultural awareness and ethnic loyalty in acculturation. In A. M. Padilla (Ed.), *Acculturation: Theory, models, and some new findings.* Boulder, CO: Westview Press.

Parham, T. A. (1989). Cycles of psychological nigrescence. *Counseling Psychologist, 17,* 187–226.

Pedersen, P. B. (1988). *A handbook for developing multicultural awareness.* Alexandria, VA: American Association for Counseling and Development.

Ruiz, R., & Padilla, A. (1977). Counseling Latinos. *Personnel & Guidance Journal, 7,* 401–408.

Sabnani, H. B., Ponterotto, J. G., & Borodovsky, L. G. (1991). White racial identity development and cross-cultural counselor training: A stage model. *Counseling Psychologist, 19,* 76–98.

Sanders, D. (1987). Cultural conflicts: An important factor in the academic failures of American Indian students. *Journal of Multicultural Counseling and Development, 15*(2), 81–90.

Shon, S. D., & Ja, D. Y. (1982). Asian families. In M. McGoldrich, J. Pearce, & J. Giordano (Eds.), *Ethnicity and family therapy.* (pp. 208–228). New York: Guilford.

Sue, D. W., Arredondo, P., & McDavis, R. (1992). Multicultural counseling competencies and standards: A call to the profession. *Journal of Counseling & Development, 70,* 477–486.

Sue, D. W., Bernier, J. E., Durran, A., Feinberg, L., Pedersen, P. B., Smith, E. J., & Vasquez-Nuttall, E. (1982). Cross-cultural counseling competencies. *Counseling Psychologist, 10*(2), 45–52.

Sue, D. W., Ivey, A. E., & Pedersen, P. B. (1996). *A theory of multicultural counseling and therapy.* Pacific Grove, CA: Brooks/Cole.

Sue, D. W., & Sue, D. (1990). *Counseling the culturally different: Theory and practice* (2nd ed.). New York: Wiley.

Vacc, N., & Wittmer, J. (1980). *Let me be me: Special populations and the helping professional.* Muncie, IN: Accelerated Development.

Part Three

Theme-Focused

Groups

~

The three chapters in this section of the text are designed to provide guidelines for those interested in leading groups that have as their focus and unifying element a single theme. Each theme demands a specific informational base and also effective techniques and approaches.

The growing prominence of self-help groups in the field of mental health is an affirmation that contact with others who are facing similar difficulties can empower individuals to act on their individual and collective needs. Chapter 9, "Group Counseling: Self-Enhancement," applies the foundational information provided in earlier chapters of this book to self-help and counseling groups with a focus on self-enhancement.

The chapter attempts to answer the questions: Why have self-help groups become so widely used? What does self-enhancement mean in relation to self-help groups? Why is self-enhancement a major focus in counseling groups? What aspects of group structure, process, and content are most effective in facilitating self-enhancement? In answering these questions, the author discusses the emphasis on individualism, individuals' responsibility to others, individual and contextual determinants of self-enhancement, and the physical and social contexts of self-enhancement as they relate to the role each plays in either supporting or complicating self-enhancement as an approach to aiding individuals in the growth process. The discussion then turns to consciousness-raising, instilling hope and commitment, and empowerment.

Chapter 10, "Group Counseling: Career and Lifestyle Issues," points out that although group counseling or therapy has grown enormously in the past 45 years, only modest attention has been given to the idea of career counseling as a theme for groups. Among the advantages of this group format are the resulting enhancement of career counseling outcomes, the support and encouragement of fellow members, efficiency in terms of time and cost, enhanced feedback, more personalizing and sharing of information, and the variety a group affords. The elements of career group counseling, applied concepts of the career literature to career group counseling, application of group theory to career group counseling, appropriate counseling skills, process, components, and techniques for career group counseling, and age-specific variations are all described in a practical, informative manner for the aspiring group work specialist.

Life entails a series of losses, and people need varying amounts of support for the grief that accompanies loss. Many of the needs resulting from a loss can be addressed within a group setting, where members can share common problems, provide mutual aid, and develop coping skills. The purpose of Chapter 11, "Group Counseling: Loss," is to provide the reader with both information and practical guidelines for leading theme-focused groups on the topic of loss.

As these chapters indicate, the effective use of group approaches is based upon a combination of knowledge and the ability to apply that knowledge in the group setting. These chapters also offer evidence that group knowledge and skill have wide application in the helping professions.

9

Group Counseling:
Self-Enhancement

Richard E. Pearson

To make self-enhancement a focal point of group counseling, though not controversial, may at first seem a bit arcane. Why not just talk about autonomy, self-direction, or self-efficacy? Why self-enhancement? The growing prominence of self-help groups as mental health resources for individuals with personal and interpersonal difficulties has highlighted the importance and utility of self-enhancement. Implicitly and explicitly, these groups point out the significance of self- and peer-based help. They affirm the view that contact with others facing similar difficulties can empower individuals to act on their individual and collective needs and interests. Self-enhancement and empowerment are major themes running through self-help and other nonprofessionally oriented helping approaches (Zimmerman, Isreal, Schulz, & Checkoway, 1992). Perhaps something is going on in these approaches to which group leaders should pay attention.

To state that groups will contribute to the personal and interpersonal competence of members is to state the obvious. But when self-enhancement becomes a central focus of group work, the meaning of "growth in clients' effectiveness" becomes narrower. It brings up the possible contradiction that counseling groups might not contribute significantly to helping members act in self-enhancing ways.

The assertion that the ability to "self-enhance" is a possible but not necessary subset of personal effectiveness suggests that we question what self-enhancement is and what place it has in the counseling process.

- What is self-enhancement?
- Why should self-enhancement be a focus in counseling intervention?
- What variations of group structure, process, and content are most effective in contributing to self-enhancement?

A View of Self Enhancement ⌇

Consider the following assertions:

- Self-enhancement consists of actions, by individuals, that represent their intention to promote their interests (e.g., well-being, rights, opportunities).
- Self-enhancement action varies as a function of individual-based (e.g., motivation, skill) and context-based (e.g., peer support, social norms) variables.
- Self-enhancement can be considered a multilevel construct, reflecting the intention to promote one's interests in social settings ranging from informal, face-to-face relationships (e.g., family, peer group) to relationships that are an aspect of one's membership in formal, distant associations (e.g., the community, the nation).
- Self-enhancement can be pursued through a wide range of actions ranging from high profile, apparent behaviors such as defiance to quieter, less noticeable actions such as biding one's time or letting small slights "roll off one's back."

Based on these assertions, self-enhancement is a construct well within the boundaries of counseling concern. Its aim of encouraging individuals toward self-direction is a familiar counseling theme. Because it is rooted in a person's attitudes and behavioral repertoires, self-enhancement is reasonably addressed by the standard array of individual and group interventions. Fostering clients' self-enhancement ability clearly is something that counselors might address. But we should also ask why.

The Significance of Self Enhancement as a Focus in Counseling ⌇

For a variety of reasons, contributing to members' self-enhancing ability might be perceived as an important outcome of a counseling group. These reasons can be viewed as clustering around two considerations: pragmatics and ideology.

Self-Enhancement as Pragmatics

From a practical position, because virtually all forms of assistance offered in counseling groups are time limited, it makes sense to prepare people for life after the group by equipping them with the attitudes, knowledge, and skills (cognitive and behavioral) that will allow them to maintain and extend the gains the group experience has helped them achieve. From this perspective, groups that operate under a "learning to learn" strategy are most effective. At the same time that individuals' presenting concerns are addressed, the individuals are enlisted as active partners in resolving those concerns. Because of this dual focus of responding to the present and preparing for the future, the nature of the process becomes just as important to the group leader as the effectiveness in resolving those concerns.

Keeping group members actively involved in resolving their concerns presumably increases the likelihood that they will acquire problem-solving strategies, knowledge, and skills and be able to bring them to bear in solving future concerns (Bond & Keys, 1993). This can be seen in the following passage from Carl Rogers' early book *Counseling and Psychotherapy* (1942), in which Rogers asserts that counselors should focus on current and future issues alike:

> The aim is not to solve one particular problem but to assist the individual to *grow*, so that he can cope with the present problem and with later problems in a better integrated fashion. If he can gain enough integration to handle one problem in more independent, more responsible, less confused, better organized ways, then he will also handle new problems in that manner. (pp. 28–29)

Self-Enhancement and the Pragmatics of Prevention   In a similar vein, strengthening self-management and self-enhancement resources, and preparing individuals to handle future life demands more effectively, can be viewed as a preventive strategy for warding off a variety of difficulties (Conyne, 1987). When viewed as prevention, counseling can help thwart acquiring dysfunctionality and ameliorate suffering. For example, acquiring effective parenting skills as a result of participating in a group for first-time parents can help a couple approach the responsibilities and pressures of child rearing in a more relaxed, effective way than they would otherwise. This could be expected to translate into a nurturing, supportive, family environment. If that translation occurs, the family will foster children who are more robust in terms of their personal and interpersonal effectiveness than might have been the case without the parents' involvement in the parenting group.

Self-Enhancement and the Conservation of Professional Help   Helping people pursue their own self-enhancement has another possible benefit: It can ease the demand for always-scarce professional helping resources. Self-enhancement can reduce the need for counseling. Professional helpers tend to view families and peer groups as hothouses for the growth of dysfunctionality (Heller, 1979), but natural networks can be reservoirs of positive assistance as well. Enhancing individuals' access to the resources of family, peer, neighborhood, and work support systems can lead to the resolution of personal and interpersonal difficulties without resorting to formal, professional assistance (Meissen, Mason, & Gleason, 1991; Pearson, 1990).

A case can be made (and many group-centered cultures and subcultures would make that case) that knowing one's place within the group, looking to it for assistance, and being willing to accept its helping efforts represent a superior general strategy for dealing with life's demands. Perhaps, after all, the preference for individual autonomy or for integration into the group is as much a matter of personal and group ideology as it is a determination of which general strategy is most efficient.

Self-Enhancement as Ideology

The importance attached to self-enhancement usually derives from individual, subjective judgments about what is good and right. These value judgments are involved in one's definition of the effective, admirable person. Fostering self-enhancement abilities can be held as a proper concern in group counseling because it moves individuals closer to widely held formulations of personal self-effectiveness.

Self-Enhancement as Personal Ideology   Observers of the American scene (such as Alexis de Tocqueville, Ralph Waldo Emerson, and Max Weber) have noted that independence and self-reliance are prized in the national ethos. Standing on one's own, and making one's own way underlie the notion of the effective, successful person (Bellah, Madsen, Sullivan, Swidler, & Tipton, 1985). To be dependent, to be unable to care for oneself, or to need reassurance and confirmation from others is to be considered weak in body or character, incompetent, unsuccessful, and even pitiable.

Given this perspective, promoting movement toward autonomy and self-direction seems to represent a reasonable outcome for counseling groups. Pragmatic considerations aside, many helping professionals in America assume that autonomy is "better" than dependence. In a careful analysis of the roots and consequences of this emphasis on individual achievement and self-direction, Bellah et al. (1985) specifically called attention to how psychotherapy "reinforces the traditional individualism of American culture, including the concept of utilitarian individuals maximizing their own interests" (p. 104).

Goble (1970) noted that the "third force" perspectives articulated by Abraham Maslow, Carl Rogers, Rollo May, and others can be understood (at least in part) as a reaction to the dominant role that psychoanalytic and behavioral perspectives had, until then, exerted in American psychology. Both psychoanalysis and behaviorism have a strong deterministic tone, viewing the individual as essentially reactive in nature and functioning in response to instinctive or environment-based forces (Allport, 1962). When extended to human service activities, these perspectives have tended to generate strategies that emphasize helper control and helped compliance (Trivette, Dunst, & Hamby, 1996). With their assumption of individuals' potential for independence and self-direction, person-centered and other third force theorists and practitioners have conceptualized the helping process as being based on respect for people's growth potential and highlighting the importance of counselor-counselee collaboration.

The emergence of self-enhancement, empowerment, and self-help constructs in professional and popular literatures might be viewed as the current face of the long-standing American propensity to prize the self-defining, competent, achieving individual as the model of personal effectiveness. Although this pragmatism draws helping professionals toward the means/ends utility of behavioral approaches, and our fascination with mysteries (what's behind the closed door?) entices us to find psychoanalytic and other "depth" perspectives intriguing, our bedrock values are most compatible with views of the helping process that speak the language of autonomy, self-direction, and personal responsibility.

Self-Enhancement as Social Ideology   At another level, self-enhancement can be viewed as central to the proper relationship between society and the individual. The

American Declaration of Independence is based on the view that governments exist to preserve the rights of individuals. One of those basic rights, specifically cited, is the freedom to pursue one's happiness (to act to further one's interests and needs). Governments that unwarrantedly restrain self-enhancement subvert their raison d'e-tre and deserve to be overthrown. Because the government is created by and for us, we as citizens have the responsibility of active involvement in the ongoing process of monitoring and shaping it to be responsive to our needs. Participation in the processes of government is, thus, not only a basic right but also a duty.

In her analysis of mutual help organizations, Marie Killilea (1976) pointed out that this widespread social phenomenon not only has deep, long-standing cultural and historical roots but it also reflects important dimensions of contemporary American life. She saw mutual help groups as expressions of the American ideal of participation and self-determination. Just as the consumer movement represents individuals' attempt to influence the production and distribution of material goods, so the mutual help movement can be considered an expression of individuals' desire to influence decisions that shape the character and delivery of mental health services.

Viewed from this perspective, the line between the personal and the political dissolves. When individuals seek out the assistance of a medical or a mental health professional, they enter a system that is as clearly defined in terms of its assumptions about power, responsibility, and rights and privileges as any explicitly "political" system. Vattano (1972) suggested that the self-help phenomenon can be understood as a reaction to a mental health establishment that has, in some respects, become unresponsive to the needs and influence of its recipients. Through self-help groups, individuals seize ownership of the helping process. Rather than being channeled into a passive "patient" role, they are able to enter into decision-making and help-delivery processes.

At a societal level, the consumerism and demand for participation that self-help groups represent can be seen as resulting in what Killilea (1976) labeled an "alternative care giving system." At an individual and immediate social network level (in this instance, the helping group), it often enables individuals to pursue their own interests and needs. In the process, they not only become empowered to "self-enhance" but also experience the boost in self-worth and personal efficacy that commonly result from having the opportunity or responsibility to assist their peers (Reissman, 1965).

Increased self-worth, heightened personal efficacy, growing self-enhancement—certainly these are outcomes of interest to the counselor who works with groups. Group leaders can learn some lessons from the structure, process, and outcome of self-help groups.

Self-Enhancement and Responsibility to Others Determining who or what to use as the standard for identifying where an individual's personal or collective interests really lie brings one into the domains of personal and social ideology with which group leaders must (or ought to) wrestle as they take on the audacious task of presuming to act as agents for others' growth and development. Given that one person's self-enhancement may be seen by another as self-indulgence or exploitive self-aggrandizement, interventions to facilitate others' ability to act in their own interests must be carried out within some social framework of understanding about the proper balance between an individual's rights and his or her responsibility to others.

Though individualism and self-enhancement can be viewed as foundational American values, these values have mixed consequences. Untrammeled individualism has been blamed for diverse contemporary social phenomena including, to mention just a few, the decline of volunteerism, dangerously high levels of personal debt, weakening of the extended and nuclear families, the escalating incidence of addiction, neglect of elders, and underfunding of the public schools. Tension between individual striving and responsibility to others is not new to American life. As Bellah et al. (1985) pointed out, however, the weakening of civic and religious traditions, which historically have acted to counterbalance individual striving, has disrupted traditional strategies for accommodating self-enhancement and responsibility toward the collective. The resulting imbalance has precipitated a range of crises that threaten the coherence and unity of American society. As noted in Bellah et al. (1985):

> The question is whether an individualism in which the self has become the main form of reality can really be sustained. What is at issue is not simply whether self-contained individuals might withdraw from the public sphere to pursue purely private ends, but whether such individuals are capable of sustaining either a public or a private life. (p. 148)

How can counseling intervention strike a balance between fostering individuality and maintaining the integrity of the collective? Person-centered theory has proposed the existence of an essentially positive human nature. If genuinely given a chance for expression, a person's most basic tendency is to "value those objects, experiences, and goals which make for his own survival, growth, and development, and for the survival and development of others" (Rogers, 1989, p. 183). From the person-centered perspective, counseling that is genuinely effective will lead to the emergence (or further emergence) of people who will (because that is their "nature") be inclined to make choices that fairly balance their own needs and interests and those of others. Thus, the challenge is not how to *make* others be responsible but, rather, how to *allow* them to be.

Others (e.g., psychoanalytic theorists) who hold a less sanguine view of the basic stuff of humanity tend to stress the importance of strengthening responsible behavior by maintaining a functional level of internalized social control. Optimum personal effectiveness occurs when the superego sets down limits of what is acceptable that are sufficiently broad to allow a reasonable array of real-world alternatives in satisfying physical and social needs while still maintaining effective control over self-gratification impulses.

Similarly, behaviorally oriented theorists and practitioners cite the necessity of ensuring that individuals are quickly confronted with, and held responsible for, the consequences of their actions. Skinner (1971), for example, asserted that much contemporary antisocial behavior (e.g., industrial pollution) is the result of too great a lag between actions and their consequences. As society becomes ever more complex, and as communities become more and more impersonal, connections between many classes of action and their consequence can become blurred. With this distortion comes a decline in the effectiveness of the process through which individuals are "taught" to behave responsibly.

Turning more specifically to groups, this matter of avoiding possible discontinuity between the consequences of individuals' self-enhancement and the needs of the collective is important, especially when focusing upon groups as vehicles to foster self-enhancement. Those who witnessed the heyday of the human potential movement of the 1970s may recall that one criticism leveled at small-group activities was that they concentrated too heavily on encouraging self-direction, self-expression, and self-preoccupation to the detriment of responsibility toward, and concern for, others. How may counseling groups in general, and groups supporting growth in members' self-enhancement ability in particular, work toward balancing individual and collective interests?

Determinants of Self-Enhancement ∿

The extent to which self-enhancement in individuals varies as a function of individual- or setting-based variables is an essential consideration. Narrow identification with sociological or psychological perspectives might cause group leaders to emphasize the importance of either contextual or individual factors in developing and maintaining attitudes and behaviors that support self-enhancement. Group leaders might see the willingness and ability to pursue one's interests as being rooted primarily in a supportive, confirming social context (family, neighborhood, school, community, nation) that presents self-assertion as normative, appropriate behavior. Conversely, they might view self-enhancement as being dependent primarily upon personal characteristics such as ego strength, self-assertion skills, or internal locus of control.

Espousing one or the other view that self-enhancement is primarily the consequence of contextual or of individual-based variables quickly translates into a preference for counseling strategies that center either on individual clients or on their social/physical contexts. An individual focus moves one toward traditional individual and group interventions that consider individuals to be separate, autonomous entities. In contrast, as Pattison (1973) noted, group leaders might consider self-enhancement (and most other behavior clusters) to be the manifestation of social forces acting upon individuals. This channels counselors and other human service workers toward interventions that, like family counseling or network therapy (Attneave, 1976; Rueveni, 1979), directly involve the social systems within which individuals lead their lives.

In the arena of counseling practice, hard-and-fast dichotomies have a way of crumbling. Group leaders have ample opportunity to see individuals being shaped by situations as well as to observe situations being transformed by the actions of individuals. Certainly, some families and neighborhoods foster hopelessness and power-lessness in their members, just as other families and neighborhoods are transformed by the growth in personal awareness and skill of their members.

In attempting to understand the presence or absence of self-enhancing behavior in group members, perhaps the most useful stance is to remain sensitive to the oper-ation of both individual- and context-based factors and to expect to find both domains functioning in an interdependent way. This willingness to consider both individual- and context-based factors in self-enhancement will, in turn, open up a wider range of counseling interventions and strategies for fostering the self-enhanc-ing ability of group members.

Individual Determinants of Self-Enhancement

What are the foundations of self-enhancement? What individual attitudes, beliefs, perceptions, or skills support or allow the expression of self-enhancement (Zimmerman et al., 1992)? Once group leaders have identified the individual-based characteristics upon which group members' self-enhancement rests, they can search for interventions that increase the group members' self-enhancement ability and activity. In helping group members develop or increase whatever prerequisite attrib-utes or skills they lack, group leaders empower them to act in their own interests.

One way of organizing the individual-based variables that can affect individu-als' willingness or ability to carry out self-enhancing actions is to consider these variables as falling into one of three categories:

1. Variables that relate to individuals' *awareness.*
2. Variables that relate to hope or *intention.*
3. Variables that relate to *knowledge or behavioral skill.*

Table 9.1 presents and elaborates on these categories and traces general strategies and specific interventions that can foster self-enhancement ability and activity.

Using the group counseling context to affect individuals' awareness, intentions, and skills is, of course, a broader matter than merely promoting self-enhancement. In this book, however, a major emphasis is on identifying how generic group coun-seling processes and activities can be put to work to further group members' ability to take actions that will improve their status vis-à-vis their needs, interests, and rights.

Contextual Determinants of Self-Enhancement

Kurt Lewin's (1951) concept of *life space* has three major components: the "me" (the individual's awareness of his or her physical and nonphysical self), the "not me" (the environment), and the "foreign hull" (those aspects of the current physical context of which the individual is not aware). Lewinian perspectives also hold that in all but the most intellectually limited or emotionally regressed individuals, the "not me" (the context) is experienced as a differentiated phenomenon. That is, parts of the environment are differentiated from one another (e.g., this chair is different from that suitcase), and the process of perceiving imposes patterns and relationships upon

Table 9.1 ~
Self-Enhancement: Determinants and Interventions

Individual-based determinant	Awareness of need for self-enhancement	Intention to take self-enhancing action	Skills required for self-enhancing
Relevant Strategy	Consciousness raising	Instilling hope and commitment	Empowerment
Focus of Specific Counseling Interventions	• Problem recognition (awareness) • Providing access to information relevant to the problem • Fostering understanding of relevant information	• Counselor encouragement and reinforcement • Contact with relevant models, case studies	• Skill acquisition • Role-playing reversal • In situ coaching

these otherwise separate parts of the context (e.g., this chair and that sofa in the other room are both furniture).

One of the most general ways to organize the context is to posit two broad categories: the physical environment and the social environment. The *physical environment* consists of the nonhuman (animate and inanimate) objects and derivative processes (e.g., weather, distance) that constitute the life space. The *social environment* is made up of human beings and their actions (e.g., my mate, social support, condemnation) that the individual perceives to be a part of the present setting.

The Physical Context and Self-Enhancement   As technology advances, people increasingly acquire the ability to transcend, or at least lessen, many of the limits formerly posed by the physical environment. For example, distances that in past eras reduced or eliminated options for action, assistance, and understanding can now be bridged through physical travel and electronic information exchange. Still, one cannot completely escape the influence of the physical setting. A malfunctioning automobile, furnace, or elevator is a quick reminder of the fragility of the technological buffer that insulates people from the demands of physical reality.

Individuals and groups with restricted access to relevant technology are most apt to be affected by limitations imposed by the physical context. For example, although living in a rural area does not necessarily eliminate alternatives for action (an automobile, fax machine, telephone, computer, and modem can put a rural dweller in touch with extensive information networks and well-placed helpers), if rural residence is accompanied by lack of access to supportive technological resources, tasks such as gaining necessary information, communicating needs and views, and locating and mobilizing the assistance of others can be problematic.

One of the unique benefits of the group setting is the opportunity it allows individuals to exchange, and pool, needed information. Isolated individuals (whether their isolation comes from the lack of transportation and communication resources accompanying rurality or from the anomie and sense of personal danger found in deteriorated urban settings) often are not even aware of the existence of others who share their concerns. Physical isolation can also cut off information about the alternatives available for constructive, self-enhancing action. The group setting, involving as it does the gathering of people, can reduce group members' physical isolation, allowing them to gain access to information about the nature, scope, and remediation of their concerns.

Social Contexts and Self-Enhancement   Although the physical environment sometimes complicates self-enhancement action, the social context usually is a more important consideration, because a person's most important primary and secondary needs typically are mediated by the characteristics and processes of the social context. For instance, in modern life, access to food is apt to depend more on a person's relationship to others (family members, employers) than on the vagaries of climate and soil conditions in the area.

Social contexts can affect self-enhancement activity in a variety of ways. Two mechanisms found in social contexts that are of particular interest to group leaders are social norms and social support.

Social Norms   Defining culture as a set of meanings that group members hold in common, Olmsted (1959) suggested that group norms can be considered an aspect of culture. Norms embody the group's position regarding the correct understanding of, and response to, situations. With regard to self-enhancement, group norms of special note are those that relate to defining what an individual's proper rights and interests are and what actions are appropriate in the pursuit of self-enhancement.

Norms relating to the nature and scope of individual rights can have a notable impact on determining when self-enhancement is appropriate. If, for example, a group's norms hold that members of a particular gender or religious or ethnic group should not work in a certain discipline, even the objects of this discrimination may not be able to perceive that their rights and interests are being usurped. Much of what has been called consciousness-raising can be understood as the process of sensitizing unaware individuals to how existing norms work against their interests. Self-help approaches to combating racism, sexism, ageism, and other forms of exploitation often begin with those affected people developing an understanding of how existing norms work against their interests. Without this awareness, the oppressed are likely to view self-enhancement as irrelevant or inappropriate. Similarly, without a change in group norms concerning the appropriate limits of rights, individuals acting upon their own view of what is proper are likely to earn such labels as "uppity," "unappreciative," "selfish," or "dangerous."

One of the most valuable functions of self-help groups is to provide individuals with a context in which the norms (unlike those of the broader social context) are more supportive of what they believe their needs and interests are. For example, self-help groups of stigmatized or exploited individuals confirm that members' difficulties are not all of their own making. Also, the self-help group can reinforce the members' view that their needs to be accepted, be treated with equity, and receive assistance are reasonable. The shifting of people's normative referents is a central part of consciousness-raising efforts.

Even when there is general acceptance of the appropriateness of self-enhancement, norms can limit and shape the actions individuals might take in furthering their rights and interests. For instance, the deliberate, circumspect process of working through channels might be considered commendable, whereas confrontive strategies such as picketing or presenting a list of nonnegotiable demands may be condemned as inappropriate. Again, being in the company of others who are in the same boat can reinforce individuals who are pursuing a confrontive, high-profile strategy to promote their interests. Collective will and support can offer members alternatives with the potential to budge the status quo and move it in the direction of needed change.

Social Support   Shumaker and Brownell's (1984) view that social support is a resource whose function is to help individuals cope with life demands overlaps many other positions found in the literature. Supporters "support" by providing resources individuals need in attempting to deal with a wide range of ordinary and extraordinary problematic life events.

Social norms can exert a powerful influence on one's willingness to offer supportive assistance. If a person's self-enhancement efforts are viewed as inappropriate, relatives and peers are apt to be indifferent to (or perhaps even oppose) entreaties for support. Thus, young adults who assert what they believe are their valid interests in the employment setting may be viewed by co-workers as troublemakers or as overstepping their "place." Rather than supporting their self-assertion, co-workers may react with ridicule or ostracism.

Further, support may not be forthcoming from the informal social network because of supporter-based deficiencies (Pearson, 1990). People in informal social networks may not only lack the inclination to be supportive, but they may also lack the skills, information, or resources needed to help individuals undertake self-enhancing activity. For example, the parents of Bob, an epileptic adolescent, might want to support his efforts to assert his interests in the face of stereotyping and discrimination in an educational setting; however, lacking information, skills, and material resources related to effective self-enhancement action, Bob's parents are likely to be limited in their ability to offer support.

Elsewhere (Pearson, 1983), I have termed support groups "surrogate support systems" that provide individuals with emotional and material support not available from the informal support network because of *network-based barriers* (e.g., supporter's lack of willingness or skills) rather than because of the operation of *barriers in those individuals* (e.g., the individual's lack of skill or information, or dysfunctional attitudes). In the latter case (i.e., support deficiency stemming from person-based barriers), I suggest that traditional individual and small-group counseling or psychotherapy interventions are appropriate.

Group Counseling and Self Enhancement ∿

The process and (to a lesser extent) content of counseling groups can be directed specifically to the goal of promoting members' movement toward effective self-enhancement. As indicated in Table 9.1, the process of group interaction can contribute to (a) increasing members' awareness of the need for self-enhancement (consciousness-raising); (b) strengthening members' intention to take self-enhancing action (instilling hope/commitment); and (c) helping members acquire or improve the knowledge and skills required for self-enhancement (empowerment). The *content* of group interaction, too, can contribute to members' self-enhancement skills. As examples, information can be provided in groups that members will find useful in pursuing their interests, and "packages" blending materials and activities that further members' skills in such domains as self-assertion, decision making, or self-esteem can be offered to strengthen self-enhancement efforts. Although the content of group interaction will vary, the process dimension of group life is generic, found across groups, whatever their content and desired outcomes.

Understanding group process requires a focus on *how* group goals are pursued, for group process is seen in the characteristics of the actions (group activities and events) through which the group seeks to achieve its purposes. For example, the process of one counseling group might be described as tightly tied to the decisions of a central leader who pursues the group's goals by closely adhering to a predetermined agenda. The process of another counseling group might be described as featuring someone who fills a position called "leader" but who really seems to exert no more influence than any other group member as the group moves from activity to activity in an apparently spontaneous, unplanned fashion.

As McLuhan (1964) and others have pointed out, characteristics of the medium through which communication takes place often contribute strongly to the impact of the communication. Similarly, the characteristics of the process through which a group pursues its ends can have a powerful influence upon group outcomes. Thus, process is not unrelated to outcome; rather, it can influence what, and to what degree, outcomes will be achieved.

Dorothy Nolte's (1989) insightful poem "Children Learn What They Live" explores the connection between the process and outcome of child rearing. Three stanzas of that poem seem particularly relevant to counseling as a means of fostering individuals' self-enhancement ability:

> *If children live with encouragement,*
> *They learn confidence.*
>
> *If children live with security,*
> *They learn to have faith.*
>
> *If children live with approval,*
> *They learn to like themselves.*
>
> *(pp. 95–96)*

In the realm of counseling, Rogers and other relationship-oriented theorists and practitioners have come to similar conclusions about the connection between process and outcome, taking the position that the process of the helping relationship should reflect the goals of those in counseling. If counseling seeks to move individuals toward greater self-acceptance, the group leader's behavior should, then, reflect a high level of acceptance of the person. Similarly, if group leaders hope for greater self-direction and autonomy in group members as an outcome of group work, the process should offer opportunities for the members to enter into decision making that determines group activity and outcome.

If group leaders accept the "process shapes outcome" thesis, the examination of group counseling as a vehicle for fostering self-enhancement logically turns to a consideration of how major elements of group process, including leadership and therapeutic mechanisms, can contribute to self-enhancement in the group counseling situation.

Leadership

In their review of the theory and research related to group leadership, Cartwright and Zander (1968) noted a movement away from considering leadership to be a specific person, or a position in a group's role structure, toward thinking of leadership as a function. In this view, leadership consists of any contribution (e.g., exerting influence, providing information, offering comfort, making suggestions) to the group's ability to achieve its goals.

The Functional Perspective   One of the most important consequences of viewing group leadership from a *functional perspective* is that it leads to the recognition that group leadership may be a *shared* function. Although it is conceivable that one person will provide all the many and varied resources a group needs to achieve its goals, a careful, unbiased examination of group life more likely will reveal that a number of members (at any given point, or across longer time frames) are actually contributing to the group's success. Even in groups that do not explicitly espouse a shared leadership pattern, members other than the designated leader quietly carry out actions that can be considered leadership from the functional perspective.

A functional view of leadership also departs from the traditional view that all leaders are a certain type of person (e.g., charismatic, powerful) doing similar things (e.g., directing, coordinating, evaluating) in all groups. Rather, the functional perspective holds that as group goals and resources vary, so will the content and structure of leadership. Thus, leadership in a task-oriented group where only one person who possesses the information and skills upon which group success rests is apt to be very different from leadership in a person-oriented group where many members have the resources needed to foster and support personal growth.

Group-centered leadership is one of the most conspicuous features of self-help groups. Even in groups that adhere to a "leader of the meeting" format, the "leader" clearly is an equal among equals, having no special prerogatives or influence (Levy, 1979; Schubert & Borkman, 1991). Designating one member as the leader does not interfere with the group's usual manner (i.e., peer-based help) of pursuing its goal.

Self-help groups, then, stand as good examples of the implementation (by design, chance, or intuition) of a function-centered, shared model of leadership. They have as their basis a self-help model of assistance that "emphasizes empowerment, self-determination, mutuality, [the] noncommodity character of help, prosumerism, antibig, antibureaucratic, and experiential wisdom, among other values" (Borkman, 1990, p. 328). That they are also powerful contributors to the development of resources relevant to self-enhancement, such as social support, hope, self-esteem, and skill acquisition, should make the leadership processes of self-help groups of interest to the leaders of counseling and other helping groups. Can any principles and practices, gleaned from an examination of the leadership function in these groups, be extrapolated to the group counseling situation in which a concern for supporting members' movement toward self-enhancement is central?

The Group Leader as Facilitator   Whether the group leader likes it or not, group members will try to be helpful to one another. Though professional eyes may see these helping efforts as ineffective (at best) or noxious (at worst), it is virtually impossible to keep members from comforting, giving advice, confronting, or otherwise taking a host of actions that their inclinations and experience cause them to believe will be helpful. Flying in the face of the assumptions of many professional help models, self-help groups place untutored peer help center stage as the method through which growth is to be achieved (Hurvitz, 1970). Most of these groups have no continuing, formal leadership structure.

Though counseling groups are characterized to varying extents by self-help, and peer-based helping processes (Schubert & Borkman, 1991), a counseling group is not a self-help group (Borkman, 1990; Pearson, 1983). However much professionally trained leaders take a group-centered stance, and stress their commonality with group members, professional ethics and (perhaps) institutional role stamp group leaders as special people, with special responsibilities, in the group. Inescapably, counseling groups have a formal, designated leader.

Even though the reality of this formal role means leaders will never be (or never ought to be) simply group members, leaders can take a range of positions regarding their extent of control in groups. A focus upon growth in clients' self-enhancement capacity as a goal for group work moves leaders toward a functionally oriented, shared view of group leadership. Such a view allows leaders to bring to counseling groups some of the benefits of self-help groups in efforts to strengthen members' self-enhancement ability. In doing so, the leader functions primarily as a facilitator, allowing members to express their self-directing and self-help resources within the group. This can be achieved by:

- communicating (implicitly and explicitly) to group members a functional, shared perspective on group leadership.
- pursuing a general strategy of power sharing by encouraging members to enter into decisions about the group's life.
- identifying existing member resources (e.g., information, feedback, accep-

tance, caring, material assistance) that can help the group move toward its goals, and encouraging members to provide those resources to the group.

- helping members fill gaps in their own resources by supporting the development of skills needed for group progress (e.g., listening skills, understanding, and skills needed for effective group management) and, again, encouraging them to contribute these newly developed resources to the group.

As a facilitator, the group leader seeks to support and empower group members (as individuals and as a group) in pursuing their growth. The leader acts as a stimulus and a resource rather than as an expert who takes responsibility for members' conduct and learning. As in self-help groups, members' ability to manage themselves and contribute to one another's growth is supported. Concomitantly, leaders expect group members to reap the benefit of the increased self-esteem typically associated with taking increased responsibility for, and initiative in, pursuit of their own growth (Reissman, 1990).

Therapeutic Mechanisms

Yalom (1985), building on an earlier schema of Corsini and Rosenberg (1955), identified 11 basic mechanisms that can be considered the source of growth in therapeutic groups. Ranging from the relatively concrete categories of "information sharing" and "development of socializing techniques" to the much more abstract "universality" (recognition that one's difficulties and concerns are shared by others), these mechanisms are basic processes in group life that promote and support members' movement toward greater effectiveness. All of the basic therapeutic mechanisms Yalom described would be expected to be observed (in some form and to some degree) in any effective personal growth-oriented group. The focus here, however, is on those processes that have the most potential in developing, or furthering, members' self-enhancement ability. Referring to the view presented in Table 9.1 that self-enhancement rests upon awareness, intention, and skill, I believe that of the therapeutic mechanisms identified by Yalom, those most central to the quest for self-enhancement are universality, instilling hope, altruism, identification/modeling, and group cohesiveness.

Universality   Perhaps even before a person can hope for change, he or she has to be aware that change is necessary. Whether one's problem comes from individual adjustment difficulties (e.g., substance abuse) or stems from external sources (e.g., racial, ethnic, sexual, or age discrimination), constructive action to resolve the problem is not apt to start until the individual acknowledges that a problem exists.

Consciousness-raising groups seek to help members recognize and affirm that the status quo is not responding to their interests and needs. The status quo may reflect the way a city government operates or how male-female relationships are structured in a marriage. Raising awareness often demands more than simply presenting data confirming a situation of exploitation, neglect, or personal dysfunction. Denial and avoidance processes operating in individuals can make it difficult for them to recognize a problem. Also, habituation can make it hard for people to step far enough out of their situations to see that a string of chronic, but minor, hassles of scattered individuals are part of a broader pattern of societal discrimination.

The group setting can contribute to consciousness-raising through a format that explicitly centers upon relating personal experience and presenting objective information about exploitive or discriminatory situations and patterns. Data about inequity in applying and enforcing laws can help people realize that individual or collective action is needed to protect their interests. Personal accounts of individuals who have recognized their disadvantage and acted to oppose it can spur group members to examine their own life situations for possible inequity and disrespect.

Even in groups that do not focus explicitly upon consciousness-raising, a considerable amount of this basic process can be expected. Voicing and exchanging life experiences are at the heart of the group process. This exchange provides a rich opportunity for individuals to observe patterns and issues that run across the experience of the separate members. As other group members tell their stories, a woman may realize that her personal experience of sexual harassment at work is not an isolated occurrence but, rather, part of a widespread pattern many women face in many different work situations. Similarly, a young girl in a support group for elementary students in divorcing families can, as member after member talks about feeling powerless and ignored, come to realize that as personal as her pain is, others share it; it is a problem whose genesis is out there and not simply of her making.

The process of universalization counteracts the sense of isolation and uniqueness that people in conflict and suffering often feel (Levy, 1979). Being with others who are in the same boat often causes people to feel that, at last, they are understood and accepted. Groups can give individuals access to new norms and points of comparison that make their concerns and difficulties seem less abnormal. In addition, the recognition of commonality can help group members become aware that their own difficulties are only a part of a broader problem. Understanding that one's problem is an instance of a more general pattern serves to demystify and deintensify the problem. It also can form the basis for individual and collective action to deal with that problem. The group setting can be a vehicle for instrumental activity, as well as a channel for expressing one's understandings, feelings, and aspirations.

Instilling Hope   The process of heightening the expectation that improvement will come is common to curing interventions across a wide range of cultural contexts (Frank, 1961). The often noted potency of placebo treatment can be traced to the patient's expectation of improvement. Frank (1961) observed that one of the most common ways of increasing hope is to have a high-prestige person sanction, or be involved in, the helping intervention. Generalizing this phenomenon to the group setting leads to the view that the ability of a group to engender hope in current or potential members would be enhanced by gaining the support and approval of influential people for the group's goals and efforts. Another strategy for increasing the hope-engendering potential of a group would be to enhance the leader's prestige and recognition in the setting.

Self-help groups are different in the sense that hope comes from observing fellow sufferers who have been able to benefit from participation in the group (Hurvitz, 1970; Levy, 1979). Self-help groups have implicit and explicit processes for building hope in group members. In groups following the 12-step model, the emphasis upon recovery as a continuing process rather than an outcome results in members' being at various stages of recovery, from the "first timer" to the veteran with many years of abstinence, at any given meeting. The opportunity for members to see and interact with peers who have gone through the same struggles implicitly teaches that people do get better, that there is hope for improvement. As Hurvitz (1970) noted: "The continued participation by those peers who have been helped by the fellowship supports the expectations of new members that they will receive the help they need and serves as a self-fulfilling prophesy" (p. 46).

More explicitly, self-help groups present direct messages of hope to members. When new members hear a veteran say, "The program does work; the fact that I have been able to turn my life around is testimony to its power—work it!" they gain hope for a way out of their seemingly insurmountable difficulties. When members of a TOPS group see the before-and-after pictures of their group leader, they are supported in their hope that the program can also help them shed their unwanted weight.

Awareness of a problem leads to despair unless that awareness is coupled with hope that there is a solution to the problem. Any counseling group that seeks to bolster members' self-enhancement resources and activities would do well to pay attention to the processes and procedures through which self-help groups instill hope in their members. Counseling groups that operate with an open-ended, continuing framework (i.e., members move into and out of the group rather than all members starting and ending the group at the same time) have a built-in possibility for new members to associate with others who are farther along in the growth process. A format that provides opportunities for "veterans" to talk about their trials and successes can make explicit the implicit message, "People can change; things can get better." Groups that have a closed format might provide for the instilling of hope by having successful "graduates" of the group return to share their stories.

Altruism   The power of altruism (contributing to the well-being of others) to promote growth in the helper has been widely noted. Frank (1961) cited the curative value of altruism as a principle common to healing procedures in a wide range of cultural settings. Reissman (1965) and Levy (1979) also highlighted the positive value of altruism to the helper, noting what might be called a "growth through helping" principle underlying the potency of self-help groups. More recently, Reissman (1990), noting that the role of "help receiver" tends to corrode individuals' feelings of competence and adequacy, suggested mutual help as an appropriate paradigm for human services in the 1990s. He asserted that in most professionally led helping interventions (e.g., counseling, psychotherapy), the help receiver is cast in a role of passivity and inadequacy:

> Besides these iatrogenic difficulties inherent in the helpee's role, the recipient of help is automatically deprived of the benefits accruing to the helper: increased status and self-esteem, the so-called "helpers high" (Luks, 1988), and all the specific helping

mechanisms involved in learning through teaching and the helper therapy principle. (p. 222)

Reissman (1990) asserted that making peer help and cooperation a central part of the ethos of the helping group strengthens the "growth through helping mechanism" of an intervention. In a counseling group, the benefits of helping can be furthered in a number of ways, some of which relate to the leader's attitudes and values, others more with procedural issues.

Perhaps the most important influence in determining the level of peer-to-peer assistance in a counseling group is the extent to which the group leader is willing to sanction and encourage peer-to-peer help rather than considering it to be an annoying, negative influence. Many group leaders neglect the possible benefits of peer help, either because they do not recognize its therapeutic potential or because they see it as a mechanism that is detrimental to their own impact upon the group.

A functionally oriented, shared model of group leadership encourages peer help. Recognition that many of the resources needed for group progress may be distributed among members can counterbalance group leaders' unexamined assumptions about the uniqueness and unmatched efficacy of help offered by professionals that preparation programs of helping professionals spawn or do little to temper (Reissman, 1990). The group leader should realistically assess the helping resources that group members have, rather than assuming that because group members "need help," they are devoid of helping resources.

Furthermore, the group leader seeking to enhance the therapeutic impact of peer help will encourage members to be involved with one another's growth and will make sure that the flow of members' helping resources is not obstructed by an assumption that the group belongs to the leader, an assumption that causes members to think their proper role is to be passive recipients of the expert's efforts. As the leader moves toward considering leadership as a group function, a process is set in motion that results in group members becoming "prosumers" (producers) in the helping process. Reissman (1990) described the prosumer model of help as promoting reciprocity, destigmatizing the negative attitude toward receiving help, empowering help receivers, and forming communities.

When the leader observes genuine gaps in members' helping resources, he or she should consider ways of helping members develop and gain access to those resources. Fostering members' helping skills may be as indirect as modeling the skills the members are lacking, with the assumption that such modeling will stimulate members to gradually acquire those skills. Fostering members' helping skills may also be done explicitly. For example, the leader might stop group interaction to give a mini-lecture on how to impart and receive feedback or to make a process observation on the characteristic decision-making strategy the group is using. Then the leader might go on to encourage members to examine the consequences of, and alternatives to, that decision-making strategy.

There are many ideology-based reasons for counseling groups to adopt self-help groups' reliance on peer help. As noted, there are also many therapeutically based reasons. As important as ideological and therapeutic considerations are, however, the group leader who holds self-enhancement as an important goal for group work believes that supporting and encouraging altruism will increase the likelihood that the group experience will be an empowering and competence-building one for group members. One broad benefit of this empowerment may well be improved attitudes, intentions, and skills members need to pursue self-enhancement.

Identification and Modeling If leaders focus primarily on the inadequacies and dysfunctionalities of group members, the possibility that those members might identify with one another, and use one another as models, will be cause for alarm. The concern that group members will "just sit around and reinforce one another's pathology" tends to accompany a view of group process in which the leader is considered the primary therapeutic resource, bearing the responsibility of countering the pathogenic possibilities of member-to-member contact.

Clearly, self-help groups take a different stance regarding peer influence. Instead of being concerned that member-to-member influence will be negative, the self-help group is founded on the assumption that peers can help one another toward resolving their difficulties. Powell (1987) pinpointed peer-based modeling as a central growth-enhancing mechanism of self-help groups. People at different levels of "recovery" (a term used here to refer to movement away from a wide range of dysfunctional conditions) demonstrate a wide range of relevant models.

> The prospective imitator usually will be encouraged by the differences among models. Variety increases the chance that he or she can match an effective pattern. The success experienced by models also encourages imitation. For even before imitation occurs, the prospective imitator-member shares vicariously in the success of the model. To the extent prospective imitators perceive important similarities to the model, they will be encouraged. (Reissman & Gartner, 1987, p. 110)

Identification and modeling in self-help groups clearly can influence a myriad of attitudes and behavior. Members can "catch" functional attitudes such as hope, perseverance, concern for others, patience, and existential equanimity. Also, members can glean from other members specific coping strategies, such as asking for help, publicly admitting failures, and substituting constructive behaviors for accustomed destructive patterns. How can identification and modeling be extrapolated to a counseling group that seeks to promote members' self-enhancement?

If counseling group members are to acquire the awareness, intentions, and skills that support self-enhancement, the group has to include individuals who can successfully model those attitudes and behaviors. A continuing, open-ended group format extends the range of models available to group members. A "self-help ethos" (Reissman & Gartner, 1987) emphasizing members' responsibility for both offering and receiving help may assist members in viewing their "work" in the group as continuing well after they have attained some success in resolving the difficulties that brought them to the group. The very presence of these successful veterans who are now getting on with their lives, looking after their interests, can provide new members with models for growth. Moreover, explicitly casting these members in the role of mentors and guides can highlight the cluster of behaviors and attitudes called self-enhancement.

The counseling group leader who works in a closed format will have to be creative in broadening the range of models available to group members. Inviting successful graduates of earlier groups to interact with current group members may be helpful. Also, the possibility of involving veterans (and other good models) in a "sponsor program," based on the practice (in 12-step groups) of linking new members with individuals who are farther along in the recovery process, might be explored. However it is done, recognizing the power of identification and modeling in self-help groups alerts group leaders to ways of getting a piece of the action in professionally led groups.

Group Cohesiveness According to Cartwright and Zander (1968), group cohesiveness varies as a function of the extent to which group members perceive the group as an effective vehicle for satisfying their needs. As members increasingly believe they need the group, they are more attracted to it. Cartwright and Zander also asserted that one of the consequences of group cohesiveness is enhanced member receptivity to group influence. Evidence of the influence of a cohesive group can be seen in group members' attitudinal and behavioral homogeneity with regard to issues and situations relevant to the group's operation. Because the group is important to its members (i.e., the satisfaction of important needs is, at least to some extent, dependent upon the group), they tend to want to meet group expectations.

By accepting, and continuing, membership in a group, individuals also accept a body of norms that often differs markedly from those of the broader social context. For example, counseling groups directly and indirectly hold that taking the risk of talking about one's inadequacies and vulnerabilities is good, even necessary. However, this norm departs widely from the everyday wisdom embodied in caution-endorsing sayings such as "Better to be quiet and thought a fool than to speak and be known as one" or "Don't air your dirty linen in public." As people enter more and more deeply into what Hurvitz (1970) called the "fellowship" of a self-help group, their membership in that group becomes a stronger influence in defining who they are, what they do, and what they will do. The group becomes a new reference group for them.

Besides this exposure to growth-enhancing influence, a cohesive group provides a strong sense of belonging. Though self-help groups can be confrontive in identifying and criticizing dysfunctional behavior, the fact that criticism comes from peers and others who are, or have been, in the same circumstances can, paradoxically, heighten the sense of being with others who really understand and care.

This is apt to be true especially if the self-help group falls into the category that Killilea (1976) characterized as an organization of "the deviant and stigmatized" (p. 61). In groups such as these, the sense of fellowship is more than just a general feeling of being with others who have problems, too. Self-help groups whose members share the experience of rejection, stigmatization, and (often) discrimination bond tightly to form a powerful new reference group, one in which individuals can compare themselves with others and gain "consensual validation leading to a reduction or elimination of members' uncertainty and sense of isolation or uniqueness regarding their problems and experiences" (Levy, 1979, p. 254).

In addition to the cohesiveness fostered by meeting members' *expressive* needs (e.g., to be accepted, or to express their feelings and beliefs openly), many self-help groups are attractive to members because they serve the *instrumental* need to change an unresponsive or noxious social context. Support groups for parents of children with handicapping conditions, for example, not only offer understanding and acceptance but also often become instruments for self-advocacy and social/political action as well. Collective action to make the community, school, or corporation more responsive to members' interests can produce a powerful sense of community that increases members' sense of belonging, self-esteem, and personal efficacy. Thus, group cohesiveness is both a contributor to and a consequence of acquiring the awareness, hope, and skill upon which self-enhancement rests.

Some groups may be composed of individuals who are collectively affected by negative attitudes and actions in the social setting (e.g., obese adolescents, women in traditionally male-dominated occupations, adults with handicapping conditions, students from recently immigrated families). These homogeneous groups may serve a dual purpose: to meet members' expressive needs and to support instrumental action. The group is a place where emotional needs are met. It also can be an impetus for members to consider, and act upon, the need to influence their nonsupportive social context.

The group solidarity that fosters sharing of a specific difficulty can heighten members' awareness that their interests are being violated, instill hope for positive change, and facilitate acquisition of knowledge and skills needed for self-enhancing activity. In groups that explore the relationship between individuals' suffering and societal influences, the line between the personal and the political tends to disappear. When members realize that much of their individual difficulty results from a system that disregards (or deliberately works against) their interests, subsequent political action, supported by collective strength, becomes an act of personal growth.

In heterogeneous groups, attraction to the group can be based on the actuality that the group helps its members meet expressive needs. These groups, though lacking the strong sense of common identity that pervades a homogeneous group, can still generate considerable cohesiveness simply by members' recognizing that amidst their diversity runs a commonality of trying to learn how to deal more effectively with life concerns.

Garden-variety, heterogeneous groups can also serve an instrumental function for their members. Even though group members have different specific goals and target their actions on different people or settings, a sense of mutuality can develop. Group members can become directly involved in one another's progress. They can be enlisted in helping one another gain the beliefs, knowledge, and skills needed for self-enhancement. The "opening go-round" ritual of some groups, in which members report on their progress or lack thereof (such as the "weighing in" procedure of weight control self-help groups) is an example of how groups can formalize member-to-member involvement in one another's progress. Progress can be reinforced, and failures can be confronted and then examined to determine what went wrong and what information, skill, or resource might be needed.

Conclusion ~

Fostering self-enhancement has an honorable place in the history of group work in the counseling field. It is still alive, well, and growing, not only because of long-standing societal prizing of independence and self-direction but also because of the vigor contributed by a more recent phenomenon—self-help groups.

The cross-fertilization of professionally led groups and peer self-help groups should be viewed as a mark of respect for the power and versatility of the self-help group movement rather than as the opening moves of a strategy of cooptation. Self-help groups do very well on their own. People make their way to them not only because these groups are often more available (physically and psychologically) than professionally led groups but also because they have virtues beyond the reach of counseling, psychotherapy, or case work groups. Self-help groups are not substitutes for, or pale reflections of, the "real thing." Among their many values is that they happen to be good vehicles for people to grow in self-enhancement ability.

Even though the process, content, and outcome of self-help groups and counseling groups may overlap considerably, the two are quite different. Group leaders who pursue the goal of promoting self-enhancement ability in members can borrow from self-help groups, make referrals to them, perhaps even act as resources for them; however, no one benefits from attempting to blur the distinctions between these two group forms.

Summary ~

Self-enhancement is a valid focus in counseling. It can be linked to some of the most fundamental theoretical, philosophical, and pragmatic underpinnings of counseling practice, especially counseling in the context of the dominant American culture. Individuals' willingness and ability to engage in self-enhancement varies as a function of their own characteristics and of properties in the physical and social contexts within which they live. The processes of formal groups (support, counseling) and informal groups (families, peers, co-workers) can inhibit or foster individuals' self-enhancement.

The growing influence of self-help groups attests to the appeal of their focus upon fostering the self-enhancement ability of group members. This can be perceived as a worthy outcome of counseling group experiences as well, so group leaders should note relevant aspects of self-help groups that might be incorporated into professionally led groups.

Increasing self-enhancement in group members is influenced by the leader's view of his or her responsibility. It can be enhanced by a view of leadership that emphasizes a facilitative, group-centered stance and maximizes the therapeutic mechanisms of universality, instilling hope, altruism, identification and modeling, and group cohesiveness. Given an acceptance of furthering members' self-enhancement ability as an important goal of group participation, self-help groups offer the professional leader useful models of content and process.

References ~

Allport, G. W. (1962). Psychological models for guidance. *Harvard Educational Review, 4,* 373–381.

Attneave, C. N. (1976). Social networks as the unit of intervention. In P. J. Guerrin (Ed.), *Family therapy: Theory and practice* (pp. 220–232). New York: Gardner Press.

Bellah, R. N., Madsen, R., Sullivan, W. M., Swidler, A., & Tipton, S. M. (1985). *Habits of the heart: Individualism and commitment in American life.* Berkeley: University of California Press.

Bond, M. A., & Keys, C. B. (1993). Empowerment, diversity, and collaboration: Promoting synergy on community boards. *American Journal of Community Psychology, 21*(1), 37–57.

Borkman, T. (1990). Self-help groups at the turning point: Emerging egalitarian alliances with the formal health care system? *American Journal of Community Psychology, 18*(2), 321–332.

Cartwright, D., & Zander, A. (1968). *Group dynamics: Research and theory* (3rd ed.). New York: Harper & Row.

Conyne, R. K. (1987). *Primary prevention counseling: Empowering people and systems.* Muncie, IN: Accelerated Development.

Corsini, R., & Rosenberg, B. (1955). Mechanisms in group psychotherapy: Processes and dynamics. *Journal of Abnormal and Social Psychology, 51,* 406–411.

Frank, J. (1961). *Persuasion and healing.* Baltimore, MD: Johns Hopkins University Press.

Goble, F. G. (1970). *The third force: The psychology of Abraham Maslow.* New York: Grossman.

Heller, K. (1979). The effects of social support: Prevention and treatment implications. In A. P. Goldstein & F. H. Kanfer (Eds.), *Maximizing treatment gains: Transfer enhancement in psychotherapy* (pp. 335–382). New York: Academic Press.

Hurvitz, N. (1970). Peer self-help psychotherapy groups and their implications for psychotherapy. *Psychotherapy: Theory, Research, and Practice, 7*(1), 41–49.

Killilea, M. (1976). Mutual help organizations: Implications in the literature. In G. Caplan & M. Killilea (Eds.), *Support systems and mutual help: Multidisciplinary explorations* (pp. 37–93). New York: Grune & Stratton.

Levy, L. H. (1979). Process and activities in groups. In M. A. Lieberman & I. D. Borman (Eds.), *Self-help groups for coping with crisis* (pp. 234–271). San Francisco: Jossey-Bass.

Lewin, K. (1951). *Field theory in social science.* New York: Harper.

Luks, A. (1988). *Helper's high. Psychology Today,* pp. 39–42.

McLuhan, M. (1964). *Understanding media: The extensions of man.* New York: McGraw-Hill.

Meissen, G. J., Mason, W. C., & Gleason, D. F. (1991). Understanding the attitudes and intentions of future professionals toward self-help. *American Journal of Community Psychology, 19*(5), 699–714.

Nolte, D. L. (1989). Children learn what they live. In Z. Zigler (Ed.), *Raising positive kids in a negative world* (pp. 95–96). New York: Ballantine Books.

Olmsted, M. S. (1959). *The small group.* New York: Random House.

Pattison, E. M. (1973). Social system of psychotherapy. *American Journal of Psychotherapy, 18,* 396–409.

Pearson, R. E. (1983). Support groups: A conceptualization. *Personnel & Guidance Journal, 61*(6), 361–364.

Pearson, R. E. (1990). *Counseling and social support: Perspectives and practice.* Newbury Park, CA: Sage Publications.

Powell, T. J. (1987). *Self-help organizations and professional practice.* Silver Spring, MD: National Association of Social Workers.

Reissman, F. (1965). The "helper" therapy principle. *Social Work, 10,* 27–32.

Reissman, F. (1990). Restructuring help: A human services paradigm for the 1990s. *American Journal of Community Psychology, 18*(3), 221–230.

Reissman, F., & Gartner, A. (1987). The surgeon general and the self-help ethos. *Social Policy, 18,* 23–25.

Rogers, C. R. (1942). *Counseling and psychotherapy: New concepts in practice.* Boston: Houghton Mifflin.

Rogers, C. R. (1989). Toward a modern approach to values: The valuing process in the mature person. In H. Kirschenbaum & V. L. Henderson (Eds.), *The Carl Rogers reader.* Boston: Houghton Mifflin.

Rueveni, U. (1979). *Networking families in crisis: Intervention strategies with families and social networks.* New York: Human Services Press.

Schubert, M. A., & Borkman, T. J. (1991). An organizational typology for self-help groups. *American Journal of Community Psychology, 19*(5), 273–293.

Shumaker, S. A., & Brownell, A. (1984). Toward a theory of social support: Closing conceptual gaps. *Journal of Social Issues, 40*(4), 11–35.

Skinner, B. F. (1971). *Beyond freedom and dignity.* New York: Knopf.

Trivette, C. M., Dunst, C. J., & Hambyu, D. (1996). Characteristics and consequences of help-giving practices in contrasting human services programs. *American Journal of Community Psychology, 24*(2), 273–293.

Vattano, A. (1972). Power to the people: Self-help groups. *Social Work, 17*(4), 7–15.

Yalom, I. (1985). *The theory and practice of group psychotherapy* (3rd ed.). New York: Basic Books.

Zimmerman, M. A., Isreal, B. A., Schulz, B., & Checkoway (1992). Further explorations in empowerment theory: An empirical analysis of psychological empowerment. *American Journal of Community Psychology, 20*(6), 707–727.

10

Group Counseling:
Career and Lifestyle Issues

Russell Miars

The phenomenal growth in group counseling during the past 45 years has been widely recognized as much needed and helpful. The premise has been well documented in many books and articles by such authors as Corey (1995), Gibson and Mitchell (1995), Gladding (1995), McAuliffe and Fredrickson (1990), Moreno (1962), and Schmuck and Schmuck (1997). Although these authors have discussed special types of groups, group counseling for the purpose of enhancing career development and launching adults into the job market has received little attention (Kivlighan, 1990; Zimpfer & Carr, 1989). Even so, group process is a valuable tool in assisting people with career decisions and transitions (Butcher, 1982; Mawson & Kahn, 1993).

Definition of Career Group Counseling ~

Career can be defined as the sequence of major positions and life roles a person accepts throughout his or her pre-occupational, occupational, and post-occupational life. It includes educational preparation, all work-related positions, such as those of student, employee, self-employed worker, and pensioner, together with complementary avocational, familial, and civic positions. Careers exist only as persons pursue them (Super, 1976) and, as such, represent patterns of self-development over the life span (Super, 1990).

Career group counseling refers to the utilization of group techniques and procedures for the purpose of enhancing people's career choices at different points in their life spans. Career group counseling may be utilized across various age levels and in a variety of work settings (Gladding, 1997) and is a cost-effective means of meeting specific needs of our rapidly changing society and world (Engels, Minor, Sampson, & Splete, 1995).

Elements of Career Group Counseling ~

Individuals have three primary needs in career group counseling: (a) input about occupations, (b) assessment data about themselves (their abilities, interests, skills, and values), and (c) exploration of personal meaning, involving identification and examination of subjective aspects of the self, feedback from others, and trying on roles (McAuliffe, 1993). This third component is what distinguishes career group counseling from group guidance (Kivlighan, 1990). A synthesis of group counseling or therapy and career group counseling establishes an environment of acceptance and openness in which group members have the freedom and opportunities to try out and integrate information about themselves and the world of work. Within this environment, participants practice and develop decision-making skills that will enable them to implement decisions. What distinguishes career group counseling from other types of group counseling or therapy are the former's use of career-related information and its emphasis on career decision making.

Use of Career-Related Information

Career group counseling makes use of information that usually is generated externally. The goal is to assist members in understanding career-related information and gaining insight about themselves and the world of work. Thus, career group counseling combines external information with personal insight development (Pyle, 1986). In this context, career group counseling is every bit as complex as other types of group counseling or therapy, and possibly more so because of the added dimension of information processing (Spokane, 1991).

Emphasis on Career Decision Making

Most theorists of career counseling have considered the skills of decision making as the core of career group counseling. Group techniques that combine decision-making concepts have been shown to stimulate occupational information-seeking behavior (Gati, 1990; Krumboltz, 1994). Gelatt, Varenhorst, and Corey (1972) set forth a decision-making strategy built around the following steps:

1. *Purpose.* A decision has to be made based on at least two options.
2. *Information.* Information about the options is identified or obtained.
3. *Possibilities.* All of the possible courses of action are identified.
4. *Results possible.* Possible consequences of each alternative are examined.
5. *Results probable.* The likelihood of each consequence is predicted.
6. *Values.* The personal desirability of each consequence is assessed.
7. *Decision.* A choice is made, either seminal or investigatory.
8. *Feedback and evaluation.* The suitability of the decision is judged by the counselee, and the counselor evaluates the effectiveness of his or her help.

Nearly all models of career group counseling use decision-making concepts to facilitate career and lifestyle planning (Fouad, 1994; Savickas, 1990; Wrenn, 1989; Zunker, 1994). Decision making is discussed in the context of group process later in this chapter.

Rationale for Career Group Counseling

The group format offers many advantages in the career process. These relate to and include (a) the enhancement of career counseling outcomes; (b) the support of group members; (c) the efficient use of time and cost-effectiveness; (d) the enhancement of feedback; (e) the personalizing of information; and (f) the enhancement of enjoyment and variety from group members (Pyle, 1986).

All counselors and therapists working with people on career decisions are interested in achieving the outcomes that are generally prescribed for the career counseling process. These include helping individuals to gain occupational information, develop decision-making skills, and, in general, make career decisions and move toward positive work adjustment (Savickas, 1990; Zunker, 1994). These outcomes are enhanced in career group counseling because peers are a major part of the process and can assist with adjustment concerns.

The group setting is also particularly conducive to the second goal, mutual support of group members (Kivlighan, 1990). By hearing others' concerns and problems, the tendency to see oneself as the only person with a career problem diminishes. Group members need to feel that their problems are not unique and that they share with others the frustrations, anxieties, and experiences of being human. The simple process of empathizing and sharing with one another is beneficial to life functioning as well as occupational functioning.

In addition, the group format allows more than one person's needs to be met within the same time frame, which has implications for cost-effectiveness and the effective use of counselor time. Given the ever increasing need for career intervention services (Reardon, 1996; Spokane, 1991), career groups represent a more practical response than individual counseling to client need.

Feedback enhancement is another benefit of career group counseling. The group leader can call upon others to help a member understand a certain aspect of himself or herself or to provide pertinent career information. The group presents a broader perspective and mirror of a person than a counselor alone can provide (Kivlighan, Multon, & Brossart, 1996). It enables people to see themselves both in others' and in their own feedback comments. The leader, therefore, has the resources of the diverse and varied personalities within the group to call upon and use in the learning process.

In an age of readily available career information, people need assistance in personalizing that information. Career counseling incorporates external information, such as assessment results and computer-generated occupational information. In the context of the group, members have the advantage of hearing others' assessment and computer-generated results, as well as their own. This helps them put the information in perspective and draw appropriate conclusions. By using techniques that enhance the affective domain, such as the expression of anxiety or frustration about career uncertainties, the leader can assist in personalizing the information. The group makes personalization even more powerful because of the influence of peers' comments, feedback, and support (Butcher, 1982).

The combination of affective and information/decision-making needs is one of the major aspects of career groups (Kivlighan, 1990; McDaniels, 1989; Pyle, 1986). All of us have heard the phrase "high-tech, high-touch," which suggests that the affective domain should be enhanced within the increasing bombardment of technology. Cold and impersonal information can be placed in the "high-tech" category, but the group leader can draw upon the humanness of the group to enhance understanding of that information. Group support, too, is usually far more significant than a counselor's suggestions and comments alone.

Dinkmeyer and Muro (1979) pointed out that groups meet a variety of needs at one time, all of which are applicable to career group counseling:

1. The need to belong, to find a place, and to be accepted as one is.
2. The opportunity for affection, to be loved and to be able to provide love; to be a part of the helping process while receiving assistance.
3. The opportunity to interact on meaningful developmental topics related to one's growth and development.
4. The opportunity to receive help in seeing that one's problem is not unique.
5. The opportunity to develop feelings of equality and acceptance without feeling that one has to "prove" himself or herself to belong.
6. The need to look at one's identity as it relates to the various social and career tasks of life.

Applied Concepts of Career Group Counseling ~

The career literature concerning career group counseling can be organized around the areas of (a) career assessment; (b) computer-assisted guidance; (c) the role of the family in career development; (d) career maturity, self-concept, and life-span development; and (e) comparative studies.

Career Assessment

Career assessment helps people answer "what" questions about themselves and the world of work. Assessment usually takes the form of interest or personality testing using standardized instruments but may also include the use of many other less formal surveys and checklists to assess interests, values, and attitudes (Bolles, 1995). Three of the most popular formal career assessment instruments administered today are the Self-Directed Search, the Strong Interest Inventory, and the Myers-Briggs Type Indicator. An overview of the benefits of using one or more of these instruments in career group counseling is provided in the following sections. The reader is referred to Seligman (1994), Spokane (1991), and Zunker (1994) for reviews of numerous other interest and ability assessment instruments that might apply to the specific purposes of a career counseling group.

Self-Directed Search (SDS)   This instrument is a self-scoring assessment of group members' vocational interests and the corresponding work environments that satisfy the expression of those interests (Holland, 1979). It can be administered and scored on the same day in the group for immediate feedback and discussion. Because the SDS is based on Holland's (1992) model of personality types and work environments, this low-cost, exploration tool is an excellent means of facilitating group members' understanding of self and the world of work. The instrument can be used equally well with adolescents, college students, and adults.

Strong Interest Inventory (SII)   This well-researched interest inventory assesses and matches group members' interest patterns with the interest patterns of people who have been satisfied with their careers for a number of years. The instrument yields a great deal of information and incorporates an overlay of Holland's (1992) model of personality/work environment types to facilitate understanding of the results. The assessment must be mailed to a scoring service for computerized scoring and requires technical knowledge of test construction for interpretation (Harmon, Hansen, Borgen, & Hammer, 1994). The cost in time and money incurred with the SII is significantly higher than the cost incurred with the SDS, but the wealth of good information the assessment can provide may be important in many career group applications. The instrument can be used with adolescents, college students, and adults.

Myers-Briggs Type Indicator (MBTI)   The MBTI assesses the strengths of group members' personality type across four bipolar dimensions. Some background study of the theory underlying the MBTI is necessary for its use (Myers & McCaulley, 1985). One of the most straightforward of the MBTI's type dimensions is Introversion-Extroversion. As these terms suggest, persons with introverted styles are more likely to be satisfied working alone, in more technical occupations, while people who are extroverted in style are more likely to need social contact and interaction with others in their work. An important feature of the MBTI is that none of the dimensions are cast as negative; instead, the dimensions are cast as people's preferred ways of perceiving and dealing with the world. A relatively low-cost, self-scoring version is available. While the MBTI can be used for personal counseling, it is widely used in career counseling to assist people in the self-exploration of their personal and interpersonal needs from work (Hammer, 1993). Results can also be combined with the SDS or SII in career group counseling to provide a more thorough exploration of self and career. One such means of combining assessment results is presented in the *Strong and MBTI Career Development Workbook* (Hammer & Kummerow, 1995), which has a number of worksheets and exercises to facilitate the career exploration process from the combined perspectives of the SII and the MBTI.

Computer-Assisted Guidance

Computers have played an increasing role in career exploration and assessment in recent years (Seligman, 1994). Comprehensive computer-assisted guidance systems such as DISCOVER and SIGI-Plus (System of Interactive Guidance—Plus) include career assessment tools, extensive occupational/career information systems, and planning and action-plan modules. These and other computer-based career information systems can be used with individuals or in groups and can be a useful aspect of career group counseling. For example, rather than spend valuable group time on information giving, the counselor might instruct group members to access, on their own time, a computer-assisted guidance system for personalized assessment and occupational information and bring the results to the next group session for discussion and personal application. With this approach, each group member benefits from the career information searches of the other members. Limitations to using computer-assisted guidance are that the systems are expensive and that they must routinely be updated to remain current.

The Role of the Family in Career Development

Career counseling will likely be enhanced if the counselor acknowledges the family as an imprint antecedent influence on the individual's career development (Whiston, 1989). Lopez and Andrews (1987) suggested that a systems perspective is essential in career decision making because young adulthood and career adjustment entail not only family values but also the other major developmental tasks of adult identity formation and psychological separation from the family. These three factors—family career values and roles, adult identity formation, and separation from family—have to be integrated in working with all career clients.

For example, young adults often come to a group with what they consider a safe presenting issue, such as "career." Yet in many cases, the issue may not be simply career. The individual may also need to process self-esteem, denial, transition identity, risk, and dreams. Career counseling requires a family systems approach, and if one or all the developmental issues facing young adults are part of career indecision, these issues have to be dealt with as part of the career counseling process (Anderson & Niles, 1995; Super, 1993).

Career Maturity, Self-Concept, and Life-Span Development

Career maturity may be defined as the "readiness to cope with vocational developmental tasks" (Savickas, 1984, p. 222). People may struggle with career maturity issues from adolescence through adulthood. Super (1957) suggested that career development is the implementation of self-concept. He also suggested that career development unfolds in five stages: growth, exploration, establishment, maintenance, and decline (Super, 1990). For each stage there is a developmental task to complete. However, a person may get stuck or struggle excessively at any of these stages over the life span. Career group counseling can help children, adolescents, young adults, and adults in career transition work through developmental tasks as they are presented at each stage. From this perspective, career group counseling has an important role to play in facilitating career development over the life span.

Comparative Studies

From their examination of the literature, Kivlighan, Hageseth, Tipton, and McGovern (1981) found several career counseling approaches, including individual, group, and self-help methods, to be effective. To date, there is not a clear research base to conclude that career group counseling is better or more effective than individual career counseling (Oliver & Spokane, 1988), although descriptive evaluations of career groups support the idea that participants like and find useful the group aspects of "being in the same boat" (universality), affective expression (catharsis), and feeling a sense of belonging and of being understood (cohesion) (Kivlighan, 1990). Mawson and Kahn (1993) found that participants in career groups for women valued both the affective (group process) and cognitive (career information) components of the group experience. The informational aspects of the group, however, had the most lasting impact at follow-up.

Applications to Career Group Counseling ∼

As mentioned earlier, career group counseling involves external information processing, distinguishing it from other forms of group counseling. Therefore, some of the process and content of the group stages are different, and career group counseling has a number of informational/cognitive goals in addition to affective goals. The end result is that frequently career group counseling tends to be more structured than other forms of group counseling (Pyle, 1986), although several authors have described a more process-oriented approach to career groups (Butcher, 1982; Kivlighan, 1990). Because of the additional content goals associated with career counseling, group size needs to remain fairly small. Small group size allows the group leader to interact individually with members as necessary and provides more time for group interaction in each of the stages.

A number of specialists in group counseling and group therapy have identified stages that counseling and therapy groups go through (Gazda, 1989; Gibson & Mitchell, 1995; Pyle, 1986; Yalom, 1985). Although the number of stages identified ranges from three to seven, the characteristics of each stage are similar in that the amount, the kind, and the timing of interventions relate to the stage of a group's development. A four-step sequence for career group counseling, with goals for each stage, is presented here.

Stage 1

Getting acquainted is the high priority of the initial stage. The group leader outlines the group's rationale and approach, and basic group rules are agreed upon. The emphasis is on members' participating and assisting one another.

Stage 2

Most career specialists call this the transition stage. The newness of the group wears off, and the leader's major role is to keep the group on task, committed, and participating. Group members self-disclose and open up to new possibilities that exist for them.

Stage 3

During this stage, members bring problems to the group and use the group process to acquire deeper self-understanding. Mawson and Kahn (1993) noted that the affective component of this stage is highly valued by group members and may deepen the impact of career group counseling. The focus is on assisting others to work out their problems; in essence, the leader does not have to be as directive as in earlier stages to bring about participation and self-disclosure. In this high-energy stage, members identify, synthesize, and realistically consider the variety and amount of career-related information that has been generated and how it applies to their personal career goals.

Stage 4

During the final stage of career group counseling, members are ready to take action on insights and ideas. They engage in activities aimed at gathering further information, or at integrating what they have already learned, to aid them with their career development. Members are more deeply aware of and more accepting of themselves, and they experience a feeling of empowerment.

Some career specialists call this stage a termination or ending phase (Gazda, 1989). Others (Johnson, 1990; Pyle, 1986; Yalom, 1985) call it an action stage, because it is when members are motivated to continue their learning independent of the group.

Appropriate Counseling Skills ~

One of the major differences between career group counseling and other forms of group counseling is the need in the former to help members understand and personalize information related to the world of work. Each group member needs to acquire certain levels of information to help him or her make good decisions and correct misconceptions or myths that are inhibiting career development. Leader skill can help these goals be realized.

Certainly all of the micro-counseling and helping relations skills are essential (Miars, Burden, & Pedersen, 1997). In addition, the career group leader should have a working knowledge of career theories and their application to a variety of populations (Spokane, 1991; Zunker, 1994) and should have counseling and group facilitation skills related to providing experiential information and information processing.

Experiential Information-Providing

Experiential information-providing is based on guided imagery and imaginal rehearsal. Rather than lecturing on occupational stereotypes, the leader might engage group members by asking them to describe what images they see after certain occupations are mentioned. By naming stereotypical careers such as teacher, nurse, social worker, accountant, doctor, or pilot, the leader can help members realize their own internalized stereotypes and can lead a discussion on the problems inherent in such limited perspectives. The discussion can focus on such questions as:

- Where did the image come from?
- To what extent does the stereotype limit the member?
- What scripts about the occupation play in the member's mind?
- How powerful is the self-concept in determining which occupation to pursue?

These are just a few of the questions that can help the group leader build awareness and insight. The critical skill here is the ability to help group members develop insight rather than simply telling them what they should know.

Information Processing

In this age of information, one of the most important skills for a group leader is information processing. Carkhuff (1967) indicated that processing, learning, and thinking skills are the critical skills of the future for counselors and that not knowing how to process all the data available will overwhelm counselors (Anthony, 1985). Within a career group format, information-processing skills can be broken down into three components (Pyle, 1986):

1. Exciting and motivating counselees with regard to the information at hand, which in turn will help them to attend to the information.
2. Helping counselees conceptualize and break down the information by asking them open-ended questions such as, "Select 5 careers from your list of 25 that you might seriously consider, and 2 that you have no interest in whatsoever. What makes you want to retain or discard each career area?"
3. Helping counselees act upon the information by motivating them to use it appropriately. For example: "What does this mean to you now? What do you need to do to act upon the information you now have?"

Process, Components, and Techniques for Career Group Counseling ~

To accomplish the stages of group development and apply the counseling skills, an overall process for facilitating career group counseling is needed. To date a limited number of career counseling processes have been conceptualized. The components and techniques that match the developmental levels of individuals as they work through the process are numerous and diverse. Age-specific variations in career group counseling are discussed in a later section of this chapter. The process described next incorporates components and techniques specifically for adult career group counseling, but it can be applied to other ages and developmental levels as well.

Adult career counseling groups should be aimed at helping members break away from their own rigid standards and outdated self-concepts and recognize their ability to make new, autonomous choices at any time. Integral to this approach is the idea that one never "arrives" but is always "on the way." Careers for adults should be seen as reflections of development phases in the life span (Seligman, 1994).

Mezerow (1978) developed a theory of "perspective transformation" that explains the need for the maturation process in adults to be "transformative."

According to this theory, adults in transition need to be liberated from previously held roles in order to frame new perspectives and live with a greater degree of self-determination.

Gould (1979) cautioned that adulthood is not a plateau; it is a dynamic and changing time. Adults who come to career groups are considering what life has been and what it could be. Forced to see the need to create one's own life rather than just live out destiny, adults become progressively freer to determine their own lives. The commitment to nurture self-growth demands an ever increasing match of talent to career while balancing the needs for security and freedom.

Adult career groups can no longer limit their goals to helping members make new career and educational decisions. They must recognize that adults in career transition need to develop a new, dynamic self-view as a result of their transformation.

A Process for Career Group Counseling

Career group counseling focuses on four major areas: self-assessment, career exploration, decision making, and taking action. The process can be structured into a six-session model, in which the content generally flows as follows.

Session 1. Group members introduce themselves and begin the process of self-disclosing how they feel about their lives and their work and life accomplishments. Participants are instructed to ask themselves specific questions to stimulate new ideas for realizing their career potential. The goal is to increase each participant's self-awareness regarding his or her unique career issues and the information he or she needs about the world of work.

Session 2. Interest inventories, values clarification tools, and personality assessments are used to help participants develop a sense of identity and define their career interests, work values, and personality preferences. Standard instruments such as the SDS, SII, and MBTI may be completed outside of the group and brought into the next group meeting for discussion.

Session 3. Information obtained from the standard assessment instruments and/or surveys are thoroughly explored and exercises are conducted to help participants learn to identify the skills they possess. Once interests and skills have been identified, discussion ensues about how to transfer existing skills to different occupations and how to identify new skills needed to enter or change careers. Strength bombardment and feedback may help members become aware of, and gain confidence in, their abilities and strengths. Group members also learn how to describe their positive attributes to potential employers.

Session 4. Group interaction continues to be used to help participants gain greater self-understanding. Career education resource materials are provided to help participants gain a better knowledge of the world of work and the variety of options open to them. Participants gather information about work settings, the nature of the work, job opportunities, and earning potential in several career fields of interest. Participants may be encouraged to use computer-assisted occupational exploration outside of the group and bring results to the next session for further group discussion.

Session 5. Goal setting and decision-making skills are discussed and practiced. As participants begin to focus on a career field or a job to pursue, they are shown how to consider and weigh their interests, work values, skills, and preferences. Specific decision-making strategies and risk-taking behaviors are examined for each individual in the group.

Session 6. Group members are encouraged to establish tentative career goals. They learn to establish short- and long-range goals and to strategize ways to ensure that they will meet their goals. Action plans for successful job hunting are reviewed, and skills and strategies for job interviews are presented. The group concludes with reinforcement of the participants' ability to carry out the career action plans they have made.

Components of Career Group Counseling

Initiating Career Counseling   During the first group session or the initial phase of later sessions, each person should be helped to feel included in the group. Participants should leave the first session confident of the possibility of resolving problems and moving toward self-fulfillment. To assist in this process, the group leader could say to each member, "So, what brings you here?" or "I understand you're looking for help in deciding about what kind of work you'll do in the future." The leader should be direct, confident, nonjudgmental, and ready to help the group members help themselves. Participants should be encouraged to take charge of career decisions and move toward self-realization in the world of work.

Determining the Members' Expectations   If a group member's expectations for career counseling differ from the leader's, the counseling process will not proceed well. The leader needs to know what each group member is really seeking. To work toward accomplishing this goal, the leader must:

- be frank and straightforward.
- describe the type of counseling that will be provided.
- explain his or her role as leader in the process.
- explain the members' role—what the members will be expected to do.
- talk about the group process.

If the leader conveys this information adequately, he or she should be able to ask at any point, "What has this got to do with what we set out to achieve?"

Establishing the Structure for Career Counseling   The leader must discuss the need for confidentiality and make absolutely clear who will have access to information generated in the group, who will use it, and how it will be used. In addition, the group process must be planned and discussed with the group members. The members play a part in structuring the counseling time, at least to the extent of setting priorities. The leader can always intervene if a member has to be refocused.

Setting Goals   The leader always thinks in terms of goals. When helping members set goals for counseling, the leader must aid them in the following areas:

- Defining present behavior.
- Discussing new behaviors that will replace old behaviors.
- Choosing goals that mean something to them.
- Selecting goals that they can attain or at least partially reach.

The counselor may ask him- or herself:

- Will the goals the members are setting allow for some early, specific successes?
- Can I help a member set his or her goals without giving the impression that I am setting them?
- Will the members be able to differentiate short-term and long-term goals?

Summarizing and Evaluating   In reviewing each session with the group, the leader should refer to members' expectations, explain the importance of various discussions, interpret members' behavior during the session, recapitulate the goals that were set, and provide a process analysis of the session. Each participant should leave every session with a clear sense of what he or she is to accomplish before the next session. This builds a firm connection between the counseling process and the rest of the person's daily life. The leader may assign specific tasks as homework, such as conducting informational interviews, researching certain organizations at a career center, or meeting with career contacts.

In his or her closing remarks at the end of a session, the leader should reinforce a sense of purpose. For example, the leader might say: "We'll talk again next week at eight o'clock. I hope you will have done some work on the matters we discussed so we will have some concrete information."

The leader must be careful to not encourage attitudes and behaviors in the group members that sustain the dependency of people in career transition. The leader must always work to empower individuals to be responsible for themselves, their choices, and their actions.

Techniques for Career Group Counseling

Techniques that are essential for career group counseling focus on members' work history, job expectations, work values, and leisure and lifestyle issues. Some examples are summarized here.

Clarifying Feelings   When appropriate, the leader should identify, clarify, and draw attention to members' feelings: "Were you aware that you had difficulty talking about changing jobs?" "Perhaps you could tell us in more detail what feelings you have when you think about changing jobs."

Interpreting Behavior   The leader should try to notice significant behavior, whether active or reactive. At times, drawing the group's attention to this behavior and its meaning will advance the counseling process: "I notice that David is smiling.

Might that mean, David, that you agree with what Margaret is saying when she talks about family career expectations?"

Encouraging Independent Thinking One goal of career group counseling is to help members think independently. Clearer, more rational thinking will result in more productive emotions and more responsible behavior: "We seem to be identifying transferable skills for one another rather than helping each person to identify skills for himself or herself more effectively."

Questioning The leaders questions should be phrased to evoke only material that is appropriate to group goals. With his or her questions, the leader should avoid being "provocative" in a haphazard way, without offering encouragement or interpretation, for that is more threatening than helpful. Further, the group will move along more effectively if questions are addressed to individuals rather than to the whole group.

Examples:

"What did you get out of being upset because you didn't finish college?"

"Can you give us an example of what you mean, Mary, when you say that no one understands you?"

"What exactly do you mean when you say you don't have time to look for a new job?"

"Randy, did you notice that Alan and Sally expressed concerns very similar to yours?"

With his or her questions, the leader continues to be accepting, supportive, and nonjudgmental, but he or she must also, at times, confront members with inconsistencies in their thinking, emotions, and behavior. The objective is to point out inconsistencies, evasions, and self-defeating behavior in a way that shows concern for the members' growth.

Information Giving Valid and reliable information are crucial in career counseling. Such information can be provided by the leader or by any member of the group. When a question comes up about businesses, training, referrals, skills, or counseling procedures, the leader has to decide whether to answer immediately or after the session, whether to refer the member to another information source (e.g., computer, data base, periodical), or whether to turn the question over to a member of the group who has some knowledge in the matter.

Through words, inflection, gestures, posture, and facial expressions, the leader can be effective, reassuring, and encouraging to members who must deal with painful issues. Though ultimately each member grapples with these issues alone, the leader's empathy and understanding make the task bearable.

Effective counselor statements include:

"Mary, some of the success myths and stereotypes that society perpetuates can be defeating for a woman returning to the workplace, can't they? Perhaps interviewing several women you consider successful in their careers might help destroy those myths."

"Robert, it's terribly difficult for you to talk about the plant closure, isn't it? You've kept all your deep feelings to yourself for a long time, and examining them here in the group is tougher than you thought it would be. You've shown how strong you are in many ways, and how deep some of the anger was. You can use this strength to deal with the past and prepare yourself for future successes. I recognize the pain this is causing you, and I respect your strength in grappling with it."

Closing and Evaluating   When further attention to an individual or to a specific issue is unlikely to be helpful, or when a discussion has become repetitive or irrelevant, the leader must help the group to move on. First, however, the leader should give a summary and sense of closure to the person who has the group's attention: "Joe, you have a firm understanding of what you've been doing that you'd like to change, and you have specific goals to work on between now and next week."

A session should not end abruptly simply because time has run out. The leader should anticipate the end of the session and provide closure by summarizing, reminding members of the homework that has been agreed upon, and creating a sense of continuity and expectation for the next session.

Closure for the final meeting of the group should tie up loose ends, appraise achievements, and allow participants to decide on developmental plans:

"We've looked at a lot of information about ourselves and the world of work and tried to understand it in terms of a career direction. I appreciate the hard work you've put into the process and hope it pays dividends for you and your future. In completing this process, you are aware that there is no final answer to career and lifestyle development. It is an ongoing process."

Age Specific Variations in Career Group Counseling ～

Counseling Children

The developmental needs of children necessitate that career counseling for children focus primarily on facilitating an awareness of work and future career choices (Gladding, 1996). Much career intervention at the elementary level is likely to be classroom based and take the form of "career education" (Brolin, 1995). If a small-group approach is used, the emphasis should be awareness of work roles, information processing of work roles, gender stereotypes, and beginning awareness of decision making and future career choices. Because concrete experiences and observations match the developmental information-processing level of children, more abstract career concepts and tasks should be deferred to later years (Zunker, 1994).

Counseling Adolescents

The adolescent years can be divided into the middle school and high school years. During the early adolescent years, children begin to develop a number of the skills that will be important to them in their future careers. For example, acquiring the basic skills of industry (organizing one's time and getting a piece of work done) are central to future school and career performance (Gibson & Mitchell, 1995). Developmentally, middle school students need to begin to relate skills to educational and occupational goals and to become more reflective about their self-identity and pursuit of future work (Zunker, 1994). Career group counseling for middle school students can begin to take on more of a process focus (including exploration of self and others at an emotional level) but still must have a central information-providing aspect since career self-concept is still developing.

The greatest need and challenge for career guidance and development programs exist at the senior high school level (Gladding, 1996). Because career self-concept and stable interest patterns are crystallizing, and the need for career information and planning is great, career group counseling has a vital role to play with this age-group. Gladding (1996) indicated that senior high school students need reassurance, information, emotional support, reality testing, attitude clarification, and career planning strategies. Although some of these needs might be met through classroom interventions, academic time pressures make it more feasible for the career intervention to be offered in a small-group format as part of the school's overall career guidance efforts.

Counseling College Students and Young Adults

The career needs of college students are an extension of those of the senior high school years. College students often revisit career exploration issues as they search for a college major, reexamining their self-identity and future work and life roles (Zunker, 1994). Thus, career exploration groups are a common career intervention service on college campuses (Sherry & Staley, 1984). They epitomize the career group counseling model presented earlier in this chapter and have been the focus of most of the research on career group counseling (Kivlighan, 1990).

Initial job placement is an issue for both college students and noncollege young adults. Placement services need to provide young adults with job market information, employment statistics, job search strategies, interview skills training, and job fairs. Although this aspect of career development is not the emphasis of the career group counseling goals outlined earlier, groups that focus more exclusively on the job search process are highly recommended for people who are job hunting (Bolles, 1995; Goldberg, 1980; Hughes, 1983; Krannich, 1983). Trimmer (1984) identified the following common elements for job search support groups:

- Exploring the hidden job market.
- Developing cohesive relationships to maintain momentum during the job search.
- Fostering individual responsibility for the search.
- Enhancing the self-image of job seekers.

Counseling Adults in Transition

Economic job insecurities make today's world of work harsh and challenging for many people (Jones, 1996; Rifkin, 1995). Many adults find themselves in unexpected and/or unplanned career transitions, either because they have voluntarily or involuntarily left a job or because their job responsibilities are changing. Therefore, the workplace and the community have become important targets for career intervention (Brown, Brooks, & Associates, 1990; McDaniels, 1989).

A variety of forces have provided the impetus for the recent interest in the workplace. Special programs for women and minorities, for example, have been instituted in response to affirmative action and equal opportunity legislation. Some company policies have evoked greater interest in promoting from within, which has increased the need to develop programs to help employees to fill human resource needs. Other programs, arising from requests from employers, undoubtedly reflect greater awareness of adult development in general and adult career behavior in particular. Lancaster and Berne (1981) observed that organizations are interested in increasing employee productivity and decreasing attrition, and they view career planning programs as possible sources of assistance.

Career group counseling in the workplace centers on placing the employees in an experimental situation in which they can rehearse new skills (such as job interviewing and selling one's ideas), can find models to imitate, and can be motivated by the stimulus of others.

Career development and the career group counseling approach have at least five possible applications in the workplace: (a) entry-level professionals; (b) midcareer workers or managers; (c) individuals preparing to leave the organization because of a cutback, firing, or retirement; (d) enhancement of the worker's present job situation; and (e) employee assistance programs (EAPs).

An additional target for career intervention with adults in transition is the community. Career intervention for displaced workers and those making midlife career changes needs to be integrated to a greater extent with community mental health counseling (Gladding, 1997). Because work/career is such a central aspect of an adult's emotional well-being (Levinson, 1978), career group counseling in community agencies needs to play a greater role in reestablishing work as a meaningful component of people's lives. Interestingly, McAuliffe (1993) found that an individual's meaning-making framework significantly contributes to his or her adaptiveness when faced with a career challenge. It is clear that personal and career issues cannot be separated, especially for adults (Anderson & Niles, 1995).

Summary ∾

John Naisbitt (1982) stated that we are living in a time of parenthesis, the time between eras. In this time of parenthesis, people have extraordinary leverage and influence—individually, professionally, institutionally—if they can only get a clear sense, a clear conception, a clear vision of the road ahead.

When done effectively, career group counseling can act as a support group for all people in most environments and across the developmental life span. The counseling profession can enrich the career and lifestyle process for people by providing a means by which dialogue, reflection, focusing, and feedback can take place.

Although group counseling and therapy have grown enormously in the past 45 years, only modest attention has been given to the idea of career counseling in groups. Among the advantages of this format are the enhancement of career counseling outcomes, the support and encouragement of fellow members, efficiency in terms of time and cost, enhanced feedback, more personalizing and sharing of information, and the variety a group affords.

Career group counseling offers members input about occupations, assessment data about their abilities, interests, skills, and values, exploration of the personal meaning of career, examination of subjective aspects of the self, and feedback from others. Career group counseling has a central theme of decision making, with a number of models to facilitate career and lifestyle planning. Computers have greatly enhanced the potential of career counseling through assessment measures, data bases, career information, and the opportunity to organize information meaningfully. Such computer-generated information can be integrated into career group counseling.

Career group counseling can be the vehicle to improve career maturity, self-concept, and attitudes toward career and jobs. This type of group generally follows the steps of getting acquainted and learning the group rules, self-disclosing and opening up to new possibilities, problem solving and exploring, and acting on insights and ideas gained.

The career group leader has to be able to provide experiential information and facilitate information processing in group members. In the latter regard, participants are encouraged to focus on self-awareness, self-assessment, skills assessment, strength seeking, career exploration, decision making, goal setting, job hunting, and reinforcing action plans. The leader's techniques include clarifying feelings, interpreting behavior, encouraging independent thinking, questioning, and providing information.

Career group counseling can be a valuable and efficient method of facilitating career development in a variety of settings and across a range of age levels. The potential of this modality has yet to be fully realized for career and lifestyle issues.

References ⌇

Anderson, W. P., & Niles, S. G. (1995). Career and personal concerns expressed by career counseling clients. *Career Development Quarterly, 43,* 240–245.

Anthony, W. A. (1985). Human and information resource development in the age of information: A dialogue with Robert Carkhuff. *Journal of Counseling & Development, 63,* 372–376.

Bolles, R. N. (1995). *What color is your parachute?* (22nd ed.). Berkeley, CA: Ten Speed Press.

Brolin, D. E. (1995). *Career education: A functional life skills approach* (3rd ed.). Englewood Cliffs, NJ: Prentice-Hall.

Brown, D., Brooks, L., & Associates (1990). *Career choice and development.* San Francisco: Jossey-Bass.

Butcher, E. (1982). Changing by choice: A process model for career group counseling. *Vocational Guidance Quarterly, 30,* 200–209.

Carkhuff, R. R. (1967). Do we have a theory of vocational choice? *Personnel & Guidance Journal, 46,* 335–345.

Corey, G. (1995). *Theory and practice of group counseling* (4th ed.). Pacific Grove, CA: Brooks/Cole.

Dinkmeyer, D. C., & Muro, J. J. (1979). *Group counseling: Theory and practice* (2nd ed.). Itasca, IL: Peacock.

Engels, D. W., Minor, C. W., Sampson, J. P., and Splete, H. (1995). Career counseling specialty: History, development, and prospect. *Journal of Counseling & Development, 74,* 134–138.

Fouad, N. A. (1994). Annual review 1991–1993: Vocational choice, decision-making, assessment, and intervention. *Journal of Vocational Behavior, 45,* 125–176.

Gati, H. (1990). Interpreting and applying career decision-making models: Comments on Carson and Mowsesian. *Journal of Counseling Psychology, 37,* 509–514.

Gazda, G. (1989). *Group counseling: A developmental approach* (4th ed.). Boston: Allyn & Bacon.

Gelatt, H. B., Varenhorst, B., & Corey, R. (1972). *Deciding.* New York: College Entrance Examination Board.

Gibson, R. L., & Mitchell, M. H. (1995). *Introduction to counseling and guidance* (4th ed.). Englewood Cliffs, NJ: Prentice-Hall.

Gladding, S. T. (1995). *Group work: A counseling specialty* (2nd ed.). Columbus, OH: Merrill.

Gladding, S. T. (1996). *Counseling: A comprehensive profession.* Englewood Cliffs, NJ: Prentice-Hall.

Gladding, S. T. (1997). *Community and agency counseling.* Upper Saddle, NJ: Prentice-Hall.

Goldberg, J. D. (1980). Counseling the adult learner: Selective review of the literature. *Adult Education, 30,* 67-81.

Gould, R. L. (1979). *Transformations: Growth and change in adult life.* New York: Simon & Schuster.

Hammer, A. L. (1993). *Introduction to type and careers.* Palo Alto, CA: Consulting Psychologists Press.

Hammer, A. L., & Kummerow, J. M. (1995). *Strong and MBTI Career Development Workbook.* Palo Alto, CA: Consulting Psychologists Press.

Harmon, L. W., Hansen, J. C., Borgen, F. H., & Hammer, A. L. (1994). *Strong interest inventory applications and technical guide.* Stanford, CA: Stanford University Press.

Holland, J. L. (1979). *Professional manual for the self-directed search.* Palo Alto, CA: Consulting Psychologists Press.

Holland, J. L. (1992). *Making vocational choices: A theory of vocational personalities and work environments.* Odessa, FL: Psychological Assessment Resources.

Hughes, R. (1983). The non-traditional student in higher education: A synthesis of the literature. *NASPA Journal, 20,* 51–63.

Johnson, D. (1990). Indecisiveness: A dynamic, integrative approach. *Career Development Quarterly, 39,* 34- 38.

Jones, L. K. (1996). A harsh and challenging world of work: Implications for counselors. *Journal of Counseling & Development, 74,* 453–459.

Kivlighan, D. M. (1990). Career group therapy. *Counseling Psychologist, 18,* 64–79.

Kivlighan, D. M., Jr., Hageseth, J. A., Tipton, R. M., & McGovern, T. V. (1981). Effects of matching treatment approaches and personality types in group vocational counseling. *Journal of Counseling Psychology, 28,* 315–320.

Kivlighan, D. M., Multon, K. D., & Brossart, D. F. (1996). Helpful impacts in group counseling: Development of a multidimensional rating system. *Journal of Counseling Psychology, 43,* 347–355.

Krannich, R. L. (1983). *Recareering in turbulent times: Skills and strategies for success in today's job market.* Manassos, VA: Impact Publications.

Krumboltz, J. D. (1994). Improving career development theory from a social learning perspective. In M. L. Savickas & R. W. Lent (Eds.), *Convergence in career development theories* (pp. 9–31). Palo Alto, CA: Consulting Psychologists Press.

Lancaster, A. S., & Berne, R. (1981). *Employer-sponsored career development programs.* Columbus, OH: ERIC Clearinghouse on Adult, Career, and Vocational Education.

Levinson, D. J. (1978). *The seasons of a man's life.* New York: Random House.

Lopez, F., & Andrews, S. (1987). Systems perspective. *Journal of Counseling & Development, 65,* 304–306.

Mawson, D. L., & Kahn, S. E. (1993). Group process in a woman's career intervention. *Career Development Quarterly, 41,* 238–245.

McAuliffe, G. J. (1993). Constructive development and career transition: Implications for counseling. *Journal of Counseling & Development, 72,* 23–28.

McAuliffe, G., & Fredrickson, R. (1990). The effects of program length and participant characteristics on group career-counseling outcomes. *Journal of Employment Counseling, 27,* 19–22.

McDaniels, C. (1989). *The changing workplace: Career counseling strategies for the 1990s and beyond.* San Francisco: Jossey-Bass.

Myers, I. B., & McCaulley, M. H. (1985). *Manual: A guide to the development and use of the Myers-Briggs Type Indicator.* Palo Alto, CA: Consulting Psychologists Press.

Mezerow, J. (1978). *Education for perspective transformation.* New York: Columbia University, Teachers College, Center of Adult Education.

Miars, R. D., Burden, C. A. & Pedersen, M. M. (1997). The helping relationship. In D. Capuzzi & D. R. Gross (Eds.), *Introduction to the counseling profession* (2nd ed., pp. 64–84). Boston: Allyn & Bacon.

Moreno, J. L. (1962). Common ground for all group psychotherapists: What is a group psychotherapist? *Group Psychotherapy, 15,* 263–264.

Naisbitt, J. (1982). *Megatrends.* New York: Warner.

Oliver, L. W., & Spokane, A. R. (1988). Career counseling outcome: What contributes to client gain? *Journal of Counseling Psychology, 26,* 447–462.

Pyle, R. (1986). *Group career counseling: Principles and practices.* Washington, DC: U.S. Office of Educational Research and Improvement.

Reardon, R. (1996). A program and cost analysis of a self-directed career decision-making program in a university career center. *Journal of Counseling & Development, 74,* 280–285.

Rifkin, J. (1995). *The end of work.* New York: Putnam.

Savickas, M. L. (1984). Career maturity: The construct and its measurement. *The Vocational Guidance Quarterly, 32,* 222–231.

Savickas, M. (1990). The career decision making course: Description and field test. *Career Development Quarterly, 38,* 275–284.

Schmuck, R. A., & Schmuck, P. A. (1997). *Group counseling in the classroom.* Madison, WI: Brown & Benchmark.

Seligman, L. (1994). *Developmental career counseling and assessment* (2nd ed.). Thousand Oaks, CA: Sage Publications.

Sherry, P., & Staley, K. (1984). Career exploration groups: An outcome study. *Journal of College Student Personnel, 25,* 155–159.

Spokane, A. R. (1991). *Career intervention.* Englewood Cliffs, NJ: Prentice-Hall.

Super, D. E. (1957). *The psychology of careers.* New York: Harper & Row.

Super, D. E. (1976). *Career education and the meanings of work.* Washington, DC: U.S. Government Printing Office.

Super, D. E. (1990). A life-span, life-space approach to career development. In D. Brown & L. Brooks (Eds.), *Career choice and development: Applying contemporary theories to practice* (pp. 197–261). San Francisco: Jossey-Bass.

Super, D. E. (1993). The two faces of counseling: Or is it three? Special Section: How personal is career counseling? *Career Development Quarterly, 42,* 132–136.

Trimmer, H. W., Jr. (1984). Group job search workshops: A concept whose time is here. *Journal of Employment Counseling, 21,* 103–116.

Whiston, S. C. (1989). Using family systems theory in career counseling: A group for parents. *School Counselor, 36,* 343–347.

Wrenn, C. (1989). The person in career counseling. *Career Development Quarterly, 36,* 337–342.

Yalom, I. (1985). *The theory and practice of group psychotherapy* (3rd ed.). New York: Basic Books.

Zimpfer, D. G., & Carr, J. J. (1989). Groups for midlife career change: A review. *Journal for Specialists in Group Work, 14,* 243–250.

Zunker, V. G. (1994). *Career counseling: Applied concepts of life planning* (4th ed.). Pacific Grove, CA: Brooks/Cole.

11

Group Counseling:
~Loss

Ann Vernon

Although we typically equate loss with death, loss is more accurately considered within the broader context of what occurs when something or someone close to us is no longer present (Locke, 1994). Loss is a prevalent theme throughout our lives, a theme intricately tied to change and growth. According to Judith Viorst (1986), "We lose not only through death, but also by leaving and being left, by changing and letting go and moving on" (p. 15). She noted that losses include separations and departures from loved ones, as well as loss of expectations, abilities, power, and freedom. Schlossberg and Robinson (1996) discussed loss associated with nonevents: the dreams that are never realized or the events that are reasonable to expect but never happen. Boss (1991) described another type of loss, ambiguous loss, which occurs when a family member is either physically or psychologically absent. Boss identified chemical dependency, child abduction, and incarceration as examples of ambiguous loss and distinguished this type of loss from other losses that involve the absence of a family member in that the former are never ritualized or officially documented. Thus, whether the loss involves a dream, a job, an absent family member, an ability, a friendship, or one's health, looks, or status, losses are inevitable. According to Viorst (1986), losses are necessary because "we grow by losing and leaving and letting go" (p. 16).

Adapting to loss and using it as a vehicle for change and growth involves adjusting to new patterns, relationships, roles, and events (Margolis et al., 1985; Volkan & Zintl, 1993). Schlossberg (1989) noted that with any loss there is a transition, which not only impacts roles, relationships, and routines but also impacts one's assessment of self. According to Locke (1994) and Rosoff (1994), the impact of a loss depends on whether the loss is temporary or permanent, the nature of the loss and how it occurred, the individual's previous history of significant losses, the psychological makeup of the individual, other life stressors, and whether the loss is visible or invisible. Worden (1991) maintained that we must understand the relationship between attachment and loss before we can fully comprehend the impact of a loss. Worden cited John Bowlby's pioneering research on attachment and loss, which proposed that attachments come from a need for security and safety, with the goal being to maintain an affectional bond. When this bond is threatened, grieflike behavior ensues. According to this theory, the greater the attachment or dependency (for safety or security), the greater the sense of loss.

Volkan and Zintl (1993) noted that how we experience loss is "as individualized as our fingerprints, marked by our past history of losses and by the particulars of the relationship" (p. 12). Despite the variability, every loss involves acceptance of the reality of the loss, a period of letting go of the loss and working through the pain, a transition and adjustment period involving adaptation to the new reality, and a new beginning (Locke, 1994; Schuchter & Zisook, 1993; Worden, 1991). Bozarth (1986) described this process as "going through a little death. In time, one comes out on the other side, a bit worn, perhaps, but in many ways brand new" (p. 90).

Although grieving a loss is a natural and necessary process, support and specific intervention can help resolve the pain of loss. Given the decline of family and religious institutions, counselors can play a significant role in helping clients deal with loss. One of the most effective approaches is group work (Price, Dinas, Dunn, & Winterowd, 1995; Spencer & Shapiro, 1993; Worden, 1991; Yalom & Vinogradov, 1988; Zimpfer, 1991).

The topics of this chapter include the mourning process, feelings associated with loss, purpose of loss support groups, considerations in conducting groups, types of loss groups, age-specific variations, and application of brief counseling or therapy related to loss.

The Mourning Process ∼

Mourning is "the psychological response to any loss or change, the negotiations we make to adjust our inner world to reality" (Volkan & Zintl, 1993, p. 2). *Grief* refers to the wide range of emotions and behaviors that accompany mourning (Locke, 1994; Volkan & Zintl, 1993; Worden, 1991). Mourning is influenced by culture, traditions, and customs (Stroebe, 1993). Volkan and Zintl (1993) stressed the importance of completing the mourning process, noting that if we are unable to mourn, "we stay in the thrall of old issues, dreams, and relationships, out of step with the present because we are still dancing to tunes from the past" (p. 3).

Worden (1991) identified four basic tasks of mourning: accepting the reality of the loss, experiencing the pain of grief, adjusting to a new "environment," and withdrawing from the lost relationship and investing emotional energy elsewhere. Staudacher (1991) and Schuchter and Zisook (1993) listed similar tasks but emphasized that while there is a general progression from one task to the next, mourning is also a fluid and overlapping process that varies from person to person.

Accepting the Reality of the Loss

Whether the loss involves control, self-esteem, ability to function, relocation, or personal autonomy, the first task of mourning is to accept the reality of the loss. This is often difficult to do, and denial is common: denying the facts of the loss, denying the meaning of the loss by making it seem less significant than it really was, practicing selective forgetting by blocking out the reality of a person or an event, or denying that the loss is irreversible (Worden, 1991). Working through this denial is essential before a person can experience the pain of grief.

Staudacher (1991) noted that it is common to "retreat psychologically" (p. 5) after a loss as a way of managing pain and anxiety. Periods of disbelief are common, but the reality of the loss must ultimately be acknowledged.

Experiencing the Pain of Grief

Although not everyone experiences the same intensity of pain or feels it in the same way, no one can lose someone or something without some pain. Schuchter and Zisook (1993) proposed that grief is a profound experience related to the pain of detachment, stressing that the acute grieving phase may last several months. Locke (1994) and Worden (1991) emphasized that pain that is not acknowledged and worked through impacts physical and mental well-being.

Grief is a highly individualized process that differs from person to person and is influenced by a multitude of variables. Schuchter and Zisook (1993) noted that there is little agreement regarding the time period for normal grief. They contended that in the case of loss involving death, many people maintain a "timeless" emotional involvement with the deceased that does not necessarily imply an unhealthy adaptation (p. 25). According to these researchers, some aspects of grief will continue for several years after the loss or will never be totally resolved.

Although grieving is a normal, healthy process that is a necessary part of healing, society is often uncomfortable with grieving and may subtly send the message that "you don't need to grieve; you are only feeling sorry for yourself" (Worden, 1991, p. 13). This may lead to denial of the need to grieve, manifested by repressing feelings or thinking only pleasant thoughts about the loss as a way to protect oneself from the discomfort.

O'Connor (1995) emphasized the importance of grieving, noting that people who choose not to grieve "remain locked in a shell of unresponsiveness, refusing to feel, and resisting the pain and tests of life" (p. 181).

Adjusting to a New Environment

Depending on the degree of attachment to the person or object of loss, adjusting to a new environment means different things and may be a multifaceted process. In the case of death, loss of a partner may mean loss of a companion, a sexual partner, a financial provider, and/or a housekeeper, depending on the roles this person played. In the case of a terminal illness, critical adjustments have to be made as a result of new medications, limited physical stamina, probable loss of employment at some point, and reactions of family and friends.

Developing new skills and assuming new roles is often accompanied by feelings of resentment or anxiety. Depending on the nature of the loss, many people are faced with the challenge of formulating a new identity or finding a new direction in life. According to Worden (1991), loss can threaten fundamental life values and beliefs.

Adjusting to a new environment implies accommodation to the reality. The primary task is to break old habits and adjust to the new reality with new patterns and interactions (Locke, 1994). This is not an easy task, and when people are unable to adapt to a loss, they may promote their own helplessness, withdraw, or be unable to develop coping skills for the new environment. These nonadaptions make the outcome of mourning more difficult.

Withdrawing and Reinvesting Emotional Energy

This task involves withdrawing from the person or object of loss and moving on to another relationship or situation. For many people, particularly after loss from death or divorce, this difficult process is associated with the fear of reinvesting emotions in another relationship and risking another loss (Locke, 1994; Worden, 1991). With other types of loss as well, a person has to successfully work through the withdrawal stage to live fully in the here and now.

The prospect of moving on often creates ambivalence, and people are often tempted to hold onto the past attachment rather than work through the feelings associated with the new reality. Worden (1991) noted that it is easy to get stuck at this point because it is so painful to give up the past reality.

Mourning can be a long-term process. Worden (1991) contended that it is impossible to set a date by which mourning should be accomplished. The acute grieving is over only when the tasks of mourning are completed and a person can regain interest in life, feel more hopeful, and adapt to new roles.

Feelings Associated With Loss ～

Following many types of loss, people experience a sense of unreality and numbness that helps them temporarily disregard the loss (Worden, 1991). But accepting the loss is important, and the people must be encouraged to talk about it and to identify and express his or her feelings. The feelings commonly associated with most types of loss are anger, guilt, sadness, anxiety, helplessness, frustration, and depression (O'Connor, 1995; Schuchter & Zisook, 1993; Staudacher, 1991).

Rando (1984) and Staudacher (1991) stressed that while these feelings may be common in most types of loss, they are not necessarily expressed by all people in the same way. Their expression is dependent on cultural and religious beliefs as well as on gender. Staudacher emphasized that men in Western cultures are expected to be strong and not openly express a wide range of feelings. They may be more reluctant to seek help and support, instead assuming full responsibility for resolving their own grief. Men in these cultures are also expected to be more in control, be able to bear the pain, and be more concerned with thinking rather than feeling. The fact remains, however, that they still experience the common feelings associated with loss, even though they might not express the feelings in the same way that others do.

Anger

Anger is linked to a loss of power and control (Staudacher, 1991). Although feeling angry over a loss is normal, many people have trouble admitting this anger because they feel ashamed (Locke, 1994). In the case of the death of a mate, survivors may be angry particularly because they are left with many responsibilities, limited finances, and necessary painful changes. At the same time, they may feel guilty because they know their mate suffered and did not want to die. In such instances, their anger may be turned inward and experienced as depression. Stern (1985) noted the importance of talking through the guilt and acknowledging the anger so it can be set aside.

With some types of loss, the anger may be more clearly directed toward the person or situation causing the anger: at the ex-mate in the case of divorce, at the employer in the case of job termination or loss of job status, at the doctor who cannot find the cure for a terminal illness, or at the adolescent who was driving while intoxicated (Locke, 1994; Sanders, 1989). Sometimes, however, identifying the anger or determining the target may be more difficult, as in life transitions. In these situations, the anger may be displaced to other people who look younger or have more physical stamina, or it may be turned inward, resulting in depression at one's personal loss (Sanders, 1989).

Guilt

Guilt plays a major role in most types of loss and can be experienced in various forms: survivor guilt—"Why him and not me?" (Schuchter & Zisook, 1993, p. 28), guilt related to responsibility for loss—"If only I had done this, had not done that, had tried harder, had tried more things..." (Stern, 1985, p. 60), and guilt over betrayal. Helplessness often accompanies guilt and leaves people feeling like they are not in control of the situation.

Guilt arises from many sources. A lot of guilt is irrational, and counselors or therapists should help people test the reality of their "if only" statements (Worden, 1991). O'Connor (1995) stressed that guilt slows down recovery and that even those people who are convinced that the loss was their fault must work on forgiveness. They may also need to reconcile the fact that they cannot change the situation.

Sadness

Some degree of sadness goes along with all types of loss. The sadness may be accompanied by tears and an awareness of how much someone or something is missed. The sadness is generally in direct proportion to the amount of attachment felt and the meaning attributed to the person or situation (Stern, 1985; Worden, 1991). Bozarth (1986) distinguished between sadness and depression, noting that sadness is highly focused in relation to the loss, whereas depression is a more general state.

Counseling professionals can support people who have experienced losses by encouraging them to express their feelings, legitimizing and normalizing these feelings, and helping them understand the meaning of the loss. Counselors or therapists also can convey the expectation that even though the situation is difficult, the person will be able to tolerate it and at some future time will have less pain and more pleasure (Larson, 1993; Rando, 1986).

Anxiety and Helplessness

After a loss, anxiety often develops, stemming from fear of the unknown and the inability to see how one will manage without the support of a partner or the security of a familiar situation or way of being. Anxiety is also related to a heightened sense of one's own vulnerability (Worden, 1991).

Individuals may have to be helped to identify the uncertainties they feel and the sources of their anxiety, as well as to recognize ways they managed situations prior to the loss and how, with some adjustment, they will be able to do so again. In the case of death or disability, survivors also become increasingly anxious about their own death or disability and must be able to articulate these fears.

Frustration

According to Sanders (1989), frustration results "when the bereaved is deprived of the things that heretofore have been expected, needed, and cherished, and when there is no hope of retrieving these resources" (p. 66). Accompanying the frustration is a sense of disappointment and emptiness that things will not be the same again. Regardless of the type of loss, individuals will be frustrated as they attempt to adjust to new situations. Because some degree of frustration is natural, counselors or therapists have to help individuals who demand that things should not be frustrating or require adaptation.

Depression

Depression is another necessary feeling in the process of expressing grief (Rando, 1986). Often, depression is connected to what is lost from the past, what one misses in the present, and the future losses one anticipates. Many symptoms accompany depression, including sleep difficulties, weight loss or gain, social withdrawal, apathy, feelings of despair, physical discomforts such as aches and pains, and feelings of being overwhelmed and out of control (O'Connor, 1995; Rando, 1986). To help individuals work through depression, counselors should encourage them to express their feelings and to identify and mourn the actual loss as well as the symbolic losses (such as opportunities, meaning, beliefs, hopes, and expectations) (O'Connor, 1995; Rando, 1986).

Even though loss involves a great deal of pain, Viorst (1986) maintained "Throughout our life we grow by giving up. We give up some of our deepest attachments to others. We give up certain cherished parts of ourselves.... Passionate investment leaves us vulnerable to loss" (p. 16). Looking at loss as it relates to growth and change can facilitate the healing process.

Purposes of Loss Support Groups ~

Any type of loss disrupts familiar patterns and relationships. The series of losses we encounter throughout our lives has consequences for our self-esteem, general sense of well-being, and emotional integrity. Whether the change is dreaded or welcomed, accidental or planned, it requires adjustment. This often results in anxiety or ambivalence.

Many of the needs resulting from a loss can be addressed effectively within a group setting. In recent years, there has been a steady increase in group work for various types of bereavement (Zimpfer, 1991).

Loss support groups allow people to share common problems and provide mutual aid, thus helping people develop new social support systems (Janowiak, Mei-Tal, & Drapkin, 1995; Price et al., 1995; Zimpfer, 1991). Groups provide emotional and educational support, characteristics that have a direct relationship to problem solving. In addition to receiving encouragement and relief, learning about resources, and mastering burdens, group members benefit from the opportunity to help others gain strength. "The group format is touted as the treatment of choice because it creates community, puts the locus of control on the individual, and emphasizes interaction and growth—all essential ingredients in bereavement" (Zimpfer, 1991, p. 47). In addition, group participation helps individuals maintain attention on the reality of the loss and prevents them from delaying or distorting the mourning process (Janowiak et al., 1995).

Zimpfer (1989) identified five purposes for loss groups: support, sharing of feelings, development of coping skills, information gathering, and consideration of existential issues.

Support

Perhaps the most important function of groups is to provide the support that comes from meeting with others who share a similar experience (Moore & Freeman, 1995; Price et al., 1995). Following a loss, people frequently feel a sense of isolation because they are reluctant to divulge their feelings with their usual support system. They may feel a need to protect others from the pain or may think others won't understand because they haven't had the same experience. Meeting with people who have had a similar experience can create a certain bonding as group members share reactions they all readily understand. Members' support comes through encouragement and helping others mobilize their inner resources to gain strength to heal and to continue life. In the group setting, members feel safe to bring up issues without avoidance, disapproval, or patronization.

Sharing Feelings

Many negative feelings surface after a loss: anger, confusion, shame, guilt, helplessness, anxiety, and depression. Within the group setting, negative feelings can be ventilated, enabling members to develop more stability and make clearer decisions (Moore & Freeman, 1995; Zimpfer, 1989).

Group leaders need to help members understand how normal their feelings are. This is extremely important because many people believe they shouldn't feel the way they do or that they shouldn't express their feelings; they should "be strong" for others. As Zimpfer (1989) noted, these "shoulds" often result in increased stress and more negative side effects.

Developing Coping Skills

The coping skills needed to survive a loss vary greatly depending on the loss. In most cases, however, how well and quickly one adjusts relates to finances, social and family relationships, independence and dependence, employment, disfiguration or physical stamina, and day-to-day living issues.

Because the coping skills needed are so varied, each group member will likely have some of the skills but not others. Group members who have dealt successfully with at least one of the problems can share experiences and offer suggestions. Hearing that others have successfully dealt with a concern one has restores a certain sense of control and instills a more positive outlook (Moore & Freeman, 1995).

Information and Education

Again, depending on the type of loss, group members may need to be educated about the normality of their reactions and feelings (Middleton, Raphael, Martinek, & Misso, 1993) as well as about issues connected with the loss: how to arrange for a funeral, how to cope with side effects of treatment, how to manage routine tasks if in a wheelchair, or where to look for a new job. Many times new role behaviors must be learned. Duhatschek-Krause (1989) noted the significant role that group members play in providing knowledge and assurance in all of these areas, making others' adjustment easier by relaying information on how to proceed and what to expect. The group leader or resource personnel also may be good sources of information because they can be objective and draw from experiences in previous leadership roles (Zimpfer, 1989).

Existential Considerations

Whether the loss involves death, dismemberment, serious illness, or change in status, loss often leads to the realization that the present is very temporary. People begin to see that ultimately they have responsibility for their lives and happiness (Zimpfer, 1989). This realization brings several results: recognizing the importance of living each day to the fullest, clarifying what is important and meaningful in life, and learning the importance of not having things left unsaid (Locke, 1994; Yalom & Vinogradov, 1988).

A group leader can facilitate discussion about the nature of loss, the meaning of the loss, and how it affects one's future. Dealing with these existential issues can help members grapple with the present loss and with its future impact. Understanding these issues can lead to positive growth and change.

Considerations in Conducting Groups ~

Members of all loss groups share the common experience of some sort of loss for which they are seeking emotional relief and a supportive atmosphere where they can discuss problems. Because group members are often at different points in grieving their loss, modeling is an important learning tool as participants share feelings and describe how they are coping. Modeling is just one of the considerations in conducting loss groups. Other leadership and membership issues must also be addressed.

Leadership

Facilitating a loss group is an intense process (Price et al., 1995). Leaders may experience their own unresolved grief issues or overidentify with group members' situations. Thus, it is helpful for a group to have co-leaders who can give each other feedback and support (Janowiak et al., 1995).

Group leadership may be facilitative or instructional. In groups that are basically informational, the leader tends to be more instructional. He or she will have expertise or experience in the specific area of loss and can dispense appropriate information as well as structure discussion or activities around predetermined topics (Zimpfer, 1989).

In *facilitative* leadership, the goal is to encourage people to share feelings and skills that enable them to cope more effectively with the loss. The facilitative leader is less likely to provide information. These groups typically do not have as much structure, nor do they have a predetermined agenda. Topics for discussion emerge from the group members, and the leader facilitates the exchange (Zimpfer, 1989).

Because people experiencing loss need information and support, both styles of leadership are often found in groups, with the dual focus of helping participants take control of their lives through problem solving and emotional support. Regardless of style, the leader has to actively set the tone for mutually sharing and exploring feelings.

Leaders should *model* respect, acceptance, nonjudgmental attitudes, and encouragement (Norberry, 1986). Group leaders also must work actively to remain open to the members' losses, avoiding the tendency to placate or protect.

Empathy is another essential leadership skill. Larson (1993) discussed empathy as "the bridge between altruism and helping" (p. 15). According to this author, empathy is the ability to feel and be sympathetically aroused by someone else's distress. Larson maintained that empathy is what transforms altruism into what he labels "caring action" (p. 15). Conveying empathy encourages further disclosure, exploration, and release of feelings.

The group leader also can encourage mourners to reminisce. Reminiscing is vital to the grieving process and can be facilitated through photos, scrapbooks, and other mementos. Telling the story of their loss helps relieve the pain and provides necessary catharsis. Group members often feel uplifted and relieved after shedding this emotional burden (Price et al., 1995).

Group leaders should continue to help members acknowledge the truth: Their loss did occur. By avoiding the truth, the grief process will be prolonged and, perhaps, incomplete (Worden, 1991).

Membership

Membership in loss groups may be open or closed (Price et al., 1995; Zimpfer, 1989). In a closed group, the same members attend for a series of sessions, which generally results in more cohesiveness. Open groups tend to continue indefinitely, with members rotating in and out depending on their needs. Open membership may offer more opportunity for modeling and sharing because of the wide range in stages of grief that are seen as new people join and others leave.

Individuals may be recommended for a loss group by a physician, a religious leader, a hospice organization, or a mental health clinic. Others may be self-referred. It is advisable to screen potential group members individually in order to discuss the purpose of the group, the individual's expectations and type of loss, and whether group or individual counseling or therapy would be most appropriate (Janowiak et al., 1995; Price et al., 1995).

Most experts recommend heterogeneous group membership, and authorities on loss groups say that this may not be much of an issue because of the natural bonding that occurs in these groups based on the need for support (Nahmani, Neeman, & Nir, 1989). Although participants in loss groups tend to be at different stages of grief, bereaved individuals are generally relieved to find a safe place to share feelings, and the group experience lessens their sense of alienation (Price et al., 1995).

Types of Loss Groups ~

Although the bereavement process involves common feelings and stages, group members get the most benefit from a group that addresses their specific kind of loss. Two of these types of groups are those providing support following the loss of a mate and those providing support following loss that results from the transition to late adult years.

Loss Group: Death of a Mate

Death of a mate is the number-one stressor of all losses, according to Holmes and Rahe (1967). Because of the bonds established within a marital relationship, Sanders (1989) maintained that it is difficult to clearly understand what is being grieved because the tasks and needs the mate provided could be endless.

Sanders (1989) emphasized the debilitating effects of the partner's death on the survivor and recommended support and intervention as means of preventing mortality or clinical depression of the bereaved mate. As Sanders noted, "Everyone needs support and social contact to deal with the frightening aspects of grief. Loss leaves the individual feeling small and empty. Social support can begin to help rebuild the person again" (pp. 218-219).

Stroebe and Stroebe (1987) cited three important functions of support groups for widows and widowers: (a) instrumental support, helping with the funeral, household tasks, and so on; (b) emotional support, helping the mourners accept the reality of the death; and (c) validational support, helping the mourners know what to expect during the period of grief and reassuring them that what they are experiencing is normal.

Specific Issues   In addition to providing a place for catharsis and for normalizing and dealing with the feelings of anger, guilt, anxiety, helplessness, sadness, and depression, the loss group can address the following specific issues:

1. *Loneliness and aloneness.* After the death of a mate, the mourner loses the daily intimacies of having someone special with whom to share significant events with and the sense of being the most important person in someone else's life. Being single rather than being part of a couple is also a difficult transition, as is the realization that part of the mourner's "history" died with the mate (Staudacher, 1991; Stroebe & Stroebe, 1993).

2. *Sense of deprivation.* According to Sanders (1989), the sense of deprivation following the death of a mate is particularly acute. Widowers and widows may feel deprived financially, socially, sexually, physically, and emotionally, in any combination. Role redefinition becomes a major task that is frequently painful and frustrating. To fill roles the mate had assumed or to learn the skills needed to fill those roles is often overwhelming (Staudacher, 1991). Survivors with children have an even greater sense of deprivation as they struggle with their own issues of grief in addition to the children's.

3. *Freedom and growth.* Despite the negative impact of loss, mourners inevitably find an awareness of freedom and the potential for change. Viorst (1986) emphasized that losses are linked to gains; loss can result in "creative transformations" (p. 326).

Helping group members recognize the strength that comes from facing and surviving a loss and coping effectively with adversity is an important step in their recovery. Encouraging participants to look at the potentials of independence and freedom is also essential. Frequently, participants enjoy the freedom of not having to adhere to a schedule, prepare meals, watch certain shows on television, or do things to please a mate (Yalom & Vinogradov, 1988). Along with this sense of freedom comes a sense of choice and a greater awareness of who one is and what one enjoys (Yalom & Vinogradov, 1988).

4. *Change.* Following the death of a partner, the survivor usually has to learn new behaviors that result in personal change: learning to cook and care for a house and children, handling repairs and financial responsibilities, making decisions alone (Yalom & Vinogradov, 1988). A major lifestyle change, such as relocation or starting a job, also may accompany loss. Even though these changes can be positive, stress and readjustment are to be expected.

5. *New relationships.* Forming a new relationship may signify readiness to put the past aside and move ahead, but this aspect of change is often difficult. Yalom and Vinogradov (1988) noted that widows and widowers often feel as if they are betraying their marriage or diminishing the love for the deceased mate by entering into a new relationship. In addition, many widows and widowers feel that their spouse is irreplaceable and they are not willing to settle for "second best" (Staudacher, 1991, p. 115). Group leaders should be sensitive to these issues but at the same time encourage participants to address the fallacy of the "perfect marriage" or the notion that they are discounting the significance of the previous relationship by forming a new one. It is also important to stress the importance of completing the necessary tasks of grieving before forming another relationship.

Leader Techniques   Unless it is a self-help support group, a loss group generally spans 8 to 12 weeks, with each weekly session ranging from 1 to 2 hours (Marmar, Horowitz, Weiss, Wilner, & Kaltreider, 1988; Yalom & Vinogradov, 1988). Typically a group has 8 to 12 members, who may be referred or who join voluntarily. They will probably be in various stages of the grief process. Sessions may be facilitated by either a co-leader team or by one leader.

Yalom and Vinogradov (1988) reported that widows and widowers frequently want human contact because of their recent loss and, therefore, have a high degree of openness from the beginning. This sense of openness frequently results in spontaneous sharing and has implications for the degree of structure imposed on the group.

In a group setting participants should, as noted by Marmar et al. (1988), have the opportunity to:

- share what bothers them instead of holding it in and trying to "be strong."
- gain insight about what they have experienced by asking questions and listening to others share their similar circumstances.
- receive support for the way they are handling their lives.
- receive advice and help with decision making on issues such as finances, how to carry out responsibilities formerly handled by the deceased partner, how to deal with friends, children, and relatives, and how to manage and settle an estate.

The following is a sample outline for a loss of mate group meeting once a week for 8 weeks. This outline is only one of several group approaches that could be used to deal with loss of this nature.

Session 1. Group members introduce themselves, and the leader facilitates a discussion on the group's purpose, soliciting participants' hopes and expectations and stressing confidentiality. The leader points out that the group is a safe atmosphere for sharing painful issues and that part of the focus will be on helping members move ahead despite the pain. During this session members are invited to describe their situation involving the loss of their mate. Because participants are usually eager to share their story with others who have gone through a similar experience, the leader generally does not have to introduce any more structure during this initial session. The sharing of experiences will most likely evoke a good deal of emotion, so the group leader will want to carefully monitor the process and intervene if a member becomes too emotional, checking to see if he or she needs to stop talking or needs other support. Depending on the group's degree of openness, the leader may ask participants at the end of the first session to bring scrapbooks or photos to the next session to stimulate discussion.

Session 2. The concept of loneliness and aloneness can be introduced to continue the grieving and expression of feelings from the first session. If group members have brought scrapbooks or photos to the session, these mementos can be used to stimulate discussion. Whether the discussion is more open-ended or is introduced by sharing photos, the focus may be on memories, what participants miss most (and least) about the deceased mate, and what being a single person in a couple-oriented society is like. The group leader encourages expression of feelings and helps members recognize the commonality of experiences.

Session 3. Depending on the issues that arose during the second session, the leader determines whether further exploration of loneliness and aloneness is necessary or whether the theme of deprivations should be introduced during this session. If the group is cohesive and the sharing is spontaneous and open, a simple invitation may be sufficient to start participants talking about ways in which they feel deprived. If this is not the case, a structured activity like the following could be introduced:

Give each member an index card and ask the group members to write the word "deprivation" across the top. Next, briefly discuss the concept of deprivation and brainstorm as a group the different kinds of deprivation that widows and widowers might experience. Following this, invite group members to write on their cards two types of deprivation they have experienced following the loss, when they experienced these, and how they feel about them. Depending on the group's cohesiveness, participants can share some of the ideas on their card with a partner or with the entire group. Debriefing should focus on the participants' feelings and how they have dealt with these deprivation experiences.

Session 4. The first three sessions were directed more toward the past, offering an opportunity to share common feelings, concerns, and experiences as an important stage in the grief process. Likewise, looking to the future and entering the healing and renewal phase are important. As a transition, the topic of freedom and growth can be introduced.

Generally, by this session, little structure is needed because participants have developed trust and rapport based on their common experiences with loss (Price et al., 1995). If necessary to stimulate discussion, the leader might introduce the following activity:

On a large sheet of newsprint, write, "What I can do or am learning to do now that I didn't or couldn't do before." Then invite group members to do some brainstorming on this topic, sharing examples of different types of freedoms they are experiencing or things they are learning to do that contribute to their growth. In debriefing this activity, help participants see that growth comes through pain and that the loss can actually provide them with the opportunity to become a more fully developed person.

Session 5. The fifth session also focuses on change and growth, but with more emphasis on some of the pragmatics of change. Because a partner assumes so many roles and responsibilities, the survivor may need to learn new behaviors to carry out these functions. By this stage, group cohesiveness will probably allow participants to openly share information and advice on new roles and responsibilities such as finances, child care, household responsibilities, settling an estate, or disposing of personal effects. The group leader may also supply information on community resources relative to these concerns.

Session 6. As widows and widowers work through the stages of grief, the concept of life changes and new relationships may have to be addressed. If group sharing is spontaneous and open, the leader may simply invite participants to share reactions, feelings, and experiences about this topic. Or the subject could be introduced through the following activity:

Give each member an index card and ask participants to select one of three future periods—a month from the present, 6 months from now, or a year from the present—ask what their life might be like in relation to (a) where they might be living, (b) how they might be spending their time, (c) who they might be spending their time with, and (d) what kinds of feelings they might have about these changes. Have them write the time period and their responses on the card. Then invite them to share their responses, focusing on their feelings concerning change and new relationships. Specific issues might include guilt about getting involved with another person, how to enter the single world, how society views new relationships, how new relationships may be a way of avoiding grief, and anxiety about change in general.

Session 7. This session may be used to allow group participants to continue exploring issues and feelings carried over from the previous session. Because members enter the group at different places in the grieving process, they are ready to make changes and enter into new relationships at different points. Encouraging discussion about anxieties and concerns may offer group members the opportunity to clarify issues and support one another in these transitions.

During this session the group might wish to discuss the meaning of life in general. For some members, marriage may have provided them with their basic sense of purpose. This loss may necessitate an examination of personal identity and life purpose. Yalom and Vinogradov (1988) suggested a structured exercise in which participants are asked to think about how they would like to be remembered and to write an obituary and share it with the group. Prior to completing this exercise, it might be helpful for group members to dialogue with a partner or the entire group about dreams or desires they might have set aside during their marriage and whether those dreams still have a place in their present life.

Session 8. In this last session, members are encouraged to deal with what has been left unsaid or unasked, and what regrets they expect to have after the group is over. This process could be loosely structured by inviting members to express an appreciation and a regret about what the group has meant to them. An exercise like this evokes powerful feelings and reinforces the idea that support from others is vital. The leader may want to encourage post-termination meetings for periodic support.

Loss From Life's Transitions

Loss occurring as a result of death is acknowledged and ritualized, unlike a great deal of the loss that occurs as a result of transitions. In reality, however, life is a series of transitions: from dependence to independence, from childhood to adulthood, from single to married, from work to retirement, from life to death. Transitions may also be promoted by illness, promotion, birth of a child, or a job relocation. Transitions are the changes, good or bad, that affect everyone and necessitate adjustment. These changes may be major or minor, anticipated or unexpected (Schlossberg, 1989).

Although people face transitions on a daily basis, Schlossberg (1989) maintained that we receive no training or preparation for dealing with them. As a result, people frequently approach transitions feeling anxious, upset, or overwhelmed. However, transitions can also be linked to growth, since the process of moving from disorientation to orientation marks a turning point involving various degrees of transformation (Merriam & Clark, 1991).

Bridges (1980) contended, "Every transition begins with an ending. We have to let go of the old thing before we can pick up the new, not just outwardly, but inwardly, where we keep our connections to the people and places that act as definitions of who we are" (p. 11). People often make external changes before recognizing that they have not yet dealt with the endings. Not until the endings have been resolved can a person move to the second phase of transition, which Bridges identified as the "lostness and emptiness" (p. 17), and continue to the third stage, a new beginning.

According to Merriam and Clark (1991), transitions often begin with a marker event, but Schlossberg (1989) suggested that while the onset may be linked to one identifiable event, transitions take time. Depending on the situation, several months to several years may pass before a major transition is completed. Schlossberg identified stages of the transition: a first stage, characterized by preoccupation with the change; a second stage of disruption as the old roles and routines are replaced with new ones; and the third stage, where the transition is finished and the individual has accommodated to the new way of life.

According to Hudson (1991), life is a Ferris wheel with ups and downs that are repeated as we continue to change with each transition. He maintained that we experience periods of stability followed by periods of transition and rejected the notion that life exists as a sequence of events within a timetable and have predictable outcomes.

Schlossberg (1989) discussed different categories of transitions: elected transitions, surprise transitions, nonevents, and sleeper transitions. Elected transitions are social milestones, such as marriage, having a child, and retirement, and individual choices, such as choosing a new job and moving to a different city. She described surprise transitions as those that are not anticipated. These unanticipated events could be good or bad, such as winning the lottery or being fired from a job. Nonevents are those events that we expect to happen but never do—for example, never becoming pregnant or never being promoted after years of hard work. Sleeper transitions are those that involve a gradual process rather than a significant identifiable beginning: gradually becoming more addicted to alcohol or gaining weight. Regardless of the category, the impact of the transition relates to whether it was gradual or sudden, permanent or temporary, reversible or irreversible, or voluntary or involuntary. The impact of the transition also depends on how relationships, routines, roles, and assumptions are affected (Schlossberg, 1984, 1989).

To successfully deal with transition, Golan (1981) felt people need to accomplish material (instrumental) tasks and psychosocial (affective) tasks. The *material tasks* include:

- Recognizing the need to do something about the old situation.
- Exploring solutions, looking at options, weighing alternatives.
- Making a choice and taking on the new role.
- Functioning under the new circumstances.

Psychosocial tasks involve:

- Dealing with the loss and the lack of security.
- Coping with anxiety, frustration, pressure, ambivalence.
- Handling the stress of taking on the new role or adjusting to the new situation.
- Adapting to shifts in status or position, which may result in feelings of inferiority, lack of satisfaction, or lack of appreciation from others.
- Learning to live with the different reality, which may involve adjusting to new standards and levels of satisfaction.

From age 60 to 65 is normally considered to be the transition period to late adulthood, but the transition may start before age 60 as individuals realize they have now lived longer than they will likely live in the future (Browers, 1991; Levinson & Levinson, 1996). At this point, people begin to think more about what their life includes and its meaning.

Although the transition to late adult years is one of the normal life cycle changes, this stage differs from earlier life cycle changes because it involves continuously adapting to decreased abilities and increased dependence (Browers, 1991). The multiple physical and emotional adjustments of this period present a challenge that individuals respond to in different ways depending on their life experiences and personalities.

The following areas may be of concern:

- Declining health and limited physical stamina.
- Adjusting to retirement.
- Role shifts/identity issues.
- Changes in living conditions/arrangements.
- Changes in looks/physical appearance.
- Financial security after employment.
- Finding a new balance with society and self.

Group work to help people deal with transitions has increased tremendously in the past several years. In the group setting, members can receive social support and factual information and can take part in emotional interactions, all of which can help them cope more effectively with the problems they may experience during transition periods (Hudson, 1991; Sanders, 1989; Worden, 1991).

The transition to late adult years is described here in further detail, with specific suggestions for incorporating this information into a 6-week group sequence, each weekly session lasting 1½–2 hours.

Session 1. The group leader begins by welcoming participants and explaining that this group will explore issues surrounding the sense of loss in the transition to late adult years. The leader explains ground rules and confidentiality. Because group members may not be in crisis as with the death of a mate, participants probably will not show as much spontaneous openness and bonding. If that is the case, the leader should instill more structure to facilitate discussion. After group members introduce themselves, the following activity is suggested:

Give each member a sheet of paper divided into four squares. Have the participants identify a positive aspect about this transition in the first square and a negative aspect in the second square. In the third space, have them describe why they chose to participate in the group and what they hope to get out of it, and in the last square, something about themselves that others can't tell by looking at them. After sharing their responses with a partner, have the partners introduce each other to the group by sharing one thing they've learned about the other person related to this transition to late adult years.

Following this sharing, lead a total group discussion about the positive and negative words participants wrote in squares one and two to elicit the range of topics that might be brought up in subsequent sessions. Record the responses on newsprint. End the session with a discussion of hopes and expectations for the group.

Session 2. The leader posts the list of positive and negative aspects of this transition generated during the first session. Group members are invited to identify the negative issue that poses the greatest problem for them and to discuss this issue with a partner.

After allowing time for discussion, the leader distributes the following questions and has the partners analyze their feelings in relation to them:

- Does this area of control represent an ending?
- If so, is this ending positive or negative?
- If this does represent an ending, is it necessary?
- Is it a choice? Or is it a myth or a tradition (such as not being as sexual during this period of life or having to retire at a certain age)?

The leader encourages sharing in the total group and challenges participants to look at what will change, how much control they have over this change, and how endings also signify beginnings.

Session 3. In this session the leader challenges participants to think about the losses connected with this transition and to identify their feelings associated with these losses. To stimulate discussion, the leader writes the following categories on newsprint and invites participants to brainstorm actual and possible losses in each area. The leader lists the responses on the newsprint.

- Physical health.
- Relationships.
- Work.
- Housing.
- Roles.
- Appearance.
- Social roles.
- Finances.

After the lists are generated, the leader invites discussion about how members have dealt, or will deal, with the actual losses and what information, resources, and support they need to deal effectively with the possible losses.

Session 4. As a follow-up to the previous session, the leader focuses on the members' feelings associated with the losses. By this time, the group likely is cohesive and members will openly discuss their feelings. If the leader senses that more structure is needed for a discussion of feelings to take place, he or she can invite members to pick one of the eight categories identified in session 3 and write down several feelings describing their reaction to the loss, which then can be shared with the total group.

Some of the members may share the negative feelings typically associated with loss, such as anger, guilt, depression, sadness, frustration, anxiety, and helplessness. But others may express relief, anticipation, or other positive feelings because the transition involves giving up some responsibilities, simplifying a lifestyle, embracing new challenges, or moving to a new location. Hearing both the positive and negative sides helps participants clarify personal feelings and, perhaps, develop a different perspective.

At this point, the leader may introduce a discussion about where feelings come from, drawing from rational-emotive therapy (Dryden & DiGiuseppe, 1990), to show group members that feelings come from thoughts about the event. To begin the discussion, the leader might point out that negative feelings associated with loss and change are the result of thinking that the event is awful, that it shouldn't happen, that it is impossible to accept, or that it somehow implies older adults are not as worthwhile. Providing a specific example, such as the following, is useful:

> Event: Having to retire.
> Feeling: Very upset, frustrated.
> Thoughts: I won't be able to stand this; I won't have anything to do; life will be boring, and that will be awful.

The degree of intensity of the upsetting and frustrating feelings could be diminished if the person were to think: How do I know I'll be bored? Isn't there anything else I could do now that I'll have free time? Lots of other people seem to like retirement, so isn't it possible that I will also? Helping group members understand where feelings come from may give them a better sense of control and a different perspective.

Session 5. This session looks at change. To introduce this concept, the leader distributes the following piece for members to read:

To everything there is a season, and a time to every purpose under the heaven;
A time to be born, and a time to die;
A time to plant, and a time to pluck up that which is planted;
A time to kill, and a time to heal;
A time to break down, and a time to build up;
A time to weep, and a time to laugh;
A time to mourn, and a time to dance;
A time to cast away stones, and a time to gather stones together;
A time to embrace, and a time to refrain from embracing;
A time to seek, and a time to lose;
A time to keep, and a time to cast away;
A time to rend, and a time to sew;
A time to keep silence, and a time to speak;
A time to love, and a time to hate;
A time for war, and a time for peace. (*Ecclesiastes*, 3:1–8, in Golan, 1981, p. viii)

After participants have finished reading, the leader gives each a sheet of paper with the following phrase written across the top: "It's a time in my life to ... ." The leader allows several minutes for the participants to complete the sentence as many times as they can and then invites discussion, highlighting the concept of endings and beginnings.

Session 6. The final session is a continuation of the fifth session, with emphasis on the individual's ability to take charge of the transition. The leader refers to the instrumental and psychosocial tasks involved in transitions, as identified by Golan (1981). Instrumental tasks involve recognizing the need to do something about the old situation, exploring alternatives and solutions, choosing to function differently, and making the change. The psychosocial tasks entail dealing with the loss, coping with the feelings, handling the stress of change, adapting to change, and learning to live with the different reality.

To facilitate discussion of these tasks and how they relate to the group members' situations, the leader might divide the group in half, giving one half a sheet listing the instrumental tasks and the other half a sheet listing the psychosocial tasks. The leader would instruct each group to discuss how these tasks relate to the life changes the members have made or anticipate making and then to summarize the issues and present them to the total group. Each participant could be invited to identify one task that he or she would like to work on and to discuss with a partner strategies for doing this.

In closing the session, the leader encourages members to relate something they have learned from participating in the group and how this knowledge will help them handle the transition.

Age-Specific Variations ∼

Children process information differently than adults. Group leaders must be aware that although children have many of the same feelings that adults do concerning loss, they may not be able to articulate those feelings as effectively. Instead, they may reflect the feelings in misbehavior or in causal reaction (Worden, 1991). Kandt (1994) noted that adolescents may also express themselves behaviorally rather than emotionally or cognitively.

Death

Children under age 2 have little conception of death (Worden, 1991), although they may react to death with confusion and separation anxiety (Norris-Shortle, Young, & Williams, 1993). Between ages 2 and 5, children are likely to see death as reversible and to assume that the loss occurred because of their bad behavior (Bertoia & Allan, 1988; Worden, 1991). They also may express concern for the physical well-being of the person who has died, because they don't understand the reality of the death. Another common occurrence is for young children to misconceive from euphemisms adults tell them. They may, for example, become fearful about taking a nap because they were told that the deceased was just taking a long nap or sleeping peacefully (Norris-Shortle et al., 1993).

By the time children reach age 5 to 7, they have a better understanding of the finality of death, so they begin to fear death. They try to avoid it or personify it as a monster. A child may assume the dead person can see or hear everything and, as a result, tries to be perfect (Gardner, 1983). From age 7 through adolescence, children approach mourning more like adults in that they have a better understanding of death and more adequate coping skills (Worden, 1991).

In conducting group sessions with children who have experienced a loss through death, the leader should use concrete techniques incorporating fairy tales, role-playing, art activities, photographs, bibliotherapy, and puppetry to deal with the children's fears, anger, sadness, and guilt (Matter & Matter, 1988; Norris-Shortle et al., 1993). Because many children have not had a chance to say good-bye to the deceased, Bertoia and Allan (1988) suggested they be encouraged to write a letter, make a tape, draw a picture, or use imagery to mentally tell the person things that were left unsaid. Children also may need facts about what happens during a funeral, how the body is prepared for burial, and so forth. Information of this sort can help alleviate fear and anxiety.

Life Transitions

Like adults, children go through many chronological transitions, including starting school, entering middle school or high school, becoming an adolescent, and leaving home after graduation. They also experience marker events, such as moving, changing schools, and parental divorce and remarriage. The usefulness of group work to facilitate these transitions is well documented (Costa & Stiltner, 1994; Masterman & Reams, 1988; Rossiter, 1988; Vernon, 1993).

In groups for children experiencing life transitions, the leader has to provide adequate structure and use concrete illustrations and activities to help the children understand the concepts. Preschoolers, for example, need a lot of play activities to help them deal with separation anxiety and to gain control of the transition of starting school. Older students may benefit from bibliotherapy, journaling, role-playing, or structured activities and games geared to the specific transition issues.

For children who have experienced loss as a result of death and those who have experienced (or anticipate experiencing) loss as a result of a life transition, group sessions can facilitate the grief process. When designing loss groups for children and adolescents, developmental issues should be considered along with the feelings, adjustments, and meaning of the specific loss (Kandt, 1994; Vernon, 1993).

Application of Brief Counseling or Therapy ∿

Since the 1970s, counselors and therapists increasingly have focused on approaches to speed up the process of client change (Littrell, Malia, & Vanderwood, 1995). Brief counseling or therapy embraces several assumptions about how meaningful change can occur within shorter periods of time than with traditional approaches. These assumptions include the following: First, time will not be spent searching for an underlying, deeper problem. The problem the client presents in counseling or therapy is the problem (O'Hanlon & Weiner-Davis, 1989). Second, clients often have the resources to resolve their problems themselves (deShazer, 1991). Third, a small change may be sufficient to interrupt clients' recurring patterns and help them act with more intention to incorporate new responses to life (deShazer, 1991).

Despite the adjective *brief*, Littrell et al. (1995) noted that brief counseling or therapy is not always short-term. Some forms of brief counseling or therapy may take 15 or more sessions, while others may be single sessions. Because the client is considered to be the expert on goal attainment, the amount of time spent is largely based on the client's assessment.

Brief therapy or counseling focuses on the exceptions—that is, it focuses on times when the problems were not occurring (Littrell, Malia, Nichols, Olson, Nesselhuf, & Crandell, 1992). It also emphasizes what can be done to change the situation in the present and future. Clients develop specific goals and steps to achieve them, as well as identify areas of competence, interest, and skill (O'Hanlon & Weiner-Davis, 1989).

At first glance, it might seem that loss issues cannot effectively be addressed through brief counseling or therapeutic approaches. Whether these approaches can be effective depends, to some extent, on the nature of the loss. However, with most loss issues, elements of brief therapy or counseling could be applicable for the following reasons:

1. The focus is on making a small change that will interrupt patterns to bring about new responses. This strategy is particularly helpful for dealing with depression, which is prevalent in most forms of loss. Taking the initiative to change something helps the client get unstuck.
2. In brief therapy, clients are encouraged to look at exceptions, as well as strengths and areas of competence. Since negative experiences are associated with many loss issues, clients frequently become more discouraged the more they talk about the problem (Yapko, 1988). Focusing on the positive is an effective way for clients to feel more hopeful.

3. With this approach, it is assumed that clients possess the resources to address the problem. This is an empowering concept, and within the group setting, empowered group members can help others access their own solutions.

Limitations of brief counseling or therapy to issues of loss include:

1. For many types of loss, "telling one's story" is an important part of the adjustment process. In many such cases, it is important to review the past through sharing memories (Locke, 1994; Worden, 1991). Brief approaches may not allow enough time for this type of catharsis.
2. Dealing with feelings is central to the grief-work process (Kandt, 1994; O'Connor, 1995; Sable, 1992). Although it is easy for clients to become more overwhelmed, depressed, or angry as they talk about loss issues, it is important for them to express their feelings and have them acknowledge. If the counselor or therapist moves too soon into the goal and the exceptions, the brief counseling or therapy approach may have limited value.

Many of the needs resulting from a loss can be addressed within a group setting, which allows people to share common problems, provide mutual aid, and develop coping skills. The leader can play an important informational and educational role, in addition to facilitating the discussion and helpful activities. The leader should model respect, acceptance, nonjudgmental attitudes, and encouragement and should be empathetic. Another function of the leader is to encourage group members to reminisce and to acknowledge the truth of the loss.

Summary ～

Life entails a series of losses, which Viorst (1986) described as necessary and having "subsequent gains" (p. 366). Although loss is inevitable, it is accompanied by grief, and people need varying amounts of support. The usefulness of groups to assist in adjustment and grieving is well documented, and groups can play a vital role in helping people of all ages effectively deal with loss (Lohnes & Kalter, 1994; Murphy & Perry, 1988; Nahmani et al., 1989; Price et al., 1995; Yalom & Vinogradov, 1988; Zimpfer, 1991).

Mourning involves accepting the reality of the loss, experiencing the pain of grief, adjusting to a new environment, and withdrawing and reinvesting emotional energy. Feelings associated with loss include anger, guilt, sadness, anxiety and helplessness, frustration, and depression.

Many of the needs resulting from a loss can be addressed within a group setting, which allows people to share common problems, provide mutual aid, and develop coping skills. The leader can play an important informational and educational role, in addition to facilitating the discusson and helpful activities. The leader should model respect, acceptance, nonjudgemental attitudes, and encouragement and should be empathetic. Another function of the leader is to encourage group members to reminisce and to acknowledge the truth of the loss.

Death of a mate is the number-one stressor of all losses because of the bonds established in a marital relationship. The survivor faces loneliness, a sense of deprivation, the possibility of freedom and growth, change, and new relationships. Another type of loss results from life transitions signified by developmental passages or marker events. To adjust to losses associated with life transitions, people have to accomplish material (or instrumental) tasks and psychosocial (or affective) tasks. The transition to late adult years involves potentially difficult losses because people are faced with adapting to diminished abilities and relinquishing social roles.

Children experience loss somewhat differently than adults according to their developmental stage. Therefore, counseling professionals have to recognize children's conceptions of loss and their manifestations. Techniques in working with children incorporate games, role-playing, puppetry, and other means to help the children deal with fears surrounding losses, probably most strongly felt as a result of death, divorce, or separation.

References ~

Bertoia, J., & Allan, J. (1988). School management of the bereaved child. *Elementary School Guidance & Counseling, 23*(1), 30–39.

Boss, P. (1991). Ambiguous loss. In F. Walsh & M. McGoldrick (Eds.), *Living beyond loss: Death in the family* (pp. 164–175). New York: Norton.

Bozarth, A. R. (1986). *Life is goodbye, life is hello: Grieving well through all kinds of loss.* Center City, MN: Hazelden.

Bridges, W. (1980). *Transitions.* Reading, MA: Addison-Wesley.

Browers, R. (1991). Retirement and aging: A lifelong view. *Counseling and Human Development, 24*(2), 1–12.

Costa, L., & Stiltner, B. (1994). Why do the good things always end and the bad things go on forever: A family change counseling group. *School Counselor, 41*(4), 300–304.

deShazer, S. (1991). *Putting difference to work.* New York: Norton.

Dryden, W., & DiGiuseppe, R. (1990). *A primer on rational-emotive therapy.* Champaign, IL: Research Press.

Duhatschek-Krause, A. L. (1989). A support group for patients and families facing life-threatening illness: Finding a solution to non-being. *Social Work With Groups, 12*(1), 55–69.

Gardner, R. A. (1983). Children's reactions to parental death. In J. E. Schowalter, P. R. Patterson, M. Tallmer, A. H. Kutscher, S. V. Gallo, & D. Peretz (Eds.), *The child and death* (pp. 104–123). New York: Columbia University Press.

Golan, N. (1981). *Passing through transitions: A guide for practitioners.* New York: Free Press.

Holmes, T. H., & Rahe, R. H. (1967). Social readjustment rating scale. *Journal of Psychosomatic Research, 11,* 213–218.

Hudson, F. M. (1991). *The adult years: Mastering the art of self-renewal.* San Francisco: Jossey-Bass.

Janowiak, S., Mei-Tal, R., & Drapkin, R. G. (1995). Living with loss: A group for bereaved college students. *Death Studies, 19,* 55–63.

Kandt, V. E. (1994). Adolescent bereavement: Turning a fragile time into acceptance and peace. *School Counselor, 41,* 203–211.

Larson, D. G. (1993). *The helper's journey: Working with people facing grief, loss, and life-threatening illness.* Champaign, IL: Research Press.

Levinson, D. J., & Levinson, J. D. (1996). *The seasons of a woman's life.* New York: Knopf.

Littrell, J. M., Malia, J. A., Nichols, R., Olson, J., Nesselhuf, D.,& Crandell, P. (1992) Brief counseling: Helping counselors adopt an innovative counseling approach. *School Counselor, 39*(3), 171–175.

Littrell, J. M., Malia, J. A., & Vanderwood, M. (1995). Single session brief counseling in a high school. *Journal of Counseling and Development, 73*(4), 451–458

Locke, S.A. (1994). *Coping with loss: A guide for caregivers.* Springfield, IL: Charles C Thomas.

Lohnes, K. L., (1994). Preventive intervention groups for parentally bereaved children. *American Journal of Orthopsychiatry, 64*(4), 594–603.

Margolis, O. S., Raether, H. C., Kutscher, A. H., Klagsbrun, S. C., Marcus, E., Pine, V. R., & Cherico, D. J. (1985). *Loss, grief and bereavement.* New York: Praeger.

Marmar, C. R., Horowitz, M. J., Weiss, D. S., Wilner, N. R., & Kaltreider, N. B. (1988). A controlled trial of brief psychotherapy and mutual-help group treatment of conjugal bereavement. *American Journal of Psychiatry, 145*(2), 203–208.

Masterman, S. H., & Reams, R. (1988). Support groups for bereaved preschool and school-age children. *American Journal of Orthopsychiatry, 58*(4), 562–570.

Matter, D. E., & Matter, R. M. (1988). Helping young children cope with the stress of relocation: Action steps for the counselor. *Elementary School Guidance & Counseling, 23*(1), 23–29.

Merriam, S. B., & Clark, M. C. (1991). *Lifelines: Patterns of work, love, and learning in adulthood.* San Francisco: Jossey-Bass.

Middleton, W., Raphael, B., Martinek, N., & Misso, V. (1993). Pathological grief reactions. In M. S. Stroebe, W. Stroebe, & R. O. Hanson (Eds.), *Handbook of bereavement: Theory, research, and intervention* (pp. 44–63). New York: Cambridge University Press.

Moore, M. M., & Freeman, S. J. (1995). Counseling survivors of suicide: Implications for group postvention. *Journal for Specialists in Group Work, 20*(1), 40–47.

Murphy, P., & Perry, K. (1988). Hidden grievers. *Death Studies, 12,* 451–462.

Nahmani, N., Neeman, E., & Nir, C. (1989). Parental bereavement: The motivation to participate in support groups and its consequences. *Social Work With Groups, 12*(2), 89–98.

Norberry, L. P. (1986). Divorce over 50: A program of support. *Journal for Specialists in Group Work, 11*(3), 157–162.

Norris-Shortle, C., Young, P. A., & Williams, M. A. (1993). Understanding death and grief for children three and younger. *Social Work, 38*(6), 736–742.

O'Connor, N. (1995). *Letting go with love: The grieving process.* Tucson, AZ: La Mariposa Press.

O'Hanlon, W. H., & Weiner-Davis, M. (1989). *In search of solutions: A new direction in psychotherapy.* New York: Norton.

Price, G. E., Dinas, P., Dunn, C., & Winterowd, C. (1995). Group work with clients experiencing grieving: Moving from theory to practice. *Journal for Specialists in Group Work, 20*(3), 159–167.

Rando, T. A. (1984). *Grief, dying, and death: Clinical interventions for caregivers.* Champaign, IL: Research Press.

Rando, T. A. (1986). *Loss and anticipatory grief.* Lexington, MA: Lexington Books.

Rosoff, B. D. (1994). *The worst loss.* New York: Henry Holt and Company.

Rossiter, A. (1988). A model for group intervention with preschool children experiencing separation and divorce. *Journal of Orthopsychiatry, 58*(3), 387–396.

Sable, P. (1992). Attachment, loss of spouse, and disordered mourning. *Journal of Contemporary Human Services, 5,* 266–273.

Sanders, C. M. (1989). *Grief: The mourning after.* New York: Wiley.

Schlossberg, N. K. (1984). *Counseling adults in transition.* New York: Springer.

Schlossberg, N. K. (1989). *Overwhelmed: Coping with life's ups and downs.* Lexington, MA: Lexington Books.

Schlossberg, N. K., & Robinson, S. P. (1996). *Going to plan B: How you can cope, regroup, and start your life on a new path.* New York: Simon & Schuster.

Schuchter, S. R., & Zisook, S. (1993). The course of normal grief. In M. S. Stroebe, W. Stroebe, & R. O. Hansson (Eds.), *Handbook of bereavement: Theory, research, and intervention* (pp. 23–43). New York: Cambridge University Press.

Spencer, A. J., & Shapiro, R. B. (1993). *Helping students cope with divorce.* West Nyack, NY: Center for Applied Research in Education.

Staudacher, C. (1991). *Men and grief.* Oakland, CA: New Harbinger Publications.

Stern, E. M. (1985). *Psychotherapy and the grieving patient.* New York: Haworth Press.

Stroebe, M. (1993). Coping with bereavement: A review of the grief work hypothesis. *Omega, 26*(1), 19–42.

Stroebe, W., & Stroebe, M. S. (1987). *Bereavement and health.* New York: Cambridge University Press.

Stroebe, M., & Stroebe, W. (1993). The mortality of bereavement: A review. In M. S. Stroebe, W. Stroebe, & R. O. Hansson (Eds.), *Handbook of bereavement: Theory, research, and intervention* (pp. 175–195). New York: Cambridge University Press.

Vernon, A. (1993). *Developmental assessment and intervention with children and adolescents.* Alexandria, VA: American Counseling Association.

Viorst, J. (1986). *Necessary losses.* New York: Simon & Schuster.

Volkan, V. D., & Zintl, E. (1993). *Life after loss.* New York: Scribner's.

Worden, J. W. (1991). *Grief counseling and grief therapy: A handbook for the mental health practitioner.* New York: Springer.

Yalom, I. D., & Vinogradov, S. (1988). Bereavement groups: Techniques and themes. *International Journal of Group Psychotherapy, 38*(4), 419–446.

Yapko, M. D. (1988). *When living hurts: Directives for treating depression.* New York: Brunner Mazel Publishers.

Zimpfer, D. G. (1989). Groups for persons who have cancer. *Journal for Specialists in Group Work, 14*(2), 98–104.

Zimpfer, D. G. (1991). Groups for grief and survivorship after bereavement: A review. *The Journal for Specialists in Group Work, 16*(1), 46–55.

Part Four

Group Work With

Special Populations

Part Four of this text covers information and techniques for working with special populations. The focus is on providing counselors and therapists with the background they need to successfully practice with clients who present with specific issues in the group setting.

Chapter 12, "Group Counseling for People with Addictions," imparts information on group construction with groups of chemically dependent members, the physiological, psychological/cognitive, and sociological factors affecting these groups, and counterproductive group processes with chemically dependent populations, among other topics. The chapter blends the idealized empirical view with the pragmatic, practice-based perspective.

Chapter 13, "Group Counseling for Individuals With Eating Disorders," deals with the specific disorders of anorexia nervosa, bulimia nervosa, and compulsive overeating. Current research regarding these disorders is presented together with the issues, implications, and applications related to group work with this population.

Chapter 14, "Group Counseling for People With Physical Disabilities," provides information on (a) the merits of group counseling with individuals who have physical disabilities, (b) the needs of those with disabilities, (c) the therapeutic factors deemed effective in working with this population, (d) the goals of groups for people with disabilities, and (e) group process and effective strategies in these groups.

Chapter 15, "Group Counseling With Gay, Lesbian, and Bisexual Clients," provides gay, lesbian, and bisexual culture-specific information. Based upon this foundation, the authors address language concerns, the culture of sexual minorities, affirmative counseling, general group approaches, and specific groups. The information provided is concrete and practical and provides an excellent resource for the group work specialist.

Chapter 16, "Group Counseling With the Elderly and Their Care Givers," overviews the history of group work with older adults, types of groups for this population, multicultural considerations, and the specifics of leading both life review groups and brief solution-focused groups.

Part Four concludes with Chapter 17, "Group Counseling for Issues Related to Suicide." This chapter begins with a discussion of the statistics on the prevalence of suicide and the significant factors that research has found to be indicative of suicidal risk. Using this information as a foundation, the author devotes the major portion of the chapter to a discussion of suicide intervention groups. The author provides a myriad of guidelines for group leaders from the perspectives of prevention, crisis-management, and postvention.

As these chapters indicate, the effective use of group approaches with special populations is based upon a combination of knowledge and the ability to practically use and apply that knowledge in a group setting. The information provided in these chapters will be highly useful to the group work specialist interested in ideas for improving his or her practice with special populations.

12

Group Counseling for
People With Addictions

Jack Clark and Melissa Blanchard

The 1990s have seen rapid and fundamental changes occur in the health care delivery system in the United States. Behavioral health, including the field of chemical dependency (CD), has not escaped these dramatic and revolutionary changes. Nelba Chavez, administrator of the Substance Abuse and Mental Health Services Administration (SAMHSA), in testimony before the Senate Committee on Labor and Human Services in 1995, cited the increasing dominance of managed care in the health care delivery system. Managed-care strategies, which are generally recognized for their short-term cost savings, are increasingly being applied in both the private and public sector across America. The widespread application of managed-care strategies in behavioral health has begun prior to the completion of any comprehensive research effort directed at understanding the long-range effect on outcome that such changes may have on the varied populations served. Recently, the Department of Health and Human Services (HHS) has initiated an attempt to study the long-term impact of managed-care strategies in the public sector (1996).

In the dramatically changing health care environment, as well as over the past three decades, group work continues to serve as the treatment of choice for addiction. The value most often associated with the role group work plays in the treatment of addiction operates on at least two basic levels: clinical efficacy and cost-effectiveness. The latter has particular significance in light of the increasing application of managed-care strategies. The addiction literature is replete with examples of the preference of the field for groups as well as of the clinical effectiveness associated with group work (Agazarian, & Peters, 1981; Brown, 1985; Flores, 1988; Khantzian, Halliday, & McAuliffe, 1990; Vannicelli, 1988; Yalom, 1985). The work by

Agazarian and Peters (1981) clearly illustrates the advantages of group over individual therapy, especially since chemically dependent individuals often express their symptoms in interpersonal terms.

Flores (1988) pointed out a potential limitation operating within groups of chemically dependent members—that the common use of a similar, defensive style may reinforce the members' denial, a central operating element in the addiction process. Attention to the presence of similar defensive styles among group members is necessary, and the group leader must be directive in the early stages of group development if he or she is to utilize this dynamic to the group's advantage. Despite the limitations of similar defensive styles, multiple benefits exist for group work in CD settings, ranging from the curative process available within the matrix of a group to the power of the group on influencing behavior.

The cost-effectiveness of groups over individual sessions is simple mathematics. A single group leader can see six to eight clients in a 1½- to 2-hour period, whereas treating corresponding numbers of clients individually would take 6 to 8 hours of counselor time. However, Zimberg, Wallace, and Blume (1985) argued that one must look at more than the number of hours the group meets, since group counseling involves other time consuming activities as well. These activities include, but are not limited to, screening, family conferences, arranging for other services members may require, record keeping, and allowing time before and after group sessions for member needs. Even taking these very real expenditures of the leader's time into account, group work remains a cost-effective method of treating the chemically dependent members' specific counseling needs. A growing presence of managed care in the addictions field has served to stimulate the continued development of cost-effective and short-term, time-limited treatment models. Gorski (1995) and Grayson (1993) described short-term, time-limited group approaches as directive rather than nondirective, goal-driven, and having specific, understandable, achievable, and measurable goals.

While it is important to recognize the role groups have played within the chemical dependency treatment community, it is also important to recognize the absence of adequate research on the application of brief, time-limited models across the diverse, complicated, and often multidrug/multiproblem clients that are represented within the total substance abuse population. Worthy of consideration is the work of Carrol, Power, Bryant, and Rounsaville (1993) that recognized a complex social and psychological profile for many substance abusers. Prochaska, DiClemente, and Norcross (1992), in their application of change theory to addictions, observed that relapse is the rule rather than the exception with addictions and subsequently revised their model of how people change from a linear model to a spiral one. Recognizing this diverse and complex population profile, with relapse as a part of the recovery/change process, raises questions about whether any single treatment offered over a relatively short period of time will have sufficient impact over the long term.

This chapter provides information relative to the following: group construction with groups of chemically dependent members, physiological, psychological/cognitive, and sociological factors affecting these groups, counterproductive group processes occurring with chemically dependent populations, the impact of learning and education within the group on group process, and tasks of the group leader. The approach blends the idealized empirical view with a pragmatic, practice-based perspective. We assume that the reader has a basic understanding of group dynamics. Based on this assumption, the information presented is not intended to be all-inclusive. Additional education, training, and experience are necessary for fully appreciating the complexities associated with group work with chemically dependent individuals.

Group Construction ~

Group construction considerations for groups of chemically dependent members are multifaceted, and effective construction requires the group leader to have a clear picture of the generalized purposes of the group. Clarification of individual client needs and goals, third-party funding source goals (feeders), time constraints, and member characteristics will aid the group leader in the development of the generalized purposes of the group.

Feeders (third parties) provide a significant amount of the funding for groups today and subsequently have influence over length of treatment, duration and type of group service purchased, and, to some degree, outcome goals. As a result of this influence, an open information exchange relative to purpose and intent between concerned parties is critical to prevent misunderstanding and confusion.

Time constraints not only include those imposed by third parties but also involve leader and member availability as well as constraints imposed by group design. For example, a third party may wish to purchase didactic groups with an awareness of chemical dependency as the outcome as opposed to groups with the purpose of increasing insight into intra/interpersonal issues. The frequency, duration, format, content, process, and so forth, of these types of groups would be designed to meet different goals and, subsequently, make different demands on members as well as leaders.

Population characteristics such as age, background, level of functioning, motivation, and individual goals for treatment require comprehensive assessment, both at the onset of the treatment experience and on an ongoing basis.

Selection and Assessment

The selection process begins with assessment and leads to the matching of clients to available services. Ongoing assessment, once the services have been implemented, allows for adjustment of services to specific client need and ensures appropriate placement of clients. The critical role that the initial, as well as ongoing, assessment plays is pointed out clearly in the work of Daley, Moss, and Campbell (1987), who stated that to develop appropriate treatment goals, an adequate assessment of the client's total functioning should be employed and viewed as ongoing.

A variety of assessment instruments are available to assist the group leader in the assessment process. Of particular value are the reliability and validity that the application of assessment instruments offers to an otherwise subjective process. One assessment instrument commonly used in the chemical dependency field is the Addiction Severity Index (ASI), which is a comprehensive clinical and research instrument useful in assessing problem severity in areas commonly present in substance abuse populations (McLellan et al., 1985). This instrument is particularly useful when readministered at regular intervals as a means of measuring clinical improvement. Another instrument that assesses a variety of problem areas is the Substance Abuse Problem Checklist (SAPC). This instrument utilizes a self-administered 377-item checklist featuring problem statements from various functional areas of life (Carroll, 1983). Additionally, the group leader may want to become acquainted with other assessment aids, such as the Michigan Alcoholism Screening Test (MAST), the Drug Abuse Screening Test (DAST), the Substance Abuse Subtle Screening Inventory—2 (SASSI–2), the Alcohol Use Inventory (AUI), and the McAndrews-Revised subscale of the Minnesota Multiphasic Personality Inventory—2 (MMPI–2) and the Minnesota Multiphasic Personality Inventory—Adolescent (MMPI–A).

The assessment process is most effective when the group leader utilizes both clinical interviews and assessment aids. The information gathered assists the leader in determining the appropriateness of placement of individuals in specific groups as well as directs the focus of treatment to areas identified as being problematic.

The placement of individuals in groups, a process referred to as *grouping,* should be done with great care. Levine (1979) stated that no single activity on the part of the group leader can influence the nature and destiny of a counseling or therapy group as much as the selection and matching of individuals for membership. Levine further stated that the potentials, limitations, and balance of a counseling or therapy group are inherent in its composition. Homogeneity (in what ways the members are similar) and heterogeneity (in what ways the members are different) are the two major considerations for mixing and matching members of a treatment group (Levine & Gallogly, 1985). Commonality of purpose, the capacity for insight, the level to which the chemical dependency has progressed, motivation to seek treatment, and degree of criminal justice system involvement all need to be considered during the grouping process.

Other factors that play a role in influencing the process within treatment groups are age differences, gender differences, racial differences, ethnic/cultural differences, socioeconomic differences, and the capacity for relationships (Levine & Gallogly, 1985). The clinical interview and the application of the assessment instruments yield valuable information that contributes to a sound clinical decision on the initial placement of an individual in a group. Ongoing assessment throughout the duration of the treatment process allows for adjustments if and when indicated. Adjustment to group structure and/or content may be necessary to fulfill the purpose of the group; adjustment of group composition may be necessary to better match individuals to groups as new client material surfaces.

Additional aspects to consider throughout the assessment process are how verbal or nonverbal a member might be and how that relates to the general composition and purpose of the group. A highly verbal, aggressive member placed in a group of withdrawn individuals will dominate the group, possibly contributing to a counterproductive process. The level to which a member appears to be able to demonstrate self-control is worthy of consideration as well. A basic understanding and some degree of tolerance for impulsivity and acting out behaviors should be collectively present in the group if any of the members have a strong propensity for such processes. Mixing members exhibiting significant differences in level of functioning can hamper group development and is generally not recommended. It should be noted that even when a group leader has to operate under less than ideal conditions, with regard to group composition with carefully applied skill he or she can often accomplish tasks consistent with available conditions.

The work of Flores and Mahon (1993) suggested that the group leader obtain information on previous positive experience in group or individual counseling or therapy, the individual's ability to form a working alliance, and any positive involvement in a 12-step program (e.g., Alcoholics Anonymous, AA; Narcotics Anonymous, NA; Cocaine Anonymous, CA; Adult Children of Alcoholics, ACOA) during the assessment process. The presence of these factors may indicate that the individual is likely to benefit from group feedback and support.

The expectations that each member has for the group, as well as the outcome each member expects, should be considered and be congruent, at least in a general sense, with group construction. Of course, there will always be some disparity of expectation as well as hidden agendas, especially with group members who are coerced into treatment. With skill, understanding, empathy, and patience, the group leader and the members of the group can often break through deception and denial, when present, and promote effective group process.

Treatment Conditions

The treatment conditions under which group work occurs are varied and tend to be arranged on a hierarchy that begins with the most restrictive level of care and ends with the least restrictive level of care. Between these two extremes are, listed here from most restrictive to least restrictive level of care, inpatient hospital care, residential treatment centers care, partial hospitalization/day care, intensive outpatient care, outpatient/traditional care, relapse prevention care, aftercare, and a host of self-help support groups. The treatment needs of the individual, his or her resources, as well as the available community resources play an integral role in the selection process. We will address the selection process in more depth later in this chapter.

Historically, addictive populations have tended to be categorized by substance of abuse (i.e., alcohol or drug), with even further subdivision by specific type of drug. Within each of these categories exist additional subgroups (i.e., adolescent, adult, elderly, and so forth). Carroll's work (1986) pointed out that when demographics of age, race, and sex are controlled, more similarities than differences exist among alcoholics, addicts, and polysubstance abusers with respect to personality needs, self-concept, psychopathology, and self-reported problems. Later work by Carrol et al. (1993) pointed out that many substance abusers have other concurrent psychiatric disorders or concurrent alcohol dependence problems that have been associated with poorer outcomes in group substance abuse treatment. It is useful for the group leader to recognize the differences that exist between the individuals seeking treatment; only with this information can the leader hope to be sensitive to the specific needs the individuals may have. Of particular importance are issues related to cultural and ethnic diversity, especially as they relate to group process. We will address these issues later in the chapter.

The purpose and subsequent goals of group work with chemically dependent individuals are varied. Included among them are personal goals of sobriety and/or other means of increasing level of functioning as well as the use of group work as a form of social control. There are many paths that lead individuals to seek treatment. However, coercion, whether directly applied via the courts or indirectly implemented through suggestion or implication, is playing an ever-increasing role in individuals' motivation to seek treatment. The role coercion plays in influencing group work is important to recognize, especially as it relates to group selection, process, and outcome. Groups that include a majority of resistant, distrustful, and angry court-referred members will certainly feature a different dynamic process, as well as outcome, than would be seen in a more heterogeneously selected group. When feeder sources supply individuals for groups, the group leader screens, selects, and then constructs groups that are consistent based upon selected outcomes. This process is most effective when similar goals are sought by all principals—that is, the feeder source, the members making up the group, and the group leader.

As was noted earlier, the intent of this chapter is to provide a balance between the ideal view and the pragmatic, practice-reality view. Thus far, we have presented the ideal view with regard to group construction. To provide some balance, we now turn to the pragmatic view. In the field, especially in agency or hospital practice, where counselors or therapists operate within a program model and under specific policies and procedures, the opportunity to freely construct groups may be limited. In these settings the group leader may be assigned previously established groups and/or be instructed to conduct a group with the clients currently registered in the program. This situation is not unusual in chemical dependency treatment programs. The leader's lack of control over group construction may present problems in group development as well as in the accomplishment of the goals and objectives of the group. Group work can occur under these conditions, and indeed does, yet may require not only an increased skill level on the part of the group leader but also modification of the goals of the group. Clearly articulated standards of care, the effective use of clinical supervision, and the utilization of clinical staff members for difficult situations are of assistance in dealing with less than ideal circumstances. Most behavioral health care organizations offer group leaders the structures and processes necessary to operate effectively and ethically.

Group Norms

Generally, the establishment of group norms is a culture-building process that takes place early in the group's development. These norms operate as a set of behavioral and ethical rules for the group. This culture-building process within groups has critical significance to the ultimate functioning level of the group. The group leader's role is to shape this culture into one that will be conducive to a therapeutic process. Yalom (1975), who has written extensively on the critical nature of culture building within groups and the group leader's role in the process, pointed out the importance of this process when he stated that, to a large extent, the group, rather than its leader alone, is the agent of change.

The idealized norms for chemical dependency groups are virtually identical to those for other types of groups: participation, nonjudgmental acceptance of others, self-disclosure, dissatisfaction with present behaviors, and the desire to change. Members should feel free to honestly express themselves, as well as to confront or question other members and the group leader. Yalom (1975) suggested that the group leader approach the important task of establishing norms "in an informed, deliberate manner" (p. 110) to prevent counterproductive norms from developing. During the early stages of group development, and often throughout a group's tenure, the leader must take a directive stance to establish and reinforce norms.

Yalom (1985) identified two basic roles the group leader must assume in the group: (a) technical expert, and (b) model-setting participant. In both of these roles the leader can influence the shaping of the group's norms. How the leader applies the roles depends on his or her particular clinical biases and personality and the group's composition and needs. In groups of chemically dependent members, the leader must shift back and forth, first providing information and guiding insight, then modeling open, empathic acceptance of others. The often discussed issue of confrontation, which is a critical aspect of chemical dependency treatment, occurs not only in the early stages of recovery, when the member is in denial, but throughout the life of the group. Confrontation gives the leader an excellent opportunity to model appropriate methods of establishing personal boundaries and limit setting.

Some norms that are specific to treatment/recovery groups relate to chemical or alcohol use. Norms must be established early in the group process to deal with issues of members coming to group sessions under the influence of chemicals or alcohol. Specifically, will slips or relapses be tolerated, and if so, under what conditions? The acting out of frustration, anger, authority issues, and other issues raised in group sessions often result in members' reverting to chemical or alcohol use. The leader must assess the role the specific incident of chemical use might be playing in the total picture of the member on both an intrapersonal and an interpersonal level and differentiate use related to a relapse and use as a form of acting out behavior. The concrete, black-and-white thinking of group members may make this task more difficult. Group members may become uncomfortable or angry when other members fail to remain sober, regardless of the reason for it.

Relapse is a reality that usually is not expected but nonetheless happens with some frequency in groups of recovering members. Group leaders may see a member's lack of total abstinence as failure and blame either the member or themselves. This kind of thinking results in anything from an increased dropout rate by members to discouraged, overly strict group leaders. The leader and the group members have to understand the reality of relapse and incorporate this understanding into their established norms for behavior within the group. A plan of support should be established for dealing with relapse. Group members and other supportive people (friends, family, employer, Alcoholics Anonymous sponsor) are some often used sources of support during relapse crises. Having a support group to bring the relapse experience back to, in order to share, understand, and ultimately extinguish or prevent future relapses, is critical to the effectiveness of the treatment group and the recovery process.

From the time of a group's inception to its closure, the evolutionary process of the group will be dictated by the members and everything they bring to the experience. The leader's personal self and professional self enter into this evolutionary process. Whether an ideal self-monitoring, freely self-disclosing, and self-valuing group evolves depends not on any one part of the whole but on the whole itself.

Physiological, Psychological/Cognitive, and Sociological Factors ~

When working with addicted populations in groups, the leader must be prepared to handle a full range of presentations, defenses, and behaviors. Although similarities stemming from the process of addiction are inherent, physiological, psychological/cognitive, and sociological factors produce many and varied presentations, defenses, and behaviors in recovering individuals. To successfully deal with these behaviors and attitudes in the group is a challenge to the leader's expertise, experience, and knowledge of addiction. Group leaders need to have thorough knowledge of addiction, sociological factors, and physiological variables with addiction. In addition, they need clinical skills to handle disruptive or antitherapeutic defenses. Flexibility and insight are useful assets for the leader, helping to keep him or her from being overwhelmed and also helping the leader organize the varied presentations, defenses, and behaviors into a meaningful assessment and viable treatment plan for each group member.

Physiological Factors

Certain variables affecting recovery are physiological in origin and likely affect a large proportion of chemically dependent individuals. These neurophysiological similarities in chemically addicted people may be present regardless of whether the drug of choice is alcohol or any other drug.

Platelet MAO   Platelet MAO (monoamineoxidase), recognized as a stable biological marker in humans, has been linked to both chemical dependency and mental illness. MAO contributes to the metabolism of certain neurotransmitters, including norepinephrine and dopamine, that allow us to experience pleasure. MAO-B is the enzyme particularly responsible for the breakdown of dopamine (Haberny et al., 1995). Studies have consistently shown lower platelet MAO levels in recovering alcoholics (Olesen, Fallon, & Mark, 1993). The net result of lower levels of MAO is to increase the available amount of norepinephrine and dopamine. People with clinical depression do not have the average amounts of these neurotransmitters. Although monoamineoxidase inhibitors may be given as antidepressants, tricyclic antidepressants are most often prescribed because of the side effects associated with monoamineoxidase inhibitors in combination with certain foods. Altered MAO level is considered a factor in bipolar disorders, and increased dopamine activity has been thought to have a significant role in schizophrenia.

With the ingestion of alcohol, more of the chemical neurotransmitters are released. Increased dopamine level is linked with amphetamine and cocaine use. Amphetamine and cocaine release dopamine. This facilitates the "high" associated with the use of these drugs. Once the dopamine is used up, depression sets in, leading to repeated use of amphetamine, cocaine, and/or alcohol. Thus, the cycle of addiction reinforces itself (Goldstein, 1994; Olesen et al., 1993).

Behaviors associated with lowered levels of MAO are increased sensation seeking, extraversion, and avoidance of monotony (von Knorring, von Knorring, Smegan, Lindberg, & Edholm, 1987). Lowered MAO levels might contribute to states of agitation, anxiety, mood disturbance, and emotionality, which clinicians often observe in newly recovering individuals (Krippenstapel, 1987). These behaviors have direct relevance to those seen in groups and are likely to be factors in relapse.

Teaching newly recovering individuals to understand their mood changes, their tendency to feel bored, and their need for stimulation and then facilitating constructive alternatives are important. The group leader should be aware of these tendencies in members and be able to recognize them when they appear. Helping the recovering members understand that biochemical reasons may underlie these discomforts helps them accept the discomforts and reduces negative and guilt-ridden self-talk. Means to manage these feelings might include attending more AA meetings, contacting others by telephone when bored, managing anger, and planning leisure time.

TIQs in the Brain   Higher levels of tetrahydroisoquinolins (TIQs) in the brain have been observed in chronic alcoholics and heroin addicts. They have not been found in normal social drinkers or other addicts (Olesen et al., 1993). These morphinelike substances ultimately replace the endorphins/enkephalins—the natural opiates—in the brain. Natural endorphine production becomes damaged, resulting in diminished ability of recovering individuals to experience enjoyment and pleasure without the drug being externally introduced (Krippenstapel, 1987). Repeated use of an opiate may turn off the production of new receptors because of the presence of excessive amounts of the neurotransmitter (Goldstein, 1994). Fewer receptors means less sensitivity to a drug, which leads to tolerance. Fewer receptors may lead to dependence due to receptor deficiency when the drug is withdrawn. TIQs are more addicting than morphine. The addict needs to keep using opiates to keep the brain producing the TIQs to which it is now addicted. TIQs stay in the brain. Any further opiate use produces more TIQs and reactivates those already there (Olesen et al., 1993).

If the group leader notices that members do not seem to experience pleasure, he or she might introduce into the group discussion ways members can improve their quality of life, such as exercise, humor appreciation, and leisure and recreational activities. We have found that when we explain underlying physical factors to newly recovering individuals, they respond with interest and are more likely to experiment with suggested alternatives. Although a faulty gene may be the ultimate cause of improper metabolism of alcohol or heroin, it remains the alcoholic's/addict's responsibility not to use the drug.

Post Acute Withdrawal   A leader in the area of relapse prevention, Terrance Gorski, wrote about the phenomenon of post acute withdrawal, describing it as a period when certain physiological processes produce episodes of decreased functioning in newly recovering individuals (Gorski & Miller, 1986). Members of support groups have known about this phenomenon for some time, as indicated by references to "dry drunks" and the "(30- 60- 90-) day syndrome."

Symptoms of post acute withdrawal include lowered ability to handle stress, poorer motor coordination, sleep and appetite disturbances, emotional overreaction or emotional "numbness," and difficulty with certain mental processes such as attention, memory, abstract reasoning, and decision-making skills. Gorski and Miller (1986) attributed these symptoms to damage to the brain from the use of chemicals in combination with less ability to handle stress. Group leaders involved with recovering members must understand this phenomenon and have a good working knowledge of the ways to manage post acute withdrawal to counter the chances of relapse.

Because stress figures so heavily in post acute withdrawal, compounded by the individual's diminished capacity to handle stress, the best way to alleviate post acute withdrawal is to lower stress. Rest, proper diet, expressing feelings, discussing fears about what is occurring, education, relaxation methods, and eliminating caffeine can all temper post acute withdrawal. Often, just knowing that post acute withdrawal is a temporary physical condition can offset much of the recovering persons' anxieties and negative self-talk about their ability to function.

Psychological/Cognitive Factors

The physiological factors that have been mentioned, plus other biological factors, both preexisting and generated as a direct result of active addiction, lead to certain observable cognitive deficits in recovering individuals. Krippenstapel (1987) reported that alcoholics generally have a higher activity level than nonalcoholics and that the incidence of hyperactivity during childhood is higher for alcoholics. Also, a direct relationship seems to exist between lowered MAO levels and mania, increased sensation seeking, and avoidance of monotony. Von Knorring et al. (1987) likewise reported lowered MAO levels, increased sensation seeking, and higher monotony avoidance among alcoholics. The implications for group work arising from these tendencies are significant.

Clinical observations support the assertion that newly recovering members are often bored and restless in groups that are lengthy or not interesting to them. Members who are not actively participating in the group are most likely to be bored and nonattentive. Although their lack of attention might be blamed on resistance or denial, certain biological reasons might be contributing. Skilled group leaders will need to be aware of this problem if they find they are losing the attention of group members.

Eliciting responses from nonattentive members, and even using appropriate dramatic or controversial techniques can help restore a nonattentive group. The group leader's charisma can be brought to bear as well. In a residential facility, for example, the residents often compare the various group leaders' approaches to groups. Leaders who are charismatic and use drama skillfully often receive fewer complaints about their groups being boring. When residents anticipate a group will be led by a "boring leader," their feelings often lead to negative self-fulfilling prophesies and heightened discomfort within the group. This is especially true with educational groups in a treatment program.

Another cognitive impairment often seen in recovering people is a problem with attention persistence. Krippenstapel (1987) pointed out that behaviors such as failing to do assignments, being at the wrong place for appointments, and in general not following instructions may in some cases be mislabeled as passive/aggressive resistance when actually they stem from attention problems. Even minor problems in this area have implications for treatment. Group leaders may have to be particularly clear in their directives. And, in our experience, repetition of significant information and ideas has usually yielded noticeably better results with alcoholics and addicts. AA has known about such attention problems for some time; to counter the problem, members repeat many sayings to newcomers, such as "Don't drink and go to meetings," "Keep it simple," and "One day at a time."

A higher level of emotionality, or the reactivity of individuals to stimulation, combined with lower levels of "soothability" after excitement, also characterizes recovering alcoholics and addicts. Somatic indications of these cognitive impairments are found in galvanic skin response, blood pressure, and heartbeat, among other responses, in diagnosed alcoholics. Recovering individuals often look for ways to reduce or avoid situations that contribute to negative responses.

Individuals in the early stages of recovery initially seem to have an absence of emotions or an absence of a range of emotions. Clinical observations and impressions seem to confirm that the emotions associated with fight/flight (such as fear, anxiety, anger, hostility, and rage) are likely to be present and are usually associated with a wider variety of situations. In addition, limitations in coping skills restrict the variety of responses to situations. Members in groups are likely to have higher levels of psychic anxiety, somatic anxiety, and muscular tension—differences that have been measured by researchers (von Knorring et al., 1987).

Gorski and Miller (1986) discussed the relationship of post acute withdrawal to stress and attributed this relationship to physiological factors such as damage to the brain resulting from chemical use (including chronic toxicity and falls/injury to the head while intoxicated or high). During periods of post acute withdrawal, individuals show an inability to handle stress and difficulty in controlling emotions. Continued research and increasing medical knowledge of the effects of addiction will likely add much to the understanding of reasons for behaviors noted in newly recovering individuals. Although observers for some time have had difficulty in agreeing upon what constitutes a pre-addictive personality with associated stable traits, more evidence exists for similarities in people after they have been actively addicted.

The emerging theories surrounding addiction and recovery maintain that the process of recovery entails much more than simply a mirror image of the decline in active stages of using addictive chemicals. The process of growth in recovery may be linked to the Piagetian process of assimilation and accommodation. Recovering alcoholics are likely to have cognitive impairments. Neuropsychological impairment is often seen in the areas of problem solving, new task learning, retaining unfamiliar material, and engaging in deductive, logical thinking relative to unfamiliar conceptual material. Neuropsychological impairment is reminiscent of the stages of cognitive development in the Piagetian model, with individuals progressing from concrete operations to formal operations.

Newly recovering individuals may have difficulty understanding certain concepts involved in the process of growth and change and in the ordering of the world around them. Cognitive distortions common among newly recovering individuals are tunnel vision, euphoric recall, and cognitive distortion of current circumstances. For example, in euphoric recall the person magnifies past, pleasant events involved with chemical use while minimizing or forgetting unpleasant consequences. In cognitive distortions of the present, the person may magnify problems of the here and now and minimize the benefits of sobriety. Tunnel vision makes the individual's entire existence seem either dismal or in the "pink cloud" that AA members often refer to in a newly recovering person. These cognitive distortions of reality unfortunately can have devastating results if they end in a relapse.

Intervention may be necessary when the group leader observes these thought patterns. The member's reality of recovery may have to be explained and reframed with more use of the concrete and less of the abstract. The group leader may have to use explanations, concepts, and words that the recovering member can comprehend and relate to. Among the reasons for the success of the book *Alcoholics Anonymous* was that it was written in language newly recovering people could understand.

Sociological Factors

Many sociological factors contribute to human functioning in social settings. In regard to chemically dependent members in groups, at least two sociological factors are relevant to group functioning: *educational background* and *economic conditions* under which individuals live. Wide disparity between group members in either of these two areas will impede the development and functioning level of the group. During the assessment and group-building processes, these two issues should be closely considered. If the leader cannot control who comes into the group, he or she must apply skill and effort toward minimizing these differences and, at the same time, try to identify areas of common experience and purpose and increase members' insight into these areas.

Counterproductive Group Process ～

Facilitating a group of chemically dependent members requires acute awareness of characterological behavior that is often defensive. Individual members can successfully defend these behaviors through a number of intellectual exercises. A group leader who is knowledgeable of and experienced with these intellectualizations can effectively intervene, using instances of these behaviors to advantage. The goal is to disrupt and lessen members' need and habit for these counterproductive behaviors.

Denial and Resistance

Phenomenologically, denial and resistance seem to interact; the strength of one enhances the other. The more a client emphatically denies or rejects the label of addict or chemically dependent or problem drinker, the stronger is his or her resistance or opposition to intervention by an outside force.

Denial can be unconscious, leading to self-deception. The client in denial may unconsciously disguise motives to avoid recognition of personal qualities or behaviors that would decrease self-esteem, which is a threat to ego structure. Denial protects a client from truth that is too painful until that truth can be confronted safely (Kearney, 1996). A paradox exists because abuse of chemicals often derives from the addict's lack of self-esteem, and by virtue of the addiction the addict perpetrates behaviors so that self-loathing is obvious to everyone, especially the abuser. Denial is lying. Denial is ignoring reality (Olesen et al., 1993).

Resistance is classically thought to be a psychological barrier keeping the unconscious impulses from conscious perception (Monte, 1980). In the group setting, according to Corey and Corey (1987), it manifests from fears of change, rejection, or dependence on the group or the group leader. Ellis (1985) also noted fears of disclosure and hopelessness.

Denial can run the gamut from (a) lack of recognition of the need for treatment to (b) disbelief in the need to cooperate with the group or (c) unwillingness or inability to accept the magnitude of the problem or (d) not admitting any problems beyond the drug abuse. An often heard statement in a group is: "I don't know what I'm doing here—I don't need treatment or anyone." Naturally, the less denial or resistance, the greater is the openness to intervention, information gathering, and willingness to ask for assistance.

Within the context of denial and resistance reside psychological defenses and behaviors well rehearsed by those who are chemically dependent. Minimizing, rationalizing, justifying, and projecting are some of the more common, entrenched, and less healthy coping mechanisms that allow for continued abuse.

Minimizing allows the addict to admit chemical use while enabling the addict to lessen or reduce its impact on his or her life. Minimizing takes many forms. For example: "I've only been using heroin for a year, so I don't have as much of a problem as others in this group."

Rationalizing means creating plausible excuses for one's behavior that are superficial and without recognition of the true motives and beliefs underlying the behavior. For example: "I'm able to control my cocaine use by buying only the purest grade, so I use it less often and less of it each time."

Justifying entails excuses that allow support of or vindication for a behavior. It grants freedom from guilt or responsibility. For example: "Cocaine gives me the edge I need to beat the competition." "I don't need to speak up in the group because I learn better by listening."

Projecting places one's own behavior or ideas or impulses onto another, particularly behaviors or ideas that are objectionable or deemed negative. For example: "All the kids in high school drank beer and smoked grass, so I had to, too."

Defensive postures are well practiced and are manifested in a variety of ways. Group leaders must use confrontation by themselves and by the group to get past these positions. The goal is for the group members to discover ways to see themselves and their behavior realistically.

The denial/resistance phenomenon has both passive and active manifestations. A group member may combine any of the defensive postures in any way to maintain unhealthy beliefs and behaviors. The following are some common passive manifestations of denial/resistance. A member may be nonparticipatory—silent and withdrawn, remarking that he or she learns best by listening and watching. In such cases, the leader may effectively intervene by encouraging involvement and by appropriately expressing how the group member's behavior affects the leader, perhaps feeling as though he or she is being kept at a distance. A member may maintain a superior "better than you other addicts" demeanor. This attitude can stop group process, because others may be unwilling to expose themselves as less perfect. A nondefensive challenge by the group leader that will refocus the group is to ask what such a superior person is doing in the group, since he or she doesn't require help. A group member acting dependent and helpless, hoping for advice and solutions from others, also exemplifies a passive stance. This member can remain feeble and effectively resist therapy and any change by not taking action. In this example, the leader would continue to admonish the group not to give answers or advice and encourage the passive member to access his or her own power from the information he or she has already gleaned in group.

Opposite of passive denial/resistance are the more active demonstrations such as open hostility to the group, the leader, or the world in general. This hostility often takes the form of caustic remarks or sarcasm. Sometimes a member uses a passive/aggressive style. For example, a male member may catch a female group member by surprise, commenting on her being a "real man-hater," and then quickly apologize or say, "Just kidding." This leaves the woman angry, hurt, intimidated. The group leader needs to explore the interaction, ask the woman about her feelings and thoughts, and then move to the man's motivation for his action (Corey & Corey, 1982).

Other forms resistance can take are members' defocusing from individual self or the group process and focusing instead on others; speaking only of superficial or inconsequential matters; and challenging the leader's competence, knowledge, or lack of personal experience with addiction (Corey & Corey, 1982). The leader must allow the resistance and challenge the denial but must not defend his or her own position or self, even though feeling threatened, angry, or inadequate in the face of the opposition. Most important, the leader must teach through example.

Boredom, impatience, avoidance of eye contact, sleeping during group, being late for group, and not coming to group are further examples of resistance. Schoenewolf (1993) discussed the issue of counterresistance of the leader to a member's or the group's resistance, which often takes similar forms to the resistance of the member or the group.

Transference

Transference is demonstrated in the reproduction of past and often repressed experiences through one's present emotions and thoughts. The original object of the repressed material is replaced by another person in the client's mind. The concept of transference can be simplified by understanding that it involves a repeat of the past that is unsuited to the present situation (Flores, 1988).

An example within the group setting is when a group member sees the leader as harsh, cold, and unreceptive yet the group reality perceives the leader as vulnerable, warm, and open. This individual group member unrealistically places a memory of an important authority figure (mother, father, grandparent) onto another important authority figure (group leader) in the present. Often, behavioral mannerisms trigger the transference. The group leader might use verbal phrases or have a physical body type, haircut, hair color, or head movement similar to the original subject. If the transference goes unrecognized by the leader and the member, the original conflict, impairment, or dysfunction is not addressed, and the group member may remain stuck in an unresolved cycle of behavior patterns of the past that reinforces his or her drug/alcohol use as a substitute or cover-up for other defects as viewed from the past.

If, after the initial stage of the leader and members learning about one another and what the group means, a group member remains hostile, withdrawn, or inappropriately angry at the leader, the leader may question whether transference may be operating. In questioning and probing the member's memories or in asking how the member experiences the leader, the leader can learn to whom the anger is really being directed. The group member might admit to existing awareness or be surprised and enlightened by the new awareness. Often the group member is surprised at the material and the feelings he or she has repressed from conscious functioning, how this repression impacts on the member's relating to the leader, and how it has generalized to other authority figures. The unresolved past continues to distort the present. After becoming aware of transference, the leader and other group members can use this knowledge to help the individual member reexperience the past in the present, view the distorted thinking and behavior patterns and modify them, and thus impact the cycle of repetitive dysfunction with the hope of stopping it.

In addition to the group leader, other group members can be objects of transference, representing sibling rivalry, jealousy, an overdeveloped sense of responsibility, and/or continual need for nurturance or approval. When the group leader suspects such transference, it is helpful for the leader to view the group as a symbol of the member's own family of origin (Brown & Beletsis, 1986), with the member's behaviors being reenacted therein, as well as viewing the group as its own uniquely defined family. The group can serve as a microcosm of the larger community within which each member lives, works, and operates outside the group. An experienced group leader remains aware of these dynamics and open to informing the group of its here-and-now behavior that might be a replay from the past. The group members can apply the dynamics with one another.

As a word of caution, the leader and the group should be careful not to use knowledge of transference as a distancing mechanism to keep worries or feelings such as inadequacy or anger at bay or to keep other group members away. Labeling problems or confrontations as transference and then dismissing them could conceivably be avoiding here-and-now events that may accurately represent the present instead of the past. A perception of the group leader as wishy-washy, unreliable, and nonsupportive may be an astute observation of the present and not a comment of disappointment surrounding a father's lack of defense of his son against a punitive mother. For change to occur, repressed and present-moment feelings must be differentiated and expressed and then worked with therapeutically (Corey & Corey, 1987).

Countertransference

Countertransference refers to feelings a group member stimulates in the leader. These feelings may come out of the past and represent unresolved issues or struggles in the leader. Countertransference may or may not be related to a member's transference issues (Gold & Nemiah, 1993). As with member transference, countertransference in the leader is at odds with the present situation. If there is to be continued healthy expression by group members, the leader must be aware of and address countertransference when it occurs. To reveal these issues to the group, however, may not always be wise or in the group's best interests. For example, a leader may be particularly attracted to or dislike a specific member. Divulging this to the group might be hurtful and embarrassing to the member and would accomplish nothing beyond exposing the leader's dubious belief that he or she had to be totally honest with the group.

A common problem confronting the leader is one of power. As substance abusers often think and react in extremes, they may hail the leader as savior, wise one, and/or expert. Quickly, members bestow their own power on the leader as they did to the parent, mate, boss, or drug. Just as quickly, the leader can be demoted and denounced when he or she fails to provide the answers or nurturance group members unrealistically expect. A leader may unconsciously keep members in a powerless position in the group and may not be able to sort out his or her own disappointment, anger, or hurt when members attack him or her as inadequate or uncaring. An unaware leader may then fall into the trap of reproducing the more verbally disagreeable members' failure patterns by punishing them.

Another common countertransference issue is the leader's belief that as a helper, he or she will be admired and loved by group members, in contrast to how others in the leader's life view him or her. The leader thus comes to depend on members as the source of nourishment and feeling good. A characteristic of substance abusers is a continual need to be nourished, approved of, cared for, or filled up, because they do not believe they can do this for themselves. If transference/countertransference issues are unrecognized or dismissed as unimportant without examination, the leader can get caught up in meeting these member needs and at the same time be appreciated (loved) for doing so. The leader is rewarded and the member is rewarded, but the result may be that no change occurs and, ultimately, the member relapses.

Finally, the group member who is holding onto intense anger, hostility, distrust, or resentment (Flores, 1988) often manifests his or her feelings in aggressive attacks on the leader. These barrages may bring forth similar reactive behaviors in group leaders who are insecure or unaware of their own personal issues related to authority or interpersonal relationships. Continued self-evaluation, ongoing education, and close processing with a clinical supervisor can bring these issues to light and diminish possible deleterious effects of countertransference with members.

Group Reinforcement

Peer pressure encourages change. As group members allow one another to change, they reinforce change. Sharing experiences and understanding the universality of behaviors create intimacy and acceptance, resulting in healing and forgiveness of oneself and others.

Although the group's capacity for healing is powerful, the group leader must be cognizant of group members' power to reinforce one another to resist change, sometimes not even consciously. For example, allowing members to dwell on how awful they are because of their days of abuse, known as telling "war stories," keeps them in the "there and then." This focus merely reinforces their hopelessness to ever change, improve, or get past their past. The leader must remember that however uncomfortable past and current addictive behavior is, it is a known quantity and gives more comfort than the fear created by facing the unknown through change.

Peer pressure in this instance discourages change. The group can reinforce itself to stay safe by remaining superficial and unwilling to move to more painful subjects. As one member begins to make a meaningful disclosure about a moving and particularly painful incident, other members, uncomfortable with the revelations, sometimes become anxious and move to block the communication by narrowing in, giving advice, or stating how they would have handled the situation better. The group begins to compete for worst story or best solution, ignoring the member's original attempts at meaningful disclosure.

Group Sessions ～

An outline of six group sessions is presented here. Following Yalom's basic structure (1983), the outline represents one of many ways to approach group counseling for people with addictions. The ideal group size is 8-12 members. The group meets once a week for approximately 1½–2 hours. Remember that many of the members may be referred by the criminal justice system and mandated to attend some form of treatment. Thus, the members may not be enthusiastic about attendance, which often results in resistance.

Session 1. The leader and co-leader introduce themselves and prepare the group members for the group experience. Preparation takes the form of discussing the purpose of group, the group norms (rules), and what is to be accomplished by the group. Group members are then encouraged to introduce themselves and state their reasons for attending the group. This part of the initial session may take some time due to the reluctance of some members to be forthcoming with strangers, especially with group leaders, whom they may regard as authority figures and potential threats to their freedom. Group leaders must continue to stress the confidential nature of the group and that the group can be a safe place to express pain and fears as well as joys and accomplishments. Upon the completion of the introductions, the leaders encourage the members' participation in formulating individual agenda topics or issues for discussion. These center around the impact of addiction in the member's life situation. Once an agenda topic is formulated, the group member involved is given time to share and the work begins. Often several members can work on personal issues during each group session. The leaders model involvement and ask for other group member involvement with the issues under discussion. A few minutes before the end of session, the group leaders briefly summarize what occurred in the group and check to see if everyone is okay to leave the session.

Session 2. The leader and co-leader reorient the group members to the purpose of the group and again ask for quick introductions of members but move quickly to the agenda section. Leaders might initiate discussion by inquiring in general how the members are doing being away from their drug of choice. This in itself may lead into an agenda issue for one or more members. If not, the leaders would question each member as to possible pressing issues. An issue is chosen (with group consensus), and work begins. The leaders need to attend to keeping the group focused on the here-and-now feelings and thoughts about how not using a drug impacts on their lives. Members may want to wander off into stories about drug use, which in turn can lead to euphoric recall, a dangerous fantasizing of how wonderful drugs are. Asking members to state positive events that have occurred since the last session can help ground the group. Again, a few minutes before the end of session, the group leaders summarize what occurred in the group and check to see if everyone is okay to leave the session. This summary is a standard for each session. By the third or fourth session, the leaders might ask the members to summarize what happened in the group.

Session 3. By this session, members are familiar with the norms of the group and one another. They need little encouragement from the leaders to begin discussion. Members once reluctant to share join the discussions, often with other members' encouragement and without the need for leader intervention. If members remain resistant to sharing issues in the group, the leaders may want to be prepared with a structured exercise on communication skills or relapse prevention material.

Structured exercises are safe ways for members to involve themselves without fear of appearing vulnerable. At any appropriate time in group sessions, leaders can inject a structured exercise. Many people with addictions know much about drug use but have little understanding of clear communication or realistic coping skills.

Session 4. In this session, leaders might point out to members the commonality of their experiences beyond the obvious experience of drug use. Members continue to share individual issues. Many will excitedly relate how their lives have improved by their remaining sober. Others may note how desperate and unhappy they feel without the use of drugs. The leaders facilitate discussions on coping mechanisms, relapse prevention strategies, and the option of involving significant others in some treatment process. They emphasize the importance of support groups. Group members may begin to rely on one another for mutual support.

Session 5. The group at this time may require little structuring by the leaders. Members know what to expect from one another and from the leaders. Confrontations are more frequent, as is supportive dialogue. Some members may show symptoms of post acute withdrawal. Leaders verbalize this phenomenon when they observe it and ask if others are experiencing similar symptoms. Members may be bored with sobriety or fearful of the success of sobriety, and relapse is a strong possibility. Leaders must discuss the possibility of relapse openly and encourage members to do the same. Group members may be feeling pressure from significant others to relapse. New roles are uncomfortable for the recovering member and the significant others. There is an awareness that the new role of sobriety has unmeasured yet concrete responsibilities. By now, the group leaders are reminding group members that the group experience is about to end. Leaders must prepare the group for the last session.

Session 6. This last session focuses on learning and termination. Members are asked to list what they have gained and lost since joining the group. Many of the losses are expressed as gains. Members express what being in the group has meant to them. Leaders underline the learning they have observed for each of the group members. The idea of termination being an ending, and thus a loss, is reframed to being simply another change. Members are encouraged to continue their support of one another and continue to attend other support groups.

Impact of Learning and Education on Group Process ~

Within the group milieu lies a vast potential for learning. As a group begins, usually with members who do not know one another and who are unaware of the biological, social, or psychological effects of addiction on themselves, learning plays a key role. Addiction is often called the disease of denial, and education regarding this disease begins to unveil the denial. Therapeutic change commences.

Information about addiction/alcoholism is shared realistically and factually in groups, relieving and erasing irrational fears or fantasy beliefs about the physiology of abuse. A foundation of knowledge is developed, staving off further denial. Along with this, education addresses the accompanying beliefs and feelings of shame and guilt imbedded in the members' minds about their inherent weakness of character, or their being recurrent life failures, because they are not able to curb the abuse alone.

Education takes on a dimension deeper than simply learning facts and fallacies. In the group setting, members have an opportunity to learn and attempt new coping mechanisms. They practice confrontation, preferably moving away from aggressive, hostile demands and accusations to assertive and clearly stated expressions of feelings and thoughts. As the group allows and accepts individual changes, self-esteem and self-acceptance increase, and self-loathing and ineffective self-rewards concurrently decrease. Group members can see how learning stimulates growth in other members, which impacts positively on the interactions in the group as well as outside the group.

Long-denied or unrecognized feelings come to the fore. Dependence on drugs/alcohol, on the group, or on the group leader abates as the sense of autonomy and control rises. Superficial verbalizations are heard less frequently, and sensitive communication develops as interaction skills improve. As the interaction among group members becomes better, the pervasive sense of isolation often accompanying addiction wanes, to be replaced by new life skills and mastery (Khantzian, 1986).

Tasks of the Group Leader ∼

Beyond the normal tasks ascribed to a group leader working with addicted populations (Yalom, 1985), a focus needs to be placed on the leader's ability to be directive, confrontive, tolerant, and nondefensive. *Directive* means being an active participant in the group by guiding discussion, using appropriate self-disclosure, and maintaining personal honesty with group members. When the group begins energizing toward someone's "war stories," the leader, rather than staying apart and letting members vent and free-associate as they will, must intervene by leading the discussion back to a present, reality-based orientation. A gentle reminder that the group is not a democratic process may be called for. In this same vein, the leader may be required to structure time and experiences in the group, doling out homework as relevant and encouraging reports on learning from previous assignments. Being directive means maintaining the focus and modeling discipline, addressing the need for self-control over low frustration tolerance while dealing with the impulsiveness often ascribed to addicted persons.

Confrontation implies challenging the group or individual members to look beyond surface issues, questioning assumptions, and disputing self-defeating patterns, mannerisms, and beliefs. Confronting can be direct, with the leader attacking the obvious denial, or it can be indirect, with a query toward what underlies the presenting behavior. Confrontation must never be at the expense of the member's sense of self-respect or cause injury to the member. This is not a power struggle with the leader as winner. No one wins.

The leader must maintain a *tolerant attitude* toward emotional raging, physical outbursts, and verbal accusations. The pain group members may feel could be attributed in part to withdrawing from drugs or alcohol as well as to facing deep issues of abandonment, rejection, separation, self-loathing, or intense anger. This recognition facilitates respect for another's beliefs or opinions without necessarily agreeing with or accepting them as one's own.

In conjunction with tolerance is an ability to remain *nondefensive* when faced with hostile and aggressive behaviors. If active transference is in progress and the group leader is aware of it, he or she can accept that the feelings are directed to a past object rather than to the group leader.

Summary ~

In this chapter, we have provided the reader with a broad outline of both clinical and administrative functions and concerns as they relate to group counseling or therapy with addicted populations. Group construction, physiological, psychological/cognitive, and sociological factors were discussed along with some of the more obvious counterproductive processes that often occur in group counseling or therapy with addicted populations.

Several issues are noticeable due to their lack of inclusion in this chapter. The subjects of co-dependency, dual diagnosis clients (those with chronically mentally ill diagnoses as well as addiction diagnoses), and combining within a group members abusing different types of chemicals were left to larger bodies of work.

It is useful to remind oneself that addictive disorders resemble other chronic medical disorders in that they are characterized by relapses and remissions. It has not been a goal of this chapter to criticize short-term, time-limited models of group work with substance abusers; however, it makes sense to consider O'Brien's (1994) observation that we are faced with the public's expectations of a "cure" for a chronic, perhaps incurable, disorder. We would add that the public also expects that the "cure" be inexpensive as well as brief.

The intent of this chapter was to focus on practical information and usable guidelines in working with a difficult, challenging, and stimulating population. We hope the intent was realized.

References ~

Agazarian, Y., & Peters, R. (1981). *The visible and invisible group.* London: Routledge & Kegan Paul.

Alcoholics Anonymous World Services, Inc., New York City, Third Edition, 1976, Fortieth Printing 1991.

Brown, S. (1985). *Treating the alcoholic: A developmental mode of recovery.* New York: Wiley.

Brown, S., & Beletsis, S. (1986). The development of family transference in groups for adult children of alcoholics. *Journal of Group Psychotherapy, 36*(1), 97–114.

Carrol, K. M., Power, M. D., Bryant, K. J., & Rounsaville, B. J. (1993). One year follow-up status of treatment seeking cocaine abusers; psychopathology and dependence severity as predictors of outcome. *Journal of Nervous & Mental Disorders, 181*(4), 71–79.

Carroll, J. F. X. (1983). *Substance abuse problem checklist.* Eagleville, PA: Eagleville Hospital.

Carroll, J. F. X. (1986). Treating alcoholics and drug abusers together in residential programs: A question of resident compatibility and staff preparedness. *Alcoholism Treatment Quarterly, 3*(1), 119–131.

Chavez, N., administrator of the Substance Abuse and Mental Health Administration. *Testimony before Senate Committee on Labor and Human Services,* July 27, 1995. Washington, DC.

Corey, G., & Corey, M. S. (1982). *Groups: Process and practice* (2nd ed.). Monterey, CA: Brooks/Cole.

Corey, G., & Corey, M. S. (1987). *Groups: Process and practice* (3rd. ed.). Pacific Grove, CA: Brooks/Cole.

Daley, C., Moss, H., & Campbell, F. (1987). *Dual diagnosis: Counseling clients with chemical dependency and mental illness.* Center City, MN: Hazelton Foundation.

Department of Health and Human Services, *Request for Proposal No. TI 96-01, No. 93.230,* June 1996.

Ellis, A. (1985). *Overcoming resistance.* New York: Springer.

Flores, P. J. (1988). *Group psychotherapy with addicted populations.* New York: Haworth Press.

Flores, P. J., & Mahon, L. (1993). The treatment of addiction in group psychotherapy. *International Journal of Group Psychotherapy, 43*(2), 143–156.

Gold, J. H., & Nemiah, J. C. (Eds.). (1993). *Beyond transference: When the therapist's real life intrudes.* Washington, DC: American Psychiatric Press.

Goldstein, A. (1994). *Addiction: From biology to drug policy.* New York: Freeman.

Gorski, T. T. (1995). *Brief strategic problem-solving group therapy.* Independence, MO: Herald House/Independence Press.

Gorski, T. T., & Miller, M. (1986). *Staying sober.* Independence, MO: Herald House/Independence Press.

Grayson, E. S. (1993). *Short term group counseling.* Arlington, TX: Kirby Lithographic.

Haberny, K. A., Walsh, S. L., Ginn, D. H., Wilkins, J. N., Garner, J. E., Setoda, D., & Bigelow, G. E. (1995). Absence of acute cocaine interactions with the MAO-B inhibitor Selegiline. *Drug and Alcohol Dependence, 39,* 55–62.

Kearney, R. J. (1996). *Within the wall of denial: Conquering addictive behaviors.* New York: Norton.

Khantzian, E. J. (1986). A contemporary psychodynamic approach to drug abuse treatment. *American Journal of Drug & Alcohol Abuse, 12*(3), 213–222.

Khantzian, E. J., Halliday, K. S., & McAuliffe, W. E. (1990). *Addiction and the vulnerable self.* New York: Guilford.

Krippenstapel, P. (1987). A fresh look at relapse. *Alcoholism Treatment Quarterly, 4*(4), 1–17.

Levine, B. (1979). *Group psychotherapy: Practice and development.* Englewood Cliffs, NJ: Prentice-Hall.

Levine, B., & Gallogly, V. (1985). *Group therapy with alcoholics: Outpatient and inpatient approaches.* Human Services Guide, Vol. 40. Newbury Park, CA: Sage.

McLellan, A. T., Luborsky, L., Cacciola, J., McGahan, P., O'Brien, C. P., & Griffith, J. (1985). *Guide to the addiction severity index.* Washington, DC: Department of Health & Human Services.

Monte, C. F. (1980). *Beneath the mask: An introduction to theories of personality* (2nd ed.). New York: Holt, Rinehart & Winston.

O'Brien, C. P. (1994). Overview: The treatment of drug dependence. *Addiction, 89*(11), 1565.

Olesen, J., Fallon, J., & Mark, L. (1993). *A manual for chemical dependency and psychiatric treatment.* Santa Fe, NM: C. L. Productions.

Prochaska, J. O., DiClemente, C. C., & Norcross, J. C. (1992). In search of how people change. *American Psychologist, 47*(9), 1102–1114.

Schoenewolf, G. (1993). *Counterresistance: The therapist's interference with the therapeutic process.* Northvale, NJ: Jason Aronson.

Vannicelli, M. (1988). Group therapy aftercare for alcoholic patients. *International Journal of Group Psychotherapy, 38*(3), 337–352.

von Knorring, L., von Knorring, A., Smegan, L., Lindberg, U., & Edholm, M. (1987). Personality traits in subtypes of alcoholics. *Journal of Studies on Alcohol, 48*(6), 523–527.

Yalom, I. (1975). *The theory and practice of group psychotherapy* (2nd ed.). New York: Basic Books.

Yalom, I. (1983). *Inpatient group psychotherapy.* New York: Basic Books.

Yalom, I. (1985). The theory and practice of group psychotherapy (3rd ed.). New York: Basic Books.

Zimberg, S., Wallace, J., & Blume, S. B. (1985). Group psychotherapy in the treatment of alcoholism. In *Practical approaches to alcoholism psychotherapy* (2nd ed.). New York: Plenum.

13

Group Counseling for Individuals With Eating Disorders

Mary Lou Bryant Frank

The constellation of eating disorders came into public awareness in the 1970s and 1980s because of the reported increase in incidence. Due to work by Boskind-Lodahl (1976) and Bruch (1973), eating disorders garnered the attention of the psychological and medical communities and precipitated early research and theorizing regarding etiology and treatment. Still in the formative stage, group counseling and therapy approaches understandably have been varied. The interpersonal nature of these disorders suggests that group treatment may offer the most potent remedy for individuals with eating disorders.

Classifications, Definitions, and Explanation

Eating disorders were first described in 1971 by Nylonder (Scarano & Kalodner-Martin, 1994) as existing on a continuum. Since then, others have also observed relationships among the primary eating disorders: anorexia nervosa, bulimia nervosa, and binge eating (Brownell & Foreyt, 1986; Fairburn & Garner, 1986; Johnson & Maddi, 1986; Russell, 1979; Squire, 1983). These three disorders are the anchors for understanding the spectrum of food and weight concerns.

Anorexia nervosa and *bulimia* were first acknowledged as diagnostic categories in the third edition of the *Diagnostic and Statistical Manual of Mental Disorders* (DSM III) (American Psychiatric Association, 1980). Seven years later, the

American Psychiatric Association changed the name bulimia to bulimia nervosa, still indicating similarities between this disorder and anorexia nervosa. The current diagnostic criteria for anorexia nervosa and bulimia nervosa are outlined in the DSM IV (American Psychiatric Association, 1994, pp. 544-550), with descriptions provided for both diagnostic categories. According to the DSM IV, anorexia nervosa may be classified as either Restricting Type or Binge-Eating/Purging Type (American Psychiatric Association, 1994, p. 541). Likewise, bulimia may be subtyped as Purging Type or Nonpurging Type (American Psychiatric Association, 1994, p. 547). Further, anorexia nervosa and bulimia nervosa share the issues of conflicted body image and overconcern about weight. The distinctions that seemed to need more focus have only become more blurred.

Binge eating disorder, previously referred to as compulsive eating, is a new diagnostic category. It is listed in the DSM IV in the section of diagnoses provided for further study (American Psychiatric Association, 1994). It has not yet been sufficiently tested to be labeled as a discrete eating disorder. Individuals with binge eating disorder have eating binges, during which they feel out of control and in distress. They do not have compensatory purging behaviors. The reason for this noticeable omission seems to be the distinction made between obesity and compulsive eating. Because of the genetic and physiological factors involved in obesity (Brownell & Foreyt, 1986), binge or compulsive eating has only earned an experimental diagnosis due to the fear of misdiagnosing a physical problem as a psychological condition.

As with all other disorders on the continua, individuals not specifically meeting the prescribed criteria for anorexia nervosa, bulimia nervosa, or binge eating but still exhibiting problems with eating are classified with the DSM IV diagnostic category of Eating Disorder Not Otherwise Specified (EDNOS).

Etiology ～

Models of etiology vary slightly for each of the eating disorders. Still, they seem to have some similar patterns, to differing degrees. The focus of this chapter is not to exhaustively explore the causes of the disorders but, instead, to look at group treatment as a means of addressing the issues that may predispose the disorders. Therefore, the following is not an exhaustive list of predisposing issues, merely a summary of themes that have evolved:

1. Developmental deficits include the individual's desire to stay a child (Bruch, 1978; Orbach, 1986), avoid femininity (Lewis & Johnson, 1985), overembrace femininity (Boskind-Lodahl, 1976; Wade, Kegan, Pettinati, & Franks, 1986), lack separation and differentiation from others (Heesacker & Neimeyer, 1990), and characteristically exhibit younger styles of reasoning, such as all-or-none thinking (Garner, 1986).

2. Societal pressures encourage individuals to adopt eating-disordered behavior to conform to current standards of body size and shape (Boskind-White & White, 1987; Brumberg, 1989; Wooley & Wooley, 1979). The media impose unrealistic standards (Kilbourne, 1994) that, it was originally

believed (Brownell & Foreyt, 1986), only Caucasian, middle-class women internalized and tried to achieve. However, it is now known that social influences to be thin impact members of minority groups (Dean & Frank, 1994; Kashubeck, Walsh, & Crowl, 1994), diverse college populations (Kashubeck et al., 1994), and men (Simon, 1995b) as well. A controversy exists about the extent to which African-American women are at risk for eating disorders. Villarosa (1994) cited research that indicates that they are as much if not more at risk than Caucasian women because of the mixed messages they receive about the value of thinness. Dolan (1991) and Powell and Kahn (1995), however, found African-American women to be less prone than Caucasian women to having an eating disorder or body image disturbance. The problem may be that some studies (Kashubeck et al., 1994) have surveyed fewer minority group members than members of the majority group and thus the data for the former are not collected. All individuals influenced by Western society are prejudiced by the value of thinness that is a precursor to eating-disordered behavior.

3. Dieting restrains the normal functions that regulate eating behavior and causes dysfunctional eating patterns. Polivy and Herman (1985) saw restraint theory as the main force behind the development of eating disorders.

4. Family systems deficits also have been designated as a precipitant to eating disorders (Sargent, Liebman, & Silver, 1985). Dysfunctional families marked by separation-individuation difficulties (Friedlander & Siegel, 1990), perfectionism (Brouwers, 1993), chaos (Root, Fallon, & Friedrich, 1986), and over- or underinvolvement (Minuchin, Rosman, & Baker, 1978) may be associated with eating-disordered behavior.

5. Several authors (Brumberg, 1989; Carruba & Blundell, 1986; Johnson & Maddi, 1986) have proposed that biological causes should be included in any integrative model.

6. Eating can also be a way to address emotional problems. Underlying a number of the predisposing issues for eating disorders are a sense of powerlessness (Bepko, 1989) and a lack of assertiveness (Ballantyne, 1991). Anderson and Holder (1989) noted:

> Eating disorders are also probably disorders of power, at some level expressing the dilemmas of women who are told to achieve but have only faulty avenues for doing so, who are told they matter but only if they're beautiful. Somewhere along the line they have lost their voices and learned to talk with their bodies. For many the process of therapy requires permission to speak, as well as help in learning how to do so. (p. 390)

As conveyed in the quotation, the voice of power is silent, hidden in self-directed shame, for many individuals with eating disorders. Other authors (Heatherton & Baumeister, 1991; Heatherton, Herman, & Polivy, 1991; Lowe & Maycock, 1988; Ruderman, 1985; Slochower & Kaplan, 1980) have pointed to the connection between stressful situations and abnormal eating. As an example, college environments and the stress of leaving home have been associated (Hotelling, 1989; Kashubeck et al., 1994) with increased eating-disordered behavior.

A review of the literature indicates that people with eating disorders share similarities and differences. Bulimics and people who binge eat indulge in overeating to fill emotional needs (Cauwels, 1983). Bulimia is seen by some (Root et al., 1986) to develop from anorexia, but qualitative differences between these two groups exist on demographic, familial, and behavioral levels. Because of the complexity of treating bulimics, any approach should acknowledge the individuals, their background, and any specific medical complications unique to their situation.

The causes of eating disorders are complex and varied. Still, people with eating disorders are usually separated by diagnostic category (Cauwels, 1983). While we acknowledge that the underlying dynamics across the eating disorders have certain similarities (Heesacker & Neimeyer, 1990), isolating the disorders facilitates group homogeneity, appropriate intervention focus, and connection.

Therapeutic Considerations ∼

Eating disorders are increasing in incidence (Brumberg, 1989; Heesacker & Neimeyer, 1990; Klesges, Mizes, & Klesges, 1987; Rodin, Silverstein, & Striegel-Moore, 1985; Sue, Sue, & Sue, 1996), but group counseling and techniques used to treat eating disorders have a very short history. Understandably, respectful treatment takes into consideration what is known about the eating-disordered population.

Individuals with eating disorders have many physical complications. Anorexia is the most lethal of all the psychological disorders (Garfinkel & Garner, 1982). After initial group screenings, medical evaluations and support are important to ensure that the individuals are medically stable for outpatient counseling or therapy or are receiving necessary attention while in inpatient treatment. At the minimum, a physician should be called on to do the medical screenings (Brownell & Foreyt, 1986) and a psychiatrist to consult regarding medication when indicated (Hudson & Pope, 1984). Individuals struggling with eating disorders who have other medical conditions present unique challenges. For instance, pregnant clients (Lacey & Smith, 1987; Stewart, Raskin, Garfinkel, MacDonald, & Robinson, 1987), athletes (Enns, Drewnowski, & Grinker, 1987; Thornton, 1990), and those with diabetes (Irvin, 1994) have special medical needs and considerations. A thorough medical evaluation screens for these complicating factors. Nutritional counseling (Kempley, 1988) and exercise counseling (Boskind-White & White, 1987) may be a needed adjunct for individuals during treatment. Bauer, Anderson, and Hyatt (1986) and Cauwels (1983) addressed these needs through a multidisciplinary team serving the dual purpose of support and direct treatment.

In addition to being checked before a group begins, the physical health of group members needs to be monitored during counseling. Inpatient settings provide the most appropriate environment for treating clients with conditions that are life-threatening. Individuals in outpatient or campus group programs will need appropriate medical referrals.

Until recently, women were the sole focus of eating disorders research. Men were considered an illusive minority (Cauwels, 1983). Still, an estimated one eighth of the individuals struggling with an eating disorder are men (Henkel, 1995). Several sports have been known to produce vocational bulimics, both male and female (Cauwels, 1983). In an article on eating-disordered athletes in the *NCAA News* (Survey on Eating Disorders, 1990), the National Collegiate Athletic Association found that eating-disordered behavior is widespread in male athletes. Because the overwhelming majority of research to date has focused on women, a bias toward women is reflected in some of the data presented in this chapter. But readers should be sensitive to this bias, which is unfounded. The need for continued research focusing on men and women with eating disorders cannot be overemphasized. Individuals express the universal needs for intimacy, acceptance, and independence through disordered eating. Men and women share these concerns. Nevertheless, as more men come into treatment, men may best be served by groups separate from women (Andersen, 1990; Cauwels, 1983).

The groups discussed in this chapter are counseling or therapy groups, not support or self-help groups. The distinction is an important one. The two types of groups have different functions and are appropriate at different stages of counseling or therapy. The decision to attend or to refer an individual to a support group versus a counseling or therapy group is addressed by an approach proposed by Hogg and Frank (1992). From their model, the most appropriate treatment modality depends on the individual's level of emotional neediness. People who have become dependent on food as an external source of selfhood are best referred to a counseling or therapy group. Individuals who have sufficient ego strength to remain separate when connected with others are best referred to a support group. Support groups are often helpful in the latter stages of treatment. Overeaters Anonymous is an example of a support group in the 12-step tradition. Its purpose is to help individuals who compulsively overeat. Support or self-help groups for anorexics and bulimics also exist. Many people have gained support, information, improved communication skills, and improved self-esteem from these groups.

Respect for individual and group boundaries is paramount in counseling and therapy group treatment for eating disorders. Some theorists have contended that women in treatment need to connect with other women (Boskind-White & White, 1987). Similarly, male identification is important to male development and identity (Doyle & Paludi, 1995). Because gender roles, stereotypes, and issues provide another layer of concerns that must be addressed, clients are often encouraged to have same-gender therapists. Some counselors or therapists have suggested male-female leader teams (Andersen, 1986). Thelen, Farmer, McLaughlin, Mann, and Pruitt (1990) suggested that women's relationships with men should be addressed before counseling or therapy is completed. Because of incest and abuse issues, women may need to reconnect with those concerns before addressing eating problems (Brody, 1984). The same would be true, for men in treatment.

The benefits of having two co-leaders for groups involving these intense issues are readily apparent. Yalom (1985) suggested that one leader generally is viewed as harmonizing and the other as questioning. Together, they can observe and intervene in the various issues that arise with eating-disordered group members.

Individual or family counseling or therapy, or both, may have to be maintained as an adjunct to group treatment. Many people realize personal issues (e.g., incest, abuse, or shame) in groups that necessitate more in-depth work than the group alone can provide. For individuals in whom the disorder developed before age 18, family counseling or therapy has yielded positive results (Russell, Szmukler, Dare, & Eisler, 1987).

Because women with eating disorders may share many of the themes and concerns that characterize women in general (Orbach, 1978; Rodin et al., 1985; Roth & Ross, 1988), approaching these issues in a way that does not overpathologize what may be the result of cultural pressures is a delicate but necessary process. At this point, men (Simon, 1995a) have not been shown to subscribe to similar stereotypes.

Finally, issues of group stability must be considered. When offering services on a school or university campus, an issue that will need to be discussed is the natural semester or quarter time limitation. Individuals with eating disorders will often develop trust within the group and want to continue in the group for additional terms. A consistent group time and place help provide an element of stability and reliability and help groups to remain intact.

Eating Disorders Counseling Groups ~

The definitive eating disorder group treatment has not been found. However in group and individual approaches, there is a need for redefining what was successful treatment. It is important for counselors to look for progress rather than a total cure (Miller, 1996). Although many group leaders (Andersen, 1986; Barth & Wurman, 1986; Boskind-White & White, 1987; Root et al., 1986; Roth & Ross, 1988) have found benefits to group counseling or therapy with individuals who have eating disorders, no one approach has emerged as universally accepted.

Models

Eating disorders groups have followed one of three general models: *cognitive* or *cognitive-behavioral* (Lee & Rush, 1986), *process focused* (Roy-Byrne, Lee-Benner, & Yager, 1984), or a *combination* of these (Love, Lewis, & Johnson, 1989; Roth & Ross, 1988). Pure cognitive-behavioral approaches focus on decreasing eating-disordered behavior and improving affective states, self-esteem, and distorted attitudes (Kempley, 1988; Lee & Rush, 1986; Roth & Ross, 1988). The process model emphasizes interpersonal relationships and the functionality of the eating disorder in meeting emotional and physical needs (Love et al., 1989). Groups combining the cognitive with the process-focused orientation are structured while still allowing members to discuss the group relationships.

Counselors and therapists have had difficulty knowing how to integrate the cognitive approach (challenging dysfunctional thoughts and behaviors) with the process-focused model (addressing group interactions and relationships) (Love et al., 1989; Roth & Ross, 1988). Some have reconciled this conflict by running the groups separately (Piran & Kaplan, 1990); others have reconciled it by starting with cognitive work and ending with the group process (Roth & Ross, 1988). The challenge has been in combining two models that are inherently at odds.

The model Yalom (1975) developed, based on Sullivan's (1953) interpersonal theory, has the dual capacity of attending to dysfunctional thoughts and behaviors while focusing on interpersonal interactions. In this model, although cognitive distortions are not explicitly taught, they are addressed when they are manifest within relationships. Yalom asserted that there is no need for group members to describe their pathology; they will act it out in the group sessions. In accordance with Sullivan's model, the group leader and the group members recognize and address the perceived distortions (Sullivan, 1953). The levels of these misperceptions and the dysfunctionality of these cognitions reflect the level of development of the pathology. When one views the cognitions or perceptual distortions as maturational and in the context of interpersonal interactions, a combined cognitive-process model is possible. Still, implementing such a model requires education and training and has not been widely discussed or adopted.

Characteristics of the Three Primary Types of Eating Disorders

An understanding of the distortions that characterize people with the different types of eating disorders is essential in order to process the distortions as they emerge in the interpersonal context. Research has yielded the following cognitive distortions characteristic of individuals with bulimia nervosa, anorexia nervosa, and binge eating disorder:

Bulimia nervosa (Bauer & Anderson, 1989, pp. 416–419)

1. Being or becoming overweight is the worst thing that can happen.
2. Certain foods are good foods; others are bad foods (good food = good person).
3. To feel safe, I must have control over all my actions.
4. I must do everything perfectly or what I do is worthless.
5. Everyone is aware of and interested in what I am doing.
6. Everyone must love me and approve of what I do.
7. External validation is everything.
8. As soon as I _____, I will be able to give up bulimia.
9. To be successful, a woman must combine the traditional values of women with the aggressive career orientation of men.

Anorexia nervosa (Brumberg, 1989; Levenkron, 1982; Orbach, 1982)

1. Fear of being/becoming overweight.
2. Feelings of inferiority.

3. Fear of intimacy.
4. Fear of criticism.
5. Fear of achievement.
6. Desire to be independent and powerful.
7. Desire for restraint and silence.

Binge eating disorder (Orbach, 1978; Roth, 1984)

1. Fear of being fat or thin.
2. Fear of being too powerful.
3. Fear of being worthy.
4. Fear of trusting.
5. Overjudging oneself.

By recognizing these underlying fears and thoughts that arise out of developmental needs (Garner, 1986) and societal pressures (Boskind-White & White, 1987), group leaders can better understand and address psychological dynamics when they are evident in group relationships.

Relationship Patterns

The following interpersonal patterns, reflective of the aforementioned cognitive distortions, can be seen in eating disorders groups (Bauer & Anderson, 1989; Brumberg, 1989; Levenkron, 1982; Orbach, 1978; Roth, 1984):

1. *Trust issues:* If I hear people laughing, I know it's about me; I wonder when it's safe to say how I really feel; Others in the group are critical of me.
2. *Power issues:* I must be dependent and subservient to others in the group; My needs are not as important as others; I'm a failure; To be fat is the worst possible thing that could happen, I compare myself, with regard to size, to the other group members; I hold myself to standards that I do not hold for others.
3. *Control issues:* If I get into my feelings, I'll lose control; I must do everything perfectly, even be a perfect client here; I'll dwell on my mistakes and ignore my successes.

In the relational context, these issues can be actively illuminated (Yalom, 1975, p. 121) with immediate interpersonal impact. Changing relational patterns within and between individuals with eating disorders is the goal of the counseling process.

Curative Factors

In the book, *The Theory and Practice of Group Psychotherapy,* Yalom (1985) listed 11 curative factors necessary for change and healing in the group process:

1. Instillation of hope.
2. Universality.
3. Imparting of information.
4. Altruism.
5. Corrective recapitulation of the primary family group.

6. Development of socializing techniques.
7. Imitative behavior.
8. Interpersonal learning.
9. Group cohesiveness.
10. Catharsis.
11. Existential factors.

Some of the curative factors have already been related directly to eating-disordered groups (Love et al., 1989; Root et al., 1986). Brief descriptions of each of the factors as they relate to these groups follow. With an understanding of the eating disorders symptomology, a knowledge of the various ways reality can be perceived or misperceived (distorted), and an understanding of the factors facilitative for growth in the group process, counselors and therapists can gain a clearer perspective of the group landscape.

Instillation of Hope   Observing that other people in the group are at varying stages of recovery provides hope and encouragement. Giving to and receiving from others have also been associated with increasing hope and self-respect (Yalom, 1985). These are crucial elements in the treatment of those who have eating disorders. People who feel little self-worth learn in the group that all is not hopeless (Barth & Wurman, 1986).

Universality   Many individuals with eating disorders feel alone and afraid (Johnson & Pure, 1986; Orbach, 1986; Roth, 1984). In a group setting, they can come to know that others share these feelings. In the group, individuals are not shamed for their behaviors or thoughts, and others learn to accept them (Yalom, 1985). Knowing that others have the same problem with food means their pain is not unique and they are not alone.

Imparting of Information   Information about the processes of counseling or therapy, about the universal concerns with food and body image, as well as about eating disorders is indispensable to group members (Orbach, 1986; Roth & Ross, 1988; Weiss, Katzman, & Wolchik, 1986). The group leader should, among other things, explain the eating disorders, explain the probability of relapse, provide information about the group model, give information about the process of the disorder, and explain the physical needs that will be addressed in treatment.

Altruism   Altruistic behavior is evident in eating disorder groups and is valuable for individuals suffering from self-directed shame and isolation. The example Yalom (1975) used to describe altruism seems written for the eating-disordered group. In this example, when shown hell, a rabbi saw starving people surrounded by adequate food but holding spoons with very long handles. The length of the spoon handles did not allow the people to feed themselves. When shown heaven, the rabbi saw the same scene but saw well-fed, happy people. The difference was that the people in heaven had learned how to feed one another. The emotional needs of eating-disordered individuals have not been met. With food all around them, they have remained unnourished emotionally. They don't yet know that to meet their needs they need to help one another (Bepko, 1989; Love et al., 1989). A group provides a context to learn how to ask for help and to help others. In learning how to give as well as receive, group members develop new tools that increase their self-esteem.

Corrective Recapitulation of the Primary Family Group   Family issues are at the core of working with the eating-disordered population. Whether working with the family (Minuchin et al., 1978) or with individuals working through family issues (Chernin, 1985; Levenkron, 1982; Root et al., 1986), the early family group experiences are evident in group counseling. When group members acknowledge that the issues of family are re-created in the group setting (Yalom, 1975), the group becomes a safe place to deal with these complex issues. The family of origin as well as the group family are healed as the layers of hurt are addressed.

Development of Socializing Techniques   Yalom (1975) asserted that learning how to tune into what is happening with others, to be helpful to others, to resolve conflict, to be less judgmental, and to be more empathic with oneself and others are potential benefits of participation in a group. Johnson and Pure (1986) identify the same interpersonal elements as vital in the curative process. Developing these socialization skills translates to aspects of healthy relatedness that will help individuals with eating disorders re-relate to themselves and others. Learning to reach out in more productive and rewarding ways allows people the rewards of connectedness.

Imitative Behavior   Modeling not just from group leaders but from other group members is essential. Women listed participant modeling as one of the most helpful factors in eating disorders treatment (White, 1985). Individuals in group counseling or therapy benefit from watching and learning from those who share the same experiences, from those who are farther along in the recovery process, as well as from those who give them a glimpse into where they have been. Working with a variety of individuals in group sessions allows group members to see not only where they have been psychologically but also where they are currently functioning and what their future may be.

Interpersonal Learning   We learn best through our relationships with others (Lerner, 1985). Sullivan's (1953) theory and Yalom's (1975) model both have a strong interpersonal focus. Group counseling or therapy is oftentimes preferred over individual counseling or therapy, primarily because the former offers more opportunities for learning (Boskind-White & White, 1987). In the group setting, members may have a corrective emotional experience (Yalom, 1975). Such an experience may entail expressing strong affect, be it positive or negative. People with eating disorders often hold in strong feelings of anger and inadequacy (Bepko, 1989). A group offers its members a safe, supportive place to begin feeling.

Group Cohesiveness   Not only is a support network a source of health and recovery, but it also has been highly correlated with success in weight studies (Brownell & Wadden, 1986). The relationships in a group are facilitative for members who need healthy intimacy and relationships (Heesacker & Neimeyer, 1990). Connecting with others in a group also allows members to reconnect with the unaccepted/unacceptable parts of themselves.

Catharsis American society has not supported women in venting thoughts and feelings regarding food and weight (Boskind-White & White, 1987; Orbach, 1978). Likewise, Western culture (Osherson, 1986) has not supported men in discussing or owning emotions other than anger. A group is an excellent environment for women and men to begin expressing these feelings, and group counseling or therapy is unequaled in its potential in this area (Hogg & Frank, 1992).

Existential Factors Few authors have delved into existential issues as related to eating disorders. The universal nature of the constructs of fairness, pain, death, aloneness, and individual responsibility (Yalom, 1975) makes these issues especially applicable to the eating-disordered population. Perhaps these struggles are particularly appropriate to people who struggle with severe, life-threatening illnesses. Further, the shame and guilt felt by those with eating disorders fit well into the existential paradigm. Group members can begin recognizing their responsibility for change (Bepko, 1989; Boskind-White & White, 1987; Chernin, 1985; Orbach, 1978), and by taking responsibility, members can become empowered.

Group Development

Within the interpersonal, process-focused model, group development requires consideration of several factors, and it moves through several phases. Counseling or therapy begins with the group screening and ends with termination of the counseling or therapy.

Screening and Composition Group screenings are critical for eating disorders groups. When group members are motivated and ready for counseling, recidivism seems to decrease. Root et al. (1986) suggested some guidelines for group screenings:

1. Members should not be using or abusing alcohol or drugs. Addiction to drugs or alcohol should be addressed before eating-disorder issues are discussed.
2. Members should share commonalities of experience as well as presenting problems (e.g., no males in groups for women and no women in groups for men; anorectics, bulimics, and binge eaters in separate groups).
3. Members should show some interest in the group process (e.g., by returning phone calls, by attending the group screening appointment, and by expressing interest and commitment to the group).
4. Members who are willing to wait for membership in a group may be even more motivated to be in the group.

Length

A 12-session, closed group model fits many campus programs. For many noncampus-based programs, treatment may extend well beyond 12 sessions. Some leaders report that members benefit from longer term group treatment (Barth & Wurman,

1986; Roth & Ross, 1988). Yalom's (1975) model suggests that instead of weeks, members work together for months. If incest issues arise during treatment, these concerns are best dealt with in individual sessions as an adjunct to the group (Kerr & Piran, 1990). The setting (inpatient, outpatient, or campus) may dictate the length of group counseling. Twelve-session or shorter term groups are not expected to progress as far as groups of longer duration.

Brief Group Approaches   Structured, short-term counseling or therapy groups are by nature and time limitations theoretically cognitive or cognitive-behavioral approaches. Several stepwise programs have emerged that have generally been aimed at individuals with bulimia nervosa or subclinical eating disorders (EDNOS). Weiss et al. (1986) formulated a 7-week (seven-session) cognitive-behavioral approach to treating bulimia. The sessions cover, sequentially, the following: information and overview, developing alternative coping strategies, addressing self-esteem perfectionism and depression, working on anger and assertiveness, cultural expectations of thinness for women, enhancing body image, and acknowledging current progress and suggesting further help. A psychoeducational program based on Weiss et al.'s (1986) work consists of eight sessions aimed at reducing dieting, fasting, and other precursors to eating-disordered behavior. An empirical study of the outcome of this program conducted by Kaminski and McNamara (1996) showed that both women with subclinical eating disorders and those with clinically diagnosable eating disorders were helped by the program. They not only decreased their dysfunctional behaviors but also showed evidence of higher self-esteem, felt that they were not criticized as much by others, and endorsed fewer body image stereotypes. Short-term treatment of clinical populations is still in its early stages. However, the studies cited suggest that psychoeducational programs can be helpful in reducing eating-disordered behaviors among bulimics and subclinical populations.

Open Groups   Open group membership is also an option, especially for outpatient, working populations (Love et al., 1989). New members are integrated as others leave. When new members join a preexisting group, the original members need to connect with the new members, and subgrouping may be proposed (Yalom, 1975). In any group—open or closed—members may choose to leave prematurely. If someone decides to leave, the leaders should discuss the issues of loss and the importance of saying good-bye. The group environment provides an optimal opportunity to bring up issues of connecting with others and separating from them, both being particular concerns of people with eating disorders (Heesacker & Neimeyer, 1990).

Stages   The *first stage* of group counseling or therapy for people with eating disorders involves orienting to the group, learning to connect, facing the reality of the eating disorder, and finding meaning from the struggle (Yalom, 1985). In the first group session, the leader should explain group rules and norms to the members. Individuals with intense shame and guilt need to be in a safe environment. Group boundaries with regard to membership and confidentiality must be discussed in the initial meeting.

Group members with eating disorders often hesitate to say the words that describe their eating-disordered behaviors. Group members with bulimia may refer to "it." Those with anorexia may be silent (Orbach, 1986). Most women will talk about their dissatisfaction with the size and shape of their body, typically exaggerating their dimensions (Wooley & Wooley, 1979). Binge eaters also may exaggerate or hide their feelings to protect themselves from pain (Orbach, 1978). The leader should normalize members' need to be hesitant in disclosure and should not encourage or reinforce their need for dependence by providing answers (Yalom, 1985). Even though food may become the topic of discussion, food is not the real issue (Orbach, 1978). The leader should also be aware of the natural tendency of group members to parentify the leader and thus recognize initial transference tendencies (Yalom, 1975). Ethically, the group leader must also discuss the limitations and potential effects of treatment. The tenor of the group begins to develop in the first session.

Their search for the meaning of their struggle leads group members to seek out the function of the eating disorder in their lives. This quest may have a broader scope as group members begin to look to their past and their future for needs and fulfillment. In the early phase of group counseling or therapy, members begin to notice common patterns and trends. A group setting offers the potential for understanding the universal nature of emotional needs.

The *second stage* of group development is characterized by conflict, dominance, and rebellion (Yalom, 1985). Groups for eating-disordered individuals begin to enter the second phase when members conflict over speaking time and show competitiveness related to attractiveness and success (Love et al., 1989). Parentification continues to surface but is more open in this second stage. Conflict and parentification are an important facet of group progress (Yalom, 1975). Although conflict is unpleasant for the parentified leader, group members learn to be honest interpersonally, confront psychodynamic and group dynamic issues (Yalom, 1975), and express anger. For example, a member may learn that he or she is expressing "I'm always disappointed in my friendships" as "I'm always disappointed in you" (Kerr & Piran, 1990, p. 35). Cognitive distortions as well as intrapersonal deficits are manifested in the interpersonal relationships of group. The leader can facilitate discussions to help members begin resolving their interpersonal conflicts and to help them connect these intrapersonal deficits to their eating-disordered behaviors.

The *third stage* of group treatment features development of cohesiveness (Yalom, 1975). Out of the conflict and storming of the previous stage evolve group integration, respect, and purpose (Yalom, 1985). A member's hidden shame and fear are potentially released in this safe environment. When group members feel a healthy closeness with one another, they no longer feel alone (Eichenbaum & Orbach, 1982). By learning to accept and appreciate others, they learn to further accept and appreciate themselves.

The *more advanced stages* of group development are difficult to map. During this period, it is no longer possible to describe discrete stages of development (Yalom, 1975). Group members face their own issues.

Subgrouping may be proposed in this phase, particularly if new members join the group or if outside-of-group contacts evolve. The challenges of integrating new members have already been discussed. With regard to extra-group contacts, although gaining support outside of a group has been viewed as helpful (Hoage, 1989), not all group leaders encourage those connections because subgrouping can promote fragmentation (Yalom, 1975). Group members should be apprised that conflicts outside of a group should be processed in the group for the therapeutic process to continue.

Termination, the final stage of group work, entails addressing separation and loss at a personal level. The group separation may provide individuals in the group their first experience in formally saying good-bye (Kerr & Piran, 1990). The termination phase generates unresolved loss and separation issues. Group members may discuss one another's progress, feelings toward one another, and their own sadness. Remissions may occur before the actual group termination because of this experience of loss (Yalom, 1985). On a more positive note, progress may continue after a group ends if the members effectively work through the termination issues.

Strategies

Because the history of treating eating disorders is relatively brief and few definitive treatments have emerged, strategies have not stood the tests of time and research validity. Several strategies, however, have met with success. Focusing on the group's interpersonal process is at the core of the group counseling or therapy process. The following strategies are suggested to supplement and facilitate that dynamic, not supplant it.

1. *Adult nomenclature.* In the group setting, identities are important. The names members use to identify themselves are important. In women's counseling or therapy groups, when members begin to refer to themselves and female friends as "women," not "girls," it is empowering. Similarly, with men in counseling or therapy, identification with "men" and not "boys" reflects a developmental awareness and acceptance of adulthood (Doyle, 1995). When the terms *women* and *men* are used in the group, a discussion might be initiated about the images group members have of women and men and what they might do if they were women or men. The topic facilitates a discussion of the fears associated with growing up and assuming the responsibilities that come with maturity. This intervention is simple and facilitates psychological development, encourages identity formation, and empowers individuals, all of which are important aspects of healing.

2. *Relaxation and hypnosis.* The use of relaxation and hypnosis for clients with eating disorders can be an effective strategy (Gross, 1983; Pettinati, Kogan, Margolis, Shrier, & Wade, 1989; Thakur, 1980) for individuals with the proper training. Teaching relaxation in the early stages of group counseling or therapy gives members another tool to use when they are alone with food. Relaxation has been helpful in creating calmness, reinforcing a positive self-image, modifying binge eating and purging behaviors, learning sensitivity to hunger, altering body image distortion, and training recognition of involuntary dissociative states associated with

binge eating (Pettinati et al., 1989). Engaging in bulimic behaviors is a stress-reducing activity (Mizes & Fleece, 1986); hence, teaching clients to relax represents a means to replace the bulimic behavior with a more facilitative behavior.

Ericksonian hypnosis has also been suggested (Bandler & Grinder, 1982). Because of the issues with control that are characteristic of many people with eating disorders (Pettinati et al., 1989), this strategy is suggested only for group members who have been briefed and are comfortable with the procedure.

3. *Body image exercises.* Body image work is a necessary adjunct to counseling or therapy for eating disorders (Hutchinson, 1985; Wooley & Kearney-Cooke, 1986). Kearney-Cooke (1989) hypothesized that body image disturbances appear in the first 3 years of life when parents disapprove of the child's body. In some groups, body image exercises may take the form of imagery exercises before the first group session really begins. Later body image exercises may evolve from the counseling or therapy process, when members compare themselves with others in the group. Using mirrors to promote self-acceptance and having members trace their image and then their real body on paper have also been recommended (Orbach, 1978). Another intervention applied to the body image disturbances and obsessions that characterize all people with eating disorders involves art, music, or dance as an adjunct to treatment (Hornyak & Baker, 1989). Finally, LeBlanc (1990) suggested that therapeutic massage, separate and apart from group counseling or therapy, may enable group members to "reclaim and feel great in" their bodies (p. 111). All of these experiential forms of treatment require skill and knowledge before being attempted with a group.

4. *Writing letters to food.* Writing letters to food (Brouwers, 1994) has been productive for bulimics specifically but also for other individuals with eating disorders. According to Brouwers (1994), writing letters fills several group tasks: building group cohesiveness through a common experience, prompting healthier attitudes toward food, developing insight into the function of food in members' lives, and initiating an exploration into the core issues behind the eating disorder (e.g., low body image, sexual abuse, family background, perfectionism).

5. *Other imagery exercises.* In recent years imagery has been used increasingly as a therapeutic tool with people who have eating disorders (Kearney-Cooke, 1989). Receiving appropriate training, having members' permission to participate, and offering an ample explanation of the imaging process are imperative for group leaders.

All imagery exercises, especially with eating-disordered groups, should begin by having members create a safe environment (in a special room, down a path, around the next corner) in their imagery world. If images get uncomfortable, they are able to return to the previously identified safe environment to process and work through threatening insights. Although selecting themes that evolve from the group content is best, several themes for imagery are suggested here as starting points:

- Imagine your mother pregnant. Imagine your parents' reaction to that pregnancy. *Goal:* to explore gender expectations and feeling of worth (Kearney-Cooke, 1989).

- Imagine yourself at a party. Imagine that your body gets larger, larger, and larger and then begins to contract and get smaller. *Goal:* to explore how body size impacts interpersonal relationships and perceptions of self (Orbach, 1978).
- Visualize the bodies of all the other women in the group and see where they fit in your lineup. *Goal:* to investigate competition and comparisons with others in the group (Kearney-Cooke, 1989).
- Imagine all the food you have at home or all the food you would ever want in the supermarket. *Goal:* to help group members recognize that needs can be filled (Orbach, 1978).
- Imagine what would happen if you woke up and felt good about your body. *Goal:* to address resistance to change (Kearney-Cooke, 1989).
- Imagine that your ideal self is accessible from the safe environment. Compare it to your real self of today. *Goal:* to help create self-acceptance and to integrate ideal aspects into the real self.
- Imagine that you are about to go on a journey. What would you want to take with you from each person in the group? *Goal:* to recognize strengths in oneself and others and to prepare for group termination.
- Imagine that the group has ended. What things do you wish you would have said or done in the group to feel completed? *Goal:* to help process termination issues and feelings toward the members of the group.

6. *Memory of meals in the family of origin.* Families have been drawn at the table, imagined at the table, and dramatized in group settings. Each approach offers aspects of the same dynamic. Exploring the early issues around food offers the individual and the group information about early feelings associated with eating and nurturing behaviors in the family. Discussing the types of food associated with childhood, as well as family traditions (or lack thereof), may be useful. From such explanation and discussion, members develop a deeper understanding of emotional needs in the family.

7. *Structured eating.* Another exercise that has been used with individuals with eating disorders is structured eating (Hoage, 1989; Sparnon & Hornyak, 1989). Structured eating is a way to desensitize group members to food and normalize the experience of eating socially. Eating in a group also provides a logical extension of the family meal exercises. Whether food is brought every week or as a one-time experience depends on the group and the process issues discussed. Once food has been discussed in the group, the leader may suggest that individuals bring their favorite food or the food they most fear (possibly the same) to the next group session. Once the food is present, the members are instructed to process it at the levels of presence, touch, smell, taste, and emotions evoked. A single taste experience can be stretched out to include food texture, taste on different parts of the tongue, feelings as the food is swallowed and goes down the esophagus, and aftertaste. When group members stretch out the eating experience, they have a model for slower, controlled eating that they can apply to other situations. After the food has been tasted

and discussed, members of some groups want to share their food with one another. Members of other groups may not want to part with their food. The information gained from this exercise gives leaders information about group and individual trust and development.

8. *Contracts.* Behavioral contracts have been recommended as a safety net during treatment. Kaplan (1990) described a verbal contract that outlines expectations for treatment, expectations concerning weight gain, expectations to give as well as receive feedback in the group, and expectations prohibiting self-harm. Written behavioral contracts are used at Arizona State University to provide consequences for students at medical risk with a pattern of manipulating treatment (Bowen, 1990). These contracts incorporate the same elements Kaplan suggested but are more explicit. The contract carries with it consequences limiting the ability to stay enrolled in the university. Just as Selzer, Koenigsberg, and Kernberg (1987) argued that explicit expectations are necessary for borderline patients, safeguards for eating-disordered clients in denial may also be needed. The overall purpose is to create an environment that is empathic but in which clear boundaries for eating behavior have been set. A contract of this nature will obviously impact group work.

9. *Workshops.* Boskind-White and White (1987) have instituted short-term, intensive group experiences that allow each participant to focus on eating issues. In a workshop format, group development will not progress through the same stages as a longer term group. The impact of disclosing personal experiences (seen in the first part of group development) will be realized and may offer relief for individuals who have never felt that anyone would understand or that their voice would be heard.

Sample Group Outline

To show how some of these techniques may be integrated into group sessions, the following is a sample outline for a pre-group screening and six group sessions for a bulimic counseling or therapy group.

Pre-Group Screening. In the first meeting between the leaders and a potential group member, the group leaders gather a complete psychological history regarding the eating disorder, family history, abuse, sexual history, drug/alcohol/shoplifting history, and so forth. They refer the potential group member for a physical evaluation and have the individual complete one or more assessment instruments. It is helpful if the group testing battery includes an eating disorder inventory (e.g., EDI–II, Eating Disorders Inventory—II), a mental status exam, a measure of depression (e.g., BDI, Beck Depression Inventory), and a measure of self-esteem (e.g., TSCS, Tennessee Self-Concept Scale) (Allison, 1995). Agency release and information forms for group counseling or therapy are signed and collected. The group leaders provide information to demystify the group experience, discuss the purpose of the group, and discuss the focus on eating disorders. They elicit and discuss any concerns the potential group member has about being in an eating disorder group. The group leaders work together to help provide information as well as to gather information as to the fit of the potential member into the counseling or therapy group.

Individuals with borderline personality disorder and narcissistic personality disorder might benefit from individual counseling or therapy before entering a group. If individuals have completed an eating-disorder contract, that also will be discussed in the pre-group screening.

Session 1. Sitting in a circle is recommended. Group members can see one another, and the group leaders are seen as part of the group rather than separate from it. Everyone introduces themselves to the group. Group members are asked to discuss their goals for the group and to say what they want or hope to get from the group experience. Group rules (confidentiality), objectives, and rights of group members are discussed. Expectations of the group leaders are also discussed. If time permits, group leaders can begin a discussion of the members' thoughts and feelings associated with bulimia. What has made it difficult for group members to change their eating-disordered behaviors? The group leaders would process reactions, comments, and methods that have been successful (and not successful) for group members. Before the end of the session, group leaders ask members to talk about their experience in the session.

Session 2. Members' reactions to returning to the group are briefly discussed. Then the group leaders introduce the idea of imagery/relaxation exercises and ask the group members if they have ever had any experiences with these techniques. A specific imagery exercise is suggested. Any resistance or concern about the exercise is discussed. (Only group leaders with training in facilitating imagery exercises should implement them.) After using a standard relaxation protocol, the group leaders begin the exercise by having the group members each imagine a safe place. It may not have always been safe, but it was at one point. It may have been outdoors, it may have been indoors. Next, the group leaders ask the members to imagine what it feels like to be in the safe place. Who else (if anyone) is there with them? What thoughts or feelings arise after being in this place? The group leaders remind the members that they can imagine this safe place whenever they want. It is always there for them. After allowing the group to experience this place for a few minutes, the leaders use a standard protocol to guide the group out of the imagery exercise. Then the group discusses the experience. What did the members experience? How did it feel? Did they go to sleep (a common response for many people)? What was it like to go to that special place? Group members may talk about their safe place, but that information is not elicited. The leaders discuss the session, making certain that everyone has an opportunity to give a reaction to the exercise and how they are feeling being in the group.

Session 3. To begin the session, the group leaders initiate discussion about what it is like to be together once more. Any issues, concerns, or thoughts that arose out of the last session's imagery exercise are discussed. The leaders ask the group members if any of them used the relaxation exercise to help them since the last group meeting. They ask the members if their safe place served as a peaceful place to imagine since the last session. The leaders ask the group for their permission to have another imagery exercise, and they lead the group through a standard relaxation/hypnosis induction. (For excellent examples and techniques, Bandler and Grinder [1981] and Fezler [1990] are recommended.)

To begin the exercise, ask the group members to, once again, imagine being in their safe place. After a few minutes, ask them to imagine a room with a door that is down a long corridor. Ask them to open this door when they are ready. Then ask them to imagine that behind the door is an image of their ideal self. Have them look at their ideal self's appearance and talk with their ideal self about how it feels to be like the person has wanted to be. What is the ideal person doing? What is his or her vocation? What about how the ideal self looks or appears any different from their regular or real self. Invite the group members to reach out to this person, touch him or her, talk with and listen to him or her. In what ways are they alike? What do the group members imagine it will take to realize or become this person? Would they like to become their ideal self? Maybe they feel better the way they are now. After giving them a few minutes to sit with this person, take them out of the room, out of the hallway, and by having them slowly become more aware of their bodily sensations, gradually use the standard protocol to ease them from the imagery exercise.

Following the exercise, the group leaders process the experiences the members relate from the imagery, connecting differences and similarities between group members' experiences. They reflect the feelings that the member's report about moving from the safe place into a place where they can experience their ideal self. The leaders initiate discussion about ways in which the members' eating patterns and behaviors are or are not a part of their ideal selves. Each group member is given the opportunity to connect with others regarding his or her experience and to discuss feelings about ending the session.

Session 4. As before, the leaders begin the session by inviting the members to discuss being together. The group members are then asked to discuss any changes they have experienced in their eating behavior. What, if any, increases or decreases have occurred in their eating-disordered behaviors, and what may be some possible explanations? The leaders then facilitate discussion about why the members want or don't want to become their ideal person. What do they feel gets them closer to or holds them back from being this person? What thoughts, feelings, or behaviors tend to keep them from realizing their goal? If the group is ready, the leaders conduct another imagery exercise:

Anchor the participants in their safe place, reminding them that they can imagine this place whenever they feel uncomfortable. Then ask them to imagine their favorite food. Have them imagine looking at it, smelling it, tasting it, feeling it in their hands. Ask them to stay with the experience of this food and to think about any other feelings, thoughts, or behaviors that come to mind when they imagine this food. Have them imagine what would normally happen after they have looked at, smelled, tasted, or felt this food and what they would like to have happen. After a few moments, gradually lead the group out of the imagery exercise.

When the group is ready, the group leaders facilitate discussion about the imagery. What foods did the member choose? What was it like for them to be alone with this food? What associations did they have with it? Were any other people involved? What would happen if they were to stay with that favorite food. The group leaders ask for the members' thoughts and reactions, encouraging discussion among the group. As an assignment, the group leaders ask the members to write a letter to their favorite food and to bring it to the next session. What would they want to say to that favorite food? What concerns of control, fear, or anxiety do they experience when thinking about this food? The leaders ensure that everyone has had a chance to discuss their food and to talk about their reactions to one another and the imagery exercise. They then end the group session.

Session 5. This session begins with a discussion about the letters to food that the group members have written. The leaders ask if the activity was difficult for anyone and, if so, why? The leaders then ask the group if they would like to bring their favorite food to the next group session. Would they want to eat the food or share it with others in the group? The members are asked how they are feeling toward other members in the group. Are there people they feel closer to or further away from given what has been said thus far. The leaders help to process individual and group relationships. Then the members are asked about their eating behaviors. Have these behaviors changed or remained the same? Do the members feel differently from or similarly to how they felt in the first session? If time permits, the leaders ask the group if they would like to have another imagery/relaxation exercise. They then conduct the following exercise.

Ask group members to use the family-of-origin meal imagery (described earlier) to imagine a meal with their family. What is happening? Who is there? Have them listen to what is being said. Have them pay attention to the food on the table. What are the smells, sounds, and tastes they experience? How much food is available? Can they eat all they want? Is anyone watching them or what they are eating? Ask them to pay attention to their feelings as they imagine this meal with their family.

After the imagery exercise is completed, the group leaders facilitate discussion about the thoughts and feelings the group members experienced around this exercise. They then prepare for the end of the session by having members discuss their reactions to and feelings about the session.

Session 6. This session begins with discussion about any residual reactions to the last session. Discussion then turns to the food that the members brought or did not bring to the session. What is it like to have food in the group? What food was brought? Members are asked to go around the group and talk about their food and any other food that is present. They are asked if they would like to sample a bite of their food. If they would, they are instructed to taste it slowly, like they have been doing when experiencing their imagery exercises. Members are instructed to smell the food, touch it and feel its texture, taste it and experience it in different parts of their mouth and tongue, swallow it and pay attention to how it feels as it travels down their throat. The group is asked to pay attention to any feelings or images they experience from this exercise. What feelings (e.g., control or lack of control, embarrassment, shame, and so forth) are evoked by having the food and tasting it? The possibility of sharing food is discussed, and food is shared if members so desire. The leaders ask if the members feel any differences (e.g., smells) in the group when food is there versus when food is discussed but not present. Some members may say they will purge the food after the session ends. This is discussed and choices to purging are provided, although purging is accepted as one possible choice. Group feelings and relationships are again discussed. The group leaders talk about the timeline for the remainder of the group. Depending on the length of the group, processing of termination issues may be initiated.

Population-Specific Considerations

Despite the common threads running through the eating disorders, some specific considerations apply to each of the three populations.

Anorexia Nervosa Groups   Problems specific to physical starvation have to be considered when working with anorectic individuals (Boskind-White & White, 1987). Boskind-White and White (1987) described anorectics as apathetic, irritable, younger and less social than bulimics, isolated, family-dependent, and less prone than people with other eating disorders to eating binges. Levenkron (1982) further described anorectics as controlling and manipulative. Group screening procedures have to assure that the physical needs of these individuals are being met. In groups, these members have limited social skills and resist treatment, so they may be challenging for the leaders.

Feminist theorists (Boskind-White & White, 1987; Chernin, 1985; Orbach, 1978) have suggested that anorexia and bulimia are more a by-product of social pressures than psychological impairments that would complicate group work. Groups have the unique ability to provide a contained environment in which anorectic members can directly confront their isolation. By realizing they are not alone, they can learn to reconnect with others and eventually connect with the fearful, silent, and hungry part of themselves.

Bulimic Groups   Bulimic group members rival anorectics in being difficult to treat (Cauwels, 1983). They are differentiated from binge eaters in that they compensate for their binge behavior with purging. Like anorectics, they have health concerns and should be monitored, but the health risk for bulimics is not generally as great as for anorectics (Boskind-White & White, 1987). Bulimic group members have more social skills than anorectics, but not without cost.

Wooley and Kearney-Cooke (1986, p. 486) noted that "bulimics tend to be compliant and make others feel at ease, their apparent warmth concealing grave difficulties in sustaining connection, avoiding anger, and preferring isolation." Bulimics may be difficult to commit to treatment, impatient when they do not recover quickly, competitive with other group members, and resistant to receiving help from others (Cauwels, 1983). Wooley and Kearney-Cooke (1986) delineated the goals of a bulimic group as (a) to be honest emotionally with one another, and (b) to make comparisons between their relationships in the group and their relationships outside the group. Yalom's (1975) model sensitively answers these two goals. Helping the bulimic person look at distancing patterns in relationships is not easy, but it is crucial for recovery.

Binge Eating Disorder Groups   Medical problems for the person with binge eating disorder also require attention but, again, do not pose as critical a threat as for the anorectic. Binge eaters share with the other eating-disorder populations an obsession with food but rely on internally directed guilt and shame to compensate. These symptoms may persist longer than similar symptoms for the other eating-disordered groups. Years of binge eating have layered the shame and guilt that distance binge eaters from others. Overeating has been correlated with anxiety and depression and, in some cases, "extreme disruptions of psychological functioning bordering on psychotic episodes" (Striegel-Moore & Rodin, 1986, p. 100). When obesity is also an issue, social discrimination (including educational and employment prejudice) is often aimed against the binge eater (Bray, 1986; Richardson, Goodman, Hastorf, & Dornbusch, 1961). Unlike people with bulimia nervosa or anorexia nervosa, those with binge eating disorder may at some point benefit from moderate and monitored exercise (Levine, Marcus, & Moulton, 1966). But it is important to remember that emotional wounds have to be addressed. Layering the pain that prompted the binge behavior with exercise will not make the problem disappear. In group counseling, an individual can begin working through the layers of shame.

Age- and Cultural-Specific Considerations

Mintz and Betz (1988) reported that 61% of their college sample had some degree of eating-disordered behavior. More significantly, they reported that only 33% of the college population they surveyed could be considered to have normal eating habits. Much of the research that has been conducted and that has been described in this chapter has focused on college campuses. Anorexia nervosa has been considered a rare disorder of young adolescents. Though it is most common in young adult college populations, it also may occur in women and men in their twenties (Garfinkel & Kaplan, 1986). Bulimia has been viewed as a phenomenon of young adult college populations, the mean age of onset being 18.4 years (Agras & Kirkley, 1986). Binge eaters may run the gamut of ages. All of these distinctions aside, eating disorders can occur at any age, among any population. Group leaders, therefore, need to consider the developmental level of group members.

Addressing younger group members entails understanding their current social situation. Whenever the person is living at home, family dynamics come to the fore. The family should be included in some manner (e.g., family counseling) to support the work of counseling or therapy. Counseling or therapy groups with older people should respect the developmental and social issues unique to that population. Couples and significant others (close friends, children, and so on) may be included in the group or in a separate group (VandenBrouke, S., Vandreycken, W., &

Vertommen, H., 1995). Again, the aim is to help heal the emotional wounds that may be manifest in individuals or systems.

A wide age span among group members provides the opportunity to speak to intragenerational issues more immediately than in age-homogeneous groups. Transference between parents and children may be faced directly in the heterogeneous group context. Although age and eating diversity have been screened out of eating disorder groups in the past (Root et al., 1986) to make the groups more homogeneous, the decision about diversity should be based on the group leaders' preference and counseling or therapy demands.

As mentioned earlier, individuals from minority cultures receive mixed messages, about thinness and beauty and ultimately this will have some impact on the group counseling or therapy process. Whether or not Afro-American women experience eating disorders appears to be an area of controversy. In an abnormal psychology text Sue et al. (1996) noted that Afro-Americans appear to be able to ignore the white media messages that equate thinness with beauty (p. 492). Conversely, Villarosa (1994) reported:

> "African-American women are at risk for and suffer from eating disorders in at least the same proportions as their White counterparts. In our community we have always been more likely than White Americans to accept large and voluptuous women. In contrast to this country's celebration of thinness, traditional African societies view full-figured bodies as a symbol of health, wealth, desire, prosperity and fertility. However, the all-encompassing worship of thinness—especially of the waif, the sickly thin model whose clothes hang off her bony frame—has taken its toll on Black women. Sadly, the insecurity and shame many of us feel about our bodies were reflected in our study." (p. 19).

Cultural and racial norms that conflict with pressures from the media would seem to add another layer of stress for many Afro-Americans. It is vital that these social and cultural pressures be addressed in group counseling or therapy. The group may be homogeneous, with other minority members (Pinkney, 1994), or heterogeneous. However, the conflicted messages that individuals of color and diverse backgrounds have had to reconcile or confront must be acknowledged and addressed.

Final Considerations

Individuals with eating disorders elicit various countertransference issues in everyone, including group leaders. Root et al. (1986) suggested that group leaders who work with these groups be experienced, recognize that new issues may arise for them, and understand the leader's role in the group. Leaders' reactions to the binge, purge, or restrictive behavior itself may be strong. The Disordered Eating Anxiety Scale (DIS-EASE), developed by Frank (1996), can be used to assess individual reactions to eating issues. The discomfort experienced by people encountering individuals with eating disorders is most often related to personal eating issues. Consequently, leaders may need to confront their own feelings about eating, competence, and authority before they will be optimally effective. Authenticity, considered an important dimension in counseling when women work with women (Brody, 1984), is important for all group leaders working with the eating-disordered population. Leaders also may have to face their own issues of power (Osherson, 1986), as they are working in a context where others look to them for answers. Yalom (1989) described how personal issues can become manifest in counseling an obese client. The following dialogue that occurred in the last session with such a client was described by Yalom:

> "Tell me, Betty,...seeing I didn't look at you or was uncomfortable with you—why did you stay? Why didn't you stop seeing me and find someone else?"
>
> "Well, I can think of at least two reasons. First, remember that I'm used to it. It's not like I expect anything more. Everyone treats me that way. People hate my looks. No one ever touches me. ... And even though you wouldn't look at me, you at least seemed interested in what I had to say—no, no, that's not right—you were interested in what I could or might say if I stopped being so jolly. Actually, that was helpful....
>
> "The second reason is that I could understand how you felt. You and I are very much alike—in one way at least. Remember when you were pushing me to go to Overeaters Anonymous? To meet other obese people—make some friends, get some dates?"
>
> "Yeah, I remember. You said you hated groups."
>
> "Well, it is true. I do hate groups. But it wasn't the whole truth. The real reason is that I can't stand fat people. They turn my stomach. I don't want to be seen with them. So how can I get down on you for feeling the same way?" (pp. 116–117)

Internalized societal values concerning fatness and thinness have impacted all of us. Perspectives differ on the amount of pathology that is present in people with eating disorders. The perceived difficulty in treating these people may be less a case of severity of pathology than of orientation, perspective, and countertransference.

Leading eating disorders groups is challenging and may be frustrating. It also has the potential to be personally and professionally rewarding. Considering the societal implications, the work may be as empowering for the group leader as for the members, but the path to change is not fully chartered. What works is not fully known. In the labyrinth of the eating disorders groups, "there is no substitute for experience, supervision, and intuition" (Yalom, 1975, p. 332).

Summary ~

In the area of eating disorders, three basic classifications have emerged: anorexia nervosa, bulimia nervosa, and binge eating disorder. Each classification has unique characteristics and implications for treatment. Although eating disorders have been earmarked as a female problem, many males are also affected. These disorders may stem from developmental deficits, societal pressures for thinness, improper dieting, family systems deficits, a sense of powerlessness, or biological causes, in any combination.

Eating disorders have health consequences and may be life-threatening. Counseling or therapy groups are at present the preferred modality for treatment because of the values gained from interacting with others who share the problem. Within a group setting, no one treatment has been found to be superior to any other; however, an interpersonal approach using Yalom's group model meets the cognitive and emotional needs specific to this population.

At the root of treatment are issues of trust, power, and control. Curative factors include instillation of hope, universality, altruism, corrective recapitulation of the primary family group, socializing techniques, imitative behavior, group cohesiveness, catharsis, and existential awareness.

Group development follows several stages, beginning with screening and progressing through orientation, conflict, cohesiveness, and termination. Strategies have included encouraging the use of and discussing adult nomenclature, relaxation and hypnosis, body image exercises, imagery activities, recalling eating memories, structured eating experiences, contracts, and workshops.

Interwoven in treatment are population-specific and age-specific considerations. In addition, group leaders are encouraged to learn about the eating disorders, know about the possible medical needs of group members, recognize societal pressures specific to women and men, and seek supervision or consultation. Group counseling with this population requires knowledge of culture, gender, and self.

References ∿

Agras, W., & Kirkley, B. (1986). Bulimia: Theories of etiology. In K. Brownell & J. Foreyt (Eds.), *Handbook of eating disorders* (pp. 367–378). New York: Basic Books.

Allison, D. (Ed.). (1995). *Handbook of assessment methods for eating behavior and weight related problems: Measure, theory, research.* New York: Columbia University.

American Psychiatric Association. (1980). *Diagnostic and statistical manual of mental disorders* (3rd ed.). Washington, DC: Author.

American Psychiatric Association. (1994). *Diagnostic and statistical manual of mental disorders* (3rd ed., rev.). Washington, DC: Author.

Andersen, A. (1986). Inpatient and outpatient treatment of anorexia nervosa. In K. Brownell & J. Foreyt (Eds.), *Handbook of eating disorders* (pp. 333–350). New York: Basic Books.

Andersen, A. (1990). *Males with eating disorders.* New York: Brunner/Mazel.

Anderson, C., & Holder, D. (1989). Women and serious mental disorders. In M. McGoldrick, C. Anderson, & F. Walsh (Eds.), *Women in families: A framework for family therapy* (pp. 381–405). New York: Norton.

Ballantyne, J. (1991, August). *Assertiveness in undergraduate women with bulimic symptom tendencies.* Paper presented at the meeting of the American Psychological Association, San Francisco.

Bandler, R., & Grinder, J. (1981). *Trans-formations.* Moab, UT: Real People Press.

Bandler, R., & Grinder, J. (1982). *Reframing.* Moab, UT: Real People Press.

Barth, D., & Wurman, V. (1986). Group therapy with bulimic women: A self-psychological approach. *International Journal of Eating Disorders, 5*(4), 735–745.

Bauer, B., & Anderson, W. (1989). Bulimic beliefs: Food for thought. *Journal of Counseling & Development,* 416–419.

Bauer, B., Anderson, W., & Hyatt, R. (1986). *Bulimia: Book for therapist and client.* Muncie, IN: Accelerated Development.

Bepko, C. (1989). Disorders of power: Women and addiction in the family. In M. Goldrick, C. Anderson, & F. Walsh (Eds.), *Women in families: A framework for family therapy* (pp. 406–426). New York: Norton.

Boskind-Lodahl, M. (1976). Cinderella's stepsisters: A feminist perspective on anorexia nervosa and bulimia. *Signs: Journal of Women in Culture & Society, 2,* 324–356.

Boskind-White, M., & White, W. (1987). *Bulimarexia: The binge/purge cycle* (2nd ed.). New York: Norton.

Bowen, D. (1990, May). *Physician's role in eating disorders team treatment.* Paper presented at American College Health Association National Convention, San Antonio.

Bray, G. (1986). Effects of obesity on health and happiness. In K. Brownell & J. Foreyt (Eds.), *Handbook of eating disorders* (pp. 3–44). New York: Basic Books.

Brody, C. (1984). Authenticity in feminist therapy. In M. Brody (Ed.), *Women therapists working with women* (pp. 11–21). New York: Springer.

Brouwers, M. (1993). Bulimia and perfectionism: Developing the courage to be imperfect. *Journal of Mental Health Counseling, 15,* 141–149.

Brouwers, M. (1994). Bulimia and the relationship with food: A letters-to-food technique. *Journal of Counseling & Development, 73,* 220–222.

Brownell, K., & Foreyt, J. (Eds.). (1986). *Handbook of eating disorders.* New York: Basic Books.

Brownell, K., & Wadden, T. (1986). Behavior therapy for obesity: Modern approaches and better results. In K. Brownell & J. Foreyt (Eds.), *Handbook of eating disorders* (pp. 180–197). New York: Basic Books.

Bruch, H. (1973). *Eating disorders: Obesity, anorexia nervosa, and the person within.* New York: Basic Books.

Bruch, H. (1978). *The golden cage: The enigma of anorexia nervosa.* New York: Vintage Books.

Brumberg, J. (1989). *Fasting girls: A history of anorexia nervosa.* New York: New American Library.

Carruba, M., & Blundell, J. (Eds.). (1986). *Pharmacology of eating disorders.* New York: Raven Press.

Cauwels, J. (1983). *Bulimia: The binge-purge compulsion.* New York: Doubleday.

Chernin, K. (1985). *The hungry self: Women, eating, and identity.* New York: Harper & Row.

Dean, K., & Frank, M. L. (1994, March). *Eating disordered behavior measured by the EDI-II: Prevalence and stereotypes among Appalachian college women.* Paper presented at the Southeastern Psychological Convention, New Orleans, LA.

Dolan, B. (1991). Cross-cultural aspects of anorexia nervosa and bulimia: A review. *International Journal of Eating Disorders, 10,* 67–69.

Doyle, J. (1995). *The male experience.* Madison, WI: Brown & Benchmark.

Doyle, J., & Paludi, M. (1995). *Sex and gender* (2nd ed.). Madison, WI: Brown & Benchmark.

Eichenbaum, L., & Orbach, S. (1982). *Understanding women: A feminist psychoanalytic approach.* New York: Basic Books.

Enns, M., Drewnowski, A., & Grinker, J. (1987). Body composition, body size estimation and attitudes towards eating in male college athletes. *Psychosomatic Medicine, 49,* 56–64.

Fairburn, C., & Garner, D. (1986). The diagnosis of bulimia-nervosa. *International Journal of Eating Disorders, 5,* 403–419.

Fezler, W. (1990). *Imagery for healing, knowledge, and power.* New York: Fireside.

Frank, M. L. (1996, March). *Meeting our fears: Anxiety about eating disorders.* Paper presented at the Southeastern Psychological Association Annual Convention, Norfolk, VA.

Friedlander, M., & Siegel, S. (1990). Separation-individuation difficulties and cognitive-behavioral indicators of eating disorders among college women. *Journal of Counseling Psychology, 37*(1), 74–78.

Garfinkel, P., & Garner, D. (1982). *Anorexia nervosa: A multidimensional perspective.* New York: Brunner/Mazel.

Garfinkel, P., & Kaplan, A. (1986). Anorexia nervosa: Diagnostic conceptualizations. In K. Brownell & J. Foreyt (Eds.), *Handbook of eating disorders* (pp. 266–282). New York: Basic Books.

Garner, D. (1986). Cognitive therapy for anorexia nervosa. In K. Brownell & J. Foreyt (Eds.), *Handbook of eating disorders* (pp. 301–327). New York: Basic Books.

Gross, M. (1983). Correcting perceptual abnormalities, anorexia nervosa and obesity by use of hypnosis. *Journal of the American Society of Psychosomatic Dentistry & Medicine, 30,* 142–150.

Heatherton, T., & Baumeister, R. (1991). Binge eating as escape from self-awareness. *Psychological Bulletin, 110,* 86–108.

Heatherton, T., Herman, C., & Polivy, J. (1991). Effects of physical threat and ego threat on eating behavior. *Journal of Personality & Social Psychology,* 138–143.

Heesacker, R., & Neimeyer, G. (1990). Assessing object relations and social cognitive correlates of eating disorder. *Journal of Counseling Psychology,* 419–426.

Henkel, J. (1995). Conditions men get, too. *FDA Consumer, 29,* 20–24.

Hoage, C. (1989). The use of in-session structured eating in the outpatient treatment of bulimia nervosa.

In L. Hornyak & E. Baker (Eds.), *Experiential therapies for eating disorders* (pp. 60–77). New York: Guilford.

Hogg, A., & Frank, M. L. (1992). Toward an interpersonal model of codependence and contra dependence. *Journal of Counseling and Development,* 371–375.

Hornyak, L., & Baker, E. (Eds.). (1989). *Experiential therapies for eating disorders.* New York: Guilford.

Hotelling, K. (1989). A model for addressing the problem of bulimia on college campuses. *Journal of Behavior Therapy and Experimental Psychiatry, 20,* 73–77.

Hudson, J., & Pope, G. (1984). *New hope for binge eaters.* New York: Harper & Row.

Hutchinson, M. (1985). *Transforming body image.* New York: Crossing Press.

Irwin, B. (1994). Disordered eating and diabetes. *On the Cutting Edge: Diabetes Care and Education, 15,* 1–3.

Johnson, C., & Maddi, K. (1986). The etiology of bulimia: Bio-psycho-social perspectives. *Annals of Adolescent Psychiatry, 13,* 1–10.

Johnson, C., & Pure, D. (1986). Assessment of bulimia: A multidimensional model. In K. Brownell & J. Foreyt (Eds.), *Handbook of eating disorders* (pp. 405–449). New York: Basic Books.

Kaminski, P., & McNamara, K. (1996). A treatment for college women at risk for bulimia: A controlled evaluation. *Journal of Counseling & Development, 74,* 288–294.

Kaplan, A. (1990). The role of the director. In N. Piran & A. Kaplan (Eds.), *A day hospital group treatment program for anorexia nervosa and bulimia nervosa* (pp. 42–60). New York: Brunner/Mazel.

Kashubeck, S., Walsh, B., & Crowl, A. (1994). College atmosphere and eating disorders. *Journal of Counseling and Development, 72*(6), 640–645.

Kearney-Cooke, A. (1989). Reclaiming the body: Using guided imagery in the treatment of body image disturbances among bulimic women. In L. Hornyak & E. Baker (Eds.), *Experiential therapies for eating disorders* (pp. 11–33). New York: Guilford.

Kempley, F. (1988). *Effectiveness of an exposure treatment for bulimia.* Unpublished doctoral dissertation, Arizona State University, Tempe.

Kerr, A., & Piran, N. (1990). Comprehensive group treatment program. In N. Piran & A. Kaplan (Eds.), *A day hospital group treatment program for anorexia nervosa and bulimia nervosa* (pp. 20–41). New York: Brunner/Mazel .

Kilbourne, J. (1994). Still killing us softly: Advertising and the obsession with thinness. In J. Fallon, M. Katzman, & S. Wooley (Eds.), *Feminist perspectives in eating disorders* (pp. 395–418). New York: Guilford.

Klesges, R., Mizes, J., & Klesges, L. (1987). Self-help dieting strategies in college males and females. *International Journal of Eating Disorders,* 409–417.

Lacey, J., & Smith, G. (1987). Bulimia nervosa: The impact of pregnancy on mother and baby. *British Journal of Psychiatry,* 777–781.

LeBlanc, D. (1990). *You can't quit 'til you know what's eating you: Overcoming compulsive eating.* Deerfield Beach, FL: Health Communications.

Lee, N., & Rush, A. (1986). Cognitive-behavioral group therapy for bulimia. *International Journal of Eating Disorders,* 599–615.

Lerner, H. (1985). *The dance of anger.* New York: Harper & Row.

Levenkron, S. (1982). *Treating and overcoming anorexia nervosa.* New York: Scribner's.

Levine, M., Marcus, M., & Moulton, P. (1966). Exercise in the treatment of binge eating disorder. *International Journal of Eating Disorders, 19*(2), 171–177.

Lewis, L., & Johnson, C. (1985). A comparison of sex role orientation between women with bulimia and normal controls. *International Journal of Eating Disorders,* 247–257.

Love, S., Lewis, L., & Johnson, C. (1989). Group therapy in the treatment of bulimia nervosa. *Advances in eating disorders* (Vol. 2, pp. 175–195). New York: JAI Press.

Lowe, M., & Maycock, B. (1988). Restraint, disinhibition, hunger, and negative affect eating. *Addictive Behavior,* 369–377.

Miller, P. (1996). Redefining success in eating disorders. *Addictive Behaviors, 21,* 745–754.

Mintz, L., & Betz, N. (1988). Prevalence and correlates of eating disordered behaviors among undergraduate women. *Journal of Counseling Psychology,* 463–471.

Minuchin, S., Rosman, B., & Baker, L. (1978). *Psychosomatic families: Anorexia nervosa in context.* Cambridge, MA: Harvard University Press.

Mizes, J., & Fleece, G. (1986). On the use of progressive relaxation in the treatment of bulimia: A single subject design study. *International Journal of Eating Disorders,* 169–176.

Orbach, S. (1978). *Fat is a feminist issue.* New York: Berkeley Books.

Orbach, S. (1982). *Fat is a feminist issue: II.* New York: Berkeley Books.

Orbach, S. (1986). *Hunger strike: The anorectic's struggle as a metaphor for our age.* New York: Norton.

Osherson, S. (1986). *Finding our fathers.* New York: Fawcett Columbine.

Pettinati, H., Kogan, L., Margolis, C., Shrier, L., & Wade, J. (1989). Hypnosis, hypnotizability, and the bulimic patient. In L. Hornyak & E. Baker (Eds.), *Experiential therapies for eating disorders* (pp. 34–59). New York: Guilford.

Pinkney, D. (1994). Afrocentric therapy. *Essence, 25,* 32.

Piran, N., & Kaplan, A. (Eds.). (1990). *A day hospital group treatment program for anorexia nervosa and bulimia nervosa.* New York: Brunner/Mazel.

Polivy, J., & Herman, C. (1985). Dieting and binging: A causal analysis. *American Psychologist, 40,* 193–201.

Powell, A., & Kahn, A. (1995). Racial differences in women's desires to be thin. *International Journal of Eating Disorders, 17,* 191–195.

Richardson, S., Goodman, N., Hastorf, A., & Dornbusch, S. (1961). Cultural uniformity in reaction to physical disabilities. *American Sociological Review, 26,* 241–247.

Rodin, J., Silverstein, L., & Striegel-Moore, R. (1985). Women and weight: A normative discontent. In T. B. Sonderegger (Ed.), *Nebraska symposium on motivation, 1984: Psychology and gender* (pp. 267–307). Lincoln: University of Nebraska Press.

Root, M., Fallon, P., & Friedrich, W. (1986). *Bulimia: A systems approach to treatment.* New York: Norton.

Roth, D., & Ross, D. (1988). Long-term cognitive-interpersonal group therapy for eating disorders. *International Journal of Group Psychotherapy, 38,* 491–510.

Roth, G. (1984). *Breaking free from compulsive eating.* New York: New American Library.

Roy-Byrne, P., Lee-Benner, K., & Yager, J. (1984). Group therapy for bulimia. *International Journal of Eating Disorders, 1*(20), 97–116.

Ruderman, A. (1985). Dysphoric mood and overeating: A test of restraining theory's disinhibition hypothesis. *Journal of Abnormal Psychology, 94,* 78–85.

Russell, G. (1979). Bulimia nervosa: An ominous variant of anorexia nervosa. *Psychological Medicine, 9,* 429–448.

Russell, G., Szmukler, G., Dare, C., & Eisler, I. (1987). An evaluation of family therapy in anorexia nervosa and bulimia nervosa. *Archives of General Psychiatry, 44,* 1047–1056.

Sargent, J., Liebman, R., & Silver, M. (1985). Family therapy for anorexia nervosa. In D. Garner & P. Garfinkel (Eds.), *Handbook of psychotherapy for anorexia and bulimia* (pp. 257–279). New York: Guilford.

Scarano, G., & Kalodner-Martin, C. (1994). A description of the continuum of eating disorders: Implications for intervention and research. *Journal of Counseling & Development, 72,* 356–361.

Selzer, M., Koenigsberg, H., & Kernberg, O. (1987). The initial contract in the treatment of borderline patients. *American Journal of Psychiatry, 144,* 927–930.

Simon, R. (1995a). Eating disorders in college men. *American Journal of Psychiatry, 152*(9), 1279–1285.

Simon, R. (1995b). Eating disorders look alike in men and women. *Psychotherapy Letter, 7,* 3.

Slochower, J., & Kaplan, S. (1980). Anxiety, perceived control, and eating in obese and normal weight persons. *Appetite, 1,* 75–83.

Sparnon, J., & Hornyak, L. (1989). Structured eating experiences in the inpatient treatment of anorexia nervosa. In L. Hornyak & E. Baker (Eds.), *Experiential therapies for eating disorders* (pp. 207–233). New York: Guilford.

Squire, S. (1983). *The slender balance.* New York: Pinnacle Books.

Stewart, D., Raskin, J., Garfinkel, P., MacDonald, O., & Robinson, G. (1987). Pregnancy associated with anorexia nervosa and starvation. *American Journal of Obstetrics and Gynecology, 129,* 698–699.

Striegel-Moore, R., & Rodin, J. (1986). The influence of psychological variables in obesity. In K. Brownell & J. Foreyt (Eds.), *Handbook of eating disorders* (pp. 99–121). New York: Basic Books.

Sue, D., Sue, D., & Sue, S. (1996). *Understanding abnormal behavior* (5th ed.). New York: Houghton Mifflin.

Sullivan, H. S. (1953). *The interpersonal theory of psychiatry.* New York: Norton.

Survey on eating disorders shows significant problem. (1990, September). *NCAA News,* pp. 1, 3, 4.

Thakur, K. (1980). Treatment of anorexia nervosa with hypnotherapy. In H. T. Wain (Ed.), *Clinical hypnosis in medicine* (pp. 147–153). Chicago: Year Book Medical.

Thelen, M., Farmer, J., McLaughlin, L., Mann, L., & Pruitt, J. (1990). Bulimia and interpersonal relationships: A longitudinal study. *Journal of Counseling Psychology, 37*(1), 85–90.

Thornton, J. (1990). Feast or famine: Eating disorders in athletes. *Physician & Sports Medicine, 18,* 116–122.

VandenBroucke, S., Vandereycken, W., & Vertommen, H. (1995). Marital communication in eating disorder patients: A controlled observational study. *International Journal of Eating Disorders, 17,* 1–21.

Villarosa, L. (1994). Dangerous eating. *Essence, 24,* 19.

Wade, J., Kogan, H., Pettinati, H. & Franks, V. (1986, April). *Sex-role self-perceptions in eating disorder patients.* Paper presented at Eastern Psychological Association, New York.

Weiss, L., Katzman, M., & Wolchik, S. (1986). *You can't have your cake and eat it too.* Saratoga, CA: R&E Publishers.

White, W. C. (1985). Bulimarexia: Intervention strategies and outcome considerations. In S. Emmett (Ed.), *Theory and treatment of anorexia nervosa and bulimia* (pp. 246–267). New York: Brunner/Mazel.

Wooley, S., & Kearney-Cooke, A. (1986). Intensive treatment of bulimia and body image disturbances. In K. Brownell & J. Foreyt (Eds.), *Handbook of eating disorders.* New York: Basic Books. 476-502.

Wooley, S., & Wooley, O. (1979). Obesity and women: I. A closer look at the facts. *Women's Studies International Quarterly, 2,* 67–79.

Yalom, I. (1975). *The theory and practice of group psychotherapy* (2nd ed.). New York: Basic Books.

Yalom, I. (1985). *The theory and practice of group psychotherapy* (3rd ed.). New York: Basic Books.

Yalom, I. (1989). *Love's executioner.* New York: Basic Books.

14

Group Counseling for
People With Physical Disabilities

Hanoch Livneh and Robert E. Pullo

The origins of group work as applied to individuals with physical disabilities can be traced to the pioneering work of Joseph Pratt, a physician at the Massachusetts General Hospital, who, as early as 1905, used group methods with tuberculous patients (Gust, 1970; Miller, Wolfe, & Spiegel, 1975). Upon noticing the role group members played in positively affecting one another's emotional adjustment to their illnesses, Pratt later expanded his work to include patients with other chronic illnesses (Durkin, 1972). Pratt's approach valued two components embedded in group methods—support and inspiration—as being of particular importance in light of the feelings of depression and isolation often associated with long-term disabling conditions.

Merits of Group Counseling ~

Group counseling with individuals who have physical disabilities has much to offer. Among its advantages are the following:

1. Groups can help people who strive toward the resolution of some common problem (e.g., accepting functional limitations, dealing with employer's prejudice) by providing them with the opportunity to learn from one another through sharing common concerns and problems and generating solutions to obstacles and difficulties (Gust, 1970).
2. Groups offer members a forum for the emotional release of burdensome per-

sonal issues in a supportive setting. Realizing that others face similar problems tends to lessen the anxiety and fear that accompany various disabling conditions.

3. The group experience can partially alleviate the stress, pain, and misery often generated by physical disability and further aggravated by social isolation, separation from family and friends, and perceived alienation from one's own body (Chubon, 1982; Jacobs, Harvill, & Masson, 1988).

4. The group experience eases the transition into the able-bodied community. Through various socialization and social skill building modeling and exercises (e.g, in assertiveness and frustration tolerance), group members learn and practice how to better deal with the outside community and its various imposed barriers (Chubon, 1982; Gust, 1970; Patterson, McKenzie, & Jenkins, 1995).

5. Through the group modality, leaders are able to more fully arrive at an accurate and comprehensive psychosocial assessment of group members (Salhoot, 1977).

Needs and Concerns of People With Disabilities

Group counseling strategies for people with disabilities have been applied to a wide range of physical and psychiatric disorders. Included are groups for those with psychosomatic conditions, such as ulcers, asthma, migraine headaches, and neurodermatitis (Scheidlinger, 1984), sensory disabilities (Seligman, 1982), and neuromuscular and orthopedic impairments (Lasky & Dell Orto, 1979; Seligman, 1982). These groups can be established in inpatient (hospitals and rehabilitation centers) as well as outpatient (community) settings. Hospital-based groups typically focus on the participants' immediate medical concerns and initial reactions to the onset of disability (e.g., dealing with medical staff and procedures and feelings of anxiety and being overwhelmed by daily stress), whereas community-based groups confront such concerns as adverse public attitudes, long-term functional limitations, and prospects of employment.

More specifically, the needs and concerns that people with disabilities customarily manifest can be conveniently classified into seven major categories:

1. Physical needs (e.g., mobility, activities of daily living, pain control).
2. Psychological needs (e.g., alleviation of anxiety and depression, anger control, frustration tolerance).
3. Social needs (e.g., appropriate interpersonal communication, assertive behavior, managing stigma).
4. Vocational needs (e.g., employment training, job interviewing, job maintenance).
5. Financial needs (e.g., disability benefits, gainful employment).
6. Environmental barriers (e.g., accessibility, transportation, shopping).
7. Attitudinal barriers (e.g., inappropriate language, social prejudice, disability-related stigma).

This wide array of needs and concerns of clients with disabilities has necessitated various therapeutic group formats. Four general group modalities seem to dominate the field:

1. *Educational groups.* These didactic groups impart factual information to participants. For example, the leader discusses and clarifies specific treatment procedures, necessary lifestyle changes, and appropriate vocational pursuits. This type of group is aimed at helping members to make appropriate decisions concerning these life issues.

2. *Social support groups.* Support groups, typically generated from self-help and peer-helper group models, provide participants with the opportunity to support one another and create a forum for exchanging ideas, concerns, and problem-solving methods.

3. *Psychotherapeutic groups.* The emphasis in psychotherapeutic groups is on the affective domain and increased self-understanding. By providing participants cathartic outlets, these groups directly address pressing emotional issues such as anxiety, depression, anger, and changes in personal identity.

4. *Coping and skill training groups.* These groups are more readily aligned with the cognitive and behavioral camps. Participants are trained to cope effectively with their disability and its implications. Specific skills are taught during group sessions and later practiced in the external environment.

Therapeutic Factors of Groups for People With Disabilities ～

Yalom's (1985) curative factors inherent in group counseling seem to be directly relevant to groups whose members have disabilities (Buchanan, 1975; Jacobs et al., 1988; Mann, Godfrey, & Dowd, 1973; Seligman, 1982; Weiner, 1988). These principles are reviewed only briefly here, in relation to disabilities, as they have been more fully explained earlier in this text.

Instillation of Hope

The expectation of recovery or of overcoming disability and the threat of future bodily deterioration, coupled with observation of the gradual progress of other group members, is a powerful motivating force. Participants perceive and vicariously identify with group members who overcome adversity.

Universality

The perception of uniqueness is dispelled in groups. Members are quick to discover that their problems, concerns, and fears are shared by others and that one does not suffer alone. The feeling of commonality tends to decrease social isolation and withdrawal.

Imparting Information

Didactic instruction (e.g., informing participants of new medical procedures; discussing anticipated psychological reactions associated with the particular impairment), as well as advice and suggestions by the group leaders, rehabilitation personnel, or other group members on the availability of health related services, job opportunities, and so on, can reduce client ignorance and anxiety about the unknown future.

Altruism

Participants learn how to be helpful and useful to others. Group members derive many personal benefits from sharing experiences, suggestions, insights, and reassurances with other members. Veterans and novices alike benefit from the mutual sharing of these experiences.

Corrective Recapitulation of the Primary Family Group

Groups for people with or without disabilities bear certain resemblances to families, both in structure and dynamics. Group leaders and members are capable of eliciting feelings and behaviors that once were directed at parents and siblings. Early family dynamics and conflicts (e.g., dependence-independence, scapegoating) can be relived in the group and corrective feedback applied to faulty perceptions and maladaptive behaviors.

Development of Socializing Techniques

In many instances, preparing individuals with disabilities to go into the community is predicated on their acquiring social skills. Group members role-play various social situations with the goal of achieving useful and constructive interpersonal behaviors.

Imitative Behavior

Emulating the behaviors of successful role models has been a cornerstone of the rehabilitation movement. Participants learn how to model their thoughts and behaviors after those of group leaders and other members who have successfully coped with their physical and social environments (e.g., gained independence, secured a job).

Group Cohesiveness

Belonging to a cohesive group produces an attitude of solidarity in the members. During group interactions, members share feelings of acceptance and mutual respect, which results in a more positive self-concept.

Groups afford their members the opportunity to ventilate strong emotions (e.g., anger, fear, loss, anxiety, joy). In the supportive social environment of the group, relieving these pent-up emotions constitutes an important curative factor. It may pave the way to gaining insight into one's problems as participants recognize their present emotional reactions and the connection to those experienced earlier with members of the nuclear family.

Goals of Group Counseling~

A review of the literature on the purposes and goals of group counseling for people with disabilities, and consideration of the problems and needs of this population, revealed that three primary group counseling goal categories seem to predominate: affective, cognitive, and behavioral goals.

Goals considered under this category pertain to those group approaches that address the client's emotional well-being (Democker & Zimpfer, 1981; Forester, Kornfeld, Fleiss, & Thompson, 1993; Henkle, 1975; Howard, 1983; Konstam, 1995; Kriegsman & Celotta, 1981; Rose, 1989; Salhoot, 1977):

1. *Provide the opportunity for emotional catharsis.* Offer group members the opportunity to express and share common feelings, experiences, and problems (e.g., depression, despair, helplessness, frustration, anger) in a safe environment.
2. *Give members emotional support.* Receiving support from peers and group leaders is a cardinal step in the process of adapting to disability.
3. *Reduce anxiety.* Overcoming initial fear and anxiety is mandatory for successful rehabilitation.
4. *Provide members with the opportunity to recognize that they are not alone.* Group members come to realize that others have similar experiences and emotional reactions.

Cognitive Goals

Cognitive goals are those directed at thought-related or perceptive processes. They are also geared toward the individual's knowledge and understanding of his or her disability and its implications for future functioning. More specifically, these goals are to (Democker & Zimpfer, 1981; Kriegsman & Celotta, 1981; Norsworthy & Horne, 1994; Singler, 1982):

1. *Assist the group member to increase self-acceptance and self-esteem.* The concept of self (self-confidence and personal worth) is intimately linked to acceptance of self with a disability and the subsequent personal adjustment.
2. *Help the person confront reality.* Clients receive opportunities to test reality and form more realistic evaluations of their assets and limitations.
3. *Provide the member with accurate and comprehensive information.* Information might include prognosis of condition, use of medication, available sexual outlets, and other facts to foster a sense of personal control and demystify the nature of the disability.
4. *Increase sense of control.* Through the use of imagery, meditation, and relaxation training, members can achieve a more positive outlook.

Behavioral Goals

The primary purpose of behavioral goals is to decrease clients' maladaptive behaviors (e.g., dependency, social withdrawal) and replace them with adaptive ones (e.g., independence, appropriate interpersonal relationships). Accordingly, behavioral goals might be to (Democker & Zimpfer, 1981; Kriegsman & Celotta, 1981; Mann et al., 1973; Miller et al., 1975; Rose, 1989):

1. Assist dependent group members in overcoming dependence (in a mutually supportive environment).
2. Increase the client's ability to cope more effectively with the disability and its associated functional limitations.
3. Provide a setting wherein group members can safely and gradually practice and rehearse new skills and behaviors.
4. Improve interpersonal communications and socialization skills.
5. Assist members in setting and implementing new and more appropriate personal, educational, and vocational goals.

The affective, cognitive, and behavioral goals listed here do not constitute a complete roster of all possible counseling goals of groups for people with disabilities. Rather, they represent the more common types of goals often suggested in the literature. Goals vary with the type of disability and the functional limitations the disability imposes, the immediate needs and concerns of each member or the group as a whole, and the leader's philosophy, knowledge, and skills (Democker & Zimpfer, 1981; Salhoot, 1977).

Phases of Group Counseling for People With Disabilities

Most authors perceive the group process as being composed of two or possibly three essential segments (Kriegsman & Celotta, 1981; Lasky, Dell Orto, & Marinelli, 1984; Mann et al., 1973; Oradei & Waite, 1974; Power & Rogers, 1979). In a three-phase model, the first phase may be construed as one of relationship building. Group members are encouraged to talk about their disability, its etiology, major presenting problems, and so on. The discussion typically evolves around issues related to factual information concerning the disability. When needed, misconceptions pertaining to the disability, its causes, its nature, and anticipated progress are clarified. Using methods such as reflection, clarification, self-disclosure, positive reinforcement, role-playing, and establishing a relaxed atmosphere, group leaders encourage participants to develop mutual trust, openness, involvement, personal awareness and responsibility, and commitment (Kriegsman & Celotta, 1981).

During these initial sessions, group leaders play a more active role earlier rather than later by initiating topics for discussion, offering support and encouragement, raising questions, and, in general, facilitating an active exchange of experiences and ideas. In more structured groups (see, for example, Lasky et al., 1984; Roessler, Milligan, & Ohlson, 1976), individual goal identification, clarification, and planning are paramount.

The second phase is normally geared toward (a) encouraging members to express and explore their feelings regarding the disability, (b) helping participants become aware that others share similar emotions, and (c) helping members develop, based on this gained awareness, a mutual understanding and closeness (Oradei & Waite, 1974; Power & Rogers, 1979). During this middle phase, group leaders shift their role from that of active structure providers and discussion guiders to a less overtly leading role in which participants are allowed to ventilate anxieties and fears about their future, and anger and frustration over interpersonal conflicts, and to initiate most discussion topics.

Attention is clearly directed to helping the participant, through ego-supportive feedback, to gain insight into his or her adjustment difficulties, while at the same time providing the opportunity for members to learn from one another's experiences and achieve a more positive outlook on life with a disability (Power & Rogers, 1979). Group leaders, therefore, pay particular attention to exploration of self, interpersonal dynamics, and the functioning of the group as a cohesive unit (Lasky et al., 1984; Mann et al., 1973).

The third and final phase of group counseling centers on the development of coping and problem-solving methods, with special emphasis on resocialization, future planning, and community reintegration. During this phase, members are assisted in assessing, selecting, and prioritizing their future needs and objectives, and are taught ways of implementing those objectives. Those who are released into the community for the first time since the onset of their disability are given emotional support and feedback on their progress. They also receive ample opportunity in the group to practice their newly learned behaviors. Group leaders and veteran participants often model community-based, adaptive behavior to clients who have recently sustained a disability. Lasky et al. (1984) viewed this final phase as directed toward "life and living," with an emphasis on creating resources that will help members apply their newly acquired skills in daily, community-based activities.

Strategies for Group Sessions ~

The strategies discussed here pertain to three groups of disabling conditions: (a) sensory disabilities (visual and auditory), (b) orthopedic and neuromuscular disabilities (spinal cord injury and cerebrovascular accident, or stroke), and (c) other physical disabilities groups. Cross-disability group strategies developed specifically for rehabilitation settings are also discussed, including (a) structured, coping-based interventions, (b) self-help group methods, and (c) vocational-related (placement-oriented) procedures.

Approaches With Sensory Disabilities Groups

The intent of this section is, first, to acquaint the reader with those relevant functional limitations (i.e., physical and psychosocial) inherent in some of the commonly encountered sensory disabilities and, second, to present specific group strategies and issues directly related to counseling these populations.

Visual Impairment Groups   The chief difficulties people with visual disabilities encounter include (Keegan, 1974; Lindemann, 1981; Van Boemel & Rozee, 1992; Vander Kolk, 1983):

- hindered mobility (restriction of freedom of movement that compromises the ability for independent living).
- dependence on the social environment.
- diminished socialization skills.
- anxiety resulting in avoidance of other people and increased isolation.
- accepting the reality of the disability and altered body image.
- coping with frustration and anger and the related lack of assertiveness.

In an early attempt to use group strategies with people who have visual impairments, Cholden (1953) sought to offer them the opportunity to verbalize and gain insight into their feelings. He argued that blind people have difficulty expressing certain feelings because of their inability to perceive visual and social cues that customarily encourage or hinder the expression of emotions during interpersonal transactions. During group sessions, members were encouraged to express and gain understanding of their personal reactions to their disability. This was followed by discussion of the means available for managing and controlling emotions. Cholden concluded that these group experiences fostered and enriched emotional communications in people who are blind.

Herman (1966) discussed the use of group therapy for blind people in rehabilitation settings. Weekly discussion topics included (a) denial of blindness and its implications, (b) depression and despair following realization of the visual loss, preventing successful adaptation, (c) dependency and low self-esteem, which work against the struggle for independence, (d) devaluation of self and guilt feelings, and (e) avoidance of social situations. Based on his clinical impressions, Herman concluded that the group experience was instrumental in bringing about closeness among the members.

Wilson (1972) and Goldman (1970) further contributed to the field's understanding of the psychological reactions of persons with visual impairments and suggested specific strategies for helping visually impaired people cope with their psychological and behavioral difficulties. Wilson (1972) discussed two types of group therapy. The first, exploratory group therapy, delves into interpersonal issues that seem to have caused the psychological and behavioral problems. The second, supportive group therapy, is geared toward providing reassurance, encouragement, education, and advice on how to manage daily problems.

Using what he termed "encounter microlabs" with a group of young people with visual disabilities, Goldman (1970) sought to encourage participants to become aware of their own and others' feelings and their own and others' bodies. Goldman viewed encounter therapy as a multifaceted concept encompassing elements of various therapeutic modalities (e.g., Gestalt, person centered, psychodynamic) in which action, holism, awareness, and self-growth are underscored. In a comprehensive discussion, he delineated five classes of techniques:

1. *Techniques to reduce initial anxiety*—exercises involving deep breathing, progressive relaxation, and corpse posture (lying down and "letting your body go").

2. *Techniques to initiate interactions*—milling exercises (moving randomly around the room, first nonverbally and then verbally, and using touch) and go-around exercises (going around to every person, touching him or her and making an "I feel" statement).

3. *Techniques for trust building*—falling and catching (falling backwards into the arms of others), lifting (being lifted up from the floor by others), and blind walk (being paired off with another member designated a "sighted guide" and together exploring the environment).

4. *Techniques for eliciting and working through problems*—a brief lecture, followed by an exercise. The lecture, covering such topics as honesty, openness, directness, and emphasizing the present, is followed by exercises including secret pool (each group member anonymously writes down a secret, about a problem he or she is experiencing and then, after each secret is read by another member, the group discusses its meaning and provides feedback) and magic shop (members are offered the opportunity to purchase anything they desire from a magic shop owned by the group leader).

5. *Guided fantasy techniques*—exercises to assist in conflict resolution and goal setting, strategies to improve perception of body and physical appearance (e.g., stretching out and relaxing, exploring internal and external body boundaries), fantasizing significant others talking about oneself, and future projection (imagining what one will be doing in the distant future).

From his studies, Goldman (1970) concluded that these exercises increase self-assertiveness and feelings of independence, in addition to self-awareness and empathy toward others.

Another concern often raised in group counseling with people who are blind centers on sexual matters (e.g., dating, marriage, sex, pregnancy). Employing group therapy with adolescent girls with multiple disabilities, Avery (1968) offered participants the opportunity to learn about sexuality issues. Through reflection of feelings, thought clarification, interpretation of emotions and behaviors, and providing answers to questions on sexual issues, Avery allowed the girls to ventilate emotional concerns in a supportive atmosphere and provided related factual information.

Still another concern revolves around interactions with sighted people (Cholden, 1953; Welsh, 1982). During these interactions, feelings of hostility and resentment are often evident. Counseling strategies geared toward appropriate assertiveness skills and developing a more positive self-concept are beneficial when these concerns arise (Welsh, 1982).

Another topic frequently encountered is how to cope with the functional limitations the visual impairment imposes. Group members might discuss the impact of these limitations on their ability to independently perform various tasks and activities in the community and how this might affect their self-concept (Inana, 1978; Welsh, 1982). Group leaders seek to facilitate acceptance of the condition, internalization of the concept of personal loss, and the development of a more realistic self-perception.

Finally, groups must attend to personal skill building. These skills may be applied in vocational training programs and in securing appropriate employment. Roessler (1978) reported on a personal achievement skill training program for visually impaired people. Participants were taught problem-solving, decision-making, and self-modification skills. They engaged in exercises and activities that enabled them to improve their communication skills, to identify and prioritize goals, and to implement and monitor the progress of those goals. This group achieved higher levels of goal attainment and self-esteem as compared to a control group.

Group counselors working with clients who have visual impairments should pay particular attention to:

1. *Periods of silence.* Periods of silence are threatening to blind people (Welsh, 1982). Silence generates discomfort, anxiety, and resentment, and may even lead to paranoid projection by some participants. Leaders must, therefore, be more verbal and directive (e.g., use audible reinforcers, invite participants to speak) rather than rely on more traditional nonverbal methods (e.g., eye contact, head nodding). Co-leadership as a means to bridge periods of silence is also recommended (Keegan, 1974; Welsh, 1982).

2. *Group structure.* When counseling people who are blind, the need for more structure of group sessions is inherent (Welsh, 1982). This is particularly important for members who are congenitally blind.

3. *Trust-building techniques.* Building trust is important in that many blind people often mistrust and resent sighted people, as well as others who are blind. Goldman's (1970) earlier discussed activities (e.g., "fall and catch," "the blind walk") are recommended (Keegan, 1974; Welsh, 1982).

4. *Selection of group members.* In choosing group participants, degree of visual impairment, its cause, and age of onset should be considered. Also, clients' levels of denial, optimism, resentment, and anxiety are important variables in establishing a well-balanced group (Routh, 1957; Welsh, 1982).

Hearing Impairment Groups   The most pervasive difficulties that beset people who have hearing impairments are (Lindemann, 1981; Ostby & Thomas, 1984):

- impaired communication.
- negotiating various environmental features that may directly impact their personal safety (e.g., inability to respond to a ringing phone or to react to honking horns or police sirens).
- experiential deprivation and isolation from significant others.
- maladaptive behavioral patterns (e.g., withdrawal, rigidity, suspiciousness, immaturity, denial) that prevent effective social interaction with hearing peers.
- handling frustrations because of inadequate communication and isolation.
- coping with overprotective and dependency-fostering parents and public.

In an early effort to apply group counseling strategies to hospital patients who were deaf, Robinson (1965), a hearing psychiatrist, employed manual communication methods in working with a group of six participants. The group proved successful in offering participants the opportunity to ventilate feelings toward other group members and the therapist. Portner (1981) described a YWCA group for deaf members that was focused on problems of living, group members' denial of impairment, projection of frustrations and anger toward hearing people, feelings of inferiority, and difficulties in communicating with mates.

As previously mentioned, a common problem of people who are deaf is their experiential deprivation and its subsequent progression into a lack of social assertiveness. In an effort to rectify their problems with assertiveness, Sedge (1982) sought to teach clients with hearing impairments to openly express their feelings and assert themselves in situations where communication barriers exist. Because prior research had demonstrated the effectiveness, for hearing-impaired people, of assertiveness training in increasing assertive behavior, improving self-concept, elevating self-confidence, improving speech fluency, and increasing interactional activities, Sedge (1982) developed an assertiveness training model for hearing-impaired servicemen that employed mini-lectures, modeling, role-playing, overt and covert behavior rehearsals, relaxation training, and homework assignments. Training goals were to discriminate between passive, assertive, and aggressive behaviors; identify and accept personal rights and those of others; exert control in situations where communication is impaired; and communicate more effectively within the environment. The training group demonstrated significant increases in level of assertiveness and in self-concept when compared to a control group.

Sarti (1993) described a mental health program for young adolescents with hearing impairments and marked ego deficits that was conducted at the Rhode Island School for the Deaf. Using what the program developers called "Prep House" group therapy, the program provided participants with both the necessary therapeutic conditions (e.g., allowing students to express their needs and conflicts in a safe atmosphere, practice in personal and social coping skills) and communicative accommodations (e.g., role-playing, "rapping," videotaping of group sessions) to enhance their egos. Reports by group therapists, teachers, parents, and participants lent support to this therapy's success in improving participants' self-concept, impulse control, and reality testing.

Concerns commonly raised and discussed in groups for people who are deaf include (Card & Schmider, 1995; Schein, 1982) feelings of isolation because of a communication handicap (e.g., difficulties associated with accurately perceiving the motives of others); appropriate expression of feelings such as anger and frustration; interpretation of symbolic behaviors, often manifested in nonverbal (e.g., facial) cues and messages (of particular importance in the prelingually deaf population); and appropriate rules and customs regarding dating and sex-oriented issues (most prevalent in individuals with prelingual deafness and those educated in restrictive residential settings).

Schein (1982) asserted that to successfully manage these concerns (e.g., isolation, lack of effective communication) as well as similar group-raised concerns, the leader should realize the importance of emotional ventilation. In a group context, emotional ventilation allows members to realize that their problems and frustrations are not unique. Furthermore, mutual expression of feelings and exchange of concerns increase self-esteem, alleviate anxiety, and reduce interpersonal awkwardness.

Card and Schmider (1995) argued that in considering group composition, group leaders should pay particular attention to participant's age of onset and severity of hearing loss, cognitive processing ability, language skills, psychosocial adjustment, and family communication patterns.

When working with deaf and hearing impaired populations, group leaders should consider the following:

1. *Arrangement of the physical setting.* In organizing the group setting, the leader should pay particular attention to the participants' seating arrangements (members must be able to see each other and the leader at the same time). Barrier-free sightlines must be ensured. Semicircular or rectangular seating patterns are often recommended (Card & Schmider, 1995; Schein, 1982). Lighting must facilitate nonverbal and manual communication, and appropriate acoustics must be ensured for members who use hearing aids (Speer & O'Sullivan, 1994).

2. *Use of sign language.* The choice of communication mode in group counseling in which most or all of the participants are hearing impaired is of utmost importance. The traditionally preferred mode has been American Sign Language (ASL) (Silberman-Miller & Moores, 1990). The leader, either hearing impaired or nonimpaired, must possess comprehensive ASL skills to function as an effective counselor (Silberman-Miller & Moores, 1990).

3. *Use of an interpreter.* Although employing a sign language interpreter is often suggested to facilitate communication in these groups, it is not without difficulties (Schein, 1982). The addition of a "third party" may adversely affect group dynamics by hindering establishment of relationships and impeding expression of many feelings and thoughts (Portner, 1981; Silberman-Miller & Moores, 1990). Also, because the interpreter cannot attend to more than one person's verbalization at a time, he or she is placed under pressure to keep pace with the messages and the group leader has to assume the role of "verbal traffic director" (Schein, 1982)

   When an interpreter is used, he or she should be easily visible to all and preferably seated next to the group leader. Ideally, even when an interpreter is used, the leader should be adept at signing, for both practical reasons (speed in communication) and psychological reasons (learning sign language is considered to be a gesture of respect for the person who is hearing impaired) (Card & Schmider, 1995; Riekehof, 1987).

4. *Eye strain.* The leader must be alert to the strain placed on members' vision as a result of their total reliance on the manual communication modality (Schein, 1982).

5. *Deaf-hearing group mixture.* The ratio of group members who are deaf to those whose hearing is normal (e.g., people with other disabilities, family members, staff members) partially dictates group communication modali-

ties, structure, and content (Schein, 1982). Group leaders should, accordingly, carefully plan the content and structure of sessions, taking into account the participants' oral and manual communication skills, degree of hearing impairment, age of onset of the impairment (prelingual versus postlingual), and social and emotional maturity.

6. *Gender and number of group leaders.* It is often recommended that groups for people with hearing impairments be co-led by members of both genders. Co-leaders can maintain better eye contact with all group participants as well as accommodate different modes of communication. If they are of different genders, they can also offer better opportunities for participants to practice gender-role issues (Card & Schmider, 1995).

Approaches With Orthopedic and Neuromuscular Disabilities Groups

Spinal Cord Injury Groups   Individuals who have sustained spinal cord injury (SCI) are primarily faced with (Crewe & Krause, 1987; Donovan, 1981):

- mobility impairment (i.e., restricted ambulation and often inaccessible environments).
- problems with personal hygiene, dressing, eating and drinking, toileting, and writing (specific impairments depend upon the nature and severity of the injury).
- difficulties (particularly in men) in sexual performance.
- feelings of depression, passivity, embarrassment, and helplessness.
- denial of the injury's degree of severity and its permanency, resulting in unwillingness to cooperate with rehabilitation efforts.
- disruption of familial, social, and vocational activities.

Mann et al. (1973), in counseling people with spinal cord injury, established four group goals: to help participants increase their self-concepts and thereby positively impact total rehabilitation efforts; to help dependent members overcome dependency in a mutually supportive environment; to provide a setting wherein interpersonal relations issues could be identified, discussed, and, when necessary, resolved; and to modify members' perceptual distortions about other people. Their groups were structured so that participants who had sustained their injuries earlier than others could assist newer clients in accepting the limitations imposed by, and adjusting to life with, their disability. In these groups, feedback and reinforcement related to progress were provided by the group leader and the other participants. Group discussion also focused on assisting clients to make maximum use of their strengths and remaining physical functions.

Reporting on short-term group counseling with SCI members, Miller et al. (1975) emphasized a more structured, didactic-informative approach. Their group was aimed at providing information on the physiology and associated problems (e.g., sexual, muscular) of spinal cord injuries. Their group members showed positive changes in self-concept as well as increases in their knowledge and understanding of the impairment.

The concern with sexuality led several clinicians to establish groups that specifically addressed this issue (Banik & Mendelson, 1978; Melnyk, Montgomery, & Over, 1979). In these groups, clients were encouraged to talk about their concerns and feelings related to sexual relations. The discussion commonly revolved around fears of rejection by sexual partners when satisfactory functioning was impaired. Using lectures and films, the group leaders disseminated specific and technical information on the psychophysiology of sex to relieve anxiety and avoidance of the issue. In general, the group leaders sought to balance informative coverage of sexual alternatives and means of expression with small-group discussion, role-playing, and behavioral rehearsal of effective partner communication, sexual adaptation, and other related concerns (Melnyk et al., 1979).

Melnyk and his co-workers developed the following weekly format for their sexual counseling groups: member introduction through "games," discussion of program goals and member problem areas; small-group work using self-guided imagery for enhancing sensuality, and large-group discussion of communication issues; verbal and nonverbal communication followed by discussion of films on sex education and techniques; and discussion of body image followed by discussion of spinal cord injuries and the use of sexual aids.

A comprehensive structured group counseling program for people with SCI was proposed by Roessler et al. (1976). Termed the Personal Achievement Skills (PAS) training program, it strived to (a) develop participants' self-awareness of their personal values and capacities and their acceptance of other group members, and (b) develop skills in such areas as communication, problem identification, goal setting, and action implementation. Typical member goals included independent community living, educational-vocational training culminating in successful job placement, identification of recreational and leisure needs and how to meet them, and family counseling focusing on sexual issues.

Bowers et al. (1987) described a structured, active mastery support group for young males who had sustained spinal cord injury. The 1-hour weekly support group meetings emphasized self-expression, especially regarding feelings about the injury and the resultant dependence upon others; the attainment of emotional independence; examination of client-staff relationships; and assessment of public attitudes toward people with physical disabilities. Structured group topics that emerged during the group meetings included developing independence (e.g., planning for work and leisure time activities and travel), role transitions (e.g., changes in social, vocational, and sexual functioning roles), self-expression (e.g., communication with friends, dealing with anger), and communication with the rehabilitation team.

Counselors who conduct group sessions with clients with SCI should pay attention to the following considerations:

1. *Appropriateness of the physical setting.* The setting for group sessions must be totally free of architectural barriers. The leader may have to make or arrange for physical modifications prior to the first session (Seligman, 1982).

2. *Attention to client fatigue.* Because fatigue plays a major role in the lives of individuals with SCI, each session should be limited to a maximum of 2 hours (Roessler et al., 1976).

3. *Knowledge of spinal cord injuries.* The group leader(s) should thoroughly understand spinal cord injuries and their functional implications (Roessler et al., 1976) and should be able to recognize and deal with emergency medical situations that might arise.

4. *Personal comfort with sexual issues.* Because a large portion of group work with this population focuses on alternative sexual outlets, sexual aids, and the like, group leaders should become familiar with these topics and personally comfortable discussing these issues in a group format.

5. *Adaptation of the group therapy modality to participants' psychosocial level of adaptation.* For example, participants who are comfortable sharing experiences with others may benefit more from a discussion-oriented group format, whereas those who are coping with earlier phases of adaptation may find structured didactic group formats more suitable for their immediate needs and concerns (Fow & Rockey, 1995).

Cerebrovascular Accident (CVA) Groups   The major physical and psychosocial difficulties associated with cerebrovascular accidents (strokes) are (Anderson, 1981; Singler, 1982):

- perceptual-spatial deficits (including problems with visual-motor coordination, visual dysfunctions, spasticity, and seizures).
- impairment of cognitive functioning (speech and language abilities, learning, abstract reasoning, memory, attention, and concentration).
- deficient affective performance (emotional reactions including anxiety, denial, depression, frustration, agitation, anger, and shame).
- behavioral involvement (increased impulsivity, restlessness, social discrimination).
- communication problems that result from deterioration in cognitive functioning (such as verbal fluency and involvement of the affective domain), causing lower frustration threshold and other emotional liability manifestations.

Because the psychophysiological implications of CVA are many, the counseling goals listed by clinicians address a wide array of concerns, issues, and problems. The two major goals D'Afflitti and Weitz (1974) identified for their patient-family, hospital-based group sessions were encouraging patients and families to (a) share feelings about the stroke to facilitate a better adjustment to the impairment and (b) use appropriate community resources and supports available to them. As expected, patients and their family members raised numerous issues during the sessions. Among them were loss of control of certain bodily parts and functions and its effect on self-esteem, attempts at denial of impairment, expression of resentment and anger by family upon realizing the magnitude of the impairment and ensuing guilt feelings, and attempts of restitution and resolution of problems by discussing life prior to the disability, accepting the loss, and adjusting to life with a disability.

D'Afflitti and Weitz (1974) reported that discussion of these issues in a group format seemed to be positively associated with facilitating communication between patient and family and creating more realistic expectations about the future, such as return to the community. Similar findings were reported by Oradei and Waite (1974), whose hospital-based stroke unit patients indicated better understanding of their impairment, its functional limitations, and how to better cope with depression and loneliness following group counseling.

Singler (1982) argued that strategies for clients who have sustained CVA must capitalize on group members' current needs and remaining strengths, such as the need to talk about oneself, the fear of future strokes, and awareness of physical losses and the resultant limitations. In developing her hospital-based group, Singler set the goals of reducing anxiety and heightening emotionalism through a supportive atmosphere and the opportunity to ventilate feelings, fostering increased self-acceptance, rebuilding damaged self-esteem, and reducing social isolation. Accordingly, group discussions centered on providing members with accurate information on strokes, the therapeutic procedures involved, and the hospital setting; sharing experiences and feelings; and identifying and confronting members' most bothersome fears and problems (e.g., fear of subsequent strokes; feelings of depression, isolation, and anger; anxiety over reactions by community members). In early sessions, the group leader was directive, guiding members and explaining life-threatening issues. In later sessions, the group leader made indirect interpretations by questioning, thus allowing members to gain insight into their problems.

An innovative approach to group counseling with stroke and other neurologically impaired clients was reported by Evans, Halar, and Smith (1985). Their short-term cognitive therapy was aimed at assisting recently discharged patients to cope with personal issues (e.g., depression, loneliness) and to interact productively with family and friends. The use of a conference-call system permitted these nonambulatory participants to engage in discussion from their homes. The group conference took place weekly and lasted an hour. The group leader directed the flow and exchange of the group members' concerns.

Briefly, the cognitive therapy format used by Evans et al. (1985) focused on task-oriented objectives geared to improving mood or modifying behavior that were based on cognitive processes that affect one's attitudes and belief system. Particularly targeted were negative and rigid cognitions leading to depression and loneliness. Leaders provided participants with feedback on circular, faulty, and destructive thought processes. Individually tailored objectives included providing accurate information on the impairment and its implications, decreasing levels of anxiety, increasing energy levels, precipitating a higher level of personal independence, and generating improved relationships with family.

Leaders of CVA groups should consider the following aspects of structuring and planning activities:

1. *Participants' speech and perceptual abilities.* Because a large number of CVA individuals have speech impairments, in addition to various other per-

ceptual, physical, and cognitive losses, the group leader has to examine the impact of these factors on the group's structure and communication modalities (Singler, 1982).

2. *Individual and group goals.* Based on the cognitive and verbal impairments of the group members and any observations of signs of frustration and anger among participants, group leaders should strive to develop specific and concrete goals to guide future group activities. Explicit, realistic, and attainable goals will most likely result in better attendance, motivation, and progress toward goal achievement.

3. *Handling denial.* Denial of their limitations by people with CVA is a rather prevalent and most disturbing phenomenon. Two strategies commonly used to diffuse the long-term impact of denial are awareness raising and gentle confrontation. Youngjohn and Altman (1989) reported on a self-awareness group that had the aim of reducing denial of deficits in stroke and head injury patients attending a rehabilitation day hospital. Patients received explanations of the cognitive and personality changes that often accompany stroke. They also were assisted in identifying their cognitive strengths and limitations by being introduced to a wide range of cognitive tasks. Similarly, confrontational strategies, were applied discreetly and cautiously (e.g., pointing out discrepancies between a client's present functional abilities and unrealistic future goals), to help penetrate the protective shield of denial.

Approaches in Other Physical Disabilities Groups

In addition, groups have been established to address the many needs and concerns of cancer patients (e.g., Cunningham & Tocco, 1989; Fawzy et al., 1990; Forester, Kornfeld, Fleiss, & Thompson, 1993; Telch & Telch, 1986), cardiac patients (e.g., Horlick, Cameron, Firor, Bhalerao, & Baltzan, 1984; Konstam, 1995; Stern, Plionis, & Kaslow, 1984; Subramanian & Ell, 1989), HIV-infected or AIDS patients (e.g., Beckett & Rutan, 1990; Norsworthy & Horne, 1994; Tunnell, 1991), chronic kidney and liver patients (e.g., Buchanan, 1975; Hollon, 1972; Stewart, Kelly, Robinson, & Callender, 1995), people with multiple sclerosis (e.g., Crawford & McIvor, 1985; Welch & Steven, 1979), and people with amputations (e.g., Fischer & Samelson, 1971; Howard, 1983; Rogers, MacBride, Whylie, & Freeman, 1977-1978).

Approaches in Rehabilitation Settings

Three types of rehabilitation-specific group strategies are discussed here. Structured Experiential Training: Rehabilitation (SET:R) is reviewed, followed by a discussion of the application of self-help and peer helper groups to rehabilitation settings. Finally, mention is made of a vocationally related group model, the job club, for people with disabilities.

Structured Experiential Training: Rehabilitation As defined by Lasky et al. (1984), "Structured Experiential Training (SET) is an eclectic group rehabilitation model which is especially designed to meet the needs of persons with physical disabilities and emphasizes group members' goal involvement, mutual concern, and accountability" (p. 317). The SET model synthesizes elements of educational, social support, psychotherapeutic, and coping skills strategies into a systematic framework to benefit people undergoing rehabilitation. People with disabilities share common concerns in the group sessions. They are afforded the opportunity to capitalize on others' strengths, benefit from role models, and gain more awareness and sensitivity to issues such as stress and stigma. This communication among group members increases mutual trust and understanding.

Methodologically, SET uses structured experiential learning, the power of the group process, and explicit goal orientation directed at acquiring skills and resolving related therapeutic issues. A variety of structured experiences related to group and personal functioning are incorporated. These structured experiences are interventions in a group's process that involve a set of specific instructions to participants. The five steps in this process are (a) experiencing an activity, (b) publishing or sharing reactions or observations about the activity, (c) processing the activity with other participants, (d) generalizing from the experience, and (e) applying this new learning behaviorally.

Group Organization   Prospective members are oriented to the expectations of the SET format, and group members are selected based on their potential to gain from the experience as well as their commitment to the SET process and the goals delineated in the initial group contract. A typical group consists of a group leader or co-leaders and 6 to 10 members. The group meets once a week for 3 hours. Group composition is limited to people who show the motivation and capability to work toward personally relevant goals. Participants are required to keep a daily record to help raise self-awareness, develop and clarify individual and group goals, and assist the group in becoming more cohesive.

Phases   The SET process involves three sequential phases (Lasky et al., 1984): personal, group, and life and living.

1. *Personal phase.* This personally oriented stage involves (a) acquainting group members with one another and with the purpose of the group; (b) selecting individual goals and determining the strategies and steps necessary to attain them; and (c) actively pursuing and implementing these goals.
2. *Group phase.* The group-oriented stage entails (a) convergence, or joint group work to identify a common goal for all members; (b) implicit mutuality, or assessing interpersonal relationships and the implications of these relationships; (c) interpersonal feedback; and (d) explicit mutuality, or the demonstration of genuine concern for other group members.
3. *Life and living phase.* The third phase, life and living, calls for (a) utilization, or the application of new knowledge and experience to daily living; (b) congruence, or the demonstration of consistent integration of thought, feeling, and action; (c) commencement, or the sharing of mutual experiences and future perspectives; and (d) reunion, or the opportunity for group members to come together to share successes and failures.

Specific structured experiential tasks are employed as interventions to facilitate development of the group, completion of each phase, and movement of the members through the SET process.

SET Focus   The consistent themes throughout the SET process are the emphases on goal involvement, mutual concern, and accountability (any of which may be the focus of any group meeting). Selected goals are expected to be relevant, understandable, performable, measurable, attainable, and time limited. The concept of mutual concern requires members to extend themselves to others in the group, to learn to rely on the group, and to provide other group members with the support and caring that are necessary for growth. Accountability takes the form of personal and interpersonal responsibility. Group members are responsible for their behavior and are not allowed to attribute personal problems to external forces.

Self-Help and Peer Help Groups   Self-help and peer help groups for individuals with disabilities have been flourishing in the past three decades. Most have been spearheaded by citizen and consumer advocacy groups sparked by the civil rights movement of the 1960s (Rhoades, 1986). Early groups were initiated by and for parents whose children had disabling conditions. Now the self-help movement is geared more directly toward people with disabilities. Peer helper programs have been established for those affected by alcoholism, heart disease, stroke, spinal cord injuries, amputations, neurological disorders, cancer, mental retardation, and many other disabling conditions.

These self-governing groups, composed of individuals who share a common condition or experience, offer direct, active, and effective interventions to the participants while allowing them to avoid the stigma frequently associated with seeking outside professional help (Lieberman & Borman, 1979). Because the person with difficulty promotes his or her own advocacy, self-help and peer helper groups afford their members a chance at a rightful and equal place in society at large (Rhoades, Browning, & Thorin, 1986).

The operational principles underlying the self-help philosophy, cogently stated by Jaques and Patterson (1974), are:

- Participants have a commonly shared personal problem or condition.
- All participants maintain an equal status (i.e., due to peer relationships).
- Peers come together with the expectation of helping themselves and one another.
- All participants seek behavioral change.
- Peers identify with the particular program developed by the group and actively support this program.
- The group process consists of participants' actively relating, owning, and sharing experiences, hopes, and problems; receiving and giving feedback to one another; and providing encouragement and criticism.
- Participants are held responsible for themselves and their behaviors.
- Group leadership develops and changes from within the group and follows the program's principles and goals.

Self-help groups serve many important functions in the lives of people with disabilities, including:

1. *Accurate knowledge.* Members can gain information (e.g., medical facts, innovative treatment and rehabilitation modalities) about their disability.

2. *Coping strategies.* Members can learn adaptive coping strategies from others who have learned to successfully live with the same or a similar disability. They also benefit from the social modeling of others who demonstrate problem-solving behaviors that are useful for life in the community and from the feedback they provide newer members (Wright, 1983).

3. *Motivation level.* Members can become more motivated to achieve their rehabilitation goals by openly sharing and communicating with others who have similar conditions and life experiences. Self-help groups provide a psychosocial support network, creating opportunities for receiving and giving emotional support and solving mutual problems (Gottlieb, 1982).

4. *Social reference group.* Groups offer identification with a social reference group, which gives members a sense of rootedness and belongingness, thereby decreasing feelings of isolation, rejection, and alienation (Plummer, 1982).

5. *Self-evaluation process.* Groups can provide members with concrete evidence of self-progress. This evaluative function is closely linked to the type of feedback received from the group leader and other members as the various phases of members' problems and coping efforts unfold (Jaques & Patterson, 1974).

6. *Active participation.* Groups enable members to surrender the role of passive recipient of services to the role of active participant. This action orientation is germane to the rehabilitation philosophy of those in rehabilitation being responsible consumers who choose among various alternatives and ultimately manage their individual rehabilitation plans and are also accountable for their results (Plummer, 1982).

The Job Club   The job club method exemplifies a behavioral group approach to vocational counseling and job placement. It centers on individual needs and uses reinforcement and peer support "to obtain a job of the highest feasible quality within the shortest feasible time period for all participating job seekers" (Azrin & Besalel, 1980, p. 1).

Each procedure employed in this approach is standardized into a consistent, intensive process for all job seekers (Azrin & Philip, 1979). Group members work together under the instruction and encouragement of a leader who provides support, information, facilities, and supplies. More than 30 procedures and activities were specified by Azrin and Besalel (1980). These include standard scripts and forms, group support from other job seekers, a buddy system, use of the telephone, emphasis on personal skills, interview training, transportation, daily progress charts, and continued assistance.

In the job club model, job search and related activities are scheduled within the club session as much as possible so immediate assistance can be given for such activities as resume and letter writing, calling friends and former employers for leads and interviews, reviewing job listings in newspapers and other available sources, and planning daily and weekly job seeking activities. The group leader's role requires a commitment to help every member obtain an appropriate job through selective placement; the leader provides job leads, encouragement, and a positive perspective focused on the member's assets, not limitations.

Before the job club is initiated, an intake group may be conducted to orient members to the job club program, basic hygiene, health and living skills, work behavior and ethics, and the world of work. Typically meeting for 810 weeks, once a week, the intake group prepares the members to apply these new knowledge areas and skills in the job club. The job club itself may meet from 1 to 5 days per week and is a continuous resource to be tapped by members, who may reenter at any time, usually for only minimal assistance.

The job club approach is efficient because it can address every participant at the same time and reinforce members' behaviors and achievements in the presence of all other members. This approach encourages others to follow examples of peer success while offering support. It also shows group members how to engage in mutual support endeavors, confront similar problems, share resources, and offer peer support. Because many of the demands of work are largely social in nature (e.g., accepting criticism, attending to directions), employers are concerned not only with the person's capacity to work but also with his or her ability to work as a team member (Johnson, Greenwood, & Schriner, 1988). Research on applying the group method to work adjustment and job placement supports the hypothesis that participants in job seeking groups are seen as more competent overall and better prepared for the jobs (Garvin, 1984; Roessler, 1986).

Recently, McWhirter and McWhirter (1996) described a group model similar to that of the job club, which they termed the *transition-to-work group*. In their group, college students with learning disabilities are prepared for dealing with the personal, professional, vocational, and legal aspects encountered upon entering the work arena. The five sessions of the group focus sequentially on the following themes: setting group format and establishing group cohesion, building self-confidence and communicating about the disability, examining and keeping records of job and market trends, discussing legal issues regarding employment and disability, and learning practical strategies to compensate for the disability in the work setting. Preliminary feedback data from group participants seem to confirm the beneficial results of the transition-to-work group experience.

Age-Specific Variations ⌇

Important considerations in groups for people with physical disabilities are the members' age and the age of onset of the disability. The latter was noted under "Strategies for Group Sessions." Here, the focus is on present age-related variables.

Considerations With Younger People

Group goals for children and adolescents differ from those for adult clients (Kennedy, 1989; Marshak, 1982), because of such factors as levels of psychosocial and cognitive functioning, self-identity, self-insight, social maturity, and attained level of independence. In general, goals in groups for children and adolescents should be narrower and should focus on solving present problems and issues (Marshak, 1982). In groups of youth with disabilities, the leader should consider the following strategies and issues:

1. Initiating and maintaining a more active style than that practiced with adults, to counteract the passive or resistant attitude commonly seen in adolescent clients (Bruce, 1975).
2. Being aware of the negative impact of long periods of silence during group sessions (Marshak, 1982). Adolescents seem to react more adversely (e.g., become anxious) to silence and to breakdowns in communication. Their adverse reactions impede the group counseling process, especially with participants who have visual and hearing impairments.
3. Self-disclosing personal feelings. Showing members that owning a wide range of feelings, rather than resorting to denying them or being overwhelmed by them, is normal can be a valuable clinical tool (Marshak, 1982).
4. Making cautious and limited use of interpretations. The aim should be behavioral and functional improvement, and setting and implementating specific and time-bound goals. Berkovitz (1972) and Marshak (1982) maintained that attempts at in-depth interpretation, and especially interpreting transference in a group setting, can have a negative impact on younger members. Also, members' level of cognitive and social maturity plays a prominent part in deciding on the type and timing of interpretation.
5. Discreetly using role-playing and psychodrama exercises. Although these strategies are often recommended in the literature (Marshak, 1982; Sussman, 1974), they are not without their pitfalls. Role-playing, especially with members who have sensory impairments, is rather common. However, before using role-playing, psychodrama, or similar techniques (e.g., music therapy, movement therapy) the group leader should weigh the members' ability to ambulate (in the case of participants with SCI, muscular dystrophy, and so forth); the members' body images (especially in the case of young adolescents, whose perception of their own bodies is precarious); and the level of group cohesiveness (e.g., in open groups, new members with body deformities may find role-playing extremely threatening, particularly in early sessions).
6. Paying special attention to the youngsters' typical concerns, which, in addition to the visible physical impairment, also include the more age-related concerns of physical appearance, peer acceptance, self-identity, sexuality, emancipation from family, and the like (Kennedy, 1989; Weinman, 1987).
7. When appropriate, requesting that parents or other family members allow the youngsters to attend the group sessions alone, without their company. If

group sessions are conducted in inpatient settings (e.g., hospital wards), parents may be requested to remain outside the room in which the sessions are held (Flynn, 1992).

The presence of a disability compromises adolescents' accomplishment of various developmental tasks (Manaster, 1977). According to Marshak (1982), the tasks most affected are (a) acquiring more mature relationships with peers of both genders, (b) acquiring feminine or masculine social roles, (c) accepting one's physique and use of body, and (d) becoming emotionally independent from parental figures. Group leaders should give equal consideration to the stresses associated with these age-related developmental tasks, the presence of physical impairment, and attitudes of parents and peers (e.g., overprotection, rejection) when selecting group strategies for adolescents with disabilities.

Considerations With Older Adults

When counseling older adults, the group leader is often required to consider an age-specific set of therapeutic goals (Kalson, 1982). The factors that exert the greatest impact on the lives of older individuals include loss of significant others; disruption of social support systems; loss of independence and control over one's life, resulting from physical deterioration; economic and financial concerns; cognitive changes (e.g., impairment of recent memory); and fear of institutionalization (Gugel & Eisdorfer, 1985; Kalson, 1982).

The group leader who works with older adults may also have to consider time constraints. Long-term goals should be carefully selected with particular attention to setting time limits on goals and their implementation (Kalson, 1982). In group counseling settings, the leader should:

1. Be brief and direct in approach (Kalson, 1982), which will expedite group cohesiveness and the development of individual and group goals.
2. Attend to members' organic conditions. Cognitive deficits related to organicity may exacerbate physical and sensory impairments (e.g., those resulting from stroke or head injuries). Kalson (1982) recommended that to assess a group member's level of organic brain involvement, the leader should arrange for tests of the member's general intelligence, short-term memory, orientation as to place and person, and judgment. If organicity is present, the counseling style should be modified to (a) allow the member more time to respond to the leader and other participants, (b) be much more concrete in content, and (c) clearly and slowly present the member with simply worded questions.
3. Be aware of the complex set of transference responses exhibited in this age-group. According to Linden (1955), two of the more common types of transference displayed by older adults are recession and sociological transference. In recession transference, social unlearning or return to repressed material occurs. This results in a series of reverse steps of psychosexual development, leading to an inversion of the parent-child relationship. The

younger leader, then, is perceived in the role of a parent. In sociological transference, the older member manifests signs of self-rejection because of identification with cultural beliefs upholding the value of youth and physical prowess. Group leaders who seek to facilitate the therapeutic effect of transference and its interpretation may heed Linden's (1954) advice to install dual-gender group leadership in an effort to replicate the original family structure.

4. Take a flexible approach in structuring and pacing sessions. Because of the numerous life crises (e.g., impaired mobility, retirement, death of mate, impending death) that beset older people with disabilities, group leaders should be prepared to deviate, when necessary, from planned group topics and address the more immediate needs of individual members.

Many authors have advocated a greater use of therapeutic group programs for people in nursing homes. Gugel and Eisdorfer (1985) posited that the functional level of older people may be improved by recreation therapy, occupational therapy, reality orientation, remotivation programs, behavior therapy, and environmental (milieu) approaches.

Summary ～

Group counseling has been applied with a wide range of people who have physical disorders including psychosomatic conditions, sensory (visual and auditory) disabilities, and neuromuscular and orthopedic impairments. The needs and concerns of these people can be generally delineated as physical, psychological, social, vocational, financial, environmental, and attitudinal. The four modalities used most often are educational, social support, psychotherapeutic, and coping and skill training groups. Goal setting addresses affective, cognitive, and behavioral areas.

People with visual impairments have concerns generally related to their reduced mobility, dependence on others, limited social skills, anxiety and avoidance of people, altered body image, and coping with the reality and limitations of the disability. Groups for people with hearing impairments focus on communication, negotiating the environment, compensating for experiential deprivation and isolation, adaptive behavior patterns, handling frustrations, and overdependency.

Neuromuscular injury groups are often geared toward individuals with spinal cord injury and those who have had cerebrovascular accidents (strokes). The former typically have difficulties with mobility, self-care, sexual performance, and affective aspects. The latter have perceptual-spatial deficits, cognitive impairments, affective problems, behavioral involvement, and communication difficulties.

In addressing all of these needs in the group setting, information providing is a fundamental strategy. Information providing is also important in approaches in rehabilitation settings, which include the Structured Experiential Training: Rehabilitation (SET:R) model, self-help and peer help groups, and the job club model.

Groups with younger people and older people are necessarily different because of developmental factors unique to each age. Other important variables are age of onset of the disability and whether the disability was present at birth or occurred later.

References ～

Anderson, T. P. (1981). Stroke and cerebral trauma: Medical aspects. In W. C. Stolov & M. R. Clowers (Eds.), *Handbook of severe disability* (pp. 119–126). Washington, DC: U. S. Department of Education.

Avery, C. (1968). Para-analytic group therapy with adolescent multi-handicapped blind. *New Outlook for the Blind, 68,* 65–72.

Azrin, N. H., & Besalel, V. (1980). *Job Club counselor's manual: A behavioral approach to vocational counseling.* Baltimore, MD: University Park Press.

Azrin, N. H., & Philip, R. A. (1979). The Job Club method for the job-handicapped: A comparative outcome study. *Rehabilitation Counseling Bulletin, 23,* 144–155.

Banik, S. N., & Mendelson, M. A. (1978). Group psychotherapy with a paraplegic group with an emphasis on specific problems of sexuality. *International Journal of Group Psychotherapy, 28,* 123–128.

Beckett, A., & Rutan, J. S. (1990). Treating persons with ARC and AIDS in group psychotherapy. *International Journal of Group Psychotherapy, 40,* 19–29.

Berkovitz, I. H. (1972). *Adolescents grow in groups.* New York: Brunner/Mazel.

Bowers, J. E., Clark-Mahoney, J. P., Forshee, T., Reiner, K. A., Schilling, J. E., & Snyder, B. S. (1987). Analysis of a support group for young spinal cord-injured males. *Rehabilitation Nursing, 12,* 313–315, 322.

Bruce, T. J. (1975). Adolescent groups and the adolescent process. *British Journal of Medical Psychology, 48,* 333–338.

Buchanan, D. C. (1975). Group therapy for kidney transplant patients. *International Journal of Psychiatry in Medicine, 6,* 523–531.

Card, K. J., & Schmider, L. (1995). Group work with members who have hearing impairments. *Journal of Specialists in Group Work, 20,* 83–90.

Cholden, L. (1953). Group therapy with the blind. *Group Psychotherapy, 6,* 21–29.

Chubon, R. A. (1982). Group practices in the rehabilitation of physically disabled persons. In M. Seligman (Ed.), *Group psychotherapy and counseling with special populations* (pp. 59–76). Baltimore, MD: University Park Press.

Crawford, J. D., & McIvor, G. P. (1985). Group psychotherapy: Benefits in multiple sclerosis. *Archives of Physical Medicine & Rehabilitation, 66,* 810–813.

Crewe, N. M., & Krause, J. S. (1987). Spinal cord injury: Psychological aspects. In B. Caplan (Ed.), *Rehabilitation psychology desk reference* (pp. 3–35). Rockville, MD: Aspen.

Cunningham, A. J., & Tocco, E. K. (1989). A randomized trial of group psychoeducational therapy for cancer patients. *Patient Education and Counseling, 14,* 101–114.

D'Afflitti, J. G., & Weitz, G. W. (1974). Rehabilitating the stroke patient through patient-family groups. *International Journal of Group Psychotherapy, 24,* 323–332.

Democker, J. D., & Zimpfer, D. G. (1981). Group approaches to psychosocial intervention in medical care: A synthesis. *International Journal of Group Psychotherapy, 31,* 247–260.

Donovan, W. H. (1981). Spinal cord injury. In W. C. Stolov & M. R. Clowers (Eds.), *Handbook of severe disability* (pp. 65–82). Washington, DC: U. S. Department of Education.

Durkin, H. E. (1972). Group therapy movement. *Psychiatric Annals, 2,* 14–23.

Evans, R. L., Halar, E. M., & Smith, K. M. (1985). Cognitive therapy to achieve personal goals: Results of telephone group counseling with disabled adults. *Archives of Medicine & Rehabilitation, 60,* 693–696.

Fawzy, F. I., Cousins, N., Fawzy, N. W., Kemeny, M. E., Elashoff, R. & Morton, D. (1990). A structured psychiatric intervention for cancer patients. *Archives of General Psychiatry, 47,* 720–725.

Fischer, W. G., & Samelson, C. F. (1971). Group psychotherapy for selected patients with lower extremity amputation. *Archives of Physical Medicine & Rehabilitation, 52,* 79.

Flynn, D. (1992). Adolescent group work in a hospital in-patient setting with spina bifida patients and others. *Journal of Child Psychotherapy, 18,* 87–102.

Forester, B., Kornfeld, D. S., Fleiss, J. L., & Thompson, S. (1993). Group psychotherapy during radiotherapy: Effects on emotional and physical distress. *American Journal of Psychiatry, 150,* 1700–1706.

Fow, N. R., & Rockey, L. S. (1995). A preliminary conceptualization of the influence of personality and psychological development on group therapy with spinal cord patients. *Journal of Applied Rehabilitation Counseling, 26,* 30–32.

Garvin, R. E. (1984). Vocational exploration and job search activities in a group setting. *Journal of Applied Rehabilitation Counseling, 15*(1), 15–17.

Goldman, H. (1970). The use of encounter microlabs with a group of visually handicapped rehabilitation clients. *New Outlook for the Blind, 64,* 219–226.

Gottlieb, B. H. (1982). Mutual-help groups: Members' views of their benefits and roles for professionals. In L. D. Borman, L. E. Borck, R. Hess, & F. L. Pasquale (Eds.), *Prevention in human services: Vol. 1. Helping people to help themselves: Self-help and prevention* (pp. 55–68). New York: Haworth Press.

Gugel, R. N., & Eisdorfer, S. (1985). The role of therapeutic group programs in a nursing home. *Rehabilitation Psychology, 30,* 83–92.

Gust, T. (1970). Group counseling with rehabilitation clients. *Rehabilitation Record, 11,* 18–25.

Henkle, C. (1975). Social group work as a treatment modality for hospitalized people with rheumatoid arthritis. *Rehabilitation Literature, 36,* 334–341.

Herman, S. (1966). Some observations on group therapy with the blind. *International Journal of Group Psychotherapy, 16,* 367–372.

Hollon, T. H. (1972). Modified group therapy in the treatment of patients on chronic hemodialysis. *American Journal of Psychotherapy, 36,* 501–510.

Horlick, L., Cameron, R., Firor, W., Bhalerao, U., & Baltzan, R. (1984). The effects of education and group discussion in the post myocardial infarction patient. *Journal of Psychosomatic Research, 28,* 485–492.

Howard, D. L. (1983). Group therapy for amputees in a ward setting. *Military Medicine, 148,* 678–680.

Inana, M. (1978). You and your body: A self-help health class for blind women. *Journal of Visual Impairment & Blindness, 72,* 399–403.

Jacobs, E. E., Harvill, R. L., & Masson, R. L. (1988). *Group counseling: Strategies and skills.* Pacific Grove, CA: Brooks/Cole.

Jaques, M., & Patterson, K. W. (1974). The self-help group model: A review. *Rehabilitation Counseling Bulletin, 18,* 48–58.

Johnson, A. J., Greenwood, R., & Schriner, K. F. (1988). Work performances and work personality: Employer concerns about workers with disabilities. *Rehabilitation Counseling Bulletin, 32,* 50–57.

Kalson, L. (1982). Group therapy with the aged. In M. Seligman (Ed.), *Group psychotherapy and counseling with special populations* (pp. 77–97). Baltimore, MD: University Park Press.

Keegan, D. L. (1974). Adaptation to visual handicap: Short-term group approach. *Psychosomatics, 15,* 76–78.

Kennedy, J. F. (1989). The heterogeneous group for chronically physically ill and physically healthy but emotionally disturbed children and adolescents. *International Journal of Group Psychotherapy, 39,* 105–125.

Konstam, V. (1995). Anger: A neglected group treatment issue with cardiac transplantation recipients and their families. *Journal for Specialists in Group Work, 20,* 189–194.

Kriegsman, K. H., & Celotta, B. (1981). Creative coping: A program of group counseling for women with physical disabilities. *Journal of Rehabilitation, 47,* 36–39.

Lasky, R. G., & Dell Orto, A. E. (Eds.). (1979). *Group counseling and physical disability: A rehabilitation and health care perspective.* North Scituate, MA: Duxbury Press.

Lasky, R. G., Dell Orto, A. E., & Marinelli, R. P. (1984). Structured experiential training: A group rehabilitation model. In R. P. Marinelli & A. E. Dell Orto (Eds.), *The psychological and social impact of physical disability* (2nd ed., pp. 304–330). New York: Springer.

Lieberman, M. A., & Borman, L. D. (Eds.). (1979). *Self-help groups for coping with crisis.* San Francisco: Jossey-Bass.

Lindemann, J. E. (1981). *Psychological and behavioral aspects of physical disability.* New York: Plenum.

Linden, M. (1954). The significance of dual leadership in gerontologic group psychotherapy: Studies in gerontologic human relations III. *International Journal of Group Psychotherapy, 4,* 262–273.

Linden, M. (1955). Transference in gerontologic group therapy: Studies in gerontologic human relations IV. *International Journal of Group Psychotherapy, 5,* 61–79.

Manaster, G. J. (1977). *Adolescent development and the life tasks.* Boston: Allyn & Bacon.

Mann, W., Godfrey, M. E., & Dowd, E. T. (1973). The use of group counseling procedures in the rehabilitation of spinal cord injured patients. *American Journal of Occupational Therapy, 27,* 73–77.

Marshak, L. (1982). Group therapy with adolescents. In M. Seligman (Ed.), *Group psychotherapy and counseling with special populations* (pp. 185–213). Baltimore, MD: University Park Press.

McWhirter, P. T., & McWhirter, J. J. (1996). Transition-to-work group: University students with learning disabilities. *Journal for Specialists in Group Work, 21,* 144–148.

Melnyk, R., Montgomery, R., & Over, R. (1979). Attitude changes following sexual counseling program for spinal cord injured persons. *Archives of Physical Medicine & Rehabilitation, 60,* 601–605.

Miller, D. K., Wolfe, M., & Spiegel, M. H. (1975). Therapeutic groups for patients with spinal cord injuries. *Archives of Physical Medicine & Rehabilitation, 56,* 130–135.

Norsworthy, K. L., & Horne, A. M. (1994). Issues in group work with HIV-infected gay and bisexual men. *Journal for Specialists in Group Work, 19,* 112–119.

Oradei, D. M., & Waite, N. S. (1974). Group psychotherapy with stroke patients during the immediate recovery phase. *American Journal of Orthopsychiatry, 44,* 386–395.

Ostby, S., & Thomas, K. R. (1984). Deafness and hearing impairment: A review and proposal. Journal of *Applied Rehabilitation Counseling, 15*(2), 711.

Patterson, J. B., McKenzie, B., & Jenkins, J. (1995). Creating accessible groups for individuals with disabilities. *Journal for Specialists in Group Work, 20,* 75–82.

Plummer, S. J. (1982). Independent living centers: A self-help group model for the severely disabled. In M. Seligman (Ed.), *Group psychotherapy and counseling with special populations* (pp. 117–142). Baltimore, MD: University Park Press.

Portner, D. (1981). Clinical aspects of social group work with the deaf. *Social Work With Groups, 4,* 123–133.

Power, P. W., & Rogers, S. (1979). Group counseling for multiple sclerosis patients: A preferred model of treatment for unique adoptive problems. In R. G. Lasky & A. E. Dell Orto (Eds.), *Group counseling and physical disability: A rehabilitation and health care perspective* (pp. 115–127). North Scituate, MA: Duxbury Press.

Rhoades, C. (1986). Different organizational models for self-help advocacy groups that serve people with developmental disabilities. *Journal of Rehabilitation, 52,* 43–47.

Rhoades, C. M., Browning, P. L., & Thorin, E. J. (1986). Self-help advocacy movement: A promising peer-support system for people with mental disabilities. *Rehabilitation Literature, 47,* 27.

Riekehof, L. L. (1987). *The joy of signing* (2nd ed.). Springfield, MO: Gospel.

Robinson, L. D. (1965). Group therapy using manual communication. *Mental Hospitals.* Washington, DC: American Psychiatric Association.

Roessler, R. T. (1978). An evaluation of personal achievement skills training with the visually handicapped. *Rehabilitation Counseling Bulletin, 21,* 300–305.

Roessler, R. T. (1986). Training for vocational coping: A method for enhancing work establishment skills. *Rehabilitation Counseling Bulletin, 29,* 258–265.

Roessler, R. T., Milligan, T., & Ohlson, A. (1976). Personal adjustment training for the spinal cord injured. *Rehabilitation Counseling Bulletin, 19,* 544–550.

Rogers, J., MacBride, A., Whylie, B., & Freeman, S. J. (1977-1978). The use of groups in the rehabilitation of amputees. *International Journal of Group Psychotherapy in Medicine, 8,* 243–255.

Rose, S. D. (1989). Coping skill training in groups. *International Journal of Group Psychotherapy, 39,* 59–78.

Routh, T. A. (1957). A study of the use of group psychotherapy in rehabilitation centers for the blind. *Group Psychotherapy, 10,* 38–50.

Salhoot, J. T. (1977). Group strategies with the severely physically handicapped. In M. Seligman (Ed.),

Group counseling and group psychotherapy with rehabilitation clients (pp. 149–172). Springfield, IL: Charles C Thomas.

Sarti, D. M. (1993) Reaching the deaf child: A model for diversified intervention. *Smith College Studies in Social Work, 63,* 187–198.

Scheidlinger, S. (1984). Group psychotherapy in the 1980s: Problems and prospects. *American Journal of Psychotherapy, 38,* 494–504.

Schein, J. D. (1982). Group techniques applied to deaf and hearing-impaired persons. In M. Seligman (Ed.), *Group psychotherapy and counseling with special populations* (pp. 143–161). Baltimore, MD: University Park Press.

Sedge, S. K. (1982). Assertiveness training with hearing-impaired persons. *Rehabilitation Counseling Bulletin, 25,* 146–152.

Seligman, M. (1982). Introduction. In M. Seligman (Ed.), *Group psychotherapy and counseling with special populations* (pp. 126). Baltimore, MD: University Park Press.

Silberman-Miller, M., & Moores, D. F. (1990). Principles of group counseling and their applications for deaf clients. *Journal of the American Deafness and Rehabilitation Association, 23,* 82–87.

Singler, J. K. (1982). The stroke group: Planning for success. In M. Seligman (Ed.), *Group psychotherapy and counseling with special populations* (pp. 43–57). Baltimore, MD: University Park Press.

Speer, D. C., & O'Sullivan, M. J. (1994). Group therapy in nursing homes and hearing deficit. *Clinical Gerontologist, 14,* 68–70.

Stern, M. J., Plionis, E., & Kaslow, L. (1984). Group process expectations and outcome with post-myocardial infarction patients. *General Hospital Psychiatry, 6,* 101–108.

Stewart, A. M., Kelly, B., Robinson, J. D., & Callender, C. D. (1995). The Howard University Hospital transplant and dialysis support group: Twenty years and going strong. *International Journal of Group Psychotherapy, 45,* 471–488.

Subramanian, K., & Ell, K. O. (1989). Coping with a first heart attack: A group treatment model for low-income Anglo, black, and Hispanic patients. *Social Work With Groups, 11,* 99–117.

Sussman, A. E. (1974). Group therapy with severely handicapped. *Journal of Rehabilitation of the Deaf, 8,* 122–126.

Telch, C. F., & Telch, M. J. (1986). Group coping skills instruction and supportive group therapy for cancer patients: A comparison of strategies. *Journal of Consulting and Clinical Psychology, 54,* 802–808.

Tunnell, G. (1991). Complications in group psychotherapy with AIDS patients. *International Journal of Group Psychotherapy, 41,* 481–498.

Van Boemel, G. B., & Rozee, P. D. (1992). Treatment for psychosomatic blindness among Cambodian refugee women. *Women and Therapy, 13,* 239–266.

Vander Kolk, C. J. (1983). Rehabilitation counseling with the visually impaired. *Journal of Applied Rehabilitation Counseling, 14*(3), 13–19.

Weiner, W. (1988). Groups for the terminally ill cardiac patient. In B. W. MacLennan, Saul, S. & Weiner, M. B. (Eds.). *Group psychotherapies for the elderly.* Madison, CT: International Universities Press.

Weinman, B. (1987). Membership retention in group therapy among adolescents who are physically disabled. *Journal of Rehabilitation, 53,* 52–55.

Welch, G. J., & Steven, K. (1979). Group work intervention with a multiple sclerosis population. *Social Work With Groups, 2,* 221–234.

Welsh, R. L. (1982). The use of group strategies with the visually impaired. In M. Seligman (Ed.), *Group psychotherapy and counseling with special populations* (pp. 163–184). Baltimore, MD: University Park Press.

Wilson, E. L. (1972). Programming individual and adjunctive therapeutic services for visually impaired clients in a rehabilitation center. *New Outlook for the Blind, 66,* 215–220.

Wright, B. A. (1983). *Physical disability—A psychosocial approach* (2nd ed.). New York: Harper & Row.

Yalom, I. D. (1985). *The theory and practice of group psychotherapy* (3rd ed.). New York: Basic Books.

Youngjohn, J. R., & Altman, I. M. (1989). A performance-based group approach to the treatment of anosognosia and denial. *Rehabilitation Psychology, 34,* 217–222.

15

Group Counseling With
Gay, Lesbian, and Bisexual
Clients

Reese M. House and Virginia Tyler

The counseling profession has been slow to respond to the mental health needs of gay, lesbian, and bisexual clients. Until 1973, the American Psychiatric Association labeled "homosexuality" a form of mental illness. The American Psychological Association did the same until 1975. Today, the official position of the counseling profession is to train counselors to adopt an enlightened stance regarding sexual orientation (Iasenza, 1989). Counseling gays, lesbians, and bisexuals is like counseling other culturally different populations in that practitioners need culture-specific preparation, which in the past most counselor trainees did not receive (Buhrke, 1989; Iasenza, 1989; McDermott, Tyndall, & Lichtenberg, 1989). Counselors need to make an effort to accurately understand the values, lifestyles, and cultural norms of gays, lesbians, and bisexuals (Gelberg & Chojnacki, 1996). Additionally, counselors need to examine their own belief systems to see whether they can offer unbiased, helpful counseling assistance to people with sexual orientations and behaviors that may be quite different from their own. Many counselor training programs are still not providing their trainees with the necessary skills. However, there are professional publications and workshops that can improve the skills of practicing professionals in this area. In the emerging gay-affirmative atmosphere in the mental health field, it is becoming easier for counselors to develop the skills and sensitivity they need to appropriately counsel lesbian, gay, and bisexual clients.

This chapter deals with language variables related to gay, lesbian, and bisexual

communities, the cultures of sexual minorities in U.S. society, heterosexism, homophobia, gay, lesbian, and bisexual affirmative counseling, general group approaches
with these populations, and specific groups for bisexuals, gays, and lesbians.

First, a Word About Words ~

Language is important for what it communicates as well as what it implies. Gays,
lesbians, and bisexuals hear biased and offensive street language such as "queer,"
"faggot," "homo," "dyke," and "queen" throughout their lives. This language affects
their self-esteem, stigmatizes gays, lesbians, and bisexuals, and is just as offensive
to these populations as ethnic slurs are to different ethnic populations.

Many individuals reject the term *homosexual* because it is used by dominant and
often oppressing groups in our culture. Though it is commonly used in the professional literature, media, and popular fiction, the term *homosexual* reflects an inac-
curately narrow, clinical focus on sexual conduct (Blumenfeld & Raymond, 1988).
It is seen by many as archaic, imprecise, and misleading (Krajeski, 1986). Generally,
homosexual is used with a pejorative connotation—those who support or affirm sexual minorities seldom use the term. *Homoerotic,* used to describe individuals who
prefer intimate emotional and physical relationships with people of the same gender,
is another clinical term that is similarly narrow (Silberman & Hawkins, 1988). For
these reasons, the terms *homosexual* and *homoerotic* should not be used to describe
individuals. To say "He is a homosexual" or "She has a homoerotic nature" is as
incomplete and negative as saying "She is a heterosexual."

Disagreement exists about what constitutes appropriate language. One difference of opinion involves the terms *sexual preference* and *sexual orientation.*
Preference implies that individuals choose to be gay, lesbian or bisexual, and *orientation* suggests that sexual predisposition is innate (Blumenfeld & Raymond, 1988).
Evidence is increasing that sexual orientation is biologically intrinsic in human
beings (Burr, 1993, 1996; Money, 1987; Ritter & O'Neill, 1989). Genetic patterns,
pre- and post-natal hormonal activity, and brain structure differences are areas being
explored as possible factors in sexual orientation (LeVay & Hamer, 1994; Money,
1987). Several researchers support the idea that genes may influence or predispose
sexual orientation but emphasize that environmental cues and social learning also
play a key role (Bailey, 1995; Byne, 1994; Johnston & Bell, 1995; LeVay & Hamer,
1994; Money, 1987).

Another area of debate involves using *gay* as an umbrella term to describe gay
men, lesbians, and bisexuals. It is common usage to refer to the "Gay Rights Parade,"
"gay marriage," or "gay-affirmative counseling." Although this usage of the term is
meant to include gays, lesbians, and bisexuals, it is not always perceived as inclusive
and tends to make lesbian women and bisexuals feel invisible. Such usage also
obscures the fact that lesbians, gay men, and bisexuals have unique identities and
issues. However, using gay as an umbrella term has a practical benefit. As an adjective, *gay, lesbian,* and *bisexual* is more than a mouthful. We have attempted to balance the defects of using gay as an umbrella term with its practical advantage by

using the umbrella term only as an adjective, not as a noun. We recognize that this compromise is not perfect and look forward to the development of an umbrella term that will be more generally inclusive and accepted.

Special consideration and care need to be taken to include the term *bisexual* in our language. Only recently have bisexuals been included in theory or research about sexual orientation (Fox, 1995). As noted by Wolf (1992), "Bisexuality has been continually attacked as a nonentity, a transitional stage from heterosexuality to homosexuality or vice-versa, and as a denial of one's homosexuality" (p. 175). However, bisexuals see themselves as having a unique identity and prefer the word *bisexual.*

We recommend that counselors be as clear as possible in their use of terminology. Group leaders need to be aware of their language choices and directly address the question of terminology with members. It is appropriate to ask: "How do you prefer to have your sexual orientation described?" "What terms would you like the group to use?" "How do you describe yourself?" These questions are respectful and imply to members that the leader is sensitive to the importance of language. This sensitivity indicates an openness in discussing issues of sexual orientation and sexual behavior.

A Cultural Overview of Sexual Minorities in U.S. Society ~

Hundreds of thousands of gay and lesbian Americans are openly integrated into our communities, families and workplaces... . A backlash against gay rights swells at the same instant we witness the widest cultural opening gay people have ever experienced; public opinion is deeply divided about how to respond to our emergence from the shadows. (Vaid, 1995, p. 1)

According to surveys, approximately 10–15% of the U.S. population, at least 20 to 25 million people are gay, lesbian, and bisexual (Betz & Fitzgerald, 1993; Fassinger, 1991; Singer & Deschamps, 1994). Some recent studies have suggested the figure is closer to 5% (Singer & Deschamps, 1994); however, as Singer and Deschamps stated, "Gross under reporting in many studies, especially those that involve face-to-face interviews with researchers, is pervasive" (p. 9). Many individuals do not report same gender activity due to the stigma attached to being nonheterosexual in U.S. society.

Whatever the exact number of gays, lesbians, and bisexuals in the United States, they are becoming more visible and active in their pursuit of equal rights. Before the 1970s, gays, lesbians, and bisexuals were a largely invisible part of the American population. Remaining invisible was, to a large extent, a survival tactic. Most gays, lesbians, and bisexuals chose to avoid the stigmatization associated with disclosing their sexual orientation. "Hostility and discrimination at the hands of an unaccepting society created a climate of secrecy that did not permit challenges to the prevailing stereotypes" (Blumstein & Schwartz, 1983, p. 9).

In the past 25 years, gays, lesbians, and bisexuals have developed a community identity to counter negative reactions from society. As evidence of this community, in 1969 there were 50 lesbian and gay organizations in the United States; today there are an estimated 3,000 lesbian, gay, and bisexual organizations active in North America (Brelin, 1996).

Nevertheless, as noted by Vaid (1995), the "new leaps in gay access, visibility, and power have not transformed the second-class status of gay, lesbian, bisexual, and transgender people" (p. xvi). In fact, the increased public visibility has provoked considerable antigay backlash throughout the United States. Some states have placed antigay initiatives on their ballots; and several cities and one state have passed antigay legislation. Many individuals and groups currently believe that gays, lesbians, and bisexuals are immoral, that they behave improperly and unnaturally, and they advocate against their rights (Vaid, 1995; White, 1995).

In only nine states do individuals perceived to be gay, lesbian, and bisexual have legal protection against discrimination in employment and housing. Career positions in teaching, the military, the police, and public office often are available only to those who pass as heterosexual. Nonheterosexual couples are not legally recognized in the United States. This lack of legal standing limits such couples in a number of significant ways, including health insurance, hospital visitation rights, child custody rights, survivorship and estate benefits, and other rights and benefits that are available only to married couples.

Despite such antigay sentiments in this country, the increasing openness of sexual minorities is mirrored by a slowly growing societal acceptance. A 1983 survey revealed that 66% of the U.S. population felt homosexuality was an unacceptable lifestyle (Blumenfeld & Raymond, 1988). Subsequent surveys have revealed a decrease in this sentiment, with between 48% and 53% of the public reporting disapproval of homosexuality ("Special Report," 1989; Wilson, 1992). There is also increasing legal support for the civil rights of gays, lesbians, and bisexuals, as demonstrated by the 1996 Supreme Court decision that ruled that Colorado's antigay Amendment 2 was unconstitutional. And, at least one state has been forced to consider legalizing same-sex marriage. A 1990 lawsuit in Hawaii, still under review when this chapter was written, challenged the denial of marriage license applications made by three same-sex couples (Berzon, 1996). However, in September 1996, Congress passed the Defense of Marriage Act, which overrides efforts by states to sanction same-sex marriage.

Although a sizable percentage of American voters do not support civil rights for gays, nearly 80% of Americans believe people should not be fired or discriminated against at work for being gay, lesbian, or bisexual (Berzon, 1996; Singer & Deschamps, 1994). Indeed, several cities, businesses, and educational institutions have adopted antidiscrimination policies that specifically include sexual orientation (Berzon, 1996; Gelberg & Chojnacki, 1996). Even though public opinion is slowly shifting toward a more tolerant attitude toward sexual minorities, U.S. society still denigrates and discriminates against gays, lesbians, and bisexuals.

Heterosexism and Homophobia

> Unless we heal the homophobia and heterosexism deep in the hearts and minds of people, legislative efforts alone will not bring about any profound or lasting social change. (Williams, 1990, p. 15)

The most serious and prevalent problem gay men, lesbians, and bisexuals must face is homoprejudice based in heterosexism and homophobia (Hancock, 1995). *Heterosexism* refers to a set of political assumptions that empowers heterosexual persons, especially heterosexual white males, and excludes people who are openly gay, lesbian, or bisexual from social, religious, and political power. It is a system that demands heterosexuality in return for first-class citizenship and forces nonheterosexuals into silence concerning the majority of their lives (Mollenkott, 1985). Heterosexism is also seen when dominant groups pity sexual minorities as poor unfortunates who cannot help being the way they are (Blumenfeld & Raymond, 1988). Heterosexism is the societal norm in the United States. It is assumed that people will marry someone of the opposite sex. The media portray only heterosexual relationships as positive and satisfying. Teachers talk in class as though all students are straight. These examples illustrate subtle and indirect ways heterosexuality is reinforced in the United States as the only viable, acceptable life option.

Homophobia, first defined by Weinberg in 1973, is an attitude of fear and loathing toward individuals perceived to be gay, lesbian, or bisexual. This belief system supports negative myths and stereotypes about these cultural minorities and maintains that discrimination based on sexual orientation is justified (Lapierre, 1990). Homophobic people downgrade, deny, stereotype, or ignore the existence of gays, lesbians, and bisexuals. Their responses range from telling or laughing at "queer" jokes to condoning, supporting, or participating in violent hate crimes committed against gays, popularly referred to as "fag" bashing. These reactions create a devalued minority in the midst of a hostile society.

Internalized Homophobia Gays, lesbians, and bisexuals often internalize the negative assumptions, attitudes, and prejudice common in the dominant culture. Internalized homophobia manifests itself in a variety of ways, including the total denial of one's sexual orientation, contempt for or mistrust of openly gay, lesbian, or bisexual people, attempts to "pass" as heterosexual, increased fear, and withdrawal from friends and families. Individuals who internalize values of otherwise credible sources (such as friends, family, religious organizations, school, and mass media) that differ from their own, experience personal dissonance and low self-esteem, which becomes a major source of distress. Acute anxiety attacks, self-destructive use of alcohol and drugs, and missed work or therapy sessions are frequent symptoms of internalized homophobia. Such self-hatred can also lead to depression, despair or suicide (Lapierre, 1990).

Counselor Homophobia Counselors are a part of the culture that denies that same-sex behaviors exist and/or teaches that they are morally repulsive and psychologically damaging. Furthermore, some of the counselors practicing today were trained in an era when homosexuality was classified as an illness. Therefore, it is not surprising that many counselors are homophobic and heterosexist and have not addressed or even recognized their own homoprejudice. Many practitioners continue to consider gays, lesbians, and bisexuals as abnormal, deviant, and in need of change (Isay, 1996). Some counselors believe the goal of counseling with these populations is to reduce or eliminate "homosexual" behavior and substitute "heterosexual" behavior (Coleman & Remafedi, 1989; Herron, Kintner, Sollinger, & Trubowitz, 1985). Some counselors assume that all of their clients are heterosexual. Other counselors are tolerant of nonheterosexuals but remain uninformed about issues pertaining to gays, lesbians, and bisexuals (Carl, 1992).

Although the counseling profession verbally supports a gay-affirmative position, counselors do not receive enough information about lesbian, gay, and bisexual issues in their counselor preparation programs to provide proper, adequate, and helpful services to sexual minorities (Betz & Fitzgerald, 1993; Buhrke, 1989; Moses & Hawkins, 1985). Practicing counselors need to reeducate themselves with regard to the particular issues and needs of their nonheterosexual clients. Counselor educators need to ensure that counselor preparation programs include information and exposure to gay, lesbian, and bisexual issues. Both trainees and educators may need to confront and overcome their own homophobic and heterosexist beliefs and behaviors. The questions in Table 15.1 can help counselors, supervisors, and counselor educators identify their own biases about sexual orientation.

Gay-Affirmative Counseling

Gay-affirmative counseling is based on six interlocking assumptions, first articulated by Schwartz and Harstein (1986): (a) Being gay, lesbian, or bisexual is not a pathological condition; (b) the origins of sexual orientation are not clearly understood or completely known; (c) gays, lesbians, and bisexuals lead fulfilling and satisfying lives; (d) there are a variety of gay, lesbian, and bisexual lifestyles; (e) gays, lesbians, and bisexuals who come to counseling with no desire to change their sexual orientation should not be coerced into doing so; and (f) gay-affirmative individual and group counseling should be available.

Counselors who are sensitive to sexual orientation issues, and who have examined and challenged their own heterosexist and homophobic attitudes, are in a powerful position to help gays, lesbians, and bisexuals recognize and accept their sexual identity, improve their interpersonal and social functioning, and value themselves while living in a predominantly heterosexual society. Counselors who are unable to meet these standards are ethically obligated to refer gay, lesbian, and bisexual clients to other professionals.

Gay, Lesbian, and Bisexual Professional Counselors

Until the late 1980s, it was assumed in the United States that heterosexuality was the only suitable orientation for counselors (Rochlin, 1985). Today, the number of publicly identified gay, lesbian and bisexual mental health professionals is growing. Many gays, lesbians, and bisexuals seek out gay, lesbian or bisexual therapists

Table 15.1 ～
Personal Values Assessment: How Homophobic Are You?

1. Do you stop yourself from certain behavior because someone might think you are gay, lesbian, or bisexual? If yes, what kinds of behavior?

2. Do you ever intentionally do or say things so that people will think you are not gay, lesbian, or bisexual? If yes, what kinds of things?

3. If you are a parent, how would you (or do you) feel about having a lesbian daughter or gay son?

4. How would you feel if you discovered that one of your parents or parent figures, or a brother or sister, were gay, lesbian, or bisexual?

5. Are there any jobs, positions, or professions that you think lesbians, gays, or bisexuals should be barred from holding or entering? If yes, why so?

6. Would you go to a physician whom you knew or believed to be gay or lesbian if that person were of a different gender from you? If that person were of the same gender as you? If not, why not?

7. If someone you care about were to say to you, "I think I'm gay," would you suggest that the person see a therapist?

8. Would you wear a button that says "Don't assume I'm heterosexual"? If not, why not?

9. Can you think of three positive aspects of being gay, bisexual, or lesbian? Can you think of three negative aspects?

10. Have you ever laughed at a "queer" joke?

The following questions apply particularly to counseling in groups and suggest how easily values and assumptions can affect group leaders.

11. Do you assume all members of your groups are heterosexual?

12. If a group member says "partner," do you assume he or she is speaking of someone of the opposite sex?

13. If a group member uses a derogatory term for a gay or lesbian, do you let the comment pass unchallenged? What do you do when a group member uses a derogatory term for a racial minority?

14. If a group member is gay, lesbian, or bisexual, do you assume that all of his or her issues are somehow related to sexual orientation? Would you make the same assumption about heterosexual group members?

15. Do you assume that all of the past partners of members of your groups have been the same gender as current partners?

Note: From *Lesbian and Gay Issues: A Resource Manual for Social Workers* (p. 153–154), 1985, Washington, DC, National Association of Social Workers. Adapted by permission.

because they are concerned that a heterosexual counselor's bias may keep the practitioner from providing appropriate care (Isay, 1996; Kus, 1990). It is becoming increasingly clear that well-trained gay, lesbian, or bisexual therapists may better meet the needs of gay, lesbian, and bisexual clients because they provide mental health services based on the premise that gay people have legitimate mental health needs, rather than on the premise that homosexuality is wrong. Gay, lesbian, and bisexual professionals who come out serve as role models, provide security for clients who want to see nonheterosexual counselors, and act as resource consultants in their professional and personal communities (Woodman & Lenna, 1980).

The Emergence of Groups in the Gay/Lesbian/Bisexual Community~

> Lesbians and gay men have worked together at the local, regional, and national levels to build viable communities, to provide needed programs and services, to cope with an unprecedented health emergency, and to build a political power base for social change. (D'Augelli & Garnets, 1995, p. 306)

As gays, lesbians, and bisexuals have become more public about their sexual orientation, organized groups within the nonheterosexual community have become more common and more open. Gays and lesbians have taken initiative and created organizations and groups to provide social support for members of their community. Organized groups are less common in the bisexual community than in the gay or lesbian community, but specific groups for bisexuals are increasing. Groups offer a counterpoint to the isolation, oppression, and alienation of being gay, lesbian, or bisexual in United States society. Groups create a mini-culture in which the homo-prejudice and homophobia gays, bisexuals, and lesbians experience in the general culture are countered by social support.

Community service centers providing speakers bureaus, hotlines, newsletters, information on community resources, referral, medical services, and other social activities such as dances and potlucks have emerged because gays, bisexuals, and lesbians often have unique and special needs that go unmet in the larger society (Blumenfeld & Raymond, 1988). Local gay newspapers list dozens of groups and organizations for bisexuals, gays, and lesbians. There are groups for women, men, racial and ethnic minorities, youth, older individuals, and persons in mixed orientation marriages (Brelin, 1996; Klein, 1990). There are groups that address coming out, relationships, career and life planning, and parenting. There are groups for the parents of gays and lesbians, their children, and their spouses. Additionally, there are groups that address issues not necessarily related to sexual orientation, such as substance abuse and personal growth. All of these diverse groups in the gay community can be divided into three primary categories: common interest, self-help, and counseling (or therapy).

Common Interest Groups

> The ultimate reward from developing a sense of community with other gay [or lesbian or bisexual] people is that you are no longer alone.... . There are people who share your values. There are people to learn from and models to emulate.... . There is the assurance of people who care and understand—people who can share familiar feelings and offer mutual support. (Clark, 1987, p. 104)

A multitude of common interest groups are available for gays and lesbians. Examples include professional support groups for lawyers, social workers, teachers, health care providers, scientists, business owners, and artists. Organizations on many university and college campuses offer a number of group activities for gay, lesbian, and bisexual students. Also, most major religious denominations have groups which allow gays, bisexuals, and lesbians a way to participate in religious activities without homophobic overtones.

   Other interest groups are organized around recreational activities, such as hiking, bowling, card games, music, or dancing. Political Action Committees (PACs) are another form of common interest group in which many gays, lesbians, and bisexuals are involved. PACs help empower the gay community and give members political strength and influence. All of these groups provide an opportunity for gays, bisexuals, and lesbians to be together and share common concerns and interests.

Self-Help Groups

> The self-help group functions for its members. It is organized around addressing a common concern. Individuals' separate agendas are transcended. Continual focusing on the common agenda leads to unity and a power base that is collectively sustaining and useful. (Eller & King, 1990, p. 330)

Self-help groups are effective for people who are stigmatized by the culture; they break down the sense of personal isolation caused by an unhealthy condition or habit and help disenfranchised individuals cope and change (Eller & King, 1990; Hall, 1985). Self-help groups are common in gay, lesbian, and bisexual communities and address a variety of issues, including alcoholism, drug addiction, incest survival, and eating disorders. Mainstream recovery groups such as Narcotics Anonymous, Cocaine Anonymous, Alcoholics Anonymous, Overeaters Anonymous, and Al-Anon often have groups specifically for gay and lesbian members. Some self-help groups address issues that are unique to the gay and lesbian experience, including coming-out groups, groups for children of gay or lesbian parents, and groups for the parents of gay or lesbian children. During the past 15 years, support groups have also developed for people living with AIDS (PLWAs) and their significant others.

Counseling Groups

> A therapy group can be a place of refuge, a place to share the most private aspects of oneself, a place to practice social skills, to get support for changing behavior. People go to groups for a variety of reasons, and that provides the diversity which makes groups so productive. (Hall, 1985, p. 68)

Gays, lesbians, and bisexuals become participants in counseling groups to address such issues as depression, anxiety disorders, panic attacks, sexual dysfunction, and personality disorders. Others join groups focused on personal growth or relationship issues. Regardless of the specialty, group counseling is particularly effective for gays, lesbians, and bisexuals because groups offer a balance to the indifference and hostility of the general culture. The feeling of safety in numbers may be the emotional condition that is needed to start a positive therapeutic process (Lapierre, 1990). In counseling groups, gays, lesbians, and bisexuals can share their experiences and feelings, and can find out how others cope with similar situations. As Lapierre (1990) noted, "Often creative forms of resolution of these kinds of negative feelings can be discovered through the group process" (p. 96).

The first decision gays, lesbians, and bisexuals must make, following the decision to participate in counseling, is whether to attend a group organized specifically for gays, lesbians, or bisexuals or a group in which sexual orientation is not the basis for selection. When internalized homophobia is a major issue, all-gay, all-lesbian, or all-bisexual groups are more appropriate for dealing with adjustment difficulties (Conlin & Smith, 1985). Even in groups that do not specifically address sexual orientation, being gay, lesbian, or bisexual is apt to be an issue in the group. Gays, lesbians, and bisexuals who attend a group that is not organized around sexual orientation will have to decide whether and how to come out in the group. Coming out always involves risks. In counseling groups, many members will be accepting, but it is common for at least one person in the group to reject and abuse nonheterosexual members. It is also not unusual for groups to become engrossed with trying to change the sexual orientation of gay, lesbian, or bisexual members (Schwartz & Harstein, 1986; Yalom, 1985).

The distinction between counseling groups and self-help groups is sometimes confusing. One important difference is that counseling groups are almost always led by credentialed counselors who take an active role in the group. Because counselors are powerful facilitators in counseling groups, they need to be sensitive to the group's attitudes and behaviors about gays, lesbians, and bisexuals. Leaders have a responsibility to recognize and confront homophobia and heterosexism among the group's members. Group leaders who fail to intervene on these issues are subtly expressing their own homophobia (Hall, 1985). Gays and lesbians frequently attend groups with a gay, lesbian, or bisexual leader or facilitator. If such groups are not available, gay-affirmative facilitators are needed to assist gays, lesbians, and bisexuals in mixed orientation groups.

Specific Gay, Lesbian, and Bisexual Counseling Groups ～

Groups are often advisable for sexual minorities who have had little or no contact with others like themselves. The group functions to "socialize" members. They typically provide a supportive atmosphere for knowledge and skill sharing about how to cope with various life problems. Groups are an important counter to the real and felt isolation which sexual minorities face in the larger social cultural milieu. (Klein, 1986, p. 28)

Groups help gay, lesbian, and bisexual members accomplish developmental tasks. They often are structured to help participants address and successfully accomplish the age-related and sexual identity developmental tasks that all people face—sexuality, career, relationships, spirituality, parenting, aging. These tasks are not unique to sexual minorities, but the lack of societal support systems for gay adults often exacerbates these issues. Counseling groups create a mini-culture where the ignorance, prejudice, oppression, and homophobia the general society directs toward gays, lesbians, and bisexuals are countered by support, acceptance, and universality. This group process allows individuals to better understand and accept the issues of being gay, lesbian, or bisexual.

Human development theories identify the development of a distinct identity and a positive construct of self-worth as necessary for growth and development. It is through an interactive process between the individual and his or her environment that people develop and define their identities and sense of self-worth. As gays, lesbians, and bisexuals question "Who am I in this world?" and "How do I relate with others?" they face challenges and controversies directly related to their sexual orientation. Specific groups, such as those discussed in the sections that follow, can help members begin to arrive at answers to these questions.

Coming-Out Groups

Being gay [or lesbian or bisexual] offers an uncommonly powerful catalyst for personal transformation. If we can stand the heat and give ourselves over to the full scope of the process of coming out, we will learn flexibility in the midst of life's chaos, paradox, and mystery. (Griffin, Wirth, & Wirth, 1986, p. 188)

The process of developing an identity as gay, lesbian, or bisexual is called coming out. As defined by D'Augelli and Garnets (1995), "Coming out is a complex sequence of events through which individuals acknowledge, recognize, and label their sexual orientation and then disclose it to others throughout their lives" (p. 302). The first step is for the individual to come out to him- or herself by acknowledging feelings for the same gender. Then the individual has to decide whether to share his or her sexual orientation with others such as parents, friends, children, employers, and co-workers. Coming out is difficult because gays, lesbians, and bisexuals typically are not born into gay, lesbian, or bisexual families. They suffer oppression alone, without benefit of advice or emotional support from relatives or friends. Most gays, lesbians, and bisexuals have few role models and no self-validating and visible culture on which to pattern themselves. Gays and lesbians often make statements like: "As I became aware of my attraction for others of the same sex, I thought I was the only one with these feelings."

Each person must decide whether to identify as gay, lesbian, or bisexual. Those who choose to keep their sexual orientation secret are said to be "living in the closet." Maintaining such a secret existence supports internalized homophobia, shame, and guilt and reinforces a negative self-image by implying that certain feelings and aspects of being gay, lesbian, or bisexual are too shameful to disclose to anyone. Closeted gays, lesbians, and bisexuals lead constricted lives, constantly monitoring their thoughts, emotions, and responses. Hiding does irreparable harm to their sense of integrity and leaves them in a stressful and dissonant position, which detracts from their mental health and well-being. Stress, depression, and substance abuse are all related clinically to maintaining a secret existence.

Individuals may decide to come out at any age. Some people have indicated that they knew they were gay or lesbian as early as age 6 or 7. If people come out during the teenage years, development of sexual identity is congruent with adolescent development. But coming out as a teenager can be particularly difficult because adolescents are most often financially and emotionally dependent on their parents. In addition, parental and peer acceptance and approval are important to young people, and adolescents take the risk of being disowned by parents or harassed by peers if they identify themselves as gay, lesbian, or bisexual (Silberman & Hawkins, 1988). Many individuals do not come out until later years and may not "enter their true adolescence until their chronological adolescence has long passed" (Coleman, 1985, p. 36). Some come out as senior citizens. Coming out is an identity crisis, and whenever it occurs, most gays, lesbians, and bisexuals will benefit from assistance with coming-out issues and developing a positive sense of self.

The stresses of addressing sexual orientation affect the function and quality of life no matter how far in or out of the closet gays, lesbians, and bisexuals are. Gays, lesbians, and bisexuals are under constant, conflicting pressure both to stay in and to come out of the closet; they face decisions about whether to come out every day. For example, when co-workers are discussing what they did on the weekend, do gay, lesbian, and bisexual workers share with whom they spent time, or do they make up appropriate other-gender partners? At holiday times, do gays, lesbians, and bisexuals bring their partners to office parties and family dinners or do they go alone and feign being unattached?

Gays, lesbians, and bisexuals frequently attend counseling groups to address coming-out issues in a supportive environment. These groups should focus on taking responsibility for the way one's life is developing. In groups, members can take steps to make connections with others and to move away from their isolation and secrecy.

No matter what stage of development a person is confronting, coming-out groups provide a place to address daily issues of being gay, lesbian, or bisexual. For example, a 45-year-old woman who has lived an active and "out" life as a lesbian may find that attending a coming-out group with people in difference stages is invaluable in assessing her current issues. Group leaders need to recognize the risk involved in sharing information about sexual orientation and remain sensitive to every member of the group.

Group leaders may find it useful to familiarize themselves with various coming-out models. Several are available that provide a framework for understanding the process of identity development for gays and lesbians (Cass, 1984; Coleman, 1985; Falco, 1987; Lewis, 1984; Sophie, 1987; Troiden, 1989). Leaders of coming-out groups, regardless of their sexual orientation, also come out when they lead such groups. Thus, they have to confront their own homophobia, face the coming out issues in their own lives, and be comfortable discussing sexual issues, including their own sexual orientation, in the group. Otherwise they may find themselves impeding rather than helping the group process.

Youth Groups

> Models of groups for gay, lesbian and bisexual youth all suggest combining education and group interaction in a safe environment. Education is particularly important, to counter the homophobic myths and stereotypes gay and lesbian adolescents have internalized. The group also provides a place in which the adolescent can safely interact with other gay or lesbian teenagers, develop socialization skills, and combat isolation. (Hancock, 1995, p. 413)

Peer groups are important for all adolescents, and a number of organizations provide teenagers with opportunities to participate in groups. However, most school, religious, and community groups do not serve the special needs of youth struggling to identify themselves as gay, lesbian, or bisexual (Gerstel, Feraios, & Herdt, 1989). In fact, there are few groups specifically organized to attract gay, lesbian, and bisexual teens (Unks, 1995). Most gay, lesbian, and bisexual teens have experienced rejection and discrimination by friends, family, church, and teachers; many have also experienced violence from their families, peers, or the community (Reynolds & Koski, 1995). The approval and inclusion that groups provide can be particularly important in helping gay, lesbian, and bisexual youth accomplish basic developmental tasks and in serving as an antidote to family difficulties, violence, hopelessness, and isolation.

Groups give gay, lesbian, and bisexual youth a chance to address issues of identifying themselves as gay, lesbian, and bisexual in society and to learn from and with other gay, lesbian, and bisexual teens. Sexual minority youth typically lack positive role models and friends during their teenage years (Kus, 1990; Unks, 1995). The chance to compare experiences with other group members who are wrestling with similar identity issues enhances self-esteem and promotes emotional growth in all the participants (Gerstel et al., 1989).

Gay, lesbian, and bisexual teens are at high risk for self-destructive behavior, including suicide. "The occurrence of suicide among adolescent homosexuals is possibly the most widely publicized data about them. That this is the case is perhaps the cruelest irony in the chronicle of the woes of gay teens" (Unks, 1995, p. 7). In 1989, the Department of Health and Human Services issued a report on teen suicide. The findings were grim: Nearly 30% of all teen suicides were gay or lesbian. One in three gay, lesbian, or bisexual teens reported making at least one self-destructive act; almost half of those teens reported repeated suicide attempts (Gibson, 1989). A youth group can act as a deterrent to suicide by providing teens with a safe place to talk about their experiences of being gay, lesbian, or bisexual in society.

Leaders of gay, lesbian, and bisexual teen groups must be prepared to address the issue of suicide in their groups. In some cases the leader may initiate the discussion to reassure members that the topic is not off-bounds. Group leaders must also be sensitive to the possibility that gay, lesbian, and bisexual teens exploring their sexual orientation may develop the misconception that suicide is the inevitable consequence of being nonheterosexual (Harbeck, 1995).

Another important issue among gay, lesbian, and bisexual adolescents is whether and how to come out to friends and family members. One quarter of gay, lesbian, and bisexual teens are homeless, and many have experienced rejection and even violence from peers and family members who were not accepting of their sexual orientation. A significant number of sexual minority teens report that they have been physically assaulted, robbed, raped, and sexually abused (Savin-Williams, 1995). Most teen counseling groups spend considerable time discussing peer and family relationships and comparing various strategies and approaches. Members can explore their own thoughts and feelings with the group and get the group's feedback. As members make and implement decisions, and share the reactions of people they disclose to, all of the group members gain new perspectives on their own choices.

Uribe (1995) described a model program developed by the Los Angeles Unified School District to address the needs of gay, lesbian, and bisexual students:

> The focus of the model is education, reduction of verbal and physical abuse, suicide prevention, and dissemination of accurate AIDS information. The method by which the model is carried out is workshops for teachers, counselors, and other support personnel, as well as support groups set up on each senior high school campus for students who are dealing with sexual orientation issues. The goal of the support groups is to improve self-esteem and provide affirmation for students who are suffering the effects of stigmatization and discrimination based on sexual orientation. (p. 204)

As this model reflects, programs focused on gay, lesbian, and bisexual teens often need to educate and involve school personnel and group facilitators as well as the teenagers. The adults in the teens' environment need to be educated, sensitized, and helped to overcome their own homophobia and heterosexism in order to offer appropriate help to teens. Without such an approach, school administrators, public officials, and religious leaders may be actively hostile to the idea of gay, lesbian, and bisexual groups for young people. These adults can create an atmosphere of fear and paranoia—an atmosphere in which sexual minority teens may hesitate to attend groups for fear of retribution and in which hostility from other teens is tolerated or even encouraged.

The Los Angeles program benefits from being located in a large, metropolitan area. Establishing and maintaining gay, lesbian, and bisexual youth groups in rural areas may be more difficult. In many small communities, such groups do not advertise their location; people are asked to phone for time and place of meetings. Further, it may be difficult in rural areas to find group facilitators who are aware of the particular issues and needs of gay, lesbian, and bisexual youth (Ryan, 1990). Facilitators may not be familiar with or have ready access to resources. In such cases, the group leaders will need to contact professional organizations, gay and lesbian task forces, and counselors more familiar with working with gays, lesbians, and bisexuals.

Leaders serve a number of different functions in counseling groups for gay, lesbian, and bisexual teens. They offer a stable hub, which is important in a group in which the membership is likely to fluctuate. They also reinforce and model the norms of confidentiality and safety within the group. These norms must be explicitly discussed whenever new people attend the group. Leaders also facilitate the group's process during discussions by modeling and reinforcing such behaviors as active listening and nonjudgmental acceptance of each individual. They can encourage linking between group members and can draw connections between what the members discuss. Leaders who are comfortable discussing their own sexual orientation in the group make a powerful statement and serve as positive role models for the members.

Group leaders may find that inevitably they have to address the community's homophobia. This can mean a number of things, from networking with school counselors about gay, lesbian, and bisexual students, to advocating at school board meetings for permission to advertise the group in the high school newspaper, to defending the group's existence in the Letters to the Editor section of local newspapers. Both group leaders and the gay, lesbian, and bisexual group members often find themselves working as activists promoting change on a community level.

Couples Groups

Many gay and lesbian individuals live with a partner. Surveys indicate that between 45% and 80% of lesbians and between 40% and 60% of gay men have steady relationships (Kurdek, 1995). With the continuation of the AIDS pandemic, more gay men are choosing to live monogamously with partners. Most often, the concerns gay couples bring to group counseling are no different from the issues in heterosexual relationships—differences in socioeconomic and family backgrounds, differences in education, religion, or values, communication problems, previous relationships, illness, financial issues, individual emotional problems, sexual dysfunction, and jealousy. Lesbian and gay couples, however, face additional relationship problems related to their sexual orientation.

Gay and lesbian couples, as Forstein (1986) noted, "do not have the social, legal or moral sanctions that sustain opposite-sex couples. Thus the development and maintenance of same-sex couples involves a commitment to a difficult process with many destructive internal and external forces in its path" (p. 105). For example, lesbian and gay couples frequently disagree about how open to be about their sexual orientation. One member of the couple may have come out to his or her family while the other has not. Gay and lesbian couples face a lack of visible role models for their relationship; they frequently express curiosity about how other couples deal with their everyday lives and bring up issues such as finances, outside relationships, families, and sex.

Group counseling gives gay and lesbian couples opportunities to explore these unique relationship issues in a safe, supportive environment. Groups can help these couples look at what happens in a relationship when one member of the couple is more out of the closet than the other. Groups also can help them realize that although there is a lack of modeling for gay and lesbian couples, which creates uncertainty about how to behave as a couple, the absence of strict, societal guidelines for same-sex couples allows for creativity in establishing ground rules for the relationship. The group leader and other group participants provide couples with mirrors of their relationship. The various group members provide each couple with a variety of role models to consider. The group leader and group members can suggest books to read, videos to view, and lectures and other community events to attend to help couples explore alternative models of behavior.

Same-sex couples face the effects of societal sex role stereotypes on their relationships. Gay couples tend to experience competition as a difficulty in relationships, while lesbian couples frequently have difficulty with fusion and separation (McCandlish, 1985; Silberman & Hawkins, 1988). Group leaders working with male couples should know about the developmental model created by McWhirter and Mattison (1984). Their six-stage model describes and identifies the tasks male couples encounter as they progress through predictable developmental stages in their relationship. Group facilitators working with lesbian couples may find the developmental model proposed by Clunis and Green (1993) helpful. Leaders might use these models in group counseling to assess whether the partners are moving at the same pace or are on different developmental tracks.

Group leaders working with gay and lesbian couples, may have to address the serious problem of violence and battering (Hammond, 1989; Hart, 1989; Island & Letellier, 1991; NiCarthy, 1986). Domestic violence is as frequent in gay and lesbian couples as it is in the society generally but has been grossly ignored and underreported (Island & Letellier, 1991). Most victims tell no one, and authorities often fail to ask. Battering has a profound impact on the victim. Closeness and equality in the relationship disappear, and fear, mistrust, and disillusionment take over. Domestic violence is a taboo topic in U.S. society, especially in gay, lesbian, and bisexual communities.

Counseling the victim and perpetrator of domestic violence in separate counseling groups is the ethical and effective way for group counselors to work with such couples. Although group couples counseling works effectively with most of the problems gay and lesbian couples face, domestic violence is an exception. As in all issues of violence, the victim's safety takes precedence over supporting the relationship or taking care of the batterer's current emotional needs. Insisting on separate groups sends the clear message that the violence is not the victim's fault or responsibility. It also underscores the seriousness of the issue: Domestic violence is a crime, and the victim has the right, as with all crimes, to be protected from the perpetrator. Even if the couple requests to continue in the same group, following disclosure of an incident of domestic violence, the leader needs to refuse this request in order to provide safety and security for the victim.

Parenting Groups

Gays, lesbians, and bisexuals are becoming partners, having and rearing children, and challenging society's definition of what "family" means. Sometimes the children of these couples are born when one parent was in a heterosexual relationship. Increasingly, however, gay, lesbian, and bisexual couples are choosing to become parents and are raising their children in redefined families. This has resulted in a "lesbian and gay baby boom" (Patterson, 1995).

Many of the difficulties of gay, lesbian, and bisexual parenting are exactly like the stresses heterosexual parents feel—jealousy, time spent with children, privacy, communication. In blended families, parenting styles and responsibilities are common points of disagreement. Other stresses are unique to gay, lesbian, and bisexual parents. The partner's inability to become a legal stepparent complicates the attempt to co-parent another's child. Same-sex couples face difficulty if they wish to adopt children. Further, many states discriminate against gays, lesbians, and bisexuals in awarding child custody and visitation rights; in some states, such parents are considered unfit. Issues that arise for gay, lesbian, and bisexual parents who are in opposite-sex marriages include concerns about coming out to a wife or husband, to children, and to other family members. Concerns about coming out also affect the children of gay and lesbian parents. Some children choose to hide their parent's sexuality from friends.

Gay Parents   Group counseling can help gay parents in several ways. Leaders may wish to introduce the group members to behavioral techniques that will teach them how to improve their child-rearing information or skill level. In the group, members are surrounded by supportive people with whom they can explore specific parenting topics. The group also can problem solve and brainstorm about parenting strategies and share information on legal and other professional resources. Groups for gay fathers and lesbian mothers exist in most urban communities and also in many rural areas.

Parents of Gay Children   Parents of gay, lesbian, and bisexual children may have difficulty accepting the sexual orientation of their children. A national organization, Parents and Friends of Lesbians and Gays (PFLAG), exists as a support and information network for these parents and coordinates local meetings at which parents share the guilt, shock, and pain that they may feel. These groups help parents overcome the cultural messages of rejection and hatred of gays and move toward acceptance and peace. The positive effects of such groups often exceed the groups' original intentions, and "the act of confronting homosexuality openly and courageously can become a source of freedom and fulfillment in the family" (Griffin et al., 1986, p. 9).

Children With Gay Parents   Children whose parents are gay, lesbian, or bisexual may have a number of issues of their own. Younger children may be confused about why their household is not like those they see in books or on television, or at their friends' homes. Older children may feel embarrassed about being different or uncertain about having friends over for fear of teasing or repercussions. Teenagers may try to make their parent(s) "pass" as heterosexual. Sometimes, other parents will restrict their children's friendships with children who live in same-sex households. All of these issues can be effectively dealt with in children's groups. In fact counselors may wish to consider running concurrent groups for children and their gay, lesbian, or bisexual parents. Such groups can meet simultaneously with facilitators who can help the children and parents process their own issues. The two groups can merge at the beginning or end of each or some sessions.

Drug and Alcohol Abuse Groups

Many mental health professionals assume that drug and alcohol abuse is quite high in the gay, lesbian, and bisexual community. However, the research in this area is sparse and contains methodological limitations (Paul, Stall, & Bloomfield, 1991). The available research does suggest that approximately 20-30% of gay men and lesbians are chemically dependent on alcohol or drugs (Clunis & Green, 1993; Kus, 1990; Lohrenz, Connely, Coyne, & Spare, 1978; Paul et al., 1991). Too often, lesbians, gay men, and bisexuals have sought and received treatment for relationship difficulties, depression, or anxiety without reporting or being asked about chemical abuse (Faltz, 1992). As a result, substance abuse problems are often unaddressed. Intake and assessment procedures with all clients should include questions about drinking and using drugs.

Internalized homophobia may explain the etiology and high incidence of alcoholism in gay men (Kus, 1987) and lesbians (Browning, Reynolds, & Dworkin, 1991). Gays, lesbians, and bisexuals tend to misuse alcohol or drugs to ameliorate their feelings related to societal rejection, alienation, and stress (Deevey & Wall, 1992). Although the substance abuse may originate with internalized homophobia, counselors cannot work on a client's self-image while the client is drinking or using drugs. Accepting oneself as gay, lesbian, or bisexual does not typically happen during periods of abuse. Leaders can work with individuals in groups only after they have successfully treated the substance abuse problem—an approach consistent with that of other substance-abusing populations.

Gays, lesbians, and bisexuals who come to treatment groups that are not specifically targeted for sexual minorities may experience heightened shame and guilt as they start this new experience. Therefore, leaders should ask questions about the group members' sexual identity and behavior in a routine and nonjudgmental manner during the first group session. By asking these questions, leaders give group members a choice about whether to reveal their sexual orientation. As noted by Finnegan and McNally (1987), "If the question [of sexual orientation] is not posed, gays or lesbians may feel heterosexuality is assumed and homosexuality is possibly unacceptable in this setting" (p. 61). Addressing sexual orientation in groups as a part of the treatment plan demonstrates sensitivity to sexual orientation issues.

Group leaders focusing on substance abuse issues should be familiar with local self-help groups and resources, and be able to make appropriate referrals, because most gay, lesbian, and bisexual individuals will need to be in both counseling and self-help groups to stay clean and sober. Leaders must encourage group members to attend gay, lesbian, or gay-lesbian self-help group meetings (such as those identified earlier in this chapter), when such meetings are available.

AIDS Groups

The response of the gay, lesbian, and bisexual community to the AIDS pandemic provides a striking example of the importance of groups in the gay community. AIDS, first identified in 1981, is a usually fatal disease for which there is no known cure or immunization. Initially, gay men were the hardest hit group in the United

States. Groups in the gay community organized the initial, desperately needed support services for those affected by AIDS, generated the earliest self-help and safer sex materials, and lobbied incessantly about the need for funds for care and research (McLaughlin, 1989). Gay men banded together, at first informally and then with increasing sophistication and organization, to provide and demand adequate, respectful care for their lovers and friends. The lesbian and bisexual communities have responded similarly and have also been actively involved in AIDS support services. Groups help with transportation, deliver meals, and run errands for people living with AIDS (PLWAs). Self-help and support groups formed as well: for people who were HIV positive; for PLWAs; for the friends and families, spouses and lovers, and grieving survivors of PLWAs; and for the health care providers, counselors, volunteers, and neighbors who care for people living with and dying from AIDS. Today, AIDS care continues to be provided by community groups that supplement existing services and in some instances substitute for the institutionalized medical and support services that do not exist for PLWAs.

Group leaders are most apt to be involved in support and therapy groups for HIV-positive individuals and PLWAs and in support groups for friends and family members. However, as with many of the issues confronting gays, lesbians, and bisexuals in our culture, group leaders may find it necessary to extend their involvement beyond these groups to the larger social and cultural factors that affect their clients. For example, they may choose to advocate for changes in drug experimentation and approval requirements, so that PLWAs will have access to treatment alternatives.

Support Groups for PLWAs, Families, and Friends   Most mental health professionals and physicians see support groups for HIV-positive people and PLWAs as an essential element of optimum care. Eller and King (1990) noted, "Another patient [sic] can do more toward relieving another's nagging fear than a host of health professionals" (p. 332). Support groups extend the participants' circle of support (Price, Omizo, & Hammett, 1986) and offer a powerful antidote to the isolation and alienation that PLWAs often encounter (Morin, Charles, & Malyon, 1984). In support groups, members can discuss problems related to their HIV status and share their feelings and thoughts.

Support groups provide friends and family members of PLWAs with the opportunity to vent their anger, frustrations, and sorrows regarding the illness and its effects on their lives in a safe and accepting environment (Martin, 1989). Friends and family often face issues that are very similar to those confronted by PLWAs. Additionally, friends and family members must deal with the exhaustion caused by physical caretaking, the anxiety of wondering "what will happen next," and the stress of financial responsibility for a disease for which long-term costs can run into the hundreds of thousands of dollars. Support groups for significant others often are led by professionals who act as facilitators or by family members who act as peer facilitators.

Counseling Groups for PLWAs   There are also counseling groups for HIV-positive people and PLWAs. In most groups, members spend time discussing their individual reactions to the diagnosis and the reactions of friends and family members. The AIDS diagnosis may force PLWAs, families, and friends to face previously avoided issues, such as sexual orientation and drug use. There are often efforts to keep the AIDS diagnosis a secret from particular family members or from people outside the family due to fears of rejection, stigma, retaliation, and isolation. Family members may try to exclude gay friends or lovers. All of these responses are brought to the group to be shared and addressed. Other issues group members may consider include anger, guilt, and grief over their own loss of health, the deaths of friends and loved ones, and their own approaching death; recurring denial about their illness; safer sex behaviors; and the need for decision making about burial and funeral matters. It is important for the counselor to be sensitive to the varying degrees of normal distress experienced by HIV-positive individuals so that he or she will neither overreact to typical expressions of grief, anger, and anxiety nor minimize or ignore statements or behaviors that indicate that an individual is in need of crisis intervention.

Counseling groups for PLWAs- and HIV-positive individuals are closed and time-limited, usually lasting 6 to 10 weeks. For people facing life-threatening illness, this group format provides stability, which reinforces their attempts to become empowered and hopeful. It also offers consistency, which is important in the development of social support, trust, and comfort within the group. Group members may look at a number of different questions, including relationship issues, existential issues raised by their illness, the challenge of making lifestyle changes, or their own death and dying. There may be differences in the health status of members: Some may be asymptomatic; others may have had medical crises but be doing well currently; still others may be having active illness symptoms or may develop them during the course of the group.

Whenever possible, group leaders should schedule a pre-group interview with each potential member to explain the goals and structure of the group and to assess for such issues as clinical depression, suicidal ideation, or substance abuse; people exhibiting these behaviors may not be appropriate for the group. Even though screening interviews are not always possible, preregistration is essential with a closed, time-limited group.

Later in this section we offer a model for a seven-session group for gay men recently diagnosed HIV positive. Groups are especially helpful for people soon after their discovery of HIV seropositivity (Rabkin, Remien, & Wilson, 1994). Positive diagnosis almost always results in personal crisis, and a group can help newly diagnosed men and women adjust by providing two important elements: information about HIV, treatments, and sources of support available locally; and the chance to talk about the experience of being HIV positive in a safe, nonjudgmental atmosphere. Research has shown that with competent counseling and support people's initial anxiety and depression over an HIV-positive diagnosis dissipate in 6-8 weeks (Perry et al., 1993).

While urban areas may have enough HIV-positive people to offer very specialized groups for newly-diagnosed gay men (e.g. HIV-positive gay men with HIV-negative partners; HIV-positive but asymptomatic gay men; and dual-diagnosis HIV-positive gay men), in many parts of the country there may not even be separate groups for gay men. In smaller communities, and in other areas with a low HIV population, groups for people newly diagnosed HIV positive may include members of all risk groups and both sexes. However, there are advantages to having gay-specific groups whenever possible. Gay men who are HIV-positive face several unique issues, including the combined stresses of the stigmatization of living with HIV and being gay; dilemmas about simultaneously disclosing sexual orientation and HIV status; and the multiple losses of large numbers of friends who are HIV positive or have AIDS. These issues are more apt to be discussed in gay-only groups than in mixed groups.

The following is a model for a seven-session group for gay men recently diagnosed HIV positive.

Session 1: Telling the Diagnosis Story. The leader welcomes everyone and discusses the ground rules and structure of the group. Confidentiality and safety are stressed at this and subsequent sessions. Each member tells the group how he came to be tested for HIV and what it was like getting the results. There will be variability in the stories. Some men may have chosen to be tested. Others may have been tested by medical care providers without their knowledge or consent. The telling of these stories is apt to be an emotionally intense experience for all the group participants. The leader needs to pace the group to be sure that each member has time to tell his story.

After the stories are told, the leader facilitates a group discussion in which each member responds to the following two statements: "The biggest change in my life since I was diagnosed is _____ " and "Right now, the hardest thing about being HIV positive is _____." It may be helpful for the leader to write the responses on a piece of newsprint posted on the wall. This helps members see their common concerns. Following this discussion, the leader can have the group build the agenda for the following six sessions. Alternatively, he or she can develop a schedule based on the needs identified by the group members.

Session 2: Decisions About Disclosing HIV-Positive Status. Disclosure is one of the most important issues facing people who are HIV positive. The group leader introduces the topic of disclosure and identifies pros and cons. Disclosure generally makes support and assistance more available (Herek, 1990), whereas secrecy tends to lead to more distress and depression (Namir, 1989). However, there are good reasons to be cautious in disclosure, because there may be negative consequences (Dworkin & Pincu, 1993; Kain, 1996). The group leader asks members to identify those people they believe it is important to tell about their HIV status—sexual partners, employers, co-workers, parents, children, other family members, neighbors, landlords.

The leader then introduces an exercise to help group members make decisions about disclosure. Each group member writes a list of 10 people and rates them along a continuum from "They already know" to "I will never tell them." They place in the middle of the continuum the names of people they may or may not tell. Group members can discuss the possible consequences of disclosing to these people and the possible results of not disclosing to them. The leader may ask group members to consider what might make it easier for them to disclose to these people by discussing how they would complete the sentence "I would tell _____ if _____ changed."

Session 3: Dealing With Emotions. In this session, participants are given a chance to focus on the range of emotional responses that are common after an HIV diagnosis. Hearing other group members express anxieties similar to their own may actually be reassuring. The discussion will probably focus on at least the following emotions: denial and disbelief; fatalism; anger; shame and guilt; and fear. The group leader can guide the group to look at how each emotion can serve a helpful function. For example, anger at the medical establishment can be helpful if it motivates a group member to become an informed consumer of medical care or to change doctors.

If positive feelings are not brought up, the group leader invites the group to discuss any positive feelings that have resulted from their diagnosis. People sometimes express relief at knowing rather than wondering if they are HIV positive and say they find it easier to plan their future. Some people who have lost many friends or family may say that being HIV positive has eliminated the survivor guilt they felt about being the only one in a circle of friends who tested negative.

Session 4: Community Resources and Financial Information. In this session, members learn about HIV-specific programs run by the health department and other local government agencies. Information is also provided about entitlement programs, including Social Security Supplemental Income (SSI), Social Security Disability (SSD), Medicaid, Medicare, and Ryan White funds. The group leader must have current data on requirements for different programs as well as basic information including phone numbers, applications, and names of individuals to contact.

The group leader might want to invite a resource person who can give accurate, comprehensive information about resources to this session. It may be best to have this presentation early in the session so the group can process the information after the expert leaves.

In larger population centers, AIDS organizations may offer resource training sessions. If such sessions are available, the group leader can recommend them to the members, and this group session can be spent on psychosocial issues instead of resources.

Session 5: Self-Care. Self-care topics such as nutrition, safer sex practices, avoiding infections, alternative therapies, choosing a physician and evaluating medical treatment, negotiating changes in work responsibilities, changing substance use behaviors, and stress reduction techniques are addressed in this session. The group leader may need to provide information or bring experts to the session to assist with these issues.

Additionally, participants are encouraged to look at their natural support systems in the context of who might be able to provide what type of assistance. The group leader encourages members to identify and/or develop a network of people who can provide practical assistance and emotional understanding and encouragement.

Session 6: Long-Term Planning. In this session, the leader introduces long-term planning issues people with serious illness need to consider, including advance health directives, power of attorney for health care, power of attorney, legal wills, long-term financial planning, and insurance options. It is particularly important for gay men to identify whom they want involved in making decisions about their care and how they want their resources used. For example, legal wills should be completed as early after diagnosis as possible, because in some instances biological family members have challenged wills to prevent gay partners from receiving inheritances.

Some professionals consider these topics "unnecessarily upsetting" (Rabkin et al., 1994, p. 149) and defer such discussion until an individual is seriously ill. However, the best time to consider these subjects and make plans is not during a serious illness (Kain, 1996). By discussing them in a group for newly diagnosed HIV-positive people, the group leader models that long-range planning is simply one more aspect of good self-care. Some group members may not be aware of some of the health care choices they have and will feel more in control of their future knowing how much say they have in their treatment throughout the course of their illness. Enough time should be allowed for the group to discuss their emotions and reactions resulting from the discussion.

At the end of this session, the leader reminds the members that the next session will be the last and encourages them to think about what they would like to say before the group ends. The group may also want to plan a celebratory element—a potluck at the beginning, or a dessert at the end, of the final group session—or a ritual to acknowledge the significance of the group.

Session 7: Facing the Future. Endings have a special poignancy for people with a life-threatening illness. For some participants, the group may have been the first place in which they could talk about their diagnosis; for some members it may still be the only place they can be completely candid. The group leader introduces a two-part exercise to help members validate the sense of loss they may be feeling. In this exercise, each member is asked to complete the sentence, "One thing I will really miss about the group is ____." After sharing their responses, each person completes this sentence: "One thing I will not miss about this group is ____."

Next, the leader facilitates a discussion of the most helpful elements of the past six sessions. The leader may find it useful to return to the exercise conducted in the first session and ask the men to complete the sentence, "Right now, the hardest thing about being HIV positive is ____." Most men will list a different concern now, underscoring how quickly changes can occur when one is living with HIV.

The leader can also encourage the members to look ahead and make appropriate plans for the future. Several different exercises can be used. Group members may discuss, as a group or in pairs, their plans for the next month, 6 months, year. The group can do goal-setting exercises, listing what they want to accomplish or what is most important to them.

At the end of this session, the leader ties up any loose ends. These may involve providing the phone number of the local AIDS hot line, the address of a pharmaceutical company that has a drug give-away program, and information on annuities. Participants are reminded of where they can get additional support and how to locate services they do not now need but may need at some future point.

Aging Groups

The assumption that aging is synonymous with decline becomes particularly negative when generalized to older lesbians, gay men, and bisexuals who have been incorrectly portrayed as lonely and pathetically miserable. Such myths and stereotypes are not substantiated by research on the lives of older gay men and lesbians. (Reid, 1995, p. 215)

It is estimated that there are approximately 3.5 million older lesbians and gay men living in the United States (Reid, 1995). Until recently, older lesbians and gay men were usually ignored by gerontologists and social scientists. Little research was available on these populations, and services geared to their special situations rarely existed (Berger, 1996; Reid, 1995). There has been a tendency by both the gay, lesbian, and bisexual community and mental health professionals to overlook the needs of elderly gays, lesbians, and bisexuals. Recently, however, "the increased visibility and demands for civil rights by the gay, lesbian, and bisexual community have directed increasing attention to the sizable numbers of older bisexuals, lesbians, and gay men living, working, and contributing to the society in which they live" (Reid, 1995, p. 217).

As we learn more about these individuals, the stereotypes and myths of older gays and lesbians living isolated and lonely lives are giving way to greater understanding. Older gay men and lesbians are not inevitably alone and unhappy. Many have created alternative families that provide friendship and support. They are most often integrated into their community as "out" gay men, lesbians, or bisexuals. As Friend (1991) pointed out, successful aging in gay men and lesbians is related to having a positive lesbian or gay identity. Those who reject the values of a homophobic culture and reconstruct a new meaning have been called "affirmative" older lesbians and gay men (Friend, 1991). Some older gays, lesbians, and bisexuals, however, choose not to be public about their homosexuality and remain in the "closet." These individuals face more challenges as they confront the last years of their lives.

Older gays and lesbians face aging issues similar to those faced by all older adults. These include the aging process and physical changes of aging, sensible nutrition, sex as an older adult, issues of ageism, managing finances, bereavement overload, and in some cases isolation and loneliness. In addition, other issues are more specifically related to aging as a sexual minority. These include legal issues because same-sex relationships are not sanctioned by law. These couples need to make specific financial plans so that when one partner dies the other will not lose possessions and property the two purchased together. Other arrangements, such as power of attorney for health care and hospital visitation agreements, have to be considered, discussed with family and lovers, and instituted.

Recently, groups for older gay men, lesbians, and bisexuals have emerged to address aging issues. Such groups provide older gays, lesbians, and bisexuals with opportunities for peer sharing, socialization, and social activities. Group leaders need to be aware of the variability among older bisexuals, gay men, and lesbians. As noted by Reid (1995), "The recipe for a successful program is not the same for all individuals... . What is needed is an increasing variety of choices of programs and services within the community (p. 230).

In urban areas, groups or programs may be in existence that address the particular needs of older gays and lesbians. The Gay Community Services Center in Minneapolis, with its Affectional Preference and Aging program, the Gay and Lesbian Outreach to Elders (GLOE) organization in San Francisco, and the Senior Action in a Gay Environment (SAGE) organization in New York City all use groups as a way to reach out to older gays and lesbians. These and similar organizations provide a variety of social activities and social support, assist with managing chronic health problems, provide transportation for homebound older adults, offer bereavement counseling, and help fight discriminatory policies in nursing homes and hospitals (D'Augelli & Garnets, 1995). In less populated areas, special programs for older gays, lesbians, and bisexuals seldom exist. Group leaders in such areas need to address these issues in the context of a mixed-orientation group.

Personal Growth Groups

Personal growth groups may be a resource and refuge for gay, lesbian, and bisexual individuals, who may receive limited support from friends, parents, siblings, or family members. In personal growth groups, members address their feelings of guilt and internalized homophobia. They learn to take responsibility for themselves rather than blaming society and the people in their lives for the awful state of "their world." Growth groups help members address the anger they feel toward society. Group members who learn to express their anger in positive ways are more apt to avoid the inward expressions of anger often associated with loneliness, substance abuse, and suicidal ideation.

Gays, bisexuals, and lesbians need to stop asking the question "Why me?" and begin to affirm their sexual orientation. Self-affirmative statements that allow members to embrace being gay, lesbian, or bisexual can be encouraged by the group. Such honest discussion in groups is liberating and lays the foundation for honest and direct interaction with other people. The ultimate reward of developing this sense of community within gay, lesbian, and bisexual personal growth groups is learning that one does not have to fight these issues alone.

Conclusion ～

Gays, lesbians, and bisexuals have a right to unbiased and professional mental health services. Group leaders must recognize and address homophobia and heterosexism in themselves, in the counseling profession, in individuals, and in groups they lead. Gay-affirmative group leaders encourage groups they facilitate to openly address sexual orientation issues by creating an atmosphere of tolerance and acceptance so that anyone who wishes to explore his or her sexual orientation can bring up concerns easily and openly. Group leaders who are sensitive to gays, lesbians, and bisexuals address the issues that are presented and do not make sexual behavior the problem if it is irrelevant to the situation. They create and model norms of nonjudgmental acceptance and tolerance of everyone in the group. Finally, gay-affirmative group leaders are knowledgeable about gay, lesbian, and bisexual culture and the resources that exist.

Summary ～

Professional groups have been slow to respond to gay, lesbian, and bisexual individuals and their unique concerns. This mirrors the attitudes of the American public, which continues to favor heterosexism. As a product of homophobia, some gays and lesbians have internalized society's negative attitudes and deny their own sexual orientation. Some counseling professionals have adopted heterosexist and homophobic attitudes.

What is needed is gay-affirmative counseling, in which leaders create an atmosphere of tolerance, acceptance, and advocacy. Such group leaders are sensitive to gay, lesbian, and bisexual concerns, openly address sexual orientation issues, and create and model norms of nonjudgmental acceptance and tolerance of all group members. Some groups, particularly couples groups, might best be led by gay, lesbian, or bisexual professional counselors.

Types of groups in which sexual minorities can find support include common-interest groups, self-help groups, and counseling groups. Specific gay, lesbian, and bisexual groups include coming-out groups, youth groups, couples groups, parenting groups, drug and alcohol abuse groups, aging groups, and AIDS groups. Self-help and support groups have developed for HIV-positive individuals; for PLWAs; for families, friends, and survivors of PLWAs; and for health care workers who care for people living and dying with AIDS.

References ～

Bailey, J. M. (1995). Biological perspectives on sexual orientation. In A. R. D'Augelli & C. J. Patterson (Eds.), *Lesbian, gay, and bisexual identities over the lifespan: Psychological perspectives* (pp. 102–135). New York: Oxford University Press.

Berger, R. M. (1996). *Gay & gray: The older homosexual man* (2nd ed.). New York: Harrington Press.

Berzon, B. (1996). *Setting them straight: You can do something about bigotry and homophobia in your life.* New York: Penguin Books.

Betz, N. E., & Fitzgerald, L. F. (1993). Individuality and diversity: Theory and research in counseling psychology. *Annual Review of Psychology, 44,* 343–381.

Blumenfeld, W. J., & Raymond, D. (1988). *Looking at gay and lesbian life.* Boston: Beacon Press.

Blumstein, P., & Schwartz, P. (1983). *American couples.* New York: William Morrow.

Brelin, C. (1996). *Strength in numbers: A lesbian, gay, and bisexual resource.* Detroit, MI: Visible Ink Press.

Browning, C., Reynolds, A. L., & Dworkin, S. H. (1991). Affirmative psychotherapy for lesbian women. *Counseling Psychologist, 19,* 177–196.

Buhrke, R. A. (1989). Incorporating lesbian and gay issues into counselor training: A resource guide. *Journal of Counseling and Development, 68,* 77–80.

Burr, C. (1993, March). Homosexuality and biology. *Atlantic Monthly,* pp. 47–65.

Burr, C. (1996). *A separate creation: The search for the biological origins of sexual orientation.* New York: Hyperion Press.

Byne, W. (1994, May). The biological evidence challenged. *Scientific American,* pp. 50–55.

Carl, D. (1992). *Counseling same-sex couples.* New York: Norton.

Cass, V. C. (1984). Homosexual identity formation: A concept in need of definition. *Journal of Homosexuality, 10,* 105–126.

Clark, D. (1987). *The new loving someone gay.* Berkeley, CA: Celestial Arts.

Clunis, D. M., & Green, G. D. (1993). *Lesbian couples.* Seattle, WA: Seal Press.

Coleman, E. (1985). Developmental stages of the coming out process. In J. C. Gonsiorek (Ed.), *A guide to psychotherapy with gay and lesbian clients* (pp. 31–43). New York: Harrington Park Press.

Coleman, E., & Remafedi, G. (1989). Gay, lesbian and bisexual adolescents: A critical challenge to counselors. *Journal of Counseling and Development, 68,* 36–40.

Conlin, D., & Smith, J. (1985). Group psychotherapy for gay men. In J. C. Gonsiorek (Ed.), *A guide to psychotherapy with gay and lesbian clients* (pp. 105–112). New York: Harrington Park Press.

D'Augelli, A. R., & Garnets, L. D. (1995). Lesbian, gay, and bisexual communities. In A. R. D'Augelli & C. J. Patterson (Eds.), *Lesbian, gay, and bisexual identities over the lifespan: Psychological perspectives* (pp. 293–320). New York: Oxford University Press.

Deevey, S., & Wall, L. J. (1992). How do lesbian women develop serenity? *Health Care for Women International, 74,* 239–247.

Dworkin, S. H., & Pincu, L. (1993). Counseling in the area of AIDS. *Journal of Counseling and Development, 71,* 275–281.

Eller, M., & King, D. J. (1990). Self-help groups for gays, lesbians, and their loved ones In R. J. Kus (Ed.), *Keys to caring* (pp. 330–339). Boston: Alyson Publications.

Falco, K. (1987). *Psychotherapy with lesbian clients: A manual for the psychotherapist.* Unpublished doctoral dissertation, Oregon Graduate School of Professional Psychology, Pacific University, Forest Grove.

Faltz, B. G. (1992). Counseling chemically dependent lesbians and gay men. In S. Dworkin & F. Gutierrez (Eds.), *Counseling gay men and lesbians: Journey to the end of the rainbow* (pp. 245–258). Alexandria, VA: American Counseling Association.

Fassinger, R. E. (1991). The hidden minority: Issues and challenges in working with lesbian women and gay men. *Counseling Psychologist, 19,* 157–176.

Finnegan, D. G., & McNally, E. B. (1987). *Dual identities: Counseling chemically dependent gay men and lesbians.* Center City, MN: Hazelden.

Forstein, M. (1986). Psychodynamic psychotherapy with gay male couples. In T. S. Stein & C. J. Cohen (Eds.), *Contemporary perspectives on psychotherapy with lesbians and gay men* (pp. 103–137). New York: Plenum.

Fox, R. C. (1995). Bisexual identities. In A. R. D'Augelli & C. J. Patterson (Eds.), *Lesbian, gay and bisexual identities over the lifespan: Psychological perspectives* (pp. 48–86). New York: Oxford University Press.

Friend, R. A. (1991). Older lesbian and gay people: A theory of successful aging. In J. A. Lee (Ed.), *Gay midlife and maturity* (pp. 99–118). New York: Haworth Press.

Gelberg, S., & Chojnacki, J. T. (1996). *Career and life planning with gay, lesbian, and bisexual persons.* Alexandria, VA: American Counseling Association.

Gerstel, C. J., Feraios, A. J., & Herdt, G. (1989). Widening circles: An ethnographic profile of a youth group. In G. Herdt (Ed.), *Gay and lesbian youth* (pp. 75–92). New York: Harrington Park Press.

Gibson, P. (1989). Gay male and lesbian youth suicide. In U.S. Department of Health and Human Services (Ed.), *Report of the Secretary's Task Force on Youth Suicide* (DHHS Publication No. ADM 89–1623, pp. 110–142). Washington, DC: U.S. Department of Health and Human Services.

Griffin, C. W., Wirth, M. J., & Wirth, A. G. (1986). *Beyond acceptance: Parents of lesbians and gays talk about their experiences.* New York: St. Martin's.

Hall, M. (1985). *The lavender couch: A consumer's guide to psychotherapy for lesbians and gay men.* Boston: Alyson Publications.

Hammond, N. (1989). Lesbian victims of relationship violence. In E. D. Rothblum & E. Cole (Eds.), *Lesbianism: Affirming nontraditional roles* (pp. 89–105). New York: Haworth Press.

Hancock, K. A. (1995). Psychotherapy with lesbians and gay men. In A. R. D'Augelli & C. J. Patterson (Eds.), *Lesbian, gay, and bisexual identities over the lifespan: Psychological perspectives* (pp. 398–432). New York: Oxford University Press.

Harbeck, K. M. (1995). Invisible no more: Addressing the needs of lesbian, gay, and bisexual youth and their advocates. In G. Unks (Ed.), *The gay teen: Educational practice and theory for lesbian, gay, and bisexual adolescents* (pp. 125–134). New York: Routledge.

Hart, B. (1989). Lesbian battering: An examination. In K. Lobel (Ed.), *Naming the violence: Speaking out about lesbian battering* (pp. 173–189). Seattle, WA: Seal Press.

Herek, G. M. (1990). Illness, stigma, and AIDS. In P. T. Costa & G. R. Vandal Boos (Eds.), *Psychological aspects of serious illness: Chronic conditions, fatal diseases, and clinical care/master lectures* (pp. 105–150). Washington, DC: American Psychological Association.

Herron, W. G., Kintner, T., Sollinger, I., & Trubowitz, J. (1985). Psychoanalytic psychotherapy for homosexual clients: New concepts. In J. C. Gonsiorek (Ed.), *A guide to psychotherapy with gay and lesbian clients* (pp. 177–192). New York: Harrington Park Press.

Iasenza, S. (1989). Some challenges of integrating sexual orientation into counselor training and research. *Journal of Counseling and Development, 68,* 73–76.

Isay, R. A. (1996). *Becoming gay: The journey to self-acceptance.* New York: Pantheon Books.

Island, D., & Letellier P. (1991). *Men who beat the men who love them: Battered gay men and domestic violence.* New York: Haworth Press.

Johnston, M. W., & Bell, A. P. (1995). Romantic emotional attachment: Additional factors in the development of the sexual orientation of men. *Journal of Counseling and Development, 73,* 621–625.

Kain, C. D. (1996). *Positive: HIV-affirmative counseling.* Alexandria, VA: American Counseling Association.

Klein, C. (1986). *Counseling our own: The lesbian/gay subculture meets the mental health system.* Renton, WA: Publication Service.

Klein, C. (1990). Gay and lesbian counseling centers: History and functions. In R. J. Kus (Ed.), *Keys to Caring* (pp. 312–320). Boston: Alyson Publications.

Krajeski, J. P. (1986). Psychotherapy with gay men and lesbians: A history of controversy. In T. S. Stein & C. J. Cohen (Eds.), *Contemporary perspectives on psychotherapy with lesbians and gay men* (pp. 9–25). New York: Plenum.

Kurdek, L. A. (1995). Lesbian and gay couples. In A. R. D'Augelli & C. J. Patterson (Eds.), *Lesbian, gay, and bisexual identities over the lifespan: Psychological perspectives* (pp. 243–261). New York: Oxford University Press.

Kus, R. J. (1987). Alcoholics Anonymous and gay American men. *Journal of Homosexuality, 14,* 253–276.

Kus, R. J. (Ed.). (1990). *Keys to caring: Assisting your gay and lesbian clients.* Boston: Alyson Publications.

Lapierre, E. D. (1990). Homophobia and its consequences for gay and lesbian clients. In R. J. Kus (Ed.), *Keys to caring* (pp. 90–104). Boston: Alyson Publications.

LeVay, S., & Hamer, D. H. (1994, May). Evidence for a biological influence in male homosexuality. *Scientific American,* pp. 44–49.

Lewis, L. A. (1984). The coming out process for lesbians: Integrating a stable identity. *Journal of the National Association of Social Workers, 29,* 464–469.

Lohrenz, L. J., Connely, J. C., Coyne, L., & Spare, K. E. (1978). Alcohol problems in several midwestern homosexual communities. *Journal of Studies on Alcohol, 39,* 1959–1963.

Martin, D. J. (1989). Human immunodeficiency virus infection and the gay community: Counseling and clinical issues. *Journal of Counseling and Development, 68,* 67–72.

McCandlish, B. M. (1985). Therapeutic issues with lesbian couples. In J. C. Gonsiorek (Ed.), *A guide to psychotherapy with gay and lesbian clients* (pp. 71–78). New York: Harrington Park Press.

McDermott, D., Tyndall, L., & Lichtenberg, J. W. (1989). Factors related to counselor preference among gays and lesbians. *Journal of Counseling and Development, 68,* 31–35.

McLaughlin, L. (1989). AIDS: An overview. In P. O'Malley (Ed.), *The AIDS epidemic: Private rights and the public interest* (pp. 15–35). Boston: Beacon Press.

McWhirter, D. P., & Mattison, A. M. (1984). *The male couple: How relationships develop.* Englewood Cliffs, NJ: Prentice-Hall.

Mollenkott, V. R. (1985). *Breaking the silence, overcoming the fear: Homophobia education.* (Available from the Program Agency, United Presbyterian Church, U.S.A., 475 Riverside Drive, Room 1101, New York, NY 10015.)

Money, J. (1987). Sin, sickness, or status? Homosexual gender identity and psychoneuroendocrinology. *American Psychologist, 42,* 384–399.

Morin, S., Charles, K., & Malyon, A. (1984). The psychological impact of AIDS on gay men. *American Psychologist, 39,* 1288–1293.

Moses, A. E., & Hawkins, R. O. (1985). Two-hour in-service training session in homophobia. In H. Hidalgo, T. Peterson, & N. J. Woodman (Eds.), *Lesbian and gay issues: A resource manual for social workers* (pp. 152–157). Silver Spring, MD: National Association of Social Workers.

Namir, S. (1989). Treatment issues concerning persons with AIDS. In L. McKusick (Ed.), *What to do about AIDS: Physicians and mental health professionals discuss the issues* (pp. 87–94). Berkeley: University of California Press.

NiCarthy, G. (1986). *Getting free: A handbook for women in abusive relationships.* Seattle, WA: Seal Press.

Patterson, C. J. (1995). Lesbian mothers, gay fathers, and their children. In A. R. D'Augelli & C. J. Patterson (Eds.), *Lesbian, gay, and bisexual identities over the lifespan: Psychological perspectives* (pp. 262–290). New York: Oxford University Press.

Paul, J. P., Stall, R., & Bloomfield, K. A. (1991). Gay and alcoholic: Epidemiologic and clinical issues. *Alcohol Health & Research World, 15*(2), 151–160.

Perry, S., Jacobsberg, L., Card, C. A., Ashman, T., Frances, A., & Fishman, B. (1993). Severity of psychiatric symptoms after HIV testing. *American Journal of Psychiatry, 150,* 775–779.

Price, R. E., Omizo, M., & Hammett, V. L. (1986). Counseling clients with AIDS. *Journal of Counseling and Development, 65,* 96–97.

Rabkin, J., Remien, R., & Wilson, C. (1994). *Good doctors, good patients: Partners in HIV treatment.* New York: NCM Publishers.

Reid, J. D. (1995). Development in later life: Older lesbian and gay lives. In A. R. D'Augelli & C. J. Patterson (Eds.), *Lesbian, gay and bisexual identities over the lifespan: Psychological perspectives* (pp. 215–240). New York: Oxford University Press.

Reynolds, A. L., & Koski, M. J. (1995). Lesbian, gay, and bisexual teens and the school counselor: Building alliances. In G. Unks (Ed.), *The gay teen: Educational practice and theory for lesbian, gay, and bisexual adolescents* (pp. 85–94). New York: Routledge.

Ritter, K. Y., & O'Neill, C. W. (1989). Moving through loss: The spiritual journey of gay men and lesbian women. *Journal of Counseling and Development, 68,* 9–15.

Rochlin, M. (1985). Sexual orientation of the therapist and therapeutic effectiveness with gay clients. In J. C. Gonsiorek (Ed.), *A guide to psychotherapy with gay and lesbian clients* (pp. 21–29). New York: Harrington Park Press.

Ryan, C. C. (1990). Accessing gay and lesbian health resources. In R. J. Kus (Ed.), *Keys to caring* (pp. 340–345). Boston: Alyson Publications.

Savin-Williams, R. C. (1995). Lesbian, gay male, and bisexual adolescents. In A. R. D'Augelli & C. J. Patterson (Eds.), *Lesbian, gay, and bisexual identities over the lifespan: Psychological perspectives* (pp. 166–189). New York: Oxford University Press.

Schwartz, R. D., & Harstein, N. B. (1986). Group psychotherapy with gay men: Theoretical and clinical considerations. In T. S. Stein & C. J. Cohen (Eds.), *Psychotherapy with lesbians and gay men* (pp. 157–177). New York: Plenum.

Silberman, B. O., & Hawkins, R. O., Jr. (1988). Lesbian women and gay men: Issues for counseling. In E. Weinstein & E. Rosen (Eds.), *Sexuality counseling: Issues and implications* (pp. 101–113). Pacific Grove, CA: Brooks/Cole.

Singer, B., & Deschamps, D. (Eds.). (1994). *Gay and lesbian stats: A pocket guide of facts and figures.* New York: New Press.

Sophie, J. (1987). Internalized homophobia and lesbian identity. *Journal of Homosexuality, 14,* 53–65.

Special report: *Gays in America.* (1989, June). San Francisco Examiner, pp. 1–78.

Troiden, R. R. (1989). The formation of homosexual identities. In G. Herdt (Ed.), *Gay and lesbian youth* (pp. 43–73). New York: Harrington Park Press.

Unks, G. (1995). Thinking about the gay teen. In G. Unks (Ed.), *The gay teen: Educational practice and theory for lesbian, gay, and bisexual adolescents* (pp. 3–12). New York: Routledge.

Uribe, V. (1995). Project Ten: A school based outreach to gay and lesbian youth. In G. Unks (Ed.), *The gay teen: Educational practice and theory for lesbian, gay, and bisexual adolescents* (pp. 203–210). New York: Routledge.

Vaid, U. (1995). *Virtual equality.* New York: Doubleday.

Weinberg, G. (1973). *Society and the healthy homosexual.* Garden City, NJ: Anchor Books.

White, M. (1995). *Stranger at the gate: To be gay and Christian in America.* New York: Penguin Books.

Williams, R. (1990). Studying sex in Sweden ... or how I spent my summer vacation. *Christopher Street, 13*(4), 11–15.

Wilson, J. D. (1992, September 14). Gays under fire. *Newsweek,* pp. 35–41.

Wolf, T. J. (1992). Bisexuality: A counseling perspective. In S. Dworkin & F. Gutierrez (Eds.), *Counseling gay men and lesbians: Journey to the end of the rainbow* (pp. 175–187). Alexandria, VA: American Counseling Association.

Woodman, N., & Lenna, H. (1980). *Counseling with gay men and women.* San Francisco: Jossey-Bass.

Yalom, I. (1985). *The theory and practice of group psychotherapy* (3rd ed.). New York: Basic Books.

16

Group Counseling
With the Elderly and Their Caregivers

M. Carolyn Thomas and Virginia Martin

At the beginning of the 20th century, persons 65 years of age or older represented about 4% (slightly more than three million people) of the U.S. population (Fowles, 1995). Little interest in this age-group was evident among mental health professionals, partly because the elderly population was so small (Gladding, 1991) but also because of prevailing negative societal attitudes toward the aging. Robert Butler, founding director of the National Institute on Aging, coined the term *ageism* to describe prejudice and discrimination against the aging population (Dickman, 1979). As late as 1975, Butler described life for many older Americans as "a tragedy, a period of quiet despair, deprivation, desolation and muted rage" (Butler, 1975, p. 2).

As we approach the 21st century, the picture has drastically changed. By 1994, the number of older Americans had increased 10-fold to 33 million, and the percentage of Americans over age 65 had more than tripled (Fowles, 1995). Ageism still exists, but mental health professionals now recognize the developmental significance of later life. Psychologist Erik Erikson (1963) pointed out that old age is a time when persons struggle to find meaning in the life they have lived, a sense of ego integrity, and satisfaction with a life well spent. Both individual and group counseling can help older persons and their caregivers find meaning during this often difficult stage of development.

The period of life designated as old age may span 30 years or more, presenting diverse counseling challenges. The issues of a vigorous, active, and involved person dealing with the transition from work to retirement, role loss, and related identity problems are very different from those of a declining older person coping with loneliness, alienation, and fear resulting from such multiple losses as death of cohorts, impaired health, and loss of autonomy. Consequently, varied counseling strategies are required to fully serve the diverse aging client population.

History of Group Work With Older Persons ~

Group work with the elderly seems to have emerged in the 1950s with the early reality orientation and remotivation groups being conducted by nursing staff or assistants in institutions. Early psychotherapy groups for older persons were also conducted, primarily with mentally ill patients in hospitals, but they were facilitated by health professionals with more training than nursing aides. Reminiscing groups, begun in the 1970s, moved groups for older people out of institutions and into the community. The types and numbers of groups quickly proliferated, once the settings and professionals conducting the groups became more diverse.

Although psychotherapy groups for senile psychiatric patients were first described by Silver (1950), Linden (1953) is most often described as the pioneer of such groups. J. Kaplan's (1953) book about a social program for older people and Kubie and Landau's (1953) book on group work with the aged strengthened the emphasis on psychotherapeutic groups for this population. Shere (1964) later described group work with the very old, and Yalom and Terrazas (1968) wrote about their work with psychotic elderly patients.

Remotivation groups were initially used by Dorothy Smith, a hospital volunteer, to restore mentally ill patients' involvement in life. In 1956, she trained a large number of Pennsylvania State Hospital staff in remotivation therapy. After the American Psychiatric Association formed a Remotivation Advisory Committee to encourage the use of remotivation therapy, training spread throughout the country. By 1967, 15,000 nurses and aides at 250 mental hospitals had been trained (Dennis, 1986).

The earliest reality orientation groups were conducted in a Topeka, Kansas, Veterans Administration Hospital as a pilot program, where Dr. James Folsom trained nursing assistants to help patients take more responsibility for their own care. Based on Folsom's work in Topeka and other work at the Mental Health Institute in Mt. Pleasant, Iowa, Folsom and Lucille Taulbee finalized the reality orientation group model at the Tuscaloosa, Alabama, Veterans Administration Hospital (Donahue, 1986; Folsom, 1968).

In the 1970s, reminiscing groups developed from individual reminiscing and life review therapy, changing the focus from offering groups for mentally ill geriatric patients in hospitals to providing help for a more diverse older population in all settings. Prior to 1960, R. G. Havighurst and others advised older people to avoid reminiscing, but by 1972 Havighurst was reporting its benefits (Havighurst & Glasser, 1972). Robert Butler (1963) is generally considered the pioneer of this change, although his early article on life review therapy did not mention reminiscing in groups. Priscilla Ebersole, a psychiatric nurse, reportedly adapted Butler's life review to include reminiscing, and began conducting reminiscing groups in 1970 (Burnside, 1978; Ebersole, 1978b). Butler and Lewis later advocated group life review in all settings (Butler & Lewis, 1977; Lewis & Butler, 1974).

Although four distinct types of groups for the elderly had emerged by the late 1970s, little had been written about their use. Butler and Lewis (1977) suggested that much more group therapy was being conducted with the elderly in and out of hospitals than was reflected in the literature. Irene Burnside (1978) also lamented the paucity of literature about group work with the elderly, noting that groups were indeed being conducted by professionals other than nurses and in settings other than institutions. Nurses first published reports about their group work, but very few such reports are found in the proceedings of national or international gerontology meetings of the 1970s. Gwen Marram's (1973) book on group work for nurses contains only a brief description of groups for the elderly. The Lewis and Butler (1974) article on psychosocial approaches for the aged also includes a small section on groups, but publications describing the groups undoubtedly being conducted for the elderly by a variety of professionals in every helping discipline and in many settings did not appear in significant numbers until the 1980s.

Irene Burnside (1978, 1986) combined the efforts and expertise of many professionals in the first comprehensive nursing text on group techniques for the elderly. She and her colleagues fully described the planning and implementation of reality orientation, remotivation, reminiscing, and psychotherapy as well as numerous topic and member-specific groups. The 1980s heralded the proliferation of group work for the elderly in the counseling profession, including an increase in numbers and types of groups outside the institutional setting. Capuzzi and Gross (1980) encouraged counselors to consider using the types of groups described by Burnside. Kaminsky (1984) edited a book on the uses of reminiscence in working with older adults. Descriptions of groups for the elderly using the arts, groups designed to help aging people with specific concerns, and groups for caregivers of the elderly appeared in the counseling journals in increasing numbers (Bledsoe & Lutz-Ponder, 1986; Burke, 1986; Capuzzi & Gossman, 1982; Cohen, 1983; Hammond & Bonney, 1983; Hawkins, 1983; Malde, 1988; Mardoyan & Weis, 1981; Zimpfer, 1987).

By the 1990s, work with older persons and their caregivers had become a major focus in the counseling profession, as evidenced by the publication of several special counseling journal issues dedicated to the topic. All of these special issues included articles on groups. Myers (1990) edited a special issue of the *Journal for Mental Health Counseling* on techniques for counseling older adults that included articles on group work. Waters (1990a) edited a special issue of *Generations* in which Capuzzi, Gross, and Friel (1990) described trends in group work with elders. Gladding and Thomas (1991) edited a special issue of the *Journal for Specialists in Group Work* focusing on group work with the aging and their caregivers. In addition, Chandras (1992) edited a special section of *Counselor Education and Supervision* in which Thomas and Martin (1992) described training considerations for group counselors of older persons and their caregivers.

Recent books by Nancy Schlossberg, Elinor Waters, and Jane Goodman provide further evidence that the counseling profession is now placing an emphasis on using individual and group counseling strategies to address the developmental, social, economic, and emotional needs of older persons. Waters and Goodman (1990) advocated using groups to empower older adults. They described appropriate groups for older persons as antidotes for loneliness, laboratories for teaching social skills, opportunities for catharsis, networks for accessing resources and developing plans of action, and sources of inspiration. Schlossberg, Waters, and Goodman (1995) provided additional information on using groups to counsel adults in transition, thoroughly describing the types of groups appropriate for older persons and their caregivers, steps in organizing groups, and considerations for accommodating cultural diversity.

The 1990s has also witnessed the publication of several group counseling texts that include chapters dedicated to groups for the elderly and their caregivers (Capuzzi & Gross, 1998; Corey & Corey, 1997; Gazda, 1989; Gladding, 1991). The inclusion of this topic in group counseling training texts validates the elderly as an important population on which to focus group counseling efforts.

Finally, specific competencies for group counselors were added to the training standards for gerontological counselors in the 1990s. Myers and Sweeney (1990) incorporated group counseling competencies in their *Gerontological Competencies for Counselors and Human Development Specialists*, which became the foundation of the national certified gerontological counselor specialty of the National Board for Certified Counselors. Myers was also instrumental in advocating and building the 1992 gerontological counseling specialty standards of the Council for the Accreditation of Counseling and Related Educational Programs (CACREP). In 1975, Salisbury reported that counseling the elderly was a neglected area in counselor education in the United States, with only 18 programs offering relevant course work. By 1988, more than half of the country's counselor education programs offered a gerontological counseling focus area, and nine offered a specialization in this area. An increased emphasis on group work training paralleled the emergence of counseling training for working with the elderly (Myers, 1989).

In summary, trends in the emergence of group work with older persons can be described as progressing from isolated groups for institutionalized persons conducted by nurses or other medical personnel to widespread groups conducted by all helping professionals in a variety of settings. Reminiscing treatment seems to have wrested groups from the hospitals and moved them into the community, which led to a proliferation in the types and topics of groups. As the gerontological counseling specialty emerged, and as group work became an increasingly important counseling strategy with the elderly, goals changed from treating severe disorders to facilitating healthy development, making transitions, finding meaning, and increasing empowerment for all older adults and their familial and professional caregivers.

Types of Groups~

Several types of groups for the elderly and their caregivers can be categorized based on topics, goals, settings, member capabilities, and counselor competencies. The most commonly cited categorization includes (a) reality orientation, (b) remotivation, (c) reminiscing and life review, and (d) psychotherapy groups (Burnside, 1986; Capuzzi et al., 1990; Thomas & Martin, 1992). Additional categories of groups include topic and theme-focused groups, groups for caregivers, and brief solution-focused groups.

Reality Orientation Groups

Reality orientation groups are designed to help regressed elderly persons suffering from dementia become more accurately oriented in time, place, and person. These groups help confused older persons correct misperceptions about their environment. Generally consisting of four or fewer members, the groups typically meet daily for periods of 30 to 40 minutes and utilize informational props. When first implemented, reality orientation groups met in hospitals or other inpatient facilities, and all institutional staff members were trained to continually reinforce reality orientation. Later, outpatient or day care groups were also found to be effective, particularly when family members and other caregivers were trained to reinforce the techniques used in the groups. The recommended schedules for meals, dates, weather, events, and other information can be displayed on boards in day care facilities or on calendars in homes as well as in institutions. Family members and paraprofessional caregivers can learn the same simple techniques and exercises used by institutional staff, such as waking people by calling their name.

Remotivation Groups

The primary goals of remotivation therapy groups are to stimulate involvement in life for those who have lost interest in the present and future, increase their communication and interaction with others, and help them progress toward resocialization. The groups historically met in classroom-type settings in hospitals and extended care facilities for 30 minutes to an hour three or four times a week for approximately 12 sessions, but variations of this organization have also proved effective (Dennis, 1986). Recommended membership usually consists of no more than 15 members who are oriented to time, place, and person. Discussion focuses on nonproblem topics, such as vacations, gardening, sports, pets, transportation, holidays, hobbies, families, or any other topic that might interest persons from diverse backgrounds. Burnside (1986) criticized the traditional remotivation group as being too rigid and disallowing feelings, leader spontaneity, touching, work-related topics, or refreshments. Group counselors and therapists conducting remotivation groups today would undoubtedly agree with Burnside. They generally utilize more flexibility and extend the groups outside institutional settings to intermediate care facilities, boarding houses, and community outpatient programs. This change in setting and membership has probably influenced the groups to decrease the classroom orientation, depend on process as well as on information, include work-focused topics, and allow discussion of feelings.

Whether the traditional or altered remotivation model is followed, the typical session covers one of the chosen topics and follows a five-step sequence of (a) creating a climate of acceptance by greetings, introductions, or other brief rapport-building exercises; (b) building a bridge to reality by encouraging members who are not sight impaired to read articles about the topic aloud; (c) developing a sense of sharing the world we all live in by using visual aids, props, and questions directly related to the topic; (d) encouraging an appreciation of the world of work and how it relates to our own work; and (e) providing a climate of appreciation by encouraging the members to express pleasure that the group has met and to plan the next meeting.

Reminiscing and Life Review Groups

Reminiscing and life review are generally considered to be synonymous, defined as a naturally occurring, universal process whereby experiences and unresolved conflicts are revived, surveyed, and reintegrated into people's views of their lives (Butler, 1963). Perhaps reminiscing, or retrieving memories from the past, is a part of life review, which adds working through unresolved conflicts and reintegrating the remembered experiences into a more meaningful view of one's life. Regardless, both result in a deepened sense of identity and connectedness with the world (Kaminsky, 1984). Reminiscing groups of six to eight members meet for 1 hour once or twice a week for six to twelve weeks. These groups originated in long-term care facilities but quickly became popular in independent environments, community settings, and nutrition centers.

Leaders of life review groups need more advanced skills in group process than do leaders of reality orientation groups or remotivation groups. Members are assumed to be more functional than members of the first two categories, but some counselors and therapists have suggested that reminiscing can also be very helpful for persons with diminishing short-term memory. A modified version of reminiscing can be used in families to help members of different generations understand central family values, behaviors, and themes, resolve learned repeated patterns that create problems, heal family wounds, and build or strengthen supportive relationships.

Psychotherapy Groups

Psychotherapy groups help older persons in institutional or community centers manage life stresses and new or ongoing unresolved, serious personal problems. Members typically have deep feelings of fear, loneliness, or anxiety that may be caused or exacerbated by aging (Capuzzi et al., 1990). Relatively small groups of six to eight members are recommended and may be conducted in institutional settings, outpatient mental health centers, or other treatment centers. Burnside (1986) noted differences between psychotherapy groups for younger and older members. In groups for the elderly, counselors and therapists often share more personal information, more physical contact is evident, silence may be more readily tolerated, greater emphasis is placed on reminiscence and life review, and the themes of loss, intergenerational conflicts, and struggling to adapt are more common. Counselors and therapists are advised to screen potential members carefully, assessing their competencies to process conflict and emotional issues. Group psychotherapists are advised to have gerontological training in addition to graduate counseling credentials.

Topic and Theme-Focused Groups

Support groups for older persons and groups with a specific focus have proliferated with the increase in these types of groups for other populations. Such groups target issues often shared by aging persons, such as health, retirement, loss, sexuality, career transitions, and spirituality. Skill-building groups help increase assertiveness, social skills, independent living competencies, and intrafamily communication skills. Counselors or therapists with specialties in psychodrama, music, art, dance, or scribotherapy may incorporate these techniques into their groups. Leaders of intergenerational groups with older persons mentoring younger persons who may be at risk need basic knowledge about developmental tasks over the life span. Most topic and theme-focused groups can be offered in a variety of settings. The size, composition, duration, and frequency of the group depend upon the group goals and member competencies.

Groups for Caregivers

Caregivers groups have typically been designed for family members, but groups for professionals working with older persons are also receiving limited attention. Since family members assume more than 80% of older persons' care, providing family members with support and information is crucial in improving the environment and quality of life for the entire family. The goals of caregivers groups for family members are to help members (a) plan safe care for the older relative, (b) obtain social support from other caregivers who understand the issues they face, (c) learn skills for dealing with the older person, (d) improve conflict management skills for use with professionals and other family members, and (e) find new ways to cope with changed roles, added responsibilities, and intensified stressors (Hinkle, 1991; Myers, Poidevant, & Dean, 1991). Because family members often have unrealistic expectations of older persons, group counseling and therapy can provide the psychoeducational forum through which they can realign their expectations with the older family member's functional level (Burnside, 1986).

Professionals also need opportunities for catharsis and support. The relationships between committed professionals and their older patients or clients may be different from the relationships between family members and their older relatives, but the bonds are often similarly strong. Nonfamilial caregivers, like family members, experience loss, guilt, stress, anger, depression, conflicts about care, burnout, and isolation. They have similar needs for networking, education, conflict resolution, and healing opportunities.

Membership in groups for caregivers varies with the goals of the group. For example, family members of persons with Alzheimer's disease may be assigned to groups based on the disease stage. Psychoeducational groups may have more members than groups for persons learning to deal with family conflicts about care. Professional caregivers groups are often small, ongoing, and open to new members.

Brief Solution-Focused Groups

Solution-focused groups may be ongoing or time limited (Coe & Zimpfer, 1996), but most solution-focused or solution-oriented groups are discussed in terms of brief counseling or therapy. Brief solution-focused groups do not necessarily constitute a distinct type of group, but they may represent a different approach in any of the previously described types, particularly the topic or theme-focused groups.

Since groups develop sequentially or cyclically over time through identifiable stages of growth (Donigian & Malnati, 1997), the term *brief group counseling or therapy* may appear to be an oxymoron or paradox to many group leaders. As the number of sessions increases, a greater sense of safety emerges, and what and how members disclose may change as a result (Donigian & Malnati, 1997). The healing capacity of groups depends upon the trust, cohesion, and congruence factors that increase as a group progresses through the stages of development (Yalom, 1985). The number of group meetings required for a specific group to achieve a significant healing potential depends upon many variables (Posthuma, 1996). Regardless of the group development model used, the healing capacity of groups is most often described as occurring after the transition or conflict stage. Unless the group regresses to an earlier stage for some reason, the healing capacity is thought to increase as group development progresses. The time it takes for healing to occur might vary according to the therapeutic factor being tracked. For instance, the educational goal of sharing information about the progression of Alzheimer's disease, or of accessing resources for older persons, may be achieved in one or a few sessions. However, developing social skills, experiencing the group as a family, or learning new behaviors to use in resolving family conflicts may occur only after trust and cohesion develop, usually following several meetings. Reality testing depends upon self-disclosure, and self-disclosure depends upon trust (Yalom, 1985). Because counselors and therapists are acutely aware of this relationship between healing and group development over time, they may fail to tap the benefits of problem-solving or solution-focused groups.

Coe and Zimpfer (1996) and LaFountain and Garner (1996, 1997) countered that solution-focused groups are not composed merely of content and that, as in longer term groups, process plays an important role. They identified stages of development in their solution-focused groups and listed clear benefits. Even Yalom (1985) described the need to sometimes regard the life of a group as a single session. He encouraged group leaders to strive to offer something useful to as many patients as possible, regardless of the number of group sessions. When the life of the group is to be only one or a few sessions, he advised counselors and therapists to avoid conflict, provide no time for issues to develop and be resolved, establish a set sequence of events, give direct support to members, and maintain moderate group structure. Hinkle (1991) recommended problem-solving approaches with caregivers of patients with Alzheimer's disease, noting that the approach enhances family relationships when families must make difficult decisions about an older family member.

Brief solution-focused groups generally meet from 1 to 6 times. The focus is always on members' competencies rather than deficits and on strengths rather than weaknesses. When issues about aging are discussed, the focus is on possibilities instead of limitations. The time focus is the future rather than the past or present (O'Hanlon & Weiner-Davis, 1989). Group leaders help members change the focus of discussions from how errors are made to how corrections are made. The goals of brief counseling and therapy are to empower the members, mobilize potentialities, reframe problems in solvable, autonomous terms, identify styles of cooperation, and create expectations of change (Talmon, 1990). Brief therapy advocates basically recommend that counselors and therapists minimize talk about problems or complaints of the past and present and maximize talk about solutions in the future (de Shazer, 1988; Walter & Peller, 1992).

Solution-focused principles can be used in a myriad of topic-specific or caregiver groups. Family members can learn to draw on their strengths and manage difficult situations with an older relative. Older persons who have lost a spouse can learn to live independently and build a new supportive network. These brief groups can serve as adjuncts to other groups designed for catharsis, ongoing support, and other long-term treatment effects. The briefer solution-focused groups may be offered concurrently with, before, or after other types of groups.

Littrell, Malia, and Vanderwood (1995) offered strong cautions for counselors and therapists planning brief groups. They advised counselors and therapists to not prematurely focus on one concern and exclude other, more serious concerns. When brief solution-focused counseling or therapy is offered as an adjunct treatment, sequencing is important. For example, when an older person has lost a spouse, grieving should not be ignored. Learning to live independently is important, but a group or other form of help to process the loss should accompany or precede the solution-focused group. They also urged counselors and therapists to remember that a brief group treatment approach is only one tool and is not appropriate in many situations. Counselors and therapists should resist using brief groups when long-term treatment is indicated, regardless of demanding client loads, third party restrictions, or administrative demands.

Multicultural Considerations ~

Although older persons share many common characteristics related to their developmental stage, their diversity mirrors the multiculturalism of the worlds in which they live. Culture consists of far more than racial or ethnic background, language, and socioeconomic status (Corey & Corey, 1997). Pedersen (1990) recommended that culture be broadly defined so that many relevant variables can be included. To consider all persons from Spanish-speaking countries as belonging to one culture ignores the rich differences between Cubans, Mexicans, Guatemalans, Panamanians, and Venezuelans and also the differences between several subcultures within those groups. Likewise, narrowly including all persons from African backgrounds in one culture may limit appreciation of the differences between people from French, Dutch, British, or American Caribbean islands or regional cultural differences among Afro-Americans.

Gillies and James (1994) encouraged professionals working with older persons, particularly those using reminiscing therapy, to pay close attention to the total experiences of the older person. Historical events, social movements, political and technological changes, and economic conditions experienced by older persons have molded their values, beliefs, behaviors, and feelings. Younger counselors or therapists can listen to older clients' stories to gain an understanding of the social and cultural contexts in which their values and behaviors were formed. Gillies and James (1994) approached counselors' need for specific cultural information by dividing the 20th century into decades and listing the important historical events that occurred in several different countries. This chronological approach gives professionals an index to culture-changing events.

Group work with older persons often presents a cultural challenge to counselors and therapists that is beyond the traditional scope of multicultural considerations. Older group members have lived through a history many counselors and therapists know only from books or media presentations. They often have come from countries and cultures that have been partly or wholly forgotten and lost in their American acculturation. In addition, the world is becoming smaller, and the activities and focus of mental health professionals are expanding to address international issues beyond the diversity challenges within U.S. borders. The older population is growing all over the world, and the cultural challenge to counselors and therapists is far greater than attending to specific populations or special interest groups. To meet the multicultural challenge of group work with older persons, counselors and therapists need to learn the history that formed the culture of their clients, understand the political, religious and economic forces that molded their differences, and recognize the clients' strengths that produced their values. Counselors and therapists may take many paths to learn about diversity, but probably the most important tack is to learn to listen to the stories of their older clients, because these stories are the living histories and the primary sources for understanding cultural diversity.

Group Examples ∼

The following are models for two types of groups, a life review group for older persons, and a brief, solution-focused group for older persons and their family caregivers who are considering changes in living arrangements for the older relative. Group structure and process are described for both models. In addition, leader skills, group goals, potential outcomes, membership, screening, settings, length, frequency, duration, size, and mobility of both models are discussed.

Life Review Group: My Life Quilt

A life review group is a reminiscing experience that helps older adults identify their life accomplishments, resolve conflicts in a nonthreatening atmosphere, and recapture meaning (Hayden & Thomas, 1990; Lewis & Butler, 1986). The group is characterized by a progressive return to the consciousness of past experiences, often resulting in a restored sense of resolution, balance, and wholeness (Butler, 1963; Ellison, 1981). Participants complete a developmental task of their life stage by taking stock of their lives and evaluating their goals, accomplishments, failures, and regrets (Kiernat, 1986).

Basically, counselors and therapists introduce open-ended topics such as a happy time, a sad time, school days, courting, holidays, family, cooking, tools, or toys. Generally, a different topic is introduced at each session, and the older participants informally relate remembrances about the topic. Their stories about the different topics become the bits and pieces that eventually converge into a meaningful, personal pattern. At first, the stories seem disconnected, and no orderly progression of memories is discernible. The stories are not organized into coherent narratives. However, the reminiscing process is ongoing, repetitious, and progressive, illuminating both conscious and unconscious material. Although the memories may seem disconnected, central values and attitudes become evident as new stories emerge and participants become more open in expressing feelings with the story content. Each new story can be seen to represent a piece of a person's life. If the pieces are put together, the person's life can be symbolically envisioned as a quilt made up of important story pieces. Perceptive group counselors and therapists can use group process to help older participants stitch their stories together in new ways to discover central themes and find the wholeness and harmony important in their search for meaning.

Pitfalls and Leader Skills   The major pitfall the leader of a life review or reminiscing group may encounter is to allow the group to become an overly structured series of stories. When this occurs, participants simply complete exercises with little or no interaction, expression of feeling, identification with other members, or introspection. Other common pitfalls include allowing competition with stories, socializing, or subgrouping; isolating members; and planning too much for single group sessions (Hayden & Thomas, 1990). Finally, failing to perceive and respond appropriately to depression and anxiety emerging from memories can create impediments to the group progress (Ellison, 1981).

Leader skills that contribute to the success of life review groups include the ability to detect central themes in the stories; understand participants' cultural histories; facilitate the accomplishments of older persons' developmental tasks; promote interaction, sharing, and the building of community; help members from diverse populations identify with one another; and use humor in the therapeutic process. Leaders of life review groups are cautioned to avoid behaviors that could be interpreted as condescending, authoritarian, stereotyping older persons, or impatience with members' limitations. Some researchers have recommended the use of mixed gender cofacilitators, because male and female leaders tend to elicit different memories (Ebersole, 1978a). However, a skilled facilitator of either gender may be sensitive to this tendency and able to counteract the gender effect.

Group Goals and Potential Outcomes   The common life review group goals are to (a) renew meaning in life by reviewing life experiences; (b) discover central themes in previously disconnected parts of life; (c) create a sense of community and belonging by sharing common concerns, experiences, and losses; (d) restore and maintain social interaction and a support network; (e) decrease isolation; (f) develop new ways of coping; (g) resolve previous life stage issues in a nonthreatening atmosphere to increase hope, wisdom, and ego integrity; (h) find order and affirmation in life patterns; and (i) discover the importance of one's uniqueness (Hayden & Thomas, 1990; Thomas, 1991; Thomas & Martin, 1997). Additional specific positive outcomes and effects of life review groups emerge as the groups progress. Members are helped to transcend difficult times and accept being older when they see how they steered through difficult times in the past. They discover wells of strength and courage and learn how to tap that strength to survive their final stage of life. They find moments of closeness with other group members when they have lost a great deal, and experience unconditional love. They enjoy the therapeutic effects of humor by sharing funny stories and lessons from mischievous escapades. They are often able to recover and heal lost relationships, make new friends, and learn to like themselves better. They are stimulated to continue growing and learning. They reap the benefits of helping and supporting others. In addition, they realize their roles as culture bearers from one generation to the next and discover the need to keep alive the values and ways of the past.

Membership, Screening, and Settings   Life review groups are appropriate for nutrition sites, domiciliary centers, adult day care centers, long-term care facilities, community agencies, and religious institutions. Membership should always be voluntary, and recruiting is best accomplished with personal group or individual presentations by the leader. The group description and goals should be concisely and clearly presented in both written and verbal communications, with positive aspects emphasized. Brief videos or role-plays may be used to show the group process to potential members. Selecting members in residential, day care, or nutrition centers should be the result of collaborative efforts with program staff.

The membership is homogeneous in that all participants are older persons, but it may be very heterogeneous with respect to cultural diversity. Depending upon the skills of the group leader, this diversity can significantly contribute to group success, goals accomplishment, community building, and interaction depth. Ebersole (1978a) recommended that groups be composed of equal numbers of male and female participants, but recent articles have also described success with single-gender reminiscing groups (Creanza & McWhirter, 1994) and with mixed groups in which there was not an emphasis on exact equal numbers (Waters, 1990b).

Some leaders may choose to implement a group screening process that is completed in the first session. Individual screening is often preferred, however, because many older persons have little experience with therapeutic groups and may be more comfortable expressing fears and asking questions in an individual screening session. Ebersole (1978a) emphasized individual screening, allowing participants to know the identity of other participants, and planning a group of compatible members. Screening also provides the opportunity to assess for special needs and provide a barrier-free setting for the participants. Members should be oriented in time and place, and they should be free from severe emotional, cognitive, or physical impairment that would significantly interfere with their ability to interact in a group. Finally, members should not be overly medicated or in crisis.

Length, Frequency, and Duration of Groups   Most reminiscing and life review groups meet for approximately 1 to 1½ hours once or twice a week for 10 to 12 weeks. Some leaders advocate reminiscing groups of much longer duration (20 or more weeks), arguing that adaptation to growing older, developing wisdom, and maintaining integrity take longer than a few weeks. Ebersole (1978a) described ongoing reminiscing groups that meet for a year or longer.

Increased illness in the fall and winter seasons often results in more absenteeism, which has led some group leaders to plan the groups for spring and summer (Kiernat, 1986). Others argue that activities are restricted in the colder months and plan fall and winter groups despite the projected absenteeism. The duration of these groups may be increased to compensate for the irregular attendance. Mid or late morning meetings are usually preferred to afternoon sessions (Kiernat, 1986). Consistency is important, and groups should always meet at the same time and place, giving members something definite to anticipate.

Group Size and Mobility   Recommended group size varies from five to nine members. Most counselors and therapists planning these groups prefer smaller groups of five or six members. Larger groups may be manageable, but the session length and membership may require adjustments to accommodate the larger size. When members have moderately impaired cognitive function, the size of the group and length of the sessions should probably be reduced.

Most groups are time limited and are closed to new members. Long-term ongoing groups are generally open, and the process and timing for adding new members are determined cooperatively by group members and group leaders.

Selecting Topics for Life Review   Topics for individual sessions can be chosen from an unlimited list by the leader or cooperatively chosen by the leader and participants. Groups may choose themes that follow a life-span or chronological order or may select random topics with no apparent pattern. Some group leaders stipulate that only positive topics or themes are appropriate, whereas other counselors or therapists argue that the inclusion of some losses, unresolved conflicts, and regrets is necessary for adequate life review. Burnside (1995) differentiated between reminiscing and life review by identifying reminiscence as including only positive memories and life review as integrating both positive and negative memories.

In selecting session themes, we recommend the following guidelines. First, include topics that elicit memories about both positive and negative experiences and feelings. Merely reminiscing happy times reduces the potential for increasing the ego integrity achievable from a more complete life review. Second, sequence the themes by beginning with stimulants for positive memories, following with topics about conflicts, regrets, or unhappy times after trust is established, and ending with topics that integrate both positive and negative memories. Third, seek a balance between more open ended topics that elicit broad discussions of memories and extremely specific topics. For instance, asking members to share memories about open-ended topics such as a very happy time or an unhappy time usually results in rich self-disclosures about values and feelings. Talking about a first toy, first kiss, or first pet can be fun, but such extremely specific topics can produce superficial levels of involvement and diminish the positive group effects. Finally, add gender, ethnic or culture-specific topics when appropriate for the membership. For example, a group of older women may benefit from relating how their roles changed during their lives. A group of older Japanese Americans could resolve some residual negative feelings about their experiences during World War II.

A model for a 10-session life review group following these guidelines is presented in the following paragraphs.

Session 1—A Happy Time. The leader begins the group with a brief get-acquainted procedure, reviews the group goals and procedures outlined during screening, and reminds the members of such group rules as maintaining confidentiality and refraining from giving advice.

Then the leader introduces the topic for the session by asking the members to think of a very happy time and to share their memories about that time with the group. If a response is very brief, the leader can add stimulants for expanded discussion by asking who was with the person, what made this a happy time, what were some long-term effects, or how the time changed the person's life.

As the members share their happy times, the leader finds connections between the past and present; attends to present feelings about the past, present, and others; includes isolated members in the discussion; fosters interaction and identification between members; points out the ongoing developmental aspects of living; and uses opportunities for closure.

Toward the end of the session, members are asked to share with other members ways in which they identify with them. Finally, the topic for the next session is introduced so the members can anticipate their next involvement.

Session 2—An Unhappy Time. Following the same procedures used in the first session, the members share an unhappy time. The leader may want to stimulate further discussion by asking about lessons learned or positive outcomes from the time, residual feelings, or how the time disclosed changed the members and their lives.

The leader begins to gradually shift responsibility to members for making the connections, looking for central themes, and finding similarities between participants. Members are encouraged to interact and help one another put their stories together. As with all other sessions, the topic for the next session is introduced.

Session 3—Holidays and Vacations. By the third session, members' stories will probably begin to reveal core values central to a their lives, and self-disclosure of deep feelings will occur. For example, when asked about the most valuable gift ever received at Christmas, one member in a life review group described a cherished item of clothing received from a very poor elderly female relative. The woman who gave the gift roamed over hills where sheep grazed and rubbed against fences, trees, and bushes to find wool. She would collect the small pieces of wool, then spin the wool and weave it into items of clothing for her family members. The man who had received the gift quietly expressed a myriad of feelings as he said he could not even remember what the woman looked like, but he would never forget the beauty of that gift, or its personal cost. This theme of doing rather than buying, and of finding gifts of love when economically poor, became evident in all of this member's stories. Questions to trigger memories about holidays or vacations could include queries about cultural customs or special foods associated with holidays, about modes of transportation, or about favorite vacations.

When introducing the next session's topic of cooking, tools, and toys, the leader may encourage members to bring old utensils, tools, or recipes to the session.

Session 4—Cooking, Tools and Toys. These more specific topics generally produce a lot of enjoyment. Members who bring old cooking utensils, tools, or toys have fun showing how they work, who used them, and how they were made. Values of ingenuity and learning to have fun, despite limited resources, usually emerge. For example, members often describe rattles made from blown-up pig bladders filled with peas or beans, or flutes made from cane. The value of not wasting emerges when members describe building furniture from cane, wood, willow branches, or discarded crates and processing clabber, butter, cream, sweet milk, or cheese from whole fresh milk.

Session 5—Historical Events. Members are asked to choose two or three historical events to share that had significant effects on their lives, their country, or society. The members' cultural histories influence the choice of topics. For example, the Depression may be meaningful for older Americans but irrelevant to those who are more recent immigrants from other countries.

Session 6—Courting and Marriage. In this, as in other sessions, members might share pictures or other mementos in relating their stories. Albums and diaries consume more time than allowed for adequate sharing, so members are encouraged to bring just one or two pictures or mementos.

Session 7—Mischievous Escapades. Family systems, communication styles, and discipline modes often become apparent in these stories. For example, a member in one life review group told how he and some other family members visited his grandfather, who had a prized buggy in a two-story barn. The boys disassembled the buggy during the night and reassembled it on top of the large barn. The grandfather was angry, but even more, he was perplexed about how to return the buggy to the ground. The dilemma was resolved after several days of frustrating problem solving and some moderate consequences for the boys, but with no apparent residual negative feelings.

Session 8—Experiences With Failure. This session provides the opportunity to integrate negative memories into a bigger picture that balances the negative and positive aspects of members' lives. Reframing failures as stepping stones to success or opportunities for learning can help resolve old intrapersonal conflicts.

Session 9—Family. Participants may share heirlooms, genograms, genealogies, or artistic representations of their families. The leader can ask many trigger questions to stimulate self-disclosure and expanded personal stories. The leader continues to assist group members in finding connections, central themes, and similarities and continues to encourage interaction. At the end of the session members are asked to take time during the next week to think about the stories they shared to date and identify the importance of each particular story in their lives.

Session 10—Closure: My Life Quilt. During this last meeting, each member is asked to put all of his or her stories together as if the stories are bits and pieces of a quilt that represents progress in the ongoing developmental aspects of living and to show how positives and negatives balance and come together to form a meaningful whole.

Finally, members are asked to relate what the group has meant to them and to evaluate the group experience. The leader may employ any appropriate evaluation measure or procedure. Leaders are strongly urged to design an evaluation that can contribute to group research.

Brief Solution-Focused Group

Many older persons, because of the loss of a spouse or diminishing health, are faced with the difficult decision of leaving their home, community, and social support systems and moving closer to their adult children or other close relatives in another location. The older person's family members are often torn between balancing jobs, raising their own children, and making frequent trips to care for the older relatives. The decision of whether an older person will remain in a familiar, comfortable environment without adequate care or move to a strange, unknown place close to family seems to be a no-win situation for both the older person and his or her family members. The following is a discussion and outline of a four-session, brief solution-focused group designed to help families prepare for this decision.

Decision Model   The basic model for the group is the Schlossberg, Waters, and Goodman (1995) 4 S model, which is a system for assessing and balancing assets and liabilities in the factors associated with any transition. The 4 S's represent (a) the situation, (b) self, (c) support, and (d) strategies. When applying this model to making decisions about the difficult transition of giving up one home for another, the *situation* is examined first. The counselor, the older person, and his or her family members discuss what triggered the transition, how timing affects the situation, how much of the situation can be controlled, the potential role changes caused by the transition, the permanence of the change, the amount of concomitant stress, previous experiences with similar transitions, and the attitudes of the family members and older person about the transition. In viewing the *self* factor, the family members and older person assess their personal and demographic characteristics, such as socioeconomic status, age, health, and stage of life. They also examine their psychological resources, such as values, ego development, and outlook. When examining the *support* factor, the family members and the older person identify assets and deficits in social support systems, such as intimate relationships, family units, friendships, community networks, and institutional programs. Finally, the family members and older person assess their *strategy*-building skills, whether they take direct action, how well they manage stress, and whether they compromise. Once the family members and older person identify their resources, they can balance the assets and liabilities and be better able to make a decision about moving. After assessing the 4 S's, they can make a decision based less on fear and more on information, strategies, possibilities, and hope.

Leadership   Co-facilitators are recommended for several reasons. First, different family units will display an array of family dynamics, and processing these dynamics might prove challenging for one leader. Second, the members will be divided into subgroups, and each subgroup will require a facilitator.

Leaders should be trained group counselors or therapists who have knowledge about family systems and solution-focused strategies. They should display warmth, empathy, democratic styles of leadership, support, and optimism. Finally, because this type of group is intergenerational, the leaders should have knowledge about the full range of human development, particularly the issues associated with aging.

Group Goals   The goals are to create options for older persons considering moving from their home and to help family members positively contribute to the decision by applying the 4 S coping resources model. Specifically, the goals are to help the families (a) identify resources and deficits in the community to which the older person may move, (b) compare resources and deficits in the old and new communities, (c) assess self and family to balance their strengths and liabilities, (d) learn new strategies for bridging transitions, and (e) form a tentative transition plan with alternatives.

Membership, Screening, and Settings   Forming this type of group would be difficult in a rural community, but gerontological counselors and therapists working in private practice, large community programs designed to help older persons in transition, and retirement communities often encounter families struggling with this decision. The group can consist of several montages of family constellations, basically two or three family units, each composed of an older relative and a few of their family members invested in the decision. Screening every potential family group member may become problematic, but adult children, older grandchildren, siblings, nieces, and nephews might be possible candidates, provided they are supportive, relatively nonjudgmental, and free of serious psychological or addictive problems. An important factor is an active and positive caring for their older relative. The older persons considering the move should be assessed for cognitive and physical functioning. This type of group would not be appropriate for persons with severe cognitive impairment but could accommodate persons with some physical deficits.

The preferred setting is the community to which the older person is considering moving. The sessions should be held in an easily reached and comfortable facility, which should also accommodate any special needs of members identified during screening.

Length, Frequency, and Duration   The recommended length of each group session is 2 hours. Depending on the size of the group, the length may be slightly shortened or extended. The frequency and duration of sessions will depend upon the members' abilities to attend. For example, if the older persons are temporarily residing in the community to which they are considering moving, or if they are on an extended visit with their family in this new community, the group may meet weekly for a month. If the older persons only occasionally visit, the group might meet monthly. Regardless of the format, ample time must be allowed between sessions for the group members to complete the homework assignments.

Group Size and Mobility   The key to determining the size of this type of brief solution-focused group is the number of family constellations. At least two separate families of varying sizes are required, and three or four family constellations are recommended. The group size could vary from 5 to 15 members. Since the group meets only four times, the group should be closed. Families wishing to join the group after the first session should be encouraged to be part of a new group.

Session 1. During the first session, the members introduce themselves and describe why the older persons are considering moving from their homes. They are encouraged to share their fears, how the move will change their roles, and their current support systems. Family members are asked to describe their views and the decision pros and cons.

The counselors or therapists will then describe the 4 S's decision model and the group goals, emphasizing the focus on a future solution rather than on present or past problems. In describing the goals, the group leaders caution members not to view the group as a vehicle for forcing a choice on anyone. The desired outcome is to help the group make more informed choices, with the empowered older person having the freedom to make as many of the decisions as possible. Appropriate group rules are also given at this time.

The group members are given community resource guides, lists of organizations, senior college and elder hostel brochures, descriptions of religious and community programs for older persons, calendars of cultural outlets, lists of opportunities for volunteer or paid work, and any additional information about resources in the new community.

Homework: The older family members are asked to thoroughly assess their social support system in their home communities and identify potentially similar resources in the new community. Family members may be asked to complete the same task, either alone or in cooperation with other family members and the older person. In the latter case, family members are cautioned not to push toward a single or final decision about the transition in living arrangements. Counselors and therapists may also have participants complete career and leisure assessment instruments or other assessment exercises.

Session 2. The group leaders begin the session by inviting the older people and their family members to share with the group those resources in the new community that they would like to more thoroughly explore. Whether older persons are considering living with or near their family members, transportation, meals, and housecleaning for the older relatives are common concerns for working family members. Older persons generally recognize similar needs but may concentrate more on friends, opportunities for social involvement, meaningful paid or volunteer work, or cultural and learning opportunities.

Assessment of personal characteristics and psychological resources that would help or hinder the transition can begin in earnest in the second session. This assessment is begun by self-disclosure and any exercise the counselors or therapists may create for self-assessment. Again, because the group is brief and solution-focused, emphasis is placed on positive characteristics that would make the transition more successful. When deficits are noted, balancing deficits with strengths is encouraged.

Homework: The older persons are asked to further explore those resources they might wish to use if they should move to the new community. The older persons are asked to visit centers of interest to them, make appointments with coordinators of any programs in which they may want to become involved, attend meetings of organizations to meet members, or visit churches, synagogues, or religious services of their choice. Family members may be given a similar assignment or may be asked to work cooperatively with the older person, again being cautioned not to push for their preferred options.

Session 3. The third session begins with the leaders subgrouping the members into one small group for the older persons from the different families and another group for the family members. Because the first steps in exploring a transition from one home to another can be discouraging, members of both subgroups are asked to share the positive and negative experiences they had while completing their assigned explorations. Negative themes may surface, such as old familial communication blocks or differences in values and attitudes. Basically, both subgroups may become acutely aware of the reality that this proposed transitional move may be far more difficult than previously anticipated. If the move from one community to another is not yet an absolute necessity, both communities can be explored to balance resource liabilities with assets.

At this juncture, regardless of the attractiveness of one choice over the other, strategies for remaining in the home community and for moving to the new community can be explored. Through the strategical planning of alternatives, compromises, and through building options, the members of each subgroup can change blocks to options. For example, older persons may devise a plan to strengthen their support and remain in their own communities. They may also move their major health care to medical facilities in their family members' community, thus removing the need for the family members to travel to the older persons' home communities during health crises. In addition, they may create a plan to alternate between living in their own community and the new community.

Homework: Members of both subgroups are asked to individually focus on possibilities and plan strategies for a variety of choices.

Session 4. The subgroups are maintained for the first part of this last session so members can share their strategies for varied ways of partially or wholly making the proposed transition from one home to another. They may incorporate others' ideas into their own strategies. Subgroups are then brought together to share their strategies.

Closure is accomplished by members having several possible options from which to select one or more plans. Members will have assessed their situations, their personal qualities, and available support. They may have devised a specific plan, but more realistically they will likely have developed a broader picture of the possibilities. What may have seemed like a trap can now be viewed as a full range of opportunities.

Closure is also accomplished by group leaders and members identifying needs for further counseling or therapy and follow-up. The older person or family members who will be most affected by the transition may want individual counseling or therapy. The single family unit may need family counseling or therapy. The older person may request help with grieving or with another aging issue. Follow-up is important, and the group leaders should make appropriate referrals, request permission to contact the group members in the future, and outline the follow-up procedures.

Training Recommendations ∿

Counseling and therapy students who intend to specialize in group work with older populations should consider training in the areas of group work and gerontological counseling and therapy in addition to training in counseling and therapy in general (Thomas & Martin, 1997). Students have several options for pursuing training. If a gerontological training program is not available, interested persons can follow an individualized plan that combines the standards of counseling or therapy, group work, and gerontology. Numerous community and mental health counseling programs accredited by the Council for the Accreditation of Counseling and Related Educational Programs (CACREP, 1994) are available throughout the country. Basic counseling and therapy competencies provide the foundation for persons working with older persons. Acquiring specific gerontological skills may present a challenge, because formal training may not be sufficiently available in many communities (Myers, 1992).

An outline of appropriate training for a gerontological specialty within community counseling programs is available in the CACREP (1994) standards, but only one accredited program is currently available. The *Gerontological Competencies for Counselors and Human Development Specialists* (Myers & Sweeney, 1990) includes minimal gerontological competencies. Those who are unable to enroll in a CACREP gerontological program can complete their basic degree program, take additional course work, and complete appropriate supervision to satisfy the requirements for the gerontological specialty certification offered by the National Board for Certified Counselors (NBCC, 1990).

The guidelines for training group specialists are specified in the Association for Specialists in Group Work's *Professional Standards for the Training of Group Workers* (ASGW, 1990). Basic knowledge and competencies for all group workers are listed, as well as required minimum course work and supervised practice. Levels of training are specified for task-work, guidance-psychoeducation, counseling-interpersonal problem solving, and psychotherapy-personality reconstruction groups. Counselors and therapists conducting groups for older persons should have achieved the level of training required for the type of group being conducted.

Until CACREP-approved gerontological programs become more widely available, persons wanting to specialize in group work with older persons will find it necessary to pursue training, certification, and supervision from several sources. In addition to receiving basic training, counselors and therapists must intensify their training in group work, human development, and gerontology. Although the National Board for Certified Counselors offers certification in gerontological counseling, courses from schools of social work or other disciplines may also be required. Several noncounseling gerontological certifications are available, but these must be combined with basic counseling or therapy training. Finally, continuing education and ongoing supervision in each of the three areas of counseling or therapy, group work, and gerontology are important in maintaining competencies.

Summary ～

A dramatic increase in the numbers and proportion of older adults in the United States during the 20th century has generated new interest in the mental health needs of this historically underserved population. Beginning in the 1950s, a number of group counseling formats emerged to meet the various emotional, physical, and social needs associated with this long developmental period.

Reality orientation groups help those suffering from dementia more accurately interpret their experiences and take increased responsibility for their own care. Remotivation groups stimulate socialization and involvement in those elderly people who are oriented but alienated. Reminiscing and life review groups foster a sense of connectedness, identity, and ego integrity for older adults in both inpatient and community settings. Psychotherapy groups focus on more intensive emotional conflicts and issues, while theme-focused groups provide support and therapy for older persons as they share a variety of specific concerns. Caregivers of the elderly, whether family members or professionals, can learn from one another and find needed support by sharing their experiences in a counseling or therapy group. Finally, a carefully planned brief solution-focused format can be successful in, among other things, helping members formulate and implement plans for change at times of transition.

Organizing the different types of groups requires specific considerations. The initial step involves assessing the appropriateness of the group mode and choosing the type of group to be conducted. Leader skills vary for each type of group. Membership, screening, and settings are different for each type of group. Decisions about group length, frequency, duration, size, and mobility must be carefully considered to maximize the attainment of potential group outcomes.

The cultural diversity of the entire country, as well as other countries, is represented in the older population. Historical differences in the life experiences of older generations from diverse backgrounds add a new dimension to multicultural awareness. This added dimension challenges group counselors and therapists to expand their knowledge and sensitivity about diversity by incorporating into their knowledge base the effects of specific historically significant events on different populations.

Working with the elderly requires training in the three areas of counseling and therapy, group skills, and gerontology. Few CACREP-approved gerontological programs are available, but there are numerous CACREP community and mental health counseling programs and medical or social work association approved gerontology programs. Persons interested in this specialty may need to develop individualized plans for receiving training in each of these areas.

As society ages, the challenges of meeting the mental health needs of the elderly will predictably increase. We hope that growing numbers of younger counselors and therapists will respond to the challenge as they come to appreciate the contributions of their living ancestors, thereby enriching their own personal and professional lives. Groups with older persons can help join the past with the present and add continuity, wholeness, balance, and meaning to the lives of participants and group leaders. Further, groups can build the bridges that create a larger community from several generations. These bridges connect the pathways we can all travel to help transform dreams into a healthy world for future generations.

References ∾

Association for Specialists in Group Work. (1990). *Professional standards for the training of group workers.* Alexandria, VA: Author.

Bledsoe, N., & Lutz-Ponder, P. (1986). Group counseling with nursing home residents. *Journal for Specialists in Group Work, 11,* 37–41.

Burke, M. J. (1986). Peer counseling for elderly victims of crime and violence. *Journal for Specialists in Group Work, 14,* 107–113.

Burnside, I. (Ed.). (1978). *Working with the elderly: Group process and techniques.* North Scituate, MA: Duxbury Press.

Burnside, I. (Ed.). (1986). *Working with the elderly: Group process and techniques* (2nd ed.). Boston: Jones & Bartlett.

Burnside, I. (1995). Themes in reminiscence groups with older women. In J. Hendricks (Ed.), *The meaning of reminiscence and life review* (pp. 159–171). Amityville, NY: Baywood.

Butler, R. N. (1963). The life review: An interpretation of reminiscence in the aged. *Psychiatry, 26*(1), 65–76.

Butler, R. N. (1975). *Why survive? Being old in America.* New York: Harper & Row.

Butler, R. N., & Lewis, M. I. (1977). *Aging and mental health: Positive psychosocial approaches* (2nd ed.). St. Louis, MO: C. V. Mosby.

Capuzzi, D., & Gossman, L. (1982). Sexuality and the elderly: A group counseling model. *Journal for Specialists in Group Work, 7,* 251–259.

Capuzzi, D., & Gross, D. (1980). Group work with the elderly: An overview for counselors. *Personnel and Guidance Journal, 59,* 206–211.

Capuzzi, D., & Gross, D. R. (Eds.). (1998). *Introduction to group counseling* (2nd ed.). Denver, CO: Love Publishing Company.

Capuzzi, D., Gross, D., & Friel, S. E. (1990). Recent trends in group work with elders. *Generations: Journal of the American Society on Aging, 14,* 43–48.

Chandras, K. V. (Ed.). (1992). Training in gerontological counseling [Special section]. *Counselor Education and Supervision, 32*(1).

Coe, D. M., & Zimpfer, D. G. (1996). Infusing solution-oriented theory and techniques into group work. *Journal for Specialists in Group Work, 21,* 49–57.

Cohen, P. M. (1983). A group approach for working with families of the elderly. *Gerontologist, 23,* 248–250.

Corey, M. S., & Corey, G. (1997). *Groups: Process and practice* (5th ed.). Pacific Grove, CA: Brooks/Cole.

Council for Accreditation of Counseling and Related Educational Programs. (1994). *Accreditation standards and procedures manual.* Alexandria, VA: Author.

Creanza, A. L., & McWhirter, J. J. (1994). Reminiscence: A strategy for getting to know you. *Journal for Specialists in Group Work, 19,* 232–237.

Dennis, H. (1986). Remotivation therapy. In I. Burnside (Ed.), *Working with the elderly: Group process and techniques* (2nd ed., pp. 187–197). Boston: Jones & Bartlett.

de Shazer, S. (1988). *Clues: Investigating solutions in brief therapy.* New York: Norton.

Dickman, I. R. (1979). *Ageism—discrimination against older people* (Public Affairs Pamphlet No. 575). (Available from Public Affairs Pamphlets, 381 Park Avenue, South, New York City, NY 10016).

Donahue, E. M. (1986). Reality orientation: A review of the literature. In I. Burnside (Ed.), *Working with the elderly: Group process and techniques,* (2nd ed., pp. 165–176). Boston: Jones & Bartlett.

Donigian, J., & Malnati, R. (1997). *Systemic group therapy: A triadic model.* Pacific Grove, CA: Brooks/Cole.

Ebersole, P. P. (1978a). Establishing reminiscing groups. In I. Burnside (Ed.), *Working with the elderly: Group process and techniques* (pp. 236–254). North Scituate, MA: Duxbury Press.

Ebersole, P. P. (1978b). A theoretical approach to the use of reminiscence. In I. Burnside (Ed.), *Working with the elderly: Group process and techniques* (pp. 139–154). North Scituate, MA: Duxbury Press.

Ellison, K. B. (1981). Working with the elderly in a life review group. *Journal of Gerontological Nursing, 7,* 537–541.

Erikson, E. (1963). *Childhood and society* (2nd ed.). New York: Norton.

Folsom, J. (1968). Reality orientation for the elderly mental patient. *Journal of Geriatric Psychiatry, 1,* 291–307.

Fowles, D. G. (1995). *A profile of older Americans: 1995.* [Online]. Washington, DC: Administration on Aging. (Available: http://www.aoa.dhhs.gov/aoa/pages/profil95.html.)

Gazda, G. M. (1989). *Group counseling: A developmental approach* (4th ed.). Boston: Allyn & Bacon.

Gillies, C., & James, A. (1994). *Reminiscence work with old people.* London: Chapman & Hall.

Gladding, S. T. (1991). *Group work: A counseling specialty.* New York: Merrill.

Gladding, S. T., & Thomas, M. C. (Eds.). (1991). Group work with the aging and their caregivers [Special issue]. *Journal for Specialists in Group Work, 16*(3).

Hammond, D. B., & Bonney, W. C. (1983). Counseling families of the elderly: A group experience. *Journal for Specialists in Group Work, 8,* 198–204.

Havighurst, R. G., & Glasser, R. (1972). An exploratory study of reminiscence. *Journal of Gerontology, 27,* 243–253.

Hawkins, B. L. (1983). Group counseling as a treatment modality for the elderly: A group snapshot. *Journal for Specialists in Group Work, 8,* 186–193.

Hayden, R., & Thomas, M. C. (1990, March). *Life review groups for the aging: Pathways to meaning.*

Paper presented at the American Association for Counseling and Development Convention, Cincinnati, OH.

Hinkle, J. S. (1991). Support group counseling for caregivers of Alzheimer's disease patients. *Journal for Specialists in Group Work, 16,* 185–190.

Kaminsky, M. (Ed.). (1984). *The uses of reminiscence: New ways of working with older adults.* New York: Haworth Press.

Kaplan, J. (1953). *A social program for older people.* Minneapolis: University of Minnesota Press.

Kiernat, J. M. (1986). The use of life review activity. In I. Burnside (Ed.), *Working with the elderly: Group process and techniques* (2nd ed., pp. 298–307). Boston: Jones & Bartlett.

Kubie, S., & Landau, G. (1953). *Group work with the aged.* New York: International Universities Press.

LaFountain, R. M., & Garner, N. E. (1996). Solution-focused counseling groups: The results are in. *Journal for Specialists in Group Work, 21,* 128-143.

LaFountain, R. M., & Garner, N. E. (1997). Solution-focused counseling groups. In S. T. Gladding (Ed.), *New developments in group counseling* (pp. 9–11). Greensboro, NC: ERIC/CASS Publications.

Lewis, M. I., & Butler, R. N. (1974). Life review therapy: Putting memories to work in individual and group psychotherapy. *Geriatrics, 29,* 165–169, 172-173.

Lewis, M. I., & Butler, R. N. (1986). Life-review therapy: Putting memories to work. In I. Burnside (Ed.), *Working with the elderly: Group process and techniques* (2nd ed., pp. 50–59). Boston: Jones & Bartlett.

Linden, M. (1953). Group psychotherapy with institutionalized senile women: Study in gerontological human relations. *International Journal of Group Psychotherapy, 3,* 150–170.

Littrell, J. M., Malia, J. A., & Vanderwood, M. (1995). Single-session brief counseling in a high school. *Journal of Counseling and Development, 73,* 451–458.

Malde, S. (1988). Guided autobiography: A counseling tool for older adults. *Journal of Counseling and Development, 66,* 290–293.

Mardoyan, J. L., & Weis, D. M. (1981). The efficacy of group counseling with older adults. *Personnel and Guidance Journal, 60,* 161–163.

Marram, G. D. (1973). *The group approach in nursing practice.* St. Louis, MO: C. V. Mosby.

Myers, J. E. (1989). *Infusing gerontological counseling into counselor preparation: Curriculum guide.* Alexandria, VA: American Association for Counseling and Development.

Myers, J. E. (Ed.). (1990). Techniques for counseling older persons [Special issue]. *Journal of Mental Health Counseling, 12*(3).

Myers, J. E. (1992). Competencies, credentialing, and standards for gerontological counselors: Implications for counselor education. *Counselor Education and Supervision, 32,* 34–42.

Myers, J. E., Poidevant, J. M., & Dean, L. A. (1991). Groups for older persons and their caregivers: A review of the literature. *Journal for Specialists in Group Work, 16,* 197–205.

Myers, J. E., & Sweeney, T. J. (1990). *Gerontological competencies for counselors and human development specialists.* Alexandria, VA: American Association for Counseling and Development.

National Board for Certified Counselors. (1990). *National certified gerontological counselor application packet.* Greensboro, NC: Author.

O'Hanlon, W. H., & Weiner-Davis, M. (1989). *In search of solutions: A new direction in psychotherapy.* New York: Norton.

Pedersen, P. (1990). The multicultural perspective as a fourth force in counseling. *Journal of Mental Health Counseling, 12,* 93–94.

Posthuma, B. W. (1996). *Small groups in counseling and therapy.* Boston: Allyn & Bacon.

Salisbury, H. (1975). Counseling the elderly: A neglected area in counselor education and supervision. *Counselor Education and Supervision, 14,* 237–238.

Schlossberg, N. K., Waters, E. B., & Goodman, J. (1995). *Counseling adults in transition* (2nd ed.). New York: Springer.

Shere, E. (1964). Group therapy with the very old. In R. Kastenbaum (Ed.), *New thoughts on old age.* New York: Springer.

Silver, A. (1950). Group psychotherapy with senile psychiatric patients. *Geriatrics, 5,* 147–150.

Talmon, M. (1990). *Single-session therapy: Maximizing the effect of the first (and often only) therapeutic encounter.* San Francisco: Jossey-Bass.

Thomas, M. C. (1991). Their past gives our present meaning: Their dreams are our future. *Journal for Specialists in Group Work, 16*(32).

Thomas, M. C., & Martin, V. (1992). Training counselors to facilitate the transitions of aging through group work. *Counselor Education and Supervision, 32,* 51–60.

Thomas, M. C., & Martin, V. (1997). Helping older adults age with integrity, empowerment and meaning through group counseling. In S. T. Gladding (Ed.), *New developments in group counseling,* (pp. 43–45). Greensboro, NC: ERIC/CASS Publications.

Walter, J. L., & Peller, J. E. (1992). *Becoming solution-focused in brief therapy.* New York: Brunner/Mazel.

Waters, E. B. (Ed.). (1990a). In-depth views of issues for aging [Special issue]. *Generations: Journal of the American Society on Aging, 14*(1).

Waters, E. B. (1990b). The life review: Strategies for working with individuals and groups. *Journal of Mental Health Counseling, 12,* 270–278.

Waters, E. B., & Goodman, J. (1990). *Empowering older adults: Practical strategies for counselors.* San Francisco: Jossey-Bass.

Yalom, I. (1985). *The theory and practice of group psychotherapy* (3rd ed.). New York: Basic Books.

Yalom, I., & Terrazas, F. (1968). Group therapy for psychotic elderly patients. *American Journal of Nursing, 68,* 190–194.

Zimpfer, D. G. (1987). Groups for the aging: Do they work? *Journal for Specialists in Group Work, 12,* 85–92.

17

Group Counseling for
Issues Related to Suicide

Ardis Sherwood-Hawes

Suicide is a universal phenomenon. The act of killing oneself transcends differences in race, gender, age, economic status, and ethnic background, and its devastating consequences can ubiquitously impact any family, any community, and any society. Adolescents and older adults are the populations most at risk for suicidal behavior. In 1988 the suicide rate for adolescents was 13.1 per 100,000, and the rate for adults who are older was 21.5 per 100,000 (Osgood & Brant, 1990).

The suicide rate in adolescents and children has increased by 300% over the past 30 years (Gilliland & James, 1988), and suicide is now the second leading cause of death in the United States for adolescents between ages 11 and 24 (Capuzzi & Gross, 1996). These data do not include children who attempt suicide or who manifest self-destructive ideation. More than 25,000 children under age 12 are hospitalized annually because they are at risk for suicide (Stiles & Kottman, 1990).

The rate of suicide is even higher among people of age 65 and older (Osgood & Brant, 1990; Saul & Saul, 1988). The ratio of completed suicides for women over 65 is double the rate for the U.S. population, and for men over 65, the ratio is four times the national average (Gilliland & James, 1988). Women who have a history of childhood sexual abuse (Davidson, Hughes, George, & Blazer, 1996) and people with AIDS (Mancoske, Wadsworth, Dugas, & Hasney, 1995) have a significantly increased risk for suicide attempts. More attempts at suicide are made by adolescents (ages 15–24) and women (ages 25–64), but older adults and men (ages 25–64) have more successful completions of suicide and choose more lethal ways to die (Henry, 1987; Saul & Saul, 1988; Vidal, 1989). People who attempt suicide are at greatest risk for a repeat attempt during the first 2-year period following the original attempt, and adolescent attempters have a high rate of repeating the attempt during the first few months after attempting suicide. Despite this dire prognosis, suicide attempters are seldom referred for further psychological services (Curran, 1987; Nordstrom, Asberg, Aberg-Wistedt, & Nardin, 1995).

Considering that suicide attempts and suicide completions are significantly underreported, the national statistics are even more alarming (Allberg & Chu, 1990; Gutstein & Rudd, 1988; Saul & Saul, 1988; Stefanowski-Harding, 1990). Due to the increasing rates of suicide across age-groups in the United States, the development and implementation of suicide prevention and intervention have become a societal priority. However, literature that scientifically examines the efficaciousness of prevention, intervention, and postvention programs is surprisingly scarce and inadequately supported (Rudd et al., 1996).

> A number of researchers note that mortality data contain intentional cover-ups by physicians or family members or misclassification as accidental death when evidence of suicide is insufficient. It has been suggested that a more accurate picture might be revealed by multiplying given statistics two-, maybe threefold. (Gutstein & Rudd, 1988, p. 5)

Assessment of Suicide Risk

Assessment or identification of a propensity toward suicidal behaviors is a complex and difficult task. A vast amount of research has been directed at identifying common denominators that cause suicidal behavior, but these investigations have failed to establish any outstanding characteristics manifested by all people who attempt or complete suicide. Researchers have agreed, however, on a number of interactional factors that are correlated with suicidality (Capuzzi & Gross, 1996; Gilliland & James, 1988). Suicide is considered to be a process, and suicide attempts and completions are the climax of this process (Bogdaniak & Coronado, 1987). A comprehensive approach that incorporates psychological, behavioral, social, and situational factors and examines the interaction among these factors can enable professionals to comprehend the common clues and patterns associated with suicidality and facilitate a competent estimation of the risk for suicide.

Suicide is rarely precipitated by a single factor. Depression is the major predictor of suicidal behavior, and vulnerability increases when both depression and impulsiveness are present (Capuzzi & Gross, 1989; Garfinkel et al., 1988). There are also significant correlations between feelings of hopelessness, depression, and suicidal behavior (Asarnow, Carlson, & Guthrie, 1987). The emotional features of depression (e.g., sadness, low self-esteem, feelings of helplessness, lack of control over situations and self, despair, self-degradation) can affect the way depressed people view the world. These feelings and beliefs can produce a frame of reference that can generate certain dysfunctional and debilitating coping mechanisms (e.g., withdrawal and isolation, anhedonia, low tolerance for frustration, dependent behaviors, inept problem-solving and communication skills, cognitive rigidity, anxiety). Depressive behaviors can reduce the ability to develop solutions to troublesome situations and amplify feelings of hopelessness. In addition, they can elicit negative reactions and rejection from other people, further diminishing weakened emotional bonds.

Inadequate coping skills lessen the chance that people who are depressed will experience positive events and receive environmental reinforcers, and lack of these skills increases the probability of aversive reinforcement. Alienation and negative experiences reinforce the nullifying emotions and concepts. The devastating effects of episodes of depression on the life circumstances of people who are depressed can lead to lasting maladaptive compromises in personal adjustment, and these perverse accommodations, which increase with successive episodes, intensify the risk of suicide. Losses (e.g., divorce, status, death, emotional ties) compound this risk (Garfinkel et al., 1988). Often, individuals who are prone to suicide have difficulty expressing their thoughts, feelings, and needs, and they are consequently unable to discuss and resolve issues that surround disappointments and losses (Capuzzi & Gross, 1996).

Research (Capuzzi & Gross, 1996; Garfinkel et al., 1988; Gutstein & Rudd, 1988; Henry, 1987; Morgan, 1981) has identified the following as crucial variables that can denote potential suicidal behavior:

- Depression.
- Psychological pain.
- Difficulty with interpersonal relationships.
- Inability to adjust and cope.
- Cognitive constriction (rigidity in thinking).
- Low self-esteem.
- Social isolation.
- Anxiety and distress.
- Hostility and rage.
- Poor communication skills.

Counselors who are assessing suicidal risk must be able to identify the warning signs of suicidality and competently determine the severity of the behaviors and clues.

Certain precipitating behaviors, events, and life circumstances increase the probability that suicide-prone individuals will actively initiate the climax of the suicide process. One of the best predictors for determining suicidal risk is a history of previous attempts at suicide (Garfinkel et al., 1988). Another major clue to the probability of overt suicidal behavior is the severity of depression the person manifests (Hatton, Valente, & Rink, 1977a). Counselors who are assessing the possibility of suicidal risk in an individual should investigate:

- the seriousness of the crisis.
- the person's coping strategies and current ability to problem solve.
- any prior history of suicide ideation.
- the individual's direct statements or indirect hints of intent to die.
- the individual's present affective or mental status.
- the individual's social resources.

- the individual's personal resources.
- the specificity of the suicide plan.

In addition, the following factors indicate future danger of suicidal risk (Bogdaniak & Coronado, 1987; Capuzzi & Gross, 1996; Garfinkel et al., 1988; Gutstein & Rudd, 1988; Hatton et al., 1977a):

- Excessive use of alcohol and/or drug dependency.
- Poor impulse control.
- History of acting out behaviors.
- Prolonged depression.
- Dramatic personality changes.
- Acts of making final arrangements.
- Family conflicts and stressors.
- Sudden mood reversal.
- Intense desire to die.
- Tendency for suicide attempts to increase on days significant to client.
- Family history of suicide.

When people at risk for suicide are given the opportunity to openly discuss and explore the possibility of suicide, they feel relieved and have less suicide ideation (Capuzzi & Gross, 1996).

Suicide Intervention Groups〜

Although the group method has been used extensively with a wide variety of mental health concerns, the traditional treatment for suicidal clients has followed the individual model (Hipple, 1982). Despite numerous indications of the positive benefits of the group approach for supporting and treating suicidal populations (Motto, 1979), counselors have been advised not to select individuals who are severely depressed or suicidal for groups (Frey, Motto, & Ritholz, 1983). This reluctance to use the group model for suicidal clients has been attributed to administrative resistance (Frey et al., 1983; Robertson & Mathews, 1989), concerns about professional competency when working with suicidal clients, and fear of legal liability in case of a suicide (Motto, 1979; Robertson & Mathews, 1989). In addition, Kaplan and Sadock (1972) have suggested that counselors may have a tendency to avoid working with these groups because some of the themes typically dealt with in the group, such as death and dying, can evoke anxiety reactions in the group leader.

During the 1970s, a movement began toward using the group approach as a remedial intervention for people who were depressed and at high risk for suicide (Asimos, 1979). Although the effectiveness of this treatment modality has been widely documented (Robertson & Mathews, 1989), most of these reports have been descriptive and impressionistic, lacking the controlled clinical trials necessary to impartially assess the therapeutic effect of group work with suicidal people (Frey et al., 1983). The literature has also seriously neglected research reports describing how to use group treatment as a primary format for suicide intervention (Hipple, 1982). The infrequent reports of controlled studies that have investigated the effectiveness of group work with suicidal clients indicate that this treatment modality is a potent intervention for people at risk for suicide.

An epidemiologic study by Billings (in Frey et al., 1983) that compared the effect of various treatment modalities (individual therapy, traditional group therapy, day treatment centers, inpatient therapy, no treatment) in reducing mortality rates in suicidal persons found that the special suicide group was the most effective intervention. In a study designed to further clarify the causal relationship between treatment and outcome with this population, Frey et al. (1983) researched the influence of a special group therapy program for people at high risk for suicide and, like Billings, reported a significant reduction in mortality rates among therapy group members when compared to people who had received outpatient services or no treatment at all. Patsiokas and Clum (1985) measured the effectiveness of three modes of intervention for suicidal persons: a problem-solving focused group, a cognitive-restructuring focused group, and a nondirective control group consisting of 10 individual unstructured therapeutic sessions. Suicide ideation scores were reduced by 60% in the problem-solving group, dropped by 43% in the cognitive-restructuring group, and were not lowered in the control group.

Counselors who use the group therapy model as their primary treatment program for suicidal individuals have been positive in their assessment of the efficacy of this approach (Asimos, 1979; Comstock & McDermott, 1975; Frey et al., 1983; Motto, 1979; Robertson & Mathews, 1989). Reports repeatedly mention the special curative factors of suicide groups, such as the social support network of the group treatment and its reparative impact for persons who feel hopeless, helpless, and isolated (Asimos, 1979). Comstock and McDermott (1975) further stated that:

> Group therapy offers appropriate means for dealing with many problems commonly found among suicidal patients, including poor impulse control, lack of future orientation, feelings of sadness and low self-esteem, inability to recognize areas of competence, and failure to accept personal responsibility. (p. 44)

The protective atmosphere of the group provides a unique environment in which members can, as noted by Robertson and Mathews (1989):

- satisfy their need to belong, to be accepted, and to give and receive love.
- become more socially integrated as group members exchange offers of support, understanding, and hope.
- disclose information about themselves and receive feedback from other group members.
- improve communication and coping skills.
- learn problem-solving techniques.
- recognize and practice positive thought patterns.
- come to understand that their concerns are not unique and that they are not alone.

In addition, the group offers an unparalleled social resource for corrective influence (Dinkmeyer, 1975). Suicide intervention groups can:

- focus on practical issues of the problems of daily living.
- eliminate the customary resistance to treatment programs (Robertson & Mathews, 1989).
- give group members an opportunity to express emotions and to vicariously experience the feelings of other group members (Goldman, 1986).
- provide a here-and-now experience that allows group members to observe one another's attitudes and behaviors (Dinkmeyer, 1975).
- be informational and educational, and motivate members to attempt new, action-oriented coping strategies (Poey, 1985).

Because the group offers many positive experiences to the suicidal person, Hipple (1982) suggested that counselors for suicidal clients seriously consider this modality as an option for treatment.

Guidelines for Group Leaders

Characteristics of the Group Leader

Potential counselors for groups that will focus on issues related to suicide should be grounded in the basic theories of group counseling, be thoroughly trained in the fundamental principles of group dynamics, and be knowledgeable about group processes and procedures. Prospective counselors also must have received extensive training in the fundamentals of working with suicidal or depressed people and be able to recognize the signs and symptoms of the presuicidal syndrome (Robertson & Mathews, 1989). Basic counselor qualities should include:

- emotional maturity.
- an exceptionally high level of self-awareness.
- accurate listening and responding skills.
- poise.
- nonjudgmental demeanor.
- a stable self-concept.
- the ability to analyze and accurately diagnose potential problems.

In addition, the following qualifications are recommended for group leaders of special suicide groups:

1. Leaders are knowledgeable about the ethical and professional issues specific to working with suicide-related groups, recognize their own individual moral beliefs, and comprehend how these values can relate to the issues of autonomy and responsibility (Clements, Sider, & Perlmutter, 1983).
2. Leaders have had personal therapy and have explored and appreciate any personal issues, biases, or unfinished business that might limit their ability to function optimally as a group leader.

3. Leaders maintain current knowledge of new research in group work and suicidality.

4. Leaders are licensed, certified, and covered by professional liability insurance.

5. Leaders obtain personal group experience by participating as a group member in a self-exploration or counseling group.

6. Leaders have the ability to effectively co-facilitate a group. Because working with suicidal people can be emotionally and physically exhausting, Hipple (1982) suggested that the group should be led by two professional counselors. Ideally, three counselors should be assigned to the group to ensure that at least two co-facilitators are present at each group session.

7. Leaders are confident in their ability to correctly diagnose an individual's degree of lethality and are willing to make an instantaneous, decisive intervention (e.g., involuntary hospitalization).

8. Leaders have a high tolerance for dependent behavior, because suicidal individuals can become extremely needy and demanding during emotional crises. In addition, because a suicide crisis can occur at any time, counselors ideally have flexible schedules so they can be present in times of crisis (Gilliland & James, 1988; Klein, 1985; Motto, 1979; Robertson & Mathews, 1989).

Role and Function of the Group Leader

Suicide intervention group members need a particularly safe milieu to talk about their feelings, concerns, thoughts, and behaviors; thus, suicide-related groups must provide participants with an environment of unconditional acceptance and complete support. To create a nonthreatening atmosphere for the group, leaders should introduce to the group as few formal expectations as possible (Hipple, 1982). These groups deal primarily with issues of life and death, and group leaders have to sensitively facilitate the group in an active, directive, and gentle confrontive style. Leaders must be comfortable in energetically managing the group process. When a member has a crisis, the condition must be discussed immediately, problem-solving techniques have to be implemented quickly, and alternative behaviors must be promptly rehearsed and adopted.

Short-Term Group Approach

The group approach as an intervention for suicidal people is generally initiated as a short-term method of treatment. This model typically ranges from 6 to 60 sessions, rarely uses psychodynamic exploration, and customarily focuses on a specific theme or treatment modality (Poey, 1985). The short-term approach is considered to be an effective intervention during and after the crisis phase of suicidal behavior. Frey et al., (1983) found that the strongest beneficial changes in short-term group interventions for people at risk for suicide occur within the first five group sessions and suggested that early treatment programs are crucial in preventing additional suicidal behaviors. They noted that "the special suicide group appears to support the natural and oftentimes slow healing that occurs after a suicide crisis" (p. 291).

Throughout this acute crisis period, the person may be out of control, disoriented, and unable to make appropriate choices. Individuals in crises may have frequent suicidal thoughts and manifest overt suicidal behaviors. They may have a limited capacity to tolerate anxiety and may not have the resources necessary for doing psychological group work. The support-oriented short-term group, directed predominately toward symptomatic relief, social maintenance from other group members, understanding the precipitating events, and developing and implementing adaptive coping strategies, more effectively meets the needs of individuals who have suicidal impulses (Hipple, 1982).

Short-Term Versus Long-Term Approach

The purpose of short-term groups is to help members meaningfully identify core conflicts and begin to examine personal implications of those issues. These groups are not designed for extensive exploration of deep-seated emotional conflicts or to help members achieve lasting structural changes in personality (Klein, 1985). Comstock and McDermott (1975) advocated a two-step approach for group intervention for suicidal clients:

1. Short-term crisis intervention is necessary to confront the suicidal behaviors and to facilitate exploration of dysfunctional emotions and actions.
2. Because the crisis interventions of the short-term approach may have a limited effect on individuals who are prone toward suicide, the additional strategies of the long-term approach are necessary to alter the self-destructive tendencies that result from ongoing, submerged psychological problems.

Suicide can be defined as a crisis situation, and suicidal behaviors are then considered to be manifestations of that crisis (Hatton, Valente, & Rink, 1977b). Crisis is a state in which intolerable barriers obstruct life goals and aspirations are perceived as no longer attainable. These obstacles, which exceed the person's resources and coping mechanisms, can arise from both developmental and situational events, and unresolved crises can generate chronic and long-term dysfunctional modes of behavior. Often the original crisis and its accompanying discomfort will disappear, and the person may feel the crisis has been resolved. In some cases, memory of the crisis may be repressed from awareness and, during times of stress, may resurface in self-destructive behaviors such as suicide attempts. Individuals may seek help during a suicidal crisis and may seem to achieve a sense of equilibrium during the counseling sessions, but unless the original crisis is resolved, the primordial trauma will often emerge the moment new stressors are presented, and the person will again have sudden, extreme anxiety, agitation, or pathology (Gilliland & James, 1988).

As individuals move out of the crisis period, their issues will change, and they will need to explore deeper levels of emotions and underlying personality disturbances. Group leaders can gradually make the transition toward the processes of the long-term approach (e.g., examination of unconscious material, less effort to avoid anxiety-provoking interactions, exploration of negative effect, less directive leadership), or they can refer the members to appropriate treatment programs (Hipple, 1982). The methods and practices of the long-term approach are beyond the scope of this chapter. The focus herein is on the procedures and processes of the short-term approach.

Structure of the Short-Term Approach

Treatment groups use both the traditional format of a closed group and the nontraditional format of an open-ended, or "drop-in," group (Motto, 1979). The closed group model does not allow new members to join after the original group has been formed. Closed groups are preferable for insight-oriented groups because they promote a stable, consistent environment that encourages the disclosure process and feelings of solidarity among group members. The open group format allows new members to join the group at any time and often gives participants the option of choosing when and how often they will attend group sessions (Motto, 1979).

Many professionals prefer the open group format for the crisis-oriented, short-term process (Asimos, 1979; Comstock & McDermott, 1975; Motto, 1979; Robertson & Mathews, 1989). During the acute phase of suicidal behavior, which is generally short in duration, the more intense therapeutic processes of exploration in the closed group may heighten the person's feelings of anxiety and depression (Asimos, 1979). The open model also ensures that anyone who is having suicidal impulses will have the opportunity to immediately join a group and benefit from it.

Asimos (1979) contended that members of suicide intervention groups will feel less threatened if there is a "deemphasis on contractual agreements and imposed expectations regarding [group] attendance and participation" (p. 110). In her groups, "members are told to come when they want to, and need to, and there are no guilt feelings if they miss a meeting because they have broken no contract" (p. 110). She further asserted that the open group format offers a benign environment of unconditional acceptance in which members learn that they are worthy of love and, thus, gradually come to understand that they can safely share their negative thoughts and emotions without loss of self-esteem or fear of rejection. Conversely, research by Rudd et al. (1996) indicated that a closed, structured, target-specific group approach is more effective in the comprehensive and persistent reduction of suicidal ideation and behavior. The researchers compared the efficacy of an intensive time-limited, small-group format that targeted the development of adequate problem-solving skills and social competence to a treatment-as-usual modality (a combination of inpatient care, outpatient care, open groups, and individual therapy). Members of the experimental group spent 9 hours a day in an outpatient treatment setting for a 2-week period. The sessions stressed the acquisition of problem-solving skills but also focused on maladaptive behaviors, cognitive restructuring, goal setting, communication, self-awareness, anger control, stress management, adaptive coping, and interpersonal relationships.

Selection of Group Members

Recruiting and selecting members for a suicide intervention group can be a formidable and complicated task. Hipple (1982) stated:

> A common myth about starting such a group is that not enough appropriate clients are available at any given time to warrant the beginning of such a special group. It is my contention that many agencies are not aware of how many clients who might profit from such a group experience are on the case role at any given time. (p. 247)

He suggested that if the group has an open, continuous format, it can be initiated with as few as two or three members. Group members then can be progressively enrolled and terminated throughout the group's existence.

When forming a group, one of the first issues that counselors face is choosing between a heterogeneous and a homogeneous composition. The heterogeneous group is composed of people who do not share a specific symptom or circumstance. Group members are dissimilar in their problems, ages, gender, personality traits, strengths, limitations, and socioeconomic backgrounds. The heterogeneous group promotes self-disclosure and has a greater potential to influence personality change and behavior modification (Klein, 1985).

In contrast, the members of a homogeneous group share a common condition, and the group focus is toward alleviating that condition. Homogeneous groups tend to be more didactic, and members are prone to superficially interact and self-disclose (Klein, 1985). In groups with a common focus, however, the members are more apt to identify with one another, quickly unite and bond with one another, attend more meetings, and offer more support to one another. The rapid development of cohesion among group members enables the group to work efficiently and effectively, and it facilitates a prompt reduction of debilitating symptoms common to members of suicide prevention groups.

Establishing a truly homogeneous group composition is extremely difficult, and leaders of suicide-related groups must remain flexible in their thinking about group composition. Group members will have different histories, unique personalities, special environmental situations, and individual responses to treatment (Frey et al., 1983; Robertson & Mathews, 1989). Robertson and Mathews (1989) suggested that selecting members according to gender is desirable in adolescent groups because the same-gender group composition accentuates members' commonality of problems and facilitates disclosure within the group. Hipple (1982) maintained that in adult groups a mixture of genders is ideal, although groups may have more women than men because of the higher incidence of suicide attempts by women.

Other guidelines for group leaders to consider during the screening process include (Frey et al., 1983; Hipple, 1982; Robertson & Mathews, 1989):

1. Potential group members should have a moderate to high rating of lethality. Those with a low risk for suicidal behavior may be adversely affected by the intense emotions and acting out behaviors of more lethal group members.
2. People who are psychotic or those who are prone to violence are generally disruptive to the group process and are considered inappropriate for a suicide intervention group.
3. Individuals who are actively involved with alcohol or drugs should be excluded from the group. Suicidal ideation and suicidal behaviors have to be the primary psychological issues for group members.

Group Limitations

During the initial session of any group, the leader or co-leaders generally discuss the goals and objectives of the group, define the rules of confidentiality, survey the members' expectations for the group experience, and take care of other "housekeeping" tasks (e.g., meeting time, place, attendance guidelines). In addition, Hipple (1982) set out the following ground rules specific to suicide intervention groups:

1. *Rule of no secrets*. Group members are encouraged to obtain assistance from people outside the group, and all interactions of external support must be shared within the group.
2. *Physical safety rule*. Group leaders advocate the release of emotions and communication about pernicious behaviors but prohibit the acting out of those behaviors in the group. Members are allowed to be angry during the group session but are not authorized to hurt themselves, threaten other group members, or destroy property. As members learn that they can vent intense emotions without indulging in physical demonstrations, they become more self-confident in their ability to be self-controlled and will generalize this more appropriate response to external environments.
3. *Confidentiality rule*. Leaders must inform group members that when they believe a member has a high probability of suicidality, it is their ethical and legal responsibility to ensure the safety of the member through immediate intervention and to report the possibility of the suicidal behavior to authorities and family members.
4. *Record-keeping issues*. Leaders of suicide-related groups should keep accurate and complete records because of the legal risk involved in facilitating this type of group. Members should be informed of any record-keeping procedures.
5. *Contract*. Leaders of special suicide groups often stipulate that a signed formal contract, in which the client agrees to stay alive, is a precondition for entry into the group. This contract serves as a powerful intervention for reducing suicidal behaviors.

Goals and Functions of the Short-Term Approach

The primary goal of the short-term approach is to confront and prevent suicidal ideation and destructive behaviors in group members. Leaders (and members) should actively respond to the immediate needs and crises of group members and should encourage expressing feelings and acquiring different, more functional behaviors (Comstock & McDermott, 1975; Robertson & Mathews, 1989). Subsequent group goals may be:

1. *Reduction of distress*. Group members with a potential for suicidal behavior are often depressed and angry. The group leaders should support and assist them in expressing their intense emotions and rage. Furthermore, the leaders should encourage members to realistically identify the source of their anger. This insight can help thwart internalization of the rage, which often

precipitates suicidal behaviors (Comstock & McDermott, 1975; Klein, 1985). Expressing emotional feelings relieves internal tension when the group member (a) has a conscious awareness of the angry feelings; (b) is aware of the reasons for suppressing the feelings of rage; and (c) does not fear rejection or loss of self-esteem by venting these threatening feelings (Robertson & Mathews, 1989).

2. *Encouragement of self-disclosure.* Group leaders seek to promote a non-threatening, supportive group environment that enables members to share personal information about themselves. Leaders model appropriate interpersonal communication skills and guide group members to reveal experiences and concerns occurring in the here and now. Personal disclosure facilitates a sense of group cohesion (members feel less isolated and lonely); a milieu of belongingness (members can perceive a commonality in problems and difficulties); feelings of acceptance and empathy toward other group members; social interest and involvement with other individuals (Dinkmeyer, 1975); self-awareness; and feelings of support. Self-disclosure also allows members to absorb, practice, and adopt competent interpersonal communication skills (Hipple, 1982).

3. *Encouragement of self-responsibility and self-management.* Group members are encouraged to become aware of, focus on, and monitor their thoughts and emotions and then connect these internal processes to their external behaviors. Insight into the relationship between thoughts, feelings, and actions can influence tendencies toward impulsive movement and can enable individuals to control dysfunctional behaviors. Members can practice new coping skills in the group and generalize them into their everyday living situations through homework assignments (Comstock & McDermott, 1975).

4. *Enhancement of self-concept.* People who are in a suicidal crisis have a tendency to focus on their negative attributes, and they fail to recognize their positive qualities. Group interactions challenge these preoccupations with the negative aspects of life and emphasize the positive essence of participants. Members are exhorted to discuss their strengths and favorable attributes within the group and are given homework assignments that highlight those characteristics (Hipple, 1982).

5. *Consideration of future goals.* Group members are encouraged to develop action plans with a positive and optimistic orientation toward the future.

6. *Development of external support systems.* Initially, the group leaders and other members may be the primary sources of support for participants. The group leaders can immediately begin to orient clients toward reaching out and seeking support from significant others, thus reducing members' dependency on the group. Members can learn by observation and practice to directly communicate their need for assistance, and homework assignments can help them achieve this external support system.

7. *Motivation of clients in the pursuit of extended therapy.* Suicidal people often manifest the dysfunctional symptoms of ongoing personality distur-

bances, and long-term therapeutic interventions are necessary to alter self-destructive tendencies. As members become capable and willing to tolerate the heightened anxieties of a more intense therapeutic process, group leaders should encourage them to seek and commit to an appropriate extended treatment program (Comstock & McDermott, 1975).

Interventions for Suicide Group Therapy ~

Problem-Solving Techniques

Feelings of hopelessness and helplessness, and deficiencies in interpersonal problem-solving skills, are highly correlated with suicidal behaviors (Asarnow et al., 1987; Patsiokas & Clum, 1985). People who attempt suicide may perceive their problems as insurmountable and may regard the act of suicide as the only solution to their predicament. The inflexible thinking process often manifested by suicide-prone individuals can negate the ability to recognize alternative possibilities.

Through a process of education and practice, group members learn problem-solving skills such as identifying the problem, investigating the facts related to the problem, concentrating on the important aspects of the situation, exploring possible solutions to the problem, and testing these solutions for effectiveness. A study by Patsiokas and Clum (1985) indicated that when individuals who are prone to suicide understand and practice appropriate methods of problem solving, their sense of hopelessness is reduced and they have a more optimistic visualization of the future. A later study that compared problem-solving group therapy and supportive group therapy found that members of the problem-solving therapy group experienced more improvement (e.g., reduction of depression and feelings of hopelessness) and rated the problem-solving approach higher in quality than did members of the supportive therapy group (Lerner & Clum, 1990; Linehan, Heard, & Armstrong, 1993). In addition, research has shown that as people acquire effective behavioral skills, their sense of self-efficacy increases and their tendency to experience extreme, dysfunctional emotional arousal during periods of distress is diminished (Lawrence & Ureda, 1990).

Cognitive Restructuring

Because depression is highly correlated with suicidal impulses (Asarnow et al., 1987; Garfinkel et al., 1988), many counselors use cognitive restructuring approaches designed to reduce depressed states in suicide-prone individuals. These interventions are based on the premise that self-defeating thinking processes are determinants in the manifestation of depression. For example, themes of suicide ideation often involve irrational beliefs about the self, life events, and how the suicide attempt will evoke favorable life changes (e.g., significant others will alter unwanted perceptions or feelings about the person) (Patsiokas & Clum, 1985).

The goal of counseling is a cognitive restructuring of erroneous, invalidating, and self-defeating perceptions, and group leaders will provocatively question, gently confront, and challenge members to relinquish and change the dysfunctional beliefs that underlie these faulty cognitions. During the entire procedure, the leaders make a conscious effort to teach and encourage members to develop self-generated rational thinking processes (Grieger & Boyd, 1980).

Self-Observation

Group members are encouraged to monitor and record their overt and covert behaviors and to reflect on the recorded behaviors (e.g., question their motives, accurately identify their emotions). Self-observation interventions are effective for two reasons. First, they increase the person's ability to understand and control behaviors, and they encourage self-responsible actions. Second, the act of monitoring brings these behaviors into conscious awareness and, thus, can decrease the frequency of the behaviors.

Action Plans

Suicidal people are often consumed with negative expectations about the future, and they commonly think about problems that have occurred in the past. This orientation toward hopelessness makes it difficult for suicidal people to have positive expectations about their existence in the future. Group members are encouraged to develop action plans that focus on future events. During periods of crisis, these agendas may have to identify day-to-day activities; as the person reestablishes emotional equilibrium, the plan of action can be extended into weeks and then months.

Challenges for Counselors ∼

Several areas of potential difficulty seem to be common to groups with suicidal and depressed populations. These include shared depressed affect in the group setting and the attempted or completed suicide of a group member.

Depressed Atmosphere

Many people who are suicidal have feelings of depression. The communication of depressive symptoms (e.g., hopelessness, helplessness, apathy, despair) can be contagious, and group members may come to project a shared sense of futility that damages the therapeutic process of the group. Leaders must be able to effectively intervene and interrupt the propensity for negativism in the group (Comstock & McDermott, 1975).

Attempted Suicide

When group leaders assess that a group member has a high risk for suicide, they must make a swift intervention to ensure the safety of the member. Leaders should establish a network of reliable emergency resources that are available during a suicide crisis (e.g., medical, family support system) and research the local requirements for involuntary hospitalization (Hipple, 1982).

Suicide of a Group Member

If a group member commits suicide, the surviving group members may have feelings of denial, guilt, anger, grief, hopelessness, and fear. In such instances, members frequently review past group interactions and ask "what if" questions. The group leaders' honest disclosure of personal reactions and emotions about the suicide can encourage members to experience and express their own feelings and apprehensions.

Leaders may have to work on the grieving process for several weeks while gradually guiding the group back to the here-and-now processes of constructive group work. Focusing on the present will allow members to become aware of how survivors are victims of suicide and how they can avoid similar self-destructive behaviors (Comstock & McDermott, 1975; Motto, 1979).

Suicide Prevention Groups ~

Public and professional education about issues and facts related to suicide is a fairly recent phenomenon. Only during the past few decades has research been directed toward establishing commonalities in suicidal behavior and empirically evaluating the effectiveness of treatment programs. The steady and dramatic increase in suicide rates in certain populations in the United States has pointed up the intense need for suicide-related literature to explicitly describe programs that can prevent suicide, intervene with people who are suicidal, and assist survivors of suicide (those who have gone through the suicidal death of a friend or loved one) (Wrobleski, 1984). In the past few years, many books and articles have been written about prevention and intervention, but little attention has been directed to the aftermath effects of a suicide. Despite a critical need for assistance programs for survivors of suicide, postvention is a seriously neglected component in the study of suicidality (Constantino, 1989; Valente, Saunders, & Street, 1988).

Bereavement is the slow process through which survivors acknowledge a death and strive to create some meaning out of the death. Mourning a death by suicide is the most difficult type of bereavement because the loss is premature and unexpected (Valente et al., 1988). Immediately after a suicide, survivors often are obsessed with a multitude of noxious emotions. Grief, horror, shock, shame, guilt, and bewilderment are thrust upon them as they simultaneously attempt to deal with the method of death (Moore & Freeman, 1995; Shelaman, 1981). This unhealthy complex of disturbing and intrusive emotions can result in depression, psychological distress, social isolation, and suicide ideation.

In comparison to survivors of other types of death, suicide survivors experience a more encompassing distress reaction, a greater number of clinical symptoms, and a higher intensity level in these symptoms (Constantino, 1989). Symptoms manifested by survivors of suicide include (Constantino, 1989; Wrobleski, 1984):

- deeper resentment and anger.
- phobias.
- debilitating fears (about death, possible harm befalling other family members).
- nightmares and dreams about the suicide.
- self-recriminations.

- excessive guilt.
- apathy.
- loneliness.
- greater risk of physical illness.
- difficulty in concentration.
- acute shame (from social stigma).

Wrobleski (1984) asserted that social stigma is the legacy the lack of education has given suicide survivors. Suicide is viewed by some people as a cowardly behavior, a mortal sin, a revengeful act, or a desperate attempt of a victim who has been wronged by significant others. Many people consider suicide to be a moral rather than a mental issue, and insurance companies have policy limitations that allow them to deny benefits to survivors of a death by suicide (Constantino, 1989). Issues of social stigma aggravate the problems of suicide survivors. Although survivors have a tremendous need to communicate their feelings, they may avoid discussing the suicide with natural sources of support because they feel shame or anticipate societal blame. Family and friends may feel threatened by the suicide and may be unable to reach out and comfort the survivor.

The subject of suicide is often avoided, and the death by suicide may be treated as a nonevent. Consequently, suicide survivors can be socially isolated, and their chances of effectively coping with the crisis are diminished (Constantino, 1989; Moore & Freeman, 1995; Wrobleski, 1984). As noted by Carter and Brooks (1990):

> The availability of external support systems is one of the most critical factors differentiating individual vulnerability from invulnerability; that is, separating individuals who survive a crisis with no harm from those who experience lasting damage. (p. 379)

Competent programs of postvention can provide the necessary support for survivors of suicide and can strengthen previously existing resources (Carter & Brooks, 1990).

Suicide survivors typically experience shock and denial. They sometimes are unaware of their need for assistance. Their social and emotional alienation reduces their ability to mourn and develop coping mechanisms, and they frequently need the structure of professional counseling to vent their feelings. They may not seek counseling, however, because they may be distrustful of postvention (Constantino, 1989). Carter and Brooks (1990) suggested that crisis counselors initiate postvention by actively pursuing survivors.

Postvention can follow several approaches, and intervention can be initiated through individual or group counseling using the formats of:

- short-term consultation (1 to 3 sessions of emergency support).
- intermediate-convergent (10 to 12 sessions focused on crisis resolution and restoration of pre-crisis functioning).
- long-term counseling (intensive therapy revolving around on insight, adaptation, primary personality change, and increased level of psychological health) (Carter & Brooks, 1990).

- grief support groups (emphasizing common problems of suicidal death, alleviation of emotional distress, acceptance, and adaptation) (Wrobleski, 1984).

Whichever format is chosen, the group approach is the preferred method of postvention in helping survivors of suicide cope with psychological distress (Carter & Brooks, 1990; Constantino, 1989; Moore & Freeman, 1995; Wrobleski, 1984).

Adolescent Postvention Group

Carter and Brooks (1990) described postvention as an opportunity for change toward positive developmental growth. For their school-based postvention program, they have used an intermediate-convergent format with a group counseling approach. They advocate this approach because it yields short-term psychological adjustments, reaches multiple survivors, and provides ample time to assess risk and to strengthen and expand external and internal support systems. They recommend that potential group leaders be trained in issues related to suicide and be qualified to work with postvention groups.

Their procedure is to immediately offer postvention services to school administrators and faculty members in the event of a student suicide. After the initial staff meetings, they conduct a rapid assessment of school resources, suicide survivor risk, and need for further interventions.

They next meet with students whom school staff members have identified as close friends of the deceased student as well as with other students who are highly distressed by the suicide. The primary purpose of this first intervention is to prevent additional deaths among the student survivors by assessing the emotional needs of the survivors, providing immediate emergency support, and establishing options for further therapeutic support. The goals of the first session are:

- to create a safe, accepting environment in which students can openly express feelings of anger and sadness.
- to offer unconditional acceptance and validation of these intense emotions.
- to assess students' support systems.
- to evaluate students' plans for obtaining support.
- to schedule additional postvention sessions.

Students who are at risk are proactively encouraged to attend the second session. If necessary, a formal postvention group is formed during the first meeting. This group might be composed of students who are survivor-victims, or it can be a multifamily group including parents, students, and other family members. Generally, the predominant theme of the group is remaining psychologically sound while coping with uncontrollable losses. The group process centers on disclosure of intimate feelings. Topics might include:

- fears surrounding the conflict between self-protection and commitment to an interpersonal relationship.

- past and future losses (e.g., divorce, death, relocation, developmental milestones).
- communication difficulties in interpersonal relationships.
- holidays and special anniversaries.
- problem-solving tactics.

Auxiliary support is crucial for counselors of postvention groups. Working with a group of adolescent suicide survivors requires a tremendous amount of responsibility, and a consultant who is not emotionally involved with the group can objectively evaluate its proceedings and increase the effectiveness of the group process.

The Suicide Survivors Grief Group

Suicide survivors have an inordinate need to verbalize their feelings, and this need to talk about the suicide lasts longer than family and friends generally are willing to listen (Wrobleski, 1984). The Suicide Survivors Grief Group (SSGG) gives people the opportunity to receive important emotional support from others who share a similar experience and, thus, begin the process of acceptance and recovery.

The SSGG (Wrobleski, 1984) is an open, ongoing postvention group that meets twice a month for 2 hours per session. People can choose their own attendance schedules, and the average number of meetings attended, over a period of 3 to 6 months, is six. The open group format is advantageous because new members can benefit from experiences of veteran survivors. People who are recovering from their grief model behaviors that reassure new members that there is hope for overcoming the intense distress reactions to the suicide.

The group leader commences each session by requesting that all members introduce themselves and state who died and how and when the death occurred. This important function of the group serves two purposes:

1. Shared experiences promote group bonding and feelings of empathy.
2. As members repeat and reproduce the narration, they gradually become desensitized to stigmatized words that surround death by suicide.

Desensitization enables them to talk more freely about the suicide, teaches them to use literal terms when they speak of suicide (e.g., killed themselves, bled to death), and promotes acceptance of the death. Leaders of these groups are empathetic (yet emotionally uninvolved to avoid burnout), are nondirective, and participate minimally in the group interaction.

The group's focus is on the common problems of suicide, and there is no agenda or predetermined topics at meetings. In an accepting and nonjudgmental milieu, people discuss the needs and problems they are dealing with that day. According to Wrobleski (1984), "The greatest need of suicide survivors is reassurance that what they are going through is "normal' " (p. 175). Disclosure, and the sharing of similar experiences, feelings, and ideas, encourages people and enables them to learn effectual ways to cope with suicide.

Age-Specific Variations for Older Adults ~

Americans 65 years and older constitute the population group with the greatest risk for suicide completion (Osgood & Brant, 1990; Saul & Saul, 1988). Adults in this age-group initiate fewer attempts at suicide, but their percentage of successful suicide completions is significantly higher than for younger people (Achté, 1988; Gilliland & James, 1988; Saul & Saul, 1988). This disproportionate vulnerability toward suicide escalates even further among people 75 years and older. Men and women over age 75 commit suicide three to four times more often than younger adults (Saul & Saul, 1988).

Researchers have uncovered several factors that may explain why a person who is older is more likely to succeed in the attempt to take his or her own life. A study by Achté (1988) revealed that only 34% of unsuccessful suicide attempters under age 25 really wanted to die, whereas 76% of adults over age 65 expressed genuine regret that the attempt had been inefficacious. This earnest desire to die is reflected by the fact that, in comparison with younger adults who attempt suicide, adults who are older use more violent and lethal methods to attempt suicide. Selecting a means that is more certain to elicit death suggests that older suicide attempters have given the matter of suicide long and careful consideration and seriously intend to die (Achté, 1988). In addition, older suicide attempters are more secretive about their intention to end their lives and are less apt to use a suicide attempt as a way to gain attention or as a disguised cry for help. Consequently, when older adults attempt suicide, they are usually successful (Saul & Saul, 1988).

Many professionals are concerned that the seriousness of the risk of suicide for adults who are older is vastly underestimated . The possibility strongly exists that the rate of suicide among people age 75 and older may be underreported and that some suicidal behavior for adults who are older may go undetected. Research data do not include the numbers of suicides from indirect life-threatening behaviors (Saul & Saul, 1988).

Osgood and Brant (1990) defined life-threatening behavior as "repetitive acts by individuals directed toward themselves, which results in physical harm or tissue damage and which could bring about a premature end of life" (p. 115). This covert form of suicide can include refusal to eat or drink, rejection of medications, propensity toward serious accidents, self-mutilation, and swallowing foreign substances or objects. Their study of suicidal behavior in long-term care facilities points to (a) a fairly high incidence of suicidal behavior among adults who are institutionalized, (b) some frequency of cases of suicide through life-threatening behavior, and (c) often unreported overt and covert suicides.

Saul and Saul (1988) conducted an extensive search for statistical information pertaining to the incidence of suicide in long-term care facilities. Their research revealed "a striking lack of information" (p. 239) and, furthermore, that long-term care facilities are often reluctant to report possible suicides or attempts at suicide. These authors proposed that the facility may feel vulnerable to punitive repercussions when a suicide is reported because:

- family members often feel guilty when placing a relative in an institution and may, through projection, blame the institution for inadequately caring for the loved one.
- due to lack of public funding, long-term care systems have many inadequacies, and social guilt may be directed toward the institution.
- the institution may actually be responsible for the death (the staff neglected the resident physically, psychologically, or emotionally).

Issues Related to Suicide Behavior in Adults Who Are Older

Separation and Loss   As people grow older, they often face an incessant series of significant losses (Leszcz, 1990). These major privations can include (Achté, 1988; Saul & Saul, 1988):

- mandatory retirement and loss of professional and social status.
- reduced sources of income.
- diminished influence among friends and within the community.
- impaired physical and mental capabilities (particularly, loss of hearing or eyesight; loss of speech or ability to walk) (Osgood & Brant, 1990).
- loss of home and separation from family, friends, and other emotional environments.
- gradual deterioration of the body and subsequent changes in physical appearance.
- loss of personal freedom and the opportunity to control one's life.

With each loss, the older individual must strive to regroup, endeavor to adjust, and attempt to adapt to the change to achieve psychological equilibrium (Achté, 1988; Leszcz, 1990). The pervasive series of deprivations, especially restrictions on freedom and sense of control, can lead to a severely damaged or altered sense of identity, a drastic loss of self-esteem, and feelings of emptiness, worthlessness, and depression (Achté, 1988; Leszcz, 1990).

Depression   Epidemiological evidence indicates that the incidence of depression does not increase with age, but depression is common among people who are older because of the major life changes in this population (Achté, 1988; Leszcz, 1990). A projected 12% to 18% of older people have a clinically significant depression, and many professionals believe the incidence of major depression is underestimated and misdiagnosed in the elderly. Older adults who are depressed are seriously at risk for suicidal behaviors. A correct diagnosis of depression and referral to treatment are extremely important because even minor depressive episodes and periods of bereavement can be life-threatening to older people (Achté, 1988; Kermis, 1986).

Groups for Adults Who Are Older

Older adults benefit greatly from peer experiences. Even though reports in professional literature neglect the prevalence and positive effects of group work with this population (Goldfarb, 1972; Zimpfer, 1987), the homogeneous group format has evolved as the principal model for counseling older adults (Kaplan & Sadock, 1972; Zimpfer, 1987).

Groups constitute an excellent means for providing services for older people. Group counseling is, of course, less expensive than individual counseling. Even more important, the special qualities of group work seem to precisely suit the requirements of older adults. Older people often suffer from loneliness, and they have fewer opportunities for social interactions. Groups furnish that social contact and offer the friendships that can thwart loneliness and rejection and, thus, help repair injuries to self-esteem.

Moreover, groups can circumvent isolation by presenting the opportunity for participants to share beliefs, information, and feelings and to receive feedback from others in similar circumstances. Groups can decrease depression in older populations by promoting mental and physical activity. Groups allow the grieving process to happen in a supportive environment, and they facilitate a structured atmosphere in which members can learn problem-solving and coping skills. Being exposed to positive modeling and practicing new skills can help older people adapt to life's changes (Leszcz, 1990; Saul & Saul, 1988; Zimpfer, 1987).

Groups for Depression   Leszcz (1990) advocated an eclectic approach incorporating psychodynamic, developmental, and cognitive-behavioral models of group counseling for treating depression in older populations. The main goal of this integrated model of group counseling is to restore a sense of mastery, competence, and purposefulness in each group member and ultimately repair the damaged sense of self. The simultaneous homogenization of these strategies generates a more powerful approach to counseling. Leszcz maintained that certain behavioral modifications are necessary for the optimal treatment of older people who are depressed. When these models are synthesized, the cognitive-behavioral interventions that promote the acquisition of specific skills advance the desired goal of psychological mastery, strengthen the psychodynamic and developmental approaches, and facilitate regeneration of the injured sense of self.

1. *Psychodynamic concerns.* Proponents of the psychodynamic approach postulate that the sense of self is strongly influenced by each individual's unique abilities, capacities, achievements, interpersonal relationships, and resources. Losses that can be associated with aging (e.g., loss of personal capability, relationships, functions, and roles) "may result in an impoverished sense of self with feelings of depletion, worthlessness, depression and helplessness" (Leszcz, 1990, p. 381). A group atmosphere that promotes belonging, cohesion, disclosure, support, and grieving can facilitate the restoration of lost self-esteem.

2. *Developmental concerns.* People who are older undergo a natural "life review" process, during which they explore, organize, and evaluate life events and reach a personal resolution regarding the positive and negative aspects of their past behaviors (Robert Butler, in Bledsoe & Lutz-Ponder, 1986). A structured group approach aimed at this reminiscent process (a) promotes a cohort effect among par-

ticipants, (b) allows participants to share significant events, (c) facilitates the resolution of interpersonal conflicts, and (d) renews feelings of self-worth through the verbalization of past achievements and personal successes (Bledsoe & Lutz-Ponder, 1986). Furthermore, reminiscing about former accomplishments can reduce apprehension and insecurities about hermetic future occurrences (Leszcz, 1990).

Reminiscence therapy groups facilitated by a nondirectional leader have a tendency to evolve into an arena in which participants become fixated on the past, and group members may generate and reinforce feelings of guilt about irreversible transgressions. Leaders can halt this harmful occurrence by consistently guiding the reminiscent process back to the here-and-now experience of the group (Leszcz, 1990).

3. *Cognitive-behavioral concerns.* Cognitive-behavioral group approaches adapt behavioral and cognitive strategies to the group setting. The major goal of this approach with people who are depressed is to identify, challenge, and change the dysfunctional attitudes and irrational beliefs that promote feelings of depression. Insight is considered to be a preliminary contingency for the working-through process, but it is not a sufficient condition for constructive change. The maladaptive cognitions that constitute the core of an individual's disturbance are usually so well practiced, reinforced, and deeply ingrained into the behavioral system that simple awareness of the situation will rarely be enough to elicit a significant modification of behavior (Leszcz, 1990).

As group members gain insight into their feelings and behaviors, their irrational beliefs can be transformed when they engage in repeated, energetic, and multimodal efforts to refute those beliefs. The group leader should (a) provocatively question and challenge the validity of the participants' depressogenic behaviors and cognitions, (b) assist members in formulating more adaptive beliefs, and (c) encourage participants to develop self-generated rational thinking processes (Grieger & Boyd, 1980).

Age-Specific Variations for Children and Adolescents ~

During the past decade, while the projected life spans of most Americans were increasing, the life expectancy rates for adolescents and children were decreasing (Kalafat, 1990; Vidal, 1989). Accidents are typically listed as the primary reason for adolescent and childhood deaths, but many professionals believe suicide is now the leading cause of death in younger populations (Allberg & Chu, 1990). It is estimated that, in the United States, a child attempts suicide every 90 seconds and an adolescent dies from the act of suicide every 90 minutes (Capuzzi & Gross, 1996).

Data imply that adolescent attempts at suicide are increasing, and the age of childhood attempters grows progressively younger each year. National surveys of schools reveal that 10% to 15% of student body members have attempted suicide. This is an extremely disturbing statistic because the probability of a completed suicide is profoundly magnified among adolescents who have attempted suicide (Kalafat, 1990). The puzzling and frightening phenomenon of cluster suicide, in which the suicide of one teenager triggers "copycat" behaviors in other teenagers, further jeopardizes the adolescent population (Garfinkel et al., 1988).

The reports on childhood and adolescent suicide behavior have shocked and disheartened adults. As noted in Allberg and Chu (1990), "No matter how often the topic is reported or discussed, it always arouses dismay, disbelief and confusion, because it defies comprehension why some adolescents choose to end their lives, and when it happens, why it creates such a ripple effect on other teenagers" (p. 342).

Public concern has stimulated extensive investigations into suicidality in children and adolescents. This research has produced various possible explanations for the increases of adolescent suicide but has not identified specific conditions, situations, or stressors that cause suicidality in younger populations (Kalafat, 1990). Research has established, however, that certain variables (e.g., depression, dysfunctional family environment, separation and loss, sexual abuse, environmental pressures, peer problems, low self-esteem, family history of suicide), when presented in a cluster of symptoms, are significantly correlated with adolescent suicide (Brent, 1995; Vanatta, 1996). An examination of the relationship among these factors will augment the understanding of adolescent suicide and facilitate the development of effective prevention and intervention programs.

Issues Related to Suicidal Behavior in Children and Adolescents

Childhood suicidal behavior usually evolves through a three-phase process. In the first stage the child encounters a stressful situation (e.g., marital conflict, illness or death in family, feelings of abandonment or rejection). During the second stage the sensations of distress intensify, and the child develops feelings of helplessness and hopelessness. In the final, crisis stage, the child perceives a profound threat to his or her well-being and becomes highly vulnerable to self-destructive behavior (Stiles & Kottman, 1990).

Most children and adolescents who show suicidal tendencies are reacting to some type of loss (Henry, 1987; Stiles & Kottman, 1990). One of the most common precipitating events for childhood suicidal behavior is the loss of a significant other through divorce, death, or chronic illness. In a vulnerable child or adolescent, even the loss of a pet can become a precursor to suicidal behavior (Capuzzi & Golden, 1988; Henry, 1987). These losses can lead to diminished self-esteem, feelings of hopelessness and helplessness, and depression (Stiles & Kottman, 1990).

Children and adolescents who have demonstrated suicidal behavior typically share the symptom of depression (Allberg & Chu, 1990). Very young children can be depressed, and children as young as age 5 have been diagnosed as having an affective disorder (Stefanowski-Harding, 1990). Diagnosing childhood and adolescent depression is extremely important because younger people who are depressed make more frequent and lethal attempts at suicide (McWhirter & Kigin, 1988). Complications in assessment can arise, however, because depression is often expressed differently in young people than in adults (Alexander, 1988; Allberg & Chu, 1990; Stefanowski-Harding, 1990). Depressed children and adolescents often do not exhibit the obvious symptoms of depression (e.g., sadness, apathy, withdrawal) and may manifest this disorder through destructive or unrealistic play or attention-getting or acting out behaviors.

Other behavioral disturbances that can mask childhood depression include anorexia nervosa, learning disabilities, psychosomatic illnesses, antisocial behavior, school failure, and alcohol and drug abuse (Allberg & Chu, 1990; Capuzzi & Gross, 1989; McWhirter & Kigin, 1988; Stefanowski-Harding, 1990; Stiles & Kottman, 1990). Most teenage suicide attempters habitually use chemical substances, and many professionals believe this destructive behavior is an attempt to self-medicate against the debilitating effects of severe depression (Allberg & Chu, 1990).

Depression is directly correlated with deficiencies in strategies for coping with life situations. Many children are not nourished by a stable and functional family atmosphere that provides support and encouragement and in which significant others model positive communication and effective coping and problem-solving skills. When parents in dysfunctional families do not demonstrate adequate or successful ways to deal with distressful events, their children may perceive their own situation as hopeless and fail to develop the necessary skills of survival (Allberg & Chu, 1990). In addition, children and adolescents who have not been exposed to self-sustaining skills may become overwhelmed by the stressful circumstances of maturation and development and may perceive suicide as a way to escape distress (Capuzzi & Gross, 1989).

Groups for Children and Adolescents

In the group setting, children and adolescents benefit from most of the same advantageous conditions that are generated by adult groups (Clouser, 1986; Robertson & Mathews, 1989), and the group model, with some modifications, is effective in the prevention, intervention, and postvention of suicidal behavior in children and adolescents (Robertson & Mathews, 1989). Because children express much of themselves through play, groups that include variations of play activities are extremely productive for children who may have difficulty expressing themselves verbally. Activities involving art, storytelling, poetry, and drama have been successfully combined with a behavioral format to (a) teach children appropriate ways to deal with destructive thoughts, (b) promote social, problem-solving, and coping skills, and (c) elevate self-esteem through reinforcement and reward systems (Clouser, 1986; Stiles & Kottman, 1990).

Developmental Counseling Groups

Counseling groups can help reduce self-destructive behavior in children and adolescents. Fairchild (1986) promoted the use of school-based prevention-oriented developmental counseling groups to facilitate self-awareness, interaction with the environment, and assimilation of positive and efficacious methods of coping with internal and external pressures. A major goal of these groups is to enable students to develop self-responsible behaviors, identify personal resources, and develop strategies for coping with potential life crises. Students are invited to join these groups and select the topics they wish to discuss. The group format is generally a function of the maturity of the participants. Older adolescent groups are given more responsibility for the content and process of the group, whereas leaders usually need to provide more structure for younger groups of children.

Groups for Children and Adolescents Dealing With Divorce-Related Issues
Goldman (1986) and others designed a school-based group intervention program for children and adolescents who have feelings of anxiety, anger, loss, and rejection associated with the crisis of divorce. These time-limited activity groups, which meet once a week for 50-75 minutes over a 6-12 week period, collaborate with administration, faculty, and parents, and have a significant and positive impact on creating constructive changes for children and their family systems. The goals of these groups are to (a) provide a safe environment in which children can develop skills that will enable them to adjust to family changes, (b) diminish children's feelings of isolation and shame, and (c) emphasize supportive aspects of the school environment. Students are referred to these groups by counselors, teachers, administration, and other school personnel, and an effort is made to keep groups as age-homogeneous as possible. Although the group model is also offered to students with long-standing school-related difficulties and no recent family change, Goldman reported that participants who have had a recent (within 2 years) family transition benefited more from the short-term group intervention format.

At the onset of the group, children are given a journal and encouraged to write about their concerns and feelings related to the group experience. This creates a sense of continuity between sessions. To introduce the concept that each child is a unique individual, participants are given a photograph of themselves to place on the cover of the journal. Photographs also are incorporated into the group's termination process, and during the group's farewell party members are given a picture of the entire group.

Activities that involve art, play, and drama facilitate discussion about divorce-related issues and encourage group members to work through conflicted emotions (e.g., guilt, rage, despair, feelings of abandonment). Goldman (1986) provided an example of the group structure and the types of interventions used at each session.

First session: Drawing of good and bad changes. The concept of change is introduced and discussed. Then participants are asked to draw a picture of a good change and one of a bad change and present these pictures to the group.

Second session: Feeling charades. The group members are each given a card with the name of a feeling written on it (e.g., happy, sad, angry, jealous) and encouraged to act out this feeling until other group members guess it.

Third session: Family change drawing. Various issues surrounding family change are introduced to the group, and children are asked to draw pictures that depict a good change and a bad change within their families over the past year.

Fourth session: Family wish drawings. Participants are asked to draw and share a picture that discloses something they wish would change in their families over the next year.

Fifth session: KKID radio broadcast. A mock radio broadcast (question-and-answer format) facilitates discussion of the children's concerns about issues related to separation and divorce.

Sixth and seventh sessions: Visitation skits. The group is separated into subgroups, each of which is asked to write and develop two skits that pertain to good and bad custodial visitations. After the skits are presented, the group leaders help children think of changes that might produce a more pleasant visitation situation and ways the children might facilitate those changes.

Eighth session: True-false game. The group leaders present prepared true-false statements to group members to assess what participants have learned about divorce and address unresolved issues.

Ninth session: Coping skills diplomas. During the last group meeting, children are given a diploma that has a coping skill written on it. An example of a coping skill could be "When your parents are fighting, you can visit a friend, ride your bike, read a book, or go outside and play ball."

Individual evaluations are conducted a month after the group has ended to evaluate participants' subjective responses to the group, discuss specific school and family problems in more depth, and offer further assistance to the children and their families. Additional individual follow-up interviews are suggested to take place 9 or 10 months after the group intervention to reassess the children's risk and, if necessary, make referrals to appropriate treatment programs.

Summary ⁓

Suicide is the ninth leading cause of death in the United States, and the populations most at risk for suicidal behavior are children, adolescents, and adults age 65 and older. The act of killing oneself is rarely precipitated by a single factor, and the phenomenon of suicide is considered to be a process. Suicidal behavior is the result of a culmination of the interactions among various psychological, behavioral, environmental, social, and situational factors.

Depression is identified as the major predictor of suicidal behavior. The emotional and behavioral features of depression (e.g., feelings of low self-esteem, helplessness, hopelessness, and despair; external locus of control; dependency; inadequate coping and problem-solving skills; poor communication skills; and withdrawal) increase the probability of negative experiences (e.g., rejection, reduced social support network) and reduce the ability to generate workable solutions to problems and adopt effective ways to cope with life events.

The group counseling approach is recommended as a treatment modality for people who are depressed and/or suicidal. It is suggested that a short-term, homogeneous, open group format best suits the special needs of people who have suicide-related issues. The benefits of a group approach are many and include (a) reduction of feelings of loneliness, isolation, and hopelessness, (b) satisfaction of the need to belong, to be accepted, to give and receive love, and to be socially integrated, (c) opportunity to disclose concerns and receive feedback, and (d) provision of a safe arena in which members can learn and practice new, effective ways to communicate, problem solve, cope, and adapt to life situations.

It is suggested that group leaders co-facilitate special suicide groups and that the leaders be thoroughly trained in psychological assessment, the basic theories of group counseling, the fundamental principles of group dynamics, the processes and procedures of group work, and the application of these maxims to therapeutic work with persons who are suicidal or depressed.

The primary goal of short-term, intervention-oriented group counseling is the confrontation and prevention of suicidal ideation and destructive behaviors in group members. Subsequent goals include reduction of stress, encouragement of self-disclosure, encouragement of self-responsibility and self-management, enhancement of self-concept, consideration of future goals, and development of external support systems.

Adults age 65 and older constitute the population group with the greatest risk for suicide completion. Groups are an excellent and practical method of providing mental health services for these adults. Members of this population often feel isolated and lonely, and groups provide peer experiences, social contact, and opportunities to receive feedback and share beliefs, information, and feelings. In addition, groups restore a lost sense of mastery and competence, help repair injuries to self-esteem, decrease depression, allow the grieving process to occur in a supportive environment, and facilitate adaptation to life's changes through the acquisition of problem-solving and coping skills.

Many professionals believe that suicide is now the leading cause of death in younger populations. Moreover, the current trend for childhood and adolescent suicide is an increased number of attempters and more attempts by younger children. The fact that the probability of a completed suicide is significantly increased among adolescent attempters compounds the seriousness of this problem. In the group setting, children and adolescents benefit from most of the same advantages offered by adult groups, and the group model, with some modifications, is an effective method of providing mental health services for younger populations. Groups that incorporate play activities, such as art, storytelling, and drama, are appropriate for children, and when combined with a behavioral format teach children effective ways to deal with destructive thoughts, promote productive social, problem-solving, and coping skills, facilitate discovery of self, and elevate self-esteem.

The increasing rate of suicide in the United States is creating another population that is at extreme risk for suicidal behavior, the survivors of suicide. Suicide attempts and completions may adversely affect the lives of over 12 million Americans annually. Postvention groups allow the grieving survivors to express their emotions, receive support from people who share a similar experience, work toward the resolution of the bereavement process, and achieve positive growth.

References ~

Achté, K. (1988). Suicidal tendencies in the elderly. *Suicide and Life-Threatening Behavior, 18*(1), 55–63.

Alexander, K. (1988, March 28-April 1). *Communicating with potential adolescent suicide through art and poetry.* Paper presented at the 66th Annual Convention of the Council for Exceptional Children, Washington, DC. (ERIC Document Reproduction Service No. ED 300 984)

Allberg, W., & Chu, L. (1990). Understanding adolescent suicide: Correlates in a developmental perspective. *School Counselor, 37*(5), 343–350.

Asarnow, J., Carlson, G., & Guthrie, D. (1987). Coping strategies, self-perceptions, and perceived family environments in depressed and suicidal children. *Journal of Consulting & Clinical Psychology, 55*(3), 361–366.

Asimos, C. (1979). Dynamic problem-solving in a group for suicidal persons. *International Journal of Group Psychotherapy, 29*(1), 109–114.

Bledsoe, N., & Lutz-Ponder, P. (1986). Group counseling with nursing home residents. *Journal for Specialists in Group Work, 11*(1), 37–41.

Bogdaniak, R., & Coronado, M. (1987). *Suicide prevention in special populations.* Paper presented at the 20th Annual Meeting of the American Association of Suicidology and the International Association for Suicide Prevention, San Francisco, CA. (ERIC Document Reproduction Service No. ED 291 026)

Brent, D. (1995). Risk factors for adolescent suicide and suicidal behavior: Mental and substance abuse disorders, family environment factors and life stress. *Suicide and Life Threatening Behavior, 25,* 52–63.

Capuzzi, D., & Golden, L. (1988). Adolescent suicide: An introduction to issues and interventions. In D. Capuzzi & L. Golden (Eds.), *Preventing adolescent suicide* (pp. 3–28). Muncie, IN: Accelerated Development.

Capuzzi, D., & Gross, D. (1996). "I don't want to live": Suicidal behavior. In D. Capuzzi & D. Gross (Eds.), *Youth at risk: A prevention resource for counselors, teachers and parents* (2nd ed., pp. 271–304). Alexandria, VA: American Association for Counseling and Development.

Carter, B., & Brooks, A. (1990). Suicide postvention: Crisis or opportunity. *School Counselor, 37,* 378–389.

Clements, C., Sider, R., & Perlmutter, R. (1983). Suicide: Bad act or good intervention. *Suicide and Life-Threatening Behavior, 13*(1), 28–41.

Clouser, W. (1986). Abused and neglected children. In T. Fairchild (Ed.), *Crisis intervention strategies for school-based helpers* (pp. 158–197). Springfield, IL: Charles C Thomas.

Comstock, B., & McDermott, M. (1975). Group therapy for patients who attempt suicide. *International Journal of Group Psychotherapy, 25*(1), 44–49.

Constantino, R. (1989, April). *Nursing postvention for suicide survivors.* Paper presented at the 22nd Annual Association of Suicidology, San Diego, CA. (ERIC Document Reproduction Service No. ED 312 548)

Curran, D. (1987). *Adolescent suicidal behavior.* New York: Hemisphere.

Davidson, J., Hughes, D., George, L., & Blazer, D. (1996). The association of sexual assault and attempted suicide within the community. *Archives of General Psychiatry, 53*(6), 550–555.

Dinkmeyer, D. (1975). Adlerian group psychotherapy. *International Journal of Group Psychotherapy, 25*(2), 219–226.

Fairchild, T. (1986). Suicide intervention. In T. Fairchild (Ed.), *Crisis intervention strategies for school-based helpers* (pp. 321–369). Springfield, IL: Charles C Thomas.

Frey, D., Motto, J., & Ritholz, M. (1983). Group therapy for persons at risk for suicide: An evaluation using the intensive design. *Psychotherapy, Theory, Research & Practice, 20*(3), 281–293.

Garfinkel, B., Crosby, E., Herbert, M., Matus, A., Pfiefer, J., & Sheras, P. (1988). *Responding to adolescent suicide.* Bloomington, IN: Phi Delta Kappa Educational Foundation. (ERIC Document Reproduction Service No. ED 301 813)

Gilliland, B., & James, R. (1988). *Crisis intervention strategies.* Pacific Grove, CA: Brooks/Cole.

Goldfarb, A. (1972). Group therapy with the old and aged. In H. Kaplan & B. Sadock (Eds.), *Group treatment of mental illness* (pp. 113–131). New York: Dutton.

Goldman, R. (1986). Separation and divorce. In T. Fairchild (Ed.), *Crisis intervention strategies for school-based helpers* (pp. 22–69). Springfield, IL: Charles C Thomas.

Grieger, R., & Boyd, J. (1980). *Rational-emotive therapy: A skill-based approach.* New York: Van Nostrand Reinhold.

Gutstein, S., & Rudd, M. D. (1988). *Adolescents and suicide. Restoring the kin network.* Austin: University of Texas Hogg Foundation for Mental Health. (ERIC Document Reproduction Service No. ED 298 409)

Hatton, C., Valente, S., & Rink, A. (1977a). Assessment of suicidal risk. In C. Hatton, S. Valente, & A. Rink (Eds.), *Suicide: Assessment and Intervention* (pp. 39–61). New York: Appleton-Century-Crofts.

Hatton, C., Valente, S., & Rink, A. (1977b). Theoretical framework. In C. Hatton, S. Valente, & A. Rink (Eds.), *Suicide: Assessment and intervention* (pp. 20–38). New York: Appleton-Century-Crofts.

Henry, C. (1987, November). *Adolescent suicide and families. A review of the literature with applications.* Paper presented at the 49th Annual Conference of the National Council on Family Relations, Atlanta. (ERIC Document Reproduction Service No. ED 292 015)

Hipple, J. (1982). Group treatment of suicidal clients. *Journal for Specialists in Group Work, 7*(4), 245–250.

Kalafat, J. (1990). Adolescent suicide and the implications for school response programs. *School Counselor, 37*(5), 359–369.

Kaplan, H., & Sadock, B. (1972). Introduction. In H. Kaplan & B. Sadock (Eds.), *Group treatment of mental illness* (pp. ix-xii). New York: Dutton.

Kermis, M. (1986). The epidemiology of mental disorder in the elderly: A response to the Senate/AARP report. *Gerontologist, 26*(5), 482–487.

Klein, R. (1985). Some principles of short-term group therapy. *International Journal of Group Psychotherapy, 35*(3), 309–330.

Lawrence, M., & Ureda, J. (1990). Student recognition of and response to suicidal peers. *Suicide and Life-Threatening Behavior, 20*(2), 164–176.

Lerner, M., & Clum, G. (1990). Treatment of suicide ideators: A problem-solving approach. *Behavior Therapy, 21*, 403–411.

Leszcz, M. (1990). Towards an integrated model of group psychotherapy with the elderly. *International Journal of Group Psychotherapy, 40*(4), 379–399.

Linehan, M., Heard, H., & Armstrong, H. (1993). Naturalistic follow-up of a behavioral treatment for chronically parasuicidal borderline patients. *Archive of General Psychiatry, 50*, 971–974.

Mancoske, R., Wadsworth, C., Dugas, D., & Hasney, J. (1995). Suicide risk among people living with AIDS. *Social Work, 40*(6), 783–787.

McWhirter, J., & Kigin, T. (1988). Depression. In D. Capuzzi & L. Golden (Eds.), *Preventing adolescent suicide* (pp. 149–186). Muncie, IN: Accelerated Development.

Moore, M., & Freeman, S. (1995). Counseling survivors of suicide: Implications for group postvention. *Specialists in Group Work, 20*(1), 40–47.

Morgan, L. (1981). The counselor's role in suicide prevention. *Personnel & Guidance Journal, 59*, 284–289.

Motto, J. (1979). Starting a therapy group in a suicide prevention and crisis center. *Suicide and Life-Threatening Behavior, 9*(1), 47–56.

Nordstrom, P., Asberg, M., Aberg-Wistedt, A., & Nardin, C. (1995). Attempted suicide predicts suicide risks in mood disorders. *Acta Psychiatrica Scandinavica, 92*(5), 345–350.

Osgood, N., & Brant, B. (1990). Suicidal behavior in long-term care facilities. *Suicide and Life-Threatening Behavior, 20*(2), 113–122.

Patsiokas, A., & Clum, G. (1985). Effects of psychotherapeutic strategies in the treatment of suicide attempters. *Psychotherapy, 22*(2), 281–290.

Poey, K. (1985). Guidelines for the practice of brief, dynamic group therapy. *International Journal of Group Psychotherapy, 35*(3), 331–354.

Robertson, D., & Mathews, B. (1989). Preventing adolescent suicide with group counseling. *Journal for Specialists in Group Work, 14*(1), 34–39.

Rudd, M. D., Rajab, M. H., Orman, D., Joiner, T., Stulman, D., & Dixon, W. (1996). Effectiveness of an outpatient intervention targeting suicidal young adults: Preliminary results. *Journal of Consulting and Clinical Psychology, 64*, 179–190.

Saul, S. R., & Saul, S. (1988). Old people talk about suicide: A discussion about suicide in a long-term care facility for frail and elderly people. *Omega, 19*(3), 237–251.

Shelaman, E. (1981). Postvention: The care of the bereaved. *Suicide and Life-Threatening Behavior, 11,* 349–359.

Stefanowski-Harding, S. (1990). Suicide and the school counselor. *School Counselor, 37*(5), 328–336.

Stiles, K., & Kottman, T. (1990). Mutual storytelling: An intervention for depressed and suicidal children. *School Counselor, 37*(5), 337–342.

Valente, S., Saunders, J., & Street, R. (1988). Adolescent bereavement following suicide: An examination of relevant literature. *Journal of Counseling and Development, 67*(3), 174–181.

Vanatta, R. (1996). Risk factors related to suicidal behavior among male and female adolescents. *Journal of Youth and Adolescence, 25*(2), 149–160.

Vidal, J. (1989). *Student suicide: A guide for intervention.* Washington, DC: National Education Association. (ERIC Document Reproduction Service No. ED 311 334)

Wrobleski, A. (1984). The suicide survivors grief group. *Omega, 15*(2), 173–185.

Zimpfer, D. (1987). Groups for the aging: Do they work? *Journal for Specialists in Group Work, 12,* 85–93.

Appendix A

Professional Standards for the Training of Group Workers

Preamble ～

All counselors should possess a set of core competencies in general group work. These basic knowledge and skills provide a foundation which specialty training can extend. Mastery of the core competencies does not qualify one to independently practice any group work specialty. Specialists in group work must possess advanced competencies relevant to a particular group work type.

The Association for Specialists in Group Work (ASGW) advocates for the incorporation of core group competencies as part of the Masters level training required in all counselor education programs. The Association also supports preparation of group counseling specialists at the Masters level. ASGW further supports the continued preparation of group work specialists at the post-Masters level (Ed.S. or Certificate, Doctoral, Continuing Education, etc.), recognizing that recommended levels of group work specialty training in many programs will need to be accomplished following completion of the Masters Degree.

This revision of the *Professional Standards for Training of Group Workers* contains two levels of competencies and related training that have been identified by the ASGW Standards Committee: (1) Core Group Competencies: The minimum core of group worker competencies and related training necessary for all counselors, including knowledge, skills, and practice (Minimum: 10 clock hours; Recommended: 20 clock hours); and (2) For Group Work Specialists: Advanced competencies that build on the generalist core in the four identified group work specialties of:

Source: From the *Professional Standards for Training of Group Workers*, revised 1990. Reprinted by permission of the Association for Specialists in Group Work (ASGW) and the American Counseling Association (ACA), Alexandria, VA.

- Task/Work groups, including knowledge, skills, and supervised practice beyond core group training (Additional minimum: 30 clock hours; Recommended: 45 clock hours);
- Guidance/Psychoeducation groups, including knowledge, skills, and supervised practice beyond core group training (Additional minimum: 30 clock hours; Recommended: 45 clock hours);
- Counseling/Interpersonal Problem-Solving groups, including knowledge, skills, and supervised practice beyond core group training (Additional minimum: 45 clock hours; Recommended: 60 clock hours);
- Psychotherapy/Personality Reconstruction groups, including knowledge, skills, and supervised practice beyond core group training (Additional minimum: 45 clock hours; Recommended: 60 clock hours

Definitions ~

Group Work

"Group work" is a broad professional practice that refers to the giving of help or the accomplishment of tasks in a group setting. It involves the application of group theory and process by a capable professional practitioner to assist an interdependent collection of people to reach their mutual goals, which may be personal, interpersonal, or task-related in nature.

Core Training in Group Work for All Counselors

All professional counselors should possess basic fundamental knowledge and skills in group work. Moreover, this set of competencies provides a basic foundation upon which specialization training in group work is built.

Core training group work competencies does not prepare a counseling professional to independently assume responsibility for conducting any of the specialty groups to be defined in these Standards. Additional focused training is required for independent practice in a specialty, as detailed below.

Group Work Specializations

The trainee may proceed beyond core training in group work to specialize in one or more advanced areas of practice. It is to be expected that all Counseling programs would provide core training in group work to all students and most would offer additional training in at least one of the other specializations.

Definitions of each specialization follow.

Task/Work Groups   Much work in contemporary Western society is accomplished through group endeavor. The task/work group specialist is able to assist groups such as task forces, committees, planning groups, community organizations, discussion groups, study circles, learning groups, and other similar groups to correct or develop their functioning. The focus is on the application of group dynamics principles and processes to improve practice and the accomplishment of identified work goals.

Guidance/Psychoeducation Groups   Education and prevention are critically important goals for the contemporary counselor. The guidance/psychoeducation group specialist seeks to use the group medium to educate group participants who are presently unaffected about a potential threat (such as AIDS), a developmental life event (such as a transition point), or how to cope with an immediate life crisis (such as suicide of a loved one), with the goal of preventing an array of educational and psychological disturbances from occurring.

Counseling/Interpersonal Problem-Solving   The group worker who specializes in counseling/interpersonal problem-solving seeks to help group participants to resolve the usual, yet often difficult, problems of living through interpersonal support and problem solving. An additional goal is to help participants to develop their existing interpersonal problem-solving competencies that they may be better able to handle future problems of a similar nature. Non-severe career, educational, personal, social, and developmental concerns are frequently addressed.

Psychotherapy/Personality Reconstruction   The group worker who specializes in psychotherapy/personality reconstruction seeks to help individual group members to remediate their in-depth psychological problems. Because the depth and extent of the psychological disturbance is significant, the goal is to aid each individual to reconstruct major personality dimensions.

Training Standards～

A. Core Group Work Training for All Counselors: Knowledge Competencies

All counselors can effectively:

1. State for the four major group work specializations identified in this document (task groups, guidance groups, counseling groups, psychotherapy groups), the distinguishing characteristics of each, the commonalities shared by all, and the appropriate instances in which each is to be used.
2. Identify the basic principles of group dynamics.
3. Discuss the basic therapeutic ingredients of groups.
4. Identify the personal characteristics of group workers that have an impact on members; knowledge of personal strengths, weaknesses, biases, values, and their effect on others.
5. Describe the specific ethical issues that are unique to group work.
6. Discuss the body of research on group work and how it relates to one's academic preparation in either school counseling, student personnel education, community counseling, or mental health counseling.
7. Define the process components involved in typical stages of a group's development (i.e., characteristics of group interaction and counselor roles).
8. Describe the major facilitative and debilitative roles that group members may take.

9. State the advantages and disadvantages of group work and the circumstances for which it is indicated or contraindicated.
10. Detail therapeutic factors of group work.
11. Identify principles and strategies for recruiting and screening prospective group members.
12. Detail the importance of group and member evaluation.
13. Deliver a clear, concise, and complete definition of group work.
14. Deliver a clear, concise, and complete definition of each of the four group work specialties.
15. Explain and clarify the purpose of a particular form of group work.

Core Group Work Training for All Counselors: Skill Competencies

All counselors are able to effectively:

1. Encourage participation of group members.
2. Observe and identify group process events.
3. Attend to and acknowledge group member behavior.
4. Clarify and summarize group member statements.
5. Open and close group sessions.
6. Impart information in the group when necessary.
7. Model effective group leader behavior.
8. Engage in appropriate self-disclosure in the group.
9. Give and receive feedback in the group.
10. Ask open-ended questions in the group.
11. Empathize with group members.
12. Confront group members' behavior.
13. Help group members attribute meaning to their experience.
14. Help group members to integrate and apply learnings.
15. Demonstrate ASGW ethical and professional standards in group practice.
16. Keep the group on task in accomplishing its goals.

Core Group Work Training

Knowledge   Core training in group work should include a minimum of one course. Contained in this course should be attention to competencies in the Knowledge and in the Skills domains.

Skills Through Supervised Practice   The Practice domain should include observation and participation in a group experience, which could occur in a classroom group.

Minimum amount of supervised practice: *10 clock hours*.
Recommended amount of supervised practice: *20 clock hours*.

B. Group Work Specializations: Knowledge, Skill and Supervised Practice Domains

The counselor trainee, having mastered the core knowledge and skill domains displayed above, can specialize in one or more advanced areas of group work practice.

These advanced specialty areas are Task/Work groups, Guidance/Psychoeducation groups, Counseling/Interpersonal Problem-Solving groups, and Psychotherapy/Personality Reconstruction groups. The advanced knowledge and skill competencies associated with each of these specialties are presented below.

Task/Work Groups ~

Knowledge Competencies

In addition to Core knowledge, the qualified Task/Work group specialist can effectively:

1. Identify organizational dynamics pertinent to task/work groups.
2. Describe community dynamics pertinent to task/work groups.
3. Identify political dynamics pertinent to task/work groups.
4. Describe standard discussion methodologies appropriate for task/work groups.
5. Identify specific ethical considerations in working with task/work groups.
6. Identify program development and evaluation models appropriate for task/work groups.
7. List consultation principles and approaches appropriate for task/work groups.

Skills Competencies

In addition to Core skills, the qualified Task/Work group specialist is able to effectively:

1. Focus and maintain attention on task and work issues.
2. Obtain goal clarity in a task/work group.
3. Conduct a personally selected task/work group model appropriate to the age and clientele of the group leader's specialty area(s) (e.g., school counseling).
4. Mobilize energies toward a common goal in task/work groups.
5. Implement group decision-making methods in task/work groups.
6. Manage conflict in task/work groups.
7. Blend the predominant task focus with appropriate attention to human relations factors in task/work groups.
8. Sense and use larger organizational and political dynamics in task/work groups.

Specialist Training: Task/Work Groups

Knowledge   Course work should be taken in the broad area of organization development, management, and/or sociology such that the student understands organizational life and how task groups function within it. Course work also should be taken in consultation.

Skills Through Supervised Practice   In addition to Core training acquired through observation and participation in a group (10 clock hours minimum; 20 clock hours recommended), practice should include:

Minimum amount of *30 clock hours* should be obtained in co-leading or leading a task/work group in a field practice setting supervised by qualified faculty or staff personnel.

Recommended amount of *45 clock hours* should be obtained in co-leading or leading a task/work group in a field practice setting supervised by qualified faculty or staff personnel.

Guidance/Psychoeducational Groups ∼

Knowledge Competencies

In addition to Core knowledge, the qualified Guidance/Psychoeducation group specialist can effectively:

1. Identify the concepts of primary prevention and secondary prevention in guidance/psychoeducation groups.
2. Articulate the concept of "at risk" in guidance/psychoeducation groups.
3. Enumerate principles of instruction relevant to guidance/psychoeducation groups.
4. Develop a knowledge base relevant to the focus of a guidance/psychoeducation group intervention.
5. List principles involved in obtaining healthy and/or at-risk group members for guidance/psychoeducation groups.
6. Describe human development theory pertinent to guidance/psychoeducation groups.
7. Discuss environmental assessment as related to guidance/psychoeducation groups.
8. Discuss principles of structure as related to guidance/psychoeducation groups.
9. Discuss the concept of empowerment in guidance/psychoeducation groups.
10. Identify specific ethical considerations unique to guidance/psychoeducation groups.
11. List advantages of guidance/psychoeducation groups and where indicated or contra-indicated.

Skills Competencies

In addition to Core skills, the qualified Guidance/Psychoeducation group specialist can effectively:

1. Plan a guidance/psychoeducation group in collaboration with "target" population members or representatives.
2. Match a relevant guidance/psychoeducation topic with a relevant (and currently "unaffected") target group.
3. Conduct a personally selected guidance/psychoeducation group model appropriate to the age and clientele of the group leader's specialty area (e.g., student personnel education).

4. Design a guidance/psychoeducation group plan that is developmentally and practically sound.
5. Present information in a guidance/psychoeducation group.
6. Use environmental dynamics to the benefit of the guidance/psychoeducation group.
7. Conduct skill training in guidance/psychoeducation groups.

Specialist Training: Guidance/Psychoeducation Groups

Knowledge   Course work should be taken in the broad areas of community psychology, health promotion, marketing, consultation, and curriculum design.

Skills Through Supervised Practice   In addition to Core training acquired through observation and participation in a group (10 clock hours minimum; 20 clock hours recommended), practice should include:

Minimum amount of *10 clock hours* should be obtained in co-leading or leading a guidance/psychoeducation group in a field practice setting supervised by qualified faculty or staff personnel.

Recommended amount of *45 clock hours* should be obtained in co-leading or leading a guidance/psychoeducation group in a practice setting supervised by qualified faculty or staff personnel.

Counseling/Interpersonal Problem-Solving Groups~

Knowledge Competencies

In addition to Core knowledge, the qualified Counseling/Interpersonal Problem-Solving group specialist can effectively:

1. State for at least three major theoretical approaches to group counseling the distinguishing characteristics of each and the commonalities shared by all.
2. Identify specific ethical problems and considerations unique to group counseling.
3. List advantages and disadvantages of group counseling and the circumstances for which it is indicated or contra-indicated.
4. Describe interpersonal dynamics in group counseling.
5. Describe group problem-solving approaches in relation to group counseling.
6. Discuss interpersonal assessment in group counseling.
7. Identify referral sources and procedures in group counseling.
8. Describe group formation principles in group counseling.

Skills Competencies

In addition to Core skills, the qualified Counseling/Interpersonal Problem-Solving group specialist can effectively:

1. Recruit and screen prospective counseling members.
2. Recognize self-defeating behaviors of counseling group members.
3. Conduct a personally selected group counseling model appropriate to the age and clientele of the group leader's specialty area(s) (e.g., community counseling).
4. Develop reasonable hypotheses about nonverbal behavior among counseling group members.
5. Exhibit appropriate pacing skills involved in stages of a counseling group's development.
6. Intervene effectively at critical incidents in the counseling group process.
7. Work appropriately with disruptive counseling group members.
8. Make use of the major strategies, techniques, and procedures of group counseling.
9. Use procedures to assist transfer and support of changes by group members in the natural environment.
10. Use adjunct group counseling structures such as homework (e.g., goal setting).
11. Work cooperatively and effectively with a counseling group co-leader.
12. Use assessment procedures in evaluating effects and contributions of group counseling.

Specialist Training: Counseling/Interpersonal Problem-Solving Groups

Knowledge   As much course work in group counseling as possible is desirable, but at least one course beyond the generalist is necessary. Other courses in the Counseling program should provide good support for the group counseling specialty.

Skills Through Supervised Practice   In addition to Core training acquired through observation and participation in a group (10 clock hours minimum; 20 clock hours recommended), practice should include:

> *Minimum* amount of *45 clock hours* should be obtained in co-leading or leading a counseling/interpersonal problem-solving group in a field practice setting supervised by qualified faculty or staff personnel.
> *Recommended* amount of *60 clock hours* should be obtained in co-leading or leading a counseling/interpersonal problem-solving group in a field practice setting supervised by qualified faculty or staff personnel.

Psychotherapy/Personality Reconstruction Groups~

Knowledge Competencies

In addition to Core knowledge, the Psychotherapy/Personality Reconstruction group specialist can effectively:

1. State for at least three major theoretical approaches to group psychotherapy the distinguishing characteristics of each and the commonalities shared by all.
2. Identify specific ethical problems and considerations unique to group psychotherapy.
3. List advantages and disadvantages of group psychotherapy and the circumstances for which it is indicated or contra-indicated.
4. Specify intrapersonal and interpersonal dynamics in group psychotherapy.
5. Describe group problem-solving approaches in relation to group psychotherapy.
6. Discuss interpersonal assessment and intervention in group psychotherapy.
7. Identify referral sources and procedures in group psychotherapy.
8. Describe group formation principles in group psychotherapy.
9. Identify and describe abnormal behavior in relation to group psychotherapy.
10. Identify psychopathology as related to group psychotherapy.
11. Describe personality theory as related to group psychotherapy.
12. Detail crisis intervention approaches suitable for group psychotherapy.
13. Specify diagnostic and assessment methods appropriate for group psychotherapy.

Skill Competencies

In addition to Core skills, the qualified Psychotherapy/Personality Reconstruction group specialist can effectively:

1. Recruit and screen prospective psychotherapy group members.
2. Recognize self-defeating behaviors of psychotherapy group members.
3. Describe and conduct a personally selected group psychotherapy model appropriate to the age and clientele of the group leader's specialty area (e.g., mental health counseling).
4. Identify and develop reasonable hypotheses about nonverbal behavior among psychotherapy group members.
5. Exhibit appropriate pacing skills involved in stages of a psychotherapy group's development.
6. Identify and intervene effectively at critical incidents in the psychotherapy group process.
7. Work appropriately with disruptive psychotherapy group members.
8. Make use of the major strategies, techniques, and procedures of group psychotherapy.
9. Provide and use procedures to assist transfer and support of changes by group psychotherapy members in the natural environment.
10. Use adjunct group psychotherapy structures such as psychological homework (e.g., self-monitoring, contracting).
11. Work cooperatively and effectively with a psychotherapy group co-leader.
12. Use assessment procedures in evaluating effects and contributions of group psychotherapy.

13. Assist individual change along the full range of development, from "normal" to "abnormal" in the psychotherapy group.
14. Handle psychological emergencies in the psychotherapy group.
15. Institute hospitalization procedures when appropriate and necessary in the psychotherapy group.
16. Assess and diagnose mental and emotional disorders of psychotherapy group members.

Specialist Training: Psychotherapy/Personality Reconstruction Groups

Knowledge   Course work should be taken in the areas of group psychotherapy, abnormal psychology, psychopathology, and diagnostic assessment to assure capabilities in working with more disturbed populations.

Skills Through Supervised Practice   In addition to Core training acquired through observation and participation in a group (10 clock hours minimum; 20 clock hours recommended), practice should include:

> *Minimum* amount of *45 clock hours* should be obtained in co-leading or leading a psychotherapy/personality reconstruction group in a field practice setting supervised by qualified faculty or staff personnel.
>
> *Recommended* amount of *60 clock hours* should be obtained in co-leading or leading a psychotherapy/personality reconstruction group in a field practice setting supervised by qualified faculty or staff personnel.

Implementation Guidelines for the ASGW Standards: Integration with CACREP Accreditation Standards

1. (a) Core group work knowledge for all counseling students can be obtained through a basic course in group theory and practice. Consistent with accreditation standards (CACREP II-J.4), study in the area of *Groups* should provide an understanding of group development, group dynamics, and group leadership styles; group leadership methods and skills; and group types, including group counseling, task groups, guidance groups, and psychotherapy groups. More explicitly, studies would include, but not be limited to the following:

   1. Principles of group dynamics including group process components, developmental stage theories, and group members' roles and behaviors.
   2. Group leadership styles and approaches including characteristics of various types of group leaders and leadership styles.
   3. Knowledge of group work types (counseling, task, guidance, and psychotherapy) including commonalities, distinguishing characteristics, and pertinent research and literature.

4. Group work methods including group leader orientations and behaviors, ethical considerations, appropriate selection criteria and methods, and methods of evaluating effectiveness.
5. Development of skills in explicit and implicit teaching, group process observation, opening and closing sessions, self-disclosing, giving and receiving feedback, modeling, focusing, protecting, managing, recruiting and selecting members, empathizing, confronting, and evaluating.

(b) Core group work training for all counseling students requires a minimum of 10 clock hours of supervised practice, and a recommended amount of 20 clock hours. These skills can be obtained through the basic course in group theory and practice mentioned in 1(a) above (which should provide for direct group participation) and through satisfying the accreditation standard II-F, which provides students with the opportunity to participate in a planned and supervised small group activity. In the latter activity, care must be taken to assure that the AACD and ASGW ethical standard relating to dual relationships is preserved.

2. Specialist group work training can occur beyond the core group work training for programs and students desiring advanced competency development. The specialist training in group work is in Task/Work groups, Guidance/Psychoeducational groups, Counseling/Interpersonal Problem-Solving groups, and/or Psychotherapy/Personality Reconstruction groups.

(a) *Specialized knowledge:* Additional course work is necessary for each of the specialty areas, as follows:

- *Task Groups:* As necessary, course work in such areas as organization development, consultation, management, or sociology so students gain a basic understanding of organizations and how task groups function in them.
- *Guidance Groups:* As necessary, course work in areas such as community psychology, health promotion, marketing, consultation, and/or curriculum design to provide working knowledge of prevention and structured groups in such areas as stress management, wellness, assertiveness training, problem solving, and smoking cessation.
- *Counseling Groups:* At least one course is necessary in group counseling. This additional course should provide opportunities for group membership and leadership, and it should advance conceptual knowledge of group work.
- *Psychotherapy Groups:* Course work in such areas as group psychotherapy, abnormal psychology, psychopathology, and diagnostic assessment.

(b) Additional supervised clinical experience is necessary for each of the specialty areas, as follows:

- *Task groups:* (30 clock hours minimum, 45 desired)
- *Guidance groups:* (30 clock hours minimum, 45 desired)
- *Counseling groups:* (45 clock hours minimum, 60 desired)
- *Psychotherapy groups:* (45 clock hours minimum, 60 desired)

For *Masters* students, in addition to courses offering content and experience related to the four group work specializations, supervised clinical experience should be obtained in practice and internship, as follows:

Masters Practicum: (CACREP standard III-H). At least 15 hours (of the 40 clock hours stipulated for direct service) should be spent in supervised leadership or co-leadership experience in a group work type designated by ASGW in Counseling, Task, Guidance, or Psychotherapy groups. At the Masters Practicum level, psychotherapy experience ordinarily would be unusual.

Masters Internship: (CACREP standard III-I). At least 90 clock hours (of the 240 clock hours stipulated for direct service) should be spent in supervised leadership or co-leadership. Approximately half of that experience (about 45 clock hours) should be spent leading counseling groups with the remaining time spent leading task, guidance, or psychotherapy groups.

Doctoral Internship: (CACREP standard O). At least 450 clock hours (of the 1200 clock hours stipulated) should be spent in supervised group work leadership or co-leadership. Approximately half of that experience (about 225 clock hours) should be spent leading counseling groups with the remaining time spent leading task, guidance, or psychotherapy groups.

National Council for Credentialing of Career Counselors
c/o NBCC
5999 Stevenson Avenue
Alexandria, Virginia 22304

National Academy for Certified Clinical Mental Health Counselors
5999 Stevenson Avenue
Alexandria, Virginia 22304

Commission on Rehabilitation Counselor Certification
162 North State Street, Suite 317
Chicago, Illinois 60601

American Association for Marriage and Family Therapy
1717 K Street, N.W., Suite 407
Washington, D.C. 22006

American Psychological Association
1200 Seventeenth Street, N.W.
Washington, D.C. 22036

American Group Psychotherapy Association, Inc.
25 East 21st Street, 6th Floor
New York, New York 10010

Appendix B
Ethical Guidelines for
Group Counselors

Preamble ~

One characteristic of any professional group is the possession of a body of knowledge, skills, and voluntarily, self-professed standards for ethical practice. A Code of Ethics consists of those standards that have been formally and publicly acknowledged by the members of a profession to serve as the guidelines for professional conduct, discharge of duties, and the resolution of moral dilemmas. By this document, the Association for Specialists in Group Work (ASGW) has identified the standards of conduct appropriate for ethical behavior among its members.

The Association for Specialists in Group Work recognizes the basic commitment of its members to the Ethical Standards of its parent organization, the American Association for Counseling and Development (AACD) and nothing in this document shall be construed to supplant that code. These standards are intended to complement the AACD standards in the area of group work by clarifying the nature of ethical responsibility of the counselor in the group setting and by stimulating a greater concern for competent group leadership.

The group counselor is expected to be a professional agent and to take the processes of ethical responsibility seriously. ASGW views "ethical process" as being integral to group work and views group counselors as "ethical agents." Group counselors, by their very nature in being responsible and responsive to their group members, necessarily embrace a certain potential for ethical vulnerability. It is incumbent upon group counselors to give considerable attention to the intent and context of their actions because the attempts of counselors to influence human behavior through group work always have ethical implications.

Source: Approved by the Association for Specialists in Group Work (ASGW), Executive Board, June 1, 1989. Reprinted by permission of the American Counseling Association (ACA), Alexandria, VA.

The following ethical guidelines have been developed to encourage ethical behavior of group counselors. These guidelines are written for students and practitioners, and are meant to stimulate reflection, self-examination, and discussion of issues and practices. They address the group counselor's responsibility for providing information about group work to clients and the group counselor's responsibility for providing group counseling services to clients. A final section discusses the group counselor's responsibility for safeguarding ethical practice and procedures for reporting unethical behavior. Group counselors are expected to make known these standards to group members.

Ethical Guidelines ～

1. *Orientation and Providing Information:* Group counselors adequately prepare prospective or new group members by providing as much information about the existing or proposed group as necessary.

    Minimally, information related to each of the following areas should be provided.

    (a) Entrance procedures, time parameters of the group experience, group participation expectations, methods of payment (where appropriate), and termination procedures are explained by the group counselor as appropriate to the level of maturity of group members and the nature and purpose(s) of the group.

    (b) Group counselors have available for distribution a professional disclosure statement that includes information on the group counselor's qualifications and group services that can be provided, particularly as related to the nature and purpose(s) of the specific group.

    (c) Group counselors communicate the role expectations, rights, and responsibilities of group members and group counselor(s).

    (d) The group goals are stated as concisely as possible by the group counselor including "whose" goal it is (the group counselor's, the institution's, the parent's, the law's, society's, etc.) and the role of group members in influencing or determining the group's goal(s).

    (e) Group counselors explore with group members the risks of potential life changes that may occur because of the group experience and help members explore their readiness to face these possibilities.

    (f) Group members are informed by the group counselor of unusual or experimental procedures that might be expected in their group experience.

    (g) Group counselors explain, as realistically as possible, what services can and cannot be provided within the particular group structure offered.

    (h) Group counselors emphasize the need to promote full psychological functioning and presence among group members. They inquire from prospective group members whether they are using any kind of drug or medication that may affect functioning in the group. They do not permit any use of alcohol and/or illegal drugs during group sessions and they discourage the use of alcohol and/or drugs (legal or illegal) prior to group meetings which may affect the physical or emotional presence of the member or other group members.

(i) Group counselors inquire from prospective group members whether they have ever been a client in counseling or psychotherapy. If a prospective group member is already in a counseling relationship with another professional person, the group counselor advises the prospective group member to notify the other professional of their participation in the group.

(j) Group counselors clearly inform group members about the policies pertaining to the group counselor's willingness to consult with them between group sessions.

(k) In establishing fees for group counseling services, group counselors consider the financial status and the locality of prospective group members. Group members are not charged fees for group sessions where the group counselor is not present and the policy of charging for sessions missed by a group member is clearly communicated. Fees for participating as a group member are contracted between group counselor and group member for a specified period of time. Group counselors do not increase fees for group counseling services until the existing contracted fee structure has expired. In the event that the established fee structure is inappropriate for a prospective member, group counselors assist in finding comparable services of acceptable cost.

2. *Screening of Members:* The group counselor screens prospective group members (when appropriate to their theoretical orientation). Insofar as possible, the counselor selects group members whose needs and goals are compatible with the goals of the group, who will not impede the group process, and whose well-being will not be jeopardized by the group experience. An orientation to the group (i.e., ASGW Ethical Guideline number 1), is included during the screening process.

Screening may be accomplished in one or more ways, such as the following:

(a) Individual interview,

(b) Group interview of prospective group members,

(c) Interview as part of a team staffing, and

(d) Completion of a written questionnaire by prospective group members.

3. *Confidentiality:* Group counselors protect members by defining clearly what confidentiality means, why it is important, and the difficulties involved in enforcement.

(a) Group counselors take steps to protect members by defining confidentiality and the limits of confidentiality (i.e., when a group member's condition indicates that there is clear and imminent danger to the member, others, or physical property, the group counselor takes reasonable personal action and/or informs responsible authorities).

(b) Group counselors stress the importance of confidentiality and set a norm of confidentiality regarding all group participants' disclosures. The importance of maintaining confidentiality is emphasized before the group begins and at various times in the group. The fact that confidentiality cannot be guaranteed is clearly stated.

(c) Members are made aware of the difficulties involved in enforcing and ensuring confidentiality in a group setting. The counselor provides examples of how confidentiality can non-maliciously be broken to increase members' awareness, and help to lessen the likelihood that this breach of confidence will occur. Group counselors inform group members about the potential consequences of intentionally breaching confidentiality.

(d) Group counselors can only ensure confidentiality on their part and not on the part of the members.

(e) Group counselors video or audio tape a group session only with the prior consent, and the members' knowledge of how the tape will be used.

(f) When working with minors, the group counselor specifies the limits of confidentiality.

(g) Participants in a mandatory group are made aware of any reporting procedures required of the group counselor.

(h) Group counselors store or dispose of group member records (written, audio, video, etc.) in ways that maintain confidentiality.

(i) Instructors of group counseling courses maintain the anonymity of group members whenever discussing group counseling cases.

4. *Voluntary/Involuntary Participation:* Group counselors inform members whether participation is voluntary or involuntary.

(a) Group counselors take steps to ensure informed consent procedures in both voluntary and involuntary groups.

(b) When working with minors in a group, counselors are expected to follow the procedures specified by the institution in which they are practicing.

(c) With involuntary groups, every attempt is made to enlist the cooperation of the members and their continuance in the group on a voluntary basis.

(d) Group counselors do not certify that group treatment has been received by members who merely attend sessions, but did not meet the defined group expectations. Group members are informed about the consequences for failing to participate in a group.

5. *Leaving a Group:* Provisions are made to assist a group member to terminate in an effective way.

(a) Procedures to be followed for a group member who chooses to exit a group prematurely are discussed by the counselor with all group members either before the group begins, during a pre-screening interview, or during the initial group session.

(b) In the case of legally mandated group counseling, group counselors inform members of the possible consequences for premature self-termination.

(c) Ideally, both the group counselor and the member can work cooperatively to determine the degree to which a group experience is productive or counterproductive for that individual.

(d) Members ultimately have a right to discontinue membership in the group, at a designated time, if the predetermined trial period proves to be unsatisfactory.

(e) Members have the right to exit a group, but it is important that they be made aware of the importance of informing the counselor and the group members prior to deciding to leave. The counselor discusses the possible risks of leaving the group prematurely with a member who is considering this option.

(f) Before leaving a group, the group counselor encourages members (if appropriate) to discuss their reasons for wanting to discontinue membership in the group. Counselors intervene if other members use undue pressure to force a member to remain in the group.

6. *Coercion and Pressure:* Group counselors protect member rights against physical threats, intimidation, coercion, and undue peer pressure insofar as is reasonably possible.

(a) It is essential to differentiate between "therapeutic pressure" that is part of any group and "undue pressure," which is not therapeutic.

(b) The purpose of a group is to help participants find their own answer, not to pressure them into doing what the group thinks is appropriate.

(c) Counselors exert care not to coerce participants to change in directions which they clearly state they do not choose.

(d) Counselors have a responsibility to intervene when others use undue pressure or attempt to persuade members against their will.

(e) Counselors intervene when any member attempts to act out aggression in a physical way that might harm another member or themselves.

(f) Counselors intervene when a member is verbally abusive or inappropriately confrontive to another member.

7. *Imposing Counselor Values:* Group counselors develop an awareness of their own values and needs and the potential impact they have on the interventions likely to be made.

(a) Although group counselors take care to avoid imposing their values on members, it is appropriate that they expose their own beliefs, decisions, needs, and values, when concealing them would create problems for the members.

(b) There are values implicit in any group, and these are made clear to potential members before they join the group. (Examples of certain values include: expressing feelings, being direct and honest, sharing personal material with others, learning how to trust, improving interpersonal communication, and deciding for oneself.)

(c) Personal and professional needs of group counselors are not met at the members' expense.

(d) Group counselors avoid using the group for their own therapy.

(e) Group counselors are aware of their own values and assumptions and how these apply in a multicultural context.

(f) Group counselors take steps to increase their awareness of ways that their personal reactions to members might inhibit the group process and they monitor their countertransference. Through an awareness of the impact of stereotyping and discrimination (i.e., biases based on age, disability, ethnicity, gender, race, religion, or sexual preference), group counselors guard the individual rights and personal dignity of all group members.

8. *Equitable Treatment:* Group counselors make every reasonable effort to treat each member individually and equally.

(a) Group counselors recognize and respect differences (e.g., cultural, racial, religious, lifestyle, age, disability, gender) among group members.

(b) Group counselors maintain an awareness of their behavior toward individual group members and are alert to the potential detrimental effects of favoritism or partiality toward any particular group member to the exclusion or detriment of any other member(s). It is likely that group counselors will favor some members over others, yet all group members deserve to be treated equally.

(c) Group counselors ensure equitable use of group time for each member by inviting silent members to become involved, acknowledging nonverbal attempts to communicate, and discouraging rambling and monopolizing of time by members.

(d) If a large group is planned, counselors consider enlisting another qualified professional to serve as a co-leader for the group sessions.

9. *Dual Relationships:* Group counselors avoid dual relationships with group members that might impair their objectivity and professional judgment, as well as those which are likely to compromise a group member's ability to participate fully in the group.

(a) Group counselors do not misuse their professional role and power as group leader to advance personal or social contacts with members throughout the duration of the group.

(b) Group counselors do not use their professional relationship with group members to further their own interest either during the group or after the termination of the group.

(c) Sexual intimacies between group counselors and members are unethical.

(d) Group counselors do not barter (exchange) professional services with group members for services.

(e) Group counselors do not admit their own family members, relatives, employees, or personal friends as members to their groups.

(f) Group counselors discuss with group members the potential detrimental effects of group members engaging in intimate inter-member relationships outside of the group.

(g) Students who participate in a group as a partial course requirement for a group course are not evaluated for an academic grade based upon their degree of participation as a member in a group. Instructors of group counseling courses take steps to minimize the possible negative impact on students when they participate in a group course by separating course grades from participation in the group and by allowing students to decide what issues to explore and when to stop.

(h) It is inappropriate to solicit members from a class (or institutional affiliation) for one's private counseling or therapeutic groups.

10. *Use of Techniques:* Group counselors do not attempt any technique unless trained in its use or under supervision by a counselor familiar with the intervention.

(a) Group counselors are able to articulate a theoretical orientation that guides their practice, and they are able to provide a rationale for their interventions.

(b) Depending upon the type of intervention, group counselors have training commensurate with the potential impact of a technique.

(c) Group counselors are aware of the necessity to modify their techniques to fit the unique needs of various cultural and ethnic groups.

(d) Group counselors assist members in translating in-group learnings to daily life.

11. *Goal Development:* Group counselors make every effort to assist members in developing their personal goals.

(a) Group counselors use their skills to assist members in making their goals specific so that others present in the group will understand the nature of the goals.

(b) Throughout the course of a group, group counselors assist members in assessing the degree to which personal goals are being met, and assist in revising any goals when it is appropriate.

(c) Group counselors help members clarify the degree to which the goals can be met within the context of a particular group.

12. *Consultation:* Group counselors develop and explain policies about between-session consultation to group members.

(a) Group counselors take care to make certain that members do not use between-session consultations to avoid dealing with issues pertaining to the group that would be dealt with best in the group.

(b) Group counselors urge members to bring the issues discussed during between-session consultations into the group if they pertain to the group.

(c) Group counselors seek out consultation and/or supervision regarding ethical concerns or when encountering difficulties which interfere with their effective functioning as group leaders.

(d) Group counselors seek appropriate professional assistance for their own personal problems or conflicts that are likely to impair their professional judgment and work performance.

(e) Group counselors discuss their group cases only for professional consultation and educational purposes.

(f) Group counselors inform members about policies regarding whether consultations will be held confidential.

13. *Termination from the Group:* Depending upon the purpose of participation in the group, counselors promote termination of members from the group in the most efficient period of time.

(a) Group counselors maintain a constant awareness of the progress made by each group member and periodically invite the group members to explore and reevaluate their experiences in the group. It is the responsibility of group counselors to help promote the independence of members from the group in a timely manner.

14. *Evaluation and Follow-up:* Group counselors make every attempt to engage in ongoing assessment and to design follow-up procedures for their groups.

(a) Group counselors recognize the importance of ongoing assessment of a group, and they assist members in evaluating their own progress.

(b) Group counselors conduct evaluation of the total group experience at the final meeting (or before termination), as well as ongoing evaluation.

(c) Group counselors monitor their own behavior and become aware of what they are modeling in the group.

(d) Follow-up procedures might take the form of personal contact, telephone contact, or written contact.

(e) Follow-up meetings might be with individuals, or groups, or both to determine the degree to which: (i) members have reached their goals, (ii) the group had a positive or negative effect on the participants, (iii) members could profit from some type of referral, and (iv) as information for possible modification of future groups. If there is no follow-up meeting, provisions are made available for individual follow-up meetings to any member who needs or requests such a contact.

15. *Referrals:* If the needs of a particular member cannot be met within the type of group being offered, the group counselor suggests other appropriate professional referrals.

(a) Group counselors are knowledgeable of local community resources for assisting group members regarding professional referrals.

(b) Group counselors help members seek further professional assistance, if needed.

16. *Professional Development:* Group counselors recognize that professional growth is a continuous, ongoing, developmental process throughout their career.

(a) Group counselors maintain and upgrade their knowledge and skill competencies through educational activities, clinical experiences, and participation in professional development activities.

(b) Group counselors keep abreast of research findings and new developments as applied to groups.

Safeguarding Ethical Practice and Procedures for Reporting Unethical Behavior

The preceding remarks have been advanced as guidelines which are generally representative of ethical and professional group practice. They have not been proposed as rigidly defined prescriptions. However, practitioners who are thought to be grossly unresponsive to the ethical concerns addressed in this document may be subject to a review of their practices by the AACD Ethics Committee and ASGW peers.

1. For consultation and/or questions regarding these ASGW Ethical Guidelines or group ethical dilemmas, you may contact the Chairperson of the ASGW Ethics Committee. The name, address, and telephone number of the current ASGW Ethics Committee Chairperson may be acquired by telephoning the AACD office in Alexandria, Virginia at (703) 823-9800.

2. If a group counselor's behavior is suspected as being unethical, the following procedures are to be followed:

   (a) Collect more information and investigate further to confirm the unethical practice as determined by the ASGW Ethical Guidelines.

   (b) Confront the individual with the apparent violation of ethical guidelines for the purposes of protecting the safety of any clients and to help the group counselor correct any inappropriate behaviors. If satisfactory resolution is not reached through this contact then:

   (c) A complaint should be made in writing, including the specific facts and dates of the alleged violation and all relevant supporting data. The complaint should be included in an envelope marked "CONFIDENTIAL" to ensure confidentiality for both the accuser(s) and the alleged violator(s) and forwarded to all of the following sources:

      1. The name and address of the Chairperson of the state Counselor Licensure Board for the respective state, if in existence.

      2. The Ethics Committee
         c/o the President
         American Association for Counseling and Development
         5999 Stevenson Avenue
         Alexandria, Virginia 22304

      3. The name and address of all private credentialing agencies that the alleged violator maintains credentials or holds professional membership. Some of these include the following:

         National Board for Certified Counselors, Inc.
         5999 Stevenson Avenue
         Alexandria, Virginia 22304

National Council for Credentialing of Career Counselors
c/o NBCC
5999 Stevenson Avenue
Alexandria, Virginia 22304

National Academy for Certified Clinical Mental Health Counselors
5999 Stevenson Avenue
Alexandria, Virginia 22304

Commission on Rehabilitation Counselor Certification
162 North State Street, Suite 317
Chicago, Illinois 60601

American Association for Marriage and Family Therapy
1717 K Street, N.W., Suite 407
Washington, D.C. 22006

American Psychological Association
1200 Seventeenth Street, N.W.
Washington, D.C. 22036

American Group Psychotherapy Association, Inc.
25 East 21st Street, 6th Floor
New York, New York 10010

Appendix C
American Counseling Association
Code of Ethics

Preamble ～

The American Counseling Association is an educational, scientific and professional organization whose members are dedicated to the enhancement of human development throughout the life span. Association members recognize diversity in our society and embrace a cross-cultural approach in support of the worth, dignity, potential, and uniqueness of each individual.

The specification of a code of ethics enables the association to clarify to current and future members, and to those served by members, the nature of the ethical responsibilities held in common by its members. As the code of ethics of the association, this document establishes principles that define the ethical behavior of association members. All members of the American Counseling Association are required to adhere to the Code of Ethics and the Standards of Practice. The Code of Ethics will serve as the basis for processing ethical complaints initiated against members of the association.

Section A: The Counseling Relationship ～

A.1. Client Welfare

  a. Primary Responsibility.
     The primary responsibility of counselors is to respect the dignity and to promote the welfare of clients.
  b. Positive Growth and Development.
     Counselors encourage client growth and development in ways that foster the

Source: Approved by The American Counseling Association (ACA), Governing Council, April 1995. Reprinted by Permission of the American Counseling Association, Alexandria, VA.

clients' interest and welfare; counselors avoid fostering dependent counseling relationships.

c. Counseling Plans.

Counselors and their clients work jointly in devising integrated, individual counseling plans that offer reasonable promise of success and are consistent with abilities and circumstances of clients. Counselors and clients regularly review counseling plans to ensure their continued viability and effectiveness, respecting clients' freedom of choice. (See A.3.b.)

d. Family Involvement.

Counselors recognize that families are usually important in clients' lives and strive to enlist family understanding and involvement as a positive resource, when appropriate.

e. Career and Employment Needs.

Counselors work with their clients in considering employment in jobs and circumstances that are consistent with the clients' overall abilities, vocational limitations, physical restrictions, general temperament, interest and aptitude patterns, social skills, education, general qualifications, and other relevant characteristics and needs. Counselors neither place nor participate in placing clients in positions that will result in damaging the interest and the welfare of clients, employers, or the public.

A.2. Respecting Diversity

a. Nondiscrimination.

Counselors do not condone or engage in discrimination based on age, color, culture, disability, ethnic group, gender, race, religion, sexual orientation, marital status, or socioeconomic status. (See C.5.a., C.5.b., and D.1.i.)

b. Respecting Differences.

Counselors will actively attempt to understand the diverse cultural backgrounds of the clients with whom they work. This includes, but is not limited to, learning how the counselor's own cultural/ethnic/racial identity impacts her/his values and beliefs about the counseling process. (See E.8. and F.2.i.)

A.3. Client Rights

a. Disclosure to Clients.

When counseling is initiated, and throughout the counseling process as necessary, counselors inform clients of the purposes, goals, techniques, procedures, limitations, potential risks and benefits of services to be performed, and other pertinent information. Counselors take steps to ensure that clients understand the implications of diagnosis, the intended use of tests and reports, fees, and billing arrangements. Clients have the right to expect confidentiality and to be provided with an explanation of its limitations, including supervision and/or treatment team professionals; to obtain clear information about their case records; to participate in the ongoing counseling plans; and to refuse any recommended services and be advised of the consequences of such refusal. (See E.5.a. and G.2.)

  b. Freedom of Choice.
  Counselors offer clients the freedom to choose whether to enter into a counseling relationship and to determine which professional(s) will provide counseling. Restrictions that limit choices of clients are fully explained. (See A.1.c.)
  c. Inability to Give Consent.
  When counseling minors or persons unable to give voluntary informed consent, counselors act in these clients' best interests. (See B.3.)

A.4. Clients Served by Others

If a client is receiving services from another mental health professional, counselors, with client consent, inform the professional persons already involved and develop clear agreements to avoid confusion and conflict for the client. (See C.6.c.)

A.5. Personal Needs and Values

  a. Personal Needs.
  In the counseling relationship, counselors are aware of the intimacy and responsibilities inherent in the counseling relationship, maintain respect for clients, and avoid actions that seek to meet their personal needs at the expense of clients.
  b. Personal Values.
  Counselors are aware of their own values, attitudes, beliefs, and behaviors and how these apply in a diverse society, and avoid imposing their values on clients. (See C.5.a.)

A.6. Dual Relationships

  a. Avoid When Possible.
  Counselors are aware of their influential positions with respect to clients, and they avoid exploiting the trust and dependency of clients. Counselors make every effort to avoid dual relationships with clients that could impair professional judgment or increase the risk of harm to clients. (Examples of such relationships include, but are not limited to, familial, social, financial, business, or close personal relationships with clients.) When a dual relationship cannot be avoided, counselors take appropriate professional precautions such as informed consent, consultation, supervision, and documentation to ensure that judgment is not impaired and no exploitation occurs. (See F.1.b.)
  b. Superior/Subordinate Relationships.
  Counselors do not accept as clients superiors or subordinates with whom they have administrative, supervisory, or evaluative relationships.

A.7. Sexual Intimacies With Clients

  a. Current Clients.
  Counselors do not have any type of sexual intimacies with clients and do not counsel persons with whom they have had a sexual relationship.

b. Former Clients.

Counselors do not engage in sexual intimacies with former clients within a minimum of two years after terminating the counseling relationship. Counselors who engage in such relationship after two years following termination have the responsibility to thoroughly examine and document that such relations did not have an exploitative nature, based on factors such as duration of counseling, amount of time since counseling, termination circumstances, client's personal history and mental status, adverse impact on the client, and actions by the counselor suggesting a plan to initiate a sexual relationship with the client after termination.

A.8. Multiple Clients

When counselors agree to provide counseling services to two or more persons who have a relationship (such as husband and wife, or parents and children), counselors clarify at the outset which person or persons are clients and the nature of the relationships they will have with each involved person. If it becomes apparent that counselors may be called upon to perform potentially conflicting roles, they clarify, adjust, or withdraw from roles appropriately. (See B.2. and B.4.d.)

A.9. Group Work

a. Screening.

Counselors screen prospective group counseling/therapy participants. To the extent possible, counselors select members whose needs and goals are compatible with goals of the group, who will not impede the group process, and whose well-being will not be jeopardized by the group experience.

b. Protecting Clients.

In a group setting, counselors take reasonable precautions to protect clients from physical or psychological trauma.

A.10. Fees and Bartering (See D.3.a. and D.3.b.)

a. Advance Understanding.

Counselors clearly explain to clients, prior to entering the counseling relationship, all financial arrangements related to professional services including the use of collection agencies or legal measures for nonpayment. (See A.11.c.)

b. Establishing Fees.

In establishing fees for professional counseling services, counselors consider the financial status of clients and locality. In the event that the established fee structure is inappropriate for a client, assistance is provided in attempting to find comparable services of acceptable cost. (See A.10.d., D.3.a., and D.3.b.)

c. Bartering Discouraged.

Counselors ordinarily refrain from accepting goods or services from clients in return for counseling services because such arrangements create inherent potential for conflicts, exploitation, and distortion of the professional relationship. Counselors may participate in bartering only if the relationship is not exploitive, if the client requests it, if a clear written contract is established, and if such arrangements are an accepted practice among professionals in the community. (See A.6.a.)

d. Pro Bono Service.

Counselors contribute to society by devoting a portion of their professional activity to services for which there is little or no financial return (pro bono).

A.11. Termination and Referral

a. Abandonment Prohibited.

Counselors do not abandon or neglect clients in counseling. Counselors assist in making appropriate arrangements for the continuation of treatment, when necessary, during interruptions such as vacations, and following termination.

b. Inability to Assist Clients.

If counselors determine an inability to be of professional assistance to clients, they avoid entering or immediately terminate a counseling relationship. Counselors are knowledgeable about referral resources and suggest appropriate alternatives. If clients decline the suggested referral, counselors should discontinue the relationship.

c. Appropriate Termination.

Counselors terminate a counseling relationship, securing client agreement when possible, when it is reasonably clear that the client is no longer benefiting, when services are no longer required, when counseling no longer serves the client's needs or interests, when clients do not pay fees charged, or when agency or institution limits do not allow provision of further counseling services. (See A.10.b. and C.2.g.)

A.12. Computer Technology

a. Use of Computers.

When computer applications are used in counseling services, counselors ensure that: (1) the client is intellectually, emotionally, and physically capable of using the computer application; (2) the computer application is appropriate for the needs of the client; (3) the client understands the purpose and operation of the computer applications; and (4) a follow-up of client use of a computer application is provided to correct possible misconceptions, discover inappropriate use, and assess subsequent needs.

b. Explanation of Limitations.

Counselors ensure that clients are provided information as a part of the counseling relationship that adequately explains the limitations of computer technology.

c. Access to Computer Applications.

Counselors provide for equal access to computer applications in counseling services. (See A.2.a.)

Section B: Confidentiality ~

B.1. Right to Privacy

a. Respect for Privacy.

Counselors respect their clients' right to privacy and avoid illegal and unwarranted disclosures of confidential information. (See A.3.a. and B.6.a.)

b. Client Waiver.

The right to privacy may be waived by the client or their legally recognized representative.

c. Exceptions.

The general requirement that counselors keep information confidential does not apply when disclosure is required to prevent clear and imminent danger to the client or others or when legal requirements demand that confidential information be revealed. Counselors consult with other professionals when in doubt as to the validity of an exception.

d. Contagious, Fatal Diseases.

A counselor who receives information confirming that a client has a disease commonly known to be both communicable and fatal is justified in disclosing information to an identifiable third party, who by his or her relationship with the client is at a high risk of contracting the disease. Prior to making a disclosure the counselor should ascertain that the client has not already informed the third party about his or her disease and that the client is not intending to inform the third party in the immediate future. (See B.1.c and B.1.f.)

e. Court Ordered Disclosure.

When court ordered to release confidential information without a client's permission, counselors request to the court that the disclosure not be required due to potential harm to the client or counseling relationship. (See B.1.c.)

f. Minimal Disclosure.

When circumstances require the disclosure of confidential information, only essential information is revealed. To the extent possible, clients are informed before confidential information is disclosed.

g. Explanation of Limitations.

When counseling is initiated and throughout the counseling process as necessary, counselors inform clients of the limitations of confidentiality and identify foreseeable situations in which confidentiality must be breached. (See G.2.a.)

h. Subordinates.

Counselors make every effort to ensure that privacy and confidentiality of clients are maintained by subordinates including employees, supervisees, clerical assistants, and volunteers. (See B.1.a.)

i. Treatment Teams.

If client treatment will involve a continued review by a treatment team, the client will be informed of the team's existence and composition.

B.2. Groups and Families

a. Group Work.

In group work, counselors clearly define confidentiality and the parameters for the specific group being entered, explain its importance, and discuss the difficulties related to confidentiality involved in group work. The fact that confidentiality cannot be guaranteed is clearly communicated to group members.

b. Family Counseling.

In family counseling, information about one family member cannot be disclosed to another member without permission. Counselors protect the privacy rights of each family member. (See A.8., B.3., and B.4.d.)

B.3. Minor or Incompetent Clients

When counseling clients who are minors or individuals who are unable to give voluntary, informed consent, parents or guardians may be included in the counseling process as appropriate. Counselors act in the best interests of clients and take measures to safeguard confidentiality. (See A.3.c.)

B.4. Records

a. Requirement of Records.

Counselors maintain records necessary for rendering professional services to their clients and as required by laws, regulations, or agency or institution procedures.

b. Confidentiality of Records.

Counselors are responsible for securing the safety and confidentiality of any counseling records they create, maintain, transfer, or destroy whether the records are written, taped, computerized, or stored in any other medium. (See B.1.a.)

c. Permission to Record or Observe.

Counselors obtain permission from clients prior to electronically recording or observing sessions. (See A.3.a.)

d. Client Access.

Counselors recognize that counseling records are kept for the benefit of clients, and therefore provide access to records and copies of records when requested by competent clients, unless the records contain information that may be misleading and detrimental to the client. In situations involving multiple clients, access to records is limited to those parts of records that do not include confidential information related to another client. (See A.8., B.1.a., and B.2.b.)

e. Disclosure or Transfer.

Counselors obtain written permission from clients to disclose or transfer records to legitimate third parties unless exceptions to confidentiality exist as listed in Section B.1. Steps are taken to ensure that receivers of counseling records are sensitive to their confidential nature.

B.5. Research and Training

a. Data Disguise Required.

Use of data derived from counseling relationships for purposes of training, research, or publication is confined to content that is disguised to ensure the anonymity of the individuals involved. (See B.1.g. and G.3.d.)

b. Agreement for Identification.

Identification of a client in a presentation or publication is permissible only when the client has reviewed the material and has agreed to its presentation or publication. (See G.3.d.)

B.6. Consultation

a. Respect for Privacy.

Information obtained in a consulting relationship is discussed for professional purposes only with persons clearly concerned with the case. Written and oral reports present data germane to the purposes of the consultation, and every effort is made to protect client identity and avoid undue invasion of privacy.

b. Cooperating Agencies.

Before sharing information, counselors make efforts to ensure that there are defined policies in other agencies serving the counselor's clients that effectively protect the confidentiality of information.

Section C: Professional Responsibility ~

C.1. Standards Knowledge

Counselors have a responsibility to read, understand, and follow the Code of Ethics and the Standards of Practice.

C.2. Professional Competence

a. Boundaries of Competence.

Counselors practice only within the boundaries of their competence, based on their education, training, supervised experience, state and national professional credentials, and appropriate professional experience. Counselors will demonstrate a commitment to gain knowledge, personal awareness, sensitivity, and skills pertinent to working with a diverse client population.

b. New Specialty Areas of Practice.

Counselors practice in specialty areas new to them only after appropriate education, training, and supervised experience. While developing skills in new specialty areas, counselors take steps to ensure the competence of their work and to protect others from possible harm.

c. Qualified for Employment.

Counselors accept employment only for positions for which they are qualified by education, training, supervised experience, state and national professional credentials, and appropriate professional experience. Counselors hire for professional counseling positions only individuals who are qualified and competent.

d. Monitor Effectiveness.

Counselors continually monitor their effectiveness as professionals and take steps to improve when necessary. Counselors in private practice take reasonable steps to seek out peer supervision to evaluate their efficacy as counselors.

e. Ethical Issues Consultation.

Counselors take reasonable steps to consult with other counselors or related professionals when they have questions regarding their ethical obligations or professional practice. (See H.1.)

f. Continuing Education.

Counselors recognize the need for continuing education to maintain a reasonable level of awareness of current scientific and professional information in their fields of activity. They take steps to maintain competence in the skills they use, are open to new procedures, and keep current with the diverse and/or special populations with whom they work.

g. Impairment.

Counselors refrain from offering or accepting professional services when their physical, mental or emotional problems are likely to harm a client or others. They are alert to the signs of impairment, seek assistance for problems, and, if necessary, limit, suspend, or terminate their professional responsibilities. (See A.11.c.)

C.3. Advertising and Soliciting Clients

a. Accurate Advertising.

There are no restrictions on advertising by counselors except those that can be specifically justified to protect the public from deceptive practices. Counselors advertise or represent their services to the public by identifying their credentials in an accurate manner that is not false, misleading, deceptive, or fraudulent. Counselors may only advertise the highest degree earned which is in counseling or a closely related field from a college or university that was accredited when the degree was awarded by one of the regional accrediting bodies recognized by the Council on Postsecondary Accreditation.

b. Testimonials.

Counselors who use testimonials do not solicit them from clients or other persons who, because of their particular circumstances, may be vulnerable to undue influence.

c. Statements by Others.

Counselors make reasonable efforts to ensure that statements made by others about them or the profession of counseling are accurate.

d. Recruiting Through Employment.

Counselors do not use their places of employment or institutional affiliation to recruit or gain clients, supervisees, or consultees for their private practices. (See C.5.e.)

e. Products and Training Advertisements.

Counselors who develop products related to their profession or conduct workshops or training events ensure that the advertisements concerning these products or events are accurate and disclose adequate information for consumers to make informed choices.

f. Promoting to Those Served.

Counselors do not use counseling, teaching, training, or supervisory relationships to promote their products or training events in a manner that is deceptive or would exert undue influence on individuals who may be vulnerable. Counselors may adopt textbooks they have authored for instruction purposes.

g. Professional Association Involvement.

Counselors actively participate in local, state, and national associations that foster the development and improvement of counseling.

C.4. Credentials

a. Credentials Claimed.

Counselors claim or imply only professional credentials possessed and are responsible for correcting any known misrepresentations of their credentials by others. Professional credentials include graduate degrees in counseling or closely related mental health fields, accreditation of graduate programs, national voluntary certifications, government-issued certifications or licenses, ACA professional membership, or any other credential that might indicate to the public specialized knowledge or expertise in counseling.

b. ACA Professional Membership.

ACA professional members may announce to the public their membership status. Regular members may not announce their ACA membership in a manner that might imply they are credentialed counselors.

c. Credential Guidelines.

Counselors follow the guidelines for use of credentials that have been established by the entities that issue the credentials.

d. Misrepresentation of Credentials.

Counselors do not attribute more to their credentials than the credentials represent, and do not imply that other counselors are not qualified because they do not possess certain credentials.

e. Doctoral Degrees From Other Fields.

Counselors who hold a master's degree in counseling or a closely related mental health field, but hold a doctoral degree from other than counseling or a closely related field, do not use the title "Dr." in their practices and do not announce to the public in relation to their practice or status as a counselor that they hold a doctorate.

C.5. Public Responsibility

a. Nondiscrimination.

Counselors do not discriminate against clients, students, or supervisees in a manner that has a negative impact based on their age, color, culture, disability, ethnic group, gender, race, religion, sexual orientation, or socioeconomic status, or for any other reason. (See A.2.a.)

b. Sexual Harassment.

Counselors do not engage in sexual harassment. Sexual harassment is defined as sexual solicitation, physical advances, or verbal or nonverbal conduct that is sexual in nature, that occurs in connection with professional activities or roles, and that either: (1) is unwelcome, is offensive, or creates a hostile workplace environment, and counselors know or are told this; or (2) is sufficiently severe or intense to be perceived as harassment to a reasonable person in the context. Sexual harassment can consist of a single intense or severe act or multiple persistent or pervasive acts.

c. Reports to Third Parties.

Counselors are accurate, honest, and unbiased in reporting their professional activities and judgments to appropriate third parties including courts, health insurance companies, those who are the recipients of evaluation reports, and others. (See B.1.g.)

d. Media Presentations.

When counselors provide advice or comment by means of public lectures, demonstrations, radio or television programs, prerecorded tapes, printed articles, mailed material, or other media, they take reasonable precautions to ensure that (1) the statements are based on appropriate professional counseling literature and practice; (2) the statements are otherwise consistent with the Code of Ethics and the Standards of Practice; and (3) the recipients of the information are not encouraged to infer that a professional counseling relationship has been established. (See C.6.b.)

e. Unjustified Gains.

Counselors do not use their professional positions to seek or receive unjustified personal gains, sexual favors, unfair advantage, or unearned goods or services. (See C.3.d.)

C.6. Responsibility to Other Professionals

a. Different Approaches.

Counselors are respectful of approaches to professional counseling that differ from their own. Counselors know and take into account the traditions and practices of other professional groups with which they work.

b. Personal Public Statements.

When making personal statements in a public context, counselors clarify that they are speaking from their personal perspectives and that they are not speaking on behalf of all counselors or the profession. (See C.5.d.)

c. Clients Served by Others.

When counselors learn that their clients are in a professional relationship with another mental health professional, they request release from clients to inform the other professionals and strive to establish positive and collaborative professional relationships. (See A.4.)

Section D: Relationships with Other Professionals ~

D.1. Relationships With Employers and Employees

a. Role Definition.
Counselors define and describe for their employers and employees the parameters and levels of their professional roles.

b. Agreements.
Counselors establish working agreements with supervisors, colleagues, and subordinates regarding counseling or clinical relationships, confidentiality, adherence to professional standards, distinction between public and private material, maintenance and dissemination of recorded information, workload, and accountability. Working agreements in each instance are specified and made known to those concerned.

c. Negative Conditions.
Counselors alert their employers to conditions that may be potentially disruptive or damaging to the counselor's professional responsibilities or that may limit their effectiveness.

d. Evaluation.
Counselors submit regularly to professional review and evaluation by their supervisor or the appropriate representative of the employer.

e. In-Service.
Counselors are responsible for in-service development of self and staff.

f. Goals.
Counselors inform their staff of goals and programs.

g. Practices.
Counselors provide personnel and agency practices that respect and enhance the rights and welfare of each employee and recipient of agency services. Counselors strive to maintain the highest levels of professional services.

h. Personnel Selection and Assignment.
Counselors select competent staff and assign responsibilities compatible with their skills and experiences.

i. Discrimination.
Counselors, as either employers or employees, do not engage in or condone practices that are inhumane, illegal, or unjustifiable (such as considerations based on age, color, culture, disability, ethnic group, gender, race, religion, sexual orientation, or socioeconomic status) in hiring, promotion, or training. (See A.2.a. and C.5.b.)

j. Professional Conduct.
Counselors have a responsibility both to clients and to the agency or institution within which services are performed to maintain high standards of professional conduct.

k. Exploitive Relationships.

Counselors do not engage in exploitive relationships with individuals over whom they have supervisory, evaluative, or instructional control or authority.

l. Employer Policies.

The acceptance of employment in an agency or institution implies that counselors are in agreement with its general policies and principles. Counselors strive to reach agreement with employers as to acceptable standards of conduct that allow for changes in institutional policy conducive to the growth and development of clients.

D.2. Consultation (See B.6.)

a. Consultation as an Option.

Counselors may choose to consult with any other professionally competent persons about their clients. In choosing consultants, counselors avoid placing the consultant in a conflict of interest situation that would preclude the consultant being a proper party to the counselor's efforts to help the client. Should counselors be engaged in a work setting that compromises this consultation standard, they consult with other professionals whenever possible to consider justifiable alternatives.

b. Consultant Competency.

Counselors are reasonably certain that they have or the organization represented has the necessary competencies and resources for giving the kind of consulting services needed and that appropriate referral resources are available.

c. Understanding With Clients.

When providing consultation, counselors attempt to develop with their clients a clear understanding of problem definition, goals for change, and predicted consequences of interventions selected.

d. Consultant Goals.

The consulting relationship is one in which client adaptability and growth toward self-direction are consistently encouraged and cultivated. (See A.1.b.)

D.3. Fees for Referral

a. Accepting Fees From Agency Clients.

Counselors refuse a private fee or other remuneration for rendering services to persons who are entitled to such services through the counselor's employing agency or institution. The policies of a particular agency may make explicit provisions for agency clients to receive counseling services from members of its staff in private practice. In such instances, the clients must be informed of other options open to them should they seek private counseling services. (See A.10.a., A.11.b., and C.3.d.)

b. Referral Fees.

Counselors do not accept a referral fee from other professionals.

D.4. Subcontractor Arrangements

When counselors work as subcontractors for counseling services for a third party, they have a duty to inform clients of the limitations of confidentiality that the organization may place on counselors in providing counseling services to clients. The limits of such confidentiality ordinarily are discussed as part of the intake session. (See B.1.e. and B.1.f.)

Section E: Evaluation, Assessment, and Interpretation∼

E.1. General

a. Appraisal Techniques.
The primary purpose of educational and psychological assessment is to provide measures that are objective and interpretable in either comparative or absolute terms. Counselors recognize the need to interpret the statements in this section as applying to the whole range of appraisal techniques, including test and nontest data.

b. Client Welfare.
Counselors promote the welfare and best interests of the client in the development, publication, and utilization of educational and psychological assessment techniques. They do not misuse assessment results and interpretations and take reasonable steps to prevent others from misusing the information these techniques provide. They respect the client's right to know the results, the interpretations made, and the bases for their conclusions and recommendations.

E.2. Competence to Use and Interpret Tests

a. Limits of Competence.
Counselors recognize the limits of their competence and perform only those testing and assessment services for which they have been trained. They are familiar with reliability, validity, related standardization, error of measurement, and proper application of any technique utilized. Counselors using computer-based test interpretations are trained in the construct being measured and the specific instrument being used prior to using this type of computer application. Counselors take reasonable measures to ensure the proper use of psychological assessment techniques by persons under their supervision.

b. Appropriate Use.
Counselors are responsible for the appropriate application, scoring, interpretation, and use of assessment instruments, whether they score and interpret such tests themselves or use computerized or other services.

c. Decisions Based on Results.
Counselors responsible for decisions involving individuals or policies that are based on assessment results have a thorough understanding of educational and psychological measurement, including validation criteria, test research, and guidelines for test development and use.

d. Accurate Information.

Counselors provide accurate information and avoid false claims or misconceptions when making statements about assessment instruments or techniques. Special efforts are made to avoid unwarranted connotations of such terms as IQ and grade equivalent scores. (See C.5.c.)

E.3. Informed Consent

a. Explanation to Clients.

Prior to assessment, counselors explain the nature and purposes of assessment and the specific use of results in language the client (or other legally authorized person on behalf of the client) can understand, unless an explicit exception to this right has been agreed upon in advance. Regardless of whether scoring and interpretation are completed by counselors, by assistants, or by computer or other outside services, counselors take reasonable steps to ensure that appropriate explanations are given to the client.

b. Recipients of Results.

The examinee's welfare, explicit understanding, and prior agreement determine the recipients of test results. Counselors include accurate and appropriate interpretations with any release of individual or group test results. (See B.1.a. and C.5.c.)

E.4. Release of Information to Competent Professionals

a. Misuse of Results.

Counselors do not misuse assessment results, including test results, and interpretations, and take reasonable steps to prevent the misuse of such by others. (See C.5.c.)

b. Release of Raw Data.

Counselors ordinarily release data (e.g., protocols, counseling or interview notes, or questionnaires) in which the client is identified only with the consent of the client or the client's legal representative. Such data are usually released only to persons recognized by counselors as competent to interpret the data. (See B.1.a.)

E.5. Proper Diagnosis of Mental Disorders

a. Proper Diagnosis.

Counselors take special care to provide proper diagnosis of mental disorders. Assessment techniques (including personal interview) used to determine client care (e.g., locus of treatment, type of treatment, or recommended follow-up) are carefully selected and appropriately used. (See A.3.a. and C.5.c.)

b. Cultural Sensitivity.

Counselors recognize that culture affects the manner in which clients' problems are defined. Clients' socioeconomic and cultural experience is considered when diagnosing mental disorders.

E.6. Test Selection

a. Appropriateness of Instruments.
Counselors carefully consider the validity, reliability, psychometric limitations, and appropriateness of instruments when selecting tests for use in a given situation or with a particular client.

b. Culturally Diverse Populations.
Counselors are cautious when selecting tests for culturally diverse populations to avoid inappropriateness of testing that may be outside of socialized behavioral or cognitive patterns.

E.7. Conditions of Test Administration

a. Administration Conditions.
Counselors administer tests under the same conditions that were established in their standardization. When tests are not administered under standard conditions or when unusual behavior or irregularities occur during the testing session, those conditions are noted in interpretation, and the results may be designated as invalid or of questionable validity.

b. Computer Administration.
Counselors are responsible for ensuring that administration programs function properly to provide clients with accurate results when a computer or other electronic methods are used for test administration. (See A.12.b.)

c. Unsupervised Test-Taking.
Counselors do not permit unsupervised or inadequately supervised use of tests or assessments unless the tests or assessments are designed, intended, and validated for self-administration and/or scoring.

d. Disclosure of Favorable Conditions.
Prior to test administration, conditions that produce most favorable test results are made known to the examinee.

E.8. Diversity in Testing

Counselors are cautious in using assessment techniques, making evaluations, and interpreting the performance of populations not represented in the norm group on which an instrument was standardized. They recognize the effects of age, color, culture, disability, ethnic group, gender, race, religion, sexual orientation, and socioeconomic status on test administration and interpretation and place test results in proper perspective with other relevant factors. (See A.2.a.)

E.9. Test Scoring and Interpretation

a. Reporting Reservations.
In reporting assessment results, counselors indicate any reservations that exist regarding validity or reliability because of the circumstances of the assessment or the inappropriateness of the norms for the person tested.

b. Research Instruments.
Counselors exercise caution when interpreting the results of research instru-

ments possessing insufficient technical data to support respondent results. The specific purposes for the use of such instruments are stated explicitly to the examinee.

c. Testing Services.

Counselors who provide test scoring and test interpretation services to support the assessment process confirm the validity of such interpretations. They accurately describe the purpose, norms, validity, reliability, and applications of the procedures and any special qualifications applicable to their use. The public offering of an automated test interpretations service is considered a professional-to-professional consultation. The formal responsibility of the consultant is to the consultee, but the ultimate and overriding responsibility is to the client.

E.10. Test Security

Counselors maintain the integrity and security of tests and other assessment techniques consistent with legal and contractual obligations. Counselors do not appropriate, reproduce, or modify published tests or parts thereof without acknowledgment and permission from the publisher.

E.11. Obsolete Tests and Outdated Test Results

Counselors do not use data or test results that are obsolete or outdated for the current purpose. Counselors make every effort to prevent the misuse of obsolete measures and test data by others.

E.12. Test Construction

Counselors use established scientific procedures, relevant standards, and current professional knowledge for test design in the development, publication, and utilization of educational and psychological assessment techniques.

Section F: Teaching, Training, and Supervision ∼

F.1. Counselor Educators and Trainers

a. Educators as Teachers and Practitioners.

Counselors who are responsible for developing, implementing, and supervising educational programs are skilled as teachers and practitioners. They are knowledgeable regarding the ethical, legal, and regulatory aspects of the profession, are skilled in applying that knowledge, and make students and supervisees aware of their responsibilities. Counselors conduct counselor education and training programs in an ethical manner and serve as role models for professional behavior. Counselor educators should make an effort to infuse material related to human diversity into all courses and/or workshops that are designed to promote the development of professional counselors.

b. Relationship Boundaries With Students and Supervisees.

Counselors clearly define and maintain ethical, professional, and social relationship boundaries with their students and supervisees. They are aware of the differential in power that exists and the student's or supervisee's possible incomprehension of that power differential. Counselors explain to students and supervisees the potential for the relationship to become exploitive.

c. Sexual Relationships.

Counselors do not engage in sexual relationships with students or supervisees and do not subject them to sexual harassment. (See A.6. and C.5.b.)

d. Contributions to Research.

Counselors give credit to students or supervisees for their contributions to research and scholarly projects. Credit is given through coauthorship, acknowledgment, footnote statement, or other appropriate means, in accordance with such contributions. (See G.4.b. and G.4.c.)

e. Close Relatives.

Counselors do not accept close relatives as students or supervisees.

f. Supervision Preparation.

Counselors who offer clinical supervision services are adequately prepared in supervision methods and techniques. Counselors who are doctoral students serving as practicum or internship supervisors to master's level students are adequately prepared and supervised by the training program.

g. Responsibility for Services to Clients.

Counselors who supervise the counseling services of others take reasonable measures to ensure that counseling services provided to clients are professional.

h. Endorsement.

Counselors do not endorse students or supervisees for certification, licensure, employment, or completion of an academic or training program if they believe students or supervisees are not qualified for the endorsement. Counselors take reasonable steps to assist students or supervisees who are not qualified for endorsement to become qualified.

F.2. Counselor Education and Training Programs

a. Orientation.

Prior to admission, counselors orient prospective students to the counselor education or training program's expectations, including but not limited to the following: (1) the type and level of skill acquisition required for successful completion of the training, (2) subject matter to be covered, (3) basis for evaluation, (4) training components that encourage self-growth or self-disclosure as part of the training process, (5) the type of supervision settings and requirements of the sites for required clinical field experiences, (6) student and supervisee evaluation and dismissal policies and procedures, and (7) up-to-date employment prospects for graduates.

b. Integration of Study and Practice.

Counselors establish counselor education and training programs that integrate academic study and supervised practice.

c. Evaluation.

Counselors clearly state to students and supervisees, in advance of training, the levels of competency expected, appraisal methods, and timing of evaluations for both didactic and experiential components. Counselors provide students and supervisees with periodic performance appraisal and evaluation feedback throughout the training program.

d. Teaching Ethics.

Counselors make students and supervisees aware of the ethical responsibilities and standards of the profession and the students' and supervisees' ethical responsibilities to the profession. (See C.1. and F.3.e.)

e. Peer Relationships.

When students or supervisees are assigned to lead counseling groups or provide clinical supervision for their peers, counselors take steps to ensure that students and supervisees placed in these roles do not have personal or adverse relationships with peers and that they understand they have the same ethical obligations as counselor educators, trainers, and supervisors. Counselors make every effort to ensure that the rights of peers are not compromised when students or supervisees are assigned to lead counseling groups or provide clinical supervision.

f. Varied Theoretical Positions.

Counselors present varied theoretical positions so that students and supervisees may make comparisons and have opportunities to develop their own positions. Counselors provide information concerning the scientific bases of professional practice. (See C.6.a.)

g. Field Placements.

Counselors develop clear policies within their training program regarding field placement and other clinical experiences. Counselors provide clearly stated roles and responsibilities for the student or supervisee, the site supervisor, and the program supervisor. They confirm that site supervisors are qualified to provide supervision and are informed of their professional and ethical responsibilities in this role.

h. Dual Relationships as Supervisors.

Counselors avoid dual relationships such as performing the role of site supervisor and training program supervisor in the student's or supervisee's training program. Counselors do not accept any form of professional services, fees, commissions, reimbursement, or remuneration from a site for student or supervisee placement.

i. Diversity in Programs.

Counselors are responsive to their institution's and program's recruitment and retention needs for training program administrators, faculty, and students with diverse backgrounds and special needs. (See A.2.a.)

F.3. Students and Supervisees

a. Limitations.

Counselors, through ongoing evaluation and appraisal, are aware of the academic and personal limitations of students and supervisees that might impede performance. Counselors assist students and supervisees in securing remedial assistance when needed, and dismiss from the training program supervisees who are unable to provide competent service due to academic or personal limitations. Counselors seek professional consultation and document their decision to dismiss or refer students or supervisees for assistance. Counselors assure that students and supervisees have recourse to address decisions made, to require them to seek assistance, or to dismiss them.

b. Self-Growth Experiences.

Counselors use professional judgment when designing training experiences conducted by the counselors themselves that require student and supervisee self-growth or self-disclosure. Safeguards are provided so that students and supervisees are aware of the ramifications their self-disclosure may have, on counselors whose primary role as teacher, trainer, or supervisor requires acting on ethical obligations to the profession. Evaluative components of experiential training experiences explicitly delineate predetermined academic standards that are separate and not dependent on the student's level of self-disclosure. (See A.6.)

c. Counseling for Students and Supervisees.

If students or supervisees request counseling, supervisors or counselor educators provide them with acceptable referrals. Supervisors or counselor educators do not serve as counselor to students or supervisees over whom they hold administrative, teaching, or evaluative roles unless this is a brief role associated with a training experience. (See A.6.b.)

d. Clients of Students and Supervisees.

Counselors make every effort to ensure that the clients at field placements are aware of the services rendered and the qualifications of the students and supervisees rendering those services. Clients receive professional disclosure information and are informed of the limits of confidentiality. Client permission is obtained in order for the students and supervisees to use any information concerning the counseling relationship in the training process. (See B.1.e.)

e. Standards for Students and Supervisees.

Students and supervisees preparing to become counselors adhere to the Code of Ethics and the Standards of Practice. Students and supervisees have the same obligations to clients as those required of counselors. (See H.1.)

Section G Research and Publication ~

G.1. Research Responsibilities

a. Use of Human Subjects.

Counselors plan, design, conduct, and report research in a manner consistent with pertinent ethical principles, federal and state laws, host institutional regulations, and scientific standards governing research with human subjects. Counselors design and conduct research that reflects cultural sensitivity appropriateness.

b. Deviation From Standard Practices.

Counselors seek consultation and observe stringent safeguards to protect the rights of research participants when a research problem suggests a deviation from standard acceptable practices. (See B.6.)

c. Precautions to Avoid Injury.

Counselors who conduct research with human subjects are responsible for the subjects' welfare throughout the experiment and take reasonable precautions to avoid causing injurious psychological, physical, or social effects to their subjects.

d. Principal Researcher Responsibility.

The ultimate responsibility for ethical research practice lies with the principal researcher. All others involved in the research activities share ethical obligations and full responsibility for their own actions.

e. Minimal Interference.

Counselors take reasonable precautions to avoid causing disruptions in subjects' lives due to participation in research.

f. Diversity.

Counselors are sensitive to diversity and research issues with special populations. They seek consultation when appropriate. (See A.2.a. and B.6.)

G.2. Informed Consent

a. Topics Disclosed.

In obtaining informed consent for research, counselors use language that is understandable to research participants and that: (1) accurately explains the purpose and procedures to be followed; (2) identifies any procedures that are experimental or relatively untried; (3) describes the attendant discomforts and risks; (4) describes the benefits or changes in individuals or organizations that might be reasonably expected; (5) discloses appropriate alternative procedures that would be advantageous for subjects; (6) offers to answer any inquiries concerning the procedures; (7) describes any limitations on confidentiality; and (8) instructs that subjects are free to withdraw their consent and to discontinue participation in the project at any time. (See B.1.f.)

b. Deception.

Counselors do not conduct research involving deception unless alternative procedures are not feasible and the prospective value of the research justifies the deception. When the methodological requirements of a study necessitate concealment or deception, the investigator is required to explain clearly the reasons for this action as soon as possible.

c. Voluntary Participation.

Participation in research is typically voluntary and without any penalty for refusal to participate. Involuntary participation is appropriate only when it can be demonstrated that participation will have no harmful effects on subjects and is essential to the investigation.

d. Confidentiality of Information.

Information obtained about research participants during the course of an investigation is confidential. When the possibility exists that others may obtain access to such information, ethical research practice requires that the possibility, together with the plans for protecting confidentiality, be explained to participants as a part of the procedure for obtaining informed consent. (See B.1.e.)

e. Persons Incapable of Giving Informed Consent.

When a person is incapable of giving informed consent, counselors provide an appropriate explanation, obtain agreement for participation and obtain appropriate consent from a legally authorized person.

f. Commitments to Participants.

Counselors take reasonable measures to honor all commitments to research participants.

g. Explanations After Data Collection.

After data are collected, counselors provide participants with full clarification of the nature of the study to remove any misconceptions. Where scientific or human values justify delaying or withholding information, counselors take reasonable measures to avoid causing harm.

h. Agreements to Cooperate.

Counselors who agree to cooperate with another individual in research or publication incur an obligation to cooperate as promised in terms of punctuality of performance and with regard to the completeness and accuracy of the information required.

i. Informed Consent for Sponsors.

In the pursuit of research, counselors give sponsors, institutions, and publication channels the same respect and opportunity for giving informed consent that they accord to individual research participants. Counselors are aware of their obligation to future research workers and ensure that host institutions are given feedback information and proper acknowledgment.

G.3. Reporting Results

a. Information Affecting Outcome.

When reporting research results, counselors explicitly mention all variables and conditions known to the investigator that may have affected the outcome of a study or the interpretation of data.

b. Accurate Results.

Counselors plan, conduct, and report research accurately and in a manner that minimizes the possibility that results will be misleading. They provide thorough discussions of the limitations of their data and alternative hypotheses. Counselors do not engage in fraudulent research, distort data, misrepresent data, or deliberately bias their results.

c. Obligation to Report Unfavorable Results.

Counselors communicate to other counselors the results of any research judged to be of professional value. Results that reflect unfavorably on institutions, programs, services, prevailing opinions, or vested interests are not withheld.

d. Identity of Subjects.

Counselors who supply data, aid in the research of another person, report research results, or make original data available take due care to disguise the identity of respective subjects in the absence of specific authorization from the subjects to do otherwise. (See B.1.g. and B.5.a.)

e. Replication Studies.

Counselors are obligated to make available sufficient original research data to qualified professionals who may wish to replicate the study.

G.4. Publication

a. Recognition of Others.

When conducting and reporting research, counselors are familiar with and give recognition to previous work on the topic, observe copyright laws, and give full credit to those to whom credit is due. (See F.1.d. and G.4.c.)

b. Contributors.

Counselors give credit through joint authorship, acknowledgment, footnote statements, or other appropriate means to those who have contributed significantly to research or concept development in accordance with such contributions. The principal contributor is listed first and minor technical or professional contributions are acknowledged in notes or introductory statements.

c. Student Research.

For an article that is substantially based on a student's dissertation or thesis, the student is listed as the principal author. (See F.1.d. and G.4.a.)

d. Duplicate Submission.

Counselors submit manuscripts for consideration to only one journal at a time. Manuscripts that are published in whole or in substantial part in another journal or published work are not submitted for publication without acknowledgment and permission from the previous publication.

e. Professional Review.

Counselors who review material submitted for publication, research, or other scholarly purposes respect the confidentiality and proprietary rights of those who submitted it.

Section H: Resolving Ethical Issues∿

H.1. Knowledge of Standards

Counselors are familiar with the Code of Ethics and the Standards of Practice and other applicable ethics codes from other professional organizations of which they are member, or from certification and licensure bodies.

Lack of knowledge or misunderstanding of an ethical responsibility is not a defense against a charge of unethical conduct. (See F.3.e.)

H.2. Suspected Violations

a. Ethical Behavior Expected.

Counselors expect professional associates to adhere to Code of Ethics. When counselors possess reasonable cause that raises doubts as to whether a counselor is acting in an ethical manner, they take appropriate action. (See H.2.d. and H.2.e.)

b. Consultation.

When uncertain as to whether a particular situation or course of action may be in violation of Code of Ethics, counselors consult with other counselors who are knowledgeable about ethics, with colleagues, or with appropriate authorities.

c. Organization Conflicts.

If the demands of an organization with which counselors are affiliated pose a conflict with Code of Ethics, counselors specify the nature of such conflicts and express to their supervisors or other responsible officials their commitment to Code of Ethics. When possible, counselors work toward change within the organization to allow full adherence to Code of Ethics.

d. Informal Resolution.

When counselors have reasonable cause to believe that another counselor is violating an ethical standard, they attempt to first resolve the issue informally with the other counselor if feasible, providing that such action does not violate confidentiality rights that may be involved.

e. Reporting Suspected Violations.

When an informal resolution is not appropriate or feasible, counselors, upon reasonable cause, take action such as reporting the suspected ethical violation to state or national ethics committees, unless this action conflicts with confidentiality rights that cannot be resolved.

f. Unwarranted Complaints.

Counselors do not initiate, participate in, or encourage the filing of ethics complaints that are unwarranted or intend to harm a counselor rather than to protect clients or the public.

H.3. Cooperation With Ethics Committees

Counselors assist in the process of enforcing Code of Ethics. Counselors cooperate with investigations, proceedings, and requirements of the ACA Ethics Committee or ethics committees of other duly constituted associations or boards having jurisdiction over those charged with a violation. Counselors are familiar with the ACA Policies and Procedures and use it as a reference in assisting the enforcement of the Code of Ethics.

Appendix D
American Counseling Association
Standards of Practice

All members of the American Counseling Association (ACA) are required to adhere to the Standards of Practice and the Code of Ethics. The Standards of Practice represent minimal behavioral statements of the Code of Ethics. Members should refer to the applicable section of the Code of Ethics for further interpretation and amplification of the applicable Standard of Practice.

Section A: The Counseling Relationship

Standard of Practice One (SP-1)
Nondiscrimination

Counselors respect diversity and must not discriminate against clients because of age, color, culture, disability, ethnic group, gender, race, religion, sexual orientation, marital status, or socioeconomic status. (See A.2.a.)

Standard of Practice Two (SP-2)
Disclosure to Clients

Counselors must adequately inform clients, preferably in writing, regarding the counseling process and counseling relationship at or before the time it begins and throughout the relationship. (See A.3.a.)

Standard of Practice Three (SP-3)
Dual Relationships

Counselors must make every effort to avoid dual relationships with clients that could impair their professional judgment or increase the risk of harm to clients. When a

Source: Approved by the American Counseling Association as revised by Governing Council, April, 1995. Effective July 1, 1995. Reprinted by permission of the American Counseling Association, Alexandria, VA.

dual relationship cannot be avoided, counselors must take appropriate steps to ensure that judgment is not impaired and that no exploitation occurs. (See A.6.a. and A.6.b.)

Standard of Practice Four (SP-4)
Sexual Intimacies with Clients

Counselors must not engage in any type of sexual intimacies with current clients and must not engage in sexual intimacies with former clients within a minimum of two years after terminating the counseling relationship. Counselors who engage in such relationship after two years following termination have the responsibility to thoroughly examine and document that such relations did not have an exploitative nature.

Standard of Practice Five (SP-5)
Protecting Clients During Group Work

Counselors must take steps to protect clients from physical or psychological trauma resulting from interactions during group work. (See A.9.b.)

Standard of Practice Six (SP-6)
Advance Understanding of Fees

Counselors must explain to clients, prior to their entering the counseling relationship, financial arrangements related to professional services. (See A.10. a-d. and A.11.c.)

Standard of Practice Seven (SP-7)
Termination

Counselors must assist in making appropriate arrangements for the continuation of treatment of clients, when necessary, following termination of counseling relationships. (See A.11.a.)

Standard of Practice Eight (SP-8)
Inability to Assist Clients

Counselors must avoid entering or immediately terminate a counseling relationship if it is determined that they are unable to be of professional assistance to a client. The counselor may assist in making an appropriate referral for the client. (See A.11.b.)

Section B: Confidentiality ~

Standard of Practice Nine (SP-9)
Confidentiality Requirement

Counselors must keep information related to counseling services confidential unless disclosure is in the best interest of clients, is required for the welfare of others, or is required by law. When disclosure is required, only information that is essential is revealed and the client is informed of such disclosure. (See B.1. a.-f.)

Standard of Practice Ten (SP-10)
Confidentiality Requirements for Subordinates

Counselors must take measures to ensure that privacy and confidentiality of clients are maintained by subordinates. (See B.1.h.)

Standard of Practice Eleven (SP-11)
Confidentiality in Group Work

Counselors must clearly communicate to group members that confidentiality cannot be guaranteed in group work. (See B.2.a.)

Standard of Practice Twelve (SP-12)
Confidentiality in Family Counseling

Counselors must not disclose information about one family member in counseling to another family member without prior consent. (See B.2.b.)

Standard of Practice Thirteen (SP-13)
Confidentiality of Records

Counselors must maintain appropriate confidentiality in creating, storing, accessing, transferring, and disposing of counseling records. (See B.4.b.)

Standard of Practice Fourteen (SP-14)
Permission to Record or Observe

Counselors must obtain prior consent from clients in order to electronically record or observe sessions. (See B.4.c.)

Standard of Practice Fifteen (SP-15)
Disclosure or Transfer of Records

Counselors must obtain client consent to disclose or transfer records to third parties, unless exceptions listed in SP-9 exist. (See B.4.e.)

Standard of Practice Sixteen (SP-16)
Data Disguise Required

Counselors must disguise the identity of the client when using data for training, research, or publication. (See B.5.a.)

Section C: Professional Responsibility ~

Standard of Practice Seventeen (SP-17)
Boundaries of Competence

Counselors must practice only within the boundaries of their competence. (See C.2.a.)

Standard of Practice Eighteen (SP-18)
Continuing Education

Counselors must engage in continuing education to maintain their professional competence. (See C.2.f.)

Standard of Practice Nineteen (SP-19)
Impairment of Professionals

Counselors must refrain from offering professional services when their personal problems or conflicts may cause harm to a client or others. (See C.2.g.)

Standard of Practice Twenty (SP-20)
Accurate Advertising

Counselors must accurately represent their credentials and services when advertising. (See C.3.a.)

Standard of Practice Twenty-one (SP-21)
Recruiting Through Employment

Counselors must not use their place of employment or institutional affiliation to recruit clients for their private practices. (See C.3.d.)

Standard of Practice Twenty-two (SP-22)
Credentials Claimed

Counselors must claim or imply only professional credentials possessed and must correct any known misrepresentations of their credentials by others. (See C.4.a.)

Standard of Practice Twenty-three (SP-23)
Sexual Harassment

Counselors must not engage in sexual harassment. (See C.5.b.)

Standard of Practice Twenty-four (SP-24)
Unjustified Gains

Counselors must not use their professional positions to seek or receive unjustified personal gains, sexual favors, unfair advantage, or unearned goods or services. (See C.5.e.)

Standard of Practice Twenty-five (SP-25)
Clients Served by Others

With the consent of the client, counselors must inform other mental health professionals serving the same client that a counseling relationship between the counselor and client exists. (See C.6.c.)

Standard of Practice Twenty-six (SP-26)
Negative Employment Conditions

Counselors must alert their employers to institutional policy or conditions that may be potentially disruptive or damaging to the counselor's professional responsibilities, or that may limit their effectiveness or deny clients' rights. (See D.1.c.)

Standard of Practice Twenty-seven (SP-27)
Personnel Selection and Assignment

Counselors must select competent staff and must assign responsibilities compatible with staff skills and experiences. (See D.1.h.)

Standard of Practice Twenty-eight (SP-28)
Exploitive Relationships with Subordinates

Counselors must not engage in exploitive relationships with individuals over whom they have supervisory, evaluative, or instructional control or authority. (See D.1.k.)

Section D: Relationship with Other Professionals ∼

Standard of Practice Twenty-nine (SP-29)
Accepting Fees from Agency Clients

Counselors must not accept fees or other remuneration for consultation with persons entitled to such services through the counselor's employing agency or institution. (See D.3.a.)

Standard of Practice Thirty (SP-30)
Referral Fees

Counselors must not accept referral fees. (See D.3.b.)

Section E: Evaluation, Assessment, and Interpretation ∼

Standard of Practice Thirty-one (SP-31)
Limits of Competence

Counselors must perform only testing and assessment services for which they are competent. Counselors must not allow the use of psychological assessment techniques by unqualified persons under their supervision. (See E.2.a.)

Standard of Practice Thirty-two (SP-32)
Appropriate Use of Assessment Instruments

Counselors must use assessment instruments in the manner for which they were intended. (See E.2.b.)

Standard of Practice Thirty-three (SP-33)
Assessment Explanations to Clients

Counselors must provide explanations to clients prior to assessment about the nature and purposes of assessment and the specific uses of results. (See E.3.a.)

Standard of Practice Thirty-four (SP-34)
Recipients of Test Results

Counselors must ensure that accurate and appropriate interpretations accompany any release of testing and assessment information. (See E.3.b.)

Standard of Practice Thirty-five (SP-35)
Obsolete Tests and Outdated Test Results

Counselors must not base their assessment or intervention decisions or recommendations on data or test results that are obsolete or outdated for the current purpose. (See E.11.)

Section F: Teaching, Training, and Supervision ～

Standard of Practice Thirty-six (SP-36)
Sexual Relationships with Students or Supervisees

Counselors must not engage in sexual relationships with their students and supervisees. (See F.1.c.)

Standard of Practice Thirty-seven (SP-37)
Credit for Contributions to Research

Counselors must give credit to students or supervisees for their contributions to research and scholarly projects. (See F.1.d.)

Standard of Practice Thirty-eight (SP-38)
Supervision Preparation

Counselors who offer clinical supervision services must be trained and prepared in supervision methods and techniques. (See F.1.f.)

Standard of Practice Thirty-nine (SP-39)
Evaluation Information

Counselors must clearly state to students and supervisees in advance of training, the levels of competency expected, appraisal methods, and timing of evaluations. Counselors must provide students and supervisees with periodic performance appraisal and evaluation feedback throughout the training program. (See F.2.c.)

Standard of Practice Forty (SP-40)
Peer Relationships in Training

Counselors must make every effort to ensure that the rights of peers are not violated when students and supervisees are assigned to lead counseling groups or provide clinical supervision. (See F.2.e.)

Standard of Practice Forty-one (SP-41)
Limitations of Students and Supervisees

Counselors must assist students and supervisees in securing remedial assistance, when needed, and must dismiss from the training program students and supervisees who are unable to provide competent service due to academic or personal limitations. (See F.3.a.)

Standard of Practice Forty-two (SP-42)
Self-Growth Experiences

Counselors who conduct experiences for students or supervisees that include self-growth or self disclosure must inform participants of counselors' ethical obligations to the profession and must not grade participants based on their nonacademic performance. (See F.3.b.)

Standard of Practice Forty-three (SP-43)
Standards for Students and Supervisees

Students and supervisees preparing to become counselors must adhere to the Code of Ethics and the Standards of Practice of counselors. (See F.3.e.)

Section G: Research and Publication

Standard of Practice Forty-four (SP-44)
Precautions to Avoid Injury in Research

Counselors must avoid causing physical, social, or psychological harm or injury to subjects in research. (See G.1.c.)

Standard of Practice Forty-five (SP-45)
Confidentiality of Research Information

Counselors must keep confidential information obtained about research participants. (See G.2.d.)

Standard of Practice Forty-six (SP-46)
Information Affecting Research Outcome

Counselors must report all variables and conditions known to the investigator that may have affected research data or outcomes. (See G.3.a.)

Standard of Practice Forty-seven (SP-47)
Accurate Research Results

Counselors must not distort or misrepresent research data, nor fabricate or intentionally bias research results. (See G.3.b.)

Standard of Practice Forty-eight (SP-48)
Publication Contributors

Counselors must give appropriate credit to those who have contributed to research. (See G.4.a. and G.4.b.)

Section H: Resolving Ethical Issues

Standard of Practice Forty-nine (SP-49)
Ethical Behavior Expected

Counselors must take appropriate action when they possess reasonable cause that raises doubts as to whether counselors or other mental health professionals are acting in an ethical manner. (See H.2.a.)

Standard of Practice Fifty (SP-50)
Unwarranted Complaints

Counselors must not initiate, participate in, or encourage the filing of ethics complaints that are unwarranted or intended to harm a mental health professional rather than to protect clients or the public. (See H.2.f.)

Standard of Practice Fifty-one (SP-51)
Cooperation with Ethics Committees

Counselors must cooperate with investigations, proceedings, and requirements of the ACA Ethics Committee or ethics committees of other duly constituted associations or boards having jurisdiction over those charged with a violation. (See H.3.)

References ～

The following documents are available to counselors as resources to guide them in their practices. These resources are not a part of the Code of Ethics and the Standards of Practice.

American Association for Counseling and Development/Association for Measurement and Evaluation in Counseling and Development. (1989). *The responsibilities of users of standardized tests* (revised). Washington, DC: Author.

American Counseling Association. (1988). *American Counseling Association Ethical Standards.* Alexandria, VA: Author.

American Psychological Association. (1985). *Standards for educational and psychological testing* (revised). Washington, DC: Author.

American Rehabilitation Counseling Association, Commission on Rehabilitation Counselor Certification, and National Rehabilitation Counseling Association. (1995). *Code of professional ethics for rehabilitation counselors.* Chicago, IL: Author.

American School Counselor Association. (1992). *Ethical standards for school counselors.* Alexandria, VA: Author.

Joint Committee on Testing Practices. (1988). *Code of fair testing practices in education.* Washington, DC: Author.

National Board for Certified Counselors. (1989). *National Board for Certified Counselors Code of Ethics.* Alexandria, VA: Author.

Prediger, D. J. (Ed.). (1993, March). *Multicultural assessment standards.* Alexandria, VA: Association for Assessment in Counseling.

Policies and Procedures for Responding to Members' Requests for Interpretations of the Ethical Standards ∼

Section A: Appropriate Requests

1. ACA members may request that the Committee issue formal interpretations of the ACA Code of Ethics for the purpose of guiding the member's own professional behavior.

2. Requests for interpretations will not be considered in the following situations:

   a. The individual requesting the interpretation is not an ACA member, or

   b. The request is intended to determine whether the behavior of another mental health professional is unethical. In the event an ACA member believes the behavior of another mental health professional is unethical, the ACA member should resolve the issue directly with the professional, if possible, and should file an ethical complaint if appropriate.

Section B: Procedures

1. Members must send written requests for interpretations to the Committee at ACA Headquarters.

2. Questions should be submitted in the following format: "Does (counselor behavior) violate Sections _____ or any other sections of the ACA Ethical Standards?" Questions should avoid unique details, be general in nature to the extent possible, and be brief.

3. The Committee staff liaison will revise the question, if necessary, and submit it to the Committee Co-Chair for approval.

4. The question will be sent to Committee members who will be asked to respond individually.

5. The Committee Co-Chair will develop a consensus interpretation on behalf of the Committee.

6. The consensus interpretation will be sent to members of the Committee for final approval.

7. The formal interpretation will be sent to the member who submitted the inquiry.

8. The question and the formal interpretation will be published in the ACA newsletter, but the identity of the member requesting the interpretation will not be disclosed.

Policies and Procedures for Processing Complaints of Ethical Violations~

Section A: General

1. The American Counseling Association, hereafter referred to as the "Association" or "ACA," is dedicated to enhancing human development throughout the life span and promoting the counseling profession.
2. The Association, in furthering its objectives, administers the Code of Ethics that have been developed and approved by the ACA Governing Council.
3. The purpose of this document is to facilitate the work of the ACA Ethics Committee ("Committee") by specifying the procedures for processing cases of alleged violations of the ACA Code of Ethics, codifying options for sanctioning members, and stating appeals procedures. The intent of the Association is to monitor the professional conduct of its members to promote sound ethical practices. ACA does not, however, warrant the performance of any individual.

Section B: Ethics Committee Members

1. The Ethics Committee is a standing committee of the Association. The Committee consists of six (6) appointed members, including two (2) Co-Chairs whose terms overlap. Two members are appointed annually for three (3) year terms by the President-Elect; appointments are subject to confirmation by the ACA Governing Council. Any vacancy occurring on the Committee will be filled by the President in the same manner, and the person appointed shall serve the unexpired term of the member whose place he or she took. Committee members may be reappointed to not more than one (1) additional consecutive term.
2. One (1) of the Committee co-chairs is appointed annually by the President-Elect from among the Committee members who have two (2) years of service remaining and serves as co-chair for two (2) years, subject to confirmation by the ACA Governing Council.

Section C: Role and Function

1. The Ethics Committee is responsible for:
   a. Educating the membership as to the Association's Code of Ethics;
   b. Periodically reviewing and recommending changes in the Code of Ethics of the Association as well as the Policies and Procedures for Processing Complaints of Ethical Violations;
   c. Receiving and processing complaints of alleged violations of the Code of Ethics of the Association; and,
   d. Receiving and processing questions.
2. The Committee shall meet in person or by telephone conference a minimum of three (3) times per year for processing complaints.
3. In processing complaints about alleged ethical misconduct, the Committee

will compile an objective, factual account of the dispute in question and make the best possible recommendation for the resolution of the case. The Committee, in taking any action, shall do so only for cause, shall only take the degree of disciplinary action that is reasonable, shall utilize these procedures with objectivity and fairness, and in general shall act only to further the interests and objectives of the Association and its membership.

4. Of the six (6) voting members of the Committee, a vote of four (4) is necessary to conduct business. In the event a Co-Chair or any other member of the Committee has a personal interest in the case, he or she shall withdraw from reviewing the case.

5. In the event Committee members recuse themselves from a complaint and insufficient voting members are available to conduct business, the President shall appoint former ACA Committee members to decide the complaint.

Section D: Responsibilities of the Committee

1. The Committee members have an obligation to act in an unbiased manner, to work expeditiously, to safeguard the confidentiality of the Committee's activities, and to follow procedures established to protect the rights of all individuals involved.

Section E: Responsibilities of the Co-Chairs Administering the Complaint

1. In the event that one of the Co-Chairs Administering the Complaint; conflict of interest in a particular case, the other Co-Chair shall administer the complaint. The Co-Chair administering the complaint shall not have a vote in the decision.

2. In addition to the above guidelines for members of the Committee, the Co-Chairs, in conjunction with the Headquarters staff liaison, have the responsibilities of:

    a. Receiving, via ACA Headquarters, complaints that have been certified for membership status of the accused;

    b. Determining whether the alleged behavior(s), if true, would violate ACA's Code of Ethics and whether the Committee should review the complaint under these rules;

    c. Notifying the complainant and the accused member of receipt of the case by certified mail return receipt requested;

    d. Notifying the members of the Committee of the case;

    e. Requesting additional information from complainants, accused members and others;

    f. Presiding over the meetings of the Committee;

    g. Preparing and sending, by certified mail, communications to the complainant and accused member on the recommendations and decisions of the Committee; and

    h. Arranging for legal advice with assistance and financial approval of the ACA Executive Director.

Section F: Jurisdiction

1. The Committee will consider whether individuals have violated the ACA Code of Ethics if those individuals:
   a. Are current members of the American Counseling Association; or
   b. Were ACA members when the alleged violations occurred.
2. Ethics committees of divisions, branches, corporate affiliates, or other ACA entities must refer all ethical complaints involving ACA members to the Committee.

Section G: Eligibility to File Complaints

1. The Committee will receive complaints that ACA members have violated one or more sections of the ACA Code of Ethics from the following individuals:
   a. Members of the general public who have reason to believe that ACA members have violated the ACA Code of Ethics.
   b. ACA members, or members of other helping professions, who have reason to believe that other ACA members have violated the ACA Code of Ethics.
   c. The Co-Chair of the Committee on behalf of the ACA membership when the Co-Chair has reason to believe through information received by the Committee that ACA members have violated the ACA Code of Ethics.
2. If possible, individuals should attempt to resolve complaints directly with accused members before filing ethical complaints.

Section H: Time Lines

1. The time lines set forth in these standards are guidelines only and have been established to provide a reasonable time framework for processing complaints.
2. Complainants or accused members may request extensions of deadlines when appropriate. Extensions of deadlines will be granted by the Committee only when justified by unusual circumstance.

Section I: Nature of Communication

1. Only written communications regarding ethical complaints against members will be acceptable. If telephone inquiries from individuals are received regarding the filing of complaints, responding to complaints, or providing information regarding complaints, the individuals calling will be informed of the written communication requirement and asked to comply.
2. All correspondence related to an ethical complaint must be addressed to the Ethics Committee, ACA Headquarters, 5999 Stevenson Avenue, Alexandria, VA 22304, and must be marked "confidential." This process is necessary to protect the confidentiality of the complainant and the accused member.

Section J: Filing Complaints

1. Only written complaints, signed by complainants, will be considered.
2. Individuals eligible to file complaints will send a letter outlining the nature of the complaint to the Committee at the ACA Headquarters.
3. The ACA staff liaison to the Committee will communicate in writing with complainants. Receipt of complaints and confirmation of membership status of accused members as defined in Section F.1, above, will be acknowledged to the complainant. Proposed formal complaints will be sent to complainants after receipt of complaints have been acknowledged.
4. If the complaint does not involve a member as defined in Section F.1., above, the staff liaison shall inform the complainant.
5. The Committee Co-Chair administering a complaint will determine whether the complaint, if true, would violate one or more sections of the ethical standards or if the complaint could be properly decided if accepted. If not, the complaint will not be accepted and the complainant shall be notified.
6. If the Committee Co-Chair administering the complaint determines that there is insufficient information to make a fair determination of whether the behavior alleged in the complaint would be cause for action by the Committee, the ACA staff liaison to the Committee may request further information from the complainant or others.
7. When complaints are accepted, complainants will be informed that copies of the formal complaints plus evidence and documents submitted in support of the complaint will be provided to the accused member and that the complainant must authorize release of such information to the accused member before the complaint process may proceed.
8. The ACA staff liaison, after receiving approval of the Committee Co-Chair administering a complaint, will formulate a formal complaint which will be presented to the complainants for their signature.
   a. The correspondence from complainants will be received and the staff liaison and Committee Co-Chair administering the complaint will identify all ACA Code of Ethics that might have been violated if the accusations are true.
   b. The formal complaint will be sent to complainants with a copy of these Policies and Procedures, a copy of the ACA Code of Ethics, a verification affidavit form and an authorization and release of information form. Complainants will be asked to sign and return the completed complaint, verification affidavit and authorization and release of information forms. It will be explained to complainants that sections of the codes that might have been violated may be added or deleted by the complainant before signing the formal statement.
   c. If complainants elect to add or delete sections of the ethical standards in the formal complaint, the unsigned formal complaint shall be returned to ACA Headquarters with changes noted and a revised formal complaint will be sent to the complainants for their signature.

9. When the completed formal complaint, verification affidavit form and authorization and release of information form are presented to complainants for their signature, they will be asked to submit all evidence and documents they wish to be considered by the Committee in reviewing the complaint.

Section K: Notification of Accused Members

1. Once signed formal complaints have been received, accused members will be sent a copy of the formal complaint and copies of all evidence and documents submitted in support of the complaint.
2. Accused members will be asked to respond to the complaint against them. They will be asked to address each section of the ACA Code of Ethics they have been accused of having violated. They will be informed that if they wish to respond they must do so in writing within sixty (60) working days.
3. Accused members will be informed that they must submit all evidence and documents they wish to be considered by the Committee in reviewing the complaint within sixty (60) working days.
4. After accused members have received notification that a complaint has been brought against them, they will be given sixty (60) working days to notify the Committee Co-Chair (via ACA Headquarters) in writing, by certified mail, if they wish to request a formal face-to-face hearing before the Committee. Accused members may waive their right to a formal hearing before the Committee. (See Section P: Hearings).
5. If the Committee Co-Chair determines that there is insufficient information to make a fair determination of whether the behavior alleged in the complaint would be cause for action by the Committee, the ACA staff liaison to the Committee may request further information from the accused member or others. The accused member shall be given thirty (30) working days from receipt of the request to respond.
6. All requests for additional information from others will be accompanied by a verification affidavit form which the information provider will be asked to complete and return.
7. The Committee may, in its discretion, delay or postpone its review of the case with good cause, including if the Committee wishes to obtain additional information. The accused member may request that the Committee delay or postpone its review of the case for good cause if done so in writing.

Section L: Disposition of Complaints

1. After Receiving the responses of accused members, Committee members will be provided copies of: (a) the complaint, (b) supporting evidence and documents sent to accused members, (c) the response, and (d) supporting evidence and documents provided by accused members and others.
2. Decisions will be rendered based on the evidence and documents provided by the complainant and accused member or others.
3. The Committee Co-Chair administering a complaint will not participate in deliberations or decisions regarding that particular complaint.

4. At the next meeting of the Committee held no sooner than fifteen (15) working days after members received copies of documents related to a complaint, the Committee will discuss the complaint, response, and supporting documentation, if any, and determine the outcome of the complaint.

5. The Committee will determine whether each Code of Ethics the member has been accused of having violated was violated based on the information provided.

6. After deliberations, the Committee may decide to dismiss the complaint or to dismiss charges within the complaint.

7. In the event it is determined that any of the ACA Code of Ethics have been violated, the Committee will impose for the entire complaint one or a combination of the possible sanctions allowed.

Section M: Withdrawal of Complaints

1. If the Complainant and accused member both agree to discontinue the complaint process, the Committee may, at its discretion, complete the adjudication process if available evidence indicates that this is warranted. The Co-Chair of the Committee, on behalf of the ACA membership, shall act as complainant.

Section N: Possible Sanctions

1. Reprinted Remedial requirements may be stipulated by the Committee.

2. Probation for a specified period of time subject to Committee review of compliance. Remedial requirements may be imposed to be completed within a specified period of time.

3. Suspension from ACA membership for a specified period of time subject to Committee review of compliance. Remedial requirements may be imposed to be completed within a specified period of time.

4. Permanent expulsion from ACA membership. This sanction requires a unanimous vote of those voting.

5. The penalty for failing to fulfill in a satisfactory manner a remedial requirement imposed by the Committee as a result of a probation sanction will be automatic suspension until the requirement is met, unless the Committee determines that the remedial requirement should be modified based on good cause shown prior to the end of the probationary period.

6. The penalty for failing to fulfill in a satisfactory manner a remedial requirement imposed by the Committee as a result of a suspension sanction will be automatic permanent expulsion unless the Committee determines that the remedial requirement should be modified based on good cause shown prior to the end of the suspension period.

7. Other corrective action.

Section O: Notification of Results

1. Accused members shall be notified of Committee decisions regarding complaints against them.

2. Complainants will be notified of Committee decisions after the deadline for accused members to file appeals or, in the event an appeal is filed, after a filed appeal decision has been rendered.

3. After complainants are notified of the results of their complaints as provided in Section O., Paragraph 2 above, if a violation has been found and accused members have been suspended or expelled, counselor licensure, certification, or registry boards, other mental health licensure, certification, or registry boards, voluntary national certification boards, and appropriate professional associations will also be notified of the results. In addition, ACA divisions, state branches, the ACA Insurance Trust, and other ACA-related entities will also be notified of the results.

4. After complainants have been notified of the results of their complaint as provided in Section O., Paragraph 2, above, if a violation has been found and accused members have been suspended or expelled, a notice of the Committee action that includes the sections of the ACA ethical standards that were found to have been violated and the sanctions imposed will be published in the ACA newsletter.

Section P: Hearings

1. At the discretion of the Committee, a hearing may be conducted when the results of the Committee's preliminary determination indicate that additional information is needed.

2. When accused members, within sixty (60) working days of notification of the complaint, request a formal face-to-face or telephone conference hearing before the Committee a hearing shall be conducted. (See Section K.6.)

3. The accused shall bear all their expenses associated with attendance at hearings requested by the accused.

4. The Committee Co-Chair shall schedule a formal hearing on the case at the next scheduled Committee meeting and notify both the complainant and the accused member of their right to attend the hearing in person or by telephone conference call.

5. The hearing will be held before a panel made up of the Committee and if the accused member chooses, a representative of the accused member's primary Division. This representative will be identified by the Division President and will have voting privileges.

Section Q: Hearing Procedures

1. Purpose
   a. A hearing will be conducted to determine whether a breach of the ethical standards has occurred and, if so, to determine appropriate disciplinary action.
   b. The Committee will be guided in its deliberations by principles of basic fairness and professionalism, and will keep its deliberations as confidential as possible, except as provided herein.

2. Notice
   a. The accused members shall be advised in writing by the Co-Chair administering the complaint of the time and place of the hearing and the charges involved at least forty-five (45) working days before the hearing. Notice shall include a formal statement of the complaints lodged against the accused member and supporting evidence.
   b. The accused member is under no duty to respond to the notice, but the Committee will not be obligated to delay or postpone its hearing unless the accused so requests in writing, with good cause reviewed at least fifteen (15) working days in advance. In the absence of such 15 day advance notice and postponement by the Committee, if the accused fails to appear at the hearing, the Committee shall decide the complaint on record. Failure of the accused member to appear at the hearing shall not be viewed by the Committee as sufficient grounds alone for taking disciplinary action.

3. Conduct of the Hearing
   a. Accommodations. The location of the hearing shall be determined at the discretion of the Committee. The Committee shall provide a private room to conduct the hearing and no observers or recording devices other than a recording device used by the Committee shall be permitted.
   b. Presiding Officer. The Co-Chair in charge of the case shall preside over the hearing and deliberations of the Committee. At the conclusion of the hearing and deliberations of the Committee, the Co-Chair shall promptly notify the accused member and complainant of the Committee's decision in writing as provided in Section O., Paragraphs 1 and 2, above.
   c. Record. A record of the hearing shall be made and preserved, together with any documents presented in evidence, at ACA Headquarters for a period of three (3) years. The record shall consist of a summary of testimony received or a verbatim transcript, at the discretion of the Committee.
   d. Right to Counsel. The accused member shall be entitled to have legal counsel present to advise and represent them throughout the hearing. Legal counsel for ACA shall also be present at the hearing to advise the Committee and shall have the privilege of the floor.
   e. Witnesses. Either party shall have the right to call witnesses to substantiate his or her version of the case.
   f. The Committee shall have the right to call witnesses it believes may provide further insight into the matter. ACA shall, in its sole discretion, determine the number and identity of witnesses to be heard.
   g. Witnesses shall not be present during the hearing except when they are called upon to testify and shall be excused upon completion of their testimony and any cross-examination.
   h. The Co-Chair administering the complaint shall allow questions to be asked of any witness by the opposition or members of the Committee if

such questions and testimony are relevant to the issues in the case.

    i. The Co-Chair administering the complaint will determine what questions and testimony are relevant to the case. Should the hearing be disturbed by irrelevant testimony, the Co-Chair administering the complaint may call a brief recess until order can be restored.

    j. All expenses associated with counsel on behalf of the parties shall be borne by the respective parties. All expenses associated with witnesses on behalf of the accused shall be borne by the accused when the accused requests a hearing. If the Committee requests the hearing, all expenses associated with witnesses shall be borne by ACA.

4. Presentation of Evidence

    a. The staff liaison, or the Co-Chair administering the complaint shall be called upon first to present the charge(s) made against the accused and to briefly describe the evidence supporting the charge. The person presenting the charges shall also be responsible for examining and cross-examining witnesses on behalf of the complainant and for otherwise presenting the matter during the hearing.

    b. The complainant or a member of the Committee shall then be called upon to present the case against the accused. Witnesses who can substantiate the case may be called upon to testify and answer questions of the accused and the Committee.

    c. If the accused has exercised the right to be present at the hearing, he or she shall be called upon last to present any evidence which refutes the charges against him or her. This includes witnesses as in Subsection (3) above.

    d. The accused will not be found guilty simply for refusing to testify. Once the accused member chooses to testify, however, he or she may be cross-examined by the complainant and members of the Committee.

    e. The Committee will endeavor to conclude the hearing within a period of approximately three (3) hours. The parties will be requested to be considerate of this time frame in planning their testimony.

    f. Testimony that is merely cumulative or repetitious may, at the discretion of the Co-Chair administering the complaint, be excluded.

5. Relevancy of Evidence

    a. The Hearing Committee is not a court of law and is not required to observe formal rules of evidence. Evidence that would be inadmissible in a court of law may be admissible in the hearing before the Committee, if it is relevant to the case. That is, if the evidence offered tends to explain, clarify, or refute any of the important facts of the case, it should generally be considered.

    b. The Committee will not consider evidence or testimony for the purpose of supporting any charge that was not set forth in the notice of the hearing or that is not relevant to the issues of the case.

6. Burden of Proof
   a. The burden of proving a violation of the ethical standards is on the complainant and/or the Committee. It is not up to the accused to prove his or her innocence of any wrong-doing.
   b. Although the charge(s) need not be proved "beyond a reasonable doubt," the Committee will not find the accused guilty in the absence of substantial, objective, and believable evidence to sustain the charge(s).
7. Deliberation of the Committee
   a. After the hearing is completed, the Committee shall meet in a closed session to review the evidence presented and reach a conclusion. ACA legal counsel may attend the closed session to advise the Committee if the Committee so desires.
   b. The Committee shall be the sole trier of the facts and shall weigh the evidence presented and assess the credibility of the witnesses. The act of a majority of the members of the Committee present shall be the decision of the Committee. A unanimous vote of those voting is required for permanent expulsion from ACA membership.
   c. Only members of the Committee who were present throughout the entire hearing shall be eligible to vote.
8. Decision of the Committee
   a. The Committee will first resolve the issue of the guilt or innocence of the accused on each charge. Applying the burden of proof in subsection (5), above, the Committee will vote by secret ballot, unless the members of the Committee consent to an oral vote.
   b. In the event a majority of the members of the Committee do not find the accused guilty, the charges shall be dismissed. If the Committee finds the accused member has violated the Code of Ethics, it must then determine what sanctions, in accordance with Section N: Possible Sanctions, shall be imposed.
   c. As provided in Section O., above, the Co-Chair administering the complaint shall notify the accused member and complainant of the Committee's decision in writing.

Section R: Appeals

1. Decisions of the ACA Ethics Committee that members have violated the ACA Code of Ethics may be appealed by the member found to have been in violation based on one or both of the following grounds:
   a. The Committee violated its policies and procedures for processing complaints of ethical violations; and/or
   b. The decision of the Committee was arbitrary and capricious and was not supported by the materials provided by the complainant and accused member.
2. After members have received notification that they have been found in violation of one or more ACA Code of Ethics, they will be given thirty (30)

working days to notify the Committee in writing by certified mail that they are appealing the decision.

3. An appeal may consist only of a letter stating one or both of the grounds of appeal listed in subsection 1 above and the reasons for the appeal.

4. Appealing members will be asked to identify the primary ACA division to which he or she belongs. The ACA President will appoint a three (3) person appeals panel consisting of two (2) former ACA Ethics Committee Chairs and the President of the identified division. The ACA attorney shall serve as legal advisor and have the privilege of the floor.

5. The three (3) member appeals panel will be given copies of the materials available to the Committee when it made its decision, a copy of the hearing transcript if a hearing was held, plus a copy of the letter filed by the appealing member.

6. The appeals panel generally will render its decision regarding an appeal which must receive a majority vote within sixty (60) working days of their receipt of the above materials.

7. The decision of the appeals panel may include one of the following:
   a. The decision of the Committee is upheld.
   b. The decision of the Committee is reversed and remanded with guidance to the Committee for a new decision. The reason for this decision will be given to the Committee in detail in writing.

8. When a Committee decision is reversed and remanded, the complainant and accused member will be informed in writing and additional information may be requested first from the complainant and then from the accused member. The Committee will then render another decision without a hearing.

9. Decisions of the appeals panel to uphold the Committee decision are final.

Section S: Substantial New Evidence

1. In the Event substantial new evidence is presented in a case in which an appeal was not filed, or in a case which a final decision has been rendered, the case may be reopened by the Committee.

2. The Committee will consider substantial new evidence and if it is found to be substantiated and capable of exonerating a member who was expelled, the Committee will reopen the case and go through the entire complaint process again.

Section T: Records

1. The records of the Committee regarding complaints are confidential except as provided herein.

2. Original copies of complaint records will be maintained in locked files at ACA Headquarters or at an off-site location chosen by ACA.

3. Members of the Committee will keep copies of complaint records confidential and will destroy copies of records after a case has been closed or when they are no longer a member of the Committee.

Section U: Legal Actions Related to Complaints

1. Complaints and accused members are required to notify the Committee if they learn of any type of legal action (civil or criminal) being filed related to the complaint.
2. In the event any type of legal action is filed regarding an accepted complaint, all actions related to the complaint will be stayed until the legal action has been concluded. The Committee will consult with legal counsel concerning whether the processing of the complaint will be stayed if the legal action does not involve the same complainant and the same facts complained of.
3. If actions on a complaint are stayed, the complainant and accused member will be notified.
4. When actions on a complaint are continued after a legal action has been concluded, the complainant and accused member will be notified.

For information on ordering the ACA Code of Ethics and Standards of Practice write to:

ACA Distribution Center
P.O. Box 531
Annapolis Junction, MD 20701-0531

or call
301-470-4ACA (301-470-4222)
toll free: 1-800-422-2648
fax: 301-604-0158

Author Index

A

Aberg-Wistedt, A., 416
Abramowitz, C. V., 107, 122
Abramowitz, S. I., 107, 118
Achenbach, T. M., 109
Achté, K., 433, 434
Adler, A., 77
Agazarian, Y., 279, 280
Agras, W., 111, 322
Albert, J., 151
Albert-Gillis, L. J., 111
Alcoholics Analymous World Services, Inc., 283, 286, 290
Alexander, K., 437
Alexander, P. C., 111
Allan, J., 270
Allberg, W., 416, 436, 437, 438
Allison, D., 317
Allport, G. W., 210
Altman, I. M., 347
American Counseling Association, (ACA), 160, 162, 172, 176, 177, 445, 457, 467, 491
American Psychiatric Association, 301, 302
American Psychological Association, 103
American School Counselor Association, 116
Anchor, K. N., 25
Andersen, A., 305, 306
Anderson, C., 303

Anderson, J., 23, 24, 25, 145
Anderson, K. J., 140
Anderson, R. F., 116
Anderson, T. P., 344
Anderson, W., 236, 246, 304, 307, 308
Andrews, S., 236
Anthony, W. A., 239
Apt, C., 111
Arbuckle, D., 20
Arciniega, G. M., 182, 188, 191
Arciniega, M., 191, 193, 198
Aries, E. J., 15, 16, 17
Armstrong, H., 111, 427
Arrendondo, P., 182, 200
Asarnow, J., 416, 427
Asberg, M., 416
Ascher, E., 25
Ashkenas, R., 24
Asimos, C., 418, 419, 423
Association for Specialists in Group Work (ASGW), 8, 52, 105, 108, 109, 159, 160, 162, 163, 177, 409, 445, 457
Atkinson, D. R., 189, 200
Attneave, C. N., 213
Austin-Murphy, J., 110
Avery, C., 339
Avila, A. L., 184
Avila, D. L., 108, 184
Axelroth, E., 141
Azim, H. F. A., 152, 153
Azrin, N. H., 350

B

Baider, L., 119
Bailey, J. M., 360
Baker, E., 315
Baker, L., 303
Baker, M., 131, 152, 155
Baker, S. B., 114, 116
Bales, R. F., 33
Ballantyne, J., 303
Baltzan, R., 347
Bandler, R., 315, 319
Banik, S. N., 344
Bardwick, J. M., 17
Barker, R. L., 102, 118
Barry, R. A., 31
Barth, D., 306, 309, 311
Bates, M., 66
Baumeister, R., 303
Bauer, B., 304, 307, 308
Bean, B. W., 25
Beasley, L., 15, 16
Beckett, A., 347
Bednar, R., 23, 24, 25, 105
Beeferman, D., 109
Beletsis, S., 293
Bell, A. P., 360
Bellah, R. N., 210, 212
Benard, B., 137, 139
Benjamin, A., 62
Benne, K. D., 6
Bennett, L. W., 112
Bennis, W. G., 33, 34
Bentley, J., 23
Bepko, C., 303, 310, 311
Berenson, B. G., 20
Berg, R., 33, 34, 36, 37, 38

Berger, R. M., 382
Bergin, A. E., 118, 119
Berkovitz, I. H., 352
Bernadett-Shapiro, S., 3, 8
Berne, E., 88
Berne, R., 246
Bertcher, H. J., 23
Bertoia, J., 270
Berzon, B., 18, 25, 362
Besalel, H., 350
Bettenhausen, K. L., 108
Betz, N., 322, 361, 364
Beutler, O. E., 107
Bhalerao, U., 347
Billingsley, A., 137, 138
Bion, R. W., 34
Blair, A. J., 111
Blatner, A., 91, 92
Blazer, D., 415
Bledsoe, N., 391, 435, 436
Bloch, S., 17
Bloomfield, K. A., 376
Blume, S. B., 280
Blumenfeld, W. J., 360, 362, 363, 366
Blumstein, P., 361
Blundell, J., 303
Bogdaniak, R., 416, 418
Bolles, R. N., 234, 245
Bond, M. A., 209
Bonney, W. C., 391
Booth, D. A., 111
Borders, L. D., 116
Bordin, E. S., 106
Borg, W. R., 103
Borgen, F. H., 235

Subject Index

DATE DUE

NOV 2 9 1999			
GAYLORD			PRINTED IN U.S.A.